Chapter 9: The Business of Banking
Commerce Bank
Tying
Fees
Fixed- versus Floating-Rate Mortgages
The Banking Crisis of the 1980s

Online Case: An Update on Bank Profits

Chapter 10: Bank Regulation
Bank Runs in Fiction and Fact
Bank Panics in the 1930s
The Keystone Scandal
Deposit Insurance and Banking Crises
Wal-Mart Bank?
Regulatory Failure in the S&L Crisis

Online Case: An Update on Capital Requirements

Chapter 11: The Money Supply and Interest Rates
The Money Multiplier and the Great Depression
Another Mistake: The Fed in 1937
The Decline of Reserve Requirements
The Monetarist Experiment

Online Case: Interest on Reserves

Chapter 12: Short-Run Economic Fluctuations
The Natural Rate in the United States
What Is a Recession?
Oil Prices and Inflation
The U.S. Economy, 1960–2007

Online Case: An Update on the U.S. Economy

Chapter 13: Economic Fluctuations, Monetary Policy, and the Financial System
Measuring the Effects of Monetary Policy on the Term Structure
Asset Prices, Banking, and the Japanese Slump
Monetary Policy, Inventories, and Small Firms
Fiscal versus Monetary Policy

Online Case: An Update on Asset Prices and Consumption

Chapter 14: Inflation and Deflation
The Free Silver Movement
The German Hyperinflation
The Worldwide Decline in Inflation
Life in Inflationary Brazil
The After-Tax Real Interest Rate
Japan's Liquidity Trap

Online Case: An Update on Worldwide Inflation

Chapter 15: Policies for Economic Stability
How Costly Is the Business Cycle?
The Fed and the Great Inflation
The Fed and the Roaring 90s

Online Case: An FOMC Meeting

Chapter 16: Monetary Institutions and Strategies
Nixon and Burns
Targeters and Nontargeters
The ECB's Two Pillars
Alan Blinder

Online Case: An Update on Fed Transparency

Chapter 17: Monetary Policy and Exchange Rates
Canadian Monetary Policy
Do Interventions Work?
The Yuan
George Soros versus the Pound

Online Case: An Update on Chinese Currency Policy

Chapter 18: Financial Crises
Disaster in the 1930s
The Financial System and the Fed, 2007–2008
Argentina's Crisis, 2001–2002

Online Case: An Update on the U.S. Financial Crisis and Policymakers' Responses

MONEY, BANKING, AND FINANCIAL MARKETS

The building on this book's cover is the Second Bank of the United States, located in Philadelphia. It operated from 1816 to 1836, serving some of the functions of the modern Federal Reserve. President Andrew Jackson vetoed legislation to extend the Bank's charter because he believed it served "moneyed interests" at the expense of common people (see Chapter 8).

The cover also shows several of the world's currencies: South Africa's rand (at top), the Japanese yen (the 500 yen coin), the euro (touching the yen coin), and a $10 bill and dime from the United States. Pictured on the $10 bill is Alexander Hamilton, Secretary of the Treasury under George Washington, who created the first national currency of the United States (see Chapter 2). The dime features President Franklin Roosevelt, whose banking and monetary policies helped end the 1930s' Great Depression (see Chapter 18). The currency that says "Washington" is a gold certificate, a type of money used in the United States in the late 19th and early 20th centuries.

MONEY, BANKING, AND FINANCIAL MARKETS

Laurence M. Ball
Johns Hopkins University

Worth Publishers

Senior Publisher: Craig Bleyer

Acquisitions Editor: Sarah Dorger

Senior Marketing Manager: Scott Guile

Market Research and Development: Steven Rigolosi

Development Editor: Barbara Brooks

Development Editor, Media and Supplements: Marie McHale

Consulting Editor: Paul Shensa

Associate Editor: Matthew Driskill

Photo Editor: Cecilia Varas

Photo Researcher: Julie Tesser

Art Director: Babs Reingold

Senior Designer, Cover Designer: Kevin Kall

Interior Designer: Lissi Sigillo

Associate Managing Editor: Tracey Kuehn

Project Editors: Dana Kasowitz
Laura Hakala, Pre-PressPMG

Production Manager: Barbara Anne Seixas

Composition: Pre-PressPMG

Printing and Binding: RR Donnelley

Cover Photos: Second Bank of the United States PHILADELPHIA USA, © Aflo Co. Ltd./Alamy
Gold certificate and coins, © Corbis Premium RF/Alamy
Euro note, Image source photography/Veer
US 10 dollars, Veer
South African rand, Veer

Library of Congress Control Number: 2008926450

ISBN-13: 978-0-7167-5934-8
ISBN-10: 0-7167-5934-9

Printed in the United States of America

First printing

Worth Publishers

41 Madison Avenue

New York, NY 10010

www.worthpublishers.com

Laurence Ball is Professor of Economics at Johns Hopkins University. He holds a Ph.D. in economics from the Massachusetts Institute of Technology and a B.A. in economics from Amherst College. Professor Ball is a Research Associate of the National Bureau of Economic Research and has been a visiting scholar at the Federal Reserve, the Bank of Japan, the Central Bank of Norway, the Reserve Bank of Australia, and the Hong Kong Monetary Authority. His academic honors include the Houblon-Norman Fellowship (Bank of England), a Professorial Fellowship in Monetary Economics (Victoria University of Wellington and Reserve Bank of New Zealand), the NBER Olin Fellowship, and the Alfred P. Sloan Research Fellowship. He lives in Baltimore with his wife, Patricia, and their son, Leverett.

To Patricia

brief contents

Preface xxvii

PART I FOUNDATIONS

1 The Financial System 1

2 Money and Central Banks 25

PART II FINANCIAL MARKETS

3 Asset Prices and Interest Rates 53

4 What Determines Interest Rates? 83

5 Securities Markets 119

6 Foreign Exchange Markets 155

PART III BANKING

7 Asymmetric Information in the Financial System 189

8 The Banking Industry 219

9 The Business of Banking 249

10 Bank Regulation 283

PART IV MONEY AND THE ECONOMY

11 The Money Supply and Interest Rates 313

12 Short-Run Economic Fluctuations 343

13 Economic Fluctuations, Monetary Policy, and the Financial System 383

14 Inflation and Deflation 413

PART V MONETARY POLICY

15 Policies for Economic Stability 443

16 Monetary Institutions and Strategies 475

17 Monetary Policy and Exchange Rates 511

18 Financial Crises 543

Glossary G-1

Index I-1

contents

Preface xxvii

PART I FOUNDATIONS

Chapter 1 The Financial System 1

1.1 Financial Markets 2
- Bonds 2
- Stocks 3

1.2 Economic Functions of Financial Markets 4
- Matching Savers and Investors 4
- Risk Sharing 5

CASE STUDY Employee Stock Ownership and the Collapse of Enron 6

1.3 Asymmetric Information 7
- Adverse Selection 8
- Moral Hazard 9

1.4 Banks 10
- What Is a Bank? 10
- Banks versus Financial Markets 11
- Why Banks Exist 11

1.5 The Financial System and Economic Growth 12
- Saving and Growth 13
- The Allocation of Saving 13
- Evidence on Growth 14

CASE STUDY Unit Banking and Economic Growth 15

CASE STUDY Microfinance 16
- Markets versus Central Planning 18

Online Case Study
An Update on Microfinance

CASE STUDY Investment in the Soviet Union 18

Summary 20

Key Terms 21

Questions and Problems 21

Appendix: Measuring Output and the Price Level 23

Chapter 2 Money and Central Banks 25

2.1 What is Money? 26

The Medium of Exchange 26

Money versus Barter 27

CASE STUDY Nineteenth-Century Visitors to Barter Economies 28

The Unit of Account 28

A Store of Value 29

2.2 Types of Money 29

Commodity Money 30

Fiat Money 31

From Commodity Money to Fiat Money 32

CASE STUDY The History of the U.S. Dollar 32

Alternatives to a National Currency 34

Online Case Study Alternative Currencies in the United States

CASE STUDY Clean and Dirty Money 35

2.3 Money Today 36

Measuring the Money Supply: M1 36

How We Spend Money 37

What About Credit Cards? 38

The Payments System 39

New Kinds of Money 40

2.4 Liquidity and Broad Money 42

The Need for Liquidity 42

Degrees of Liquidity 42

Measuring Broad Money: M2 43

CASE STUDY Sweep Programs 45

2.5 Functions of Central Banks 46

Clearing Payments 47

Monetary Policy 47

Lending 47

Bank Regulation 47

CASE STUDY The Fed and September 11 47

2.6 The Rest of this Book 48

Financial Markets 49

Banking 49

Money and the Economy 49

Monetary Policy 50

Summary 50

Key Terms 51

Questions and Problems 51

PART II FINANCIAL MARKETS

Chapter 3 Asset Prices and Interest Rates 53

3.1 Valuing Income Streams 54

Future Value 54

Present Value 55

3.2 The Classical Theory of Asset Prices 57

The Present Value of Income 57

What Expectations? 58

What Interest Rate? 59

3.3 Fluctuations in Asset Prices 60

Why Do Asset Prices Change? 60

CASE STUDY The Fed and the Stock Market 60

Which Asset Prices Are Most Volatile? 62

3.4 Asset-Price Bubbles 63

How Bubbles Work 63

CASE STUDY Tulipmania 64

Looking for Bubbles 65

CASE STUDY The Millennium Boom 66

Online Case Study An Update on the Stock Market

3.5 Asset-Price Crashes 68

How Crashes Work 68

CASE STUDY The Two Big Crashes 69

Crash Prevention 70

3.6 Measuring Interest Rates and Asset Prices 71

Yield to Maturity 71

The Rate of Return 72

Returns on Stocks and Bonds 73

Rate of Return versus Yield to Maturity 74

3.7 Real and Nominal Interest Rates 74

Real Interest Rates: Ex Ante versus Ex Post 75

CASE STUDY Inflation and the Savings and Loan Crisis 77

Inflation-Indexed Bonds 77

Summary 78

Key Terms 79

Questions and Problems 80

Chapter 4 What Determines Interest Rates? 83

4.1 The Loanable Funds Theory 84
Saving, Investment, and Capital Flows 85
Effects of the Real Interest Rate 86
The Equilibrium Real Interest Rate 87
4.2 Determinants of Interest Rates in the Loanable Funds Theory 89
Shifts in Investment 89
Shifts in Saving 91
CASE STUDY Budget Deficits and Interest Rates 93
Shifts in Capital Flows 94
Nominal Interest Rates 95
4.3 The Liquidity Preference Theory 97
The Market for Money 98
The Equilibrium Interest Rate 98
Changes in Interest Rates 100
Relating the Two Theories of Interest Rates 102
4.4. The Term Structure of Interest Rates 102
The Case of Certainty 103
The Expectations Theory of the Term Structure 104
Accounting for Risk 105
The Yield Curve 106
Online Case Study The Recent Behavior of the Yield Curve
CASE STUDY Inverted Yield Curves 109
4.5 Default Risk and Interest Rates 110
Default Risk on Sovereign Debt 110
CASE STUDY The Paradox of Japanese Interest Rates 111
Default Risk on Corporate Debt 112
CASE STUDY General Motors Bonds 112
CASE STUDY The High-Yield Spread 114
4.6 Two Other Factors 115
Liquidity 115
Taxes 115
Summary 116
Key Terms 117
Questions and Problems 117

Chapter 5 Securities Markets 119

5.1 Participants in Securities Markets 120

Individuals 120

Securities Firms 121

Other Financial Institutions 122

Online Case Study An Update on Investment Banks

5.2 Stock and Bond Markets 123

Primary Markets 123

CASE STUDY Google's IPO 125

CASE STUDY Treasury Bill Auctions 126

Secondary Markets 127

Finding Information on Security Prices 130

5.3 Firms' Capital Structure 130

Is Capital Structure Irrelevant? 131

Why Capital Structure Does Matter 132

Debt Maturity 133

5.4 What Assets Should Savers Hold? 133

The Risk-Return Trade-off 133

Choosing the Mix 136

CASE STUDY Age and Asset Allocation 138

5.5 Which Stocks? 138

The Efficient-Markets Hypothesis 139

Two Kinds of Mutual Funds 140

Can *Anyone* Beat the Market? 141

CASE STUDY The Oracle of Omaha 143

5.6 Derivatives 144

Futures 145

Options 145

Hedging with Derivatives 146

Speculating with Derivatives 147

CASE STUDY Derivative Disasters 148

New Frontiers 149

Summary 150

Key Terms 151

Questions and Problems 152

Chapter 6 Foreign Exchange Markets 155

6.1 Currency Markets and Exchange Rates 156
- The Trading Process 156
- Measuring Exchange Rates 158

6.2 Why Exchange Rates Matter 160
- Effects of Appreciation 160

CASE STUDY The Politics of the Dollar 162
- Hedging Exchange-Rate Risk 163
- Real versus Nominal Exchange Rates 164
- The Trade-Weighted Real Exchange Rate 166

CASE STUDY Exchange Rates and Steel 167

6.3 The Long-Run Behavior of Exchange Rates 169
- Purchasing Power Parity 169
- How Reasonable is PPP? 170
- Evidence for PPP 170

6.4 Real Exchange Rates in the Short Run 172
- Net Exports and Capital Flows 172
- Effects of the Real Exchange Rate 173
- The Equilibrium Exchange Rate 173

6.5 Fluctuations in Exchange Rates 174
- Shifts in Net Capital Outflows 174

Online Case Study An Update on Exchange Rates

CASE STUDY The Euro versus the Dollar 176
- Shifts in Net Exports 178
- Nominal Rates Again 180

6.6 Currency Speculation 180
- Forecasting Methods 182

CASE STUDY More on Technical Analysis 183

Summary 185

Key Terms 186

Questions and Problems 186

PART III BANKING

Chapter 7 Asymmetric Information in the Financial System 189

7.1 Adverse Selection 190

The Lemons Problem 191

Lemons in Securities Markets 192

A Numerical Example 193

7.2 Moral Hazard 195

Moral Hazard in Stock Markets 196

CASE STUDY Dennis Kozlowski 196

Moral Hazard in Bond Markets 197

The Numerical Example Again 198

7.3 Reducing Information Asymmetries 198

Information Gathering 199

The Free-Rider Problem 199

Information-Gathering Firms 200

Boards of Directors 200

CASE STUDY International Differences in Shareholder Rights 202

Private Equity Firms 203

7.4 Regulation of Financial Markets 205

Information Disclosure 205

Insider Trading 207

CASE STUDY Some Inside Traders 208

7.5 Banks and Asymmetric Information 209

Screening Borrowers 209

Collateral and Net Worth 210

Covenants and Monitoring 211

Interest Rates and Credit Rationing 211

CASE STUDY The Five C's of Business Lending 212

CASE STUDY Traditional Home Mortgages 212

7.6 Banks and Transaction Costs 214

Reducing Costs to Savers 214

Reducing Costs to Investors 214

Summary 215

Key Terms 216

Questions and Problems 216

Online Case Study
An Update on Financial-Markets Regulation

Chapter 8 The Banking Industry 219

8.1 Types of Banks 220

Commercial Banks 221

Thrift Institutions 222

Finance Companies 223

8.2 Dispersion and Consolidation 223

Why So Many Banks? 223

CASE STUDY The Politics of Banking in U.S. History 224

Consolidation in Commercial Banking 226

International Banking 228

Consolidation Across Businesses 228

CASE STUDY Citigroup 229

8.3 Securitization 231

The Securitization Industry 231

Why Securitization Occurs 232

8.4 Subprime Lenders 233

Finance Companies 233

Online Case Study An Update on the Mortgage Crisis

CASE STUDY The Subprime Mortgage Fiasco 234

Payday Lenders 236

CASE STUDY Is Payday Lending Predatory? 237

Pawnshops 239

Illegal Loan Sharks 239

8.5 Government's Role in Lending 239

Mortgage Agencies 240

Loan Guarantees 241

CASE STUDY Student Loans 241

The Community Reinvestment Act 243

Government-Owned Banks 244

Summary 245

Key Terms 246

Questions and Problems 247

Chapter 9 The Business of Banking 249

9.1 Banks' Balance Sheets 250
- Liabilities and Net Worth 251
- Assets 252

9.2 Off-Balance-Sheet Activities 253
- Lines of Credit 253
- Letters of Credit 254
- Asset Management 254
- Derivatives 254
- Investment Banking 254

9.3 How Banks Make Profits 255
- Melvin Opens a Bank 255
- The Income Statement 256
- Profit Rates 257

9.4 The Evolving Pursuit of Profits 258
- Sources of Funds 258

Online Case Study
An Update on Bank Profits

CASE STUDY Commerce Bank 261
- Seeking Income 262

CASE STUDY Tying 264

CASE STUDY Fees 265

9.5 Managing Risk 266
- Liquidity Risk 267
- Credit Risk 269
- Interest-Rate Risk 270

CASE STUDY Fixed- versus Floating-Rate Mortgages 273
- Market and Economic Risk 274
- Interactions Among Risks 274

9.6 Insolvency 275
- An Example 275
- The Equity Ratio 275

CASE STUDY The Banking Crisis of the 1980s 277

Summary 278

Key Terms 280

Questions and Problems 280

Chapter 10 Bank Regulation 283

10.1 Bank Runs 284
How Bank Runs Happen 284
An Example 285
Suspension of Payments 285

CASE STUDY Bank Runs in Fiction and Fact 286
Bank Panics 288

CASE STUDY Bank Panics in the 1930s 288

10.2 Deposit Insurance 290
How Deposit Insurance Works 290
Deposit Insurance in the United States 290

10.3 Moral Hazard Again 291
Misuses of Deposits 291

CASE STUDY The Keystone Scandal 292
The Problem with Deposit Insurance 293
Limits on Insurance 294

CASE STUDY Deposit Insurance and Banking Crises 294

10.4 Who Can Open a Bank? 295
Chartering Agencies 296
Obtaining a Charter 296
The Separation of Banking and Commerce 296

CASE STUDY Wal-Mart Bank? 297

10.5 Restrictions on Balance Sheets 299
Who Sets Regulations? 299
Restrictions on Assets 300
Capital Requirements 300

Online Case Study
An Update on Capital Requirements

10.6 Supervision 303
Information Gathering 303
CAMELS Ratings 303
Enforcement Actions 305

10.7 Closing Insolvent Banks 305
The Need for Government Action 305
Forbearance 306

CASE STUDY Regulatory Failure in the S&L Crisis 307
Deciding on Closure 308
The Closure Process 308

Summary 309
Key Terms 310
Questions and Problems 310

PART IV MONEY AND THE ECONOMY

Chapter 11 The Money Supply and Interest Rates 313

11.1 The Federal Reserve System 314

11.2 The Fed and the Monetary Base 315

- The Monetary Base 315
- Creating the Base 315
- The Fed's Balance Sheet 317

11.3 Commercial Banks and the Money Supply 317

- An Economy Without Banks 318
- A Bank Creates Money . . . 318
- . . . and More Money 320
- Limits to Money Creation 321

11.4 A Formula for the Money Supply 322

- Deriving the Formula 322
- Changes in the Money Supply 323
- The U.S. Money Multiplier 324

CASE STUDY The Money Multiplier and the Great Depression 324

11.5 The Fed's Monetary Tools 326

- Open-Market Operations 326
- Lending Policies 327
- Reserve Requirements 328

CASE STUDY Another Mistake: The Fed in 1937 328

CASE STUDY The Decline of Reserve Requirements 329 — Online Case Study: Interest on Reserves

11.6 Money Targets versus Interest-Rate Targets 330

- Two Approaches to Monetary Policy 331
- Does the Choice Matter? 332
- The Fed's Choice 333

CASE STUDY The Monetarist Experiment 334

11.7 Interest-Rate Policy 335

- The Federal Funds Rate 335
- The Federal Open Market Committee 336
- Implementing the Targets 336

Summary 339

Key Terms 340

Questions and Problems 341

Chapter 12 Short-Run Economic Fluctuations 343

12.1 The Business Cycle 345

Long-Run Output and Unemployment 345

CASE STUDY The Natural Rate in the United States 346

Booms and Recessions 347

CASE STUDY What Is a Recession? 350

Aggregate Expenditure 351

12.2 What Determines Aggregate Expenditure? 352

The Components of Expenditure 352

The Role of the Interest Rate 352

Monetary Policy and Equilibrium Output 353

Expenditure Shocks 354

Countercyclical Monetary Policy 357

12.3 Fluctuations in the Inflation Rate 358

Expected Inflation 358

What Determines Expected Inflation? 358

The Effect of Output 360

Supply Shocks 363

CASE STUDY Oil Prices and Inflation 366

12.4 The Complete Economy 367

Combining the Two Curves 367

The Economy Over Time 369

Online Case Study An Update on the U.S. Economy

JUMBO CASE STUDY The U.S. Economy, 1960–2007 373

Conclusion: What Causes the Business Cycle? 375

12.5 Long-Run Monetary Neutrality 376

Long-Run Output and Unemployment 376

A Permanent Boom? 376

The Neutral Real Interest Rate 377

Summary 378

Key Terms 379

Questions and Problems 379

Appendix: The Loanable Funds Theory and the Neutral Interest Rate 381

Chapter 13 Economic Fluctuations, Monetary Policy, and the Financial System 383

13.1 Monetary Policy and the Term Structure 384

The Term Structure Again 384

A Policy Surprise 385

Expected Policy Changes 387

CASE STUDY Measuring the Effects of Monetary Policy on the Term Structure 389

13.2 The Financial System and Aggregate Expenditure 390

Changes in Asset Prices 391

Online Case Study An Update on Asset Prices and Consumption

Changes in Bank Lending Policies 392

CASE STUDY Asset Prices, Banking, and the Japanese Slump 393

The Investment Multiplier 396

13.3 The Monetary Transmission Mechanism 397

Effects in Financial Markets 398

Effects on Bank Lending 398

Effects on Expenditure 398

Multiplier Effects 398

Some Lessons 399

CASE STUDY Monetary Policy, Inventories, and Small Firms 399

13.4 Time Lags 400

Lags in the AE Curve 401

Lags in the Phillips Curve 401

Evidence 402

13.5 Time Lags and the Effects of Policy 403

A Disinflation 403

Countercyclical Policy 405

CASE STUDY Fiscal versus Monetary Policy 406

Summary 409

Key Terms 410

Questions and Problems 410

Chapter 14 Inflation and Deflation 413

14.1 Money and Inflation in the Long Run 414

Velocity and the Quantity Equation 414

Deriving the Inflation Rate 415

The Data 416

The Phillips Curve Again 417

14.2 What Determines Money Growth? 419

Commodity Money 419

CASE STUDY The Free Silver Movement 420

Fiat Money and Inflation 421

The Output–Inflation Trade-off 421

Seigniorage and Very High Inflation 422

CASE STUDY The German Hyperinflation 424

CASE STUDY The Worldwide Decline in Inflation 425

Online Case Study An Update on Worldwide Inflation

14.3 The Costs of Inflation 427

The Inflation Fallacy 427

Very High Inflation 428

CASE STUDY Life in Inflationary Brazil 429

Moderate Inflation 430

CASE STUDY The After-Tax Real Interest Rate 432

14.4 Deflation and the Liquidity Trap 433

Money Growth Again 433

The Liquidity Trap 433

CASE STUDY Japan's Liquidity Trap 437

Summary 438

Key Terms 439

Questions and Problems 439

PART V MONETARY POLICY

Chapter 15 Policies for Economic Stability 443

15.1 Choosing the Long-Run Inflation Rate 444
- The Case for Zero Inflation 444
- The Case for Positive Inflation 445
- Current Practice 446

15.2 Inflation and Output Stability 446
- Inflation Stability 447
- Output Stability 447
- Balancing the Goals 448

CASE STUDY How Costly Is the Business Cycle? 448

15.3 The Taylor Rule 449
- Martin's Metaphor 450
- Taylor's Formula 450
- Applying the Rule 451
- The Rule in Action 451

15.4 The Taylor Rule in the AE/PC Model 452
- An Example 453
- Choosing the Coefficients 453

15.5 Uncertainty and Policy Mistakes 454
- A Mistake About the AE Curve 455
- Mismeasurement of the Output Gap 457

CASE STUDY The Fed and the Great Inflation 460

CASE STUDY The Fed and the Roaring 90s 462
- Coping with Uncertainty 463

15.6 Making Interest-Rate Policy 464
- Monitoring the Economy 465
- Forecasts 466
- Policy Options 467
- The FOMC Meeting 467 — Online Case Study: An FOMC Meeting

15.7 Monetary Policy and Financial Events 468
- Responses to Financial Crises 468
- Responses to Bubbles 470

Summary 471

Key Terms 472

Questions and Problems 472

Chapter 16 Monetary Institutions and Strategies 475

16.1 Time Consistency and Inflation 476

Rational Expectations and the Phillips Curve 476

The Time-Consistency Problem 477

How the Time-Consistency Problem Increases Inflation 478

Solving the Time-Consistency Problem 481

16.2 Central Bank Independence 483

The Independent Federal Reserve 483

Independence Around the World 484

Opposition to Independence 485

The Traditional Case for Independence 486

Independence and Time Consistency 487

Evidence on Independence and Inflation 488

16.3 Monetary Policy Rules 489

Two Approaches to Policy 489

Traditional Arguments for Rules 490

CASE STUDY Nixon and Burns 491

Time Consistency Again 492

Money Targets 492

16.4 Inflation Targets 493

How Inflation Targeting Works 494

The Spread of Inflation Targeting 495

The Case for Inflation Targeting 497

Opposition to Inflation Targeting 499

CASE STUDY Targeters and Nontargeters 500

CASE STUDY The ECB's Two Pillars 501

16.5 Communication by Central Banks 502

Reputation 502

CASE STUDY Alan Blinder 503

Online Case Study An Update on Fed Transparency — Transparency 504

Summary 507

Key Terms 508

Questions and Problems 508

Chapter 17 Monetary Policy and Exchange Rates 511
17.1 Exchange Rates and Stabilization Policy 512
Exchange Rates and Aggregate Expenditure 512
Offsetting Exchange-Rate Shocks 513
CASE STUDY Canadian Monetary Policy 515
17.2 Costs of Exchange-Rate Volatility 516
Exchange Rates and Risk 516
Risk and Economic Integration 517
17.3 Exchange-Rate Policies 517
Interest-Rate Adjustments 518
Foreign-Exchange Interventions 519
CASE STUDY Do Interventions Work? 522
Capital Controls 523
Policy Coordination 525
CASE STUDY The Yuan 526
Online Case Study An Update on Chinese Currency Policy
17.4 Fixed Exchange Rates 528
Mechanics of Fixed Exchange Rates 528
Devaluation and Revaluation 529
Loss of Independent Monetary Policy 529
Controlling Inflation 530
The Instability of Fixed Exchange Rates 531
CASE STUDY George Soros versus the Pound 533
A Brief History of Fixed Exchange Rates 534
17.5 Currency Unions 535
The Euro 535
The Economics of Currency Unions 538
The Politics of Currency Unions 539
More Currency Unions? 540
Summary 540
Key Terms 541
Questions and Problems 541

Chapter 18 Financial Crises 543

18.1 The Mechanics of Financial Crises 544

Events in the Financial System 544

Financial Crises and the Economy 545

CASE STUDY Disaster in the 1930s 547

18.2 Policy Responses to Financial Crises 549

Expansionary Monetary Policy 549

Liquidity Crises and the Lender of Last Resort 550

Bailouts of Insolvent Institutions 551

Online Case Study An Update on the U.S. Financial Crisis and Policymakers' Responses

JUMBO CASE STUDY The Financial System and the Fed, 2007–2008 553

18.3 Financial Crises in Emerging Economies 558

Capital Flight 558

Capital Flight and Financial Crises 559

CASE STUDY Argentina's Crisis, 2001–2002 561

The Role of the IMF 564

Summary 566

Key Terms 566

Questions and Problems 566

Glossary G-1

Index I-1

preface

Perhaps the greatest challenge facing teachers of economics is connecting the theories we present to the real world. Students have a natural interest in the economic events they see in the news and the economic problems they face in their lives, but they often have trouble seeing the relevance of the graphs and equations in economics textbooks.

A course on money, banking, and financial markets is an ideal opportunity for closing this gap. The topics of the course fill today's headlines: the behavior of the stock market, banking crises, Federal Reserve policies, and the causes of recessions, for example. At the same time, a real understanding of these issues requires a foundation in economics, including some of the major theoretical advances of recent decades.

- Problems in securities markets and the banking system stem from asymmetric information between borrowers and lenders. To analyze these problems, students need to understand the fundamental concepts of moral hazard and adverse selection.
- Economic fluctuations and Federal Reserve policy involve the interplay of interest rates, output, and inflation. We can best analyze fluctuations using the framework of modern macro theorists, in which the interest rate is the Fed's policy instrument.
- In the last two decades, central banks around the world have become more independent, their policymaking has become more transparent, and many have adopted inflation targeting. A major motivation for these changes has been academic research on the dynamic consistency problem in monetary policy.

THIS BOOK'S APPROACH

My goal in *Money, Banking, and Financial Markets* is to link great economic ideas to real events and policies in a manner accessible to undergraduates. My approach is based on three related principles:

- *Present core theory simply but rigorously.* I never use a formal model when a commonsense verbal explanation does the job just as well. At the same time, I don't shy away from models when they allow me to present ideas more crisply. One case is the analysis of asymmetric information in Chapter 7. I use precise numerical examples to show

how moral hazard and adverse selection can cause loan markets to break down.

- *Emphasize the relevance of theory to reality.* This book does *not* include a stand-alone segment on "monetary theory." Instead, I seek to integrate theory and applications in every chapter. To this end, the book features 81 case studies. Examples throughout the text also emphasize the connection between economic models and actual events. Like most texts, this one presents graphs and discusses the factors that cause curves to shift. For every curve shift, I have asked myself what historical episode the shift explains. When I don't have an answer, I'm likely to skip the exercise.
- *Strip away unnecessary material.* To better focus on core principles and their application, I have worked to eliminate nonessential coverage. While the book delves into important historical topics, it avoids "standard" but outdated material. I also aim for a lean discussion of the financial system, conveying what's important while avoiding encyclopedic coverage of every type of financial institution and instrument. Focusing on the key material has produced a book of 18 chapters, one that is approximately 100 pages shorter than a standard money and banking text.

CASE STUDIES CLOSE THE GAP BETWEEN THEORY AND REALITY

Multiple case studies in each chapter help students examine the book's topics from a variety of perspectives:

The Viewpoint of Financial Firms When I discuss how banks raise funds, I present a case on Commerce Bank, which has been unusually successful in attracting deposits. A case on Citigroup illustrates the consolidation of financial institutions. The discussion of exchange rates includes a case on the strategies of currency traders.

The Viewpoint of Aggregate Economies Case studies discuss Germany's hyperinflation in the 1920s and Japan's deflation in the 1990s and 2000s. Cases cover financial crises from the Great Depression to the breakdown of Argentina's currency board to the subprime mortgage fiasco. Some cases address current controversies around the world, such as China's exchange-rate policy. Others discuss episodes that students have read about in history books—money and banking in the days of Alexander Hamilton, Andrew Jackson, and William Jennings Bryan.

The Viewpoint of Economic Policymakers Cases discuss issues facing financial regulators, ranging from insider trading to the separation of banking and commerce. (Should Wal-Mart be able to open a bank?) Other cases address controversies about monetary policy. Does inflation targeting improve economic performance? Should central banks try to dampen asset-price bubbles?

The Viewpoint of Individuals Confronting the Financial System Many case studies address questions that are likely to arise in students' lives. How should people allocate their wealth, and how should this allocation change with age? Should you finance a home with a fixed-rate or adjustable-rate mortgage? And most pressing to many students, how is the government's student loan program changing?

Online Case Studies Will Keep the Book Current

The topics discussed in this book are changing rapidly. To keep the material fresh, the text is supplemented by 18 online case studies, one per chapter, that will be updated regularly. One online case reports on the Federal Open Market Committee's actions in recent months. Others discuss areas in which major changes are anticipated, such as investment banking. Still others cover events that were breaking news as the text went to press, such as the government's response to the U.S. financial crisis.

AN OVERVIEW OF THE TEXT

The book's 18 chapters are organized into five parts.

PART I: Foundations

Chapters 1 and 2 outline the basic purposes of the financial and monetary systems. Chapter 1 describes how the financial system channels funds from savers to investors and its role in economic growth. It also introduces the problem of asymmetric information and banks' role in overcoming this problem. Chapter 2 introduces students to money—what it is, why we need it, and how it's changing—and to central banks and their multiple functions.

PART II: Financial Markets

Chapters 3–6 describe markets for stocks, bonds, derivatives, and currencies. Who participates in these markets? What are these players trying to do? What determines asset prices, interest rates, and exchange rates?

These financial markets chapters emphasize important controversies. For example, when asset prices rise, does this reflect news about the assets' fundamental values, or is an irrational bubble occurring? Are there bubbles in U.S. stock and real estate prices? What about 17th century tulip prices?

PART III: Banking

Chapters 7–10 discuss the roles of banks and other financial intermediaries. Chapter 7 explains why banks exist, Chapter 8 describes the structure of the banking industry, Chapter 9 explains how banks seek profits, and Chapter 10 discusses why and how they are regulated.

Part III starts with a detailed treatment of asymmetric information. The concepts of adverse selection and moral hazard are tied to practical topics such as the Enron scandal and the Sarbanes-Oxley Act. The discussion of banking ranges from the growth of subprime lending to banks' increased reliance on fee income to the merging of commercial and investment banking.

PART IV: Money and the Economy

I believe that students need to see how the Fed affects the economy before discussing what the Fed ought to do. Thus, one innovation of this book is to present basic theories of money and economic fluctuations before turning to monetary policy debates. Chapters 11–14 analyze fluctuations—booms and recessions, inflation and deflation.

The centerpiece of Part IV is a short-run model of the economy based on an Aggregate Expenditure (AE) curve and a Phillips curve. In the model, the central bank sets an interest rate-target; the AE curve shows how the interest rate and expenditure shocks determine output; and the Phillips curve shows how output and supply shocks determine the inflation rate. This AE/PC model is a more natural tool for analyzing modern monetary policy than the traditional AD/AS model. The AE/PC model fits better both with academic research and with discussions of economic events in the news media. In Chapter 12, an extended case study uses the model to interpret U.S. economic history from 1960 to the present.

PART V: Monetary Policy

Chapters 15–18 survey central banking and debates about monetary policy and institutions. The discussion starts with theoretical issues, such as the dynamic consistency problem, and then moves to a wide range of practical questions. How does the FOMC decide when to change interest rates? Why did Ben Bernanke advocate inflation targeting when he was a professor, and what will he do about it as Fed chair? What policy mistakes produced the economic instability of the 1970s? Why did European countries abolish their national currencies and create the euro?

Chapter 18, the book's capstone, examines financial and banking crises—how they happen and how policymakers should respond. An extended case study reviews the dramatic events in the United States over 2007–2008. To understand crises, students need to understand financial markets, banks, monetary policy, and the overall economy—all the major subjects of this book. By illuminating the topic of financial crises, Chapter 18 shows students the payoff from a course on money, banking, and financial markets.

ALTERNATE USES OF THIS BOOK

Although this book contains just 18 chapters, there is more than enough material for a money and banking course. Most instructors will want to emphasize some parts of the text and touch more lightly on others. I suggest that any course cover Chapters 1–2, the foundations part of the book, and Chapters 3–4, which present core concepts about interest rates and asset prices. Most instructors will also want to delve into Chapter 7, which discusses why banks exist, and Chapters 11–12, the core material on money and economic fluctuations. I recommend leaving some time for Chapter 18, given the importance of the topic of financial crises.

Otherwise, the best chapters to cover depend on the emphasis of a course. Here are a few examples:

A course emphasizing the financial system: The key material for this course is Chapter 5 on securities markets and Part III (Chapters 7–10) on banking. I also recommend Chapter 13, which shows how the financial system influences economic fluctuations.

A course emphasizing the behavior of the aggregate economy: This course should cover Part IV (Chapters 11–14) on money and the economy and as much as possible of Part V (Chapters 15–18) on monetary policy.

A course emphasizing monetary policy: This course should cover Part V in detail.

A course with an international perspective: The key material is Chapter 6 on foreign-exchange markets and Chapter 17 on international monetary policy. I also recommend two chapters that emphasize cross-country comparisons: Chapter 14 on inflation and Chapter 16 on monetary institutions.

SUPPLEMENTS AND MEDIA ACCOMPANYING THIS BOOK

INSTRUCTOR SUPPLEMENTS

Instructor's Manual with Solutions Manual Prepared by Jane Himarios (University of Texas–Arlington), for each chapter in the textbook the Instructor's Manual provides:

- *Brief Chapter Summary*: summarizing the contents of the chapter.
- *Detailed Section Summaries*: detailed lecture notes including coverage of all case studies and references to online case studies.
- *Inside* and *Outside the Classroom Activities*: problems, exercises, and discussion questions relating to lecture material, designed to enhance student learning.
- *Detailed Solutions*: to all end-of-chapter questions and problems; prepared by Doris Geide-Stevenson (Weber State University).

Printed Test Bank Prepared by Robert (Tino) Sonora (Fort Lewis College), the Test Bank provides questions ranging in levels of difficulty and format to assess students' comprehension, interpretation, analysis, and synthesis skills. Containing roughly 100 questions per chapter, the Test Banks offers a variety of multiple-choice, true/false, and short-answer questions.

Computerized Test Bank The printed test bank will be available in CD-ROM format for both Windows and Macintosh users. With this flexible, test-generating software, instructors can easily create and print tests as well as write and edit questions.

Instructor's Resource CD-ROM Using the Instructor's Resource CD-ROM, instructors can easily build classroom presentations or enhance online courses. This CD-ROM contains all of the text figures and tables (in JPEG and PPT formats), PowerPoint lecture presentations prepared by James Butkiewicz (University of Delaware), and detailed solutions to all end-of-chapter questions in the textbook prepared by Doris Geide-Stevenson (Weber State University).

STUDENT SUPPLEMENTS

Study Guide Prepared by Richard Stahl (Louisiana State University), the Study Guide complements the textbook by providing students additional opportunities to develop and reinforce lessons learned in the money and banking text. For each chapter of the textbook, the Study Guide provides:

- *Brief Chapter Summary*: summarizing the contents of the chapter.
- *Key Terms:* listed and defined, with space for students to write in the definitions in their own words.
- *Detailed Section Summaries with Student Tips and Concept-Related Questions*: including coverage of all case studies, tips to help students with difficult concepts, and 3–5 questions per section to reinforce learning of key concepts.
- *Self-test End-of-Chapter Questions*: 15–20 application-oriented, multiple-choice questions.
- *Worked-out Solutions*: including solutions to all Study Guide review questions.

COMPANION WEB SITE FOR STUDENTS AND INSTRUCTORS:

http://www.worthpublishers.com/ball

The companion site is a virtual study guide for students and an excellent resource for instructors. For each chapter in the textbook, the tools on the site include:

Student Tools:

- *Practice Quizzes*: a set of 20 questions with feedback and page references to the textbook. Student answers are saved in an online database that can be accessed by instructors.
- *Online Case Studies*: one per chapter; resembling the case studies in the text, these case studies will be updated to keep up with current events beyond the publication of the text; prepared by Charles Weise (Gettysburg College).
- *Key Economic Data and Web Links to Relevant Research*: related to chapter content and end-of-chapter questions.

- *SimEcon*: Prepared by Neil Garston and Anne Bresnock (California State University-Pomona), SimEcon provides students with a set of topic-specific modules in which they are expected to put economic course material to work and "learn by doing." The modules allow students to make decisions about different economic variables, view the results of their actions, and improve their decisions based on the results.

Instructor Resources:

Quiz Gradebook: The site gives instructors the ability to track students' interaction with the practice quizzes via an online gradebook. Instructors may choose to have student results e-mailed directly to them.

- *PowerPoint Lecture Presentations*: These customizable PowerPoint slides, prepared by James Butkiewicz (University of Delaware), are designed to assist instructors with lecture preparation and presentation by providing learning objectives, figures, tables, and equations from the textbook, key concepts, and bulleted lecture outlines.
- *Illustration PowerPoint Slides*: A complete set of figures and tables from the textbook in JPEG and PowerPoint formats.
- *Images from the Textbook*: Instructors have access to a complete set of figures and tables from the textbook in high-res and low-res JPEG formats.

eBOOK

Students who purchase the Money & Banking eBook have access to interactive textbooks featuring:

- quick, intuitive navigation
- customizable note-taking
- highlighting
- searchable glossary

With the Money & Banking eBook, instructors can:

- Focus on only the chapters they want. You can assign the entire text or a custom version with only the chapters that correspond to your syllabus. Students see your customized version, with your selected chapters only.
- Annotate any page of the text. Your notes can include text, web links, and even photos and images from the book's media or other sources. Your students can get an eBook annotated just for them, customized for your course.

WEBCT

The Ball WebCT e-pack enables you to create a thorough, interactive, and pedagogically sound online course or course Web site. The e-pack provides you with online materials that facilitate critical thinking and learning, including preprogrammed quizzes and tests. This material is preprogrammed and fully functional in the WebCT environment.

BLACKBOARD

The Ball BlackBoard Course Cartridge allows you to combine BlackBoard's popular tools and easy-to-use interface with the Ball text-specific, rich web content, including preprogrammed quizzes and tests. The result is an interactive, comprehensive online course that allows for effortless implementation, management, and use. The files are organized and prebuilt to work within the BlackBoard software. They can be easily downloaded from the BlackBoard content showcases directly onto your department server.

EconPortal—*AVAILABLE FOR SPRING 2010*

EconPortal is the digital gateway to Ball's *Money, Banking, and Financial Markets*, designed to enrich your course and improve your students' understanding of economics. EconPortal provides a powerful, easy-to-use, completely customizable teaching and learning management system complete with the following:

- *An Interactive eBook with Embedded Learning Resources:* The eBook's functionality will allow for highlighting, note-taking, graph and example enlargements, a full searchable glossary, as well as a full text search. Embedded icons will link students directly to resources available to enhance their understanding of the key concepts.
- *A Fully Integrated Learning Management System:* The EconPortal is meant to be a one-stop shop for all the resources tied to the book. The system will carefully integrate the teaching and learning resources for the book into an easy-to-use system. The EconPortal's Assignment Center will allow instructors to select their preferred policies for scheduling, maximum attempts, time limitations, feedback, and more! A wizard will guide instructors through the creation of assignments. Instructors can assign and track any aspect of their students' EconPortal. The Gradebook will capture students' results and allow for easily exporting reports.

The ready-to-use course can save many hours of preparation time. It is fully customizable and highly interactive.

ACKNOWLEDGMENTS

Scores of people provided invaluable help as I wrote this book, from research assistants and students who commented on draft chapters, to academic colleagues and practitioners in the world of money and banking, to the exceptional team at Worth Publishers. To thank everyone properly in this preface would grossly violate my principle of writing a concise book.

I must, however, single out my development editor, Barbara Brooks, for service beyond the call of duty.

I want to acknowledge the economics teachers who shaped the book by reviewing chapters and participating in focus groups:

Burton Abrams
University of Delaware

Douglas Agbetsiafa
Indiana University at South Bend

Francis Ahking
University of Connecticut at Storrs

Ehsan Ahmed
James Madison University

Jack Aschkenazi
American InterContinental University

Cynthia Bansak
San Diego State University

Clare Battista
California Polytechnic State University

Peter Bondarenko
University of Chicago

Michael Brandl
University of Texas at Austin

James Butkiewicz
University of Delaware

Anne Bynoe
Pace University

Tina Carter
Florida State University

Jin Choi
DePaul University

Peter Crabb
Northwest Nazarene University

Evren Damar
Pacific Lutheran University

Ranjit Dighe
State University of New York at Oswego

Aimee Dimmerman
George Washington University

Ding Du
South Dakota State University

John Duca
Southern Methodist University

Fisheha Eshete
Bowie State University

Robert Eyler
Sonoma State University

Imran Farooqi
University of Iowa

David Flynn
University of North Dakota

Yee-Tien Fu
Stanford University

Doris Geide-Stevenson
Weber State University

Ismail Genc
University of Idaho

David Hammes
University of Hawaii at Hilo

Jane Himarios
University of Texas at Arlington

David Hineline
Miami University

Aaron Jackson
Bentley College

Nancy Jianakoplos
Colorado State University

Frederick Joutz
George Washington University

Bryce Kanago
University of Northern Iowa

John Kane
State University of New York at Oswego

Elizabeth Sawyer Kelly
University of Wisconsin

Kathy Kelly
University of Texas at Arlington

Faik Koray
Louisiana State University

John Krieg
Western Washington University

Kristin Kucsma
Seton Hall University

Mary Lesser
Iona College

David Macpherson
Florida State University

Michael Marlow
California Polytechnic State University

W. Douglas McMillin
Louisiana State University

Perry Mehrling
Barnard College

Jianjun Miao
Boston University

John Neri
University of Maryland

Rebecca Neumann
University of Wisconsin at Milwaukee

Robert Pennington
University of Central Florida

Ronnie Phillips
Colorado State University

Dennis Placone
Clemson University

Ronald Ratti
University of Missouri

Robert Reed
University of Kentucky

Joseph Santos
South Dakota State University

Mark Siegler
California State University at Sacramento

Robert Sonora
Fort Lewis College

Richard Stahl
Louisiana State University

Frank Steindl
Oklahoma State University

James Swofford
University of South Alabama

Behrouz Tabrizi
Saint Francis College

Sven Thommesen
Auburn University

Brian Trinque
University of Texas at Austin

Kristin Van Gaasbeck
California State University at Sacramento

Rubina Vohra
New Jersey City University

John Wade
Eastern Kentucky University

Qingbin Wang
University at Albany

Charles Weise
Gettysburg College

Raymond Wojcikewych
Bradley University

Paul Woodburne
Clarion University

Bill Yang
Georgia Southern University

Most of all, I want to thank my family, whose support made this book possible.

Laurence M. Ball
Baltimore, September 2008

chapter one 1

The Financial System

- 1.1 FINANCIAL MARKETS
- 1.2 ECONOMIC FUNCTIONS OF FINANCIAL MARKETS
- 1.3 ASYMMETRIC INFORMATION
- 1.4 BANKS
- 1.5 THE FINANCIAL SYSTEM AND ECONOMIC GROWTH
- APPENDIX: MEASURING OUTPUT AND THE PRICE LEVEL

The financial system is part of your daily life. You buy things with debit or credit cards, and you visit ATMs to get cash. You may have borrowed money from a bank to buy a car or pay for college. You see headlines about the ups and downs of the stock market, and you or your family may own shares of stock. If you travel abroad, you depend on currency markets to change your dollars into local money at your destination.

The financial system is also an important part of the overall economy. When the system works well, it channels funds to investment projects that make the economy more productive. For example, companies use bank loans to build factories, which produce new goods for consumers and new jobs for workers. The financial system helps the economy to grow and living standards to rise.

At times, however, the financial system malfunctions, damaging the economy. In the United States, the most traumatic example is the Great Depression. In October 1929, the stock market fell by more than 25 percent in one week, wiping out many fortunes. After the stock market crash, people lost confidence in the financial system. They rushed to their banks to withdraw money, and banks ran out of cash. Nearly half of all U.S. banks were forced out of business in the early 1930s.

KIERANTIMBERLAKE ASSOCIATES LLP

The financial system channels funds to investment projects that make the economy more productive. An example is this factory in New Hampshire. It belongs to Bensonwood Homes, which produces "eco-friendly" houses that save energy and other resources. Here a worker at the factory stands atop a master-bathroom module.

These events triggered an economic disaster. The nation's output fell by 30 percent from 1929 to 1933, and the unemployment rate rose to 25 percent. Millions of Americans were impoverished.

This book explores financial systems in the United States and around the world. We discuss the different parts of these systems, such as banks and stock markets, and their economic functions. We discover how a healthy financial system benefits the economy, and why the system sometimes breaks down. We discuss what governments can do to strengthen their countries' financial systems.

This book also discusses money. Money is another part of your daily life: you may have dollar bills in your pocket right now. Like the financial system, money is critical to the health of the economy. Another cause of the 1930s' depression was a sharp fall in the U.S. money supply. Throughout the book we discuss the effects of the money supply and how economic policymakers determine this variable.

Part I of this book lays a foundation for discussing all these topics. Chapter One introduces the financial system, and Chapter Two introduces money. We begin with an overview of the financial system's two main parts, financial markets and banks.

1.1 FINANCIAL MARKETS

In economics, a market consists of people and firms who buy and sell something. The market for shoes includes the firms that manufacture shoes and the consumers who buy them. The market for labor includes workers who sell their time and firms that buy it. **Financial markets** are made up of people and firms that buy and sell two kinds of assets. One kind is currencies of various economies, such as dollars and euros. The second kind, which we'll focus on in this chapter, is securities.

Financial market A collection of people and firms that buy and sell securities or currencies

A **security** is a claim on some future flow of income. Traditionally, this claim was recorded on a piece of paper, but today most securities exist only as records in computer systems. The most familiar kinds of securities, the ones you've probably heard of and those we will discuss the most, are stocks and bonds.

Security Claim on some future flow of income, such as a stock or bond

Bonds

A **bond** is also called a *fixed-income security*. It promises to pay predetermined amounts of money at certain points in the future. For example, you might pay $100 for a bond that pays $6 a year for 10 years, and then pays back the $100. To introduce some terms, the *face value* of this bond is $100, and the *coupon payment* is $6; the bond's *maturity* is 10 years.

Bond (*fixed-income security*) Security that promises predetermined payments at certain points in time. At *maturity*, the bond pays its *face value*. Before that, the owner may receive *coupon payments*.

Corporations issue bonds to finance investment projects, such as new factories. Governments also issue bonds when they need funds to cover budget deficits. When a corporation or government issues bonds, it essentially borrows money from those who buy the bonds. The issuer receives funds immediately and makes future payments in return. Reflecting these facts, bonds are called *debt securities* as well as fixed-income securities.

Almost always, the total payments promised by a bond—the face value plus all coupon payments—exceed the price that a buyer pays for the bond. This means that bonds pay **interest:** the issuer pays buyers for the use of their funds, in addition to repaying the price of the bond.

Interest Payment for the use of borrowed funds

Bonds differ in their maturities, which range from a few months to 30 years or more. Bonds with maturities of less than a year have special names: they are called *commercial paper* when issued by corporations and *Treasury bills* when issued by the U.S. government.

Bonds also differ in the stream of payments they promise. For example, a *zero-coupon bond* yields no payments until it matures. To attract buyers, it sells for less than its face value. For example, you might pay $80 for a zero-coupon bond that pays $100 at maturity.

In our world, promises are not always kept. This includes promised payments on bonds. Sometimes a bond issuer **defaults:** it fails to make coupon payments or pay the face value at maturity. A corporation defaults on its bonds if it declares bankruptcy and goes out of business. A government defaults if it doesn't have enough revenue to make bond payments.

Default Failure to make promised payments on debts

The risk of default varies greatly for different bonds. This risk is small for bonds issued by the U.S. government or by large and successful corporations. Default risk is larger for new corporations with unknown prospects or corporations that are losing money. These companies may go bankrupt and stop making bond payments.

In Chapters Four and Five, we discuss how firms and governments decide what kinds of bonds to issue and how people decide what kinds of bonds to buy. We also discuss how buyers and sellers interact in the bond market, determining the prices of bonds and the interest they pay.

Stocks

A **stock,** or *equity*, is an ownership share in a corporation. As of 2007, General Motors had issued about 600 million shares of stock. If you own 6 million of these shares, you own 1 percent of GM and its factories. You are entitled to 1 percent of the company's future profits.

Stock *(equity)* Ownership share in a corporation

Companies issue stock for the same reason they issue bonds: to raise funds for investment. Like a bond, a share of stock produces a flow of income—but a different kind of flow. A bondholder knows exactly how much the bond will pay (unless the issuer defaults). The earnings from a company's stock are a share of profits, and profits are unpredictable. Consequently, buying stocks is usually riskier than buying bonds. People buy stocks despite the risk because stocks often produce higher returns.

Since stock is an ownership share, stockholders have ultimate control over a corporation. Stockholders elect a corporation's Board of Directors, which oversees the business and hires a president to run it day-to-day. In contrast, bondholders do not have any control over a corporation; a bond is simply a promise of future payments.

Like bond markets, stock markets generate lots of challenging questions. How do firms decide how much stock to issue, how do people decide which stocks to buy, and what determines the prices of stocks? One big issue for both firms and individuals is the choice between stocks and bonds. Which should a firm issue to raise funds? Which should a person buy? We return to these questions in Chapters Three through Five.

1.2 ECONOMIC FUNCTIONS OF FINANCIAL MARKETS

What is the purpose of stock and bond markets? Why do people participate in them, and why are they important for the economy? There are two main answers. First, securities markets channel funds from savers to investors with productive uses for the funds. Second, these markets help people and firms share risks.

Matching Savers and Investors

We can illustrate the first purpose of securities markets with an example. Consider a young man named Britt. Unlike most people, Britt can throw a baseball 95 miles an hour—and he has a good curve ball too. For these reasons, a baseball team pays him $10 million a year to pitch. Britt happens to be a thrifty person, so he does not spend all his salary. Over time, he accumulates a lot of wealth. He asks himself, "What should I do with all my savings?"

Britt's first thought is to accumulate cash and put it in a safe. However, he quickly realizes that this would mean his wealth will not grow. In fact, if there is inflation, the value of his money will fall over time. Can't Britt use his wealth to earn more wealth?

Britt's friends tell him he should use his savings to start a business. However, Britt knows little about the business world, and he doesn't have any ideas for new products that consumers might buy. Anyway, he doesn't have time to start a business: he spends all his free time working on his changeup, the third pitch he needs for a Hall of Fame career.

So must Britt resign himself to putting his money in a safe? Fortunately, no, because of Harriet. Harriet owns a software company, and she is a person of great vision. Harriet realizes that the next big thing in her industry will be software that sends smells over the Internet.

Harriet wants to develop this software, which will let people send perfumes to their sweethearts and rotten-egg smells to their enemies. She knows this product, eSmells, will be highly profitable. Unfortunately, it is expensive to buy the computers and hire the programmers needed for Harriet's project. Her current business does not generate enough profits to finance this investment. Harriet fears that she won't be able to develop her great idea.

You should see the solution to everyone's problems. Harriet should get the funds for her investment from Britt and people like him. She can do so through financial markets. Harriet's company can issue new stock, which people like Britt will buy in the hope of sharing in Harriet's future profits. Harriet can also raise funds by selling bonds; she can use part of her future profits to make the payments promised by the bonds.

This is a win-win outcome. Harriet develops the exciting new software she has dreamed of. Britt earns large returns on the stocks and bonds that he buys. Harriet's workers earn the high wages that a profitable business can afford to pay. People around the world have fun exchanging eSmells.

This simple example captures the primary role of all the trillion-dollar financial markets in the real world. At any point in time, some people earn more than they spend, producing savings. Other people know how to use these savings for investments that earn profits and benefit the economy. When they work well, financial markets transfer funds from the first group of people to the second, allowing productive investments to take place.

A note on terminology: We will use the word **savers** for people like Britt who accumulate wealth by spending less than they earn. We will use the word **investors** for people like Harriet who start or expand businesses by building factories, buying equipment, and hiring workers.

Savers People who accumulate wealth by spending less than they earn

Investors People who expand the productive capacity of businesses

This terminology is common among economists, but the term "investor" is often used differently in common parlance. Britt might say he is "investing" when he buys stocks or bonds from Harriet. But for us, purchasing securities is a form of saving. Harriet does the investing when she buys computers and hires programmers. With this terminology, the primary role of financial markets is to move funds from savers to investors.

Risk Sharing

Financial markets have another important role in the economy: they help people share risks. Because of this role, we would need financial markets even if investors could finance their projects without them.

To see this point, let's change our example of Harriet the software entrepreneur. Suppose that Harriet happens to be wealthy. If she uses most of her wealth, she could finance the expansion of her business without getting funds from anyone else. She would not have to sell stocks or bonds in financial markets. She would retain full ownership of her firm and keep all the profits from eSmells.

But this strategy is probably unwise. The software business, like any industry, is risky. Harriet's new software will probably be profitable, but there is no guarantee. It's possible that another firm will produce a better version of the software, or that consumers will tire of computer gimmicks and go back to reading books.

In these cases, Harriet might not sell much software, and she could lose the funds she invested. Since those funds were a large part of her wealth, she would have to cut back on the lavish lifestyle she enjoys. Putting money in a safe may start to look attractive: it probably means giving up high software profits, but it is less risky.

Fortunately, Harriet does not have to choose between hoarding money or risking everything on her company. Thanks to financial markets, she can fund her new investment, at least in part, by issuing stocks and bonds. This reduces the amount of her own wealth that Harriet must put into the firm. She shares the risk from her business with the buyers of her securities.

Diversification The distribution of wealth among many assets, such as securities issued by different firms and governments

Harriet can use the wealth she doesn't spend on eSmells to buy stocks and bonds issued by other companies. She can also buy bonds issued by the U.S. and other governments. Such behavior is an example of **diversification,** the distribution of wealth among many assets.

Diversification reduces the risk to a person's wealth. Most of the time, some companies do well and others do badly. The software industry might boom while the steel industry loses money, or vice versa, and one software company may succeed while another fails. If a person's wealth is tied to one company, he loses a lot if the company is unsuccessful. If he buys the securities of many companies, bad luck and good luck tend to average out. Diversification lets savers earn healthy returns from securities while minimizing the risk of disaster.

This book discusses some sophisticated ideas about diversification. We discuss recent developments in risk sharing, such as markets for futures and options. At its core, however, the idea of diversification is common sense. The late James Tobin won the Nobel Prize in Economics in 1981 largely for developing theories of asset diversification. When a newspaper reporter asked Tobin to summarize his Nobel-winning ideas, he said simply, "Don't put all your eggs in one basket."

But just because a principle is common sense doesn't mean that people follow it. The following case study offers an example of people who failed to heed James Tobin's advice, with disastrous consequences.

CASE STUDY

Employee Stock Ownership and the Collapse of Enron

Many Americans save for their retirement through "401(k)" plans, named for the Congressional act that created them. A 401(k) plan is a savings fund administered by a company. A worker can put money in the 401(k) plan run by her employer. People have an incentive to save this way because they receive a tax deduction. In addition, some companies match employee contributions to 401(k) plans.

Mutual fund Financial institution that holds a diversified set of securities and sells shares to savers

When a person puts money in a 401(k) plan, she can buy a variety of assets. Usually the choices include shares in **mutual funds.** A mutual fund holds a large number of different stocks and bonds. Buying mutual fund shares is one way to follow Tobin's advice about diversification.

However, many employees make a different choice: they put much of their 401(k) savings in the stock of the company they work for. This is nondiversification. There seem to be several reasons for this behavior. Some employers encourage it, believing that workers are more loyal if they own company stock. Many workers are confident about their companies' prospects, so they view company stock as less risky than other securities. People are influenced by success stories such as Microsoft, where employees grew rich from company stock.

But putting all your eggs in one basket is disastrous if someone drops the basket. A poignant example is Enron, the huge energy company that went bankrupt in 2001. At Enron, 58 percent of all 401(k) funds—and all the savings of some workers—was devoted to Enron stock. During 2001, as an accounting scandal unfolded, Enron's stock price dropped from $85 to 30 cents. This wiped out the retirement savings of many employees. One 59-year-old man saw his 401(k) account fall from $600,000 to $11,000.

The disaster was even worse because Enron laid off most of its employees. Workers lost their life savings at the same time they lost their jobs. Many suffered hardships such as the loss of their homes.

A year after Enron's collapse, a similar disaster occurred at WorldCom: again, employees had put too much of their wealth in company stock and lost it when the company went bankrupt. Since these episodes, financial advisors have urged greater diversification in 401(k) plans, and some people have taken this advice to heart. One study estimates that, averaging over all companies, the percentage of 401(k) funds in company stock fell from 19 percent in 1999 to 11 percent in 2006.

The government has encouraged this trend through the Pension Reform Act of 2006, which limits companies' efforts to promote employee stock ownership. Before the act, some companies contributed their stock to 401(k) plans on the condition that workers hold on to the stock. Now employees must be allowed to sell company stock at any time and put the proceeds in other assets.

Despite these changes, economists worry that far too much 401(k) wealth is still in company stock. At some large companies, such as General Electric, Pfizer, and Proctor and Gamble, the percentage of 401(k) funds in company stock is 60 percent or more—higher than the level at Enron. If these companies get in trouble, their workers will be hurt badly. Companies like General Electric may seem safe—but so did Enron before its collapse.

Some economists think the government should take stronger action to address this problem. They propose a cap on the percentage of 401(k) money that goes to company stock. At this writing, however, no new laws appear imminent.*

* For more on Enron's workers, see "Workers Feel Pain of Layoffs and Added Sting of Betrayal," *New York Times*, January 20, 2002. For recent trends in 401(k) plans, see Sarah Holden and Jack VanDerhei, "401(k) Plan Asset Allocation, Account Balances, and Loan Activity in 2006," Issue Brief #308, Employee Benefit Research Institute, August 2007.

1.3 ASYMMETRIC INFORMATION

When financial markets work well, they channel funds from savers to investors, and they help people reduce risk. But financial markets don't always work well. Sometimes they break down, harming savers, investors, and the economy. The problems of financial markets can be complex, but many have the same basic source: **asymmetric information.** In general, this means that one side of an economic transaction has more information than the other side. In financial markets, the sellers of securities know more than the buyers.

Asymmetric information
The problem that one side of an economic transaction knows more than the other

Two types of asymmetric information exist in financial markets. First, sellers of securities know more than buyers about their own characteristics,

FIGURE 1.1 Asymmetric Information in Financial Markets

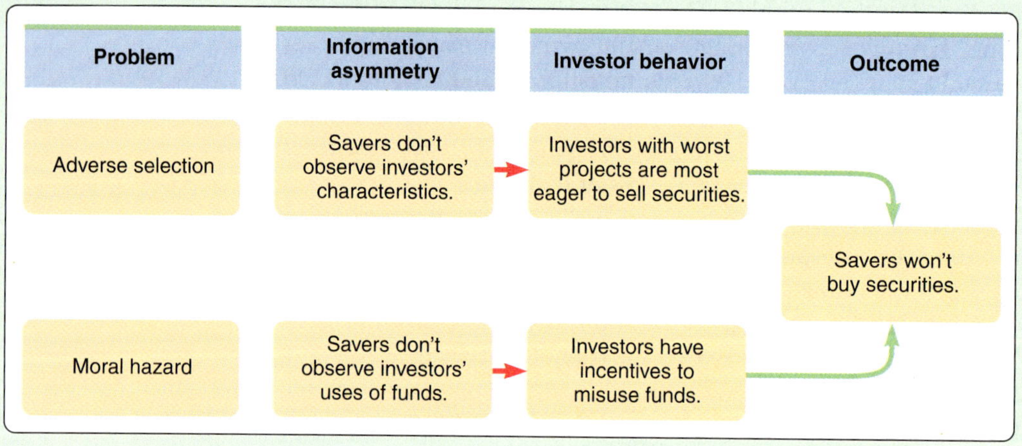

which affect the value of the securities. This asymmetry produces the problem of adverse selection. Second, after investors sell securities, they know more than security holders do about their uses of funds. This produces the problem of moral hazard. These two concepts are outlined in **Figure 1.1.** Let's discuss them in turn.

Adverse Selection

Adverse selection The problem that the people or firms who are most eager to make a transaction are the least desirable to parties on the other side of the transaction

In general, **adverse selection** means that the people or firms who are most eager to make a transaction are the least desirable to parties on the other side of the transaction. In securities markets, firms are most eager to issue stocks and bonds if they are a bad deal for buyers. This is a problem for buyers because they lack information about the real value of the securities.

To illustrate adverse selection, we return to the story of Harriet and Britt. Let's add a third character, Martha. Like Harriet, Martha runs a software firm, and she would like to develop e-smells technology. But Martha is not as gifted as Harriet. There are technical glitches in Martha's plans for the software. Also, Martha is a poor manager. She is disorganized, and her abrasive personality produces high employee turnover. For all these reasons, if Martha invests in e-smells, she is less likely than Harriet to develop a successful product.

Both Martha and Harriet would like to finance investment by selling securities to Britt. If Britt knew that Harriet is more talented than Martha, he would prefer to buy Harriet's securities. Harriet's stock will probably produce higher earnings than Martha's, and Harriet is less likely to go bankrupt and default on her bonds.

But remember: Britt's expertise is baseball, not software or business. He doesn't know Martha or Harriet, and he can't evaluate their talents. The two women have equally glib sales pitches for their products. Britt doesn't know the likelihood that each will succeed, so he doesn't know whose securities are more valuable.

The story gets worse. Martha and Harriet understand their businesses, so they *do* know the value of their securities. They have more information than Britt. This fact produces adverse selection: Martha, the less skilled investor, wants to issue more securities than Harriet. To see this, think about the decision to issue stock. Harriet knows that shares in her company are worth a lot. She wants to sell some stock for diversification but keep a relatively large amount for herself. Martha is more eager to sell stock because she gives up less in future profits.

Britt doesn't understand computers, but he does understand adverse selection. He realizes that somebody is most eager to sell something if it is not worth much. When firms offer securities, Britt worries that most are a bad deal. So he decides after all to put his money in a safe—he won't earn anything, but at least he won't get ripped off. Consequently, neither Harriet nor Martha can finance investment. In Martha's case, this is no great loss. But Harriet's inability to invest harms the many people who would benefit from her project: Harriet, savers such as Britt, Harriet's workers, and consumers.

Moral Hazard

In general, **moral hazard** is the risk that one party to a transaction takes actions that harm another party. In securities markets, investors may take actions that reduce the value of the securities they have issued, harming buyers of the securities. The buyers can't prevent this because they lack information on investors' behavior.

Moral hazard The risk that one party to a transaction takes actions that harm another party

To understand moral hazard, let's once again change the Britt-and-Harriet story. In this version, we ignore adverse selection. Harriet is the only investor—there is no Martha. And everyone, including Britt, knows that Harriet is brilliant. If Harriet can finance her investment, there is no doubt she is capable of producing great software. So far it seems Britt would be smart to buy Harriet's securities.

The problem here involves how Harriet uses Britt's funds. Software is a tough, competitive industry. Harriet has the skills to succeed, but only with hard work. And to earn profits, she must keep her costs low. Unfortunately, as a human being, Harriet faces temptations. She would like to pay high salaries to herself and the friends who work for her. She would love to have some nice Post-Impressionist paintings on her office wall. She thinks it would be fun to have company parties at trendy clubs—and to leave work at 2:00 PM to get the parties started.

If Harriet succumbs to these temptations, her costs rise and productivity falls, and her firm is less profitable. It could even go bankrupt if the partying gets out of hand. If Harriet financed her business with her own wealth, she would have incentives for prudence. The cost of artwork and parties would come out of her own pocket. But these incentives disappear if Harriet's firm is financed by Britt. If Britt buys the firm's stock, then it is he, not Harriet, who loses if profits are low. If Britt buys bonds, it is he who loses if the firm goes bankrupt and defaults.

Once again, Britt is not a business wizard, but he is no fool. He understands human nature and realizes that Harriet might misuse his funds. So he refuses to buy Harriet's securities. Once again, Harriet cannot finance investment, even though she has a great idea for a new product.

Asymmetric information underlies this example of moral hazard. Harriet knows how she runs her business and Britt doesn't. Before buying securities, Britt might make Harriet promise to work hard and spend money wisely. But this promise would be meaningless, because Britt can't tell whether Harriet lives up to it. If Britt could somehow see everything Harriet does, he could demand his savings back the first time she leaves work early. He could cancel her orders at fancy caterers. But Britt is busy at the baseball stadium and doesn't see what happens at Harriet's office.

1.4 BANKS

The story of Britt and Harriet has taken a bad turn. Because of asymmetric information, financial markets have failed to channel funds from savers to investors. But now a hero arrives on the scene: a bank. Britt deposits his money in the bank and earns interest. The bank lends money to Harriet for investment. Ultimately, Britt's savings find their way to Harriet, and both people benefit.

Why can Harriet get money from a bank if she can't get it from financial markets? The answer is that banks reduce the problem of asymmetric information. Let's discuss how, after a little background on banks.

What Is a Bank?

Financial institution (*financial intermediary*) Firm that helps channel funds from savers to investors

Bank Financial institution that accepts deposits and makes private loans

A bank is one kind of **financial institution.** A financial institution, also known as a *financial intermediary*, is any firm that helps channel funds from savers to investors. A mutual fund is another example of a financial institution, as it sells shares to savers and uses the proceeds to purchase securities.

A **bank** is a financial institution defined by two characteristics. First, it raises funds by accepting deposits. These include checking deposits that people and firms use to make payments. They also include savings deposits that earn more interest than checking deposits.

Private loan Loan negotiated between one borrower and one lender

Second, a bank uses its funds to make loans to companies and individuals. These loans are **private loans:** each is negotiated by one lender and one borrower. In this way, they differ from the borrowing that occurs when companies sell bonds to the public at large.

We'll see in this book that modern banks engage in many financial businesses. They trade securities, sell mutual funds and insurance, and much more. Still, what makes them banks are their deposits and loans.

There are several types of banks. For example, *Savings and Loan Associations* are usually small, and much of their lending is to people buying homes. *Commercial banks* can be very large, and they lend for many purposes. We discuss the various types of banks in Chapter Eight.

Another note on terminology: in everyday language, the term "bank" is used more broadly than we have defined it. Some institutions are called banks even though they don't accept deposits or make loans. One example is an *investment bank*, a financial institution that helps companies issue new stocks and bonds. An investment bank is not really a bank in economists' sense of the term.

Banks versus Financial Markets

Banks play the same basic role as financial markets: they channel funds from savers to investors. Funds flow through a bank in a two-step process: savers deposit money in the bank, and then the bank lends to investors. In financial markets, savers provide funds directly to investors by buying their stocks and bonds. For these reasons, channeling funds through banks is called **indirect finance** and channeling through financial markets is **direct finance. Figure 1.2** illustrates these concepts.

Indirect finance Savers deposit money in banks that then lend to investors

Direct finance Savers provide funds to investors by buying securities in financial markets

Why Banks Exist

Indirect finance is costly. The interest that banks charge on loans is higher than the interest they pay on deposits: banks take a cut of the funds they transfer to investors. Nonetheless, people like Britt and Harriet use banks because asymmetric information hinders direct finance. Banks overcome the problem by producing information. They reduce both adverse selection and moral hazard.

Reducing Adverse Selection Banks reduce adverse selection by screening potential borrowers. If both Harriet and Martha want money, Britt can't tell who has a better investment project. But a good banker can figure it out.

When the two investors apply for loans, they must provide information about their business plans, past careers, and finances. Bank loan officers are trained to evaluate this information and decide whose project is likely to

FIGURE 1.2 The Flow of Funds from Savers to Investors

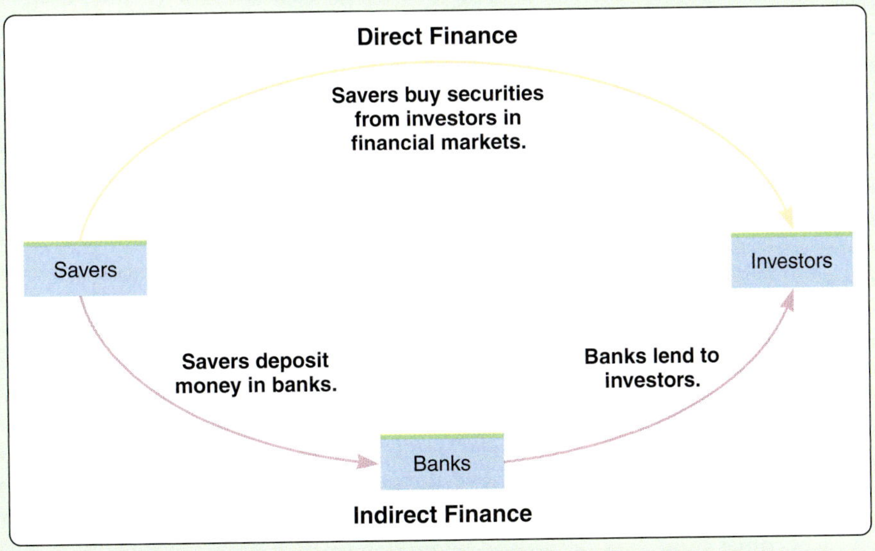

succeed. They care because a firm with a bad project may go bankrupt, and bankrupt firms default on bank loans as well as on bonds.

Loan officers may detect flaws in Martha's plans or see that her past projects have lost money. They turn down Martha and lend money to Harriet, whose application is perfect. Because the bank has gathered information, funds flow to the most productive investment.

Covenant Provision in a loan contract that restricts the borrower's behavior

Reducing Moral Hazard To combat moral hazard, banks include **covenants** in loan contracts. A covenant is an agreement about the borrower's behavior. For example, Harriet's lender might include a covenant requiring that she spend her loan on computers—not parties at trendy clubs.

Banks monitor their borrowers to make sure they obey covenants and don't waste money. Harriet must send her bank periodic reports on her spending. If Harriet misuses her loan—thereby increasing the risk of bankruptcy—the bank demands its money back. With this monitoring, it is safe for the bank to finance Harriet's investment.

Banks help Harriet to expand her business. They also help Britt by providing an outlet for his savings. The interest that Britt earns from his bank is less than Harriet pays for her loan. But it's more than Britt would earn by putting his money in a safe.

Who Needs Banks? In reality, some firms can raise funds by issuing securities; others can't, and depend on bank loans. The asymmetric information problem explains why. If a firm is large and well established, savers know a lot about it. Everyone knows something about General Motors or Microsoft. And it's easy to find out more: an industry of securities analysts studies prominent firms and provides information to savers. This information reduces moral hazard and adverse selection, allowing the firms to issue securities.

Savers know less about newer or smaller firms. Someone who starts a company can't immediately issue securities, because savers can't judge the company's prospects. Your local pizza parlor can't issue securities, even if it has been in business a long time, because few savers know it. Startups and small businesses need banks to finance investment.

Another group that can't issue securities is individual people. Again, the reason is asymmetric information. When I bought a house, I couldn't finance it by issuing bonds. Most savers have heard of Microsoft but know little or nothing about me. Fortunately, individuals like me can borrow from banks. A bank lent me money after gathering information, such as my income and credit history.

1.5 THE FINANCIAL SYSTEM AND ECONOMIC GROWTH

Economic growth Increases in productivity and living standards; growth in real GDP

We have seen how the financial system helps individual savers and investors, such as Britt and Harriet. Financial markets and banks also benefit the economy as a whole. When funds flow to good investment projects, the economy becomes more productive and living standards rise. A strong financial system spurs this **economic growth.**

Saving and Growth

If you have studied macroeconomics, you learned about economic growth. Economists define it as the growth of **real gross domestic product (real GDP),** the measure of an economy's total output of goods and services. If economic growth is 3 percent in 2020, this means that real GDP is 3 percent higher in 2020 than in 2019. If you need more review on GDP, see the Appendix on page 22.

Real gross domestic product (real GDP) The measure of an economy's total output of goods and services

When real GDP rises, an economy produces more goods and services, and the people in the economy can consume more. Therefore, a high level of economic growth causes living standards to rise rapidly.

In your macro class, you probably learned that economic growth depends on saving rates. The more people save, the more funds are available for investment. With high saving, companies can build factories and implement new technologies. They produce more, leading to higher profits and higher wages for workers.

Differences in saving rates help explain why some economies grow faster than others. One famous example is the "East Asian miracle," the rapid growth of countries such as Taiwan, Singapore, and South Korea. In 1960, these countries were among the world's poorest; by the 1990s, their living standards approached those in the most developed countries. A major reason was high saving. In South Korea, for example, saving averaged more than 20 percent of GDP over the period 1960–1995. By contrast, the United States saved 7 percent of its GDP over that period.

The Allocation of Saving

Your macro course was right to stress the benefits of saving. However, it likely ignored the issues discussed in this chapter. Basic macro theories assume that saving flows automatically to investors with productive projects. In fact, the right investors get funds only if the economy has a well-functioning financial system. An economy can save a lot and still remain poor if saving is not channeled to its best uses.

Financial systems vary across countries. Some countries, including the United States, have large stock and bond markets and banks with ample funds. In these countries, it is relatively easy for good investors to raise funds. In other countries, the financial system is underdeveloped. Investors have trouble financing their projects and this retards economic growth.

What explains these differences? We address this question in detail in later chapters. To preview the discussion, one factor is government regulation.

Some governments regulate securities markets to reduce the problem of asymmetric information. In the United States, for example, companies that issue securities must publish annual reports on their investments and earnings. This information makes savers less wary of adverse selection and more willing to buy securities. Some countries lack such regulations.

Government policies also affect banks. In the United States, the government provides insurance for bank deposits, encouraging savers to channel funds through banks. Not all countries have such insurance.

Evidence on Growth

Many economists have studied the effects of financial systems on economic growth. Much of this research has occurred at the World Bank, a large international organization that promotes economic development. The research finds that differences in financial systems help explain why some countries are richer than others.

Figure 1.3 presents a portion of World Bank data drawn from 124 countries between 1996 and 2005. Figure 1.3A shows *stock market capitalization* in several groups of countries. This variable is the value of all stocks issued by corporations, as a percentage of GDP. For example, a figure of 50 percent means the total value of stocks is half a year's output. Stock market capitalization measures investors' success in raising funds through the stock market.

Figure 1.3B shows total bank loans, again as a percentage of GDP. This variable measures banks' success in channeling funds to investors.

The figure divides countries into four groups based on their real GDP per person. The "high-income" group contains a quarter of all countries, those with the highest real GDP per person. "Upper-middle-income" countries are the next quarter, and so on. For each group, the figure shows the average levels of stock market capitalization and bank loans.

Figure 1.3 has a simple message. Richer countries—those with higher real GDP per person—tend to have more developed financial systems than

FIGURE 1.3 Financial Development and Economic Growth, 1996–2005

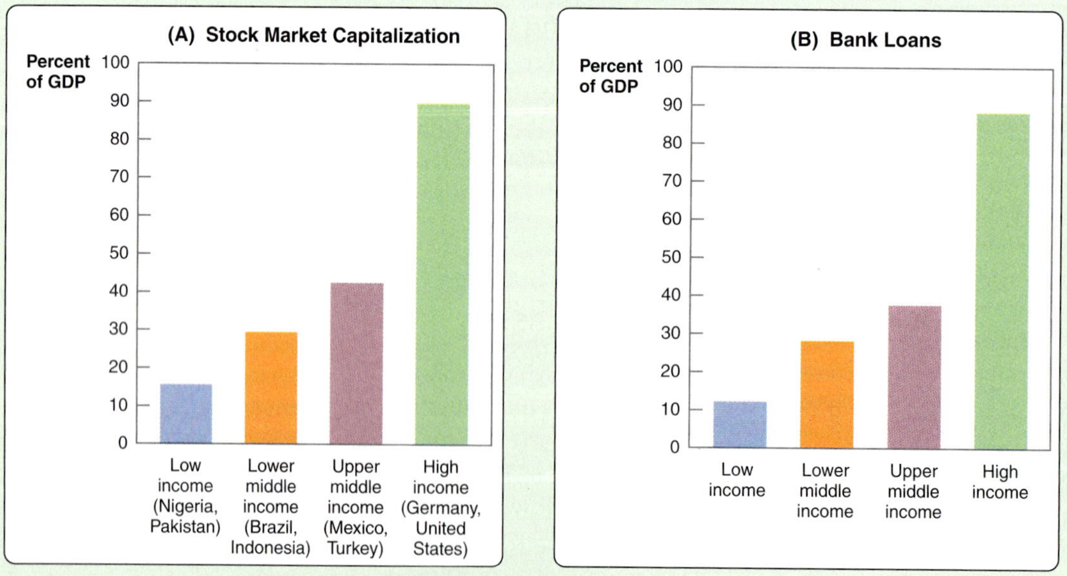

This figure compares financial development in four groups of countries, from the quarter with the lowest real GDP per capita to the quarter with the highest. Examples of countries in each group appear in parentheses in Panel A. Richer countries have higher levels of stock market capitalization and bank loans than poorer countries.

Source: World Bank

poorer countries. Rich countries have larger stock markets and more bank loans. These facts support the view that financial development aids economic growth.

By themselves, these graphs are not conclusive. They show a correlation between financial development and income levels, but correlation does not prove causation. Financial development could cause economic growth, but the opposite is also possible: perhaps countries grow rich for some other reason, such as good educational systems or robust foreign trade, and this growth causes them to develop larger financial systems. Or perhaps some third factor causes both economic growth and financial development.

Much of the World Bank's research addresses the question of causality. One strategy is to compare countries with strong and weak financial systems in some past period, such as the 1960s. Researchers find that countries with stronger systems during the 1960s had faster economic growth in the decades *after* the 1960s. This suggests that financial development comes first and causes growth, rather than vice versa.[1]

Let's examine two cases that illustrate how the financial system affects growth. The first, from U.S. history, discusses an unwise government policy that interfered with the financial system. The second discusses recent efforts to expand the financial systems of poor countries.

CASE STUDY

Unit Banking and Economic Growth

Today, large banks conduct business throughout the United States. You can find branches of Bank of America, for example, in most U.S. cities. This has not always been true. Before World War II, a bank was allowed to operate in only one state. Some states went further and restricted each bank to a single branch. A bank's customers could make deposits or seek loans at only one location. This restriction was called *unit banking*.

Proponents of unit banking believed that multiple branches would allow banks to become too large and powerful. Large banks might drive smaller banks out of business and exploit customers. Unit banking was most common in the Midwest, the home of the Populist political movement of the nineteenth century. Populists were angry at banks for seizing property from farmers who defaulted on loans.

In retrospect, most economists think unit banking was a mistake. It hurt both banks and their customers, for several reasons:

- Large banks benefit from *economies of scale*. They operate more efficiently than small banks. Unit banking increased banks' costs by keeping them small.
- With unit banking, a bank operated in only one town. If the town's economy did poorly, many borrowers defaulted on loans. The bank

[1] Much of this research is summarized in *Finance for Growth: Policy Choices in a Volatile World*, a book published in May 2001 by the World Bank/Oxford University Press.

lost money and might be forced out of business. Having branches in different towns is a form of diversification: it reduces risk.

- Under unit banking, many small towns had only one bank, which operated as a monopoly. Customers had nowhere else to go if the bank charged high interest rates or provided poor service. In states that allowed multiple branches, banks from throughout the state could enter a town and increase competition.

For all these reasons, unit banking reduced the number of banks and their efficiency. The policy impeded the flow of funds from savers to investors. The result was lower economic growth.

The effects of unit banking are analyzed in a 2007 study by two economists, Rajeev Dehejia of Columbia University and Adriana Lleras-Muney of Princeton University. The study compares states with unit banking to states that allowed multiple branches during the period from 1900 to 1940. As you might expect, the volume of bank loans was higher in states that permitted branching, confirming that branching helps move funds from savers to investors. Most important, the study also finds effects on the overall economy, including both the agricultural and manufacturing sectors.

In states with branching, farms were larger in acres, and the value of farm machinery per acre was higher. Apparently the less-constrained banking systems provided more funds for farmers to expand their farms and make them more productive. States with branching had higher employment in manufacturing industries and higher manufacturing wages. Again this suggests that, when allowed branching, banks were better able to channel funds to investors, in this case firms that wanted to build new and more productive factories. The study provides a concrete example of how policies that promote banking can contribute to a prosperous economy.*

*The Dehejia-Lleras-Muney study is "Financial Development and Pathways of Growth: State Branching and Deposit Insurance Laws in the United States from 1900 to 1940," *Journal of Law and Economics*, 2007.

CASE STUDY

Microfinance

Poor countries have severe shortages of jobs that pay decent wages. As a consequence, many people seek to support themselves by starting rudimentary businesses—making furniture or clothes, running small restaurants or shops. In many countries, women are especially likely to start businesses because discrimination limits their other opportunities.

A business requires an initial investment; for example, a furniture maker must buy tools and raw materials. Often the necessary funds are small by Western standards but still exceed the wealth of would-be entrepreneurs. Most banks shy away from lending to the very poor, because they fear high default rates and because the interest payments on tiny loans do not cover the costs of screening and monitoring borrowers. Discrimination can make it especially difficult for women to get loans.

Without bank loans, many people are unable to start businesses that might lift them out of poverty. Others borrow from village money lenders at exorbitant interest rates—sometimes 10–20 percent per *day*.

Microfinance seeks to fill this gap in developing countries' banking systems by providing small loans to poor people. The idea was pioneered by Mohammed Yunus, an economics professor in Bangladesh, who founded the Grameen Bank in the village of Jobra in 1974. Since then, microfinance institutions (MFIs) have sprung up in Africa, Asia, Latin America, Eastern Europe, and even poor areas in the United States.

Microfinance Small loans that allow poor people to start businesses

MFIs are initially funded by governments, international organizations such as the World Bank, and private foundations. Their loans can be as small as $25, but they are large enough to fund simple businesses. Microfinance has grown spectacularly since its beginnings in a single village. As of 2007, a total of 10,000 MFIs had about 100 million borrowers around the world.

MFIs try to overcome the problems that make conventional banks wary of lending to the poor. For example, some MFIs require that people borrow money in groups. The Grameen Bank lends to five would-be entrepreneurs at a time. This practice reduces the bank's costs. In addition, it reduces the problem of moral hazard—the risk that borrowers will squander their loans and default. Credit is cut off to all five borrowers if any one defaults, creating peer pressure to use loans prudently.

Many MFIs lend primarily to women. In part this reflects the institutions' desire to serve a group that faces discrimination elsewhere. But MFIs also cite their self-interest: they report that women default on loans less often than men. Overall, default rates on microloans are low—less than 2 percent at many institutions.

Many people think that microfinance has helped reduce poverty. In 2006, Mohammed Yunus and the Grameen Bank were awarded the Nobel Peace Prize. Yunus is the first economist to win a Nobel Prize in an area other than economics. In explaining its choice, the Nobel committee said that "loans to poor people without any financial security had appeared to be an impossible idea," but "Yunus and Grameen Bank have shown that even the poorest of the poor can work to bring about their own development."

Mohammed Yunus, the founder of Grameen Bank, discusses microfinance during a 2004 visit to Kalampur village in Bangladesh.

AP Photo/Pavel Rahman

The microfinance industry is changing as it grows. Most MFIs are nonprofit organizations supported by donations. In recent years, however, for-profit commercial banks have taken an interest in microfinance. These banks have observed the success of MFIs, especially the low default rates on their loans, and decided that microfinance can be profitable. Commercial banks have started making microloans in countries such as India, Colombia, and Senegal. Elsewhere, commercial banks support microfinance indirectly by lending money to MFIs.

Many supporters of microfinance welcome the involvement of commercial banks, as it increases the availability of microloans. Some worry, however, that the "commercialization" of microfinance will lead to loan decisions based on profitability rather than the needs of borrowers.

Online Case Study: An Update on Microfinance

Markets versus Central Planning

Another way to grasp the importance of the financial system is to ask what happens if an economy lacks one entirely. Imagine a country with an economy run by the government. No private firms exist; everybody works for the government, which decides what goods and services to produce and who receives them. The government also decides what investment projects are worthwhile and orders that they be undertaken. No one raises funds for investment through financial markets or private banks.

Centrally planned economy *(command economy)* System in which the government decides what goods and services are produced, who receives them, and what investment projects are undertaken

This is not a fanciful idea, but rather a basic description of a **centrally planned economy,** also known as a *command economy*. This was the economic system under Communist governments in the Soviet Union and Eastern Europe, which held power until the early 1990s. Centrally planned economies still exist in fairly pure form in Cuba and North Korea.

If you have studied microeconomics, you learned that its central idea is the desirability of allocating resources through free markets. Market prices provide signals about what firms should produce and consumers should buy, guiding the economy to efficiency. Microeconomists take a dim view of central planning because a modern economy is too complicated for government officials to run without the help of markets.

These basic principles about free markets apply to the financial system. In upcoming chapters, you will learn how prices in financial markets, such as stock prices and interest rates, help channel funds to the most productive investments. This process does not work perfectly, but it beats the alternative of central planning. History shows that government officials do a poor job of choosing investment projects. To illustrate this point, the next case examines history's most famous example of central planning.

CASE STUDY

Investment in the Soviet Union

In 1917, a Communist revolution led by V. I. Lenin overthrew Czar Nicholas II of Russia. Lenin established the Soviet Union, which eventually grew to include Russia and 14 other "republics," from Ukraine in the West to Uzbekistan in Central Asia. The economy of the Soviet Union was centrally planned.

Initially, the Soviet economy was mainly agricultural, and most of its people were poor. After Lenin's death in 1924, Josef Stalin took control of the government and began a push to "industrialize." Stalin and the leaders who succeeded him hoped to achieve rapid economic growth through investment in factories and modern technologies. Because Soviet planners controlled the economy's resources, they could dictate high levels of investment. From the 1930s to the 1980s, investment as a percentage of GDP was more than twice as high in the Soviet Union as in the United States and Western Europe.

At first, high investment did produce rapid economic growth. In the 1950s and 1960s, Soviet planners predicted—and Western leaders feared—that the Soviet Union would become the world's most productive economy. But growth slowed in the 1970s and 1980s. Despite high investment, the Soviet Union fell further and further behind the West. Partly because of economic disappointment, the Soviet Union broke apart in the early 1990s. Russia and the other former republics shifted to economic systems based on free markets.

What went wrong with the Soviet Union? In retrospect, an important factor was a misallocation of investment. Soviet planners chose projects poorly, so high investment did not lead to high output. Economic historians point to a number of mistakes:

- Planners put too many resources into prestige sectors of the economy that symbolized economic development. These sectors were mainly in heavy industry. The Soviets built too many factories to produce steel and too few to produce consumer goods. They invested in an unsuccessful effort to develop large airplanes. Starting in the 1950s, they spent heavily on their space program, which boosted national pride but strained the economy.
- Soviet planners overemphasized *short-run* increases in productivity. They were too hasty in trying to reach Western output levels. In 1931, Stalin said, "We are fifty or a hundred years behind the advanced countries. We must make good the distance in ten years. Either we do it or they will crush us." This attitude caused planners to neglect investments that were important for the long term. For example, they skimped on maintenance of roads and other infrastructure. This had little immediate effect, but over time the crumbling infrastructure became a drag on productivity.
- A related problem was that factory managers were evaluated based on annual production quotas. Managers focused on meeting current quotas rather than increasing long-run productivity. For example, they were reluctant to retool factories to use new technologies because this might disrupt production temporarily.
- The power of government bureaucrats reduced efficiency. Plant managers were rewarded for following orders, not for thinking of innovative ways to raise output. In addition, managers competed for investment

funds by lobbying the government. Those who were well connected or talented at lobbying received more resources than they needed, while other managers received too few.*

* For more on Soviet investment, see Gur Ofer, "Soviet Economic Growth, 1928–1985," *Journal of Economic Literature*, 1987. This article was published shortly before the breakup of the Soviet Union.

Summary

- The financial system has two central parts, financial markets and banks.

1.1 Financial Markets

- Financial markets are markets for currencies and for securities, such as stocks and bonds.
- A bond is a fixed-income security: it promises predetermined payments at certain times. Corporations and governments issue many types of bonds with different maturities and default risk.
- A stock or equity is an ownership share in a corporation. A stockholder receives a share of the corporation's earnings.

1.2 Economic Functions of Financial Markets

- The primary function of financial markets is to channel funds from savers to investors with productive uses for those funds.
- Financial markets also help people diversify their asset holdings. This reduces risk. People who don't diversify, such as many Enron employees, can suffer disaster.

1.3 Asymmetric Information

- Financial markets can malfunction because of asymmetric information: sellers of securities know more than buyers.
- Adverse selection arises from asymmetric information about investors' characteristics. Investors with low chances for success are the most eager to sell securities.
- Moral hazard arises from asymmetric information about investors' actions. Investors have incentives to misuse the funds they receive from savers.

1.4 Banks

- A financial institution is a firm that helps channel funds from savers to investors.
- A bank is one kind of financial institution. Banks raise funds by accepting deposits and use the funds for private loans.
- Banks gather information about borrowers, reducing the problems of adverse selection and moral hazard. As a result, people and firms that can't issue securities can get bank loans.

1.5 The Financial System and Economic Growth

- Saving can spur economic growth—but only if the financial system channels savings into productive investment.
- Differences in financial systems help explain why some countries are richer than others. Richer countries tend to have higher stock market capitalization and more bank loans.
- Poorly conceived government policies can harm the financial system, reducing economic growth. An example from U.S. history is unit banking. Programs that expand the financial system, such as microfinance, can spur growth and alleviate poverty.
- Central planning is a poor system for allocating investment funds, as illustrated by the history of the Soviet Union.

Key Terms

adverse selection, p. 8
aggregate price level, p. 23
asymmetric information, p. 7
bank, p. 10
bond, p. 2
centrally planned economy, p. 18
covenant, p. 12
default, p. 3
direct finance, p. 11
diversification, p. 6
economic growth, p. 12
financial institution, p. 10
financial market, p. 2
indirect finance, p. 11
inflation rate, p. 23
interest, p. 3
investors, p. 5
microfinance, p. 17
moral hazard, p. 9
mutual fund, p. 6
nominal GDP, p. 23
private loan, p. 10
real gross domestic product (real GDP), p. 13
savers, p. 5
security, p. 2
stock, p. 3

Questions and Problems

1. When financial markets channel funds from savers to investors, who benefits? Explain.
2. Suppose an owner of a corporation needs $1 million to finance a new investment. If his total wealth is $1.2 million, would it be better to use his own funds for the investment or to issue stock in the corporation? What if the owner's wealth is $1 billion?
3. Suppose you were required to put all your retirement savings in the securities of one company. What company would you choose, and why? Would you choose the company you work for? Would you buy stock or bonds?
4. Suppose there are two investors. One has a project to build a factory; the other has a project to visit a casino and gamble on roulette. Which investor has a greater incentive to issue bonds? Which investor's bonds are a better deal for savers?
5. Suppose a company raises funds by issuing short-term bonds (commercial paper). It uses the funds to make private loans. Such a firm is called a *finance company*. Is a finance company a type of bank?
6. Firms such as Moody's and Standard & Poor's study corporations that issue bonds. They publish "ratings" for the bonds—evaluations of the likelihood of default. Suppose these rating companies went out of business. What effect would this have on the bond market? What effect would it have on banks?
7. National credit bureaus collect information on people's credit history. They are likely to know whether you ever defaulted on a loan. Suppose that a new privacy law makes it illegal for credit bureaus to collect this information. What effect would this have on the banking industry?

8. When a bank makes a loan, it sometimes requires borrowers to maintain a checking account at the bank until the loan is paid off. What is the purpose of this requirement?

9. Microfinance institutions argue that (a) many traditional banks discriminate against women in lending and (b) women have lower default rates than men on loans from MFIs. Discuss how point (a) could explain point (b).

Online and Data Questions

www.worthpublishers.com/ball

10. The text Web site contains World Bank data on financial development. Using these data, compare bank loans as a percentage of GDP in two groups of countries: those in East Asia (8 countries) and those in sub-Saharan Africa (16 countries). For each group, compute the average of the bank-loan variable for three time periods: 1976–1985, 1986–1995, and 1996–2005.
    a. Which of the two regions has a higher level of bank loans? How has the level of loans changed over time in each region?
    b. What might explain the differences between East Asia and Africa that you found in part (a)? How do you think these differences have affected the economies of the two regions?

11. In the World Bank data, examine bank loans as a percentage of GDP in the United States, Germany, and Japan. Is the level of bank loans relatively high or low in the United States? What might explain this fact? (*Hint*: See the data on stock market capitalization in the three countries.)

12. Link through the text Web site to the site of Planet Rating, a French organization that calls itself "the global microfinance rating agency." (Click on "English" unless you are a French major.) What is the main function of Planet Rating? How might its work help the microfinance industry to grow?

A Small Research Project

13. Do you know someone (such as a parent) who is working and saving for retirement? Does he or she have money in a 401(k) plan? What securities does the person hold through the plan? Does he or she follow the principle of diversification?

APPENDIX: MEASURING OUTPUT AND THE PRICE LEVEL

This appendix reviews the basic macroeconomic concept of real GDP. To define this term, we must first define nominal GDP and the aggregate price level.

Nominal GDP is the total value of all final goods and services produced in an economy in a given period. For example, in the United States, nominal GDP was $14 trillion in 2007. If we add up all the $20,000 cars produced in 2007, all the $5 hamburgers, $15 haircuts, and so on, the total is $14 trillion.

Nominal GDP The total value of all final goods and services produced in an economy in a given period

The **aggregate price level** is an average of the prices of all goods and services. It is a weighted average: some prices have a bigger influence than others. The weights are based on the amount of spending on each item. For example, car prices have a large weight because consumers spend a lot on cars. Toothpick prices have a small weight because relatively little is spent on toothpicks.

Aggregate price level An average of the prices of all goods and services

There are several different measures of the price level. The best known are the *consumer price index* (CPI) and the *GDP deflator*. These variables differ in subtle ways, such as the methods for choosing weights. The details are not important for our purposes: we will simply interpret the aggregate price level as an average of all prices.

The **inflation rate** is one of the best known economic variables. It is the percentage change in the aggregate price level over a period of time, typically a year. As measured by the GDP deflator, for example, the inflation rate over 2007 was 2.6 percent. This means the price level was 2.6 percent higher at the end of 2007 than at the beginning.

Inflation rate Percentage change in the aggregate price level over a period of time

We can now define real GDP as nominal GDP divided by the aggregate price level:

$$\text{real GDP} = \frac{\text{nominal GDP}}{\text{aggregate price level}}$$

As we discuss in Section 1.5, economists use real GDP to measure an economy's output of goods and services. Economic growth is the growth of real GDP.

Why is real GDP defined this way? This variable is a measure of output that is not distorted by inflation. Suppose the prices of all goods and services double but there is no change in what the economy produces. Nominal GDP doubles because everything is worth twice as much in dollars. The aggregate price level also doubles. In the formula for real GDP, both the numerator and the denominator double, so real GDP does not change. The constancy of real GDP captures the fact that output has not changed.

chapter two 2

Money and Central Banks

- 2.1 WHAT IS MONEY?
- 2.2 TYPES OF MONEY
- 2.3 MONEY TODAY
- 2.4 LIQUIDITY AND BROAD MONEY
- 2.5 FUNCTIONS OF CENTRAL BANKS
- 2.6 THE REST OF THIS BOOK

Mark Gertler is an economics professor at New York University. While he is well respected in academic circles, he usually receives little attention in the mass media. Yet on the afternoon of October 24, 2005, Gertler received phone calls from NBC, CBS, ABC, CNN, and more than 50 print journalists, all seeking interviews. What was the occasion?

On that day, President Bush had appointed Ben Bernanke, formerly an economics professor at Princeton University, as Chair of the Federal Reserve System. Everyone was eager to learn about Bernanke's beliefs and character, but the Bush administration had asked him not to speak to the media. So reporters sought out anyone who knew him. Gertler was a leading target because he had coauthored a number of research papers with Bernanke and briefly shared a house with him.

Reporters were not the only people who reacted quickly to Bernanke's appointment. At the New York Stock Exchange, traders responded by bidding up stock prices. When the president made his announcement, the Dow Jones Index of stock prices was at 10,216. Within a few minutes, traders pushed the Dow to 10,333, a rise of more than 1 percent. The value of stocks in U.S. corporations jumped by billions of dollars.

Doug Mills/The New York Times/Redux

October 24, 2005: Ben Bernanke enters the Oval Office at the White House for the announcement of his appointment as Chair of the Federal Reserve System. Bernanke is followed by Alan Greenspan, who was retiring after 18 years as Fed Chair.

Federal Reserve System (the Fed) Central bank of the United States

Central bank Institution that controls an economy's money supply

Why was Ben Bernanke's appointment such big news? Why did it cause stock prices to jump? The short answer is that the **Federal Reserve System,** or **Fed,** is the central bank of the United States. A **central bank** controls an economy's money supply, which has strong effects on the financial system and the economy. Thus Bernanke and other Fed officials have great economic power. Their decisions help determine the economy's levels of output, unemployment, and inflation.

What is the money supply? How does it affect the economy? How do central banks control it? These questions are major topics in this book, and this chapter introduces them. Our main focus here is the concept of money—what it is, how it's measured, how people use it, and its economic functions.

2.1 WHAT IS MONEY?

"Money" is a word that economists use differently from most people. In everyday speech, "money" is often used as a synonym for income or wealth. Someone might remark that "neurosurgeons make a lot of money," meaning their annual incomes are high. Or you might hear that "Bill Gates has a lot of money" because his wealth—the total value of his assets—is $30 billion. Gates's wealth includes assets such as Microsoft stock, other securities, and real estate.

Money Class of assets that serves as an economy's medium of exchange

For economists, by contrast, **money** is a narrow class of assets with special properties. Money serves the economy as the medium of exchange, the unit of account, and a store of value.

The Medium of Exchange

Medium of exchange Whatever people use to purchase goods and services

While money serves several functions, it is defined by its primary role: people use it as the **medium of exchange.** That is, people use money to purchase goods and services. Money is whatever a grocery store or movie theater accepts as payment.

In today's economy, dollar bills are one form of money. The balances in people's checking accounts are also money, because many goods and services can be bought by writing a check or debiting an account electronically. Stocks and bonds are *not* money because you can't walk into a store and trade them for groceries.

People with wealth must choose what assets to hold—how to divide their wealth among stocks and bonds, real estate, money, and other assets. People with substantial wealth usually hold only a small fraction of it in money. The reason is that money yields a poor return compared to other assets, such as bonds. A dollar bill pays no interest. Some checking accounts pay interest, but the interest rates are lower than those on bonds.

Nonetheless, everybody holds *some* wealth in the form of money because of its unique role as the medium of exchange. Rich people keep most of their wealth in securities and real estate, but they keep enough in cash and checking accounts to buy groceries, pay for haircuts, and otherwise purchase the goods and services they desire.

The amount of wealth that people choose to hold in money is called **money demand.** In Chapter Four we discuss the factors that determine money demand, such as interest rates on other assets. For now, the crucial point is that people benefit greatly from holding some money. To see why, let's discuss how an economy would operate if money didn't exist.

Money demand Amount of wealth that people choose to hold in the form of money

Money versus Barter

In any economy, people produce goods and services and trade them for other goods and services. In the absence of money, this trade occurs through **barter,** which means that one good or service is traded directly for another. Barter was the means of trade in early societies. Often it took place in a village market. A dairy farmer might bring milk to the market and trade it to a weaver for cloth or to a potter for a bowl.

Barter System of exchange in which goods and services are traded directly, with no money involved

Barter is cumbersome. For it to work, individuals must experience a **double coincidence of wants.** This means I have something that you want *and* you have something I want. If a dairy farmer wants a piece of cloth, it is not enough to find a weaver; he must find a weaver who is thirsty for milk. If the weavers he encounters are looking for other things, the farmer cannot make the trade he desires.

Double coincidence of wants Condition needed for barter: each party to a transaction must have something the other wants

Probably a dairy farmer in a simple village will eventually find a thirsty weaver. The farmer can trade for what he wants because many people need milk. The double-coincidence problem is more severe in highly developed economies. These economies have large numbers of goods and services, many of which are consumed by small parts of the population. Economic specialization makes barter more difficult.

To see this point, consider Tom the music teacher. Tom produces a specialized service: viola lessons. One day Tom notices his hair is getting long and decides to get a haircut. Let's suppose Tom lives in an economy without money and therefore must acquire his haircut through barter. He must offer the barber a deal: "If you give me a haircut, I'll teach you the viola part in Mozart's Quartet Number 1 in G major."

You may see the problem. Some people, including some barbers, don't want music lessons. Even if they do, their instrument may be the clarinet, not the viola. Tom's proposal is likely to be turned down by many barbers. Tom might spend the whole day traveling around town before he finds a hair-cutting viola student.

Tom's life is easier if his economy has money. Tom can give lessons to anyone who wants to learn the viola. His students may not know how to cut hair, but that doesn't matter. They pay Tom with money, and Tom uses the money to buy a haircut. Even if the barber hates stringed instruments, he knows he can spend Tom's money on things he does like. Trade no longer requires a double coincidence of wants: the people Tom teaches and the people who give him haircuts need not be the same.

CASE STUDY

Nineteenth-Century Visitors to Barter Economies

Probably no one has really tried to trade a viola lesson for a haircut. However, William Stanley Jevons—the nineteenth-century economist who coined the "double coincidence" term—recorded some true stories about the inconveniences of barter. These stories involve Europeans who were accustomed to using money but visited Pacific islands in which barter was the means of exchange.

One of Jevons's anecdotes concerns Mademoiselle Zelie, a well-known French singer on a world tour. In the Society Islands, near Tahiti, she agreed to give a concert in return for one-third of the receipts from tickets. Jevons reports, "When counted, her share was found to consist of three pigs, twenty-three turkeys, forty-four chickens, five thousand cocoa nuts, besides considerable quantities of bananas, lemons, and oranges." These were the commodities exchanged for concert tickets under the local barter system.

In Parisian markets, these livestock and fruits could have sold for around 4000 francs—a good payment for a concert. However, nobody in the Society Islands had money to buy the goods. Mlle. Zelie had no means of shipping her possessions to France, and she did not have time during her visit to eat much of the pork, poultry, or fruit. She had to leave them behind and therefore gained little from her singing. (Before leaving, she fed the fruit to the pigs and chickens.)

Jevons also tells of a Mr. Wallace, who traveled in the Malay Archipelago. People there did not use money, so Mr. Wallace had to barter for his dinner each night. Unfortunately, sometimes the people with food did not desire any of Mr. Wallace's possessions: there was no double coincidence of wants. To reduce the risk of going hungry, Mr. Wallace began traveling with a collection of goods, such as knives, cloth, and liquor, that he hoped would appeal to the local people. This made his suitcase heavier, but it raised the odds that he could make a trade.

Fortunately, in the twenty-first century, money is used almost everywhere. Thanks to money, touring singers can be paid, and travelers can buy dinner wherever they go.*

* Jevons tells the stories of Mlle. Zelie and Mr. Wallace in his book *Money and the Medium of Exchange*, D. Appleton and Company, 1875.

The Unit of Account

Unit of account Measure in which prices and salaries are quoted

In addition to serving as the medium of exchange, money has another, related role in the economy. Money is the **unit of account.** This means that prices, salaries, and levels of wealth are measured in money. Dollar bills are money in the United States and so prices are quoted in dollars.

To see why this measurement function is important, think again of an economy without money. In this world, prices would have to be set in units of goods or services. Different prices might be set in different units, making it hard to compare them.

For example, suppose you live in this economy and you need a new washing machine. You want to buy it as inexpensively as possible. You see that one store sells a machine for 500 loaves of bread. Another store sells the same model for 30 pairs of men's loafers. It would be hard to figure out which deal is better—you would have to know the prices of bread and shoes. To make matters worse, you might find that bread prices are quoted in apples and shoe prices in oranges. You literally would have to compare apples and oranges!

Once again, money makes life easier. If dollars are the unit of account, you will see that one store charges $500 for the washing machine and the other charges $400. You know immediately that the second price is lower. You can shop wisely for a washer without researching the prices of other goods.

A Store of Value

Traditionally, economists have cited a third function of money, besides its roles as the medium of exchange and unit of account. Money is a **store of value**—a form in which people can hold wealth.

Store of value Form in which wealth can be held

To understand this function, think again about a dairy farmer. If his farm is unusually productive one year, he may want to set something aside for the next year, when times could be harder. However, the farmer can't save the extra milk he produces—it will spoil, making it worthless. Milk is not a good store of value. The solution is to sell the milk for money. If the farmer keeps the money in a safe place, he will have it next year when he needs it.

Money's store-of-value function has become less important in developed economies. We have already discussed why: the financial system has produced assets with higher returns than money. In most economies today, holding money is better than holding milk, but holding bonds is better still, because bonds pay more interest. People with financial savvy use money as a medium of exchange, but they hold most of their wealth in other assets.

Exceptions occur, mainly in poor countries. In some places the financial system functions so poorly that few assets are more attractive than money. People hold much of their wealth in cash. But there is a twist: most of this cash is foreign currency—U.S. dollars or euros—rather than the local money. This currency switch results from inflation, as we discuss later in this chapter.

2.2 TYPES OF MONEY

Money is defined by what it does, not by what it is. Money is whatever people use as the medium of exchange. Today, certain greenish pieces of paper are money because people use them to buy goods and services. But money could be anything else that people use to buy things.

Over human history, many objects have served as money—everything from seashells to whiskey to animal skins. (That is why we still call our dollars "bucks," for buckskins.) Regardless, all kinds of money fall into two broad categories, commodity money and fiat money.

Commodity Money

Commodity money Valuable good that serves as the medium of exchange

Commodity money is a valuable good that also becomes the medium of exchange. To see how this works, think again of a village of farmers and artisans. Even in this village, barter is cumbersome. A dairy farmer who wants a shirt must find a thirsty weaver, and a shoemaker who wants chicken must find a barefoot poultry farmer.

So the village adopts a better system. When someone trades her product, she does not insist on receiving what she wants at the moment. Instead, everyone provides goods and services in return for a particular commodity—grain, for example. People accept grain even if they don't need it because they know others will accept it. The shirtless dairy farmer trades milk for grain and then uses the grain to acquire a shirt.

In this system, grain becomes the medium of exchange, just as dollar bills are a medium of exchange today. In addition, people start setting prices in grain—a shirt might cost two bushels. So grain becomes the unit of account. A commodity has taken on the key functions of money.

This example is not fanciful. Grain really was used as money in ancient Egypt. Another agricultural product—tobacco—served as money in the British colonies of Maryland and Virginia.

While many goods have been used as money, the most common commodity moneys are gold and silver. These metals are used for purposes such as jewelry making. They are also good choices for money because they are durable—they don't fall apart or go sour. In addition, precious metals have high value relative to weight. Pieces of gold or silver can purchase a lot of goods and services, while still being light enough to carry.

Coins At first, the precious metals used as money were unmarked lumps of various sizes. Coins appeared in China around 1000 BCE and in Greece around 700 BCE. Governments produced metal coins with standard weights and purities. This made it easier to buy and sell things, as people exchanging coins didn't have to weigh them or examine them carefully.

Coins had markings stamped on them for identification. For example, the city-state of Athens issued silver coins with the goddess Athena on the front and an owl on back. Alexander the Great, who had a large ego, put pictures of himself on his empire's coins. This started the tradition of money with pictures of political leaders.

Gold and silver coins circulated throughout the world until the middle of the twentieth century. But today, they have been replaced by other kinds of money.

Origins of Paper Money Paper money appeared around the year 1000 in China and between 1500 and 1700 in Europe. Originally, it was a version of commodity money, because it was backed by commodities. A piece of paper money was essentially an ownership certificate for a certain amount of gold or silver—or, in Maryland and Virginia, a certain amount of tobacco.

People carried paper money because it was more convenient than coins. In Europe, paper money was issued first by private banks and later by governments. Anyone who held money could turn it in to the issuer and demand the commodity that the money represented. This backing limited the amount of paper money that banks or governments could create.

One hundred years ago in the United States, money was backed by gold. Paper money looked fairly similar to the currency of today, but the phrase "Gold Certificate" was printed on each bill. This meant that the money could be exchanged for gold coins. A $20 bill, for example, could be traded for 20 gold dollar coins, each weighing 0.0484 ounces.

In an economy with commodity money, people may trade goods or services for something they do not wish to use. They accept gold or gold certificates even if they have no interest in making jewelry. However, the money they accept has value for someone. Today, we use a different kind of money.

Fiat Money

Money is no longer backed by gold. In the United States, the "Gold Certificate" label on paper money has been replaced by "Federal Reserve Note." What does that mean?

It means that today's currency is **fiat money**—money with no intrinsic value. Fiat money cannot be made into jewelry, baked into bread, or otherwise put to use. And fiat money is *not* backed by any commodity. No government or bank has promised to exchange anything for your $20 bills. These bills are money "by fiat," which means the government has simply declared them money. "Gold Certificate" means that money can be traded for gold, but "Federal Reserve Note" doesn't really mean anything. This phrase is just a label for a worthless piece of paper.

Fiat money Money with no intrinsic value

ANA Money Museum

The $20 bill on the top, a Gold Certificate from 1928, is commodity money; the $20 bill on the bottom, a Federal Reserve Note from 2006, is fiat money. The two bills have similar appearances but differ in their fine print. Look carefully at the Gold Certificate, and you may be able to make out a complete sentence. It begins in the top line with "This certifies that there have been deposited in the Treasury of" and continues in the banner, "The United States of America," then picks up at the bottom of the bill, "twenty dollars" and below that, "in gold coin payable to the bearer on demand." The Federal Reserve Note features the phrase "twenty dollars," but it doesn't mention anything payable to the bearer.

From one point of view, it might seem odd that people trade goods and services for fiat money. Take your textbook author, for example. I work hard all day on writing and teaching and endure long meetings of faculty committees. And what do I get in return? Nothing I can eat or wear or play with. All my university gives me is a bunch of worthless pieces of paper. Why do I bother to work?

The answer, of course, is that I can trade my worthless pieces of paper for things I value. The grocer will give me bread for my worthless paper because he knows that others will accept the paper from him. With commodity money, people accept a commodity they might not want because everybody else accepts it. With fiat money, people accept paper that is worthless to *everyone* because everybody else does. Thanks to this behavior, dollar bills serve their purpose as a medium of exchange.

From Commodity Money to Fiat Money

Fiat money evolved out of the original paper money, which was backed by commodities. Governments realized that people were happy to use paper money and rarely demanded the commodities behind it. So they started cheating, in a sense. They promised to redeem money for commodities, but they issued more money than they had commodities to back up. This was possible as long as people didn't try to trade in all the money at once.

Once people became accustomed to paper money, governments took the next step and stopped promising to redeem the money for commodities. Thus paper money became fiat money. The pioneers in this area were countries that needed to pay for wars, such as Britain during the Napoleonic Wars. Because money was not backed by anything, governments could print as much as they needed.[1]

In the United States, the nature of money has evolved through twists and turns. The dollar has sometimes been commodity money, sometimes fiat money, and sometimes in between, as we discuss in the next case study.

CASE STUDY

The History of the U.S. Dollar

Before the American Revolution, each colony issued its own money. The first national currency was created by the Continental Congress in 1776, shortly after it declared independence from Britain. This money was the Continental dollar.

The Continental Dollar The new currency was fiat money. Like other governments, Congress printed large amounts to pay for the Revolutionary War.

Congress worried that people would think the dollar worthless, as it was not backed by anything. To encourage acceptance of the money, a congressional resolution appealed to patriotism:

[1] For more on the development of money, see Glyn Davies, *A History of Money from Ancient Times to the Present Day,* University of Wales Press, 1994.

> *Any person who shall hereafter be so lost to all virtue and regard for his country as to refuse Bills or obstruct and discourage their currency or circulation shall be deemed published and treated as an enemy of the country. . . .*

This appeal didn't work for long. As we discuss in Chapter Fourteen, when governments print money rapidly, inflation is the inevitable outcome. During the Revolution, prices rose so much that Continental dollars became almost worthless.

Money in the New Republic Alexander Hamilton became the first secretary of the Treasury in 1789. He earned his current spot on the $10 bill through wise economic policies. Hamilton wanted American money to have a stable value, so he created dollar coins. A dollar was either 0.056 ounces of gold or 0.84 ounces of silver. The government allowed people to trade in 100 Continental dollars for one of the new dollar coins, which was generous to the holders of Continentals.

Paper money also developed, but unevenly. At times the government established a national bank, a precursor to the modern Federal Reserve. The First Bank of the United States operated from 1791 to 1810, and the Second Bank from 1816 to 1836. One function of the banks was to issue "national bank notes," which were paper money backed by gold and silver coins.

▶ Section 8.2 discusses the politics that led to the opening and closing of the First and Second Banks of the United States.

Private banks also issued notes. These banks, like the national banks, promised to redeem the notes for coins. However, private banks sometimes went out of business, reneging on their promises. Because of this risk, people refused notes issued by some banks and accepted others for less than their face value.

This system ended with the Civil War in the 1860s. Once again, war prompted the government to issue large amounts of fiat money. This currency was called "Greenbacks," because it was the first American money of that color. As usual, rapid creation of money caused high inflation.

The Classical Gold Standard In 1879, the government reestablished commodity money. It set the value of a dollar at 0.0484 ounces of gold. To say the same thing a different way, the government declared that an ounce of gold was worth $1/(0.0484) = 20.67$ dollars. The primary type of money was gold certificates like the one pictured on page 31.

During this period, the government did not control the amount of money in the economy. It passively issued gold certificates to anyone who turned in gold and gave back gold to anyone who turned in the certificates. This system lasted until 1913, when the Federal Reserve System was established.

To the Present Today, dollars are fiat money—there is no link to gold. The tight link under the gold standard was relaxed in several steps, beginning in 1913 when Congress instructed the Fed to create an "elastic currency." The Fed was required to hold gold reserves equal to at least 40 percent of the money it created. However, as long as it obeyed this constraint, the Fed could expand or contract the money supply as it chose. The gold standard was still in effect in the sense that people could trade dollars for gold, or vice versa.

The next big step occurred during the Great Depression of the 1930s. In 1933, President Franklin Roosevelt temporarily broke the link between the dollar and gold. It was reestablished in 1934 but with major changes. The value of a dollar was reduced from 0.0484 ounces of gold to 0.0286 ounces, allowing more dollars to be printed.

▶ Before 1971, governments traded dollars for gold as part of the world system for fixing exchange rates between currencies. We discuss this system in Chapter Seventeen.

Most important, Americans could no longer exchange money for the gold that theoretically backed it. Only foreign governments had the right to trade dollars for gold. Indeed, it became illegal for private citizens to own gold, except small amounts for uses such as jewelry making. All other gold had to be sold to the government. This restriction lasted until 1974.

In 1945, the Fed's required gold reserves were reduced from 40 percent of the money it issued to 25 percent. In 1965, the minimum was abolished entirely. The final step came in 1971, when President Nixon eliminated the right of foreign governments to trade dollars for gold. Since then, gold and dollars have had no connection to one other.

Alternatives to a National Currency

In most countries, a central bank issues fiat money, which serves the economy as a medium of exchange, unit of account, and store of value. Exceptions of several kinds exist, however.

Dollarization In some countries, the national currency is replaced by foreign currency. Most often this currency is the U.S. dollar, so this phenomenon is called **dollarization.**

Dollarization Use of foreign currency (often U.S. dollars) as money

Dollarization sometimes arises informally, without any action by the government. People and businesses decide to use dollars rather than the local money. Usually the reason is high inflation, which makes local currency lose value rapidly. Informal dollarization was common in Latin America in the 1980s and in former Soviet republics in the 1990s. Inflation rates in these countries often exceeded 100 percent per year or even 1000 percent.

One aspect of dollarization is that people in other nations use U.S. currency as a store of value. More than half of U.S. currency is held abroad, mostly in $100 bills. In addition, banks in some countries offer accounts in which people can deposit dollars rather than local money. The value of these deposits is not affected by local inflation.

Sometimes the dollar replaces the local currency as the unit of account, and prices are quoted in dollars. In the 1980s, for example, many stores in Argentina set prices in dollars rather than Argentine pesos. Dollar prices were easier to understand, because the value of the peso was changing rapidly during those inflationary times. Sometimes, people paid for things with pesos—dollar prices were converted to pesos using the current exchange rate. Other times, people paid with dollars, meaning that dollars became the medium of exchange as well as the unit of account.

More recently, some countries have "officially" dollarized. This means the government steps in and completely abolishes the local currency. Dollars become the only money throughout the country. Ecuador's government dollarized in 2000, and El Salvador's in 2001. Officials acted out of frustration with high inflation. Unable to stabilize their currencies, they got rid of them.

Currency Boards Another variation on money is created when a government establishes a **currency board,** an institution that issues money backed by a foreign currency. If the foreign currency is U.S. dollars, for example, then people can trade their money for dollars at a fixed rate. The currency board must hold enough dollars to buy back all the money it has created.

Currency board Institution that issues money backed by a foreign currency

Economies with currency boards include Bulgaria, where each Bulgarian lev can be traded for 0.515 euros, and Hong Kong, where each Hong Kong dollar can be traded for 0.115 U.S. dollars. (Hong Kong has maintained this arrangement despite its political integration into China.) Argentina established a currency board in 1991, but it broke down amid a financial crisis in 2001.

Like dollarization, currency boards are usually prompted by high inflation. Inflation erodes the value of a country's money. A currency board seeks to preserve this value by tying the money to a stable currency.

A currency board is the closest thing to commodity money in the world today. A currency board issues money that is exchangeable for something of value. The twist is that this something is not a commodity, but a well-respected fiat money issued by another country.

Currency Unions Sometimes a group of countries forms a **currency union.** They agree to abolish their national monies and create a single currency for the group. They also create a central bank to issue the common currency. Note that this differs from dollarization, when one country unilaterally adopts the money of another.

Currency union Group of countries with a common currency

Currency unions exist in several parts of the world, including West Africa and the Carribean. The best known is in Europe. In 1999, 11 European countries abolished their national currencies, including the French franc and German mark, and created a new currency, the euro. In 2008, Europe's currency union had 15 members, and it is likely to grow further as Eastern European countries join. Euros are issued by the European Central Bank (ECB) in Frankfurt, Germany.

Why a currency union? Briefly, the hope is to increase trade and other economic links within the union. It is easier to travel and do business if everyone uses the same currency. In the case of the euro, a single currency is also a symbol of political unity. Chapter Seventeen has more about the pros and cons of currency unions.

We have seen the great diversity in money. The next case study, based on a personal experience, offers an odd twist on dollarization, one that helps us understand the nature of fiat money.

Online Case Study: Alternative Currencies in the United States

CASE STUDY

Clean and Dirty Money

We have discussed the puzzle of fiat money: people provide goods and services in return for worthless pieces of paper. The resolution of this puzzle is that people accept fiat money because everybody else accepts it.

Economic theorists have pointed out that such a system might break down. If everybody else *refuses* to accept money, then you will too: you won't work for green pieces of paper if the grocer won't take them from you, and the grocer won't take them if people won't accept them from her. A common belief that nobody will accept money implies that nobody does accept it, just as a belief in acceptance produces acceptance.

The idea of people refusing money may seem far-fetched, but it has actually happened. In 1996, I visited Uzbekistan, a country in central Asia, to help teach an economics course for young government officials. At the time, Uzbekistan suffered from high rates of inflation, and this led to substantial dollarization. For example, the stipends for students in the course were paid in U.S. dollars, and people used dollars for major purchases.

However, an odd custom developed. Uzbeks would accept U.S. currency for goods and services only if it was clean and unwrinkled. A $100 bill that looked worn out or smudged could not be used to buy things. I was surprised by this behavior. Often people refuse to buy goods if they are in poor condition; you wouldn't buy shoes if the soles were worn out. But we usually think that money is money, even if it is wrinkled. Why did people in Uzbekistan turn down certain bills?

The answer is that each person turned down worn bills because everybody else did. Once the custom of refusing certain bills somehow got started, it was self-perpetuating. This is a real example of how the acceptance of fiat money can break down if people expect it to break down.

A student in our course had a $100 bill in his pocket, along with a pen. The pen broke, producing a large ink spot next to the picture of Benjamin Franklin. This flaw meant that people were unlikely to accept the bill. The student was crestfallen—it was as if his $100 had disappeared—$100 is a lot of money, especially in a poor country like Uzbekistan.

But there is a happy ending. I had a clean, new $100 bill in my wallet, and I knew that nobody in the U.S. cares about inkspots on money. So I traded my $100 bill for the student's $100 bill, which I took home and spent. This made the student happy and cost me nothing. (I thought about offering only $90 for the imperfect $100 bill, but I managed to resist this greedy impulse.)

2.3 MONEY TODAY

Money supply Total amount of money in the economy

Let's now leave Uzbekistan and focus on money in the United States today. We introduce how the Federal Reserve measures the **money supply,** which is the total amount of money in the economy. We also discuss the ways that people use money to purchase goods and services. The ways that money is spent are evolving rapidly.

Measuring the Money Supply: M1

Monetary aggregate Measure of the money supply (M1 or M2)

M1 The Federal Reserve's primary measure of the money supply; the sum of currency held by the nonbank public, checking deposits, and traveler's checks

Each month the Federal Reserve reports data on the **monetary aggregates,** which are measures of the money supply. The Fed reports on two different aggregates, called M1 and M2. **M1** is the Fed's primary measure of the money supply and the measure we use most often in this book.

The idea behind M1 is that money is the medium of exchange—it's what people use to purchase goods and services. Today, people purchase things mainly with two assets: currency and the deposits in their checking accounts. So these two assets are the major components of M1. Currency is included in M1 only if it is held by the nonbank public. Currency sitting in banks' vaults or ATMs isn't part of the money supply.

M1 also includes a third component, traveler's checks. These are dying out because travelers can get cash from ATM networks worldwide, but the Fed still keeps track of them.

To summarize,

$$\text{M1} = \text{currency} + \text{checking deposits} + \text{traveler's checks}$$

In March 2008, total currency held by the nonbank public was about \$762 billion. Deposits in checking accounts were \$604 billion, and traveler's checks were \$6 billion. Adding these three numbers, M1 totaled \$1372 billion.

▶ A small detail: as measured by the Fed, the traveler's-check component of M1 includes only traveler's checks issued by institutions other than banks. Traveler's checks issued by banks are included in checking deposits. Don't ask me why.

\$1372 billion is about 10 percent of U.S. GDP. This may sound like a lot, but the level of M1 is small compared to other assets. By comparison, the total value of the stock of U.S. companies is over 100 percent of GDP. As we've discussed, people hold relatively little of their wealth in money because it yields low returns. Nonetheless, we will see that changes in the money supply have big effects on the economy, because of money's role as the medium of exchange.

How We Spend Money

There is only one way to spend currency—hand it over at the register. But there are several ways to spend the money in checking accounts. The traditional way is to write a paper check—that's how checking accounts got their name. As you probably know from experience, though, people can also spend checking deposits electronically. Funds are taken from your checking account when you swipe a debit card at a store. You can also transfer funds over the Internet, commonly to pay monthly bills such as utilities. Many firms make electronic payments, such as direct deposits of paychecks.

As technology develops, electronic payments are becoming more common. In the United States, the volume of payments by paper check peaked in the mid-1990s and has declined since then. **Figure 2.1** presents data on payment methods from a survey that the Federal Reserve conducts every 3 years. The number of payments by check was 42 billion in 2000 and 31 billion in 2006. Over the same period, electronic payments rose from 15 billion to 41 billion. Economists debate whether check usage will level off in the future or checks will eventually disappear.

Is this trend important for the economy? Yes and no. It is important in reducing costs for banks. It costs close to a dollar to send a paper check through the banking system; processing electronic payments is much cheaper. Electronic payments are one of the many ways computers have made the economy more efficient.

On the other hand, these innovations don't really change the nature of money. M1 is still defined as currency and checking deposits, regardless of

FIGURE 2.1 The Shift to Electronic Payments

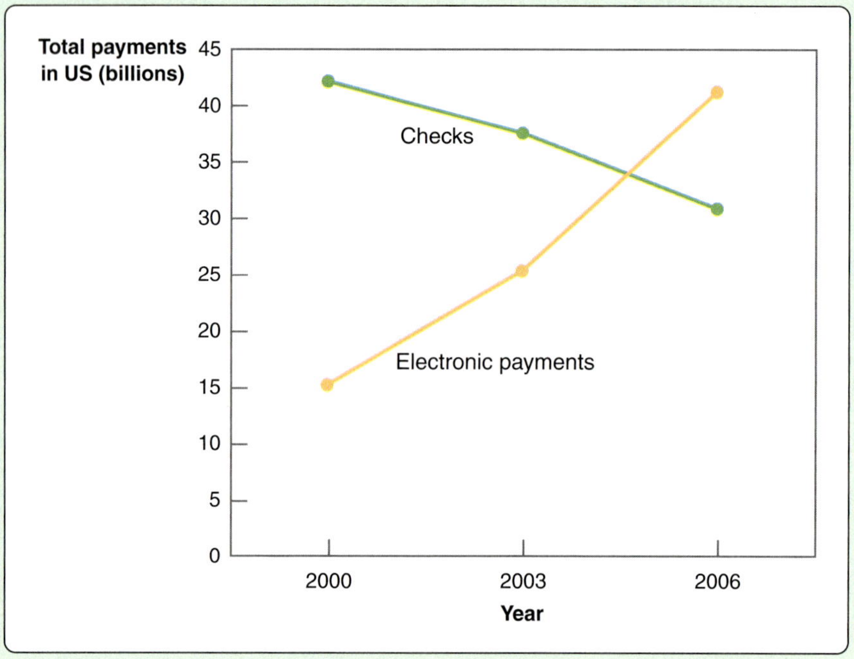

In 2000, payments by paper check were almost three times as common in the United States as electronic payments. By 2006, electronic payments exceeded checks. Electronic payments are made with debit cards or over the Internet. They do not include purchases with credit cards, which are not final payments.

Source: 2007 Federal Reserve Payments Study

how the deposits are spent. And changes in payment methods have little effect on the principles we will discuss governing what determines the money supply and how it affects the economy.

What About Credit Cards?

At this point, you may think we have left something out. When you make purchases, you don't use just cash and checking accounts. Probably you also use credit cards. A credit card looks similar to a debit card, but it works differently. Nothing is taken directly from your checking account; instead, you receive a credit card bill each month.

Even though people buy things with credit cards, economists ignore them in measuring the money supply. The rationale is that you don't really pay for something when you use a credit card. Instead, you buy the item on credit, that is, by borrowing. You pay for your purchase later, when you pay your credit card bill. And you use the funds in your checking account to pay this bill, either by writing a check or by electronic transfer. Your checking account is the ultimate way you pay for your purchase, just as when you write a check at the store.

The Payments System

We've discussed how people pay for goods and services. Now let's discuss how sellers of goods and services receive payment. This might sound like the same topic, but it's not. Suppose you give your landlady a rent check, for example. From your point of view, you've paid money. But your check is not money for the landlady: she can't trade it for groceries. Somehow the check must be transformed into money that the landlady can spend.

This happens through the **payments system.** A purchase sets off a series of transactions that ends with the seller receiving money. The details depend on the initial method of payment. Let's start with paper checks.

Payments system Arrangements through which money reaches the sellers of goods and services

Check Clearing Suppose your rent is $500. You give your landlady, Julia, a check for that amount, and she deposits it in *her* checking account. Then different things can happen. The story is simplest if you and Julia happen to have accounts at the same bank. When the bank receives the check, it reduces your balance by $500 and adds that amount to Julia's balance. Julia has received $500 that she can spend.

Now suppose that you and Julia have accounts at different banks. For Julia to receive payment, your check must travel from her bank, where she deposits it, to yours. This trip usually includes a stop at another institution—one where both your bank and Julia's have accounts. This could be a third private bank, but most often it is a branch of the Federal Reserve. All banks hold accounts at the Fed and use them for processing checks.

Figure 2.2 shows what happens. You give your check to Julia (step 1) and she deposits it in her bank account (step 2). Then Julia's bank deposits the check in *its* account at the Federal Reserve (step 3). The Fed adds $500

FIGURE 2.2 The Travels of Your Rent Check

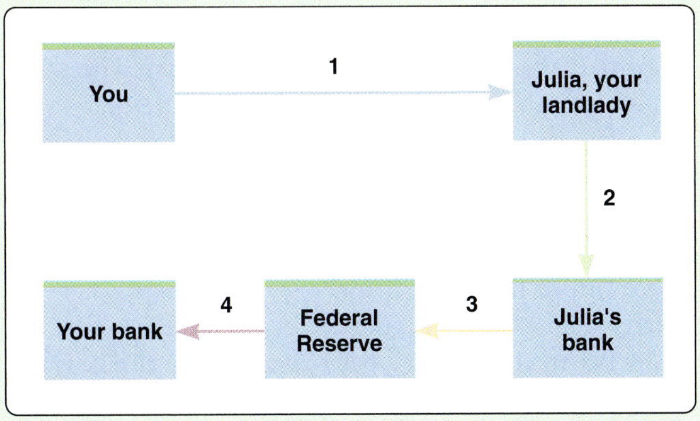

If you and Julia, your landlady, have different banks, paying your rent triggers a series of transactions. You give your rent check to Julia (step 1), and she deposits it in her bank (step 2). Julia's bank deposits the check in *its* account at the Federal Reserve (step 3), and the Fed debits your bank's account. Finally, the Fed sends the check to your bank (step 4), and your bank debits your account.

to this account and deducts \$500 from your bank's account. The Fed also sends the check to your bank (step 4). When your bank receives the check, it deducts \$500 from your account.

When Julia deposits your check (step 2), her account balance does not rise immediately. Her bank waits until it knows that the check is good—that you have at least \$500 in your account. Julia's bank learns this at the end of the process, after the check reaches your bank and your account is debited (step 4). At that point, Julia's checking account balance rises by \$500. Julia has finally received money that she can spend.

The Shift to Check Imaging Traditionally, paper checks traveled through the payments system by truck and airplane. This was a legal requirement in many states: to debit your account for a check you wrote, your bank had to receive the original check. Transportation accounted for much of the cost of check processing.

All this changed under a 2004 federal law called Check21, which allows digital imaging of checks. Now a merchant who receives a paper check can scan it and send it to his bank electronically. Or, if he sends in the paper check, the bank can convert it to an image at that point. The check image travels between the computers of banks and the Federal Reserve; no airplanes are needed.

Many, but not all, banks have adopted the technology for check imaging. At present, your landlady's bank might create an image of your check at step 2 in Figure 2.2, but if your bank can't receive the image, the Federal Reserve will have to convert it back to paper at step 4. It is likely, however, that imaging will eventually spread to all banks. The cost savings might slow the decline of checks as a means of payment.

Processing Electronic Payments Electronic deposits and withdrawals also trigger a series of transactions among banks and the Federal Reserve. These occur through networks that link computers at the different institutions.

Suppose you swipe your debit card at the grocery store. The machine that reads your card first checks with your bank to ensure that you have sufficient funds for your purchase. For merchants, this is an advantage over paper checks, which they have to take on faith.

If funds are available, your bank debits your account by the amount of your purchase. Your bank also sends a message to the Fed asking that funds be transferred from its Fed account to that of the grocer's bank. (The same transfer would occur if the Fed were processing a check from you to the grocer.) When the grocer's bank receives the funds, it credits the grocer.

New Kinds of Money

As technology evolves, so does money. Two new ways of purchasing goods and services, stored-value cards and e-money, are less common than electronic transfers from checking accounts. However, they are potentially more important, in the sense that they may change what counts as money in the definition of M1.

Stored-Value Cards A **stored-value card** looks like a debit or credit card. The difference is that it is "prepaid." For example, you might pay $100 in cash and receive a card with that balance. When you buy things with the card, the balance is reduced. Some cards can be "reloaded"—you make additional payments to increase the balance.

Stored-value card Card issued with a prepaid balance that can be used for purchases

Many stored-value cards can be used for only one purpose. Common examples include calling cards issued by telephone companies, "gift cards" issued by stores, and fare cards issued by transit systems.

Multipurpose stored-value cards are issued by banks. Since 1999, many of these cards have been associated with the Visa and MasterCard networks. They can be used for purchases anywhere that accepts these credit cards. Stored-value cards can be bought at many locations, such as convenience stores and Western Union offices; in some places, machines dispense them.

Banks charge fees for stored-value cards. Their customers include people without checking accounts and parents who buy the cards to budget their teenagers' spending. (Stored-value cards are sometimes called "teen cards.") Cards can be replaced if lost, an advantage over cash.

In the United States, the use of stored-value cards is low compared to debit and credit cards but appears to be rising. (We don't know how fast because there isn't much data.) Stored-value cards are popular in Asia—except they are not always cards. In countries such as Japan, you can load money on your cell phone and buy things by waving the phone over a reader, as shown in the accompanying photo. It's not yet clear whether this technology will catch on in the United States.

We can think of stored-value cards as electronic versions of traveler's checks. Traveler's checks are also prepaid, usable for purchases, and replaceable if lost. Recall that traveler's checks are included in the M1 measure of the money supply. By the same logic, M1 should include the balances on stored-value cards—or at least multipurpose cards. These balances are media of exchange.

Currently, the Federal Reserve ignores stored-value cards when it measures money. It doesn't matter much today, as card balances are small compared to total M1. However, this could change.

A new way to buy things.

AP Photo/Itsuo Inouye

e-money Funds in an electronic account used for Internet purchases

▶In 2006, Google introduced a new process for online purchases, Google Checkout. Although it's often compared to PayPal, Google Checkout does *not* involve e-money. Rather, it is a system for storing credit card information and making it easier to buy with credit cards.

Liquidity Ease of trading an asset for money

Electronic Money **E-money** is yet another variation on the medium of exchange. Currently, the main issuer of e-money is PayPal, a subsidiary of eBay. You can establish a PayPal account and deposit money electronically either by transferring it from a bank account or by charging a credit card. To purchase goods, you transfer funds from your PayPal account to the account of the online merchant.

As with stored-value cards, there is an argument for adding e-money to M1, but this has not happened so far. Some economists doubt that e-money will become a major means of payment. It is not essential for Internet commerce, as people can use credit and debit cards online. As of 2007, PayPal was used for only 10 percent of online purchases.

2.4 LIQUIDITY AND BROAD MONEY

Now that we've introduced money, we can define another of this book's key concepts: **liquidity.** An asset is liquid if it can be traded for money easily and inexpensively.

The Need for Liquidity

To see why liquidity is important, recall our friend Britt, the star pitcher, whom you met in Chapter One. Britt has considerable wealth, and he must decide how to divide it among various assets. Britt would be unwise to keep a large part in money because, as we discussed earlier, other assets yield higher returns. Britt decides to hold only the minimal amount of money he needs to purchase goods and services.

But Britt has a problem: he doesn't know how much money he will need. He has a monthly budget, but he doesn't always follow it. Sometimes Britt sees a new electronic toy that he must have and spends an extra $200. Once his car's transmission failed, producing an unexpected expense of $1000. And there's always the risk of an emergency, such as a medical problem, that would cost much more.

So Britt faces a dilemma. If he holds enough money for any possible spending, much of his wealth will be diverted from higher-earning assets. On the other hand, if he holds too little money, he may run out if he has large bills to pay.

Liquid assets are the solution to Britt's dilemma. Many liquid assets produce higher returns than money. These assets can't be spent, but if necessary, they can be traded quickly for assets that *can* be spent. If Britt holds a substantial level of liquid assets, he can earn good returns on his wealth and still be ready for unexpected expenses.

Degrees of Liquidity

The liquidity of assets varies widely. **Figure 2.3** illustrates this point by comparing several types of assets.

By definition, the most liquid assets are money that people can spend directly, including currency and checking deposits. Some other kinds of bank deposits, such as savings deposits, are almost as liquid. You can't spend

FIGURE 2.3 Degrees of Liquidity

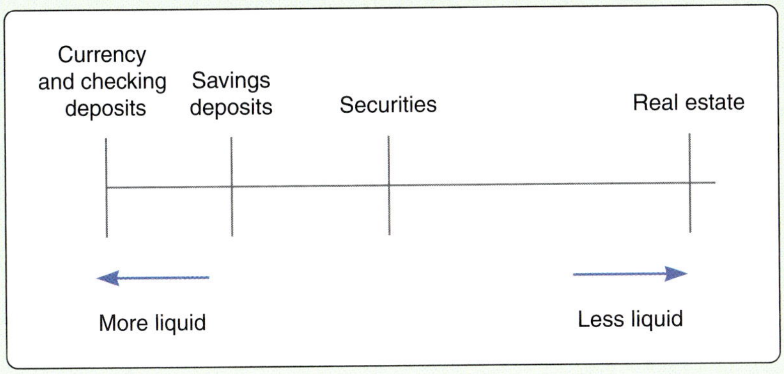

the balance in a savings account, but it takes just a few minutes at an ATM to withdraw these funds or transfer them to a checking account. Thus savings deposits can easily be turned into money. For this reason, savings deposits are sometimes called *near money*.

Securities are less liquid than savings deposits. If you own a stock or bond, you can't trade it for cash at an ATM. To sell the security, you must call a broker or contact one online. You must pay a fee, and you may not get your money until the next day.

▶We discuss how securities are traded in Chapter Five.

Still, securities are more liquid than many assets. Real estate, for example, is illiquid. A house can be traded for money, but the process is time-consuming and expensive. The seller must hire a real estate agent, show the house to prospective buyers, and negotiate a price. It can take months to make a deal. If a house must be sold quickly, the seller may have to accept less than the house is really worth.

Sometimes a trade-off exists between the returns on assets and their liquidity. For example, checking deposits earn less interest than savings deposits, or even no interest, but they are more liquid. Savings deposits earn less interest than bonds. Given this trade-off, many people hold a mixture of assets with different degrees of liquidity.

Britt, for example, keeps money in a checking account for routine spending, such as trips to the grocery store. He also maintains a savings account. If he wants to make a special purchase, he transfers funds from savings to checking—this is not hard, but it would be a nuisance to do it every time he visits a store.

Britt keeps most of his wealth in securities. He usually doesn't touch these assets, but he can sell some in an emergency—or when he buys a new Hummer. It is worth paying occasional broker's fees to earn the high potential returns on securities.

Measuring Broad Money: M2

We previously discussed one of the Federal Reserve's measures of the money supply, M1. The concept of liquidity helps us understand the other

M2 Broad measure of the money supply that includes M1 and other highly liquid assets (savings deposits, small time deposits, and retail money-market mutual funds)

measure, **M2.** This monetary aggregate includes the assets in M1 plus other assets that are highly liquid, such as savings deposits. M2 is sometimes called *broad money* because it includes more than M1.

To see the idea behind M2, remember the definition of money: it can be used to purchase goods and services. Only the assets in M1—mainly currency and checking deposits—are used *directly* for purchases. For practical purposes, however, liquid assets such as savings deposits are almost as useful as M1 for making purchases. To spend the funds in your savings account, you need only stop at an ATM on the way to the store. Thus some economists think that a measure of money should include savings deposits and assets with similar liquidity. The M2 aggregate is such a measure.

TABLE 2.1 The Monetary Aggregates

	Levels in March 2008 (Billions of dollars)
Components of M1	
Currency	761.7
Checking deposits	604.1
Traveler's checks	6.2
Total M1	1372.0
Components of M2 = M1 +	
Savings deposits	4007.3
Small time deposits	1217.0
Retail money-market mutual funds	1065.3
Total M2	7661.6

Source: Federal Reserve

The Federal Reserve's definition of M2 includes several types of assets, which are listed in **Table 2.1.** Notice that the level of M2 is more than five times the level of M1. Besides the assets in M1, M2 has three components: savings deposits, small time deposits, and retail money-market mutual funds.

Savings Deposits This component is about two-thirds of M2. As we've discussed, savings deposits earn higher interest than checking deposits. Usually savings deposits can't be spent directly, but they can be withdrawn at any time.

One kind of savings account is a money-market deposit account (MMDA). The existence of MMDAs blurs the line between checking and savings deposits because it is possible to write checks on MMDAs. However, depositors are limited to six checks a month, and people don't make purchases with MMDAs very often. The Fed treats MMDAs as savings rather than checking accounts, so they are included in M2 but not in M1.

Small Time Deposits A time deposit is also known as a certificate of deposit, or CD. It is like a savings account, except that deposits are made for a fixed period (usually between 6 months and 3 years). There is a penalty for early withdrawal from a time deposit.

"Small" time deposits are those worth less than $100,000. This covers most CDs held by individuals. Larger-denomination time deposits, which are held mainly by firms and financial institutions, are not included in M2.

Some economists think that *no* time deposits should be included in a measure of the money supply. The restriction on withdrawals reduces the liquidity of time deposits, limiting their usefulness for purchasing goods and services. However, the Federal Reserve has judged that small time deposits are liquid enough to belong in M2.

Retail Money-Market Funds This is the only component of M2 that is not a bank account. A money-market fund is a mutual fund that holds bonds with maturities of less than a year: Treasury bills and commercial paper. The "retail" part of money-market funds covers shares that are purchased for less than $50,000. Once again, this restriction is meant to capture assets held by individuals.

Shares in money-market funds are highly liquid; they can be cashed in quickly without a fee. Some funds allow limited check writing, like money-market deposit accounts at banks.

CASE STUDY

Sweep Programs

Most of the assets included in M1 and M2 are bank accounts, so innovations in banking influence these aggregates. An important example is **sweep programs,** in which banks shift funds between customers' checking accounts and their money-market deposit accounts (MMDAs). This practice is invisible to consumers, but it has greatly reduced the levels of M1 calculated by the Federal Reserve.

Sweep program Banking practice of shifting funds temporarily from customers' checking accounts to money-market deposit accounts

Sweep programs began in 1994, when a change in Federal Reserve regulations made them legal. In a sweep program, computer software identifies funds in people's checking accounts that they are not likely to spend soon, based on their past behavior. This money is automatically "swept" into MMDAs. Funds are periodically moved back to the checking accounts to cover withdrawals and checks written on the accounts.

The motivation for sweep programs arises from Fed regulations. The Fed requires banks to hold reserves equal to a certain percentage of their total checking deposits. A bank's reserves consist of the cash in its vault and deposits it makes at the Fed. MMDAs have no reserve requirements, so moving funds from checking accounts to MMDAs reduces a bank's required level of reserves. This benefits the bank because reserves pay little interest: sweep programs free up funds for more profitable uses.

Checking deposits are part of M1 and MMDAs are not; as a type of savings deposit, MMDAs count only in M2. Therefore, when banks sweep funds from checking accounts to MMDAs, M1 falls. We can see this effect in **Figure 2.4,** which shows the behavior of M1 over time. Normally, M1 rises, since people hold more money as the economy grows. But M1 fell for several years after 1994, when sweep programs started.

Most consumers are unaware that their checking deposits may be swept into other accounts. Bank brochures mention this only in the fine print. Consumer ignorance of the practice doesn't matter, as funds that are swept out of checking accounts are always swept back in when they are needed.

Recall that M1 is meant to measure media of exchange—the funds available to buy goods and services. People can spend all the money they deposit in checking accounts, even funds that have moved temporarily to MMDAs. Therefore, a growing number of economists argue that the definition of M1 should be revised to include funds swept out of checking accounts.

FIGURE 2.4 Sweep Programs and M1

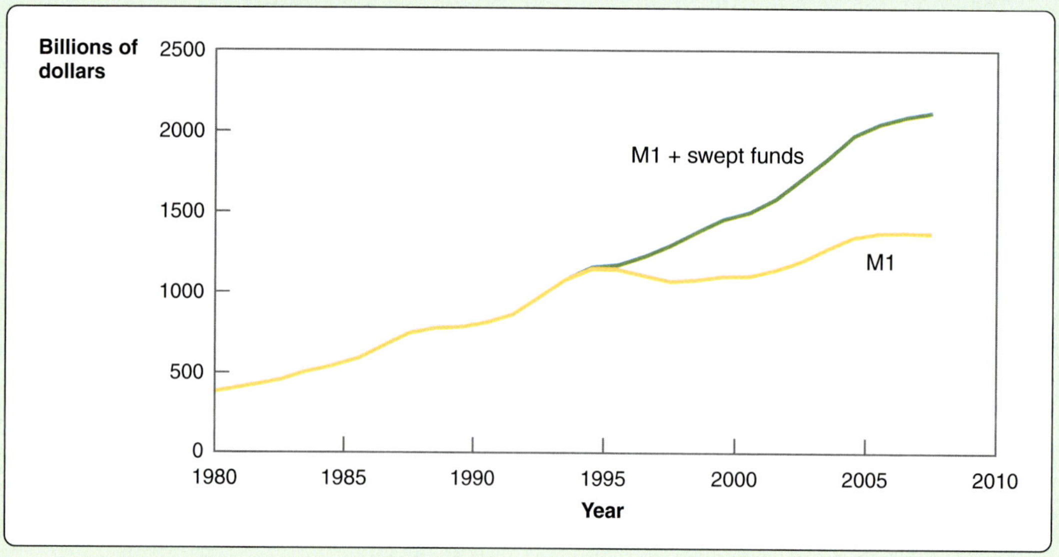

Since 1994, banks' sweep programs have moved funds from checking accounts, which are part of M1, to money-market deposit accounts, which are not. Consequently, M1 fell from 1994 to 1997 and its subsequent growth has been slow. Data on M1 would show faster growth if the aggregate were redefined to include swept funds.

Source: sweepmeasures.com (maintained by Barry E. Jones of the State University of New York at Binghamton)

Changing the definition of M1 would make a big difference. In Figure 2.4, the green line shows M1 plus swept funds—what M1 would total if its definition were changed. With this adjustment, M1 grows steadily rather than dipping after 1994. At the beginning of 2008, M1 was 56 percent higher with swept funds included than without.*

*The Federal Reserve does not collect data on swept funds, but economists have produced estimates of this variable, which we use in Figure 2.4. See Donald Dutkowsky, Barry Z. Cynamon, and Barry E. Jones, "U.S. Narrow Money for the 21st Century," *Economic Inquiry*, January 2006.

2.5 FUNCTIONS OF CENTRAL BANKS

To complete our introduction to money, let's discuss the institution that controls the money supply: the central bank. As we discussed in the chapter introduction, the central bank of the United States is the Federal Reserve System. This system includes 12 Federal Reserve Banks spread across the country. Overseeing the system is a Board of Governors in Washington, D.C. The most powerful individual at the Fed is the Chair of the Board of Governors—currently, Ben Bernanke.

A central bank has many roles in the economy. Let's outline the most important functions, which are summarized in **Table 2.2.**

TABLE 2.2 Major Functions of Central Banks

1. Clearing checks and electronic payments
2. Monetary policy (managing the money supply)
3. Emergency lending to banks
4. Bank regulation

Clearing Payments

We mentioned this role of central banks in our discussion of the payments system. Every private bank has an account at the Federal Reserve Bank for its region. Banks use these accounts to clear checks and process electronic payments (see Figure 2.2). The Fed is sometimes called the "banks' bank" because banks have accounts there.

Monetary Policy

The best-known function of central banks is **monetary policy,** or management of the money supply. These policy decisions have strong effects on the economy, which we discuss at many points in this book.

Monetary policy Central banks' management of the money supply

How does a central bank control the money supply? After all, M1 is mainly currency and deposits in checking accounts. A central bank chooses how much currency to issue, but it does not directly determine checking deposits. These are created by banks and their customers. Nonetheless, central banks have developed ways to manipulate how much money is created. We discuss how this works in Chapter Eleven.

Lending

Central banks lend money to private banks. This lending occurs primarily during financial crises, which threaten banks with failure. During crises, banks need loans to survive, and they cannot get funds from private sources. So the central bank steps in: it is the **lender of last resort.** Chapter Eighteen examines financial crises and central banks' responses.

Lender of last resort Central bank's role as emergency lender to banks

Bank Regulation

In most countries, central banks regulate private banks. Regulators try to reduce the risk of bank failure by restricting banks' activities. For example, banks are discouraged from making loans with high default risk. In the United States, the Federal Reserve shares bank regulation duties with other government agencies. We discuss bank regulation in Chapter Ten.

We discuss the policies of central banks throughout this book. As a preview, the next case study reviews the actions of the Federal Reserve following the terrorist attacks on September 11, 2001. In addition to the direct human cost, the attacks threatened America's financial system and economy. The Fed responded quickly to contain these threats and to minimize the economic trauma. Its actions involved all four central bank functions that we have outlined.

CASE STUDY

The Fed and September 11

The attacks on the World Trade Center and the Pentagon immediately interrupted the payments system. Since airplanes were grounded, checks stopped traveling among banks. In addition, the attacks knocked out electronic communications in Manhattan's financial district. Many banks could not make electronic payments that they had promised.

Consequently, some banks did not receive payments they expected and ran short of money. This could have had a domino effect. When banks are worried about a money shortage, they are reluctant to send money elsewhere; they delay payments and refuse to make loans. This means that other banks don't receive expected funds. Everybody starts hoarding money, and the payments system can break down.

Without a payments system, people can't buy or sell goods and services. So a serious breakdown in payments could have disrupted the whole economy, slowing growth and raising unemployment. The Fed took several actions to prevent this outcome.

- The Fed adjusted the rules governing payments. Normally, the Fed charges overdraft fees to banks with negative balances in their Fed accounts. These fees were suspended from September 11 to September 21. This policy encouraged banks to keep making payments even if incoming funds were delayed, pushing their balances negative.
- The Fed acted as a lender of last resort. At 11:45 on September 11, 3 hours after the initial attack, it issued a press release saying, "The Federal Reserve System is open and operating" and ready with emergency loans. Lots were needed: on September 12 the Fed had $45 billion of loans out to banks, about 200 times the normal level.
- The Fed relaxed bank regulations. It allowed loans that it would normally prohibit. For example, the Fed encouraged banks to lend to securities dealers, which it usually considers risky. Many dealers needed money because, like banks, they didn't receive expected payments.

Besides disrupting payments, the 9/11 attacks threatened the economy in other ways. A higher demand for money raises interest rates. Banks' scramble for money could have raised rates, which in turn would have slowed economic growth. However, starting on September 11, the Fed increased the money supply to match money demand. This action kept interest rates stable.

On Monday, September 17, the Fed went a step farther. It decided the economy needed not stable interest rates, but *lower* rates. It decided to push short-term rates from 3.5 percent to 3 percent, which it accomplished by increasing the money supply.

The Fed acted because it feared a decline in economic growth. Growth was threatened by problems in certain industries, such as airlines and travel, and by reduced consumer spending caused by general uncertainty. Lower interest rates encouraged consumers and firms to spend, helping to offset the factors reducing growth.

2.6 THE REST OF THIS BOOK

We have now finished the introduction to this book. Chapter One introduced the central parts of the financial system—financial markets and banks—and their roles in the economy. Chapter Two has discussed money—what it is, how it is measured, how it is spent—and how central banks can manage the money supply.

The rest of this book expands on this foundation. Before diving into the details, let's look at where we're going. The rest of the book is divided into four major parts, on financial markets, banking, money and the economy, and monetary policy.

Financial Markets

Part II examines financial markets in detail. We first discuss the prices and returns on securities, such as stocks and bonds. Why do stock prices sometimes rise and sometimes fall? Why are some interest rates high and some low?

We then discuss firms' decisions to issue securities, and savers' decisions about which securities to buy. When you accumulate wealth, should you buy stocks or bonds? Which firms' securities are the best buy?

Part II also discusses the markets for "derivative" securities, such as futures and options. We will see how some people and firms use these markets to reduce risk while others use them to gamble. Finally, we discuss the markets for foreign currencies. We will see why currency values fluctuate and how these fluctuations affect the economy.

Banking

Part III turns to the banking industry. We expand on the primary reason that banks exist: the problem of asymmetric information in securities markets. This problem lies behind financial scandals such as insider trading and dishonest accounting by corporations. We will see how banks can help to reduce the problem.

Part III also discusses the business of banking—how banks earn profits from accepting deposits, making loans, and other activities. We will see that banking can be a risky business and that bank failures are costly to the economy. This leads to the topic of government regulation, which aims to reduce the risk of bank failure.

Money and the Economy

Part IV returns to the topic of money. We discuss how central banks such as the Federal Reserve control the money supply. We then discuss economic fluctuations—the ups and downs of output, inflation, and unemployment. Central banks' decisions about the money supply are a central factor in these fluctuations.

This discussion builds on the earlier parts of the book. We will see that central banks' power stems from their influence on the financial system. Changes in the money supply affect financial variables such as interest rates, asset prices, and the level of bank lending. Then changes in financial variables affect the rest of the economy.

Monetary Policy

Part V turns to monetary policy. How should central banks use their power? We examine the strategies that central banks pursue to stabilize the economy and their successes and failures.

Part V also explores financial crises. We examine episodes ranging from the Great Depression, to the recent subprime mortgage debacle, to exchange-rate crises in developing countries. Preventing financial crises is one of the most controversial issues in economic policy.

Summary

- An economy's money supply is controlled by the central bank. The Federal Reserve System is the central bank of the United States.

2.1 What Is Money?

- Money is, first, the medium of exchange, the assets people use to purchase goods and services.
- Money offers an alternative to barter as a means of trading goods and services. Barter is inefficient because it requires a double coincidence of wants: when two people trade, each must have something the other wants.
- Money serves as the unit of account, that is, the measure in which prices are quoted. Money is also a store of value, a form in which wealth can be held.

2.2 Types of Money

- Commodity money is a medium of exchange with intrinsic value, such as gold coins or paper money exchangeable for gold.
- Fiat money, the kind of money used today, is intrinsically worthless pieces of paper. Each person accepts fiat money only because others do.
- Fiat money evolved from commodity money over time. The U.S. dollar has sometimes been commodity money, sometimes fiat money, and sometimes in between.
- Dollarization occurs when a country adopts a foreign currency as its money. A currency board issues a local money backed by a foreign currency. A currency union, such as the euro area, is a group of countries that creates a common money.

2.3 Money Today

- M1 is a measure of the money supply based on the idea that money is the medium of exchange. It includes assets that people use to purchase goods and services: cash, balances in checking accounts, and traveler's checks. New forms of money, such as stored-value cards and e-money, are not currently included in M1.
- Technology is rapidly changing how money is spent. Debit cards and Internet payments are replacing paper checks.
- Sellers of goods and services receive money through the payments system, a system of transactions among banks and the Federal Reserve.

2.4 Liquidity and Broad Money

- An asset's liquidity is the ease of trading it for money. The liquidity of assets ranges from high (e.g., savings accounts) to medium (e.g., securities) to low (e.g., real estate).
- Holders of liquid assets can earn higher returns than they would from money while still being ready for unexpected spending.
- M2 is a broad measure of the money supply. It includes the components of M1 and other highly liquid assets, such as savings deposits.
- Banks' sweep programs have shifted funds out of checking accounts, reducing the measured level of M1.

2.5 Functions of Central Banks

- The Federal Reserve System is the central bank of the United States. This system includes 12 Federal Reserve Banks located around the country and a Board of Governors in Washington, D.C.
- The primary functions of central banks are payments processing, monetary policy, emergency lending to banks, and bank regulation.

2.6 The Rest of This Book

- The four remaining parts of this book build on the foundation laid in Chapters One and Two. They detail the workings of financial markets and the banking system, how money influences the economy, and the policies of central banks.

Key Terms

barter, p. 27
central bank, p. 26
commodity money, p. 30
currency board, p. 35
currency union, p. 35
dollarization, p. 34
double coincidence of wants, p. 27
e-money, p. 42
Federal Reserve System, p. 26
fiat money, p. 31
lender of last resort, p. 47
liquidity, p. 42
M1, p. 36
M2, p. 44
medium of exchange, p. 26
monetary aggregate, p. 36
monetary policy, p. 47
money, p. 26
money demand, p. 27
money supply, p. 36
payments system, p. 39
store of value, p. 29
stored-value card, p. 41
sweep program, p. 45
unit of account, p. 28

Questions and Problems

1. The U.S. government owns about 4500 tons of gold, stored mainly at Fort Knox in Kentucky. Why did the government accumulate this gold? Should it continue to hold the gold, or sell it?
2. In the 1964 movie *Goldfinger*, the title character schemes to increase the price of gold. He plans to drop an atomic bomb on Fort Knox, making the gold there radioactive. His operation is financed by North Korea, which hopes to make the dollar worthless, disrupting the U.S. economy. If James Bond hadn't thwarted Goldfinger's plan, what effects might it have had on the monetary system and economy in 1964?
3. Scientists believe that the Sun will explode some billions of years from now. According to

some economic theorists, this means that nobody should accept money today. What is the logic behind this idea?

4. The U.S. population is approximately 300 million. Using the information in Table 2.1, calculate the average amount of U.S. currency per citizen. Do most Americans hold that much cash? If not, where is it?

5. Suppose that technology completely eliminates the use of cash. People buy newspapers by putting debit cards in the newspaper box. They use the Internet to pay babysitters. With no cash, does the nature of money change? Should the Federal Reserve change the definition of M1?

6. Explain how each of these events affects the amount of M1 that people hold:
   a. ATMs are invented.
   b. Credit cards are invented.
   c. Debit cards are invented.
   d. Stored-value cards are invented.
   e. Interest rates on bonds rise.

7. Is your checking account a sweep account? Find out from your bank. How much of the money you deposit is actually in the account on a typical day, and how much has been swept into an MMDA?

8. Recall the transactions that are triggered when you pay your rent (see Figure 2.2). Now suppose your check bounces because you don't have enough funds in your account. How does this change the series of transactions?

9. For a citizen of the United States, how liquid is each of the following assets? Explain each answer.
   a. Bonds issued by the U.S. government
   b. Bonds issued by corporations
   c. Post-Impressionist paintings
   d. British pounds

Online and Data Questions

www.worthpublishers.com/ball

10. Using the data on the text Web site, compute the ratio of M1 to GDP and the ratio of M2 to GDP. These ratios show how much money people hold relative to total spending in the economy. Plot these ratios over the last 40 years. Have the ratios been steady, or have they risen or fallen? What might explain these trends?

11. Figure 2.4 shows that sweep programs have reduced the level of M1. How do you think sweeps have affected M2? Do the M2 data on the text Web site support your answer?

12. The text Web site has links to several sites with information about stored-value cards. Some are maintained by card issuers, others by government agencies or consumer advocates. After visiting some of these sites, discuss the pros and cons of multipurpose stored-value cards. Who, if anybody, would be wise to use them?

chapter three 3

Asset Prices and Interest Rates

- 3.1 VALUING INCOME STREAMS
- 3.2 THE CLASSICAL THEORY OF ASSET PRICES
- 3.3 FLUCTUATIONS IN ASSET PRICES
- 3.4 ASSET-PRICE BUBBLES
- 3.5 ASSET-PRICE CRASHES
- 3.6 MEASURING INTEREST RATES AND ASSET RETURNS
- 3.7 REAL AND NOMINAL INTEREST RATES

AP Photo/Fox Business

What explains the numbers on this screen?

Suppose you turn on a financial news channel. You learn that the interest rate on 3-month Treasury bills is currently 4.5 percent, and the rate on 30-year government bonds is 5.2 percent. You also learn that the price of Microsoft stock has risen from $63 per share to $65, while General Motors is unchanged at $43. A dollar can buy 122 yen or 0.85 euros in foreign currency markets.

These facts may raise questions in your mind. As an inquisitive student, you wonder what determines the various interest rates, asset prices, and exchange rates you hear about. What economic forces cause these numbers to move around?

As someone who hopes to be wealthy, or at least will need to manage your own retirement account, you wonder about which assets you should buy. Which is a better deal, 5.2 percent interest on a 30-year bond or 4.5 percent on a 3-month bill? Is $65 a good price for Microsoft? Should you look into Japanese or European securities?

Part II of this book helps you answer questions like these about financial markets. This chapter discusses how assets are valued and how interest rates are measured. Chapter Four takes a closer look at the different interest rates in an economy and how they are determined.

Chapter Five examines the workings of securities markets, firms' decisions about issuing securities, and savers' decisions about which securities to buy. Chapter Six discusses foreign-currency markets and the determinants of exchange rates.

What determines the prices of assets? How are asset prices related to interest rates? This chapter discusses some basic principles and applies them to different types of assets, such as stocks and bonds. Economists' approach to asset pricing rests on a fundamental concept: the present value of an income stream. So our first task is to understand what present value means.

3.1 VALUING INCOME STREAMS

A financial asset yields a stream of income in the future. The owner of a bond receives a payment when the bond matures and may receive coupon payments before then. The owner of a firm's stock receives part of the firm's future earnings. To find the value of an asset, we must determine the value of these income streams.

In doing this, the key principle is that payments have different values depending on when they are received. A dollar today is worth more than a dollar in the future. The reason is that you can take today's dollar, put it in the bank, and receive interest. This transforms one dollar today into more than one dollar in the future.

Future Value

Future value Value of a dollar today in terms of dollars at some future time; \$1 today = $\$(1 + i)^n$ in n years

To compare payments at different times, economists begin with the concept of **future value.** The future value of a dollar is how many dollars it can produce in some future year. To understand this concept, suppose that banks pay an interest rate of 4 percent. If you deposit a dollar today, it grows to \$1.04 in a year. Thus the future value of a dollar today is \$1.04 in 1 year.

If you keep your money in the bank for a second year, it grows by another 4 percent. When \$1.04 grows by 4 percent, it becomes \$(1.04) (1.04), or $\$(1.04)^2$. So a dollar today is worth $\$(1.04)^2$ in 2 years. If you keep the money in the bank for a third year, it grows by 4 percent again, becoming $\$(1.04)^3$.

You should see the pattern. With a 4 percent interest rate, a dollar left in the bank for n years, where n is any number, grows to $\$(1.04)^n$. A dollar today is worth $\$(1.04)^n$ in n years.

The same principle applies to interest rates other than 4 percent. Let i be any interest rate expressed in decimal form. (In decimal form, 4 percent is 0.04). A dollar today grows to $\$(1 + i)$ in a year, $\$(1 + i)^2$ in 2 years, and $\$(1 + i)^n$ in n years. So the future value of a dollar is given by

FUTURE VALUE

$$\$1 \text{ today} = \$(1 + i)^n \text{ in } n \text{ years} \qquad \textbf{(3.1)}$$

Present Value

We've seen how much a dollar today is worth in the future. Now let's turn this relation around to see how much a *future* dollar is worth *today.* This is the **present value** of the future dollar.

Present value Value of a future dollar in terms of today's dollars; \$1 in n years = $\$1/(1 + i)^n$ today

We can understand present value with a little algebra. We start by turning around the equation for future value:

$$\$(1 + i)^n \text{ in } n \text{ years} = \$1 \text{ today}$$

Now divide both sides of the equation by $(1 + i)^n$:

$$\frac{\$(1 + i)^n}{(1 + i)^n} \text{ in } n \text{ years} = \frac{\$1}{(1 + i)^n} \text{ today}$$

The left side of this equation simplifies, giving us a key formula:

PRESENT VALUE

$$\$1 \text{ in } n \text{ years} = \frac{\$1}{(1 + i)^n} \text{ today} \qquad \textbf{(3.2)}$$

A dollar in n years is worth $1/(1 + i)^n$ dollars today.

With a 4 percent interest rate, the present value of a dollar in n years is $\$1/(1.04)^n$. For example, the present value of a dollar in 3 years is $\$1/(1.04)^3 = \$0.889$. The present value of a dollar in 20 years is $\$1/(1.04)^{20} = \$0.456$.

Equation (3.2) has a key implication: *a higher interest rate reduces the present value of future money.* A higher rate means a saver can trade a dollar today for more future dollars; turning this around, a future dollar is worth less today. Mathematically, a higher i reduces present value because it raises the denominator in the formula.

If the interest rate rises from 4 percent to 6 percent, the present value of a dollar in 3 years falls from \$0.889 to $\$1/(1.06)^3 = \$0.840$. The present value of a dollar in 20 years falls from \$0.456 to \$0.312.

A Series of Payments We can extend our reasoning to value a flow of money over multiple years. Suppose someone promises you \$3 in 2 years and \$5 in 4 years. Each dollar in 2 years is worth $\$1/(1 + i)^2$, so the \$3 are worth $\$3/(1 + i)^2$. The \$5 in 4 years are worth $\$5/(1 + i)^4$. Altogether, the present value of the future payments is $\$3/(1 + i)^2 + \$5/(1 + i)^4$.

To get a general formula, suppose you receive X_1 in one year, X_2 in two years, and so on up to X_T in T years. The present value of this flow of money is

$$\text{present value} = \frac{X_1}{(1 + i)} + \frac{X_2}{(1 + i)^2} + \cdots + \frac{X_T}{(1 + i)^T} \qquad \textbf{(3.3)}$$

To practice using this formula, let's calculate the present value of a contract signed by baseball star Alex Rodriguez. After the 2000 season, the Texas Rangers agreed to pay A-Rod \$25.2 million per year for 10 years, from 2001 through 2010. Let's assume an interest rate of 4 percent. In this case, the present value of the salary, as of 2000, was

$$\$25.2 \text{ million}/(1.04) + \$25.2 \text{ million}/(1.04)^2 + \cdots$$
$$+ \$25.2 \text{ million}/(1.04)^{10}$$

If you plug these numbers into a calculator, you will find that the present value of A-Rod's salary in 2000 was \$204.4 million.

▶After the 2003 season, the Rangers realized they couldn't afford Rodriguez and traded him to the New York Yankees. After the 2007 season, A-Rod and the Yankees cancelled the last three years of the 2000 contract and made a new agreement covering the period 2008–2017. The present value of A-Rod's new deal as of 2007 was \$226.8 million.

Payments Forever Some assets provide income indefinitely—there is no year T when the last payment is made. For example, a share of stock entitles the holder to a stream of earnings with no endpoint. A rare type of bond called a *perpetuity* pays interest forever.

One can derive the present value of such an income stream if the payment is the same every year. If the annual payment is Z, the present value is

$$\text{present value} = \frac{Z}{(1+i)} + \frac{Z}{(1+i)^2} + \frac{Z}{(1+i)^3} + \cdots$$

where the "..." at the end means the series continues forever. This equation simplifies to

$$\text{present value} = \frac{Z}{i} \tag{3.4}$$

For example, if the interest rate is 4 percent, a payment of \$100 per year forever has a present value of \$100/(0.04) = \$2500.

Deriving the last equation requires calculus, but the equation itself is simple. For perpetual payments, a higher annual payment means a higher present value. And, as always, a higher interest rate means a lower present value.

Table 3.1 summarizes the key principles about present values that we have derived.

TABLE 3.1 Present Values of Some Common Types of Payments

Payment (dollars)	Present Value (dollars)
1 in n years	$\frac{1}{(1+i)^n}$
A series of annual payments: $X_1, X_2, \ldots, X_T$	$\frac{X_1}{(1+i)} + \frac{X_2}{(1+i)^2} + \cdots + \frac{X_T}{(1+i)^T}$
An annual payment of Z forever	$\frac{Z}{i}$

3.2 THE CLASSICAL THEORY OF ASSET PRICES

We can now return to the question we raised earlier: what determines the price of an asset, such as a stock or bond? Economists usually answer this question with the **classical theory of asset prices.** This theory is based on several ideas involving present values.

Classical theory of asset prices The price of an asset equals the present value of expected income from the asset

The Present Value of Income

An asset produces a flow of income. This flow might be a series of fixed payments (in the case of bonds) or a share of a company's profits (in the case of stock). According to the classical theory, the price of an asset equals the present value of the income that people expect to receive:

$$\text{asset price} = \text{present value of expected asset income}$$

Notice the word "expected" in the theory. In many cases, nobody knows exactly how much income an asset will produce. For example, nobody is certain of a company's future profits, which determine the income from stock. Given this uncertainty, the classical theory says that asset prices depend on people's expectations, or best guesses, of asset income.

The rationale for the classical theory is simple. People purchase an asset because it yields a stream of income. The present value tells us how much this income is worth, so people are willing to pay that much for the asset.

Suppose an asset's price were *below* the present value of income. Say the present value is \$100 and the asset price is \$80. This situation wouldn't last long. At a price of \$80, the asset is a great deal: buyers pay less than the asset is worth. Lots of savers will purchase the asset, and high demand will push up the price. This continues until the price rises to \$100.

Conversely, if an asset price exceeds the present value of income, then sellers receive more than the asset is worth. In this situation, the asset's owners will rush to sell, pushing down the price.

The classical theory applies to many types of assets. For example, it says that the price of an apartment building equals the present value of net rental income from the building. Let's look more closely at the theory's implications for two classes of assets, bonds and stocks.

Bond Prices The income from a bond includes the periodic coupon payments (if any) and the face value received at maturity. Let's say a bond has a maturity of T years, a face value of F, and an annual coupon payment of C. Assuming no chance of default, bondholders expect to receive all the promised payments. The payments are C in years 1 through $T-1$ and $C+F$ in year T. The bond price is the present value of these payments. Using Equation (3.3), this present value is

$$\text{bond price} = \frac{C}{(1+i)} + \frac{C}{(1+i)^2} + \cdots + \frac{(C+F)}{(1+i)^T} \qquad \textbf{(3.5)}$$

For example, suppose a bond's maturity is 3 years, so $T = 3$. Annual coupon payments are \$5 and the face value is \$100. Assume the interest rate is 4 percent. In this case, Equation (3.5) tells us

$$\text{bond price} = \frac{\$5}{1.04} + \frac{\$5}{(1.04)^2} + \frac{\$105}{(1.04)^3}$$
$$= \$102.78$$

Stock Prices According to the classical theory, there are two ways to determine stock prices. The first is based on the fact that stockholders own firms, so firms' earnings belong to them. If a company issues 1 million shares of stock, then each share entitles the holder to one-millionth of the company's earnings. The price of a share is the present value of these earnings. If expected earnings per share are E_1 in the next year, E_2 in the year after that, and so on, then

$$\text{stock price} = \frac{E_1}{(1+i)} + \frac{E_2}{(1+i)^2} + \frac{E_3}{(1+i)^3} + \cdots$$

Dividend Payment from a firm to its stockholders

Alternatively, we can look at the income that flows directly to stockholders. Firms periodically make payments to stockholders called **dividends.** A company with 1 million shares might announce a dividend of \$2 per share, paying a total of \$2 million. A stock's price is the present value of expected dividends. If expected dividends per share are D_1 in the next year, D_2 in the year after that, and so on, then

$$\text{stock price} = \frac{D_1}{(1+i)} + \frac{D_2}{(1+i)^2} + \frac{D_3}{(1+i)^3} + \cdots$$

At first, the two ways of writing a stock price might look contradictory. In any year, a firm's earnings and dividends can be quite different. For example, some companies have healthy earnings but choose not to issue any dividend. How then can both equations be correct?

The answer is that earnings and dividends have the same present value. Eventually, a firm distributes all its earnings to shareholders. If dividends are less than earnings in one year, the firm builds up funds, allowing it to pay higher dividends later. In the long run, the dividends the firm can afford are determined by earnings, so its stock price can be computed from either flow.

What Expectations?

An asset price depends on the present value of *expected* asset income. What determines what people expect? The classical theory assumes that people's expectations are the best possible forecasts of asset income based on all public information. This assumption is called **rational expectations.**

Rational expectations Theory that people's expectations are the best possible forecasts based on all public information

To understand the concept of rational expectations, consider Harriet's software company, eSmells, which we discussed in Chapter One. The price of the company's stock depends on its expected earnings. Rational expectations of earnings are based on all public information about the company. For example, if Harriet announces a new product, expected earnings rise to reflect the product's likely impact. If the economy enters a recession, expected earnings adjust based on how Harriet's firm will be affected. Expected earnings also account for the costs of producing software, the number of competitors the firm faces, and all other relevant factors.

Rational expectations may not be correct expectations. Unpredictable events can cause actual earnings to differ from what people expect. However, rational expectations means these differences are as small as possible. Expectations incorporate all relevant information, so there is no way to make them more accurate.

What Interest Rate?

Asset prices depend on interest rates, which determine the present value of asset income. What determines these interest rates? In the classical theory, different interest rates are relevant for different assets. The riskier an asset, the higher the interest rate.

To see this point, recall our initial discussion of present value, where we saw that a dollar today is worth $1 + i$ dollars in a year. In this discussion, i is an interest rate that savers receive for sure—say, from a safe bank account. From now on, we will call this rate the **safe interest rate,** or *risk-free rate.* We use the symbol i^{safe} for the safe interest rate.

Safe interest rate (i^{safe}) Interest rate that savers can receive for sure; also, *risk-free rate*

Our discussion of present value also assumes that future payments are known with certainty. A dollar today is worth a certain $\$(1 + i^{safe})$ in a year, because you receive that amount by saving the dollar.

When determining asset prices, however, we often have to value uncertain payments. For example, suppose the expected earnings from a share of stock are \$10. This is the best forecast, but earnings could range between \$8 and \$12 per share. People dislike such risk. Therefore, the earnings from the stock are worth less than a certain \$10.

Risk affects present values. A dollar today is worth $1 + i^{safe}$ certain dollars next year. This means a dollar today is worth *more* than $1 + i^{safe}$ risky dollars next year, because risky dollars are less valuable than certain dollars. To put it differently, a dollar today is worth $1 + i^{safe} + \varphi$ risky dollars in a year, where φ (the Greek letter phi) is a **risk premium.** A risk premium is a payment on an asset that compensates the owner for taking on risk.

Risk premium (φ) Payment on an asset that compensates the owner for taking on risk

The same reasoning applies to risky income at any point in the future. A dollar today is worth $(1 + i^{safe} + \varphi)^n$ risky dollars in n years. Turning this around, the present value of a risky dollar in n years is $1/(1 + i^{safe} + \varphi)^n$. In our equations for asset prices, the interest rate, i, is $i^{safe} + \varphi$. In words, the interest rate is the sum of the safe rate and the risk premium.

Assets carry varying degrees of risk. The greater the risk, the higher the risk premium. For example, stocks have higher risk premiums than bonds because, as we discuss in Section 3.6, the income from stocks is more volatile. A higher risk premium raises the interest rate in the present value formula, reducing the present value of expected income. Therefore, a higher risk premium reduces an asset's price.

TABLE 3.2 The Classical Theory of Asset Prices

- An asset price equals the present value of expected income from the asset.
- Rational expectations: Expected income is the best possible forecast based on all public information.
- The interest rate in the present value formula is the safe interest rate plus a risk premium: $i = i^{safe} + \varphi$.

Table 3.2 summarizes the ideas behind the classical theory of asset prices.

3.3 FLUCTUATIONS IN ASSET PRICES

If you watch your financial news channel every night, you will notice that asset prices move around a lot. Stock and bond prices rise and fall, providing ample subject matter for TV analysts. What are the basic forces behind these price movements?

Why Do Asset Prices Change?

The classical theory says an asset price is the present value of expected income from the asset. This present value changes if expected income changes or if interest rates change.

Stock prices change frequently because of changes in expected income from the stock. These changes occur when there is news about a company's prospects, either good or bad. If a drug company patents a new wonder drug, rational expectations of the company's earnings rise. Its stock price rises accordingly. If a car company's new model proves unpopular with consumers, its expected earnings and stock price fall. If there are signs that the whole economy is entering a recession, expected earnings and stock prices are likely to fall for many companies.

Such news has less effect on bond prices than on stock prices. Recall that the income from a bond is fixed as long as the issuer does not default. As a result, news about companies' prospects often has little effect on the expected income from bonds.

Changes in interest rates, however, affect the prices of both stocks and bonds. A higher interest rate reduces asset prices because it reduces the present value of any income flow. Recall that the relevant interest rate is the economy's safe rate plus a risk premium ($i^{safe} + \varphi$). An asset price falls if either the safe rate rises or the risk premium rises. The risk premium might rise because of greater uncertainty about income from the asset.

CASE STUDY

The Fed and the Stock Market

In Chapter Two we described the excitement around Ben Bernanke's appointment as Federal Reserve Chair in 2005. We can now see one

FIGURE 3.1 The Fed and the Stock Market

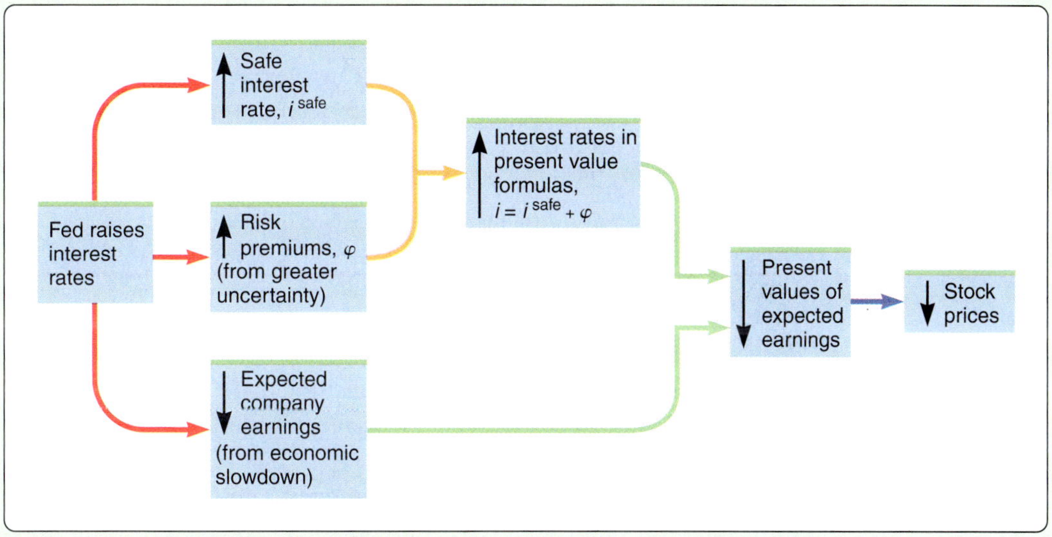

When the Fed *raises* interest rates unexpectedly, a series of effects reduces stock prices. When the Fed *lowers* rates unexpectedly, opposite effects occur and stock prices rise.

reason the Fed is so important: monetary policy has strong influences on asset prices. When the Fed adjusts the money supply to push interest rates up or down, its actions cause jumps in asset prices.

The classical theory helps explain these effects. Let's focus on the behavior of stock prices. When the Fed raises interest rates, the stock market is affected in several ways, which are summarized in **Figure 3.1:**

- One rate determined by the Fed is the economy's safe interest rate. A higher safe rate reduces the present value of companies' earnings.
- Higher rates also reduce spending by consumers and firms. The economy slows, reducing expected earnings for many companies.
- Some economists think there is a third effect: higher risk premiums. A slower economy not only reduces expected earnings but also raises uncertainty, because it is hard to predict the effects of the slowdown. Higher risk premiums raise the interest rates that determine present values.

All three effects reduce the present value of earnings. So stock prices fall when the Fed raises interest rates. If the Fed reduces rates, the three effects work in reverse, and prices rise.

A qualification: Fed actions have large effects only when they are unexpected. If people know the Fed is going to change rates, stock prices are likely to adjust in advance, so nothing happens when the Fed moves. In contrast, surprise rate changes cause sharp jumps in stock prices.

Ben Bernanke understands all this. Bernanke studied the effects of Fed policies during his career as an economics professor. He estimated the effects of interest-rate changes on the stock market in a 2005 paper with Kenneth Kuttner of Oberlin College.

Bernanke and Kuttner examined the period from 1989 to 2002. They measured changes in stock prices on days when the Fed made surprise announcements about interest rates. On average, a rise in rates of 0.25 percent—say, from 4.0 percent to 4.25 percent—caused stock prices to drop suddenly by about 1 percent. A decrease in rates had the opposite effect: a cut of 0.25 percent *raised* stock prices by 1 percent.*

* See Ben Bernanke and Kenneth Kuttner, "What Explains the Stock Market's Reaction to Federal Reserve Policy?" *Journal of Finance*, June 2005.

Which Asset Prices Are Most Volatile?

All asset prices change over time, but some fluctuate more than others. Let's discuss why some asset prices are especially volatile.

Short versus Long Bonds Changes in interest rates are the primary reason for changes in bond prices. (As noted earlier, expected income flows are constant unless default risk changes.) If interest rates in an economy rise, then all bond prices fall. But the size of the effect differs depending on bond maturities. *A change in interest rates has a larger effect on prices of long-term bonds than on prices of short-term bonds.*

The reason is that short-term bonds provide income only in the near future, while most payments on long-term bonds come later. The present value of a payment is affected more strongly by the interest rate if the payment comes later.

For example, suppose the interest rate rises from 4 percent to 6 percent. The present value of a dollar in 1 year goes from \$1/(1.04), which equals \$0.961, to \$1/(1.06), which equals \$0.943. This is a decrease in value of about 2 percent. The value of a dollar in 20 years goes from $\$1/(1.04)^{20} = \$0.456$ to $\$1/(1.06)^{20} = \$0.312$, a decrease of 32 percent. If much of the income from a bond is received in 20 years, then a rise in interest rates can wipe out a large part of the bond's value.

To illustrate this point further, **Table 3.3** compares bonds with maturities ranging from 1 year to 30 years. Each bond has a face value of \$100 and coupon payments of \$5 per year. The table shows the prices of the bonds when the interest rate is 4 percent and when it is 6 percent. The longer a bond's maturity, the greater the percentage fall in the price when the interest rate rises.

Bonds versus Stocks Prices for stocks are more volatile than prices for bonds, even long-term bonds. Stock prices fluctuate greatly for two reasons. First, like long-term bonds, stocks yield income far into the future—a firm's earnings continue indefinitely. Changes in interest rates have large effects on the present value of this income. Second, as we've discussed, news about firms causes changes in expected earnings. These changes

TABLE 3.3 Bond Prices, Maturity, and Interest Rates

This table shows how much bond prices fall when the interest rate (i) rises from 4% to 6%. All bonds have a face value of $100 and annual coupon payments of $5. The change in the interest rate has larger effects on prices of long-term bonds than on prices of short-term bonds.

Years to Maturity	Price if i = 4%	Price if i = 6%	Percentage Fall in Price from Increase in i
1	$100.96	$99.06	1.89
2	101.89	98.17	3.65
3	102.78	97.33	5.30
4	103.63	96.53	6.85
5	104.45	95.79	8.29
10	108.11	92.64	14.31
15	111.12	90.29	18.75
20	113.59	88.53	22.06
25	115.62	87.22	24.57
30	117.29	86.24	26.48

cause fluctuations in stock prices, adding to the fluctuations caused by changes in interest rates.

3.4 ASSET-PRICE BUBBLES

The classical theory says an asset price equals the present value of expected income from the asset. Is this really true? Is it just a theoretical idea, or does it explain asset-price movements in the real world?

This is a controversial issue. Clearly there are elements of truth in the theory. We have seen, for example, that it helps explain how stock prices react to Federal Reserve policies. However, many economists believe that changes in asset prices can occur for reasons outside the classical theory—reasons besides changes in interest rates or expected income.

One possible reason is an **asset-price bubble.** In a bubble, asset prices rise rapidly even though there is no change in interest rates or expected income to justify the rise. Let's discuss how bubbles can occur and the debate over their relevance.

Asset-price bubble Rapid rise in asset prices that is not justified by changes in interest rates or expected asset income

How Bubbles Work

When a bubble occurs, an asset price rises simply because people *expect* it to rise. To see how this might happen, suppose a famous stock analyst tells his TV audience that the stock of Acme Corporation is hot: the stock price is likely to rise rapidly in the future. Let's assume the expert doesn't really have a good reason for this view; he is just trying to get attention with a bold prediction. Nonetheless, many people believe the expert and rush to buy Acme. This demand pushes up the price of the stock. The expert looks smart, and a bubble has begun.

Once a bubble begins, it feeds on itself. When Acme's price starts rising, more and more people decide the stock is hot. They buy Acme stock, pushing the price higher still. The stock looks even hotter, more buyers rush in, and so on.

As the bubble expands, Acme's price rises far above the level dictated by the classical theory: the present value of earnings per share. People pay more for the stock than it is really worth. They buy it because they expect the price to rise even higher in the future, allowing them to sell the stock for a profit.

The problem with bubbles is that they eventually pop. At some point Acme's price rises so high that people begin to doubt whether price increases can continue. They stop buying the stock, and this causes the price to fall. The price heads back toward the level dictated by the classical theory. People who buy Acme at the height of the bubble can lose a lot when the bubble bursts.

▶ Many economists believe a bubble occurred in U.S. real estate prices from roughly 2001 to 2006. Later chapters discuss this episode, the collapse of the bubble after 2006, and the repercussions for the economy.

Bubbles can arise in many kinds of asset prices. History has seen bubbles in stocks, bonds, real estate, foreign currencies, precious metals, and commodities such as coffee and sugar. The next case study discusses one famous bubble.

CASE STUDY

Tulipmania

A dramatic asset-price bubble occurred in Holland in the 1630s. Oddly enough, the asset was tulip bulbs. Holland was growing wealthy from foreign trade. Merchants showed off their new wealth by building estates, which included fancy gardens. The tulip, originally from Turkey, reached Holland in 1593, and its dramatic colors made it the most popular flower. Certain rare varieties were especially prized for their intricate patterns. These tulips became status symbols.

The supply of tulips was limited, as they reproduce slowly; a tulip yields only one or two new bulbs in a year. The combination of high demand and low supply meant that bulb prices rose rapidly. In 1633, someone traded three rare bulbs for a house. In 1634, someone offered 3000 guilders, roughly the annual income of a wealthy merchant, for one bulb. The offer was turned down.

Initially, such prices reflected the true value of tulips, in the sense that people were willing to pay that much to plant bulbs in their gardens. But at some point—historians differ on when—a bubble emerged. People without gardens started buying bulbs. They planned to make money by reselling the bulbs after prices rose even higher.

In 1636, tulipmania swept Holland. Word spread that tulip bulbs were the way to get rich quickly. People mortgaged their property to borrow money and buy bulbs. Groups met regularly in taverns to trade bulbs.

The bubble started in prices of rare bulbs but then spread to common tulips, which had previously been inexpensive. Prices for common bulbs exploded in the winter of 1636–37. The price of one variety, the Switser tulip, rose from 1 guilder in January 1637 to 30 guilders in February.

February 1637 was the peak of the bubble. At that point, the government started discussing measures to end it, such as giving tulip buyers the right to renege on contracts. This development shook people's confidence in tulips, and they stopped buying. Prices for many bulbs fell by more than 90 percent in February and stayed low. In 1722, a Switser bulb cost one-twentieth of a guilder.*

* For more on this episode, see Mike Dash, *Tulipmania: The Story of the World's Most Coveted Flower and the Extraordinary Passions It Aroused,* Weidenfeld and Nicholson Publishers, 1999.

Looking for Bubbles

Economists often debate whether bubbles are occurring in asset prices. Discussions of stock prices sometimes focus on **price-earnings ratios.** This variable—the **P/E ratio** for short—is the price of stock divided by earnings per share. Earnings are measured over the recent past. Economists compute P/E ratios for individual companies and also the average P/E ratio for the stock market. Some think that high P/E ratios are evidence of bubbles.

Price-earnings ratio (P/E ratio) A company's stock price divided by earnings per share over the recent past

To see why, recall the classical theory: a stock price equals the present value of expected earnings per share. It is difficult to test this theory, because we can't directly measure expectations of future earnings. But some economists argue that earnings in the recent past are a good guide to the future. If a stock price is unusually high compared to past earnings—if the P/E ratio is high—then the price is probably high compared with future earnings. The price is higher than it should be under the classical theory, suggesting a bubble.

According to the classical theory, high P/E ratios could be explained by low interest rates. Low rates raise the present value of future income, pushing up stock prices. In practice, however, stocks' P/E ratios sometimes rise without changes in interest rates. These cases may be explained by bubbles.

A high P/E ratio cannot be definitive proof of a bubble. It indicates a bubble only if recent earnings are a good predictor of future earnings. This is not true if earnings are expected to grow rapidly. For example, suppose a company is developing a promising new product. The company's current earnings are low, but earnings are expected to rise a lot when the product is introduced. According to the classical theory, high expected earnings imply a high stock price. With current earnings low, the classical theory predicts a high P/E ratio.

Economists have tried to determine the correct interpretation of P/E ratios. Do high ratios usually signal a bubble? Or are they more likely to reflect expectations of high earnings growth? Some researchers address this issue by examining what happens to stock prices *after* a period of high P/E ratios. Remember that bubbles eventually end. If a bubble has pushed up the P/E ratio, stock prices are likely to fall later. In contrast, if a high P/E ratio reflects high expected earnings, there is no reason to expect falling prices. Examining later price movements helps to isolate why the P/E ratio was high.

FIGURE 3.2 Evidence for Bubbles?

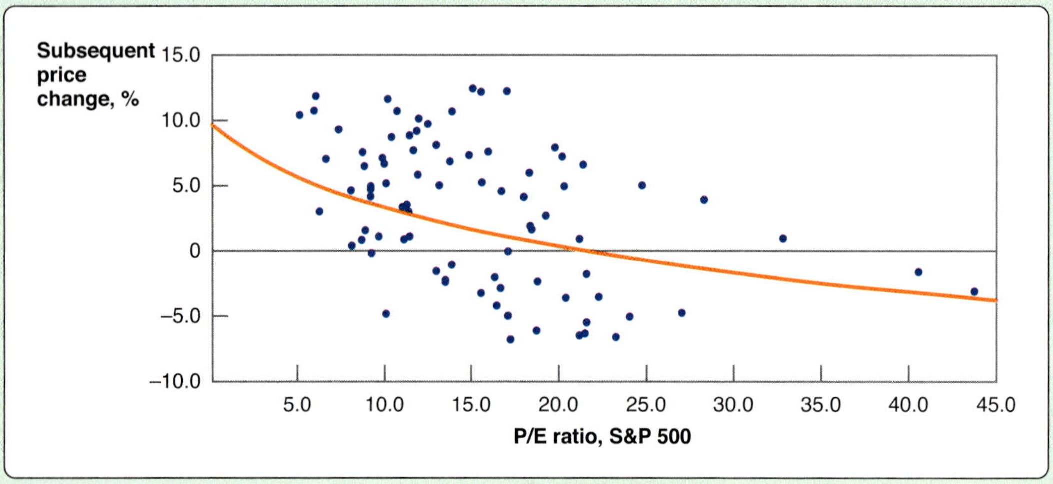

Each point in this graph represents a year between 1918 and 2000. The horizontal axis is the price-earnings ratio for stocks in the S&P 500, based on average earnings over the previous 10 years. The vertical axis is the average percentage change in S&P prices over the following 10 years, adjusted for inflation. (The 10-year changes after 1999 and 2000 are estimated with data through 2008.) When the P/E ratio is high, stock prices are likely to grow slowly or fall over the following 10 years.

Source: Robert Shiller, Yale University (www.econ.yale.edu/~shiller/data.htm)

This approach was introduced in a 1997 paper by John Campbell of Harvard University and Robert Shiller of Yale University. Campbell and Shiller examined the P/E ratio for a large group of companies, the S&P 500. For a given year, they defined P as the average stock price for the group and E as average earnings per share over the past 10 years. Campbell and Shiller compared the P/E ratio to the change in stock prices over the following 10 years.

Figure 3.2 makes Campbell and Shiller's comparison for the period from 1918 through 2000. In this graph, the horizontal axis is the P/E ratio and the vertical axis is the average percentage change in stock prices over the next 10 years. We see a negative relationship: when the P/E ratio is high, stock prices are likely to fall. Campbell and Shiller concluded that high P/E ratios are usually caused by bubbles that dissipate in the future.

Campbell and Shiller's research was stimulated by a rapid rise in stock prices during the 1990s. The next case discusses this episode and its aftermath.

CASE STUDY

The Millennium Boom

The green curve in **Figure 3.3** shows the Dow Jones index of stock prices from 1990 through 2007. The Dow rose from about 2500 at the start of this period to over 6000 in 1997, when Campbell and Shiller wrote. The index continued to rise after that, peaking at 11,497 in the summer of 2000.

FIGURE 3.3 U.S. Stock Prices, 1990–2007

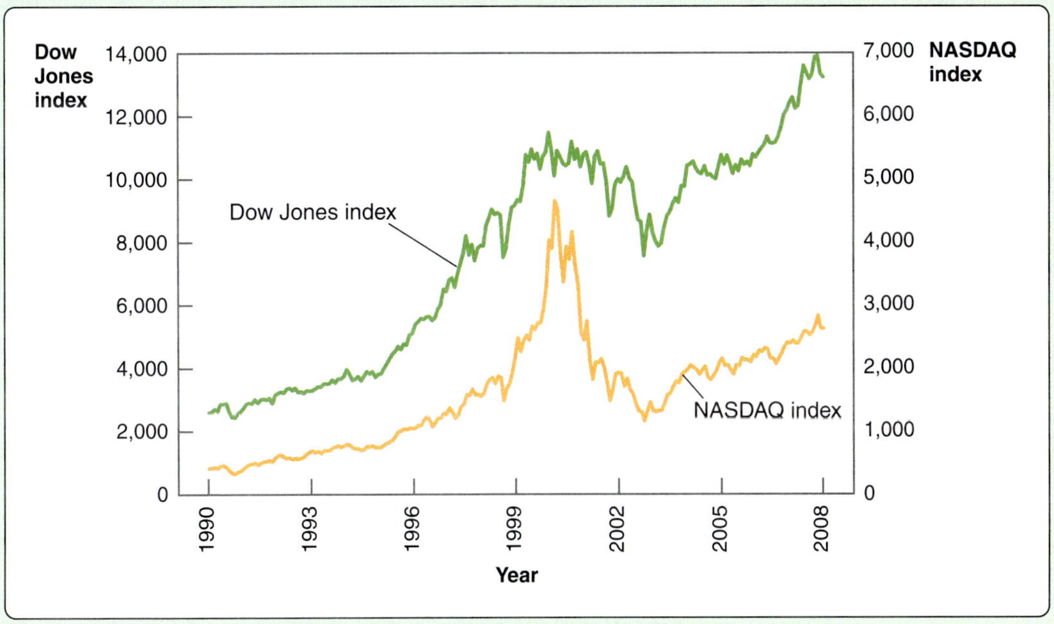

U.S. stock prices rose rapidly in the late 1990s and then fell in the early 2000s. This pattern was especially pronounced for the tech stocks that dominate the NASDAQ index. Some economists interpret the late-90s experience as an asset-price bubble.

Source: finance.yahoo.com

Price increases were especially rapid for stocks of "tech" companies—those involved with computers, software, and the Internet. The NASDAQ stock index (named for the National Association of Securities Dealers) is based mainly on tech stocks. As shown by the orange curve in Figure 3.3, this index rose from 330 in 1991 to almost 4700 9 years later.

Companies' earnings rose during the 1990s, but not as fast as stock prices. This meant rising P/E ratios. From 1960 to 1995, the average P/E ratio for the Dow Jones index was about 15. This ratio rose above 40 in 2000. For many tech companies, the P/E ratio exceeded 100.

During the 1990s, many economists argued that a stock market bubble was underway. Federal Reserve Chair Alan Greenspan supported this idea in a famous 1996 speech. Greenspan suggested that stock prices had been "unduly escalated" by "irrational exuberance," meaning prices had risen above the levels dictated by the classical theory.

Others defended the accuracy of the classical theory. They argued that developments during the 1990s made it rational to expect rapid growth in companies' earnings. As we discussed earlier, expectations of high earnings growth imply a high P/E ratio in the classical theory.

Optimism about earnings was based on the new technologies of the 1990s—the rapid spread of computers and the Internet. These technologies raised productivity and reduced costs in many industries. Stock analysts predicted these trends would continue, raising firms' profits.

In 2000, stock prices peaked, and they fell for the next 3 years. The Dow Jones index fell below 8000 in 2003; the NASDAQ reached 1172, less than a quarter of its peak level. Believers in a stock market bubble claimed vindication. They interpreted the price declines as the bursting of the bubble and evidence that stocks were never really worth the prices of the late 1990s.

But again, not everyone is convinced. Believers in the classical theory point to several pieces of bad news that arrived between 2000 and 2003. These included the terrorist attacks of September 11, 2001; the discovery of false accounting at companies such as Enron; and the recession of 2001–2002. These events reduced companies' expected earnings, possibly explaining the fall in stock prices. So the debate over stock bubbles continues.

Online Case Study: An Update on the Stock Market

Stock prices began rising again in 2003. As shown in Figure 3.3, the Dow passed its 2000 peak in 2006. The NASDAQ, however, has remained far below its peak level.

3.5 ASSET-PRICE CRASHES

Believers in asset-price bubbles think that bubbles eventually end and prices fall. Sometimes this occurs gradually, as in the U.S. stock market over 2000–2003. Other times a bubble ends with an **asset-price crash:** prices plummet over a very short period.

Asset-price crash Large, rapid fall in asset prices

We saw earlier that Holland's tulip bubble ended with a crash in 1637. In U.S. history, the most famous crashes have occurred in the stock market. In both 1929 and 1987, stock prices fell dramatically within a single day. Let's discuss how such crashes occur.

How Crashes Work

Crashes are hard to explain with the classical theory of asset prices. Under that theory, prices fall sharply only if there is a large drop in the present value of expected asset income. This requires either a rise in interest rates or bad news about future income, and crashes often occur without such events; for example, the stock market crashed on October 19, 1987. Interest rates were stable on that day, and there was no significant news about companies' earnings.

A crash is easier to explain if it is preceded by an asset-price bubble. At some point during a bubble, people start worrying that it will end. They would like to hold assets as long as prices rise but sell before the bubble bursts. So they watch alertly for the end of the bubble.

At some point, a few asset holders get especially nervous and decide to start selling. Others notice this and fear that the bubble may be ending. They sell, too, hoping to dump assets before prices fall too much. These actions push down prices. Pessimism about prices is self-fulfilling, just as optimism was self-fulfilling during the bubble.

Once a crash starts, it can accelerate rapidly. As prices fall, panic sets in, and lots of asset holders try to sell at the same time. Prices plummet. Eventually, prices fall far enough to make the assets attractive again. At this point, prices may be *below* the present value of expected income, so it is more profitable to hold assets than to sell them. The rush to sell abates, and prices stabilize.

According to this reasoning, a crash is a risk whenever an asset-price bubble is underway. However, nobody knows how to explain why crashes occur on particular days. Sometimes there is a small piece of news, such as a report of low company earnings, that increases the nervousness of asset holders. But often the timing of a crash appears arbitrary. Even in retrospect, we do not know why the 1987 crash occurred on October 19 rather than some other day.

CASE STUDY

The Two Big Crashes

Stock prices rose rapidly during the "Roaring Twenties": the Dow Jones Industrial Average climbed from 70 in 1921 to 365 in September 1929. This performance reflected excitement about new technologies, such as cars, radios, and electric appliances. The demand for stocks was also fueled by people's ability to "buy on margin," that is, to buy stock on credit, with only a small down payment.

In retrospect the 1920s' experience looks like a classic bubble, but economists did not recognize this at the time. On October 17, 1929, economist Irving Fisher of Yale University commented that "stock prices have reached what looks like a permanently high plateau."

As usual, it is not clear why the crash occurred just when it did. Increases in interest rates in early 1929 may have made stockholders nervous, since they reduced the present values of company earnings. In any case, the stock market fluctuated erratically for several months and then plummeted. The largest one-day decline occurred on "Black Monday," October 28, when the Dow dropped by 13 percent. This crash was followed by a series of smaller declines. In July 1932, the Dow reached a low of 41.

The 1987 crash was in some ways a repeat of 1929. It followed a rapid rise in prices: the Dow climbed from 786 in 1980 to 2655 in August 1987. Some observers suggested that a bubble was underway, but again the crash was unexpected. The market started falling on October 14, and the bottom fell out on October 19, the second Black Monday. That day the Dow dropped 23 percent, easily beating the 1929 record for a one-day drop.

October 19, 1987: Traders at the New York Stock Exchange work frantically as stock prices plummet.

AP Photo/Peter Morgan

The 1987 crash was exacerbated by the use of computers to trade stocks. Computers sped up trading, so prices fell more quickly than in 1929. Moreover, in 1987 large stockholders such as mutual funds had systems of *program trading,* in which computers automatically sold stock if the market fell by a certain amount. These systems were designed to get rid of stocks quickly if a crash were underway. When the crash occurred, program trading worsened the vicious cycle of falling prices and heavy selling.

Despite the similarities between the two crashes, their aftermaths differed. After October 1929, stock prices stayed depressed. The Dow did not climb back to its precrash level until 1954. In 1987, the market bounced back quickly. The Dow reached its precrash level in 1989 and kept rising through the 1990s.

The two crashes also had different effects on the overall economy. The 1929 crash contributed to the Great Depression of the 1930s, while economic growth was strong after the 1987 crash. Part of the explanation is the different responses of the Federal Reserve to the two crashes.

Crash Prevention

Is there any way to prevent crashes? Both the government and stock exchanges have imposed rules for stock trading to make crashes less likely. Let's discuss two rules, one adopted after the 1929 crash and one after the 1987 crash.

Margin requirements Limits on the use of credit to purchase stocks

Margin Requirements

After the 1929 crash, Congress gave the Federal Reserve authority to establish **margin requirements.** These are limits on the amount that people can borrow to buy stock. Margin requirements have varied over time, but in recent years they have been around 50 percent. This means that stock purchasers must pay at least 50 percent of the cost with their own money.

This regulation tries to curtail the buildup of stock price bubbles that precede crashes. As we have discussed, the practice of buying on margin helped fuel the stock market boom of the 1920s. Margin requirements make such a price run-up less likely. When prices don't rise as high, there is less danger they will fall sharply.

Circuit breaker Requirement that a securities exchange shut down temporarily if prices drop by a specified percentage

Circuit Breakers

After the 1987 crash, some securities exchanges established **circuit breakers,** requirements to shut down trading temporarily if prices fall sharply. These rules are motivated by the view that crashes are a vicious cycle of panic and falling prices. A circuit breaker stops this process; it gives people time to calm down and remember the true value of their assets. If this works, the rush to sell subsides and prices stabilize when the exchange reopens. (In other words, panicky asset traders are like naughty 4-year-olds: they behave more rationally after a "time out.")

At the New York Stock Exchange, current rules mandate a suspension of trading if the Dow Jones Average falls 10 percent within a day. The length of the suspension depends on the size of the fall and the time of day. For example, trading halts for an hour if prices fall 10–20 percent before 2 PM. Larger decreases can halt trading for the rest of the day.

So far, trading on the New York Stock Exchange has been interrupted only once, on July 27, 1997. At that time the rules set smaller price declines as triggers for circuit breakers. The Dow Jones Average fell 7 percent, which was enough to shut down the exchange for the rest of the day.

3.6 MEASURING INTEREST RATES AND ASSET RETURNS

We can use what we have learned so far to define two central concepts in financial markets: a bond's yield to maturity and the rate of return on a stock or bond. We will use these concepts frequently in future chapters.

Yield to Maturity

Buying a bond means lending money to the company or government that issues the bond. To decide whether to buy, people must compare the interest they will receive to other interest rates, such as rates on bank accounts.

However, the interest rate on a bond is not always obvious. Consider a bond with a \$100 face value, 3 years to maturity, and coupon payments of \$5 per year. You can buy the bond for a price of \$95. If you do, what interest rate do you earn?

Economists answer this question by calculating the bond's **yield to maturity.** This concept is based on the classical theory of asset prices. Earlier, we used this theory to derive Equation (3.5), which gives the price of a bond:

Yield to maturity Interest rate that makes the present value of payments from a bond equal to its price

$$P = \frac{C}{(1+i)} + \frac{C}{(1+i)^2} + \cdots + \frac{(C+F)}{(1+i)^T}$$

where C is the coupon payment, F is the face value, and T is the maturity. This equation says the price of a bond equals the present value of payments from the bond.

Previously, we used this equation to determine a bond's price, assuming we know the payments from the bond (C and F) and the interest rate i. When we measure yield to maturity, we turn this calculation around. We know the payments and the bond's price, P, and we use the equation to derive an interest rate. This interest rate is the one that makes the present value of the bond's payments equal to P. It is the yield to maturity.

Recall the example of a bond with a 3-year maturity, a \$100 face value, and \$5 coupon payments. If the bond's price is \$95, Equation (3.5) becomes

$$95 = \frac{5}{(1+i)} + \frac{5}{(1+i)^2} + \frac{105}{(1+i)^3}$$

The yield to maturity is the interest rate i that solves this equation. The solution is $i = 0.069$, or an interest rate of 6.9 percent.

(A technical note: Usually, there is no easy way to solve equations like the last one. You have to use trial and error, plugging in different values for i until you find one that makes the right side equal to the 95 on the left. Fortunately, a computer or financial calculator can do this for you quickly.)

Recall that the classical theory implies that asset prices move inversely with interest rates. In the case of bonds, this principle is true by definition: it follows from how we measure the yield to maturity. If the price on the left side of our equation goes up, the interest rate on the right must go down for the equation to hold.

In our example of a 3-year bond, if the price rises from \$95 to \$98, the yield to maturity falls from 6.9 percent to 5.8 percent. If this happens, you might hear on the news that "bond prices rose" or that "interest rates on bonds fell." These are two ways of saying the same thing.

The Rate of Return

Suppose you buy a stock or bond and hold onto it for a year. How much have you earned by holding the security? You have potentially increased your wealth in two ways:

1. The security may pay you directly. A bond may yield a coupon payment. If you own a company's stock, you do not directly receive the company's profits, but you may receive a dividend.
2. The price of the security may change. If the price rises, you own a more valuable asset, so your wealth rises. This is called a **capital gain.** Of course the price may also fall, causing a **capital loss.**

Capital gain Increase in an asset holder's wealth from a change in the asset's price

Capital loss Decrease in an asset holder's wealth from a change in the asset's price

Return Total earnings from a security; the capital gain or loss plus any direct payment (coupon payment or dividend); return = $(P_1 - P_0) + X$

Rate of return Return on a security as a percentage of its initial price; rate of return = $(P_1 - P_0)/P_0 + X/P_0$

The total amount you gain from holding the security is the capital gain or loss plus any direct payment you receive. This total is called the **return** on the security:

$$\text{return} = (P_1 - P_0) + X$$

where P_0 is the initial price of the security, P_1 is the price after you hold it for a year, and X represents a direct payment. (X can be a coupon payment, C, or a dividend, D.)

The **rate of return** on a security is the return as a percentage of the initial price. It is calculated by dividing the return by the price:

AN ASSET'S RATE OF RETURN

$$\text{rate of return} = \frac{\text{return}}{P_0}$$

$$= \frac{(P_1 - P_0)}{P_0} + \frac{X}{P_0} \quad (3.6)$$

▶ In the case of a bond, the second term in the rate-of-return formula is the coupon payment divided by the initial price, C/P_0. This variable is called the *current yield* on the bond.

The rate of return has two parts. The first is the percentage change in the security price, and the second is the direct payment divided by the initial price.

Suppose in 2020 you buy a bond for \$80. In 2021, the bond makes a coupon payment of \$4 and the price rises to \$82. Plugging these numbers into the formula, the rate of return is

$$\frac{(82 - 80)}{80} + \frac{4}{80} = 0.075, \text{ or } 7.5\%$$

If the bond makes a coupon payment of \$4 but the price falls from \$80 to \$75, the rate of return is

$$\frac{(75-80)}{80}+\frac{4}{80}=-0.013, \text{ or } -1.3\%$$

As this example illustrates, the rate of return can be negative if there is a large enough capital loss.

Returns on Stocks and Bonds

Figure 3.4 traces some data on rates of return. It shows the average rates of return on U.S. stocks and Treasury bonds from 1900 through 2007. You can see immediately that stock returns are more volatile than bond returns. This reflects the fact that stock prices fluctuate more than bond prices, as we discussed in Section 3.2. Changes in stock prices cause large swings in the rate of return.

On the other hand, the *average* rate of return is higher for stocks than for bonds. Averaging over 1900–2007 produces a rate of about 11 percent for stocks and 5 percent for bonds. This fact should make sense. As we discussed earlier, savers choose assets with more uncertain income only if they are compensated with a risk premium—a higher average return.

FIGURE 3.4 Stock and Bond Returns, 1900–2007

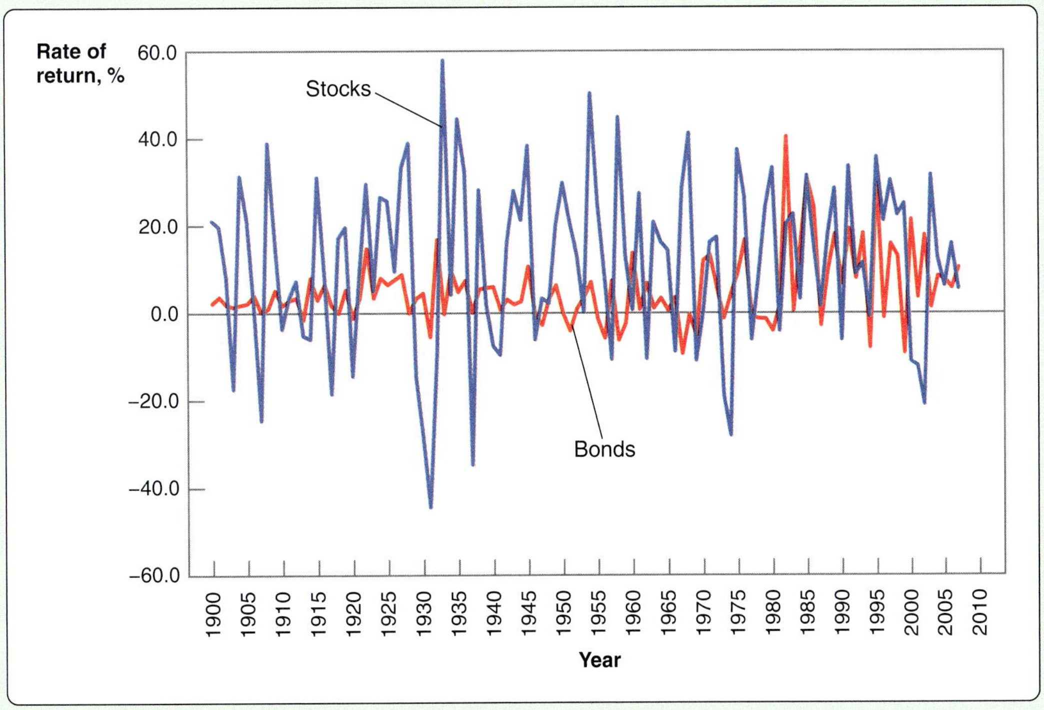

Rates of return on U.S. stocks are more volatile than rates of return on Treasury bonds.
Source: Jeremy Siegel, University of Pennsylvania (jeremysiegel.com)

Rate of Return versus Yield to Maturity

People are often confused about the difference between the rate of return on a bond and the yield to maturity. Both variables tell us something about how much you earn by holding the bond. But they can behave quite differently. For example, a sharp rise in the yield to maturity may mean a *negative* rate of return, because the bond's price falls. If you are thinking of buying a bond, which variable should you care about?

The answer depends on how long you are likely to hold the bond. If you hold the bond until it matures, the yield to maturity tells what interest rate you receive. Fluctuations in the bond's price, which affect the rate of return, are irrelevant if you never sell the bond.

On the other hand, if you sell the bond after a year, you will receive the rate of return for the year. The yield to maturity does not matter if you don't hold the bond to maturity. As we will see in Chapter Five, these facts help us understand who buys different kinds of bonds.

3.7 REAL AND NOMINAL INTEREST RATES

We now introduce a crucial distinction between two kinds of interest rates, nominal interest rates and real interest rates. The interest rates we have discussed so far are nominal rates, but we'll see that real rates are more important for economic decisions. What is the difference?

Nominal interest rate (i) Interest rate offered by a bank account or bond.

Real interest rate (r) Nominal interest rate minus the inflation rate; $r = i - \pi$

A **nominal interest rate** is the interest rate offered by a bank account or a bond. If a sign at your bank says "savings accounts now paying 4.2%," then 4.2 percent is a nominal interest rate. If you calculate that a bond's yield to maturity is 5.8 percent, that is also a nominal rate.

The **real interest rate** is the nominal rate minus the inflation rate. Economists use the letter r for the real rate, i for the nominal rate, and π for the inflation rate. Thus we can write

$$r = i - \pi \qquad \textbf{(3.7)}$$

If your bank pays a 5 percent nominal interest rate and the inflation rate is 3 percent, then the real interest rate is $5\% - 3\% = 2\%$.

What's the meaning of the real interest rate? Suppose again that the nominal rate is 5 percent and the inflation rate is 3 percent. You put \$100 in the bank and it grows to \$105 after a year. Does that mean you are 5 percent richer? Not really, because the value of your money has been eroded by inflation.

A 3 percent inflation rate means that each of your dollars is worth 3 percent less than a year ago. The bank has given you 5 percent of your initial deposit, but inflation has taken away 3 percent of its value. Subtracting your loss from your gain, the value of your deposit has risen 2 percent. This 2 percent is the real interest rate.

Generally, economists think the behavior of consumers and firms depends on real interest rates, not nominal rates. For example, real rates help determine how much people save out of their incomes. Savers care how much their wealth will grow after accounting for the losses from inflation.

Figure 3.5 graphs real and nominal interest rates from 1960 through 2007. The green line shows a nominal rate, the yield to maturity on 3-month Treasury bills. The orange line shows the real rate, measured as the nominal rate minus inflation over the previous year.

The graph shows that real and nominal interest rates can move quite differently. In the 1970s, nominal rates were high, but inflation was also high, so real interest rates were low or negative. Since the 1980s, nominal rates have been lower than they were in the 1970s, but real rates have usually been higher.

As well as distinguishing between nominal and real interest rates, economists define nominal and real versions of asset returns. The rate of return in Equation (3.6) is the *nominal rate of return*. The *real rate of return* is the nominal rate minus the inflation rate. For example, if the nominal rate of return on a stock is 10 percent and inflation is 3 percent, the stock's real rate of return is $10\% - 3\% = 7\%$.

Real Interest Rates: Ex Ante versus Ex Post

Let's now make our definition of the real interest rate more precise. Suppose in 2020 you buy a bond with a 10-year maturity and a nominal interest rate

FIGURE 3.5 Real and Nominal Interest Rates, 1960–2007

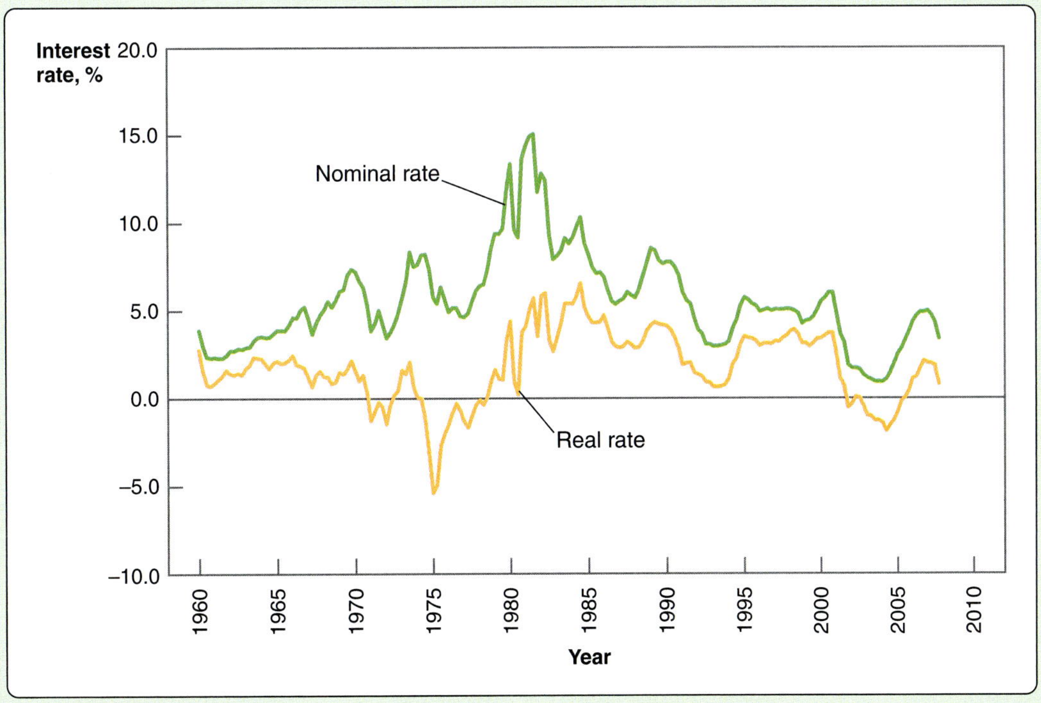

This graph plots the nominal and real interest rates on 3-month Treasury bills. The real rate is the nominal rate minus the inflation rate over the previous year.

Source: Federal Reserve Bank of St. Louis

(the yield to maturity) of 7 percent. To find the real interest rate, you must subtract the inflation rate from 7 percent. This raises a question: over what time period should you measure the inflation rate?

The relevant time period is the life of the bond. For a 10-year bond issued in 2020, this is the period from 2020 to 2030. Inflation over this period determines how much of the earnings on the bond are eroded in real terms.

You should see a problem. If you are thinking about buying a bond in 2020, you would like to know the real interest rate that it pays. You can calculate the nominal rate, but you don't have a crystal ball to say what inflation will be from 2020 to 2030. What, then, is the real interest rate?

Economists answer this question in two different ways. They define two versions of the real interest rate, *ex ante* and *ex post*. In Latin, *ex ante* means "from before" and *ex post* means "from after." The **ex ante real interest rate** is the nominal rate minus the inflation rate that people *expect* when a bond is sold:

Ex ante real interest rate ($r^{\text{ex ante}}$) Nominal interest rate minus expected inflation over the loan period; $r^{\text{ex ante}} = i - \pi^{\text{expected}}$

EX ANTE REAL INTEREST RATE

$$r^{\text{ex ante}} = i - \pi^{\text{expected}} \qquad (3.8)$$

In our example, suppose that people's best guess is that inflation will average 2 percent per year over the period 2020–2030. In this case, the ex ante real interest rate is the nominal rate of 7 percent minus 2 percent, or 5 percent.

The **ex post real interest rate** is the nominal rate minus the *actual* inflation rate.

Ex post real interest rate ($r^{\text{ex post}}$) Nominal interest rate minus actual inflation over the loan period; $r^{\text{ex post}} = i - \pi^{\text{actual}}$

EX POST REAL INTEREST RATE

$$r^{\text{ex post}} = i - \pi^{\text{actual}} \qquad (3.9)$$

Suppose people expect inflation of 2 percent per year over 2020–2030, but unexpected events cause actual inflation to average 4 percent. The ex post real interest rate is $7\% - 4\% = 3\%$.

When people borrow or lend funds, their decisions depend on the ex ante real interest rate; they don't yet know the ex post rate. In the end, however, the ex post rate determines what borrowers really pay and lenders receive. The ex post rate is lower than the ex ante rate if inflation turns out higher than expected:

$$\pi^{\text{actual}} > \pi^{\text{expected}} \rightarrow r^{\text{ex post}} < r^{\text{ex ante}}$$

The reverse happens if inflation is lower than expected:

$$\pi^{\text{actual}} < \pi^{\text{expected}} \rightarrow r^{\text{ex post}} > r^{\text{ex ante}}$$

In our example, actual inflation turns out to be 4 percent, higher than the expected level of 2 percent. This means the ex post real rate is 3 percent, lower than the ex ante rate of 5 percent.

The difference between ex ante and ex post real interest rates can cause problems for the financial system. The next case study recounts a famous example.

CASE STUDY

Inflation and the Savings and Loan Crisis

In the early 1960s, U.S. inflation rates averaged less than 2 percent per year. This situation appeared stable, so people expected low inflation to continue in the future. However, inflation rose rapidly in the late 1960s and 1970s. Because actual inflation over this period was higher than expected, ex post real interest rates were lower than ex ante rates. In real terms, lenders received less from borrowers than they expected to receive when they made loans.

Losses to lenders were greatest for long-term loans, especially home mortgages. In 1965, the nominal interest rate on 30-year mortgages was under 6 percent. This rate was locked in until 1995. Since inflation was expected to be less than 2 percent, the ex ante real interest rate was positive. However, inflation averaged 7.8 percent over the 1970s, implying negative ex post rates.

Negative real interest rates on mortgages were a great deal for homeowners. But they caused large losses for banks that specialized in mortgages, such as savings and loan associations. These losses were one reason for the "S&L Crisis" of the 1980s, when many savings and loans went bankrupt. We return to this episode in Chapters Nine and Ten.

Inflation-Indexed Bonds

The preceding case study illustrates a general point: *uncertainty about inflation makes it risky to borrow or lend money.* This is true for bank loans, and also when firms borrow by issuing bonds. In both cases, borrowers and lenders agree on a nominal interest rate but gamble on the ex post real rate. Borrowers win the gamble if inflation is higher than expected, and lenders win if inflation is lower than expected.

Can borrowers and lenders avoid this gamble? One tool for reducing risk is **inflation-indexed bonds.** This type of bond guarantees a fixed ex post real interest rate. Unlike a traditional bond, it does not specify a nominal interest rate when it is issued. Instead, the nominal rate adjusts for inflation over the life of the bond, eliminating uncertainty about the real rate.

Inflation-indexed bond Bond that promises a fixed real interest rate; the nominal rate is adjusted for inflation over the life of the bond

For example, an indexed bond might promise an ex post real interest rate of 2 percent. This means the nominal rate (i) is 2 percent plus inflation over the life of the bond (π^{actual}). If inflation turns out to be 3 percent, the nominal rate is 5 percent. If inflation is 4 percent, the nominal rate is 6 percent. Either way, the ex post real rate, $i - \pi^{\text{actual}}$, is 2 percent. Higher inflation doesn't benefit borrowers at the expense of lenders, or vice versa.

Economists have long advocated the creation of inflation-indexed bonds. The government of the United Kingdom began issuing indexed bonds in 1975, and the U.S. Treasury followed in 1997. The U.S. bonds are called TIPS, for Treasury Inflation Protected Securities. (Not coincidentally, an economics professor, Harvard's Lawrence Summers, was Deputy Treasury Secretary when TIPS were created.)

Yet indexed bonds have not proved very popular. Currently, TIPS account for less than 10 percent of Treasury securities, as most savers prefer to buy traditional bonds. No corporations issue inflation-indexed bonds. Economists find this situation puzzling, since indexed bonds reduce risk, both for borrowers and for lenders. Some suggest that most savers simply don't understand the benefits of indexation.

Summary

3.1 Valuing Income Streams

- The future value of a dollar is how many dollars it can produce in some future year. The future value of a dollar in n years is $\$(1 + i)^n$, where i is the interest rate.
- The present value of a future dollar is its worth in today's dollars. The present value of a dollar in n years is $\$1/(1 + i)^n$. We can use this formula to find the present value of a stream of income.
- A perpetual payment of Z per year has a present value of Z/i.

3.2 The Classical Theory of Asset Prices

- The classical theory says an asset price equals the present value of expected future income from the asset.
- The price of a share of stock is the present value of *either* company earnings per share or dividends per share.
- The classical theory assumes that expectations are rational: expected asset income is the best possible forecast, given all public information.
- The interest rate used to compute an asset price is the safe rate plus a risk premium. The risk premium rises with uncertainty about asset income.

3.3 Fluctuations in Asset Prices

- A rise in expected asset income raises asset prices. A rise in interest rates reduces asset prices.
- Actions by the Federal Reserve have strong effects on stock prices because they influence companies' earnings, the safe interest rate, and risk premiums.
- The prices of long-term bonds are more volatile than those of short-term bonds because they respond more strongly to changes in interest rates. Stock prices are more volatile than bond prices because they respond strongly both to interest-rate changes and to changes in expected company earnings.

3.4 Asset-Price Bubbles

- Some economists believe that asset prices are influenced by bubbles. This means that prices rise above the present value of asset income. People pay high prices for assets because they expect prices to rise even higher.
- Bubbles occur in many types of asset prices, including stock prices and real estate prices. In the seventeenth century, Holland experienced a bubble in the prices of tulip bulbs.
- Some economists think that high price-earnings ratios signal bubbles in the stock market. When P/E ratios are high, returns on stocks are usually low over the next decade.
- Stock prices in the United States rose rapidly in the 1990s and then fell in the early 2000s. Some economists interpret this episode as a bubble and its collapse. Others explain the experience with

the classical theory; they cite good news about company earnings during the 1990s and bad news after 2000.

3.5 Asset-Price Crashes

- An asset-price bubble may end with a crash: prices plummet in a short period of time. A crash occurs when asset holders lose confidence, sparking a vicious cycle of selling and declining prices.
- U.S. stock prices crashed on two "Black Mondays": October 28, 1929 and October 19, 1987.
- To reduce the risk of crashes, the government has established margin requirements, which limit borrowing to buy stock. Securities exchanges have created circuit breakers: trading is suspended if prices fall sharply.

3.6 Measuring Interest Rates and Asset Returns

- The interest rate on a bond is measured by the yield to maturity, the interest rate that makes the present value of the bond's payments equal to its price.
- The return on an asset is the change in its price plus any current payment (a coupon payment or stock dividend). The rate of return is the return as a percentage of the initial price.
- The rate of return on stocks is more volatile than the rate of return on bonds, but it is higher on average.
- A bond's rate of return shows what someone earns by holding the bond for a year and then selling it. The yield to maturity shows the earnings from holding the bond to maturity.

3.7 Real and Nominal Interest Rates

- The interest rates we observe in financial markets are nominal rates (i). A real interest rate (r) is a nominal rate minus the inflation rate (π).
- The ex ante real interest rate on a loan or bond is the nominal rate minus the inflation rate *expected* over the life of the loan or bond. The ex post real rate is the nominal rate minus the *actual* inflation rate over the period.
- When inflation is higher than expected, ex post real interest rates are lower than ex ante rates, benefiting borrowers at the expense of lenders. The reverse occurs when inflation is lower than expected. The rise in inflation in the 1970s produced negative ex post rates, which helped cause the savings and loan crisis of the 1980s.
- Inflation-indexed bonds guarantee fixed real interest rates. The nominal interest rate adjusts for inflation, eliminating the effect of inflation on the ex post real rate.

Key Terms

asset-price bubble, p. 63

asset-price crash, p. 68

capital gain, p. 72

capital loss, p. 72

circuit breaker, p. 70

classical theory of asset prices, p. 57

dividend, p. 58

ex ante real interest rate, $r^{\text{ex ante}}$, p. 76

ex post real interest rate, $r^{\text{ex post}}$, p. 76

future value, p. 54

inflation-indexed bond, p. 77

margin requirements, p. 70

nominal interest rate, i, p. 74

present value, p. 55

price-earnings (P/E) ratio, p. 65

rate of return, p. 72

rational expectations, p. 58

real interest rate, r, p. 74

return, p. 72

risk premium, φ, p. 59

safe interest rate, i^{safe}, p. 59

yield to maturity, p. 71

Questions and Problems

1. Suppose you win the lottery. You have a choice between receiving $100,000 a year for 20 years or an immediate payment of $1,200,000.
   a. Which choice should you take if the interest rate is 3 percent? If it is 6 percent?
   b. For what range of interest rates should you take the immediate payment?
2. Suppose a bond has a maturity of 3 years, annual coupon payments of $5, and a face value of $100.
   a. If the interest rate is 4 percent, is the price of the bond higher or lower than the face value? What if the interest rate is 6 percent?
   b. For what range of interest rates does the price exceed the face value? Can you explain the answer?
3. Suppose that people expect a company's earnings to grow in the future at the same rate they have grown in the past. Does this behavior satisfy the assumption of rational expectations? Explain.
4. Describe how each of the following events affects stock and bond prices.
   a. The economy enters a recession.
   b. A genius invents a new technology that makes factories more productive.
   c. The Federal Reserve raises its target for interest rates.
   d. People learn that major news about the economy will be announced in a few days, but they don't know whether it is good news or bad news.
5. Consider two bonds. Each has a face value of $100 and matures in 10 years. One has no coupon payments, and the other pays $10 per year.
   a. Calculate the price of each bond if the interest rate is 3 percent and if the interest rate is 6 percent.
   b. When the interest rate rises from 3 percent to 6 percent, which bond price falls by a larger percentage? Explain why.
6. Suppose a company's stock has current earnings of X per share. People expect the earnings to grow by a fraction g each year: earnings will be $X(1+g)$ next year, $X(1+g)^2$ the year after that, and so on forever. The interest rate is i.
   a. Write a formula for the price of the stock according to the classical theory. The formula should show an infinite number of terms added together.
   b. [***Advanced***] Can you reduce the formula for the stock's price to a single term involving X, g, and i?
   c. Use the answers to parts (a) and (b) to explain why the high price-earnings ratios of the 1990s might be consistent with the classical theory.
7. Suppose a bond has a face value of $100, annual coupon payments of $4, a maturity of 5 years, and a price of $90.
   a. Write an equation that defines the yield to maturity on this bond.
   b. If you have the right kind of calculator or software, find the solution for the yield to maturity.
8. Suppose the price of the bond in Problem 7 falls from $90 to $85 over a year. Calculate the bond's rate of return over the year.
9. Suppose the yield to maturity on a 1-year bond is 6 percent. Everyone expects inflation over the year to be 3 percent, but it turns out to be 5 percent. What is the nominal interest rate on the bond, the ex ante real rate, and the ex post real rate?
10. "I just bought my first house. Economists are predicting low inflation in the future, but

I sure hope they're wrong!" Why might it make sense for someone to say this?

11. "Buying an inflation-indexed bond is risky. If I buy a conventional bond, I know what interest rate I will receive. With an indexed bond, the rate can rise or fall depending on inflation. Risk-averse savers should prefer conventional bonds." Discuss.

Online and Data Questions

www.worthpublishers.com/ball

12. The text Web site contains data from the Bernanke–Kuttner paper on the Fed and the stock market (see p. 60). The data cover 68 days from 1995 through 2002 when the Fed either changed interest rates or decided not to change them. For each of these days, the data include the change in a short-term interest rate and the percentage change in stock prices. The data also include the interest-rate change that participants in financial markets expected before the Fed acted. (The expected change is measured using data on interest-rate futures, which we discuss in Chapter Five).
    a. Make a graph with the change in the interest rate on the horizontal axis and the percentage change in stock prices on the vertical axis. Plot a point for each day in the data set.
    b. Now compute the *unexpected* change in the interest rate — the actual change minus the expected change. Redo the graph in Part (a) with this variable on the horizontal axis.
    c. Which has a stronger effect on stock prices, the change in the interest rate or the unexpected change? Explain your finding.

13. The text Web site links to bloomberg.com, which provides daily data on the Dow Jones stock index. Find a day within the last year when the index rose or fell by at least 1 percent. Consult news reports for that day and discuss why stock prices might have changed. Was the change consistent with the classical theory of asset prices?

14. The text Web site contains data on interest rates for Treasury bonds. For the most recent data, compare the rates on 10-year conventional bonds and 10-year inflation-indexed bonds. What do these rates tell us about expectations of future inflation?

chapter four 4

What Determines Interest Rates?

- 4.1 THE LOANABLE FUNDS THEORY
- 4.2 DETERMINANTS OF INTEREST RATES IN THE LOANABLE FUNDS THEORY
- 4.3 THE LIQUIDITY PREFERENCE THEORY
- 4.4 THE TERM STRUCTURE OF INTEREST RATES
- 4.5 DEFAULT RISK AND INTEREST RATES
- 4.6 TWO OTHER FACTORS

Low interest rates have helped American citizens. It's helped them buy a home. It's helped them refinance if they own a home. It's put more money in circulation, which is good for job creation.

—*George W. Bush, 2003*

Lower interest rates have made it easier for businesses to borrow and to invest and create new jobs. Lower interest rates have brought down the cost of home mortgages, car payments, and credit cards to ordinary citizens.

—*Bill Clinton, 1996*

I think that if the interest rates had been lowered more dramatically that I would have been reelected President....

—*George H. W. Bush, 1998*

Getty Images/Blend Images

Low interest rates help families buy new homes.

These statements from three presidents illustrate the importance of interest rates. These rates affect the lives of individuals and the growth of the overall economy. They can help determine the outcomes of elections.

Chapter 3 discussed how real and nominal interest rates are measured. This chapter asks what factors determine interest rates. Why do some bonds and bank loans have higher rates than others? Why do rates rise in some time periods and fall in others?

Figure 4.1 on page 84 illustrates the behaviors that we want to understand. For the period from 1960 to 2007, the figure shows the paths of several interest rates: the rates on 90-day Treasury bills, 10-year Treasury

FIGURE 4.1 U.S. Real Interest Rates, 1960–2007

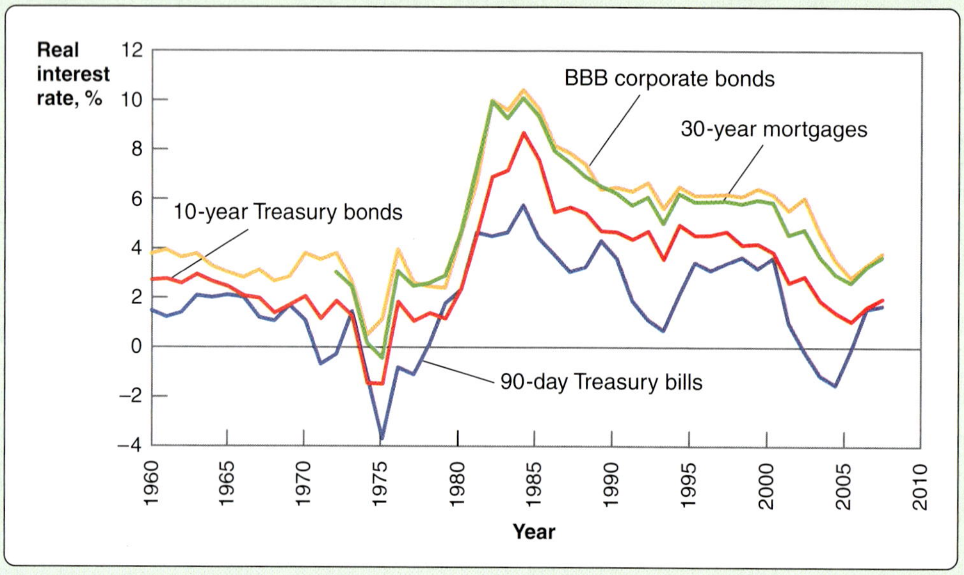

This graph shows the behavior over time of four real interest rates in the United States. Each real rate is a nominal rate minus inflation over the previous year. The broad movements in the four interest rates are similar.

Source: Federal Reserve Bank of St. Louis

bonds, moderate-risk corporate bonds, and 30-year home mortgages. Each interest rate is a real rate, r, defined as the nominal rate, i, minus inflation, π, over the previous year (review Equation 3.7).

The various interest rates in the figure generally move together. Rates fell in the 1970s, rose sharply in the early 1980s, and have mostly fallen since then. This chapter presents two theories that help explain these movements. In one theory, interest rates are determined by the supply and demand for loans. In the other, rates are determined by the supply and demand for money.

Figure 4.1 reveals differences among individual interest rates. Notice, for example, that the corporate bond rate is always higher than the Treasury bond rate. The Treasury bond rate is *usually* higher than the Treasury bill rate, but it dips below the T-bill occasionally. This chapter reviews the reasons behind such differences in rates. It turns out that two factors are most important: the term of a bond or loan and the risk of default by the borrower.

4.1 THE LOANABLE FUNDS THEORY

Loanable funds theory Real interest rates are determined by the supply and demand for loans

The first theory of interest rates that we'll examine is the **loanable funds theory,** which states that the real interest rate is determined by the supply and demand for loans. This theory is based on the central idea of Chapter 1: the financial system channels funds from savers to investors. The loanable funds theory assumes that funds are transferred in a simple way. An economy's savers and investors meet in a market for loans, where the savers lend to the investors.

The interest rate is the price of a loan—what investors pay savers for using their funds. Economists generally believe that prices are determined by supply and demand, and the loan market is no exception. The interest rate is determined by the supply and demand for loans.

Like all economic models, the loanable funds theory simplifies reality. The theory assumes there is only one type of loan and one interest rate; it ignores the diversity of rates illustrated in Figure 4.1. The theory also assumes that savers lend directly to investors, which ignores the role of banks. Nonetheless, the loanable funds theory offers us many insights into the forces determining interest rates.

Saving, Investment, and Capital Flows

What determines the supply and demand for loans? We have assumed that loans are used to finance investment. Therefore, the demand for loans is the level of investment in the economy. If investors decide to undertake more projects, they must borrow more:

$$\text{demand for loans} = \text{investment}$$

The supply of loans is a bit more complicated. Investors borrow from savers, which suggests that the supply of loans equals the level of saving. This is the end of the story if the economy is "closed"—it does not interact with the economies of other countries. However, real-world economies are open, with loans flowing across national borders. An economy's supply of loans depends on these flows as well as on its saving.

Loans can flow in two directions. First, a country's investors can borrow from abroad. For example, a U.S. company that wants to build a new factory can sell bonds to Europeans as well as to Americans. Funds raised from foreign savers are called **capital inflows.** An economy's supply of loans includes these inflows as well as saving within the economy.

Conversely, a country's savers can lend to foreign investors. U.S. savers might buy bonds issued by European companies. Funds sent abroad are called **capital outflows.** These funds are a part of a country's saving that is *not* lent to that country's investors.

To summarize, an economy's total supply of loans is its saving *plus* capital inflows *minus* capital outflows. Economists use the term **net capital inflows** for capital inflows minus outflows. The supply of loans can be written as

$$\begin{aligned}\text{supply of loans} &= \text{saving} + \text{capital inflows} - \text{capital outflows}\\ &= \text{saving} + \text{net capital inflows}\end{aligned}$$

Capital inflows can be greater or less than outflows, so net capital inflows can be either positive or negative. Positive net inflows raise the supply of loans above the level of saving, while negative net inflows do the reverse.

Capital inflows Funds provided to a country's investors by foreigners

Capital outflows Funds provided to foreign investors by a country's savers

Net capital inflows Capital inflows minus capital outflows

Effects of the Real Interest Rate

Now that we know what constitutes the demand and supply for loans, let's discuss how these variables are affected by the price of loans—the interest rate.

Recall the distinction between real and nominal interest rates from Chapter 3. The relevant interest rate here is the ex ante real rate—the nominal interest rate minus expected inflation. The real rate measures the true cost of borrowing and the true earnings from lending. Loan decisions depend on the ex ante real rate, not the ex post rate, because only the ex ante rate is known when loans are made.

Effects on Loan Demand The demand for loans equals the level of investment. To see how the real interest rate affects this variable, consider a firm with a possible investment project, say, a new factory. In deciding whether to build the factory, the firm compares the costs to the revenues the factory is likely to produce. The costs include the interest payments on the loans that finance the project. A rise in the real interest rate means higher costs, making it less likely the firm will decide to build the factory.

This reasoning applies to investment projects throughout the economy. A higher real interest rate makes investment more costly, so fewer projects are undertaken. Lower investment means that investors want fewer loans.

LOAN DEMAND

↑ real interest rate → ↓ investment → ↓ quantity of loans demanded

Effects on Supply The real interest rate affects both components of loan supply, saving and net capital inflows. A higher interest rate means higher returns to savers. Saving becomes a better deal: the money you put aside grows more rapidly. Thus a higher interest rate encourages people to save more:

↑ real interest rate → ↑ saving

To see how the interest rate affects capital flows, consider a foreign saver who plans to purchase bonds and is choosing among bonds issued in different countries. For example, a French saver is choosing between bonds issued by French corporations and U.S. corporations. If the real interest rate rises in the United States, then U.S. bonds become more attractive. Everything else equal, the saver will buy more U.S. bonds. Thus the higher interest rate increases capital inflows to the United States.

A higher U.S. interest rate also influences U.S. savers. It encourages them to buy bonds in their own country rather than send money abroad. So a higher interest rate decreases capital outflows. The combination of higher inflows and lower outflows raises net capital inflows:

↑ real interest rate → ↑ capital inflows and ↓ capital outflows
→ ↑ net capital inflows

To summarize, a higher real interest rate raises both saving and net capital inflows. Both effects raise the quantity of loans supplied:

LOAN SUPPLY

↑ real interest rate → ↑ saving and ↑ net capital inflows
→ ↑ quantity of loans supplied

The Equilibrium Real Interest Rate

Figure 4.2 summarizes our analysis with a graph. It shows how the quantity of loans supplied and the quantity demanded depend on the real interest rate. The graph gives specific numbers as examples.

In the figure, the downward-sloping line is the demand curve. This curve shows how investment falls as the real interest rate rises, reducing the

FIGURE 4.2 The Loan Market

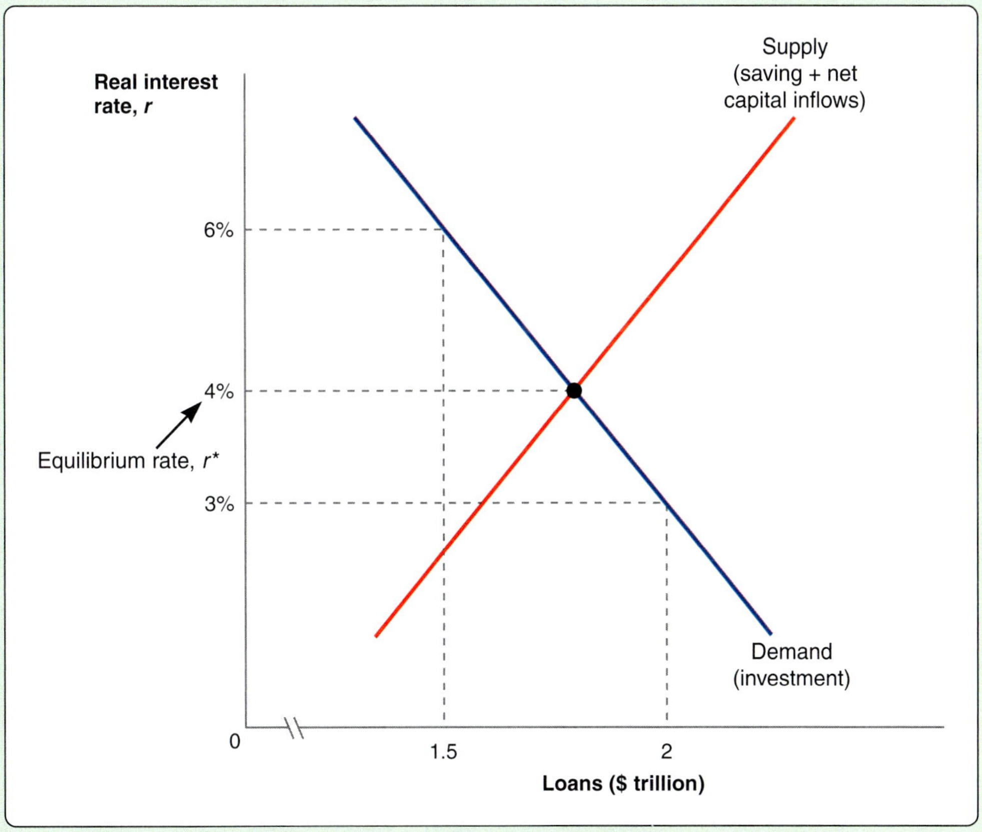

The demand for loans equals investment. A higher real interest rate reduces investment and therefore reduces the quantity of loans demanded. The supply of loans equals saving plus net capital inflows. A higher interest rate raises both factors and therefore raises the quantity of loans supplied. Here, the equilibrium real interest rate, r^*, where the supply and demand curves intersect, is 4 percent.

quantity of loans demanded. If the interest rate is 3 percent, investment is \$2 trillion. If the rate rises to 6 percent, investment falls to \$1.5 trillion in this example.

The upward-sloping line is the supply curve. It shows that a higher interest rate raises the sum of saving and net capital inflows and therefore raises the quantity of loans supplied.

In this market, what interest rate will be charged for loans? The answer is the interest rate at which the supply and demand curves intersect. This is the *equilibrium* real interest rate, r^*. In our graph, the curves intersect at a rate of 4 percent, so this is the equilibrium rate.

To understand why the interest rate is 4 percent, suppose it were higher—say, 7 percent. This rate would attract high levels of saving and net capital inflows but discourage investment. As shown in **Figure 4.3,** the quantity of loans supplied would exceed the quantity demanded. As a

FIGURE 4.3 Adjustment to Equilibrium

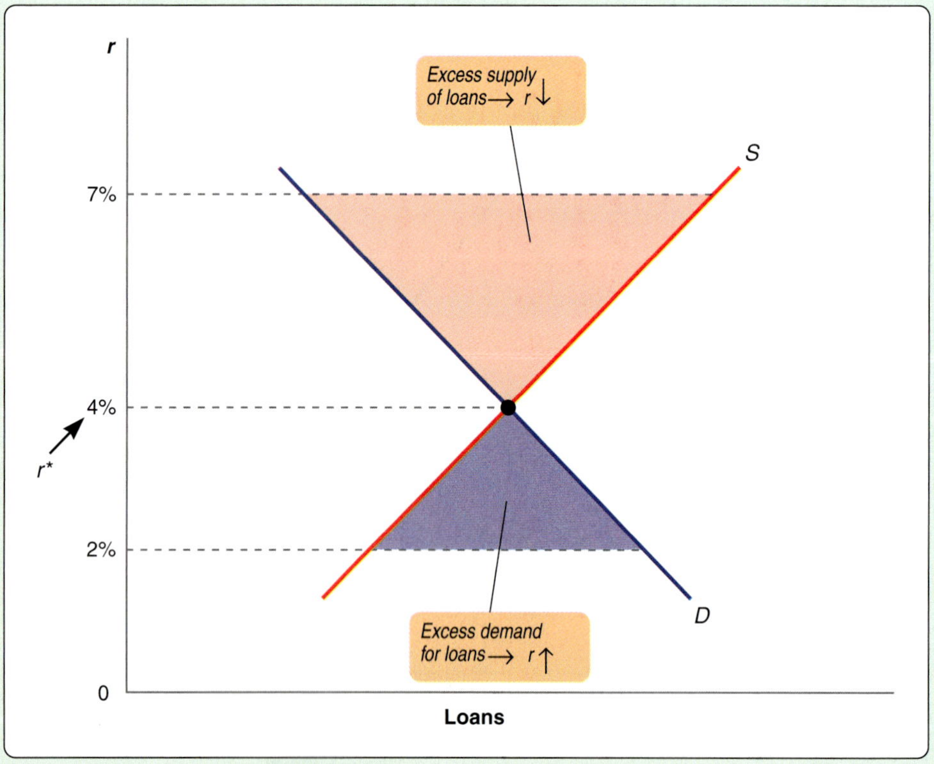

In this example, the equilibrium real interest rate, r^*, is 4 percent. A higher interest rate, say 7 percent, creates an excess supply of loans: not all lenders can find borrowers to take their funds. In this situation, lenders offer lower interest rates to attract borrowers, pushing rates down toward 4 percent. A real interest rate lower than the equilibrium level, say 2 percent, creates an excess demand for loans: not all borrowers can find lenders. In this case, borrowers offer higher rates to attract lenders, pushing rates up toward 4 percent.

result, not all lenders would be able to find borrowers to take their funds. In competing to attract borrowers, lenders would start offering lower interest rates. Rates would fall until they reached the equilibrium rate of 4 percent.

Conversely, if the interest rate were 2 percent, the quantity of loans demanded would exceed the quantity supplied. Borrowers would compete to acquire scarce loans, pushing the interest rate up to 4 percent.

4.2 DETERMINANTS OF INTEREST RATES IN THE LOANABLE FUNDS THEORY

Now that we have developed the loanable funds theory, let's put it to work. We can use the theory to analyze the effects of various events and economic policies on the real interest rate. The theory says the interest rate changes when there is a shift in the supply or demand for loans.

Economists distinguish between shifts in supply and demand curves and movements *along* the curves. Changes in the real interest rate cause movements along the curves; a higher rate raises the quantity of loans supplied and reduces the quantity demanded. A curve shifts when supply or demand changes for a reason *besides* changes in the interest rate. Such an event affects the equilibrium interest rate.

Supply and demand for loans are determined by investment, saving, and net capital inflows. A number of factors cause these variables to change, shifting the supply and demand curves. **Table 4.1** lists some important factors detailed in the following sections.

Shifts in Investment

The demand for loans shifts if a change occurs in the level of investment at a given interest rate. For example, suppose someone invents a machine that makes factories more productive. Many firms want to buy this new machine, so investment rises.

Figure 4.4 illustrates this shift in the demand curve. Before the machine was invented, investment was \$2 trillion if the interest rate was 3 percent.

TABLE 4.1 Loanable Funds Theory: Factors That Can Change the Real Interest Rate

Shifts in Investment	Shifts in Saving	Shifts in Net Capital Inflows
New technologies Changes in investors' confidence	Changes in private saving Changes in government budget deficits	Changes in foreign savers' confidence Changes in foreign interest rates

FIGURE 4.4 An Increase in Investment

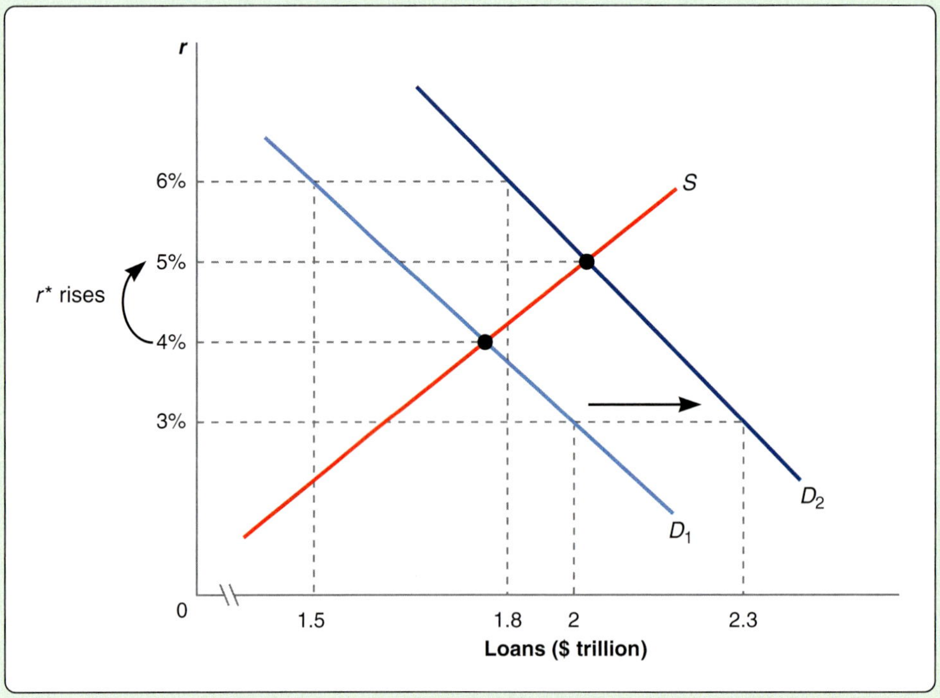

Here a new technology raises the level of investment at each real interest rate. A rise in investment shifts the demand for loans from D_1 to D_2, and r^* rises from 4 percent to 5 percent.

Now, because of the invention, a 3 percent interest rate produces $2.3 trillion of investment. Before, a 6 percent interest rate produced $1.5 trillion of investment; now it produces $1.8 trillion. After the invention, investment still depends negatively on the interest rate but is higher at each rate. In Figure 4.4, the demand curve for loans shifts to the right, from D_1 to D_2.

Understanding this shift makes it easy to see what happens to the equilibrium interest rate. Before the new machine was invented, supply and demand intersected at a real interest rate of 4 percent. After the shift, the intersection occurs at 5 percent. This interest rate is the new equilibrium.

Generally, any event that encourages investment shifts the demand curve for loans to the right, raising the equilibrium interest rate. Any event that makes investment less attractive does the reverse: the demand curve shifts to the left and the interest rate falls.

In real economies, why might investment change for a given interest rate? The example of a new machine is not fanciful: sometimes investment shifts because new technologies are invented. One example is the development of the Internet and related computer applications in the late 1990s. These innovations led to a surge in investment as companies bought new computers.

Another factor is investors' confidence in the economy—their expectations about future economic growth. Strong growth raises the demand for companies' products, making it profitable to increase output. To produce more, companies invest in new factories and machines. Therefore, if good economic news raises expected growth, investment rises for a given interest rate. The demand curve for loans shifts to the right. The opposite happens if bad news reduces expected growth.

Shifts in Saving

The supply of loans shifts when a change occurs in the behavior of saving or net capital inflows. Let's consider saving first. Suppose people become more thrifty: they save more at a given interest rate. This change raises the sum of saving and net capital inflows at a given interest rate, shifting the supply curve for loans to the right.

Figure 4.5 gives an example. If the real interest rate is 3 percent, a higher level of saving raises the quantity of loans supplied from \$1.6 trillion to \$1.8 trillion. At a rate of 6 percent, the quantity supplied rises from \$2 trillion to \$2.2 trillion. The shift in the supply curve reduces the equilibrium interest rate from 4 percent to 3.5 percent.

FIGURE 4.5 An Increase in Saving

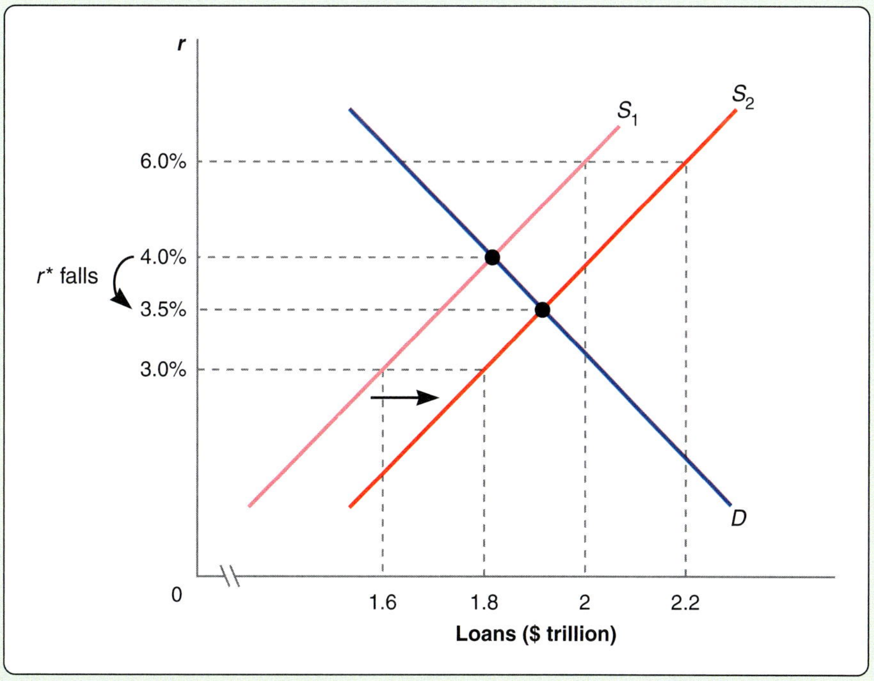

When people become more thrifty, they save more at each real interest rate, increasing the supply of loans. In this example, the supply curve for loans shifts from S_1 to S_2, and r^* falls from 4 percent to 3.5 percent.

Private saving Saving by individuals and firms

Public saving Saving by the government (tax revenue minus government spending)

Why might the level of saving change for a given interest rate? An economy has two kinds of saving, **private saving** and **public saving.** The first is saving by individuals and firms, and the second is saving by the government. Total saving is the sum of the two:

$$\text{saving} = \text{private saving} + \text{public saving}$$

To understand changes in saving, let's examine the two components in turn.

Private Saving The level of private saving can change considerably over time. In the first half of the 1980s, private saving in the United States averaged 20 percent of GDP. Then saving started to decline, and from 2000 to 2007 it averaged 14 percent of GDP. Low saving shifted the supply curve for loans to the left, causing interest rates to be higher than they otherwise would be.

Economists are not sure why private saving fell. One possible explanation is that it became easier for consumers to borrow. From the 1980s to the 2000s, credit cards spread through the economy. So did home equity loans, which allow homeowners to borrow against the equity they've built up in their houses. Easier access to credit may encourage people to spend more, reducing private saving.

Public Saving This part of saving is better understood. The government saves if it takes in tax revenue and doesn't spend it all. That is,

$$\text{public saving} = \text{tax revenue} - \text{government spending}$$

This component of saving is determined by political decisions about taxing and spending.

Budget surplus A positive level of public saving

Budget deficit A negative level of public saving

Public saving can be either positive or negative. We say there is a **budget surplus** when public saving is positive (tax revenue exceeds government spending) and a **budget deficit** when it is negative (spending exceeds revenue). Deficits have been the norm in recent history. Since 1970, the U.S. government has run surpluses in only four years.

Economists often advise governments to reduce budget deficits. The loanable funds theory captures one reason why: deficits raise the real interest rate. Suppose, for example, that the government starts with a deficit and then cuts taxes. The tax cut raises the deficit, which means it reduces public saving—that component of saving becomes more negative. Assuming no big change in the behavior of private saving, total saving falls for a given interest rate. As illustrated in **Figure 4.6,** the supply curve for loans shifts to the left, and the real interest rate rises.

To understand the consequences of this change, recall the quotations from past presidents at the start of this chapter. Higher interest rates make it harder for people to buy houses, borrow for college, or pay off their credit cards. Higher rates also reduce investment in factories and machines, hurting the future productivity of the economy. Lower productivity reduces the incomes of both workers and firms.

FIGURE 4.6 A Rise in the Government Budget Deficit

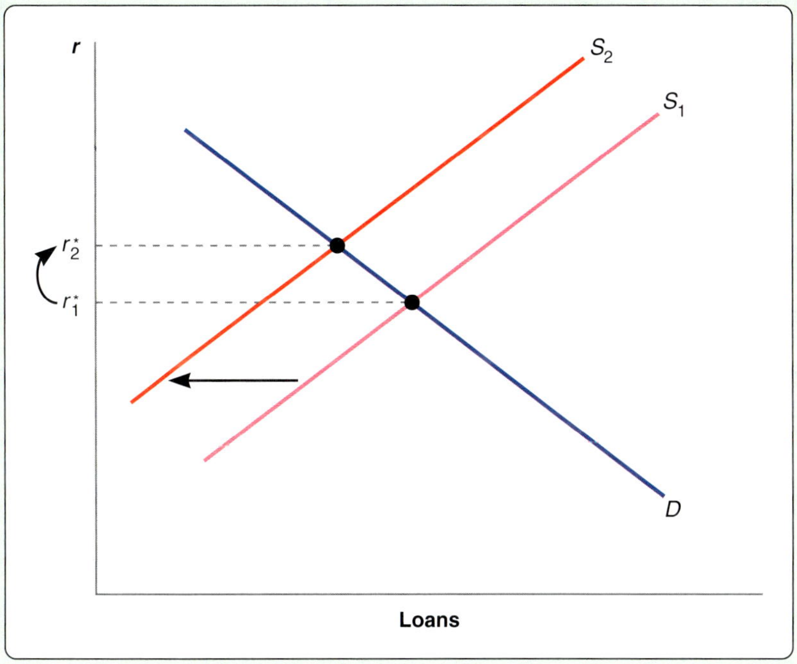

A rise in the government budget deficit is a fall in government saving. This event reduces total saving in the economy. The supply of loans shifts from S_1 to S_2, raising the equilibrium real interest rate from r_1^* to r_2^*.

CASE STUDY

Budget Deficits and Interest Rates

Our theory tells us that budget deficits raise interest rates, but it does not tell us the size of this effect. For example, U.S. budget deficits averaged around 3 percent of GDP over the period 2003–2007. How does a budget deficit of that size affect interest rates?

A 2007 study by Thomas Laubach of the Federal Reserve estimates the effects of U.S. budget deficits. Laubach examines forecasts of deficits made by two government agencies, the Office of Management and Budget (OMB) and the Congressional Budget Office (CBO), over the period 1976–2006. Laubach focuses on forecasts of the deficit five years into the future (e.g., forecasts in 2000 of the deficit in 2005). The goal is to capture long-term movements in the deficit, which are likely to have larger effects than year-to-year fluctuations.

Laubach estimates the effects of deficits on the interest rate on 10-year Treasury bonds. He finds that, on average, a rise in the forecasted deficit of 1 percent of GDP raises the interest rate by about 0.25 percent. Therefore, the total effect of a 3 percent deficit, compared to a balanced budget, is to raise the interest rate by 0.75 percent (say from 5 percent to 5.75 percent).

We've seen that different interest rates in the economy tend to move together (see Figure 4.1). If Laubach's results are accurate, the budget deficit is likely to raise many interest rates by similar amounts. To get a sense of the cost, suppose you have a student loan with a balance of \$20,000. If the interest rate on this loan rises by 0.75 percent, your current interest charges rise by \$150 per year ($0.0075 \times \$20{,}000 = \$150$).*

* See Thomas Laubach, "New Evidence on the Interest Rate Effects of Budget Deficits and Debt," unpublished paper, 2007; forthcoming in *Journal of the European Economic Association*.

Shifts in Capital Flows

A final factor that causes changes in interest rates is shifts in net capital inflows. **Figure 4.7A** shows what happens if net capital inflows rise for a given interest rate. The effects are similar to those of higher saving (see Figure 4.5). The sum of saving and net capital inflows rises, shifting the supply curve for loans to the right. This shift reduces the equilibrium interest rate.

Changes in Confidence Why might capital flows shift? One reason is changes in confidence about an economy's performance. A dramatic example occurred in 1997–1998 in East Asian countries such as Taiwan, South Korea, and Indonesia. These countries had previously received large capital inflows. Foreigners bought bonds issued by East Asian governments, and they lent money to the region's banks to finance the banks' loans to companies.

In the late 1990s, these economies and banking systems experienced problems, and foreign savers began to fear that their loans would not be

FIGURE 4.7 Shifts in Capital Flows

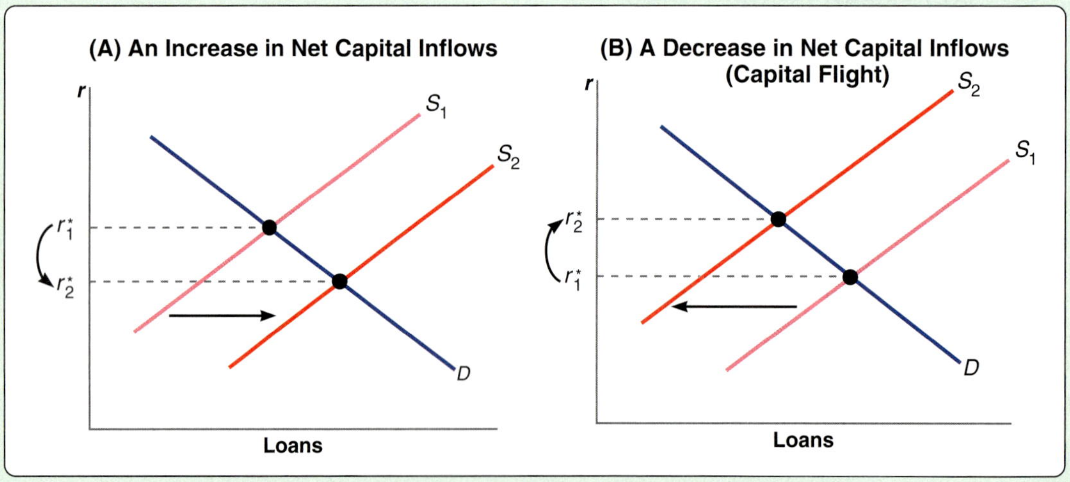

(A) Net capital inflows rise at each real interest rate, shifting the supply of loans from S_1 to S_2. The equilibrium real interest rate falls from r_1^* to r_2^*. (B) Net capital inflows fall at each real interest rate, shifting the supply of loans from S_1 to S_2. The equilibrium real interest rate rises from r_1^* to r_2^*.

repaid. This led to a sharp drop in capital inflows. Net capital inflows (inflows minus outflows) shifted from positive to negative. A shift of this type is called **capital flight.**

Capital flight Sudden decrease in net capital inflows that occurs when foreign savers lose confidence in an economy

The fall in net capital inflows meant the supply of loans in East Asian countries shifted to the left, as shown in **Figure 4.7B**. These shifts raised interest rates sharply. In South Korea, for example, short-term rates jumped from 12 percent in November 1997 to 31 percent in December.

Foreign Interest Rates Another factor behind a country's capital flows is interest rates in *other* countries. Let's think about net capital inflows to the United States. A saver choosing between U.S. bonds and those of another country, say France, compares interest rates in the two countries. If the French interest rate rises, French bonds become more attractive. Savers in France buy more French bonds and fewer U.S. bonds, reducing capital inflows to the United States. U.S. savers also buy more French bonds, raising capital outflows from the United States. Lower inflows and higher outflows both reduce net capital inflows.

Once again, a fall in net capital inflows reduces the supply of loans at a given U.S. interest rate. The supply curve shifts to the left, raising the equilibrium real interest rate.

This analysis implies that interest rates in different countries are connected: they tend to move in the same direction. An event that raises the interest rate in one country, such as a higher budget deficit, reduces net capital inflows to other countries. The supply of loans falls in the other countries, so their interest rates rise too.

Figure 4.8 presents evidence that supports our analysis. The figure shows the real interest rates on short-term government bonds in the United States, Canada, and France for the period 1960–2006. From year to year, these rates bounce around in different ways. But they all follow the broad pattern that we saw in Figure 4.1 for U.S. real rates: a fall in the 1970s, a rise in the 1980s, and a downward drift since then.

Nominal Interest Rates

The loanable funds theory helps us understand the ex ante real interest rate. Let's now return to the subject of nominal interest rates—the rates posted at banks and the bond yields reported in financial media. What determines these rates?

To answer this question, we start with the definition of the ex ante real interest rate: $r = i - \pi^e$, where r is the real interest rate, i is the nominal rate, and π^e is expected inflation. If we turn this equation around, we get

FISHER EQUATION

$$i = r + \pi^e \qquad \textbf{(4.1)}$$

This relation is called the **Fisher equation** because it was developed by the economist Irving Fisher, whom you met in Section 3.5, where we discussed his failure to foresee the 1929 stock crash.

Fisher equation The nominal interest rate equals the real rate plus expected inflation; $i = r + \pi^e$

FIGURE 4.8 International Real Interest Rates, 1960–2006

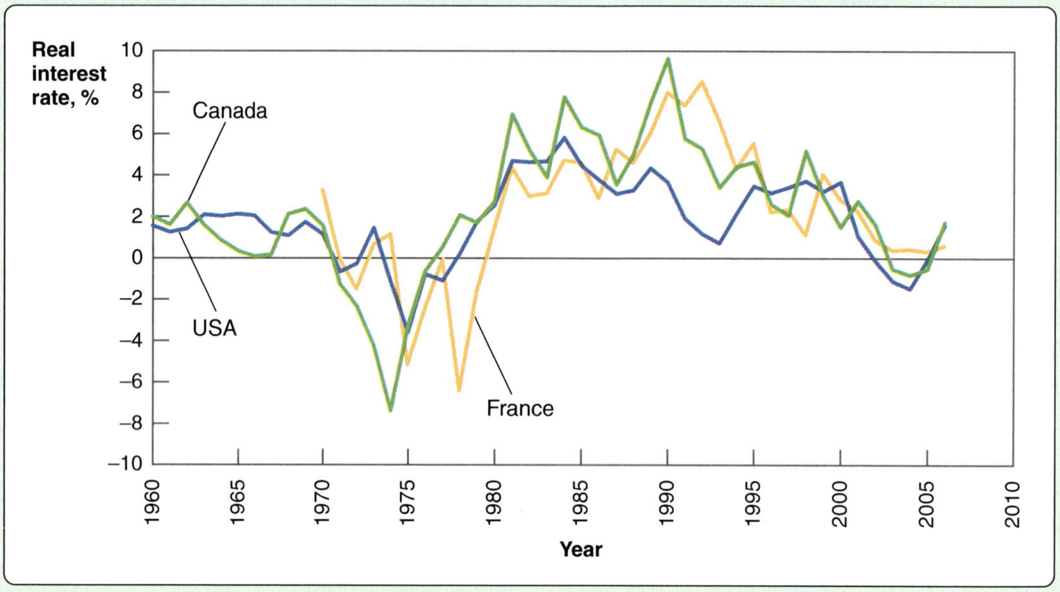

Real interest rates in the three countries examined here follow the same broad pattern over time. (The real interest rate for each country is the nominal rate on 3-month government bonds minus inflation over the previous year.)

Sources: International Monetary Fund; Banque de France

According to the Fisher equation, a rise in the real interest rate (r) raises the nominal rate (i). So the various factors that shift real rates—the items in Table 4.1 on page 89—shift nominal rates too. In addition, for a given real rate, the nominal rate rises and falls with expected inflation, π^e. A rise in π^e of one percentage point raises i by one percentage point.

Adaptive expectations Theory that people's expectations of a variable are based on past levels of the variable; also, *backward-looking expectations*

What determines expected inflation? Economists have not settled this question, but many think a reasonable assumption is **adaptive expectations.** This means that expected inflation is based on inflation rates in the recent past. If annual inflation has run at 3 percent recently, people expect inflation near 3 percent in the future. If inflation rises to 4 percent, people start expecting 4 percent. This assumption is also called *backward-looking expectations*.

▶ Recall that we made a different assumption, rational expectations, in analyzing asset prices (see Section 3.2). We also assume rational expectations in analyzing the term structure of interest rates (Section 4.4). Chapters 12 and 16 discuss economists' debate over the behavior of expectations.

With adaptive expectations, observed inflation rates influence nominal interest rates. An increase in inflation raises expected inflation, which raises the interest rate implied by the Fisher equation.

This *Fisher effect* explains much of the behavior of nominal interest rates. **Figure 4.9** presents data on nominal rates and inflation for 41 countries during the 1990s. As the Fisher equation implies, countries with higher inflation have higher interest rates.

FIGURE 4.9 Inflation and Nominal Interest Rates Across Countries

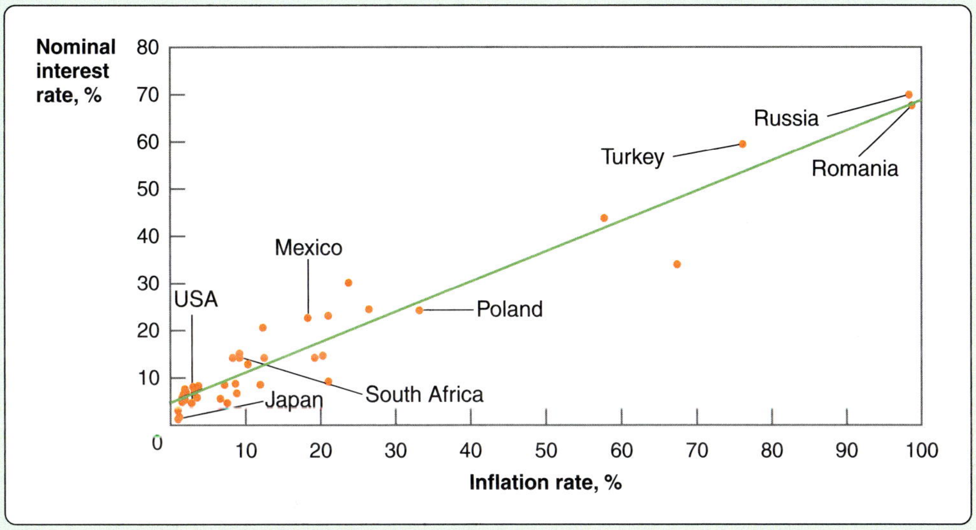

For the 1990s, this graph plots average inflation and the average nominal interest rate on 3-month government bonds in 41 countries. The graph illustrates the Fisher effect: higher inflation raises the nominal interest rate.

Source: International Monetary Fund

4.3 THE LIQUIDITY PREFERENCE THEORY

In the loanable funds theory, interest rates are determined by the supply and demand for loans. We now turn to the **liquidity preference theory,** where interest rates are determined by the supply and demand for money. The demand for money is sometimes called "liquidity preference" because money is the most liquid asset (review Figure 2.3).

Liquidity preference theory The nominal interest rate is determined by the supply and demand for money

In the liquidity preference theory, the supply and demand for money determine the *nominal* interest rate. This is one difference from the loanable funds theory, which explains the *real* interest rate; when we use that theory, we must use the Fisher equation to find the nominal rate. We'll compare our different theories of interest rates after we develop the liquidity preference theory.

In the liquidity preference theory, the key simplifying assumption is that only two kinds of assets exist, money and bonds. All wealth is held in one of these forms. The assets differ in two ways:

1. Money is the medium of exchange (see Section 2.1). People use money to purchase goods and services; they can't use bonds.
2. Bonds pay interest but money does not. This assumption is fairly realistic. In modern economies, money consists mainly of cash and checking accounts (see Section 2.3). Cash doesn't pay interest. Some checking accounts do pay interest, but only small amounts.

The Market for Money

Using these assumptions, let's discuss the key concepts in the liquidity preference theory: money supply and money demand.

Money Supply

The money supply is the total amount of money in the economy. It is controlled by the central bank—in the United States, the Federal Reserve (see Section 2.5).

For our current purposes, we can assume the central bank controls the money supply in a simple way. If it wants to increase the money supply, it first prints new money. It uses this money to purchase bonds, putting the money into circulation in the economy. If the central bank wants to reduce the money supply, it takes in money by selling some of the bonds that it owns. It puts this money in a paper shredder.

In reality, central banks control the money supply through a more complicated process. We discuss the details in Chapter 11. For now, the key point is simply that the central bank chooses the economy's money supply.

Money Demand

In the liquidity preference theory, people choose how to split their wealth between the economy's two assets, money and bonds. Money demand is the amount of wealth that people choose to hold in the form of money.

When people choose their money holdings, they face a trade-off. Since money is the medium of exchange, holding a large amount makes life more convenient. If you carry lots of cash and keep a high balance in your checking account, you can buy things whenever you want. If you hold less cash, a purchase may require a trip to an ATM. If your checking balance is low, you may have to sell bonds to buy something expensive.

On the other hand, holding money reduces your interest income. Each dollar of wealth held in money is a dollar less in interest-bearing bonds. This means that a key determinant of money demand is the nominal interest rate on bonds. Since money pays a nominal rate of zero, the interest rate on bonds tells us how much you give up by holding money. If bonds pay 5 percent, you lose 5 percent by holding money. In economic language, the nominal interest rate on bonds is the *opportunity cost* of money.

When the interest rate rises, the opportunity cost of money is higher. This leads people to hold less money and to place more of their wealth in bonds. Holding less money makes it more cumbersome to buy things, but people accept this inconvenience if bonds pay high interest rates. Therefore,

$$\uparrow i \rightarrow \downarrow \text{quantity of money demanded}$$

The Equilibrium Interest Rate

Figure 4.10 summarizes our discussion. It shows how money supply and money demand are related to the nominal interest rate. Money demand is

FIGURE 4.10 The Market for Money

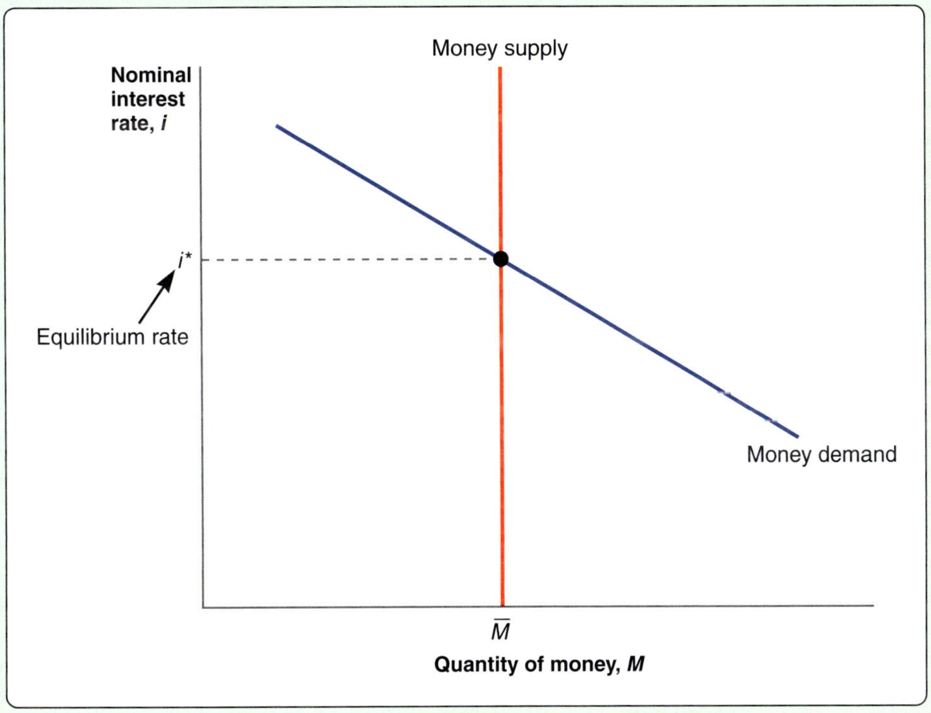

A rise in the nominal interest rate reduces the quantity of money demanded. The quantity of money supplied is fixed at $\overline{M}$, a level chosen by the central bank. The equilibrium nominal interest rate, i^*, is the rate where the supply and demand curves intersect.

captured by a downward-sloping curve: a higher interest rate reduces the quantity of money demanded. The money supply is fixed at a level chosen by the central bank, regardless of the interest rate. This means the money supply curve is vertical. We use the symbol $\overline{M}$ to denote the money supply chosen by the central bank.

The equilibrium nominal interest rate, i^*, is the rate where the supply and demand curves intersect. Market forces push the interest rate to i^*. To understand this process, suppose the interest rate is below i^*. In this case, the quantity of money demanded exceeds the quantity supplied. In other words, the amount of money that people want to hold is greater than the amount the central bank has created.

In this situation, people try to get more money. They do so by selling bonds, which pushes down the price of bonds. As we learned in Chapter 3, lower bond prices mean higher interest rates, so i rises toward i^*.

Conversely, if the interest rate is above i^*, the quantity of money demanded is less than the quantity supplied. People try to reduce their money holdings by purchasing bonds, which pushes bond prices up and the interest rate down.

Changes in Interest Rates

In the liquidity preference theory, changes in equilibrium interest rates are caused by shifts in money supply and money demand. **Table 4.2** lists some reasons for these shifts.

TABLE 4.2 Liquidity Preference Theory: Factors That Can Change the Nominal Interest Rate

Shifts in Money Supply
Decisions by the central bank
Shifts in Money Demand
Changes in aggregate spending
Changes in transaction technologies

Shifts in Money Supply The central bank can choose to change the money supply, $\overline{M}$. **Figure 4.11** shows what happens when $\overline{M}$ increases. The money supply curve shifts to the right, reducing the equilibrium nominal interest rate.

This effect on i is often the motive for changes in the money supply. Central banks act when they believe that changes in interest rates would benefit the economy. For example, after the 9/11 terrorist attacks in 2001, the Federal Reserve raised the money supply to reduce interest rates and stimulate the economy (see Section 2.5). In 2007–2008, the Fed did the same thing to offset economic weakness arising from the subprime mortgage crisis.

FIGURE 4.11 An Increase in the Money Supply

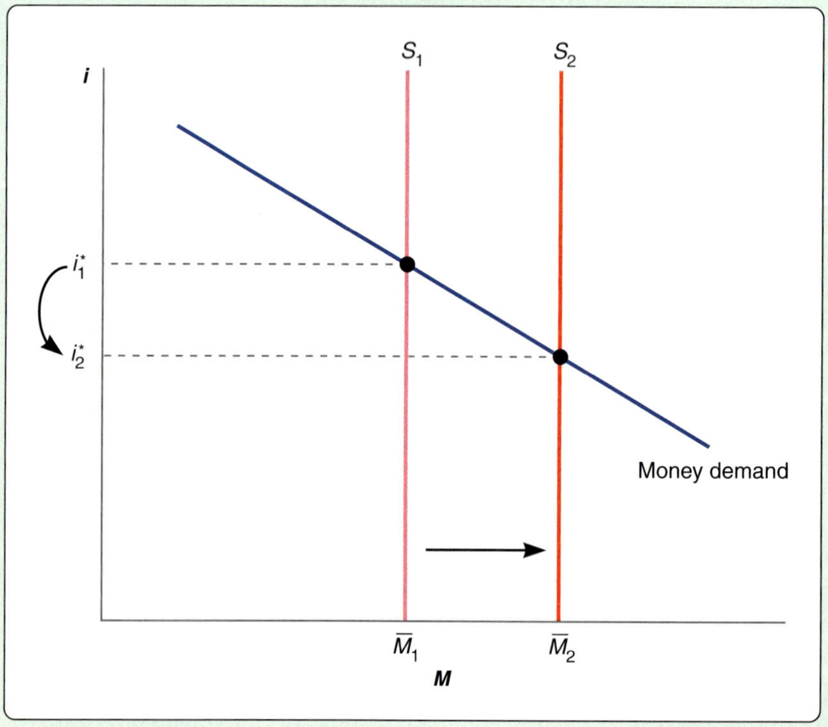

Here the central bank raises the money supply from $\overline{M}_1$ to $\overline{M}_2$. The money supply curve shifts from S_1 to S_2, reducing the equilibrium nominal interest rate from i_1^* to i_2^*.

Shifts in Money Demand The money demand curve shifts if people change the level of money they hold at a given interest rate. **Figure 4.12** illustrates an increase in money demand. The demand curve shifts to the right, raising the equilibrium interest rate.

Why might money demand shift? One reason is a change in aggregate spending on goods and services. Since the purpose of money is to facilitate purchases, people hold more money when they spend more. A person planning a shopping spree needs more cash and checking deposits than a more frugal person. For the economy as a whole, the demand for money rises when total spending rises.

An economy's total spending is nominal GDP. This variable is the product of real GDP and the aggregate price level:

$$\text{nominal GDP} = \text{real GDP} \times \text{aggregate price level}$$

Real GDP measures the quantity of goods and services purchased, and the price level measures the cost of these items. An increase in nominal GDP can result *either* from a rise in real GDP (economic growth) or from a rise in the price level (inflation). In either case, higher spending shifts money demand to the right, raising the equilibrium interest rate, as shown in Figure 4.12.

▶ If you need to review the concepts of real GDP and the aggregate price level, see the appendix to Chapter 1.

FIGURE 4.12 An Increase in Money Demand

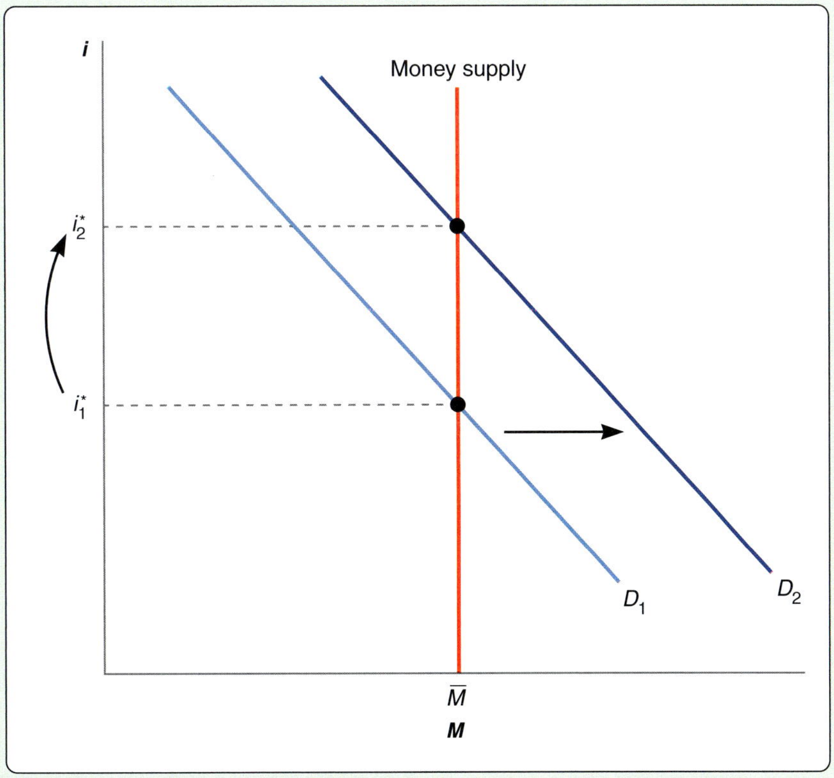

An increase in people's money holdings at a given nominal interest rate shifts money demand from D_1 to D_2. The equilibrium nominal interest rate rises from i_1^* to i_2^*.

Another source of money-demand shifts is changes in *transaction technologies*. This term refers to the methods that people use to obtain money and spend it. Transaction technologies evolve over time, changing the amount of money that people wish to hold.

For example, suppose that ATMs spread to more locations. People may decide to carry less cash in their wallets, because cash is easily available at ATMs. This change reduces the quantity of money demanded at a given interest rate. The money demand curve shifts to the left, which reduces the equilibrium nominal interest rate.

Relating the Two Theories of Interest Rates

Earlier in this chapter we described the loanable funds theory, where the real interest rate is determined by the supply and demand for loans. The nominal rate is determined by the Fisher equation: it is the equilibrium real rate plus expected inflation (see Equation (4.1)).

In the liquidity preference theory, the nominal interest rate is determined by the supply and demand for money. It is natural to ask how this theory relates to the loanable funds theory. Which is more relevant for the interest rates we see in the real world?

The full answer to this question is complex. We will return to the question in Part IV of this book, which includes some necessary background on economic fluctuations. We'll see that the two theories complement one another, capturing different aspects of interest-rate behavior.

A brief preview: For explaining the *long-run* behavior of interest rates, the loanable funds theory is the best framework. The supply and demand for loans determines the average real interest rate over periods of, say, 5 or 10 years. The liquidity preference theory is most useful for explaining the *short-run* behavior of interest rates—the ups and downs from year to year. These movements mainly reflect central banks' decisions about the money supply.

4.4 THE TERM STRUCTURE OF INTEREST RATES

Both the loanable funds theory and the liquidity preference theory assume that an economy has a single interest rate. In reality, there are many different rates on different bonds and bank loans. At any point in time, some rates are higher than others, as we saw in Figure 4.1. The balance of this chapter discusses differences among interest rates. The main factors behind these differences are listed in **Table 4.3.**

TABLE 4.3 Factors That Explain Differences Among Interest Rates

Maturity (term)
Default risk
Liquidity
Taxation

One factor is the term of a bond or a loan. *Term* is another word for time to maturity. Bond maturities range from a few months to 30 years or more. Different maturities usually imply different interest rates, even for bonds issued by the same borrower. Similarly, banks charge different interest rates on loans of different durations.

Term structure of interest rates Relationships among interest rates on bonds with different maturities

The relationships among interest rates on bonds with different maturities are called the **term structure of interest rates.** Let's discuss what determines the term structure—why interest rates differ across maturities, and how these differences change over time.

The Case of Certainty

To understand the term structure, we analyze savers' decisions about what bonds to buy. For now, let's make a major simplifying assumption: savers know the interest rates on all bonds, both today and in the future. For example, they know the rates on bonds that will be issued a year from now. We'll derive a theory of the term structure using this assumption, and then we'll address the complications arising from uncertainty about future interest rates.

We start with an example involving 1-year and 2-year bonds. Suppose it is 2020, and someone plans to save money for two years, until 2022. This person is considering two ways to save: by purchasing 1-year bonds and by purchasing 2-year bonds. Let's compare the interest that the saver receives in the two cases.

Suppose first that the saver buys 2-year bonds, and let $i_2(2020)$ denote the annual interest rate on 2-year bonds issued in 2020. The saver receives this interest rate for two years, for a total of $2i_2(2020)$. For example, if the interest rate is 4 percent, the saver receives a total of $2(4\%) = 8\%$ of his initial wealth.[1]

Now suppose the saver buys 1-year bonds. She purchases these bonds in 2020 and they mature in 2021. At that point she can use the proceeds to buy new 1-year bonds, which mature in 2022. The interest rates on 1-year bonds purchased in 2020 and 2021 are $i_1(2020)$ and $i_1(2021)$, so the saver receives total interest of $i_1(2020) + i_1(2021)$. Recall that we're assuming certainty, so the saver knows both 1-year rates in advance.[2]

In this case, we can derive a relationship between 1- and 2-year interest rates. The interest earnings from a 2-year bond issued in 2020 must equal the total earnings from 1-year bonds issued in 2020 and 2021. That is,

$$2i_2(2020) = i_1(2020) + i_1(2021)$$

This equation must hold if borrowers issue both 1- and 2-year bonds. If the 2-year bonds offered more interest, savers would buy only 2-year bonds. Issuers of 1-year bonds would have to raise interest rates to attract buyers. If 2-year bonds paid less, issuers of these bonds would have to raise rates. In the case of certainty, competition to sell bonds equalizes the interest payments for different maturities.

---

[1] This calculation uses an approximation. To see this, let's compute the earnings on a 2-year bond exactly. If someone saves a dollar at an interest rate i_2, his wealth grows to $1+i_2$ dollars after a year. His wealth after two years is $(1+i_2)^2$ (see the discussion of future value in Section 3.1). The quantity $(1+i_2)^2$ equals $1+2i_2+(i_2)^2$. Subtracting off the saver's initial dollar yields his total earnings: $2i_2+(i_2)^2$.

We've assumed that the earnings on a 2-year bond are simply $2i_2$, which means we ignore the $(i_2)^2$ term. Economists often use this approximation because $(i_2)^2$ is small. For an interest rate of 4 percent (or 0.04 in decimal form), $(i_2)^2$ is 0.16% (0.0016). The total earnings on a 2-year bond are $2i_2+(i_2)^2 = 8\% + 0.16\% = 8.16\%$. Our approximation yields 8 percent, which is accurate enough for present purposes.

[2] Once again we've used an approximation. The exact earnings from the 1-year bonds are $i_1(2020) + i_1(2021) + [i_1(2020)] \times [i_1(2021)]$. We ignore the last term (the product of the two rates), which is small.

If we divide the last equation by 2, we get a formula for the 2-year interest rate:

$$i_2(2020) = \frac{1}{2}[i_1(2020) + i_1(2021)]$$

The 2-year rate is the average of the current 1-year rate and the 1-year rate in the following year. For example, if the 1-year rate is 3 percent in 2020 and 5 percent in 2021, the 2-year rate in 2020 is 4 percent.

Our example concerns 2020, but the logic applies to any year. Let $i_2(t)$ be the interest rate on a 2-year bond issued in year t; $i_1(t)$ is the rate on a 1-year bond issued in t, and $i_1(t + 1)$ is the 1-year rate in the following year. Then we have

$$i_2(t) = \frac{1}{2}[i_1(t) + i_1(t + 1)]$$

The 2-year rate in year t is the average of the 1-year rates in t and $t + 1$.

This formula also holds for periods other than a year. If t is a *month* and $t + 1$ is the following month, the formula says that the 2-month interest rate is the average of two 1-month rates.

Our logic extends beyond one- and two-period bonds to longer-term bonds. If $i_3(t)$ is the interest rate on a *three*-period bond, then

$$i_3(t) = \frac{1}{3}[i_1(t) + i_1(t + 1) + i_1(t + 2)].$$

The three-period interest rate is the average of the one-period rates in the current period, t, and the next two periods, $t + 1$ and $t + 2$.

The rationale for this equation is similar to our reasoning about two-period bonds. Someone saving for three periods can buy either a three-period bond or a series of three one-period bonds. These strategies must produce the same earnings if savers buy both kinds of bonds. Equal earnings implies our formula for $i_3(t)$.

Finally, we can write a general formula for any maturity. Let $i_n(t)$ be the interest rate on an n-period bond in period t. The maturity n can be four periods, five periods, or anything else. The formula is

$$i_n(t) = \frac{1}{n}[i_1(t) + i_1(t + 1) + \cdots + i_1(t + n - 1)] \qquad \textbf{(4.2)}$$

The n-period interest rate is the average of one-period rates in the current period and the next $n - 1$ periods. For example, the 10-year interest rate in 2020 is the average of the 1-year rates in 2020 and the next nine years, 2021 through 2029.

The Expectations Theory of the Term Structure

So far, we have assumed that savers know the interest rates on all bonds, including bonds issued in the future. Of course this assumption is not realistic. In 2020, savers know the current interest rates for all maturities, but they do not know the rates in 2021 or later.

To account for this fact, economists analyze the term structure with the **expectations theory of the term structure.** In this theory, savers do not know the future with certainty, but they have expectations about future interest rates. These expectations are rational: they are the best possible forecasts given current information. Savers choose among bonds based on their rational expectations about interest rates.

Expectations theory of the term structure The n-period interest rate is the average of the current one-period rate and expected rates over the next $n - 1$ periods.

In the expectations theory of the term structure, bonds of different maturities must produce the same *expected* earnings. If they don't, nobody will buy the bonds with lower expected earnings. This reasoning leads to the following term structure equation:

▶ See Section 3.2 for a review of rational expectations.

EXPECTATIONS THEORY OF THE TERM STRUCTURE

$$i_n(t) = \frac{1}{n}[i_1(t) + Ei_1(t+1) + \cdots + Ei_1(t+n-1)] \quad \textbf{(4.3)}$$

where E means "expected." This equation is the same as Equation (4.2), except it replaces actual future interest rates with expected rates. The n-period interest rate is the average of the current one-period rate and expected rates from $t + 1$ to $t + n - 1$.

Accounting for Risk

The expectations theory assumes that savers choose bonds based only on expected interest rates. This assumption ignores the role of uncertainty. Modifying the theory to account for risk makes it more realistic. As we discussed in Chapter 3, savers are risk averse. When asset returns are uncertain, savers demand higher expected returns as compensation.

To see the implications for the term structure, recall another point from Chapter 3: long-term bond prices are more volatile than short-term bond prices. Long-term prices respond more strongly to changes in interest rates. This means that holders of long-term bonds may experience large capital gains or losses, and this risk makes the bonds less attractive to savers.

Therefore, it is *not* true that long- and short-term bonds yield the same expected earnings, as the basic expectations theory assumes. If they did, savers would buy only short-term bonds, which are less risky. To attract buyers, long-term bonds must offer higher expected earnings.

Economists capture this idea by modifying the expectations theory of the term structure, adding a **term premium** to the formula for long-term interest rates. This premium, denoted by τ (the Greek letter tau), is the extra return that compensates for a long-term bond's riskiness. Equation (4.3) becomes

Term premium (τ) Extra return on a long-term bond that compensates for its riskiness; τ_n denotes the term premium on an n-period bond

THE EXPECTATIONS THEORY WITH A TERM PREMIUM

$$i_n(t) = \frac{1}{n}[i_1(t) + Ei_1(t+1) + \cdots + Ei_1(t+n-1)] + \tau_n \quad \textbf{(4.4)}$$

where τ_n is the term premium for an n-period bond. This equation says that the n-period interest rate is the average of expected one-period rates *plus* the term premium.

Bonds of different maturities have different term premiums. The quantity τ_2 is the premium for two-period bonds, τ_3 is the premium for three-period bonds, and so on. The longer a bond's maturity, the higher its term premium; for example, $\tau_3 > \tau_2$ and $\tau_4 > \tau_3$. A longer maturity means a more variable bond price, requiring greater compensation for risk.

The Yield Curve

Yield curve Graph comparing interest rates on bonds of various maturities at a given point in time

The term structure of interest rates can be summarized in a graph called the **yield curve.** The yield curve shows interest rates on bonds of various maturities at a given point in time.

Figure 4.13 shows a hypothetical yield curve for January 1, 2020. On that day, bonds with longer maturities have higher interest rates. For example, the 3-month interest rate is 4 percent, the 1-year rate is 5 percent, and the 10-year rate is 6 percent.

Yield Curve Shapes The yield curve looks different at different points in time. The shape of the curve depends on expectations about future interest rates. **Figure 4.14** shows four possibilities. All assume the same one-period rate, but different expectations about future rates produce different interest rates at longer maturities.

FIGURE 4.13 A Yield Curve

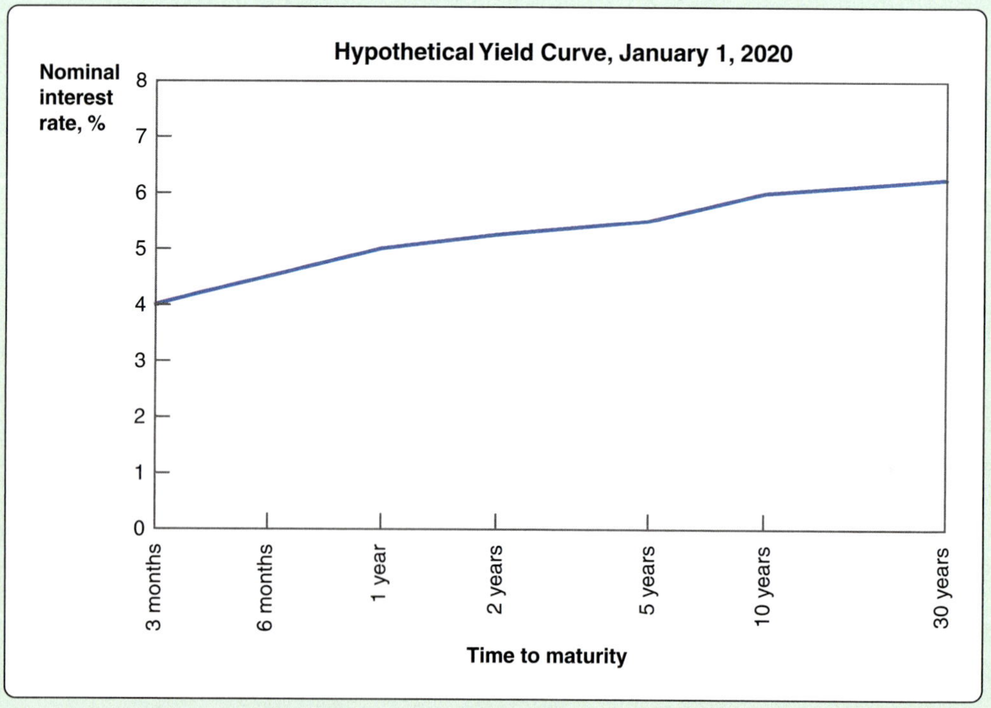

This hypothetical yield curve shows the nominal interest rates on bonds of various maturities on January 1, 2020. On that day, the 3-month interest rate is 4 percent, the 1-year rate is 5 percent, and the 10-year rate is 6 percent.

FIGURE 4.14 Four Possible Yield Curves

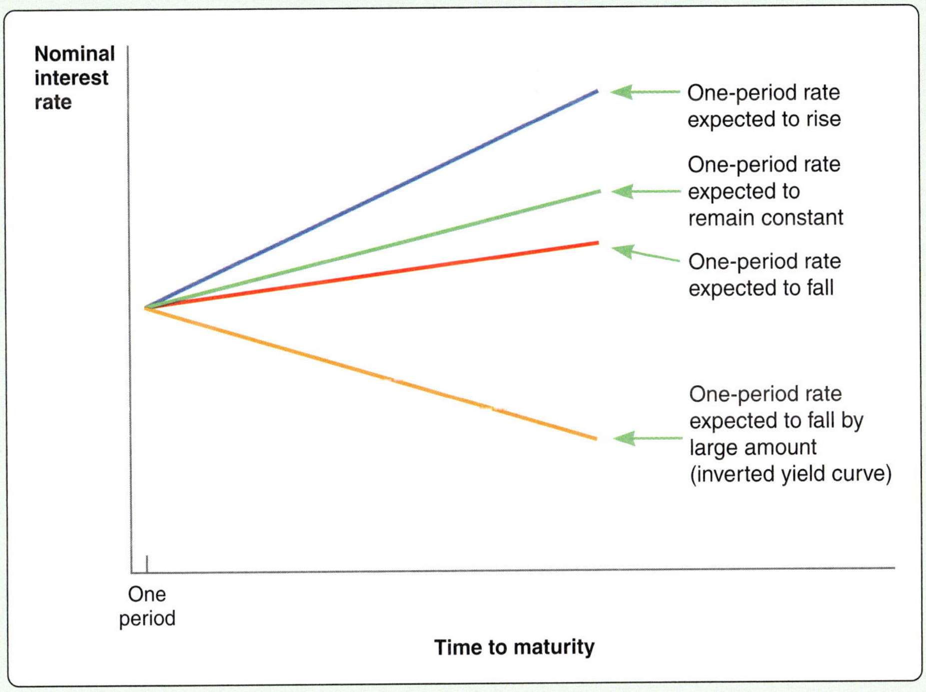

The current one-period interest rate is the same on each of these yield curves. The slopes of the curves depend on expectations of future one-period rates.

As a first example, suppose that people expect the one-period interest rate to stay constant. The expected future rates, $Ei_1(t+1)$, $Ei_1(t+2)$, and so on, all equal the current rate $i_1(t)$. Substituting this assumption into the formula for the n-period rate, Equation (4.4), yields

$$i_n(t) = \frac{1}{n}[i_1(t) + i_1(t) + \cdots + i_1(t)] + \tau_n$$

which simplifies to

$$i_n(t) = i_1(t) + \tau_n$$

With the one-period rate expected to stay constant, the average of expected future rates equals the current one-period rate. The n-period rate is the one-period rate plus a term premium.

Recall that the term premium τ_n rises with a bond's maturity, n. Therefore, the last equation implies that the interest rate $i_n(t)$ rises with n. This case is captured by the green line in Figure 4.14. Rising term premiums cause the yield curve to slope upward.

The other lines in the figure are cases where the one-period interest rate is *not* expected to stay constant. The blue line is an example in which people expect the one-period rate to rise in the future. The average of expected future rates exceeds the current rate, pushing up long-term interest rates: they exceed the one-period rate by more than the term premium. In our graph, the yield curve is steep.

The red line is an example in which people expect the one-period interest rate to fall. The average of expected future rates is less than the current rate, reducing long-term rates and flattening the yield curve.

Inverted yield curve Downward-sloping yield curve signifying that short-term interest rates exceed long-term rates

Finally, the orange line is an example of an **inverted yield curve,** a curve that slopes down. This case arises when people expect an unusually large fall in the one-period interest rate. This expectation reduces long-term rates by more than term premiums raise them, so long-term rates lie below the current one-period rate.

Some Examples **Figure 4.15** graphs actual yield curves for U.S. Treasury bonds at three points in time: January 1981, October 1992, and June 1999. These cases illustrate some of the possible yield curves that we've discussed.

Notice first that interest rates were high at all maturities in 1981. Inflation was high at that time, producing high nominal interest rates through the Fisher equation, $i = r + \pi^e$.

For our current discussion, the key features of the yield curves are their slopes. The yield curve for June 1999 has a common shape—a moderate upward slope. The interest rate is 4.6 percent at a maturity of 3 months, 5.6 percent at 2 years, and 6.0 percent at 30 years. The curve for October 1992 is unusually steep, going from 2.9 percent at 3 months to 7.5 percent

FIGURE 4.15 Some Examples of Yield Curves

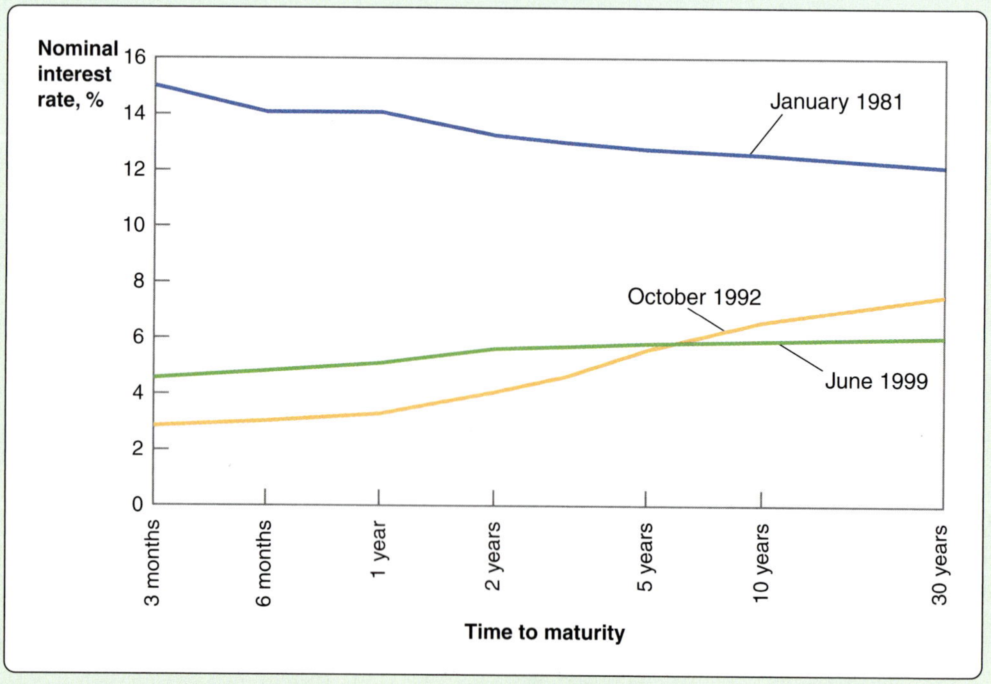

This graph shows the yield curves for U.S. Treasury bonds at three points in time.
Source: Federal Reserve Board

at 30 years. Finally, the yield curve for January 1981 is inverted: rates fall with maturity over most of the curve.

Forecasting Interest Rates The expected path of interest rates determines the yield curve. Turning this relation around, the yield curve tells us about the expected path of rates. An unusually steep curve, such as October 1992, means that short-term interest rates are expected to rise. An inverted curve, such as January 1981, means rates are expected to fall sharply.

These facts imply a use for the yield curve: to forecast interest rates. Suppose you are thinking of borrowing money in the future, so you would like to know future interest rates. You can't know these rates for sure, but you can estimate them with the yield curve. The yield curve reveals the expectations of people who trade bonds. These are good forecasts because bond traders are well informed about interest rates.

CASE STUDY

Inverted Yield Curves

Because of term premiums, the yield curve usually has an upward slope. An inverted curve occurs only if short-term interest rates are expected to fall by a large amount. Why might this expectation arise?

Historically, most inverted yield curves have been caused by the Federal Reserve's monetary policy—specifically, by efforts to reduce inflation. To fight inflation, the Fed slows the growth of the money supply. This action raises short-term interest rates, as we can see with the liquidity preference theory (Section 4.3). Higher interest rates reduce economic growth temporarily, and slower growth reduces inflation.

▶ Chapter 12 details the effects of monetary policy on economic growth and inflation.

In such an episode, short-term interest rates rise temporarily. People expect the central bank to end its policy in the future, reducing short-term rates. In fact, these rates are likely to fall by more than they have risen, ending up lower than they were before the central bank acted. The reason is that inflation will probably fall, reducing nominal interest rates through the Fisher equation. The expected decrease in rates may be large enough to invert the yield curve.

In Figure 4.15, we saw that the yield curve for Treasury securities was inverted in 1981. At that time inflation had been running near 10 percent, and the Federal Reserve was determined to reduce it. The Fed slowed money growth, raising the 3-month Treasury bill rate to 15 percent. The yield curve inverted because people expected large decreases in inflation and interest rates. Expectations turned out to be correct: the 3-month T-bill rate fell to 8 percent in 1983 and 6 percent in 1986.

Another inverted yield curve occurred at the end of 2000. The Fed was worried that inflation might rise, because output had been growing at an unusually rapid pace. The Fed raised short-term interest rates to contain inflation, and the yield curve mildly inverted. In December 2000, the 3-month rate was 6.0 percent, the 1-year rate was 5.7 percent, and the 30-year rate was 5.4 percent.

Online Case Study: The Recent Behavior of the Yield Curve

4.5 DEFAULT RISK AND INTEREST RATES

The governments and corporations that issue bonds sometimes default; that is, they don't make the payments they have promised. The risk of default varies across bonds, leading to differences in interest rates. Bonds with higher risk pay higher rates. The reason is simple. Default risk makes bonds less attractive to savers. If bonds with different risk promised the same interest rate, savers would prefer the bonds with lowest risk. Issuers of high-risk bonds must offer high interest rates to attract buyers.

Default Risk on Sovereign Debt

Sovereign debt Bonds issued by national governments

Many national governments issue bonds to cover their budget deficits. These bonds are called **sovereign debt.** Default risk on these bonds varies greatly across countries.

The U.S. government has never defaulted on its bonds. People generally assume this record will continue, so the bonds' default risk is close to zero. As a consequence, the interest rates on U.S. government bonds are always among the lowest for a given maturity.

The story is different elsewhere. Governments in other countries have defaulted on bonds. Two examples are Russia in 1998 and Argentina in 2001. In each case, the government ran up debt through years of high spending. Weak economies in both countries made it difficult to collect enough taxes to pay off the debt. Eventually, the government stopped making promised payments on its bonds.

Bond rating agencies Firms that estimate default risk on bonds

Because of such experiences, purchasers of sovereign debt pay close attention to default risk. They are assisted by **bond rating agencies,** such as Moody's Investor Services and Standard & Poor's (S&P). These firms study the political and economic situations in different countries and estimate the chances that governments will default.

Rating agencies summarize their judgments with a grade for each country's debt. For example, Standard & Poor's gives ratings from AAA (the highest) to D (the lowest). Sometimes a plus or minus is added to the letter grade. **Table 4.4** shows the different S&P ratings, the corresponding ratings from Moody's, and examples of countries with these ratings in 2008.

TABLE 4.4 Sovereign Debt Ratings, April 2008

Standard & Poor's	Moody's	Risk	Examples
AAA	Aaa	Lowest Risk	USA, Germany
AA	Aa	Low Risk	Chile, Japan
A	A	Low Risk	Italy, China
BBB	Baa	Medium Risk	Colombia, India
BB, B	Ba, B	High Risk	Nigeria, Ecuador
CCC, CC, C	Caa, Ca, C	Highest Risk	Lebanon
D	C	In Default	

A low rating usually means that a country must offer high interest rates to sell its debt.

Sovereign debt from the richest countries, such as the United States and Germany, usually receives a AAA rating. A few rich countries slip to AA or A because of high government debt. For example, Italy's rating in 2008 was A+, or slightly above A, because its debt was 100 percent of a year's GDP. (In the United States, government debt was 44 percent of GDP.)

Poorer countries usually have lower debt ratings. Such countries have defaulted in the past, and analysts worry that economic or political crises will produce future defaults. Colombia's rating in 2008 was BBB+ and Nigeria's was BB.

The bottom of the ratings scale covers countries with serious problems. In 2008, Ecuador had a B- rating, reflecting the fact that it defaulted on debt in 2001. Lebanon had the world's lowest rating, CCC+. Analysts were wary of Lebanon because of a political crisis that left the country without a president.

CASE STUDY

The Paradox of Japanese Interest Rates

Japan is the world's second-largest economy. Its debt had a AAA rating from 1975, when Standard & Poor's first examined it, until 2001. Then the rating started to slide: in 2001 it fell to AA+ and then AA, and in 2002 it reached AA−. The AA− rating ranked Japanese bonds below such countries as Chile and Slovenia. Japan's rating stayed at AA− until 2007, when it edged up to AA.

Japan's ratings reflect growth in its government debt. The underlying problem is an economic slump that started in the early 1990s. The weak economy reduced tax revenue, creating large budget deficits in Japan. Debt grew from about 30 percent of GDP in 1995 to 90 percent in 2007. The economy improved somewhat at the end of this period and the growth of debt slowed, accounting for the slight rise in the bond rating in 2007.

Low bond ratings usually produce high interest rates, but Japan is an exception. In 2007, the nominal interest rate on 10-year government bonds was 1.7 percent. From 2002 to 2006, the period of the AA− rating, the 10-year bond rate averaged 1.4 percent. These interest rates are unusually *low*. Why hasn't default risk produced higher rates?

Part of the answer is the inflation rate. In much of the 2000s, Japanese inflation was negative; over 2002–2006, it hovered around −1 percent. So the real interest rate on government debt, $i-\pi$, was about $1.4\% - (-1\%) = 2.4\%$. A real rate of 2.4 percent is not unusually low.

Still, one might expect default risk to push the real rate higher. In Japan, the effect of default risk has been offset by two factors that push interest rates down. Both are part of the loanable funds theory of interest rates.

The first factor is high saving. Over 2002–2006, private saving in Japan averaged 26 percent of GDP, compared to 15 percent in the United States. As a result, total saving was high despite government budget deficits. High saving raises the supply of loans, reducing the real interest rate.

The other factor is investment. Japan's slump eroded confidence in the economy, reducing firms' desire to invest. Low investment means a low demand for loans, which also reduces the real interest rate.

Default Risk on Corporate Debt

Corporations sometimes declare bankruptcy and default on their bonds. Bond rating agencies study corporations and estimate default risk, using the same grading scale as for sovereign debt.

AAA ratings go to well-known corporations with successful track records. Examples include Exxon, General Electric, and Johnson & Johnson. Bonds issued by these companies are considered safe—but not quite as safe as U.S. government bonds. In recent years, AAA corporate bonds have paid interest rates about one percentage point above Treasury bonds.

Companies with problems receive lower bond ratings. For example, in 2007, the media conglomerate Time Warner had a rating of BBB+. This rating reflected a high level of debt, accumulated when Time Warner bought other companies, such as Adelphia Communications. The rating also reflected weak earnings at some of Time Warner's subsidiaries, such as AOL.

Junk bond Corporate bond with an S&P rating below BBB

Corporate bonds with ratings below BBB are called **junk bonds** to indicate their high risk. Junk bonds pay interest rates at least seven or eight points above Treasury bonds. In 2007, this category included many airlines. Continental, Delta, and United had ratings of B, and US Airways had a B−.

Link through the text Web site to the Standard & Poor's site, which has current bond ratings for thousands of companies

A company's fortunes can change over time, changing the risk of bankruptcy and default. Rating agencies watch companies and adjust bond ratings for the latest developments. The next case study gives an example.

CASE STUDY

General Motors Bonds

One company whose bond rating has fluctuated is General Motors. GM is the world's largest carmaker and a big issuer of bonds: in 2007, its outstanding bonds totaled $50 billion. **Figure 4.16** shows the evolution of GM's rating by Standard & Poor's.

GM was first rated in 1953, receiving S&P's top grade of AAA. It maintained this rating until 1981. During this period, GM was considered one of country's strongest companies.

The 1980s were a hard time for U.S. carmakers, including GM. The deep recession of the early 1980s reduced car sales. In addition, competition from foreign companies, especially Honda and Toyota, reduced the market shares of U.S. firms. GM's profits fell, and rating agencies started to question its financial health. S&P downgraded GM bonds to AA+ in 1981. Five more downgrades followed, and GM's rating reached BBB+ in 1993.

GM's business rebounded in the 1990s. Its SUVs and pickup trucks became popular, raising sales and profits. S&P responded by raising GM's rating to A− in 1995 and A in 1998.

FIGURE 4.16 General Motors' Bond Rating

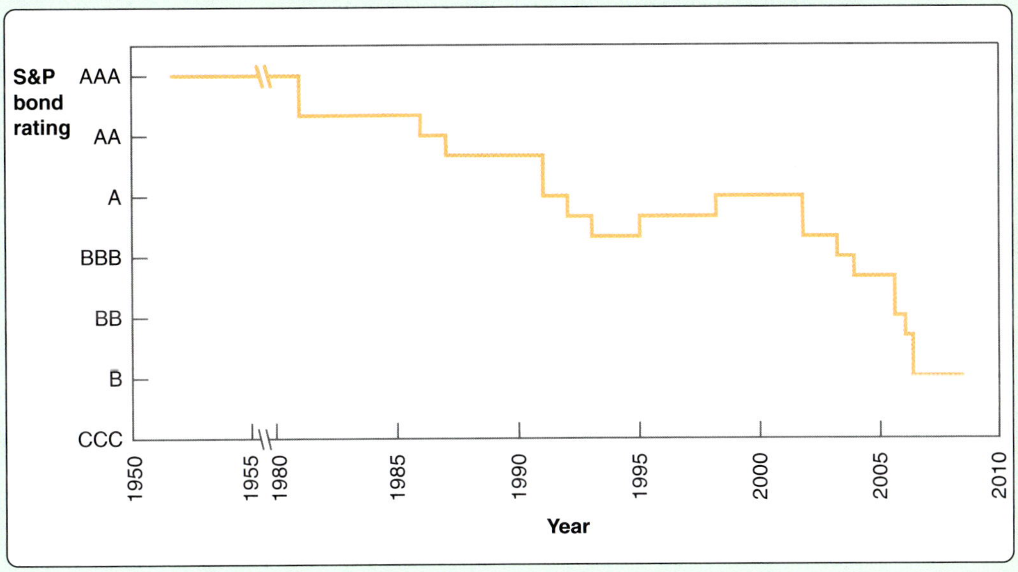

This graph shows the changes over time in Standard & Poor's rating for GM bonds. The rating rises in periods when the company is successful and falls when the company has problems.

Sources: New York Times, Standard & Poor's

Then the company was hit with new problems. Sales of SUVs and pickups fell in the early 2000s, partly because Japanese companies entered this market and partly because consumers shifted toward fuel-efficient cars. GM's overall sales have stagnated in the 2000s, and profits have been negative in some years. From 2005 to 2007, GM suffered total losses of $51 billion.

Rating agencies have also become worried about employee benefits. Traditionally, GM's contracts with the United Auto Workers have included generous pensions and health insurance for retirees. The cost of these benefits is rising rapidly because the number of GM retirees is rising. In 2007, GM's payments to retirees were about $750 per vehicle sold. In that year, GM and the UAW reached an agreement to reduce benefit costs, but rating agencies question whether this deal went far enough.

Because of these problems, GM's bond rating started falling in 2001. In May 2005, the rating reached BB, meaning GM bonds became junk bonds. In December 2005, the rating fell to B, reflecting strong fears about the company's future. Asked whether GM might go bankrupt, an auto analyst for Standard & Poor's replied, "At this juncture it's our feeling that this isn't a far-fetched conclusion, if the deterioration we've seen is continuing." GM's bond rating remained at B in early 2008.

CASE STUDY

The High-Yield Spread

Bond ratings affect the interest rates that corporations must pay. How big is this effect? How much extra interest do savers demand as compensation for default risk? The answer varies over time, depending on the state of the economy.

High-yield spread Difference between interest rates on BBB and AAA corporate bonds with 10-year maturities

To illustrate this point, **Figure 4.17** presents data on the **high-yield spread.** This variable is the difference between two interest rates: the rates on corporate bonds with BBB ratings and with AAA ratings (both with maturities of 10 years). AAA bonds are safe, whereas BBB bonds have significant default risk; a BBB rating is just above the junk-bond level. The high-yield spread is the extra interest that compensates for default risk on BBB bonds.

In many years, the high-yield spread is 1 percentage point or less. But the spread rises sharply in certain periods. There are large spikes in the 1970s and 1980s, and smaller increases in the early 1990s and early 2000s.

FIGURE 4.17 The High-Yield Spread, 1960–2007

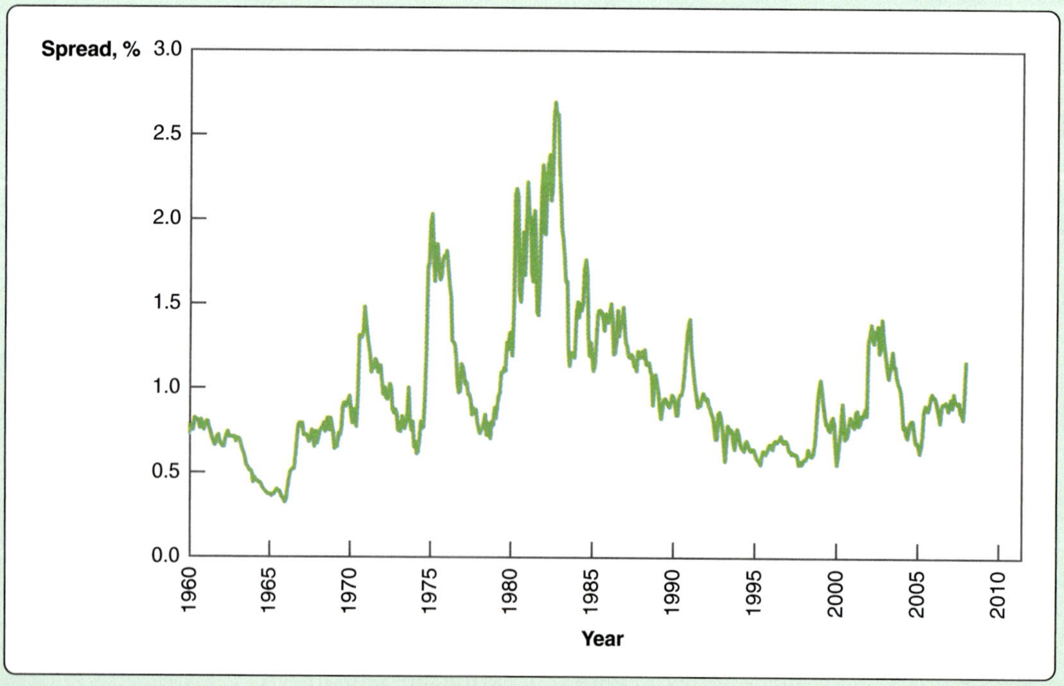

This graph shows the behavior of the high-yield spread—the difference between interest rates on AAA and BBB corporate bonds with 10-year maturities. The high-yield spread rises around the time of recessions.

Source: Federal Reserve Bank of St. Louis

The causes of these peaks are no mystery: they all occur near recessions, when the economy's output falls. When a recession occurs, many firms see their earnings fall. Firms with AAA ratings are strong enough to survive these episodes. But BBB firms, which were shaky to start with, may be driven into bankruptcy. Default risk rises for BBB bonds, so savers demand greater compensation for this risk.

The biggest rises in the high-yield spread occurred in the mid-1970s and early 1980s. The recessions of those periods were the two worst since World War II. Recessions have been milder since the 1980s, so the high-yield spread hasn't risen as much as before.

Economists monitor the high-yield spread because of its relation to recessions. During these episodes, the spread often starts rising before other data indicate that a recession has begun. So a rising spread may be an early signal of a recession.

4.6 TWO OTHER FACTORS

We have discussed the two biggest reasons for differences in interest rates, maturity and default risk. Two other factors, liquidity and taxes, are worth a mention.

Liquidity

Remember the concept of liquidity: an asset's liquidity is the ease of converting it to money. Asset holders value liquidity because they might need to raise money quickly in an emergency.

Bonds vary in their liquidity. U.S. government bonds are highly liquid, because bond dealers trade large quantities every day. People can sell government bonds in this market whenever they want.

Corporate bonds are less liquid. A particular company, say General Electric, issues far fewer bonds than the government, and the bonds are not traded as often. Someone who wants to sell a GE bond may not find a buyer quickly.

Recall that corporate bonds pay higher interest rates than U.S. government bonds. One reason is default risk, as we have discussed. Another is liquidity: savers demand an extra return on corporate bonds to compensate for the difficulty of selling them. The interest-rate spread between government bonds and the highest-rated corporate bonds (AAA) largely reflects liquidity, as default risk on AAA corporate bonds is almost as low as default risk on government bonds.

Taxes

Taxation affects interest rates. This factor is most relevant for interest rates on **municipal bonds**—bonds issued by state and local governments in the United States. Interest income from U.S. government bonds is taxed at the same rate as wages and salaries, but interest on municipal bonds is tax-free.

Municipal bonds Bonds issued by state and local governments

This tax difference encourages savers to buy municipal bonds. As a result, these bonds pay lower interest rates than U.S. bonds, even though default risk is a bit higher. (Unlike the federal government, states and localities have occasionally defaulted.)

Typically, interest rates on municipal bonds are about a quarter or half a percentage point below rates on federal government bonds with the same maturity. For people in most tax brackets, this difference is smaller than the tax savings from municipal bonds. So municipal bonds offer higher earnings after taxes.

U.S. government bonds are bought largely by nonprofit institutions, which don't pay taxes. For example, universities hold these bonds as part of their endowments. Untaxed institutions have no incentive to accept the lower interest rates on municipal bonds.

Summary

- This chapter surveys the determinants of interest rates. It analyzes the overall level of interest rates and differences among rates on different bonds and loans.

4.1 The Loanable Funds Theory

- In the loanable funds theory, the real interest rate is determined by the supply and demand for loans.
- The demand for loans equals investment. A higher interest rate reduces the quantity of loans demanded.
- The supply of loans equals saving plus net capital inflows. A higher interest rate raises both parts of this sum, so it increases the quantity of loans supplied.
- The equilibrium real interest rate, r^*, is the rate at which the supply and demand for loans intersect.

4.2 Determinants of Interest Rates in the Loanable Funds Theory

- Shifts in the supply and demand for loans cause changes in the equilibrium real interest rate. These shifts result from changes in investment, saving, and net capital inflows.
- The causes of investment shifts include new technologies and changes in investor confidence. Shifts in saving arise from changes in private saving and public saving (the budget surplus or deficit). Net capital inflows shift because of changes in confidence and changes in foreign interest rates.
- The nominal interest rate is the equilibrium real interest rate plus expected inflation. Countries with high inflation have high nominal interest rates.

4.3 The Liquidity Preference Theory

- In the liquidity preference theory, the nominal interest rate is determined by the supply and demand for money.
- The supply of money is the amount created by the central bank. The demand for money is the amount that people choose to hold. A rise in the nominal interest rate reduces the quantity of money demanded.
- The equilibrium nominal interest rate, i^*, is the rate at which money supply and money demand intersect. It changes when the central bank changes the money supply, or when money demand shifts. Shifts in money demand arise from changes in aggregate spending or changes in transaction technologies.

4.4 The Term Structure of Interest Rates

- The term structure is the relationship among interest rates on bonds of different maturities (terms).
- According to the expectations theory of the term structure, the interest rate on an n-period bond is the average of the current one-period rate and the expected rates for the next $n - 1$ periods.
- The interest rates on long-term bonds include term premiums that compensate for the risk of price changes. Term premiums rise with a bond's maturity.
- The yield curve summarizes the term structure at a point in time. The shape of the yield curve depends on expectations about future interest rates. Economists use the yield curve to forecast future rates.

- An inverted yield curve occurs when people expect an unusually large fall in short-term interest rates. This can happen when the central bank raises rates temporarily to fight inflation.

4.5 Default Risk and Interest Rates

- Interest rates on bonds increase with the level of default risk. This risk is low for bonds issued by the U.S. government but high for some other governments. Default risk also varies for corporate bonds.
- Agencies such as Moody's and Standard & Poor's rate the default risk on countries' and corporations' bonds.
- The high-yield spread is the difference between interest rates on BBB and AAA corporate bonds. This spread rises in recessions.

- In the 2000s, interest rates on Japanese government bonds have been low despite significant default risk. This fact is explained by low inflation, high private saving, and low investment.

4.6 Two Other Factors

- Corporate bonds are less liquid than U.S. government bonds. This fact helps explain why corporate bonds pay higher interest rates than government bonds do.
- Interest on municipal bonds is tax-free, so these bonds pay slightly lower interest rates than U.S. government bonds.

Key Terms

adaptive expectations, p. 96

bond rating agencies, p.110

budget deficit, p.92

budget surplus, p.92

capital flight, p.95

capital inflows, p.85

capital outflows, p.85

expectations theory of the term structure, p.105

Fisher equation, p.95

high-yield spread, p.114

inverted yield curve, p.108

junk bond, p.112

liquidity preference theory, p.97

loanable funds theory, p.84

municipal bonds, p.115

net capital inflows, p.85

private saving, p.92

public saving, p.92

sovereign debt, p.110

term premium, τ, p.105

term structure of interest rates, p.102

yield curve, p.106

Questions and Problems

1. Using the loanable funds theory, show in a graph how each of the following events affects the supply and demand for loans and the equilibrium real interest rate:
   a. A war leads the government to increase spending on the military. (Assume taxes do not change.)
   b. Wars in *other* countries lead to higher government spending in those countries.
   c. Someone invents a new kind of computer that makes firms more productive. Many firms want to buy the computer. Higher productivity also increases people's confidence in the economy, so consumers see less need to save.
   d. The same things happen as in part (c). In addition, increased confidence in the economy raises net capital inflows.

2. Suppose the real interest rate rises. Using the loanable funds theory, discuss whether this event is likely to reflect good economic news or is a sign of trouble.

3. Comment on this statement: "People care about real interest rates, not nominal rates. Therefore, money demand should depend on the difference between the real rates on money and bonds, *not* the nominal rate on bonds."

4. Suppose that discount brokers make bonds more liquid. It becomes quick and inexpensive to sell bonds. In the liquidity preference theory, how does this development affect money demand and the interest rate?

5. Suppose again that discount brokers make bonds more liquid. What should the central bank do if it doesn't want the interest rate to change? Explain your answer.

6. Suppose it is 2020 and the 1-year interest rate is 4 percent. The expected 1-year rates in the following four years (2021 to 2024) are 4 percent, 5 percent, 6 percent, and 6 percent.
   a. Assume the expectations theory of the term structure, with no term premiums. Compute the interest rates in 2020 on bonds with maturities of 1, 2, 3, 4, and 5 years. Draw a yield curve.
   b. Redo part (a) with term premiums. Assume the term premium for an *n*-year bond, τ_n, is $(n/2)$ percent. For example, the premium for a 4-year bond is $(4/2)\% = 2\%$.

7. Suppose it is 2020, the 1-year interest rate is 8 percent, and the 10-year rate is 6 percent.
   a. Draw a graph showing a likely path of the 1-year rate from 2020 through 2029.
   b. Why might people expect such a path for the 1-year rate?

8. Using the pure expectations theory, derive a formula giving the 4-year interest rate in 2020 as a function of *2-year* rates in 2020 and the future.

9. Suppose that some event has no effect on expected interest rates, but raises uncertainty about rates. What happens to the yield curve? Explain.

10. Suppose a Treasury bond costs $100 and promises a payment of $105 in one year. A bond from the Acme Corporation costs $100 and promises $107 in a year. Assume that Acme pays the $107 with probability *p*. With probability $1-p$, Acme defaults and pays nothing. What are likely values of *p*? Explain.

Online and Data Questions

www.worthpublishers.com/ball

11. From the text Web site, link to the site of the Federal Reserve Bank of St. Louis; also, see the "Guide to St. Louis Fed Data." Get data on the inflation rate and the interest rate on 90-day Treasury bills. Compute the average T-bill rate and average inflation for each decade from the 1960s to the 2000s. Make a graph showing the relationship between the two variables across decades, and explain your results.

12. From the text Web site, link to the St. Louis Fed site for data on the high-yield spread and on the unemployment rate. Make a graph with unemployment on the horizontal axis and the spread on the vertical axis, with a point for each year from 1970 to the present. What do you learn from this graph?

13. From the text Web site, link to the online *Economic Report of the President* for the current year. Look up recent interest rates on municipal bonds and long-term Treasury bonds. Taking taxes into account, which type of bond would produce higher income for a college student without a job? Which would produce higher income for someone in the top tax bracket? Explain.

14. Link through the text Web site to the "Ratings" page of the Standard & Poor's Web site. Find a country or corporation whose debt rating has recently changed and explain why S&P made the change.

chapter five 5

Securities Markets

- 5.1 PARTICIPANTS IN SECURITIES MARKETS
- 5.2 STOCK AND BOND MARKETS
- 5.3 FIRMS' CAPITAL STRUCTURE
- 5.4 WHAT ASSETS SHOULD SAVERS HOLD?
- 5.5 WHICH STOCKS?
- 5.6 DERIVATIVES

UPI Photo/Monika Graff/Landov

Traders conduct business on the floor of the New York Stock Exchange on July 17, 2007, when the Dow Jones stock index rose above 14,000 for the first time.

If you are a college student, you may not be a saver right now. But someday you probably will be. Perhaps your brilliance and hard work will make you rich. Even if your income is modest, you will probably set some of it aside for retirement. Either way, you will have to choose what to do with your savings.

Should you put your money in a bank? Should you buy securities such as stocks and bonds? Which securities are best? How about mutual funds?

People around the world face this problem, the choice of **asset allocation.** So do financial institutions that hold assets, such as banks and pension funds. Decisions about asset allocation produce the activity that we see in financial markets—the daily trading of securities worth billions of dollars.

This chapter discusses securities markets. We first meet the participants in these markets, including a variety of financial institutions. Then we discuss how the markets work—how governments and firms issue securities and how securities are traded. Much securities trading occurs at exchanges such as the New York Stock Exchange, pictured here.

Asset allocation Decisions by individuals or institutions about what assets to hold

Next we analyze the key choices facing securities-market participants. These include firms' decisions about what securities to issue and savers' choices of asset allocation. Savers must decide how to split their wealth among broad classes of assets, such as stocks and bonds. They must also choose among individual securities, such as the stocks of different companies.

We turn last to another class of securities: derivatives. Markets for derivatives, which include futures and options, have grown rapidly in the last few decades. We discuss what derivative securities are, why they are traded, and the risks they can create.

The behavior of securities markets is a vast subject. This chapter's overview highlights key issues and ideas. If you take courses in finance, you will study some of these topics in detail. The goal here is to give you a broad understanding of what happens in securities markets.

5.1 PARTICIPANTS IN SECURITIES MARKETS

TABLE 5.1 Major Institutions in Securities Markets

Securities Firms
Mutual funds
Hedge funds
Brokers
Dealers
Investment banks
Other Financial Institutions
Pension funds
Insurance companies
Commercial banks

The players in securities markets include individual savers like you and me, and many kinds of financial institutions. The key institutions are listed in **Table 5.1.** Some own large quantities of securities; some help people and firms to trade securities; some do both.

Before diving into the details, let's review an issue of terminology. In the financial world, the purchase of securities is often called "investment." People who buy securities are "investors," and institutions that buy securities are "institutional investors." You will encounter this terminology in the media, and you will hear it if you talk to a stockbroker.

In economics, however, the term *investment* has a different meaning. Investment is the production of physical capital, such as factories and machines. When Exxon builds an oil well, it is investing. When you buy Exxon's securities, you are saving, *not* investing. We will stick with this economic terminology throughout the book.

Individuals

Some securities are owned by individual people. In 2007, U.S. citizens directly owned 28 percent of the stock of U.S. companies. They also owned most shares in mutual funds, which held another 25 percent of U.S. corporate stock.

Over time, stock ownership has spread to a larger fraction of the U.S. population. In 1983, only 19 percent of households owned any stock, either directly or indirectly through mutual funds. In 2005, 50 percent of households owned stock. One reason for this trend is the growth of 401(k) plans, which channel workers' retirement savings into securities.

While many people own stock, a few hold disproportionately large amounts. In 2004, the wealthiest 1 percent of U.S. households owned 37 percent of stock held by individuals. The top 10 percent in wealth owned 79 percent.

Securities Firms

Among the financial institutions that participate in securities markets, one broad category is **securities firms.** These companies' primary purpose is to hold securities, trade them, or help others trade them. There are several types of securities firms: mutual funds, hedge funds, brokers and dealers, and investment banks.

Securities firm Company whose primary purpose is to hold securities, trade them, or help others trade them; includes mutual funds, hedge funds, brokers and dealers, and investment banks

Mutual Funds We defined *mutual funds* in Section 1.2 as financial institutions that hold a diversified set of securities and sell shares to savers. In effect, each shareholder owns a small part of all the securities in a fund. Buying mutual fund shares is an easy way for savers to diversify their assets, which reduces risk.

About 8000 separate mutual funds exist in the United States. Most are run by large mutual fund companies such as Fidelity, Vanguard, and American Funds. Each company offers a menu of funds with different sets of securities. Some funds hold a wide variety of stocks and bonds; others specialize. For example, some funds hold only Treasury bonds and some hold only corporate bonds. Some specialize in stocks issued by large firms and some specialize in small firms. Some funds hold only U.S. securities and some hold foreign securities.

Hedge Funds Like mutual funds, **hedge funds** raise pools of money to purchase securities. Unlike mutual funds, they cater only to wealthy people and institutions. Most hedge funds require clients to contribute $1 million or more. In the 2000s, lots of money has flowed into hedge funds; in 2007, their total assets were almost $3 trillion.

Hedge fund Variant of a mutual fund that raises money from wealthy people and institutions and is largely unregulated, allowing it to make risky bets on asset prices

A key difference between hedge funds and mutual funds involves government regulation. To protect small savers, the government limits the risks that mutual funds can take with shareholders' money. Hedge funds are largely unregulated; the government assumes that the funds' rich customers can look out for themselves. Light regulation means that hedge funds can make risky bets on asset prices. These bets sometimes produce large earnings, and sometimes large losses.

One common tool of hedge funds is **leverage:** funds borrow money from banks and use it to increase their security holdings. Larger security holdings magnify the funds' gains and losses when security prices change. Mutual funds aren't allowed to use leverage to buy securities. Another risky practice of hedge funds, forbidden to mutual funds, is trading derivative securities. We discuss derivatives in Section 5.6.

Leverage Borrowing money to purchase assets

Brokers and Dealers These firms help securities markets operate. A **broker** buys and sells securities on behalf of others. For example, if you want to acquire a share of Microsoft, a broker will buy it for you in a stock market. You pay a fee to the broker for this service.

Broker Firm that buys and sells securities for others

You can choose between two types of brokers. A *full-service broker* has advisors who help clients choose which securities to buy. Leading full-service brokers include Merrill Lynch, Smith Barney, and Dean Witter. A *discount broker* provides less advice, or none at all; customers must choose securities on their own. This category includes Charles Schwab, TD Waterhouse, and online brokers such as E*Trade.

Dealer Firm that buys and sells certain securities for itself, making a market in the securities

A **dealer** buys securities for itself, not others, and earns profits by reselling them at higher prices. Typically, a dealer specializes in a narrow set of securities, such as Treasury bills or the stocks of certain companies. It holds an inventory of these securities and "makes a market" for them. The dealer stands ready to buy the securities when someone else wants to sell, and to sell when someone else wants to buy.

Investment Banks This type of securities firm includes well-known names such as Goldman Sachs, Morgan Stanley, and Credit Suisse. An **investment bank** is not really a bank in economists' sense of the term, because it does not take deposits. Instead, investment banks have several functions in securities markets.

Investment bank Financial institution that serves as an underwriter and advises companies on mergers and acquisitions

Underwriter Financial institution that helps companies issue new securities

One function is underwriting. As an **underwriter,** an investment bank helps companies issue new stocks and bonds. It advises the companies and markets the securities to potential buyers. We discuss the underwriting process in Section 5.2.

Investment banks also help companies buy other companies or merge with them. This business is called *mergers and acquisitions*, or M&A. Investment banks research their client companies' potential profits from these deals. They advise their clients about which deals to make and what prices to pay.

Finally, investment banks buy and sell securities. Like hedge funds, they try to make money through risky bets on asset prices. Many investment banks trade derivatives.

Online Case Study: An Update on Investment Banks

Industry Consolidation We have discussed several types of securities firms. In practice, these categories overlap, because many firms are in more than one business. For example, Merrill Lynch is a broker and also provides investment banking services such as underwriting. Mergers have produced large securities firms with multiple functions. For example, Salomon Smith Barney was formed in 1997 by the merger of Salomon Brothers, an investment bank, and Smith Barney, a broker.

Other Financial Institutions

Besides securities firms, several other financial institutions are important participants in securities markets, because they buy large quantities of stocks and bonds. Let's describe these institutions briefly.

Pension Funds Employers, both private firms and governments, establish pension funds to provide income to retired workers. Employers contribute money to the funds, and sometimes workers also make contributions. Pension funds use this money to purchase securities, and earnings from the securities provide retirement benefits.

Insurance Companies These companies sell life insurance and insurance for property, such as houses and cars. Purchasers of insurance pay premiums, which the companies use to buy securities. Earnings from the securities pay for insurance claims.

Commercial Banks As discussed in Section 1.4, commercial banks are institutions that accept deposits and make loans. Their primary assets are the loans—the money they are owed by borrowers. However, commercial banks also own securities, mainly government bonds. Banks hold bonds for liquidity: they can sell the bonds easily if they need cash.

More Industry Consolidation Mergers have created conglomerates that combine diverse financial institutions, including securities firms and commercial banks. For example, Citigroup was created in the 1990s through mergers of several institutions, including Salomon Smith Barney, the consolidated broker/investment bank we mentioned earlier, and Citi corp, a commercial bank. Citigroup (which started calling itself "Citi" in 2007) is a commercial bank, an investment bank, a mutual fund company, and a broker.

▶A wave of consolidation was occurring as this book went to press. In September 2008, Bank of America agreed to purchase Merrill Lynch, and both Goldman Sachs and Morgan Stanley announced plans to establish commercial banks as subsidiaries of their firms. This Chapter's online case study and Chapter 8 discuss the reasons behind financial-industry consolidation.

5.2 STOCK AND BOND MARKETS

Having introduced the players in securities markets, let's discuss how they interact with one another. Savers and financial institutions participate in two kinds of markets. Firms and governments issue new securities in **primary markets,** and existing securities are traded in **secondary markets.**

Primary markets Financial markets in which firms and governments issue new securities

Secondary markets Financial markets in which existing securities are traded

Primary Markets

When a firm is founded, it can get funds from the owners' personal wealth and from bank loans. It may also attract funds from *venture capital firms*, which finance new companies in return for ownership shares. Up to this point, the firm is a *private company* with a small number of owners.

As a firm grows, it may need more funds than it can raise as a private company. At that point, it turns to securities markets. It becomes a **public company,** a firm that issues securities that are traded in financial markets. A firm becomes public by issuing stock. Its first sale of stock is called an **initial public offering,** or **IPO.** Purchasers of the stock receive ownership shares in the firm. In return, the firm receives funds that it can use for investment.

Public company Firm that issues securities that are traded in financial markets

Initial public offering (IPO) Sale of stock when a firm becomes public

IPOs are underwritten by investment banks. Usually a company issuing stock hires a lead investment bank, which enlists other investment banks in a *syndicate*. The syndicate members purchase the company's stock and resell it immediately to financial institutions, such as mutual funds and pension funds. Shares are not offered to individual savers. Typically, investment banks sell the stock for 5–10 percent more than they pay.

An IPO is announced in a formal document called a *prospectus*, which describes the stock being offered and the price. The prospectus also provides detailed information on the company issuing the stock, including financial statements and biographies of managers. The company's investment banks help prepare the prospectus. They also market the stock by sending their representatives around the country on *road shows*. The investment bankers make presentations about the stock to potential purchasers, such as mutual fund managers.

After a firm goes public, it returns to securities markets periodically to raise funds for investment. The firm can issue new stock, spreading ownership of the firm. It can also borrow money by issuing bonds. Investment banks underwrite these security issues, just as they underwrite IPOs.

The Need for Investment Banks Investment banks earn large profits from underwriting. They receive a significant chunk of the money that firms raise by issuing securities. Why do investment banks earn so much? Why can't firms cut out investment banks and sell securities directly to the final purchasers?

The answer is that investment banks reduce the problem of adverse selection. This problem arises from asymmetric information (review Figure 1.1). Adverse selection prevents brand-new companies from issuing securities. To go public, a firm needs a track record to help people judge the value of its stock. Even then, potential purchasers of securities are wary because they know less about the firm's business than the firm does. They fear that bad companies will try to sell securities at inflated prices.

Investment banks reduce this worry. They research the firms whose securities they underwrite. They try to ensure that the firms are sound and that the securities are priced reasonably. Investment banks convince other institutions of the securities' value by putting their own reputations on the line. If the Acme Corporation hires Goldman Sachs to underwrite its IPO, mutual fund managers may not have heard of Acme. But they've heard of Goldman Sachs, and they know that Goldman has a history of underwriting good securities.

Because reputation is so important, investment banking is a concentrated industry—it is dominated by a small number of institutions. In the 2000s, 10 investment banks have underwritten more than half of the securities issued around the world. It is hard for lesser-known underwriters to enter the business. If your friend Joe started Joe's Discount Investment Bank, he would probably have trouble selling securities. Mutual fund managers don't know Joe, so they would fear a ripoff.

The high earnings from underwriting are rewards for investment banks' reputations. These earnings help produce high compensation for investment bankers. For example, in 2006 the 26,000 employees of Goldman Sachs earned a total of $16.5 billion in salaries and bonuses, an average of $600,000 per person.

Criticism of Underwriters Since the late 1990s, some economists have criticized the practices of investment banks. The main complaint is that investment banks "underprice" stock in IPOs: they sell the stock for less than its true value. Underpricing reduces revenues for the firms issuing stock.

The evidence for underpricing is that a stock's price often jumps up right after an IPO, when the stock starts trading on secondary markets. A jump suggests that the initial price was too low. Price jumps were especially large during the stock market boom of the 1990s. In 1999 and 2000, the average new stock jumped by 64 percent in the first day of trading. Over 2001–2007 the jump averaged 12 percent, but it was much higher for some companies.

Why do investment banks underprice? Critics suggest the following story. People who buy underpriced stocks earn large, quick profits when the prices jump. So everyone wants to buy these stocks. Investment banks choose who receives the stocks they underwrite. So they can do favors for people they do other business with—people who can return the favors.

For example, many investment banks are parts of conglomerates that also include stock brokers. The investment banks grant IPO shares to mutual funds that hire the brokers to make trades. This favor encourages the mutual funds to provide more business to the brokers.

This practice falls into a grey area legally. It is not necessarily illegal for investment banks to allocate IPO shares to their friends. It *is* illegal if the allocation is tied directly to something the investment bank receives in return. Several investment banks have been prosecuted for crossing this line.

For example, in 2002 the government accused Credit Suisse of trading IPO shares for brokerage commissions. Institutions that received IPO shares made numerous stock trades with Credit Suisse brokers, trades that were made simply to generate commissions—and the commissions were a dollar per share for trades that normally cost six cents. The government interpreted these payments as kickbacks in return for IPO allocations. Credit Suisse did not admit guilt, but it paid the government $100 million to settle the charges.

Whether or not it involves illegal behavior, underpricing hurts the owners of a company going public. They receive less than they could for selling part of their business. One company responded by reducing the role of investment banks in its IPO, as we see in the next case study.

For more on underpricing, link from the text Web site to the site of Jay Ritter of the University of Florida. Ritter is a leading critic of investment banks.

CASE STUDY

Google's IPO

In 1998, two graduate students, Sergei Brin and Larry Page, founded Google in a friend's garage. The rest is history. The company went public in 2004, issuing $1.7 billion worth of stock. In announcing the IPO, Brin and Page said, "Google is not a conventional company. We do not intend to become one." They backed up this statement by selling stock in an unorthodox way.

Google hired two investment banks, Morgan Stanley and Credit Suisse, to run the IPO. But these firms did not set the stock price or allocate shares. Instead, following Google's instructions, they ran an online auction for the new stock. Both financial institutions and individuals submitted bids, saying how many shares they wanted and what they were willing to pay. The stock was sold to the highest bidders.

Google chose this approach for several reasons. First, the auction was less costly than a traditional IPO. The investment banks did not have to research to choose a stock price, and there was no road show to market the stock. As a result, the investment banks' fees were only 3 percent of the IPO revenue, less than their usual share of 5–10 percent.

Second, Google sought to avoid underpricing. It believed that bidding would produce a price close to the true value of the stock. Most observers judge the auction as fairly successful on this score. Google's stock rose 18 percent on the first day of trading, suggesting some underpricing. But this increase was modest compared with IPOs for other tech companies.

Finally, Google's leaders cited an idealistic motive for the auction. Brin and Page argued that it was more "fair" and "inclusive" than traditional IPOs, because small savers could bid along with financial institutions. You could buy stock even if you weren't a favorite customer of an investment bank.

Google was able to modify the traditional IPO because it was an unusually well-known, successful company. Its reputation reduced the adverse selection problem. Many people were eager to buy Google stock, so the company didn't need the usual help from investment banks.

One issuer of securities has never hired an investment bank: the U.S. government. The government is even better known than Google, so it can sell bonds directly to savers and financial institutions. Most government bonds are issued through auctions run by the Treasury Department. These auctions are designed to produce the highest possible prices for the bonds. Many details of Google's auction were patterned after Treasury auctions. The next case study describes how some of these auctions work.

CASE STUDY

Treasury Bill Auctions

Every Monday, the U.S. Treasury auctions T-bills with maturities of 13 weeks and 26 weeks. Each T-bill has a face value of $1000, which it pays at maturity. It is a zero-coupon security, meaning it pays nothing before maturity.

A few days before each auction, the Treasury examines its needs for cash and decides how many bills to issue. It announces this figure and invites bids, which are due by 1:00 PM on the auction day.

Link through the text Web site to the TreasuryDirect site to see how individuals bid for T-bills. If you have a spare $1000, you can buy a T-bill next Monday.

There are two kinds of bidders. Noncompetitive bidders simply state how many T-bills they wish to buy, without specifying a price. These bidders are mainly small savers. Any saver can establish an account with the Treasury and submit bids through the TreasuryDirect Web site. The minimum purchase is a single $1000 T-bill.

Competitive bidders are bond dealers and other financial institutions, which often buy millions of dollars worth of T-bills. Each competitive bidder states a desired quantity of bills *and* the price it is willing to pay. Many bids are submitted just seconds before the 1:00 PM deadline.

Once all the bids are in, the Treasury determines who gets the available T-bills. First, T-bills are allocated to all the noncompetitive bidders. Then the competitive bidders are ranked by the prices they submitted. The bidder with the highest price is awarded the number of bills it wants, then the bidder with the second-highest price, and so on until no bills are left.

All the T-bills are sold for the same price—the lowest price offered by any bidder who receives bills. Bidders who submitted higher prices pay less than they bid. This system is called a "unitary price auction."

Let's look at a specific example. On Monday, March 31, 2008, the Treasury auctioned $24 billion worth of 13-week T-bills. It received approximately $1.5 billion in noncompetitive bids and $53.9 billion in competitive bids. The noncompetitive bidders received their requested $1.5 billion, leaving $22.5 billion for the competitive bidders with the highest bids.

The median of successful bids was $996.76 (half the successful bids were above this level and half below). The lowest successful bid was $996.36, so all the bills were sold for that price. A price of $996.36 for a $1000 T-bill implies a yield to maturity of 0.365 percent over 13 weeks. This is equivalent to an annual yield of about 1.5 percent.

Before 1998 the Treasury used a different kind of auction, called a "discriminatory auction." Under this system, each bidder paid whatever price it bid. In our example, an institution that submitted the median bid of $996.76 would have paid that price rather than $996.36.

It might appear that discriminatory auctions raise more revenue for the government than uniform price auctions. However, economists believe that uniform price auctions produce higher bids. A bidder is less leery of overpaying, because it won't pay its full bid if the bid is unusually high. The Treasury experimented with different kinds of auctions during the 1990s and decided that uniform price auctions raise the most money.

Secondary Markets

After securities are issued in primary markets, their buyers often resell them in secondary markets. Then the securities are traded repeatedly among institutions and individual savers.

To understand this process, we first discuss how brokers help people enter securities markets. Then we discuss the main types of secondary markets: exchanges and over-the-counter (OTC) markets. OTC markets can be divided into dealer markets and electronic communication networks (ECNs).

▶ Secondary markets can also be categorized as "money markets" or "capital markets." Money markets are markets for bonds with maturities below 1 year (Treasury bills and commercial paper). Capital markets are markets for longer-term bonds and for stocks.

The Role of Brokers A financial institution can buy securities directly from other institutions. Individual savers can buy bonds directly from the government in auctions. However, to buy stocks or corporate bonds, individuals need assistance from brokers.

If you want to buy securities, the first step is to establish an account with a broker. You can use a traditional broker, such as Merrill-Lynch, or an online broker, such as E*trade. You deposit money in your account, and it is available to buy the securities you choose.

When you want to buy or sell, you contact your broker by phone or over the Internet. You place an order—let's say you want to buy 100 shares of Boeing, the aircraft manufacturer. You can place a *market order,* which tells the broker to buy Boeing for the best price he can find. Or you can place a *limit order,* telling him to buy only if the price reaches a certain level. The broker fills your order in different ways, depending on which type of secondary market he uses.

Exchange A physical location where brokers and dealers meet to trade securities

Exchanges Your broker may fill your order at an **exchange,** a physical location where brokers and dealers meet. Exchanges are used mostly to trade stocks, not bonds. The world's largest securities exchange is the New York Stock Exchange (NYSE), located on Wall Street in lower Manhattan. The stocks of roughly 3000 companies are traded on the NYSE. Other cities with large stock exchanges include London, Frankfurt, Tokyo, and Sao Paolo.

Figure 5.1 illustrates how stocks are traded on the NYSE. You have asked your broker, Merrill-Lynch, to buy 100 shares of Boeing. Merrill has a *seat* on the exchange, allowing it to trade there. The person you contact at Merrill sends your order to one of the firm's *commission brokers,* who work on the floor of the exchange.

Specialist Broker-dealer who manages the trading of a certain stock on an exchange

The commission broker walks to the *trading post* for Boeing stock. The trading post is a desk staffed by a broker-dealer called a **specialist.** The NYSE chooses one securities firm to provide a specialist for each stock (the specialist for Boeing works for Spear, Leeds, and Kellogg). The specialist manages the trading of that stock.

Brokers tell the specialist how many shares of Boeing they want to buy or sell, and what prices they will accept. The specialist records this information and arranges trades. Sometimes the specialist matches a broker who wants to buy stock with another who wants to sell. Other times, the specialist acts as a dealer, trading with brokers on behalf of her own firm. Either way, her job is to help brokers make the trades ordered by their customers.

Link through the text Web site to the NYSE's Web site for more information on stock trading.

FIGURE 5.1 Purchasing Boeing Stock on the NYSE

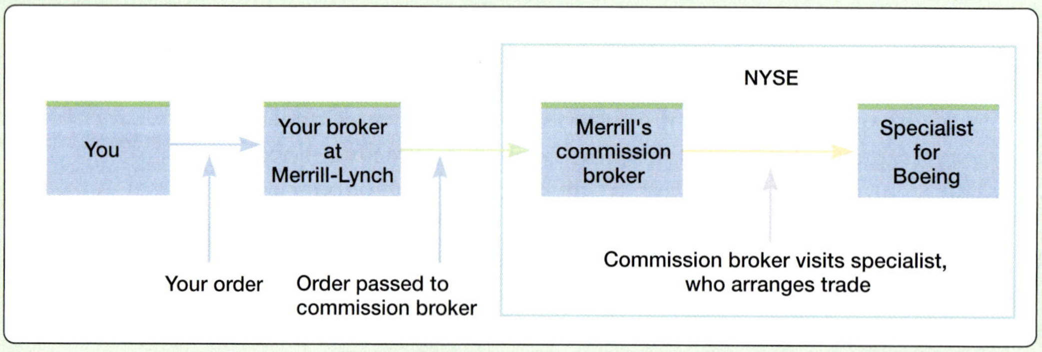

Dealer Markets A secondary market that has no physical location—one that is not an exchange—is an **over-the-counter (OTC) market.** One type of OTC market is a **dealer market,** in which all trades are made with dealers. A computer network connects the dealers to brokers and other financial institutions that want to trade. Each dealer posts "bid" prices at which it will buy certain securities and "ask" prices at which it will sell.

Over-the-counter (OTC) market Secondary securities market with no physical location.

Dealer market OTC market in which all trades are made with dealers

The largest dealer market for stocks is the NASDAQ network. The initials stand for National Association of Securities Dealers Automated Quotation. Roughly 3000 stocks are traded on the NASDAQ, the same number as on the NYSE. NASDAQ companies tend to be smaller, and many are in high-tech industries.

Within the NASDAQ network, 20 or more firms may be dealers in a particular stock. All the dealers post bid and ask prices. If you tell your broker to trade a stock for you, he looks for the dealer with the best price.

Link through the text Web site to the NASDAQ Web site for more information on that market.

Most bonds, both corporate and government bonds, are traded on dealer markets. Again, computer networks link dealers with other financial institutions that want to make trades. The biggest bond dealers are divisions of financial conglomerates such as Citi and JP Morgan Chase.

Dealers make profits from the **bid-ask spread**—the gap between the prices at which they buy and sell a security. The size of these spreads varies greatly. Spreads are smaller for more liquid securities—those that are easy to trade because there are many buyers and sellers. For the most liquid, Treasury securities, spreads are well under 0.1 percent of the price. Dealers can profit from small spreads by purchasing lots of securities and reselling them immediately.

Bid-ask spread Gap between the prices at which a dealer buys and sells a security

Bid-ask spreads are higher for stocks, and higher still for corporate bonds. Spreads on these bonds can be several percentage points. The bond of a particular company may not be traded frequently. If a dealer buys the bond, it might take awhile to sell it, and the price could fall in the meantime. The bid-ask spread compensates the dealer for this risk.

ECNs An alternative to exchanges and dealer markets is an **electronic communications network (ECN).** An ECN is an over-the-counter market in which trading doesn't require dealers. Financial institutions such as brokers and mutual funds trade directly with one another. Institutions that want to trade submit offers to the ECN. They say what securities they want to buy or sell and the prices they will accept. The electronic system automatically matches buyers and sellers who submit the same price. Traders pay a small fee for each transaction.

Electronic communications network (ECN) OTC market in which financial institutions trade securities with one another directly, rather than through dealers

The advantage of trading through an ECN is that there is no bid-ask spread. The seller of a security receives the full price paid by the ultimate buyer. Dealers don't take a cut.

The first ECN, Instinet, was created in 1969. As of 2008, about a dozen ECNs operated in the United States, including Instinet, Direct Edge, and Arca (an ECN owned by the NYSE). Trading has grown rapidly since the mid-1990s, especially for NASDAQ stocks. Nearly half of all trades in these stocks occur through ECNs rather than the NASDAQ dealer network.

Finding Information on Security Prices

Suppose you are adding up your wealth, so you want to know the current prices of stocks and bonds. Daily newspapers such as the *Wall Street Journal* report prices from the previous day. A number of Web sites provide information that is updated more frequently. One popular site is Bloomberg (www.bloomberg.com). The Bloomberg company was founded in 1981 by Michael Bloomberg (more recently mayor of New York City). Its Web site reports prices for many types of stocks and bonds, both U.S. and foreign. It also reports prices of shares in leading mutual funds.

The text Web site has a link to the Bloomberg site and a guide to using it.

Figure 5.2A presents a page from the Bloomberg site, one that covers the 30 stocks in the Dow Jones index. During trading, this page is updated about every 20 minutes. It reports the price of each stock, the change in the price since the start of the day, and the number of shares traded. Clicking on a company symbol leads to more detailed information on the company, including past movements in its stock price, the price-earnings ratio, and dividend payments. **Figure 5.2B** shows this information for Boeing.

Stock market index An average of prices for a group of stocks

Each day the prices of some stocks rise and others fall. The overall behavior of prices is measured by **stock market indexes.** An index is an average of prices for a group of stocks.

The Dow Jones is the oldest and most famous stock index. However, since the Dow covers only 30 stocks, it may not capture the movements of the whole market. The Standard & Poor's (S&P) 500 index is better for this purpose, as it covers the 500 largest U.S. companies. The Wilshire 5000 index is even broader. The NASDAQ index covers all the companies that are traded in that market. It is influenced strongly by the prices of tech stocks. As we saw in Figure 3.3, the NASDAQ has been highly volatile, with a big run-up in the 1990s and a collapse in the early 2000s.

Web sites such as Bloomberg provide data on a variety of stock market indexes. In Figure 5.2A, information on the Dow appears above the prices of individual stocks. The Bloomberg site also provides indexes for sectors of the economy, such as transportation and utilities, and indexes for foreign stocks.

5.3 FIRMS' CAPITAL STRUCTURE

So far we've discussed the mechanics of security trading. Now we turn to the behavior of market participants—their decisions about which securities to buy and sell. We start with firms' decisions about issuing new securities.

The basic reason that firms issue securities is to raise funds for investment. The question here is *which* kind of securities. A firm can raise funds by issuing either stocks or bonds. How does it choose between the two?

Capital structure Mix of stocks and bonds that a firm issues

The mix of stocks and bonds that a firm issues is called its **capital structure.** Economists have long debated which capital structure is best. Let's discuss some of the key ideas.

FIGURE 5.2 Stock Prices on Bloomberg.com

(A)

DOW JONES INDUS. AVG SNAPSHOT

1 YEAR

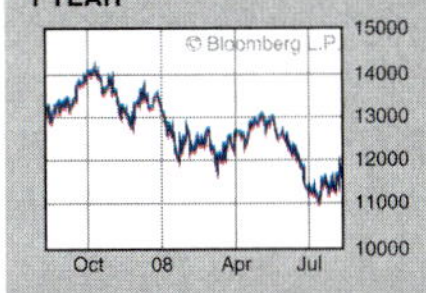

VALUE	11,520.67
CHANGE	–121.8
% CHANGE	–1.05
TIME	10:27
TOTAL MEMBERS	30
UP	7
DOWN	23
UNCHANGED	0

INDEX PROFILE

The Dow Jones Industrial Average is a price-weighted average of 30 blue-chip stocks that are generally the leaders in their industry. It has been a widely followed indicator of the stock market since October 1, 1928. See DIA US Equity <GO> for the tradeable equivalent.

DOW JONES INDUS. AVG MEMBERS

COMPANY	PRICE	CHANGE	%CHANGE	VOLUME	Time
3M CO	72.72	–0.88	–1.20	392,134	10:12
ALCOA INC	31.00	0.04	0.13	1,866,549	10:12
AMER INTL GROUP	22.06	–0.79	–3.46	10,011,271	10:12
AMERICAN EXPRESS	36.97	–1.08	–2.84	2,273,065	10:12
AT&T INC	31.41	–0.24	–0.75	2,611,372	10:12
BANK OF AMERICA	29.78	–1.35	–4.34	17,125,871	10:12
BOEING CO	64.90	–1.03	–1.56	1,199,207	10:12
CATERPILLAR INC	69.15	–2.66	–3.70	2,690,594	10:12
CHEVRON CORP	83.46	–0.10	–0.12	1,421,509	10:12
CITIGROUP INC	18.08	–0.46	–2.48	15,634,047	10:12
COCA-COLA CO	55.04	0.26	0.47	968,175	10:12
DU PONT (EI)	44.74	–1.05	–2.29	989,902	10:12
EXXON MOBIL CORP	77.09	0.21	0.27	2,926,212	10:12
GENERAL ELECTRIC	29.36	–0.38	–1.29	5,336,761	10:12
GENERAL MOTORS	11.00	–0.10	–0.90	2,600,818	10:12
HEWLETT-PACKARD	45.98	0.30	0.66	1,469,374	10:12
HOME DEPOT INC	26.78	–0.70	–2.55	4,012,806	10:12
IBM	126.15	0.93	0.74	828,187	10:12
INTEL CORP	24.39	–0.13	–0.53	6,620,439	10:12
JOHNSON&JOHNSON	71.48	–0.22	–0.31	1,074,814	10:12
JPMORGAN CHASE	37.24	–0.68	–1.79	8,851,938	10:12
MCDONALDS CORP	63.45	–0.49	–0.77	1,911,604	10:13
MERCK & CO	36.41	0.24	0.66	1,821,390	10:12
MICROSOFT CORP	28.26	0.14	0.50	6,578,176	10:11
PFIZER INC	19.71	–0.01	–0.05	5,318,742	10:12
PROCTER & GAMBLE	69.69	–0.65	–0.92	1,484,337	10:12
UNITED TECH CORP	65.67	–0.84	–1.26	493,093	10:12
VERIZON COMMUNIC	34.69	–0.13	–0.37	1,383,766	10:12
WAL-MART STORES	58.17	–1.08	–1.82	2,953,190	10:12
WALT DISNEY CO	31.86	–0.30	–0.93	1,272,595	10:12

(B)

BA:US

Boeing Co

Industry: Aerospace/Defense

Add Security to your Watch List ›

10:24 New York Currency: USD

Price	Change	% Change	Bid	Ask	Open
64.780	–1.150	–1.744	N.A.	N.A.	66.070
Volume	**High**	**Low**	**52-Week High**	**52-Week Low**	**1-Yr Return**
1,504,013	66.230	64.750	107.15 (10/02/07)	60.77 (08/01/08)	–33.911%

EARNINGS

Earnings Past 12 Months	Quarter Est. EPS(09/08)	Quarter Est. EPS(12/08)	Year Est. EPS(12/08)
5.740	1.39	1.63	5.81
Price/Earnings (Trailing)	**Relative P/E**	**Earnings Growth Rate**	**Estimated P/E**
11.298	0.439	10.500	11.300

FUNDAMENTALS

Shares (Millions)	Market Cap (Millions)	Float (Millions)	Return on Equity
740.245	48,004.900	738.571	59.288
Short Interest	**Last Dividend Reported**	**Dividend Yield (Trailing 12mo.)**	**Relative Dividend Yield**
9,648,137.000	0.400 Regular Cash	2.360	0.998

Price for BA:US **SECTOR COMPARATIVE RETURNS**

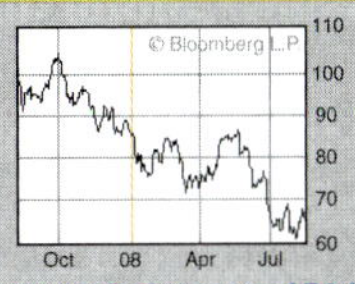

Chart the Performance of BA:US

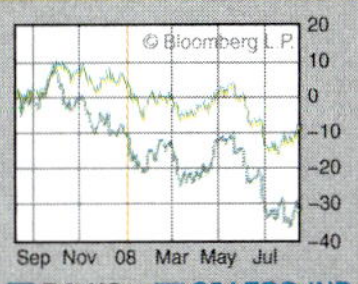

COMPANY PROFILE

The Boeing Company, together with its subsidiaries, develops, produces, and markets commercial jet aircraft, as well as provides related support services to the commercial airline industry worldwide. The Company also researches, develops, produces, modifies, and supports information, space, and defense systems, including military aircraft, helicopters and space and missile systems.

(A) A page downloaded from bloomberg.com on 8/18/08 reports data on the 30 stocks in the Dow Jones index. For each stock, the page shows the current share price (in dollars), the change in the price since the start of the day (both the change in dollars and the percentage change), the number of shares traded (labeled "volume"), and the time at which these numbers were last updated. The top of the page provides information on the overall Dow index. Clicking on "BOEING CO" leads to the page shown in (B), which gives detailed information on Boeing, including past movements in the stock price, the price-earnings ratio, and dividends. For detailed definitions of the variables on these pages, visit the "Guide to Bloomberg" on the text Web site.

Is Capital Structure Irrelevant?

The starting point for analyzing capital structure is the **Modigliani-Miller Theorem (MM Theorem).** This idea was proposed in 1958 by Franco Modigliani and Merton Miller, who both went on to win the Nobel Prize in Economics. The MM view of capital structure is simple: capital structure doesn't matter. Stocks and bonds are equally good ways for firms to raise funds.

Modigliani-Miller Theorem (MM Theorem) Proposition that a firm's capital structure doesn't matter

In making their argument, MM assume that firms operate for the benefit of their stockholders. Stockholders give something up when a firm issues securities. If the firm issues new stock, current stockholders lose part of their ownership of the firm. They receive smaller shares of the firm's future earnings. If the firm issues bonds, stockholders retain full ownership, but part of their earnings goes to interest payments. When firms issue securities, MM argue, they should choose the type that minimizes the costs to current stockholders.

To determine these costs, MM use the classical theory of asset prices. The classical theory says that the price of any security, whether a stock or a bond, equals the present value of expected income from the security (review Section 3.2).

The classical theory leads quickly to the conclusion that capital structure doesn't matter. Suppose a firm sells a share of new stock for \$100. The present value of expected earnings that the buyer receives—and current stockholders give up—is \$100. If the firm sells a bond for \$100, the future payments again have a present value of \$100. Either way, it costs \$100 in present value to raise \$100. Stocks and bonds are equally good deals for their issuers.

Why Capital Structure Does Matter

The MM Theorem implies that firms shouldn't care which securities they issue. However, few people take this idea literally. The theorem ignores several practical differences between stocks and bonds. Some of these factors encourage firms to issue stocks, and some favor bonds. As a result, most firms issue a mixture of the two.

Taxes Corporations pay taxes on their profits at rates up to 35 percent. In computing profits, corporations can deduct interest payments on bonds. Therefore, the more bonds a firm issues, the lower its taxes. In contrast, issuing stock does not affect corporate taxes.

These tax rules change the relative costs of securities. Ignoring taxes, the MM Theorem says it is equally costly to issue stocks and bonds. But the costs of bonds are partly offset by their tax benefits, making them a cheaper way to raise funds.

Bankruptcy While issuing bonds has tax benefits, it also has a disadvantage: the risk of bankruptcy. When a firm sells bonds, it promises certain payments to bondholders. If the firm's earnings are low, it may not be able to make the payments. It defaults, leading to bankruptcy. The more bonds a firm issues, the greater this risk.

Bankruptcy is costly. It triggers a legal process that requires expensive lawyers and accountants. And often a bankrupt firm is forced to shut down. Its business is destroyed, eliminating opportunities for future profits.

Firms can reduce bankruptcy risk by issuing stocks rather than bonds. If a firm's earnings are low, then stockholders receive low returns. The stockholders are disappointed, but the firm has not defaulted. Stocks don't require payments that the firm might have trouble making.

Adverse Selection As we discussed earlier, savers fear that firms will try to sell securities for more than their true value. This adverse selection problem affects capital structure because it is more severe for stocks than for bonds.

To see why, remember that adverse selection is caused by asymmetric information: buyers of securities know less than sellers. This asymmetry may be small when firms issue bonds. Buyers know exactly how much a bond pays as long as the issuer doesn't default, and they may know that default is unlikely. In contrast, stock purchasers are always uncertain about how much they will earn. This uncertainty creates scope for adverse selection.

The consequence is that some firms can issue bonds more easily than stock. To sell stock to nervous savers, these firms would have to accept low prices—less than the stock is really worth. Adverse selection is another reason to issue bonds, in addition to the tax advantages discussed earlier.

Debt Maturity

So far, we've focused on the choice between stocks and bonds. When firms issue bonds, they must also choose the bonds' maturity. Firms can issue long-term bonds, which typically have maturities of 5 or 10 years, or commercial paper, with maturities under a year.

Generally, firms choose bond maturities based on their ability to pay off the bonds. A long-term investment project, such as a new factory, takes years to produce revenue. Firms finance these projects with long-term bonds, which they can pay off after revenue starts arriving.

Firms issue commercial paper when they need to borrow for short periods. This need often arises from the time lag between production and sales. For example, a swimwear company might produce bathing suits in the winter and sell them in the spring. It can issue 3-month commercial paper to cover its winter production costs until it receives revenue in the spring.

5.4 WHAT ASSETS SHOULD SAVERS HOLD?

We now turn from the issuers of securities to the buyers. Savers and institutions must choose their asset allocation, that is, how they split their wealth among different types of assets. We discuss the main factors in these decisions, focusing on the choice between stocks and bonds. We also touch on bank deposits, another asset held by savers.

The Risk-Return Trade-off

Our discussion of stocks and bonds builds on Section 3.6, where we discussed the rates of return on these securities. We saw that stocks have a higher average return over time. From 1900 through 2007, the nominal rate of return averaged about 11 percent for U.S. stocks and 5 percent for Treasury bonds. We can find average *real* returns by subtracting the inflation rate, which averaged 3 percent over 1900–2007. The real rate of return averaged 8 percent for stocks and 2 percent for bonds.

We also saw that stock returns are more volatile than bond returns (see Figure 3.4). A saver can earn a lot on stocks, but she can also lose a lot.

From 1900 through 2007, there were 16 years when nominal stock returns were less than −10 percent, including 6 with returns below −20 percent. In contrast, returns on Treasury bonds have never been less than −10 percent.

When a saver chooses between stocks and bonds, she chooses between average return and safety. The choice is not all-or-nothing, however. The saver can split her wealth between the two assets, seeking a high return on part of it and keeping the rest safe. A key decision is the fraction of wealth to put into stocks. Raising this fraction raises the average return on total assets, but it also increases risk.

Calculating the Trade-off Suppose that bonds have a real return of 2 percent (the actual average since 1900). Assume that this return is constant, so bonds are safe assets. (In reality bond returns vary somewhat, but we assume this variation is small enough to ignore.) Stocks, by contrast, have variable returns. Assume that half the time the real return is 22 percent, and half the time it is −6 percent. The average return on stocks is

$$\frac{1}{2}(22\% + (-6\%)) = 8\%$$

This average exceeds the return on bonds, but stocks are risky.

You have some wealth, say \$100, to split between stocks and bonds. We'll use the letter s to denote the fraction of wealth you put in stocks. The fraction in bonds is $1 - s$. If $s = 0.6$, for example, you put \$60 in stocks and \$40 in bonds. The overall return on your wealth is a weighted average of stock and bond returns with weights of s and $1-s$. That is,

$$\begin{aligned}\text{return on wealth} &= s(\text{return on stocks}) \\ &\quad + (1-s)(\text{return on bonds}) \qquad \textbf{(5.1)}\end{aligned}$$

As long as s is positive (you hold some stock), the return on your wealth is variable. It depends on whether stock returns are high (22 percent) or low (−6 percent). If stock returns are high, Equation (5.1) becomes

$$\begin{aligned}&\text{return on wealth if stock returns high} \\ &\quad = s(22\%) + (1 - s)(2\%) \\ &\quad = s(22\%) + 2\% - s(2\%) \\ &\quad = 2\% + s(20\%) \qquad \textbf{(5.2)}\end{aligned}$$

By similar reasoning,

$$\begin{aligned}&\text{return on wealth if stock returns low} \\ &\quad = s(-6\%) + (1-s)(2\%) \\ &\quad = s(-6\%) + 2\% - s(2\%) \\ &\quad = 2\% - s(8\%) \qquad \textbf{(5.3)}\end{aligned}$$

Expressions (5.2) and (5.3) are your return on wealth for the two possible stock returns. Using these formulas, we can see how the choice of s, the fraction of wealth in stock, affects your average return and risk. Your average return is the simple average of (5.2) and (5.3):

average return on wealth

$$= \frac{1}{2}[2\% + s(20\%)] + \frac{1}{2}[2\% - s(8\%)]$$
$$= 1\% + s(10\%) + 1\% - s(4\%)$$
$$= 2\% + s(6\%) \tag{5.4}$$

The last line shows that a rise in s raises your average return.

Risk can be measured in several ways. We will use one simple measure: the difference between your two possible returns, expressions (5.2) and (5.3). This difference shows how much your wealth varies based on stock returns:

difference between high and low returns on wealth

$$= [2\% + s(20\%)] - [2\% - s(8\%)]$$
$$= s(28\%)$$

A rise in the fraction s raises risk.

Figure 5.3 shows the trade-off you face. It shows the risk and average return that result from different levels of s. If $s = 0$ (you buy no stock), your

▶ Economists often use another measure of risk, the standard deviation of returns. You know what this means if you have studied statistics. In our example, the standard deviation of the return on wealth is $s(14\%)$. An increase in s raises this standard deviation, as well as raising the difference in returns that we use to measure risk.

FIGURE 5.3 The Risk-Return Trade-off

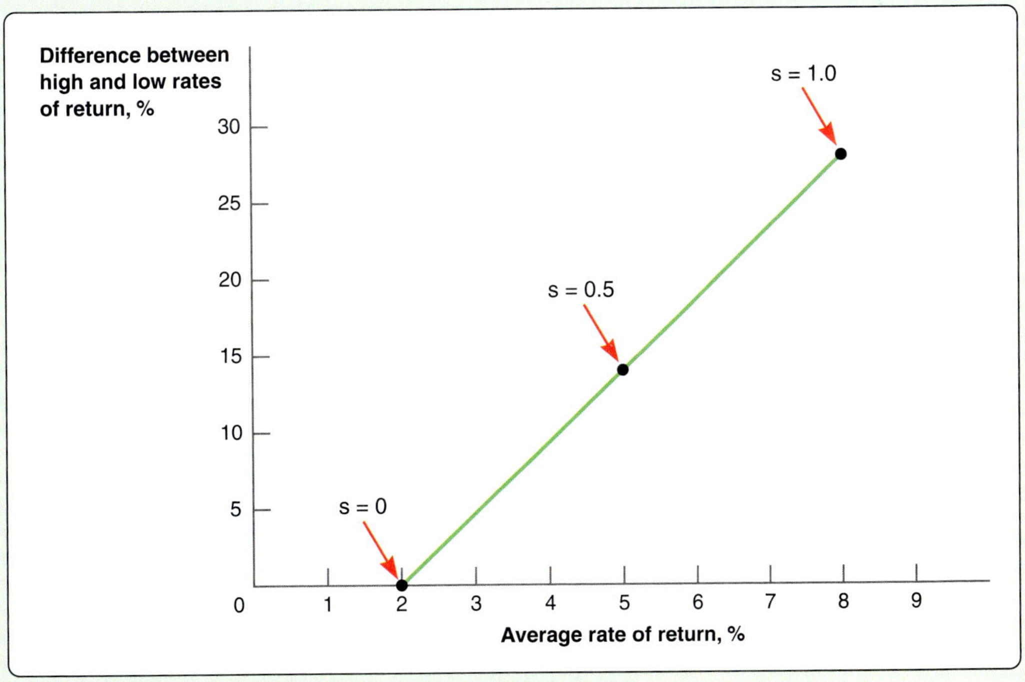

In this example, bonds have a constant real return of 2 percent. The real return on stocks is 22 percent half the time and is −6 percent half the time. Savers face a trade-off between the average return on wealth and risk, measured here by the difference between the returns on wealth when stock returns are high and low. An increase in s, the fraction of wealth in stock, raises both the average return and risk.

average return is only 2 percent, but you face no risk. Both risk and return rise as s rises, reaching their highest levels at $s = 1$ (you buy only stock).

What About Bank Accounts? Buying stocks and bonds isn't the only way to save. Many people deposit some or all of their wealth in bank accounts. How do bank accounts fit into the issue of asset allocation?

For present purposes, the answer is that bank accounts are similar to bonds. Bank accounts produce lower average earnings than stocks, but they are safe. In the example we just discussed, you can think of your holdings of "bonds" as your total safe assets, including both bonds and bank accounts. Your key decision is how to split your wealth between these safe assets and risky stock.

In reality, bank accounts and bonds are not exactly the same. Chapter 7 expands on their differences. We'll see that bonds pay somewhat higher interest rates than bank accounts do, but are less liquid. For now we ignore these issues and lump bonds and bank accounts together as safe assets.

Choosing the Mix

How should you respond to the risk-return trade-off? Should you put a large fraction of your wealth in stock, accepting risk to seek high returns? Or should you play it safe and put most of your wealth in bonds and bank accounts?

Attitudes Toward Risk The asset-allocation question does not have an absolute answer. The right allocation depends partly on personal preference—how you feel about risk.

Perhaps you are very *risk-averse*. You worry a lot about worst-case scenarios, and you would find it painful to lose money. If so, you should hold most of your wealth in safe assets: you should accept low returns to avoid risk. On the other hand, if you don't mind risk, you should put most of your wealth in stock.

Risk aversion is a personality trait that varies across people. Social scientists have tried to measure it. For example, a University of Michigan study measured risk aversion by asking people whether they would accept various monetary gambles. The researchers found that risk aversion helps explain behavior. People with lower risk aversion are more likely to engage in risky activities such as smoking, drinking, and going without insurance. These people also put a larger fraction of their wealth in stock.[1]

Economists' Advice Suppose you are a typical person, with an average level of risk aversion. What asset allocation should you choose?

Most economists agree on an answer: you should hold more stocks than bonds. Financial planners who advise savers say the same thing. A common rule of thumb is that savers should hold 2/3 of their wealth in stocks and 1/3

---

[1] This study is "Preference Parameters and Behavioral Heterogeneity," by Robert Barsky and others, *Quarterly Journal of Economics*, May 1997.

in bonds. In 2005, *Money* magazine analyzed asset allocation for a typical person who is in the middle years of a career and is saving for retirement. The magazine recommended that such a saver put 86 percent of her wealth in stock—even more than the usual 2/3.

Precise numbers such as 86 percent are based on complex calculations. However, two basic factors underlie the advice to hold mostly stocks. First, historically, average returns are not just higher for stocks than for bonds, but *much* higher. Over long periods, the differences in returns add up. If you put $100 in bonds and they produce their average real return of 2 percent, your wealth grows to $181 in 30 years. If you put $100 in stocks and they earn 8 percent, you end up with $1,006.

Second, stocks are not really as risky as they first appear. We've seen that the returns on stock vary greatly from year to year. However, these fluctuations tend to average out over time, as good years offset bad years. People who hold stock for long periods, say 20 or 30 years, are quite likely to do well overall.

This point was popularized by a 1994 book, *Stocks for the Long Run*, by Jeremy Siegel of the Wharton Business School at the University of Pennsylvania. Siegel compared stock and bond returns over every 30-year period since 1871 (1871–1901, 1872–1902, and so on). Siegel found that stocks had higher returns than bonds over every one of these periods.

Do People Listen? Some people take economists' advice to hold stock, but many don't. While stockholding has grown, about half of U.S. savers still own no stock. Many of these people have significant wealth in safe assets.

Economists are puzzled by this behavior. Many think that savers are making a mistake. People see fluctuations in stock returns and conclude that stocks are too risky. They don't realize that fluctuations average out over time or that the average return on stocks is so high.

On the other hand, some economists suggest that savers might have good reasons to avoid stock. Perhaps stocks really *are* risky. So far, stockholders haven't lost money over any 30-year period, because bad years have been followed by good years. But the future might differ from the past. A run of bad luck could produce large losses for stockholders.

A long period of losses could result from some national crisis. Perhaps the financial system will break down, or a war will destroy much of the economy. Such events would drive many companies into bankruptcy, making their stocks worthless. Even if these disasters are unlikely, the risk might lead people to avoid stocks.[2]

Economists' advice to hold stocks has one important qualification, which we discuss in the next case study.

---

[2] This idea is discussed by Robert Barro of Harvard University in "Rare Disasters and Asset Markets in the Twentieth Century," *Quarterly Journal of Economics*, August 2006.

CASE STUDY

Age and Asset Allocation

Economists such as Jeremy Siegel argue that stocks are not very risky. However, the risks from stockholding grow with age, so older people should hold less stock than younger people.

Recall Siegel's point: stocks are safe because high and low returns average out over time. This argument applies to people who hold stocks for long periods. An older person has a shorter saving horizon: he is likely to start selling his assets soon to finance retirement. If this person holds stock, a few bad years can reduce his wealth significantly, and he won't have a chance to recoup these losses.

Another difference between young and old savers is that the young expect more future income from working. This prospect reduces the risk of holding stock. To see this point, suppose a 30-year-old puts all his savings in stock and the market crashes. Even if this person's wealth is wiped out, this event is not a disaster. The 30-year-old has several decades to earn money, rebuild his savings, and finance retirement. In contrast, a current retiree who loses his wealth is in trouble, because he can't fall back on future earnings.

For these reasons, financial advisors tell savers to change their asset allocation as they age. You should start by holding mostly stock, and then shift gradually toward bonds. One rule of thumb is that the percentage of your wealth in stock should be 100 minus your age—70 percent at age 30, 60 percent at age 40, and so on.

Recall that *Money* magazine suggests an 86 percent allocation to stock. This advice applies if you are more than 10 years from retirement. The magazine suggests that you reduce stock to 66 percent when you are close to retirement, and 55 percent during retirement.

5.5 WHICH STOCKS?

So far, we have discussed the allocation of wealth among broad asset classes. A saver must also choose specific assets within each class. We now consider this decision, focusing on the choice among stocks issued by different companies.

We have already discussed one key principle: *diversification*. Holding too much of one company's stock can be disastrous, as we saw with the Enron case study in Section 1.2. To reduce risk, savers should split their wealth among a sizable number of stocks. One way to do this is to buy shares in a mutual fund.

By itself, the principle of diversification does not pin down which stocks to buy. A saver can achieve diversification with around 30 or 40 stocks; with that many, one company's misfortune can't hurt too much. Thousands of companies issue stock, so the possible combinations of 30 or 40 are vast. Someone—either you or a mutual fund manager—must choose which stocks to buy.

The Efficient-Markets Hypothesis

Suppose you graduate from college and get a job at a mutual fund. Your boss asks you to recommend stocks for the fund to purchase. With little experience, you're not sure what to suggest. Fortunately, you remember a friendly finance professor. You decide to consult her, figuring that a finance professor must know how to pick stocks.

You may be surprised at the professor's advice. She is likely to tell you that it doesn't matter which stocks you pick. Rather than sweating over your decision, you can choose stocks randomly. Write the names of companies on pieces of paper, put them in a hat, close your eyes, and pull out your selections.

Is your professor joking? Is she hiding her true secrets for stock picking? No, her advice is probably sincere, because she believes the **efficient-markets hypothesis (EMH).** The EMH says that no stock is a better buy than any other, which justifies random choices. The EMH is a central tenet of finance theory.

Efficient-markets hypothesis (EMH) The price of every stock equals the value of the stock, so no stock is a better buy than any other.

The EMH follows from another finance principle, the classical theory of asset prices. To see the connection, think about how you would choose stocks if you *don't* draw names from a hat. You should look for good deals—stocks that are worth a lot relative to their prices. A stock's worth is the present value of expected earnings, so you should buy stocks with prices below this level. In Wall Street lingo, you should buy stocks that are **undervalued assets.**

Undervalued asset Asset with a price below the present value of expected earnings

But the classical theory says that a stock price always equals the present value of expected earnings. And recall that the theory assumes rational expectations: expected earnings are the best possible forecasts. Thus the price of a stock always equals the best estimate of the stock's value. Undervalued stocks do not exist, so it's futile to look for them.

Prices Follow Random Walks To see this point another way, let's think about movements in stock prices. When you pick stocks, you might try to forecast future price changes. If you can identify stocks with prices that are likely to rise, you can buy these stocks and earn capital gains when the increases occur. Your returns will exceed those on a random selection of stocks.

Once again, the EMH says your strategy won't work. A stock price reflects forecasts of earnings based on all public information. The price changes when new information arrives, changing the forecasts. This information must be a surprise—say, an announcement of higher-than-expected sales. If the information were anticipated, it would already be accounted for in earnings forecasts.

By definition, you can't predict surprises. Since only surprises affect stock prices, changes in these prices are unpredictable. In statistical language, each price follows a **random walk.** You never know which prices are likely to rise, so once again stock picking is futile.

Random walk the movements of a variable whose changes are unpredictable

The Critique of Stock Picking The efficient-markets hypothesis is controversial. It is popular among finance professors, but there are many doubters at securities firms. Analysts for mutual funds and brokers think they can do what the EMH says is impossible: identify undervalued stocks.

These analysts don't think that stock prices always reflect the best possible forecasts of earnings. So they study companies and produce their own forecasts. These forecasts are based on many factors: companies' past performances, their current investment projects, competition in their industries, and so on. When forecasts for a company's earnings are high compared to its stock price, analysts recommend the stock. The securities firms they work for buy the stock and/or recommend it to clients.

Thousands of firms perform this analysis, and they put lots of resources into it. They pay high salaries to attract talented, hardworking analysts. The analysts gather lots of data and use sophisticated statistical techniques. They monitor companies continuously, so their forecasts account for the latest news.

Analysts argue that this effort pays off with good stock picks. But EMH supporters disagree. Ironically, the fact that analysts try so hard to pick stocks is a reason to believe that stock picking doesn't work. Analysts' research and the resulting stock trades actually are forces that make the market efficient.

We can see this point with an example. Assume that, initially, the price of Boeing stock equals the present value of expected earnings. The stock is neither under- nor overvalued. Then Boeing announces some good news: United Airlines has ordered 50 new planes. Analysts who follow Boeing read its news release and realize that the order will raise the company's earnings. At the current stock price, Boeing is undervalued. Analysts tell their firms to buy the stock.

This happens simultaneously at many firms, creating a surge in demand for Boeing. High demand causes the stock price to jump up. The price quickly reaches a level that equals the new present value of earnings, accounting for the United order. At that point, Boeing is no longer an especially good buy. Analysts' efforts to identify undervalued stocks have caused undervaluation to disappear.

Two Kinds of Mutual Funds

Actively managed fund Mutual fund that picks stocks based on analysts' research

Index fund Mutual fund that buys all the stocks in a broad market index

The EMH is important for a decision facing many savers: the choice among mutual funds. There are two types of funds. An **actively managed fund** employs analysts who do the kind of research on companies that we have discussed. These funds buy and sell stocks frequently based on the analysts' recommendations.

In contrast, an **index fund** doesn't try to pick stocks. Instead, it buys *all* the stocks in a broad market index, such as the S&P 500. An index fund doesn't hire analysts to study companies—someone just looks up which stocks are in the index. The fund buys these stocks and then holds onto them, so it doesn't trade as often as an actively managed fund.

If you believe the EMH, you should prefer index funds. The EMH says that stocks picked by analysts will do no better, on average, than an index. And actively managed funds have the disadvantage of high fees. To pay analysts and traders, the funds usually charge shareholders 1 percent or more of their assets each year. Many index funds charge around a quarter of a percent. Once fees are deducted, returns are likely to be higher for index funds than for actively managed funds.

Many economists have examined returns on mutual funds. Generally, their data support the view that index funds produce higher returns, on average, than actively managed funds. This finding suggests that the EMH has a large element of truth.

For example, about 1300 actively managed stock funds operated over the decade 1995–2005. Averaging these funds together, the rate of return was 8.2 percent. Over the same period, the return on the S&P 500 was 10.0 percent. Of the individual mutual funds, 15 percent had a higher return than the S&P 500, and 85 percent had a lower return.

Notice that *some* funds beat the S&P index. What accounts for this success? There are two possible answers. One is that the managers of successful funds—the top 15 percent—are unusually talented. They can identify undervalued stocks even though the average manager can't. Given this interpretation, it might make sense to buy shares in actively managed funds. You should do so if you can figure out which funds have the best managers.

Believers in the EMH have a different view: successful fund managers are lucky. Different funds buy different sets of stocks. There is no good reason to prefer one portfolio to another. Nonetheless, over any period, news about companies will cause some stocks to perform better than others. Mutual funds that happen to own these stocks will have above-average returns.

According to this view, it's impossible to predict which mutual funds will beat a market index. You can see which funds have done so in the past. But since these funds were just lucky, there is no reason to think their success will continue. You should reject all managed funds and put your wealth in a low-cost index fund.

Once again, research supports the predictions of the EMH. A number of studies have examined mutual funds with above-average returns over periods of 1 to 5 years. The studies ask whether these funds beat an index in subsequent years, and generally find that they don't.

Can *Anyone* Beat the Market?

Some economists interpret the EMH as an absolute law: anyone who tries to beat a stock market index is wasting his time. Yet other economists have a less extreme view. They think that beating the market is difficult but not impossible, because exceptions to market efficiency exist. In any case, people keep trying to beat the market—to succeed where the average mutual fund fails. Many would-be market beaters fall into one of three categories, which we now discuss.

Fast Traders One strategy for beating the market relies on speed. To understand this approach, recall the logic behind the EMH. If there is good news about a company's earnings, demand rises for the company's stock. Higher demand pushes the stock price to a level reflecting current expectations about earnings.

The EMH assumes that stock prices respond instantly to news. In reality, price adjustment takes a little time. For example, suppose there is good news about a NASDAQ stock. This news prompts buy orders to dealers who trade the stock. These dealers see decreases in their inventories and realize that demand has risen. They respond by raising their ask prices for the stock.

This process may not take long. Dealers can respond to demand shifts within minutes or even seconds. But there is a brief period before a stock price adjusts to news when the stock is undervalued. Traders can profit if they get their orders in quickly.

Many investment banks have departments that specialize in fast trading. Traders sit in front of several computer screens, some that report news and others connected to securities dealers. When news arrives about a stock, traders can buy or sell it almost instantly.

Behaviorists Fast trading exploits brief deviations from market efficiency. Another strategy is based on the view that inefficiencies persist: some stocks are undervalued for long periods. People who identify these stocks can beat the market even if they aren't especially fast. This view is held by believers in **behavioral finance.**

Behavioral finance Field that uses ideas from psychology to study how deviations from rational behavior affect asset prices

Recall that stock prices depend on expectations about company earnings. The EMH assumes rational expectations: people who forecast earnings, such as stock analysts, do as well as they can given their information. Behaviorists dispute this assumption. They argue that forecasters regularly make certain kinds of mistakes, leading to over- or undervaluation of stocks.

This idea has become popular in the last 20 years. One leader of the behavioral school is Richard Thaler of the University of Chicago. Researchers such as Thaler try to identify common mistakes in earnings forecasts. They base their work on theories from psychology as well as finance.

One mistake stressed by behaviorists is "anchoring" of forecasts. They argue that stock analysts form opinions about companies and then are reluctant to change them. If analysts have predicted that a company will do badly, they resist evidence to the contrary. If the company reports good news, analysts grudgingly raise their earnings forecasts, but not as much as they should. With earnings forecasts too low, the company's stock is undervalued.

Some hedge funds pick stocks based on behavioral theories. One of the first was founded by Thaler and others in 1993. Behavioral funds try to find examples of common mistakes, such as anchored forecasts. If they succeed, they can tell that certain stocks are undervalued.

Since behavioral funds are fairly new, we can't yet judge their success. Some have beaten stock indexes in recent years, but we need more data to tell whether this record reflects good strategies or good luck.

Link through the text Web site to Richard Thaler's Web site for more on behavioral finance.

Geniuses? Many stock pickers are neither fast traders nor behaviorists. They just study companies, forecast earnings, and decide which stocks are undervalued. We have seen that most people who follow this approach can't beat the market. But maybe a few can.

In recent history, a handful of stock pickers have gained notoriety for beating the market repeatedly. One is Peter Lynch, who ran Fidelity's Magellan

Fund from 1978 to 1990. Magellan's average return during this period was 29 percent. Also famous is William Miller of Legg Mason, whose fund beat the S&P 500 for 15 straight years, from 1991 through 2005. (Miller's star waned a bit when his fund underperformed the market in 2006 and 2007).

Hard-core believers in the EMH say that Lynch and Miller were lucky. If so, they were *very* lucky. The EMH implies that a mutual fund has no better than a 1/2 probability of beating an index each year. The probability of winning 15 years in a row is at most $(1/2)^{15} = 0.00003$. Many observers doubt that anyone beats these odds through luck alone. They conclude that people such as Lynch and Miller really can pick stocks.

How do they do it? EMH supporters stress that everyone has the same information about companies. Lynch and Miller read the same annual reports as other mutual fund managers and receive the same news releases. But perhaps some people have unusual skill in *interpreting* information. If a company creates a new product, for example, everyone hears about it. But a few geniuses have special insights about the product's likely success. They can forecast earnings better than the rest of the market.

When people name the best stock pickers, Peter Lynch and William Miller are often on the list. But one man is always at the top: Warren Buffett.

CASE STUDY

The Oracle of Omaha

Warren Buffett was born in Omaha, Nebraska in 1930, the son of a stockbroker. He earned a master's degree in economics and then worked in New York for Benjamin Graham, a famous stock picker of the 1940s and 1950s. In 1957, Buffett returned to Omaha and started a fund, Buffett Partnership Ltd. Its initial wealth was $105,000 from family and friends plus $100 of Buffett's own money. Buffett bought stocks through this company and a successor, Berkshire Hathaway.

The rest is history. From 1965 to 2007, the return on Berkshire Hathaway stock averaged 21.1 percent, compared to 10.3 percent for the S&P 500. If you put $10,000 in the S&P in 1965, you would have had about $600,000 in 2007. If you put $10,000 in Berkshire Hathaway, you would have $31 million.

As of 2008, Buffett owned about 30 percent of Berkshire Hathaway's stock. In that year, his total wealth reached $62 billion, and he passed Bill Gates to become the richest person in the world. (But he still lives in a house that he bought for $32,000 in 1957.) At age 77, Buffett was still running Berkshire Hathaway full-time.

How does Buffett pick stocks? He says he buys "great companies" with high earnings potential. In looking for such companies, Buffett "sticks with businesses we think we understand. That means they must be relatively simple and stable in character." This principle leads Buffett to avoid tech companies such as Microsoft, whose businesses change rapidly.

Buffett puts great weight on the quality of companies' managers. He looks for people who are smart and dedicated to making money for shareholders.

When Warren Buffett buys a stake in a company, he likes to get acquainted with its managers. In 2006, Buffett (left) toured Jerusalem's Old City with Eitan Wertheimer, Chairman of Israel's Iscar Metalworking.

AP/Wide World Photos

He is leery of "empire builders"—managers who maximize their companies' size rather than profits. Buffett likes to meet managers personally to judge their abilities.

One example of Berkshire Hathaway's success was its purchase of Coca-Cola stock starting in 1988. Coke's earnings had been mediocre and analysts predicted that its business would stagnate. Its stock price was $11. Buffett realized that Coke had untapped potential for expanding overseas, using its world-famous brand name. After he bought the stock, Coke did expand overseas, and others raised their earnings forecasts. The stock price was $75 in 1993.

For more on Warren Buffett's stock picking, link through the text Web site to Berkshire Hathaway's Web site and to buffettsecrets.com.

Berkshire Hathaway has had many other successes. It bought large stakes in the *Washington Post* in 1973, GEICO in 1976, and Gillette in 1989. All these companies had problems that held down their stock prices—but all did well after Buffett bought shares. As with Coca-Cola, Buffett somehow saw potential profits that others didn't see.

5.6 DERIVATIVES

Derivatives Securities with payoffs tied to the prices of other assets

So far, this chapter has discussed two kinds of securities, stocks and bonds. We now turn to another kind, **derivatives.** The payoffs from these securities are tied to the prices of other assets (the securities are "derived" from the other assets). The most common types of derivatives are futures and options.

We first define futures and options and describe how they are traded. Then we discuss the uses of derivatives, which vary widely. As you will see, some savers and financial institutions use derivatives to reduce risk. Others use derivatives to make risky bets on asset prices.

Futures

A **futures contract** is an agreement to trade an asset for a certain price at a future point in time. One party agrees to sell the asset and another agrees to buy. The oldest futures contracts are those for agricultural products, such as grain and cotton. Farmers have traded these contracts for centuries. Futures also exist for nonagricultural commodities, such as oil and natural gas.

Futures contract Agreement to trade an asset for a certain price at a future point in time

Futures contracts for securities, called *financial futures*, were invented in the 1970s. The most common are futures for Treasury bonds and for stock indexes. Each contract states a "delivery date" when a transaction will be made. These dates are usually between 1 and 9 months in the future. For example, you might agree to pay $100 to receive a 10-year Treasury bond 6 months from now.

Some futures contracts, such as those for Treasury bonds, literally require the seller to deliver securities to the buyer. Other contracts specify cash payments based on security prices. For example, a seller of futures on the S&P 500 does *not* deliver shares of the 500 stocks. Instead, for each future, she pays an agreed-upon "multiplier" times the S&P index on the delivery date. If the multiplier is $10 and the index is 1000, she pays ($10) × (1000) = $10,000.

Trading futures can produce either gains or losses. Generally, one side of a contract earns money at the expense of the other. Who wins depends on the price in the futures contract and the current price of the asset on delivery day.

Let's consider an example. On January 1, 2020, Jack sells a Treasury-bond future to Jill. The delivery date is July 1, and the price is $100. When July 1 arrives, it turns out that Treasury bonds are trading for $110. Jill is in luck. She pays Jack $100 for a bond, as they agreed 6 months before. She can resell the bond for the current price of $110, yielding a profit of $10. Jack, on the other hand, receives only $100 for a bond worth $110. He loses $10.

Now let's change the story. Jack and Jill make the same deal on January 1, but the price of T-bonds on July 1 is $90. In this case, Jack wins: he receives $100 for a bond worth $90, gaining $10. Jill pays $100 for a $90 bond, losing $10.

Futures are traded on exchanges such as the Chicago Board of Trade and the Chicago Mercantile Exchange. People who want to trade hire brokers who work at the exchanges. A broker whose client wants to sell a certain contract looks for a broker whose client wants to buy. When the brokers meet, they arrange a trade.

When a trade occurs, both buyer and seller must post deposits with the futures exchange. These deposits are called *margins*. The purpose is to ensure that both parties fulfill their contract on the delivery day. A typical margin is 10 percent of the futures price. On January 1, when Jack and Jill trade a $100 bond future, each must deposit $10 with the exchange.

Options

A futures contract requires a transaction at the delivery date. An **option,** as the name suggests, may or may not produce a later transaction. If Jack sells Jill an option, she gains the right to trade a security with him—but not an obligation. Jill pays Jack a fee to receive the option.

Option The right to trade a security at a certain price any time before an expiration date

Call option An option to buy a security

Put option An option to sell a security

▶The options we discuss are "American" options, the most common type in the United States. A "European" option is a little different. It can be exercised only on a single day in the future, not any time before expiration.

A **call option** allows its owner to *buy* a security at a certain price, called the "strike price." The option holder can make this purchase at any point before an expiration date, which is set in the contract. If he buys the security, he is said to "exercise" the option. A **put option** allows its owner to *sell* a security. Like a call option, it specifies a strike price and an expiration date.

Call and put options are sold for Treasury bonds and stock indexes. They are also sold for individual stocks. Expiration dates are usually between 1 and 6 months in the future.

Options are traded on exchanges such as the Chicago Board of Options Exchange. As on futures exchanges, brokers for buyers and sellers meet to make deals. An option buyer immediately pays a fee to the seller. The seller makes a margin deposit to guarantee his performance if the buyer exercises the option.

Options also come from another source. Many companies create call options on their own stock and give them to executives. These options are part of the executives' pay. Options are valuable if stock prices rise, as the following example illustrates.

It is January 1, 2020. The current price of Google stock is $400. You buy a call option on one share of Google, with a strike price of $450 and an expiration date of July 1. You pay $20 for this option.

As long as Google's price is below $450, you don't exercise the option. You don't choose to buy the stock for more than it's worth. If July 1 arrives and the price is still below $450, the option expires. The $20 you paid for the option is a loss.

On the other hand, suppose that Google's stock rises to $500 on April 1. At that point, you might exercise the option. You can buy the stock for $450 and resell it for $500. You come out ahead, even accounting for the $20 you paid initially.

▶Problem 5.11 explores the dilemma of when to exercise an option.

It is tricky to choose when to exercise an option. In our example, you earn a profit by exercising on April 1. But you might do even better by waiting. If the stock reaches $600 on May 1, you will earn more by exercising then. On the other hand, the stock might fall after April 1. If that happens, you will wish you had cashed in when the stock was high.

Hedging with Derivatives

Hedging Reducing risk by purchasing an asset that is likely to produce a high return if another of one's assets produces low or negative returns

Why do people trade derivatives? One purpose is to reduce risk through **hedging.** To hedge is to purchase an asset that is likely to produce a high return if another of one's assets produces a low or negative return. Derivatives can be used for many types of hedging; let's look at some examples.

Hedging with Futures Hedging was the original purpose of agricultural futures. Imagine a farmer growing wheat and a miller who will buy the wheat when it is harvested in 6 months. Both parties face risk from fluctuations in the price of wheat. If the price is high in 6 months, the farmer will earn extra income, but the miller's costs will rise. The reverse happens if the price is low.

Wheat futures eliminate this risk. The farmer can sell a contract for wheat in 6 months and the miller can buy this contract. The contract locks in a price for both parties.

Like commodities futures, financial futures can reduce risk. The owners of securities experience gains and losses when security prices change. To hedge, security holders make derivatives trades that produce profits if they suffer losses elsewhere.

For example, commercial banks hold large quantities of Treasury bonds. They stand to lose a lot if bond prices fall. A bank can reduce this risk by selling Treasury bond futures. If bond prices do fall, the bank earns profits from its sale of futures (like Jack in our earlier example). The profits on futures cancel the losses on bonds. If prices rise, the bank loses on futures but gains from its bond holdings. Either way, the bank's total profits are insulated from bond-price movements.

Other institutions hedge by *buying* futures rather than selling them. Suppose a pension fund expects a large contribution in 3 months and plans to use this money to buy Treasury bonds. The pension fund faces risk because it doesn't know how much the bonds will cost. It can lock in a price by purchasing T-bond futures with a delivery date in 3 months, just as a miller can use futures to lock in a price for wheat.

Hedging with Options Security holders can also reduce risk by trading options. One hedging strategy is a "protective put." This means a purchase of put options on securities you own. It protects against big losses on the securities.

For example, suppose you own shares in a mutual fund that holds the S&P 500. The current level of the S&P index is 1000. The index is likely to rise, but you worry about the possibility of a stock market crash. You might sleep better if you buy puts on the index, say with a strike price of 900. In effect this option lets you sell stocks for 90 percent of their current value, even if prices fall lower. Your potential losses are limited.

You must pay for the put options, and you never use them if the S&P index stays above 900. Nonetheless, it may be prudent to purchase the puts. They are essentially insurance: you pay fees to reduce risk.

Speculating with Derivatives

Derivatives are also useful for **speculation.** This practice is the opposite of hedging, which reduces risk. Speculators use financial markets to make bets on asset prices, earning a lot if they are right and losing a lot if they are wrong.

Speculation Using financial markets to make bets on asset prices

Suppose the current price of a Treasury bond is $100. Most people expect this price to stay constant, so the 6-month futures price is also $100. You, however, are more insightful than most people. You realize that the Federal Reserve is likely to lower its interest-rate target, pushing up bond prices. You can bet on this belief by purchasing the $100 Treasury bond futures. You will profit if T-bonds are selling for more than $100 in 6 months.

You can also bet on Treasury bonds simply by purchasing the bonds themselves. However, buying futures has the advantage that you need less money up front. You need only post margin, not pay full price, for the bonds you bet on. As a result, you can make larger bets.

For example, suppose you have $1000 available to bet on bond prices. At the current price of $100, you can buy 10 bonds. If the price in 6 months is $110, you earn $10 per bond, for a total of $100. Your initial $1000 rises by 10 percent. If the bond price is $120, you earn $200, a return of 20 percent.

Now suppose that you buy bond futures. If the margin requirement is 10 percent, you must deposit $10 for every $100 future. Depositing your $1000 lets you buy 100 futures. Now if the bond price in 6 months is $110, you earn $10 per future, for a total of $1000. The return on your initial $1000 is 100 percent. If the price in 6 months is $120, your return is 200 percent. Thanks to futures, you have profited greatly from your understanding of the Fed and bond prices.

You can also use options to bet on T-bonds. If you think the price will rise, you might sell put options on the bonds, say with a strike price of $100. As long as the actual price stays above $100, nobody exercises the options. The fees you receive for the options are pure profit. Once again, you need only a modest margin deposit to try this strategy.

The catch, of course, is that speculation requires you to predict asset prices better than other people. The efficient-markets hypothesis says that's not possible. If it's really likely that the Fed will lower interest rates, everyone knows it. The prices of futures and options have already adjusted to this information, eliminating profit opportunities. According to the EMH, speculation is pure gambling; you might as well play the slots.

Nonetheless, many financial institutions speculate with derivatives. Leading players include investment banks and hedge funds. The term *hedge fund* is a misnomer, because hedge funds don't hedge, they speculate.

As one might expect, some speculators have made large profits and others have lost a lot. The next case study discusses some examples of speculation gone wrong.

CASE STUDY

Derivative Disasters

One famous fiasco occurred in 1995 at Barings LLC, a prestigious bank based in Britain. Nick Leeson, 27, was a low-level trader in Barings's Singapore office. Without anyone's permission, Leeson started making risky bets with derivatives.

One of Leeson's strategies was to sell "straddles" on Japan's Nikkei stock index. This means selling call options with a strike price above the current level of the index *and* selling put options with a price below the current level. The bet is that the index stays between the two strike prices, so neither the calls nor the puts are exercised. For a while this strategy worked, and Leeson produced large profits for Barings.

Unfortunately, the Kobe earthquake triggered a sharp fall in the Nikkei in February 1995. The put options were exercised, meaning Barings was forced to buy stock for prices well above the current market. Leeson lost more than $1 billion through this and similar strategies, and Barings went bankrupt. Leeson went to jail for trying to cover up his losses.

In 2008, the financial world was reminded of the Barings episode by a similar debacle at Societé Generale, a large investment bank in France. Once again, a low-level trader—Jerome Kerviel, 31—made large bets on stock markets. Starting in 2006, Kerviel bought futures on European stock indexes, such as France's CAC and Germany's DAX, hoping to profit from rising stock prices. He falsified trading records to hide his activities from his supervisors.

In 2007–08, fears of a financial crisis in the United States spread around the world. European stock markets fell, so Kerviel's bets produced losses. By the time Societé Generale's management discovered Kerviel's trades, he had lost 4.9 billion euros ($7.2 billion). Like Leeson, Kerviel was arrested for fraud.

Derivative disasters have also occurred in the United States. In the early 1990s, many speculators bet that bond prices would stay constant or rise, but prices fell in 1994 when the Fed raised interest rates unexpectedly. In addition to private firms, the losers in this episode included the government of Orange County, California. Its treasurer, Robert Citron, lost $2 billion of tax receipts on derivatives. This loss led Orange County, one of the country's wealthiest counties, to default on its debt.

Small savers have also been burned by derivatives. In the 1980s, some stockbrokers advised clients to sell puts on stock indexes. This strategy was advertised as safe, because the puts would be exercised only if stocks fell sharply, which was considered very unlikely. Disaster arrived on October 19, 1987, the day of the big crash discussed in Section 3.5.

A *Wall Street Journal* article tells the story of a small business owner who sold puts on the stock market. He hoped to earn $1000 per month to help pay for his children's college education. This man lost more than $100,000 on the day of the 1987 crash. The *Journal* does not report whether his kids made it to college.

Such episodes have hurt the reputation of derivatives. Warren Buffett is a critic: he calls derivatives "financial weapons of mass destruction." (One company that Buffett owned suffered large losses from derivatives.) Defenders respond that the problem is not derivatives themselves, but their misuse. People should be more cautious, and financial institutions should supervise traders like Leeson and Kerviel more closely.

New Frontiers

Most of the derivatives we've discussed were invented in the 1970s. Since then, financial engineers have created many others.

One is futures on weather, which have been traded on the Chicago Mercantile Exchange since 1999. Payoffs depend on temperatures in various cities. For example, you can buy a future that pays $20 times the difference between 65 and Boston's average winter temperature in degrees

Farenheit. In 2007, $19 billion of weather futures were traded. Agricultural and energy companies, whose profits depend on temperatures, use these securities to hedge.

In 2006, the Chicago Mercantile Exchange introduced house-price derivatives. Like weather derivatives, these securities are created for different cities. They yield "dividends" that rise or fall depending on indexes of local house prices. So far, not many of these securities have been traded, but some economists predict the market will grow. Homeowners can potentially use house-price derivatives to hedge: they can buy securities that yield high payoffs when the value of their houses fall.

The list of derivatives goes on and on. You can buy securities with payoffs tied to economic statistics, such as aggregate employment. Or securities tied to votes in presidential elections, or batting averages of baseball players. In many cases, it's dubious that the securities are useful for hedging. They are bought by speculators who think they are good at forecasting the economy, politics, or sports—or who simply enjoy betting.

Summary

5.1 Participants in Securities Markets

- Securities firms are companies whose primary purpose is to hold securities, trade them, or help others trade them. These firms include mutual funds, hedge funds, brokers, dealers, and investment banks.
- Other financial institutions that own large quantities of securities include pension funds, insurance companies, and commercial banks.

5.2 Stock and Bond Markets

- Corporations and governments issue securities in primary markets. Investment banks underwrite corporations' securities, reducing the problem of adverse selection.
- The U.S. government sells bonds through auctions. Google used a similar auction when it first issued stock in 2004.
- After securities are issued, they are traded in secondary markets. These markets include exchanges, such as the New York Stock Exchange, and over-the-counter markets, which have no physical location. OTC markets include dealer markets and electronic communications networks.
- Information on securities prices is available in newspapers such as the *Wall Street Journal* and on Web sites such as bloomberg.com.

5.3 Firms' Capital Structure

- Firms can finance investment by issuing either stocks or bonds. The mix of the two that a firm chooses is called its capital structure.
- The Modigliani-Miller Theorem states that a firm's capital structure is irrelevant. Stocks and bonds are equally good ways for firms to raise funds.
- In reality, issuing bonds rather than stock reduces a firm's taxes. It also lessens the adverse selection problem. On the other hand, issuing bonds raises the risk of bankruptcy. Because of these trade-offs, most firms issue a mixture of stock and bonds.

5.4 What Assets Should Savers Hold?

- Savers must choose how to split their wealth among different classes of assets, such as stocks and bonds. Stocks have higher average returns than bonds, but they are also riskier.
- Economists and financial planners advise savers to hold most of their wealth in stock. They argue that the gains in average return outweigh the risk. Yet many people ignore this advice: they hold most of their wealth in safe assets, including bonds and bank accounts.
- Financial planners also advise savers to shift their wealth from stock to safe assets as they grow older.

5.5 Which Stocks?

- According to the efficient-markets hypothesis, every stock's price equals the best estimate of its value, so no stock is a better buy than any other. It is futile to look for stocks that will produce higher-than-average returns.
- Actively managed mutual funds employ analysts who select stocks; index funds hold all the stocks in a broad market index. Most actively managed funds underperform index funds, a fact that supports the EMH.
- The EMH may not be completely true: some stock pickers may be able to beat the market. Some people try to beat the market by reacting quickly to news, some employ behavioral theories of finance, and some try to predict companies' prospects better than others can. Warren Buffett has been hugely successful with the last approach.

5.6 Derivatives

- Derivative securities include futures contracts and options. A futures contract is an agreement to trade an asset for a certain price at a future point in time. An option is a right (but not an obligation) to trade a security at a certain price before an expiration date.
- Some people and institutions use derivatives to hedge. They purchase derivatives that will produce high returns if other assets they own produce low or negative returns.
- Other people and institutions use derivatives to speculate. They make bets on asset prices that sometimes produce large profits and sometimes lead to disaster.
- Financial engineers continually create new derivatives, such as securities tied to weather or to house prices.

Key Terms

actively managed mutual fund, p. 140
asset allocation, p. 119
behavioral finance, p. 142
bid-ask spread, p. 129
broker, p. 121
call option, p. 146
capital structure, p. 130
dealer, p. 122
dealer market, p. 129
derivatives, p. 144
efficient-markets hypothesis (EMH), p. 139
electronic communications network (ECN), p. 129
exchange, p. 128
futures contract, p. 145
hedge fund, p. 121
hedging, p. 146
index fund, p. 140
initial public offering (IPO), p. 123
investment bank, p. 122
leverage, p. 121
Modigliani-Miller Theorem, p. 131
option, p. 145
over-the-counter (OTC) market, p. 129
primary markets, p. 123
public company, p. 123
put option, p. 146
random walk, p. 139
secondary markets, p. 123
securities firm, p. 121
specialist, p. 128
speculation, p. 147
stock market index, p. 130
undervalued asset, p. 139
underwriter, p. 122

Questions and Problems

1. When investment banks underwrite IPOs, they typically sell stock for 5–10 percent more than they pay for it. When they underwrite new stock for companies that are already public, the typical markup is 3 percent. What explains this difference?

2. As in Section 5.4, assume that bonds pay a real return of 2 percent. Stocks pay 22 percent half the time and −6 percent half the time. Suppose you initially have wealth of $100, and let X be your wealth after 1 year. What fraction of your wealth should you hold in stock under each of the following assumptions?
   a. You want to maximize the average value of X.
   b. You want to maximize the lowest-possible value of X.
   c. You want to be certain that X is at least $100 (that is, you don't lose any of your initial wealth). Subject to that constraint, you maximize the average value of X.

3. Suppose two people are the same age and have the same level of wealth. One has a high-paying job and the other has a low-paying job. Who should hold a higher fraction of his or her wealth in stock? Explain.

4. Chapter 3 presented the classical theory of asset prices. In this chapter, we discussed two ideas that follow from the classical theory: the Modigliani-Miller Theorem, and the efficient-markets hypothesis. How well do these two ideas fit real-world financial markets? Where does each fit on a spectrum from literally true to completely unrealistic?

5. Suppose everyone in the world becomes convinced that the efficient-markets hypothesis is true. Will it stay true? Explain.

6. Research around 1980 showed that stocks of small firms had higher average returns than stocks of large firms. This finding gained much attention, as it seemed to contradict the efficient-markets hypothesis. It suggested a simple way to beat the market: purchase only small-firm stocks.
   a. Can you explain this deviation from market efficiency? (*Hint:* Think about the behavior in financial markets that leads to efficiency, and why this behavior might not occur.)
   b. Would you guess that small stocks have done better than large stocks since 1980? Why or why not?

7. Recall that U.S. mutual fund companies offer about 8000 separate funds. Suppose each fund has a 50 percent chance of beating the S&P 500 each year.
   a. Over a 5-year period, how many funds will beat the market in every year? How about a 15-year period?
   b. Based on the performance of William Miller's mutual fund from 1981 through 2005, would you say Miller is a genius? Explain.
   c. Does Miller's record in 2006 and 2007 change your answer to part (b)?

8. In 1989, the economist Paul Samuelson rated Warren Buffett the greatest stock picker in the country. Yet Samuelson warned against buying Berkshire Hathaway stock. He wrote that "knowledge of Buffett's skills may be already fully discounted in the marketplace. Now that B-H has gone up more than a hundredfold, it is at a premium."
   a. Explain Samuelson's reasoning in your own words.
   b. People who followed Samuelson's advice have regretted it, because the returns on B-H stock since 1989 have been similar to earlier returns. What does this tell us about Buffett and/or the efficient-markets hypothesis?

9. On its Web site, one mutual fund company describes its "disciplined and sophisticated investment strategies." (The term *investment* is used to mean the choice of securities.) Let's

change the company's name to "Smith." With this alteration, the site says:

> *At the center of Smith's investment process is the Smith Investment Committee. It consists of a select group of senior investment professionals who are supported by an extensive staff. This staff provides multilevel analyses of the economic and investment environments, including actual and projected corporate earnings, interest rates, and the effect of economic forecasts on market sectors, individual securities, and client portfolios.*

Does this statement convince you to buy Smith mutual funds? Why or why not?

10. Suppose you hold most of your wealth in stock. What kinds of options should you buy or sell in each of the following circumstances?
    a. You think the stock market will probably do well, but you worry about a crash.
    b. You want to get a steady return on your assets. You don't care whether you get rich from a big rise in the market.
    c. You think there will soon be big news about firms' earnings, but you don't know whether the news will be good or bad.

11. Suppose you buy call options on Microsoft stock. Each option costs $2 and has a strike price of $40 and an expiration date of July 1. Discuss whether you would exercise the options in each of the following situations, and why:
    a. It is March 1 and Microsoft's stock price is $30.
    b. It is March 1 and the stock price is $40.10.
    c. It is March 1 and the stock price is $50.
    d. It is June 30 and the stock price is $50.
    e. It is June 30 and the stock price is $40.10.

12. Suppose company A has a stable stock price. The price is not likely to change much in the next year. Company B has an uncertain stock price: it could either rise or fall by a lot. Would you pay more for a call option on A's stock or B's stock? Explain.

Online and Data Questions

www.worthpublishers.com/ball

13. Use bloomberg.com to answer the following questions:
    a. Which has done better over the last year, the U.S. stock market or the Brazilian stock market?
    b. Which have done better over the last year, the stocks in the Dow Jones index or the NASDAQ index?
    c. What is the rate of return on Boeing stock over the last year?

14. The text Web site provides data on rates of return for selected mutual funds. Choose 20 actively managed funds and rank them by their average returns over the period 1998–2002. Then rank the same funds by their average returns over 2003–2007. What is the relationship between the two rankings? Are the results surprising? Explain.

15. Link through the text Web site to buffettsecrets .com and study Warren Buffett's principles for choosing stocks. Do you think you could beat a stock index by following these principles? Explain.

chapter six

Foreign Exchange Markets

- 6.1 CURRENCY MARKETS AND EXCHANGE RATES
- 6.2 WHY EXCHANGE RATES MATTER
- 6.3 THE LONG-RUN BEHAVIOR OF EXCHANGE RATES
- 6.4 REAL EXCHANGE RATES IN THE SHORT RUN
- 6.5 FLUCTUATIONS IN EXCHANGE RATES
- 6.6 CURRENCY SPECULATION

The currency of South Africa is the *rand*. **Figure 6.1** on p. 156 shows the value of this currency as measured by the *exchange rate* between the rand and the U.S. dollar. This variable, known more formally as the **nominal exchange rate (*e*),** is the price of one currency in terms of another.

In recent years, the value of the rand has fluctuated a lot. At the start of 2000, 1 rand was worth about 0.16 dollars (16 cents). The exchange rate fell rapidly over the next two years, reaching a low of 0.09 in 2002. Then the trend reversed, and the exchange rate climbed to 0.17 in 2005. It drifted down after that, and was 0.15 at the beginning of 2008.

Why did the rand lose value from 2000 to 2002? Why did it recover after that? And why do these movements matter? Is it better for South Africans if the exchange rate rises, or if it falls?

Economists ask similar questions about exchange rates around the world. This chapter tackles these issues. We start by discussing the markets in which currencies are traded. Then we discuss how exchange rates affect economies, the factors that cause exchange rates to fluctuate, and how speculators try to profit from exchange-rate movements.

ALASTAIR MILLER/BLOOMBERG NEWS/Landov

South Africa's currency is the rand. This 100-rand note features Cape buffaloes and the name of South Africa's central bank in both English and Afrikaans. At the beginning of 2008, 100 rand were worth about 15 U.S. dollars.

FIGURE 6.1 South Africa's Nominal Exchange Rate, 2000–2007

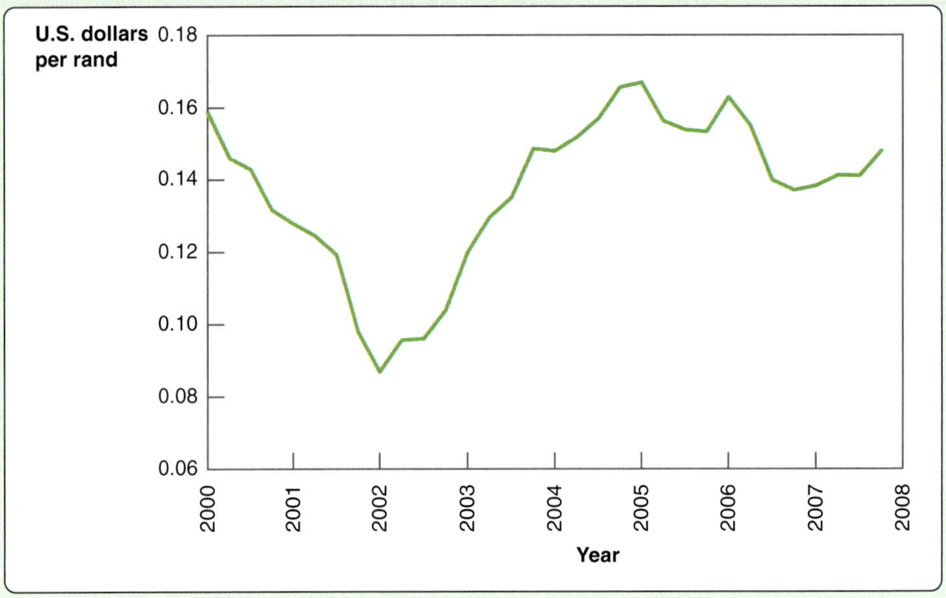

This graph shows the exchange rate between South Africa's rand and the U.S. dollar. From 2000 through 2007, the value of the rand fluctuated between 0.09 dollars and 0.17 dollars.

Source: Federal Reserve Bank of St. Louis

Nominal exchange rate (*e*) Price of one unit of a currency in terms of another currency

One purpose of this chapter is to lay foundations for other parts of the book. Monetary policy has strong effects on exchange rates, so exchange-rate behavior is central to many debates about policy. We discuss these debates in later chapters, especially Chapter 17.

6.1 CURRENCY MARKETS AND EXCHANGE RATES

Every day, people and firms exchange trillions of dollars worth of currencies. They need foreign currencies to make two kinds of transactions. One is purchases of goods and services from other countries. For example, some Americans like to buy French wine, which French vineyards sell for euros. To buy this wine, American importers must first trade dollars for euros.

The other kind of transaction is purchases of foreign assets. These purchases are called *capital outflows* (review Section 4.2). For example, some U.S. mutual funds buy stock in European as well as American companies. The European stock is sold for euros, so the funds must trade dollars for euros before buying the stock.

The Trading Process

How does someone trade dollars for euros? It depends who you are and how much you are trading.

The Interbank Market Large currency trades occur in the "interbank" market. As the name suggests, participants are large commercial banks, such as JP Morgan Chase, and investment banks, such as Deutsche Bank. These institutions are dealers, trading currencies for themselves, and also act as brokers for companies and individuals. The minimum trade on the interbank market is $1 million worth of currency.

The interbank market is an over-the-counter market—it has no physical location. Most trades occur through two electronic networks, Reuters and Electronic Broking Services (EBS), where dealers post bid and ask prices for currencies. Dealers are located in many time zones, so trading goes on 24 hours a day. (The trading week starts at 3 PM on Sunday, Eastern Time—Monday morning in Sydney, Australia—and ends at 4:30 PM on Friday.)

Over 100 currencies are traded in the interbank market. In most trades, the U.S. dollar is exchanged for one of the other currencies. Traders use dollars because this currency is highly liquid—there are many buyers and sellers. Institutions buy dollars even if they ultimately want a different currency. If a bank wants to exchange South African rand for Swiss francs, the easiest way is to trade rand for dollars and then trade the dollars for francs.

▶ Notice that the word "rand" is like the word "sheep": the plural form is the same as the singular, with no "s" added.

As you might imagine, currency traders do not ship bundles of cash around the world. Instead, they exchange bank deposits. If an institution trades dollars for euros, it receives a credit in an account holding euros. It also has an account holding dollars, which is debited.

The Retail Market Most companies and individuals can't trade in the interbank market. If they want foreign currency, they must use a bank as a broker.

Suppose a clothing store in the United States needs euros to buy dresses from a French designer. The store has an account at JP Morgan Chase. It asks the bank to take dollars from its account and use them to purchase euros. The euros are either deposited in another account or paid directly to the French clothier. JP Morgan profits by charging the store a bit more for the euros than it pays on the interbank market.

Recall that only large banks trade in the interbank market. Small banks trade currencies through accounts at large banks. Say your business has an account at First Bank, a small bank in your town. First Bank has an account at JP Morgan Chase. If you need euros, First Bank transfers funds from your account to its account at JP Morgan, and JP Morgan buys the euros.

Your Week in Paris You encounter small-scale currency markets when you travel abroad. Dealers have offices in airports and tourist spots where you can trade dollars for foreign currency. However, these trades are expensive. Dealers set large spreads between their bid and ask prices—often about 10 percent. So the exchange rates you get are significantly worse than interbank rates.

It is less expensive to get currency from ATMs. ATMs in many countries accept U.S. bank cards. You receive foreign currency, and dollars are deducted from your account based on the interbank rate. You pay a small fee to the bank that owns the ATM.

If you use your credit card in foreign countries, charges are converted to dollars on your bill. The exchange rate is the interbank rate, but your card issuer is likely to add a 1–2 percent fee for foreign purchases. It's usually cheaper to buy your souvenirs with cash from ATMs.

Measuring Exchange Rates

An exchange rate involves two currencies. A nominal exchange rate can be expressed as the price of either currency in terms of the other. For example, the dollar–rand exchange rate on January 2, 2008 can be stated as 0.147 dollars per rand. It can also be stated as 6.803 rand per dollar. The second version of the exchange rate is the inverse of the first ($6.803 = 1/0.147$).

When this book discusses an economy, we express its exchange rate as the amount of foreign currency that buys one unit of the local currency. When we analyze South Africa, for example, we treat the United States as a foreign country. We state the exchange rate as 0.147, because it takes that many dollars to buy one rand.

South Africa has other exchange rates with currencies such as the euro and the Japanese yen. Again, when we study South Africa, we state these rates as foreign currency per rand. On January 2, 2008, the rates were 0.100 euros per rand and 16.126 yen per rand. (It's just a coincidence that the euro–rand rate was a round number.)

When we study the U.S. economy, we state exchange rates as foreign currency per dollar. The rates are euros per dollar, yen per dollar, and so on. In this case, the exchange rate with South Africa is stated as 6.803 rand per dollar.

Appreciation Rise in a currency's price in terms of foreign currency

Depreciation Fall in a currency's price in terms of foreign currency

Changes in Exchange Rates

An **appreciation** of a currency is a rise in its price. Each unit of the currency is worth more foreign currency. For example, the rand appreciates against the dollar if the exchange rate rises from 0.15 dollars per rand to 0.20. A **depreciation** is a fall in a currency's price. The rand depreciates if the exchange rate falls from 0.15 dollars per rand to 0.10.

When people discuss exchange rates, they often use the terms "strong" and "weak." Saying that a currency has become stronger means that it has appreciated. A currency is weaker if it has depreciated.

Information on Exchange Rates

Exchange rates fluctuate from minute to minute, just like stock and bond prices. Many newspapers and Web sites report nominal exchange rates. One good source is bloomberg.com.

Bloomberg's main exchange-rate page, shown in **Figure 6.2A,** covers eight major currencies. This page reports the prices of each currency in terms of the other seven. These rates come from the interbank market and are updated every 15 minutes.

Bloomberg also reports exchange rates between the U.S. dollar and many currencies. The page shown in **Figure 6.2B** gives the prices of a U.S. dollar in Canadian dollars, Mexican pesos, and other currencies of the Americas. This page reports the levels of the exchange rates and changes since the start of the day.

FIGURE 6.2 Exchange Rates on Bloomberg.com

(A)

Benchmark Currency Rates

	USD	EUR	JPY	GBP	CHF	CAD	AUD	HKD
HKD	7.8109	11.4631	0.0711	14.5254	7.1112	7.3294	6.7674	
AUD	1.1542	1.6939	0.0105	2.1464	1.0508	1.0831		0.1478
CAD	1.0657	1.564	0.0097	1.9818	0.9702		0.9233	0.1364
CHF	1.0984	1.612	0.01	2.0426		1.0307	0.9516	0.1406
GBP	0.5377	0.7892	0.0049		0.4896	0.5046	0.4659	0.0688
JPY	109.876	161.2518		204.3287	100.0337	103.1032	95.1966	14.067
EUR	0.6814		0.0062	1.2671	0.6204	0.6394	0.5904	0.0872
USD		1.4676	0.0091	1.8596	0.9104	0.9384	0.8664	0.128

Above is a chart designed to display the cross rates of eight major world currencies. Scan across the chart to find the rate of exchange between any two of these currencies.

Currency key

USD:	U.S. Dollar	**CAD:**	Canadian Dollar
GBP:	British Pound	**EUR:**	Euro
CHF:	Swiss Franc	**AUD:**	Australian Dollar
HKD:	Hong Kong Dollar	**JPY:**	Japanese Yen

Unless indicated otherwise: intraday data is at least 15 minutes delayed; mutual fund NAVs are updated at the close of every market day; all prices are in the local currency; Time is ET.

(A) A table downloaded from bloomberg.com on 8/19/08 reports exchange rates among eight major currencies. Each column gives the price of one currency in terms of the other seven. For example, the first column shows that 1 U.S. dollar (USD) is worth 7.81 Hong Kong dollars (HKD) or 1.15 Australian dollars (AUD) or 1.07 Canadian dollars (CAD).

(Continued)

FIGURE 6.2 *Continued*

(B)

World Currencies

AMERICAS | ASIA/PACIFIC | EUROPE/AFRICA/MIDDLE EAST

CURRENCY	VALUE	CHANGE	% CHANGE	TIME
USD-CAD	1.0654	0.0010	0.0892%	10:23
USD-MXN	10.1930	0.0185	0.1818%	10:23
USD-BRL	1.6438	0.0028	0.1706%	10:23
USD-CLP	523.7000	4.4500	0.8570%	10:23
USD-COP	1899.3000	24.6250	1.3136%	10:23
USD-PEN	2.9362	0.0108	0.3675%	10:19
USD-VEF	2.1473	0.0000	0.0000%	01:46
USD-CRC	552.0000	−0.1800	−0.0326%	20:42
USD-ARS	3.0312	0.0018	0.0578%	10:23

Currency Calculator ▸

When the U.S. dollar is listed first, the valuation is expressed as the number of the units of the other currency per U.S. dollar. When another currency is listed first, the valuation is expressed as the number of U.S. dollars per currency unit.

Currency key

USD:	U.S. Dollar	**CAD:**	Canadian Dollar
MXN:	Mexican Peso	**BRL:**	Brazilian Real
CLP:	Chilean Peso	**COP:**	Colombian Peso
PEN:	Peruvian New Sol	**VEF:**	Venezuelan Bolivar
CRC:	Costa Rican Colon	**ARS:**	Argentine Peso

Unless indicated otherwise: intraday data is at least 15 minutes delayed; mutual fund NAVs are updated at the close of every market day; all prices are in the local currency; Time is ET.

(B) Another bloomberg page reports exchange rates between the U.S. dollar and other currencies in the Americas. It shows the price of 1 U.S. dollar in terms of each currency, the change in the price since the start of the day, the percentage change, and the time when these numbers were last updated.

6.2 WHY EXCHANGE RATES MATTER

Exchange rates get a lot of attention. The financial media highlight fluctuations in the dollar along with stock prices and interest rates. Why do we care about exchange rates?

Effects of Appreciation

Suppose the dollar appreciates against the euro. The exchange rate rises from 0.8 euros per dollar to 0.9. This event is neither entirely good nor entirely bad for the United States. Some Americans benefit from the appreciation, and others are hurt. These mixed effects can make exchange rates a controversial topic.

TABLE 6.1 When the Dollar Appreciates . . .

Imports become less expensive	⟶	benefits U.S. consumers
	⟶	hurts U.S. firms that compete with imports
U.S. goods become more expensive to foreigners	⟶	hurts U.S. firms that export
Foreign assets become less valuable in dollars	⟶	hurts U.S. owners of foreign assets

Table 6.1 summarizes the effects of a dollar appreciation on Americans. As the following sections detail, the effects fall on consumers, firms and their workers, and owners of foreign assets.

Cheaper Imports The first effect is beneficial. When the dollar appreciates against the euro, European goods and services become less expensive for American consumers.

Suppose you visit Paris and stay in a hotel that costs 100 euros per night. You have dollars and trade them for euros to pay your bill. If a dollar buys 0.8 euros, then a full euro costs 1/0.8 dollars, or \$1.25. To get 100 euros to pay the hotel, you need \$125. If the dollar appreciates to 0.9 euros, you need only 1/0.9 dollars, or about \$1.11, for each euro. The hotel room costs \$111, so the appreciation saves you money on your trip.

You don't need to travel to benefit from a dollar appreciation. A stronger dollar means that American wine importers need fewer dollars to buy wine from French vineyards. Lower costs to importers lead to lower prices at your local wine store. You can more often afford a nice chardonnay with dinner.

Lower Sales for Domestic Firms While an appreciation is good for consumers, it hurts many U.S. firms because it becomes harder to sell their goods and services. In popular jargon, an appreciation hurts the firms' "competitiveness." Two types of firms are hurt.

One type is firms whose products compete with imports. We saw that a dollar appreciation makes French wine less expensive for Americans. This price change causes consumers to switch from California wines to French wines, reducing the sales of California vineyards. Similarly, hotels in Florida lose business when a strong dollar attracts tourists to Paris.

The other type of firms hurt by an appreciation are exporters. U.S. goods become more expensive for Europeans, reducing sales in Europe. Suppose a U.S. company exports clothes to France. It sells a pair of jeans for \$50. If the exchange rate is 0.8 euros per dollar, a French consumer must pay $(0.8)(50) = 40$ euros for the jeans. If the exchange rate is 0.9, the cost of the jeans rises to $(0.9)(50) = 45$ euros. Fewer jeans are sold.

When U.S. firms lose sales, their profits fall, hurting stockholders. The firms' employees are also hurt, because lower sales can lead to wage cuts or layoffs.

Losses to Holders of Foreign Assets A final group affected by the exchange rate is Americans who own foreign assets. An appreciation hurts this group because it reduces the dollar value of the assets.

Suppose you own a bond issued by the French government that will soon pay 100 euros. You plan to trade the euros for dollars to spend in your hometown. If the exchange rate is 0.8 euros per dollar, the 100 euros will buy you $100/0.8 = 125$ dollars. If the rate rises to 0.9 before you receive the bond payment, you end up with only $100/0.9 = 111$ dollars.

CASE STUDY

The Politics of the Dollar

A strong dollar has both pluses and minuses for the United States. Most economists believe that, overall, a weaker dollar is desirable in some circumstances. These situations include recessions, when firms' sales are low and unemployment is high. A depreciation increases the competitiveness of U.S. firms, so they sell more goods and hire more workers.

Nonetheless, government officials rarely admit that a weak dollar can be good. During the Clinton administration, Treasury Secretary Robert Rubin was often asked his views on exchange rates. He would say only, "I believe a strong dollar is in our nation's interest." Journalists started calling this statement a "mantra."

Lawrence Summers succeeded Rubin as treasury secretary in 1999. When asked for *his* opinions on exchange rates, Summers responded, "a strong dollar is in our interest."

In 2001, President Bush's first treasury secretary, Paul O'Neill, made a surprising statement. He declared, "we are not pursuing, as it is often said, a policy of a strong dollar." This comment provoked widespread criticism. The *Wall Street Journal* charged that O'Neill had "tried to trash the value" of his country's currency. O'Neill responded that he had been misinterpreted. A week after his initial comment he said, "I believe in a strong dollar and I'm not ever going to change." But the damage was done. O'Neill's waffling on the dollar contributed to a reputation for unwise remarks, and he lost his job in 2002.

What's wrong with questioning the strong dollar? The answer involves terminology rather than substance. The word *strong* has positive connotations, and *weak* has negative connotations. The public wouldn't like a defense secretary who advocated a weak military. They wouldn't like a U.S. Olympic coach who promised to field a weak team. Noneconomists often assume that a weak dollar must somehow be bad for the nation's well-being or pride.

The next treasury secretary, John Snow, took a novel approach to this issue. In 2003, he said he didn't mind a recent depreciation of the dollar.

That attitude made sense, as unemployment was high and the Bush administration was trying to reduce it. Snow cited the fact that "when the dollar is at a lower level, it helps exports."

Snow denied, however, that he was abandoning support for a strong dollar. Instead, he invented a new definition of the term. He declared that a currency is "strong" if it is "a good medium of exchange . . . something people are willing to hold . . . hard to counterfeit, like our new $20 bill." The dollar can be strong by this definition even if the exchange rate is low.

Snow later reverted to the Rubin–Summers approach. In 2006, he said—you guessed it—"a strong dollar is in our nation's interest." Snow's successor as treasury secretary, Henry Paulson, said exactly the same thing in 2007. Let's hope, however, that people start interpreting a "strong dollar" policy as opposition to counterfeiting. Then politicians can support depreciations when necessary without appearing wimpy.

Hedging Exchange-Rate Risk

We've seen that an appreciation of the dollar helps some groups and hurts others (Table 6.1). A depreciation has the opposite effects: it hurts American consumers and helps firms and holders of foreign assets. Overall, fluctuations in exchange rates create risk. Anyone affected by exchange rates can win or lose depending on whether the dollar strengthens or weakens.

As we stress throughout this book, people generally dislike risk. They can reduce the risk arising from exchange-rate fluctuations by trading futures contracts for currencies.

Currency Futures and Hedging Section 5.6 discussed futures contracts for stocks and bonds. Currency futures work in a similar way. Two parties agree to trade currencies at a certain exchange rate on a future delivery date. Currency futures are traded on the Reuters and EBS networks, where the underlying currencies are also traded.

Firms use currency futures to hedge exchange-rate risk. The basic method is the same as hedging in security markets: firms make futures trades that produce profits if they suffer losses elsewhere.

For example, a firm that exports to Europe can hedge exchange-rate risk by selling euro futures. Let's say the firm agrees to sell euros at a rate of 0.8 per dollar in 6 months. If the exchange rate in 6 months turns out to be 0.9, the firm profits. Under the futures contract, it trades 0.8 euros for dollars that are now worth 0.9. The gains from this transaction offset losses from the strong dollar, which hurts the firm's European sales.

If the exchange rate in 6 months is 0.7, the firm loses on its futures trades. But these losses are offset by profits from higher European sales. The firm is protected against both rises and falls in the dollar.

Asset holders also hedge exchange-rate risk. A U.S. mutual fund that holds French securities is likely to sell euro futures. Once again, this transaction produces profits if the dollar strengthens, offsetting the fall in the dollar value of the securities.

Limits to Hedging Hedgers can't eliminate exchange-rate risk entirely. The use of currency futures is limited because contracts rarely have delivery dates more than 6 months in the future. Hedgers can protect themselves against short-lived movements in exchange rates, but not changes that last more than 6 months.

Suppose it is January and the exchange rate is 0.8 euros per dollar. The rate is expected to stay at this level. To guard against unexpected changes, an exporter has sold euro futures at 0.8, with delivery dates ranging from February to July. In February, something happens that raises the exchange rate to 0.9, and now this rate is expected to persist. The stronger dollar reduces the exporter's sales and profits. Until July, these losses are offset by gains on futures contracts, but not after that.

The exporter can keep selling 6-month euro futures. In February it can sell contracts for delivery in August, and in March it can sell contracts for September. However, with the exchange rate at 0.9 and expected to stay there, the futures rate also rises to 0.9. The exporter doesn't profit from futures unless the dollar rises even more. It can't undo the damage from the appreciation from 0.8 to 0.9.

Changes in exchange rates often last longer than 6 months. We saw in Figure 6.1, for example, that South Africa's exchange rate rose throughout the period from 2002 to 2005. South Africa's exporters couldn't have hedged against this appreciation.

Real versus Nominal Exchange Rates

We've outlined the major effects of exchange rates on people and firms. To make our analysis precise, we must discuss a nuance that we've ignored so far: the distinction between nominal and real exchange rates.

We defined the nominal exchange rate, e, in the introduction to this chapter. It is the price of a unit of currency in terms of a foreign currency. The **real exchange rate (ε)** is a more subtle concept. It measures the relative prices of domestic and foreign goods.

Real exchange rate (ε) Measure of the relative prices of domestic and foreign goods ($\varepsilon = eP/P^*$)

Defining the Real Exchange Rate To understand the real exchange rate, remember why exchange rates matter: they affect the costs of goods and services in different countries. If the dollar appreciates against the euro, a Paris hotel costs Americans less.

The costs of goods and services also depend on the prices that firms charge in their local currencies. If the Paris hotel cuts its room rate from 100 euros to 90, American tourists save 10 percent on their lodging costs. The effect is the same as if the dollar appreciated by 10 percent.

▶ The appendix to Chapter 1 reviews the concept of the aggregate price level.

The real exchange rate measures the relative prices of goods in different countries, accounting both for the nominal exchange rate *and* for local prices. The definition of the real exchange rate uses the concept of the aggregate price level. An economy's price level is an average of prices of all its goods and services. We denote a country's price level by P and the foreign price level by P^*.

For now, let's focus on the U.S. real exchange rate against the euro. When we calculate this variable, the nominal exchange rate e is measured in euros per dollar. P is the U.S. price level and P^* is the European price level. Each economy's price level is measured in its own currency: P is in dollars and P^* is in euros.

To find the real exchange rate ε, we must compare the prices of American and European goods. This requires that we measure these prices in the same currency. Let's measure them in euros.

Suppose first that someone wants to buy American goods with euros. She must trade the euros for dollars and then use the dollars to buy the goods. Each dollar costs e euros (the nominal exchange rate), and the goods cost P dollars (the U.S. price level). The cost of the goods in euros is e times P:

$$\text{cost of American goods in euros} = eP$$

If someone wants to buy European goods with euros, she doesn't need to trade currencies. The cost of the goods is simply P^*, the European price level:

$$\text{cost of European goods in euros} = P^*$$

The real exchange rate is the ratio of the two costs:

$$\begin{aligned}\varepsilon &= \frac{\text{cost of U.S. goods}}{\text{cost of European goods}} \\ &= \frac{eP}{P^*} \qquad (6.1)\end{aligned}$$

Suppose the nominal exchange rate (e) is 0.8. The U.S. price level (P) is 150 and the European price level (P^*) is 100. Then the real exchange rate (ε) is $(0.8)(150)/(100) = 1.2$. This means that U.S. goods are 1.2 times as costly as European goods.

Changes in Real Exchange Rates The formula for the real exchange rate shows that this variable rises if the nominal rate rises. Holding price levels constant, a nominal appreciation raises the cost of American goods relative to European goods. Suppose again that $P = 150$ and $P^* = 100$. If $e = 0.8$, the real exchange rate is 1.2. If e rises to 0.9, the real exchange rate rises to $(0.9)(150)/(100) = 1.35$.

The real exchange rate also changes if P or P^* changes. For example, a rise in P^*, the European price level, reduces the real exchange rate. The dollar becomes weaker in real terms. Say that P^* rises from 100 to 110. In other words, Europe experiences 10 percent inflation. Assume that e stays constant at 0.8 and P stays at 150. In this case, the U.S. real exchange rate falls from 1.2 to $(0.8)(150)/(110) = 1.09$.

To understand why the dollar weakens, think of an American who buys euros. As long as e is constant, he gets the same number of euros for each dollar. But a higher European price level means the euros have less purchasing power. A dollar is worth less in terms of the foreign goods it can buy.

Which Exchange Rate Matters? Earlier we discussed how an appreciation affects American consumers and firms. Now we can be more precise: these effects follow from a rise in the *real* exchange rate. The real rate determines the costs of imports. It also determines the costs of American goods in Europe and, hence, the competitiveness of U.S. exports.

In our earlier examples, we asked what happens if the nominal exchange rate rises from 0.8 to 0.9. These examples implicitly assume that price levels are constant, which means a higher nominal rate raises the real rate as well. This assumption is fairly realistic for the United States and Europe today, because the price levels in these two economies are stable. We return to this issue in Section 6.5.

The Trade-Weighted Real Exchange Rate

The United States has many real exchange rates. In addition to the dollar–euro rate, there are rates between the dollar and the yen, the dollar and the British pound, and so on. These rates can move in different directions. Sometimes the dollar appreciates against one currency while depreciating against another.

Trade-weighted real exchange rate Weighted average of a country's real exchange rates, with weights proportional to levels of trade

Economists often summarize a country's exchange rates with a **trade-weighted real exchange rate.** This variable is a weighted average of real

FIGURE 6.3 U.S. Real Exchange Rates, 1980–2007

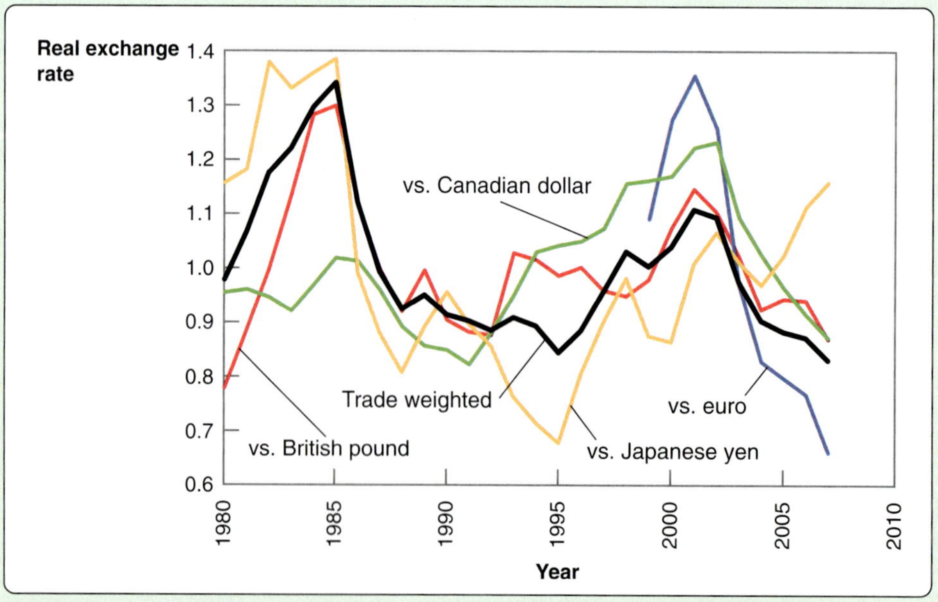

This graph shows U.S. real exchange rates against several currencies. It also shows the trade-weighted real exchange rate, which measures the overall strength of the U.S. dollar. (The scale of each series is adjusted so the average value from 1980 through 2007 is 1.0).

Sources: OECD; Bank for International Settlements

exchange rates with all foreign currencies. The weight on each country's currency is proportional to the level of trade with that country.

In the trade-weighted real exchange rate for the United States, the dollar–euro rate has the largest weight. In 2007, this weight was 0.18, because 18 percent of U.S. trade was with euro countries. The weight means that a 1 percent rise in the dollar–euro exchange rate raises the trade-weighted rate by 0.18 percent. Other weights include 0.09 for the dollar–yen rate and 0.05 for the rate between the dollar and the British pound. The trade-weighted exchange rate measures the overall strength of the dollar.

Figure 6.3 shows U.S. real exchange rates from 1980 through 2007. It includes the U.S. rates against several currencies and the trade-weighted rate (the thick black line). The figure shows that real exchange rates fluctuate considerably over time.

CASE STUDY

Exchange Rates and Steel

U.S. companies are hurt by a strong dollar if they export their products or compete with imports. Steel companies do both. They compete with foreign firms both at home and abroad, so exchange rates have large effects on their sales.

Figure 6.4 shows the total output of the U.S. steel industry from 1980 through 2004. The figure also shows the U.S. trade-weighted real exchange

FIGURE 6.4 The Exchange Rate and Steel, 1980–2004

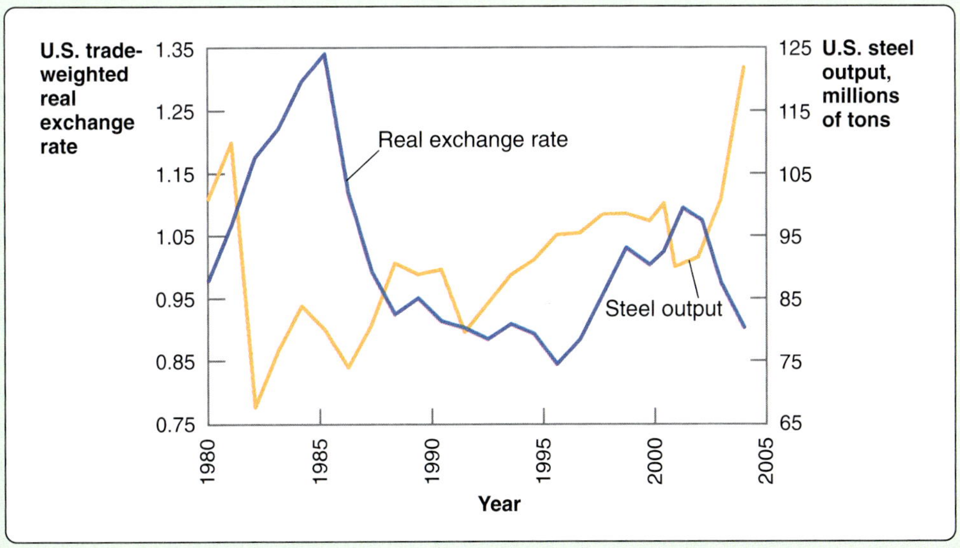

A stronger dollar reduces U.S. steel output and a weaker dollar increases steel output.

Sources: Bank for International Settlements; International Iron and Steel Institute

▶What about the period since 2004? In recent years, U.S. steel manufacturers have faced rapidly growing competition from one country, China. As a result, the key exchange rate for the industry has been the rate between the dollar and the Chinese yuan, which has behaved differently from the trade-weighted rate that we discuss here. The dollar has been strong against the yuan, hurting the steel industry, as we discuss in Chapter 17.

rate from Figure 6.3. Fluctuations in the exchange rate help explain the ups and downs of the steel industry.

In the 1980s, the U.S. steel industry faced a crisis. Its annual output fell from 110 million tons in 1981 to an average of 77 million over 1982–1986. Steel companies laid workers off, and some economists suggested the industry was dying.

The initial fall in steel output reflected the U.S. recession of 1981–1982. However, output stayed low as the rest of the economy recovered in the mid-1980s. Exchange rates were the main reason. The trade-weighted real exchange rate rose by 37 percent from 1980 to 1985, hurting the competitiveness of U.S. steel.

Then the situation improved. Steel output started rising in 1987, and this trend continued for a decade (except for an interruption during the recession of 1990–1991). A 1996 book on the industry was called *The Renaissance of American Steel.* This turnaround resulted partly from innovations in manufacturing. U.S. steel companies moved from large factories to "mini-mills" where costs were lower. However, exchange rates also helped revive the industry. The dollar fell over the late 1980s and then stabilized at a moderate level.

The "renaissance" was followed by another troubled period. Steel output leveled off in the late 1990s despite a booming economy, and output fell sharply from 2000 to 2002. Once again, layoffs were widespread, and more than 30 steel companies went bankrupt.

As you can see from Figure 6.4, the main culprit was the exchange rate. The trade-weighted rate rose by 31 percent from 1995 to 2001. And once again, the crisis passed when the appreciation was reversed. The dollar started falling in 2003 and steel output rose rapidly.

In tough times, the steel industry often seeks help from the government. To protect their sales, companies advocate restrictions on imports of foreign steel. Such policies are controversial. Typically, they are supported by congressional members from steel-producing areas but opposed by economists, who believe in free trade.

During the 1980s steel crisis, the Reagan administration negotiated "voluntary restraint agreements" with European countries and Japan. Under pressure, these countries agreed to reduce their sales of steel in the United States. The agreements were allowed to lapse in the early 1990s as U.S. steel companies recovered.

In the late 1990s, the Clinton administration again tried to reduce steel imports by negotiating with foreign governments. In March 2002, at the height of the most recent crisis, the Bush administration imposed steel tariffs. *Tariffs* are taxes on imports; in this case, foreign steel was taxed at rates up to 30 percent.

The steel tariffs angered foreign governments. U.S. companies that purchase steel, such as auto firms, also criticized them. The recovery of the domestic steel industry after 2002 reduced support for the tariffs, and they were rescinded in December 2003.

6.3 THE LONG-RUN BEHAVIOR OF EXCHANGE RATES

So far we've focused on how exchange rates affect people and firms. The rest of the chapter discusses what determines exchange rates and why they change over time.

When economists ask, "what determines variable X?" they often give two sets of answers—one for the long run and one for the short run. Exchange rates behave differently over these two time horizons, so we develop separate short-run and long-run theories of exchange rates. We start with the long run. Economists don't define the long run as a precise time span. But roughly speaking, you can think of long-run exchange-rate movements as trends over a decade or more, not year-to-year fluctuations.

Purchasing Power Parity

The leading theory of long-run exchange rates is called **purchasing power parity (PPP).** This theory's key idea is that a currency can purchase the same quantities of goods and services in different countries. Let's discuss this idea and its implications for exchange rates.

Purchasing power parity (PPP) Theory of exchange rates based on the idea that a currency purchases the same quantities of goods and services in different countries; implies that real exchange rates are constant over time

Law of one price Theory that an identical good or service has the same price in all locations

The Law of One Price PPP starts with a basic idea from microeconomics: the **law of one price.** This law says that an identical good or service should sell for the same price everywhere. If a certain kind of hammer costs $10 at a hardware store in Boston, it should also cost $10 at a store in Kansas City or San Diego.

To see the rationale for this idea, suppose it's not true. A hammer costs $10 in Boston but $11 in San Diego. This difference creates opportunities for people to make money. Someone can buy hammers for $10 in Boston, ship them to San Diego, sell them for $11, and earn profits. This strategy is called *arbitrage*.

Arbitrage eliminates price differences. It raises the demand for hammers in Boston, pushing up the price in that city. It raises supply in San Diego, pushing down the price there. This process continues until the two prices reach the same level, perhaps $10.50.

You can probably see that the law of one price is not 100 percent realistic. But let's assume for the moment that the law holds and see where it leads us.

The Law Across Borders PPP applies the law of one price across national borders. The price of a hammer should be the same not only in Boston and San Diego but also in Paris. Otherwise, someone could make money shipping hammers across the Atlantic. Suppose again that a hammer costs $10 in Boston. If the nominal exchange rate is 0.8 euros per dollar, then $10 is worth 8 euros. The law of one price says a hammer must cost 8 euros in Paris.

In this theory, what's true for hammers is true for all goods and services. Everything costs the same in the United States and Europe. Remember that we measure the overall cost of goods and services with the aggregate price level. The cost in Europe, measured in euros, is P^*. The cost in the United States is P in dollars and eP in Euros, where e is the nominal exchange rate. So

$$eP = P^*$$

This equation has strong implications for exchange rates. If we divide both sides by P^*, we get

$$\frac{eP}{P^*} = 1$$

Here, the left side is the real exchange rate. PPP says this variable must always equal 1. It is constant. The law of one price rules out changes in the relative prices of U.S. and European goods.

Rearranging again, we get an expression for the nominal exchange rate:

$$e = \frac{P^*}{P} \quad \textbf{(6.2)}$$

Under PPP, the nominal exchange rate equals the ratio of price levels in Europe and the United States.

How Reasonable is PPP?

PPP is not exactly true. In reality, goods can sell for different prices in different countries. And the real exchange rate changes over time, as we saw in Figure 6.3.

PPP can fail because arbitrage isn't perfect. It is costly to ship hammers around the world. If hammer prices vary by modest amounts, the earnings from arbitrage may be less than the shipping costs. In this case, differences in hammer prices can persist.

The limits to arbitrage are clear if we look beyond hammers. Some things are very hard to transport, especially services. If a haircut costs more in Paris than in Boston, the law of one price says someone will hire Boston barbers and fly them to Paris. This doesn't really happen.

On the other hand, PPP contains a large grain of truth. The assumption of arbitrage captures the idea that market forces push prices toward each other. Differences in prices produce flows of goods that cause the differences to diminish.

Suppose U.S. goods are more expensive than European goods. In other words, the U.S. real exchange rate is high. Imports are cheap for Americans, so goods flow from Europe to the U.S. The demand for U.S. products is low, putting pressure on U.S. firms to reduce their prices. Across the ocean, the strong dollar means booming sales for European firms. In this environment, the firms are likely to raise prices. Over time, falling American prices and rising European prices reduce the real exchange rate, pushing it toward the PPP level.

Evidence for PPP

Now that we've discussed the logic behind PPP, let's turn to evidence that supports it. We'll see that long-run movements in exchange rates fit well with the theory.

First we need a little math. PPP says the nominal exchange rate equals a ratio of price levels: $e = P^*/P$. To study exchange-rate movements over time, we take percentage changes:

$$\%\text{ change in } e = \%\text{ change in } \frac{P^*}{P}$$

The right side of this equation can be rewritten using a common approximation: the percentage change in a ratio equals the change in the numerator minus the change in the denominator. This implies

$$\%\text{ change in } e = (\%\text{ change in } P^*) - (\%\text{ change in } P)$$

▶Note to math majors: We are using a first-order Taylor approximation.

To interpret this equation, recall that the percentage change in a country's price level defines its inflation rate. The percentage change in the foreign price level, P^*, is the foreign inflation rate. So we can write

$$\%\text{ change in } e = \pi^* - \pi \tag{6.3}$$

where π stands for the inflation rate. The percentage change in a country's exchange rate is the difference between foreign inflation and domestic inflation. For example, if $\pi^* = 5\%$ and $\pi = 3\%$, the exchange rate rises by $5 - 3 = 2\%$.

Equation (6.3) fits exchange-rate movements over long periods. **Figure 6.5** shows changes in the U.S. exchange rate against 29 foreign currencies over

FIGURE 6.5 Inflation and Nominal Exchange Rates

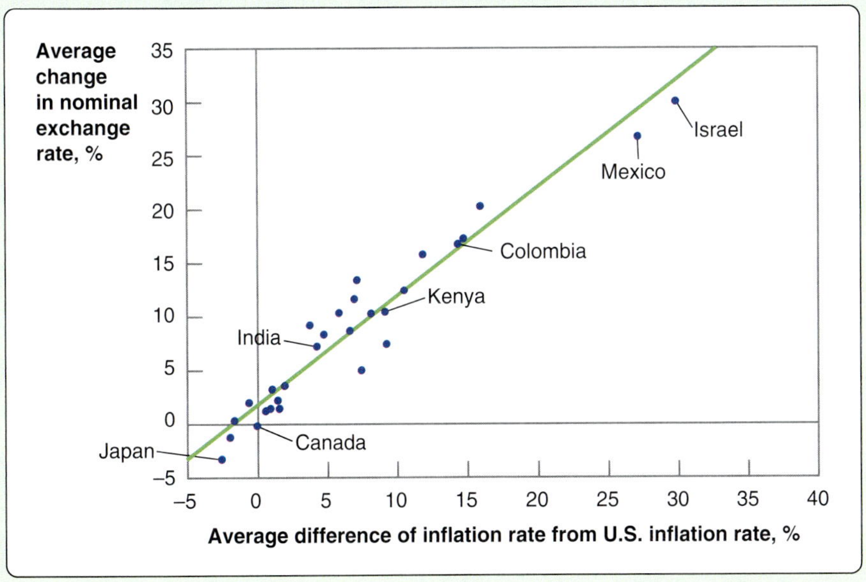

In this scatterplot, each point represents a country during the period 1980–2006. The horizontal axis is the average difference between the country's annual inflation rate and the U.S. inflation rate, and the vertical axis is the average percentage change in the U.S. exchange rate against the country's currency. As predicted by PPP, inflation differences explain changes in nominal exchange rates.

Source: International Monetary Fund

the period 1980–2006. For each currency, the figure plots the average annual change in the nominal exchange rate, *e*, against the difference between foreign and U.S. inflation.

For example, the point in the lower left is the Japanese yen. Over 1980–2006, the dollar's value in yen changed by −3.1 percent per year. The average difference between the Japanese and U.S. inflation rates was −2.6 percent. (Inflation averaged 1.3 percent in Japan and 3.9 percent in the United States.)

Figure 6.5 confirms a close relationship between inflation and changes in nominal exchange rates. Japanese inflation was lower than U.S. inflation, so the dollar depreciated against the yen. The difference between Canadian and U.S. inflation was close to zero, implying little change in the U.S.–Canada exchange rate. Mexico and Israel had high inflation, so the dollar appreciated strongly against the Mexican peso and the shekel.

6.4 REAL EXCHANGE RATES IN THE SHORT RUN

While PPP explains long-run changes in exchange rates, it doesn't fit the short-run picture well. Contrary to PPP, real exchange rates fluctuate considerably from year to year. We now develop a theory of these short-term fluctuations. For the moment, let's focus on the overall level of the U.S. real exchange rate, as measured by the trade-weighted rate.

This exchange rate is determined in the currency markets we discussed in Section 6.1. It is the price of a dollar in these markets. Economists generally believe that prices are determined by supply and demand, and the exchange rate is no exception. So we will examine what determines the supply and demand for dollars.

Net Exports and Capital Flows

The supply of dollars comes from Americans who trade dollars for foreign currencies. Recall that Americans sell dollars for two reasons: to buy foreign goods and services and to buy foreign assets. Purchases of foreign goods and services are imports, and purchases of assets are capital outflows. The supply of dollars is the total amount that must be sold for these purposes:

$$\text{supply of dollars} = \text{imports} + \text{capital outflows}$$

The demand for dollars comes from foreigners. They buy dollars to purchase American goods and services and to purchase American assets. Foreign purchases of goods and services are exports for the United States, and the purchases of assets are capital inflows. Therefore,

$$\text{demand for dollars} = \text{exports} + \text{capital inflows}$$

We assume the exchange rate adjusts to equalize supply and demand:

$$\text{supply of dollars} = \text{demand for dollars}$$

Substituting in the previous equations, we get

$$\text{imports} + \text{capital outflows} = \text{exports} + \text{capital inflows}$$

To understand the last equation, it helps to rearrange the terms. We can rewrite the equation as

$$\text{exports} - \text{imports} = \text{capital outflows} - \text{capital inflows}$$

The left side of this equation, exports minus imports, is called **net exports (*NX*).** The right side, capital outflows minus capital inflows, is **net capital outflows (*NCO*).** Using these terms, we can write the equation more compactly:

Net exports (*NX*) Exports minus imports

Net capital outflows (*NCO*) Capital outflows minus capital inflows

$$NX = NCO \tag{6.4}$$

Net exports can be either positive or negative. They are positive if exports exceed imports, creating a *trade surplus,* and negative if imports exceed exports, creating a *trade deficit*. Similarly, net capital outflows can be either positive or negative. Either way, net exports and net capital outflows must be equal to balance the supply and demand for dollars.

You might recall that Section 4.1 discussed net capital *inflows*. This variable is capital inflows minus capital outflows. The term we use here, net capital *outflows,* is the reverse. In the last equation, we could replace net capital outflows with −(net capital inflows), and the equation would say the same thing.

Effects of the Real Exchange Rate

Now the real exchange rate enters the story. Remember that a rise in this variable means that U.S. goods become more expensive compared with foreign goods. This change leads foreigners to buy fewer U.S. goods, so U.S. exports fall. Americans also switch from U.S. to foreign goods, so imports rise. Both lower exports and higher imports reduce net exports:

$$\begin{aligned} \uparrow \varepsilon &\rightarrow \downarrow \text{exports}, \uparrow \text{imports} \\ &\rightarrow \downarrow \text{net exports} \end{aligned}$$

We assume that the exchange rate does *not* affect net capital outflows. This variable is determined by factors such as interest rates and confidence in the economy.

The Equilibrium Exchange Rate

Figure 6.6 summarizes our discussion. This graph shows the relationships among net exports, net capital outflows, and the real exchange rate. Net exports and net capital outflows are measured in dollars. The downward-sloping curve shows the behavior of net exports. A higher real exchange rate reduces net exports. The vertical line captures the behavior of net capital outflows, which do not change as the real exchange rate changes.

We have seen that net exports must equal net capital outflows. This happens only if the real exchange rate is at the level marked ε^* in the graph, where the two curves intersect. This level is the equilibrium real exchange

FIGURE 6.6 The Real Exchange Rate in the Short Run

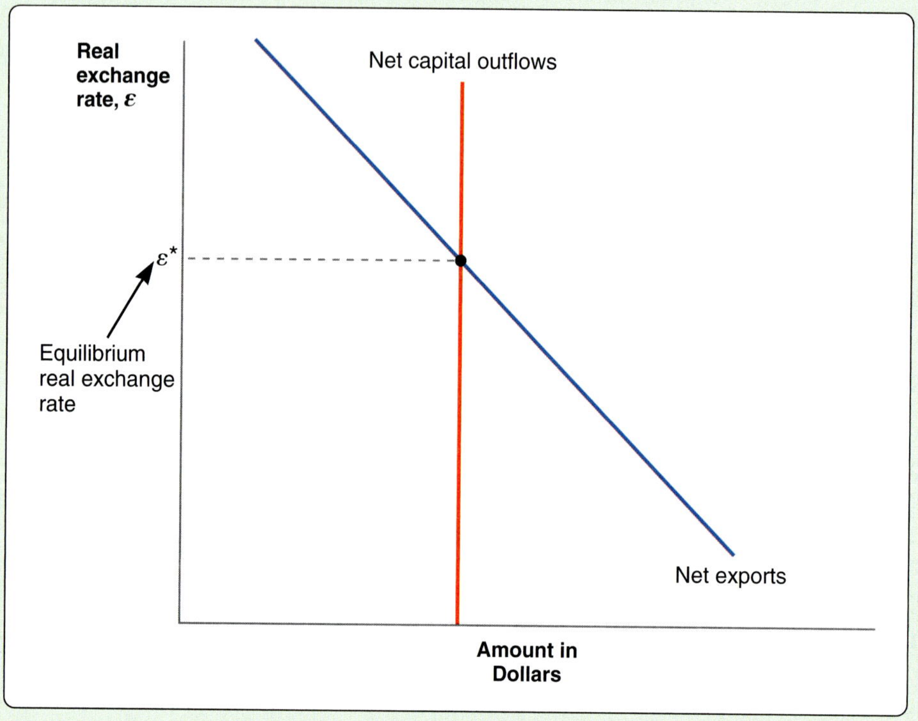

A rise in the real exchange rate reduces net exports. The equilibrium real exchange rate, ε^*, is the rate at which net exports equal net capital outflows.

rate. Supply and demand in currency markets push the exchange rate to equilibrium.

6.5 FLUCTUATIONS IN EXCHANGE RATES

We can use Figure 6.6 to explain short-run fluctuations in the real exchange rate. These movements are caused by shifts in the two curves in the figure, net exports and net capital outflows. The main reasons for such shifts are summarized in **Table 6.2.**

TABLE 6.2 Why Do Real Exchange Rates Fluctuate?

Shifts in net capital outflows because of . . .
Changes in real interest rates (causes include changes in monetary policy or in budget deficits)
Changes in confidence
Changes in expected future exchange rates
Shifts in net exports because of . . .
Foreign recessions
Changes in commodity prices

Shifts in Net Capital Outflows

Many changes in exchange rates are caused by shifts in net capital outflows. **Figure 6.7A** shows what happens when *NCO* rises. The vertical curve in our graph shifts to the right, reducing the equilibrium exchange rate. **Figure 6.7B** shows the opposite case of a fall in *NCO*, which raises the exchange rate.

FIGURE 6.7 Shifts in Net Capital Outflows

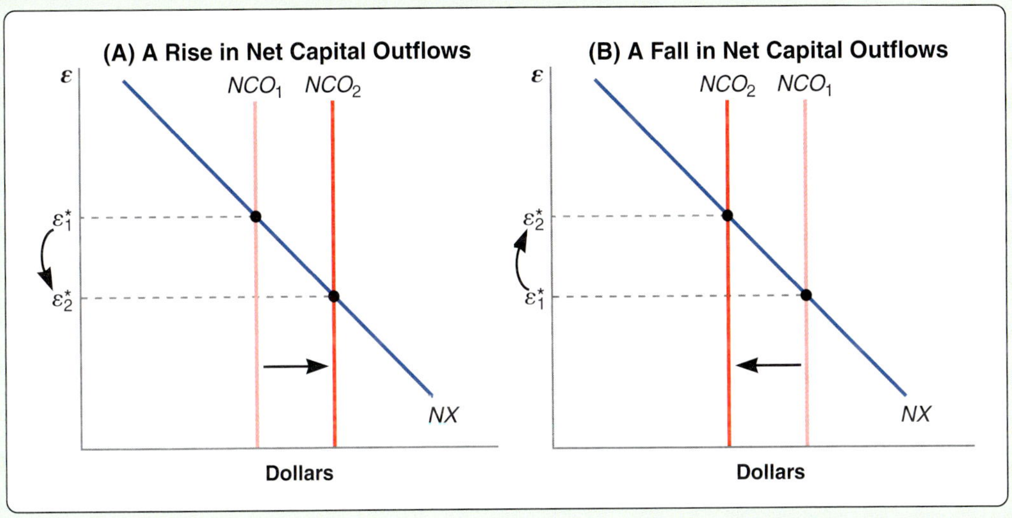

(A) Net capital outflows rise, shifting the *NCO* curve to the right. The equilibrium real exchange rate falls from ε_1^* to ε_2^*.
(B) Net capital outflows fall, shifting the *NCO* curve to the left. The equilibrium real exchange rate rises from ε_1^* to ε_2^*.

To understand these effects, remember that a rise in capital outflows (Figure 6.7A) means Americans buy more foreign assets. To do so, they must first trade dollars for foreign currency. The supply of dollars rises, pushing down the price of the dollar.

Chapter 4 discussed several reasons that capital flows can fluctuate, including changes in interest rates and changes in confidence. Let's review these factors and examine their effects on exchange rates.

Changes in Interest Rates A key factor is the real interest rate, *r*. If *r* rises in the United States, U.S. assets become more attractive. Capital outflows fall as Americans keep more of their wealth at home, and capital inflows rise. Both effects reduce net capital outflows. In our graph, the vertical line shifts to the left, raising the real exchange rate (Figure 6.7B).

This analysis tells us that *factors that influence the real interest rate also affect the real exchange rate.* For example, a tightening of monetary policy raises the real interest rate in the short run. This action raises the real exchange rate as well.

The real interest rate is also influenced by government budget deficits. For example, deficits during the Reagan administration contributed to high real interest rates in the mid-1980s, which in turn caused an appreciation of the dollar. We saw the effects of this appreciation in the case study on the U.S. steel industry.

Changes in Confidence Another key factor is confidence in the economy. A drop in confidence can provoke capital flight—a shift toward foreign assets. This means a rise in net capital outflows. In Figure 6.7A, the vertical line shifts to the right, reducing the real exchange rate.

Section 4.2 discussed the capital flight from East Asian countries in 1997–1998. Applied to this episode, our theory predicts decreases in East Asian exchange rates—depreciations against the dollar and other currencies outside the region. This prediction is correct. In Korea, for example, the value of the won fell from 0.11 dollars in October 1997 to 0.06 the following January.

Changes in confidence also help explain the behavior of South Africa's rand (see Figure 6.1). The sharp depreciation of the rand over 2000–2002 resulted from worries about South Africa's political and economic future. These involved a variety of problems, including an investigation of government corruption, the failure to privatize state-owned industries, and the AIDS epidemic.

Confidence in South Africa was also damaged by events in other countries. In neighboring Zimbabwe, disastrous government policies produced an economic collapse in the early 2000s. People worried that this crisis would somehow spill over into South Africa. In addition, Argentina's debt default in 2001 shook confidence about developing countries around the world.

▶ Chapter 18 discusses the Argentine financial crisis of 2001.

Confidence in South Africa improved after 2002. Some worries faded, such as the fears created by Argentina's default. Confidence also rose as South Africa reduced inflation and government budget deficits. Rising confidence helps explain the appreciation of the rand over 2002–2005. The rand was also strengthened by a rise in South African interest rates relative to U.S. and European rates.

Changes in Expected Exchange Rates A final factor is expectations about future exchange rates. Suppose the real exchange rate is low, but people learn it is likely to rise in the future. For example, the central bank indicates it will tighten monetary policy, pushing up the exchange rate. The expectation of this event shifts capital flows, changing the exchange rate immediately. The exchange rate reacts before the central bank actually does anything.

To see why, recall that an appreciation hurts the owners of foreign assets, because it reduces the value of these assets in domestic currency. When people expect the exchange rate to rise in the future, they expect losses on foreign assets. This discourages them from buying the assets, so net capital outflows fall. As usual, a decrease in net capital outflows raises the real exchange rate.

This effect helps explain the volatility of exchange rates—why they jump up and down so frequently. Exchange rates can jump without changes in the variables that affect them directly, such as interest rates. It is enough for news to arrive that changes expectations about the future.

CASE STUDY

The Euro versus the Dollar

The euro was created on January 1, 1999, and as of 2008 it was the currency for 15 European countries. Since the euro was launched, its value has been a subject of intense interest to European economists, politicians, and ordinary citizens. This interest partly reflects the importance of a "strong" euro to European pride.

Figure 6.8 shows the European real exchange rate against the U.S. dollar over the euro's first 9 years. The exchange rate is defined from the point of view of Europe, so an increase means the euro is more valuable and the dollar less valuable. The figure shows that the euro fell from 1999 to 2001 and then rose from 2001 through 2007.

At least two factors help explain the initial fall in the euro. One was the attitude of the European Central Bank (ECB). When the euro was created, Wim Duisenberg, the ECB president, stated that he was mainly concerned with controlling inflation and did not have any "exchange rate aim." Commentators interpreted this statement to mean the ECB might allow the exchange rate to fall. As we have discussed, expectations of a lower exchange rate cause higher capital outflows, and hence an immediate fall in the exchange rate.

▶Chapters 16 and 17 discuss the workings of the European Central Bank.

Another factor was growing confidence in the U.S. economy. The late 1990s were the "new economy" period in which U.S. productivity grew rapidly and the stock market soared. U.S. assets became more attractive, raising net capital outflows from Europe. This shift exacerbated the fall in the euro.

The euro's turnaround in 2001 is also partly explained by events in the United States. In that year new-economy euphoria ebbed as the stock market fell and the U.S. entered a recession. Net capital outflows from Europe decreased and the euro rose.

FIGURE 6.8 The Euro versus the Dollar

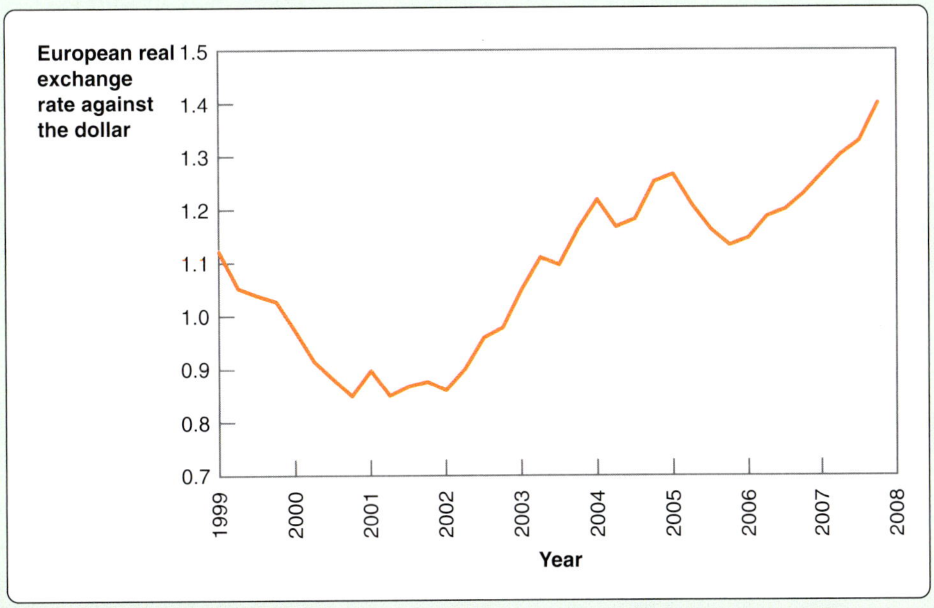

The euro depreciated against the U.S. dollar from 1999 to 2001 and then appreciated from 2001 through 2007. These exchange-rate movements reflect shifts in capital flows.

Sources: Federal Reserve Bank of St. Louis; OECD

In addition, the Federal Reserve responded to the 2001 recession by easing monetary policy. It reduced real interest rates and kept them low, while interest rates in Europe stayed relatively high. This difference made European assets more attractive. It was another reason for lower net capital outflows and a stronger euro.

In 2005, some of the conditions underlying the euro's appreciation were reversed. U.S. economic growth was strong, bolstering confidence in the U.S. economy, and the Fed raised interest rates. These developments increased net capital outflows from Europe, weakening the euro.

But this episode was short-lived. The euro started rising again in early 2006, and it was still rising at the start of 2008. Several factors contributed to this trend:

- In the United States, large trade deficits and government budget deficits reduced confidence in the economy.
- In 2007, confidence in the U.S. took a sharp hit from the subprime mortgage crisis.
- The Fed reduced U.S. interest rates in response to the subprime crisis.
- The ECB, concerned about inflation, raised European interest rates over 2006 and the first half of 2007.

▶ Upcoming chapters detail the major events in the U.S. economy over 2006–2008.

All these developments made European assets more attractive compared with American assets. Europe's net capital outflows fell and the euro rose.

Online Case Study: An Update on Exchange Rates

Shifts in Net Exports

Another source of exchange-rate fluctuations is shifts in net exports. For example, suppose U.S. goods become more fashionable in Europe. Everyone in France and Germany wants the latest American clothes and a new iPod. For a given exchange rate, U.S. net exports are higher. **Figure 6.9A** shows what happens in the U.S. economy. The *NX* curve shifts to the right, raising the real exchange rate.

Once again, this result makes sense if we think about currency markets. To buy more U.S. goods, foreigners need more dollars. Higher demand for the dollar pushes up its price.

Figure 6.9B shows the opposite case. Here, European goods become more popular, reducing U.S. net exports. The *NX* curve shifts to the left, reducing the real exchange rate.

Shifts in preferences for countries' goods are one reason net exports might shift. Let's discuss two other reasons that are often important: foreign recessions and changes in commodity prices.

Foreign Recessions Net exports depend on the strength of foreign economies. Suppose that Europe and Japan enter recessions. Incomes fall in those economies, so people reduce their spending, including spending on U.S. goods. From the U.S. point of view, net exports fall at any exchange rate. As in Figure 6.9B, the *NX* curve shifts to the left, reducing the real exchange rate.

FIGURE 6.9 Shifts in Net Exports

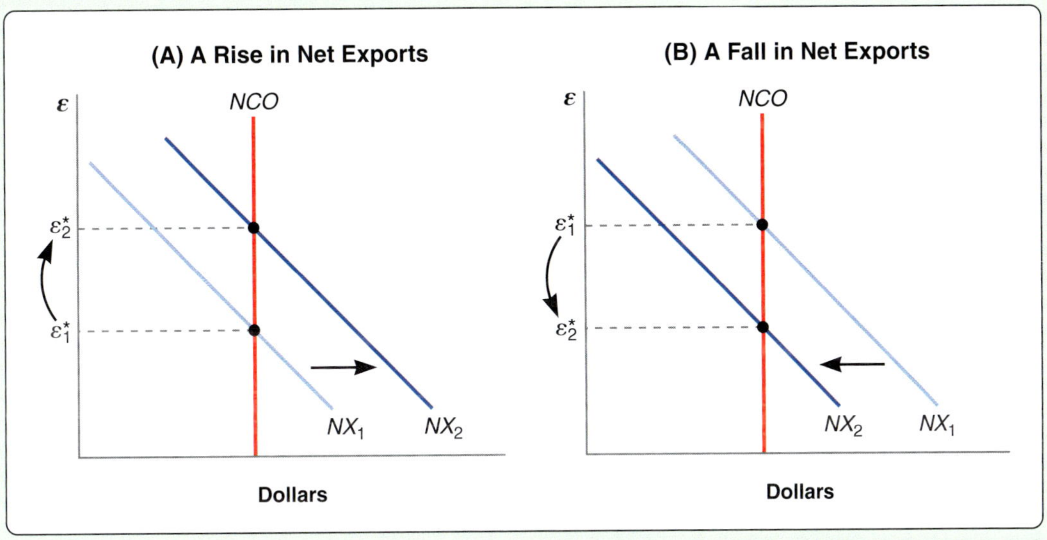

(A) Net exports rise for each real exchange rate, shifting the *NX* curve to the right. The equilibrium real exchange rate rises from ε_1^* to ε_2^*.
(B) Net exports fall for each real exchange rate, shifting the *NX* curve to the left. The equilibrium real exchange rate falls from ε_1^* to ε_2^*.

The effect of a foreign recession is largest when the level of trade with the foreign country is high. Consider Canada. Roughly 30 percent of Canada's GDP is exported to the United States. When the U.S. enters a recession, Canadian exports are hit hard, pushing down the exchange rate. For example, during the U.S. slowdown of the early 2000s, the Canadian dollar fell from 0.69 U.S. dollars in 2000 to 0.63 in 2002. In contrast, the United States exports less than 3 percent of its GDP to Canada. So fluctuations in Canada's economy do not greatly affect the United States.

Commodity Prices The main exports from some countries are commodities such as oil or agricultural products. For these countries, changes in the real exchange rate arise largely from fluctuations in commodity prices.

Norway, for example, exports oil from its North Sea wells. These exports are 15–20 percent of Norwegian GDP. The price of oil in U.S. dollars is determined by world supply and demand. If oil prices rise, Norway's net exports rise for a given exchange rate. Norway may ship the same quantity of oil, but it counts as higher exports because the oil is more valuable. The net exports curve shifts to the right, raising the value of the Norwegian kroner.

Similarly, copper is a large part of Chile's exports. So fluctuations in the world price of copper affect the value of Chile's peso. Australia and New Zealand have large agricultural exports, so fluctuations in agricultural prices affect the Australian dollar and the New Zealand dollar.

Nominal Rates Again

Our short-run theory explains fluctuations in real exchange rates. Remember that the exchange rates reported in the news are nominal rates. What determines the short-run behavior of these rates?

To answer this question, we start with the definition of the real exchange rate: $\varepsilon = (eP)/P^*$. Rearranging this equation yields an expression for the nominal rate:

$$e = \varepsilon\left(\frac{P^*}{P}\right) \tag{6.5}$$

Our long-run theory, PPP, assumes that ε is constant. So changes in the nominal exchange rate are determined by changes in P and P^*.

We've seen, however, that the real rate fluctuates in the short run. And often P and P^* do *not* change much in the short run. These price levels are stable if domestic and foreign inflation rates are low. In this case, fluctuations in real exchange rates produce parallel fluctuations in nominal rates.

For example, **Figure 6.10A** compares the real and nominal exchange rates between the euro and the dollar. From 1999 through 2007, Europe and the United States had similar, low inflation rates. The ratio of price levels, P^*/P, did not change much. Thus the nominal exchange rate closely tracked the real rate.

Figure 6.10B compares the South African rand's real and nominal exchange rates against the dollar. The two rates diverge a bit more in this case than they do for Europe. The real rate has risen compared to the nominal rate because South Africa's inflation rate has exceeded the U.S. inflation rate. Nonetheless, the two exchange rates have followed the same broad pattern.

6.6 CURRENCY SPECULATION

Now that we've discussed how exchange rates are determined, let's turn to another aspect of currency markets: speculation. In Section 5.6, we saw how speculators place bets on movements in stock and bond prices. Speculators also bet on exchange rates. They forecast changes in rates, buy currencies they think will appreciate, and then resell the currencies. They profit if their forecasts are correct.

Currency speculators include commercial banks, investment banks, hedge funds, and individuals. Speculators trade both currencies and currency futures. We saw in Section 6.2 that futures are useful for hedging exchange-rate risk. They are also useful for speculation, because little money is needed up front to place bets.

Of course it's not easy to predict exchange rates. The efficient-markets hypothesis applies to currencies as well as to stocks and bonds. The EMH says there can't be good reasons to expect profits from a currency purchase. If there were, traders would already have bought the currency, pushing up the price. The market quickly eliminates profit opportunities, just as the stock market eliminates undervaluation of companies (review Section 5.5).

FIGURE 6.10 Real and Nominal Exchange Rates Against the Dollar, 1999–2007

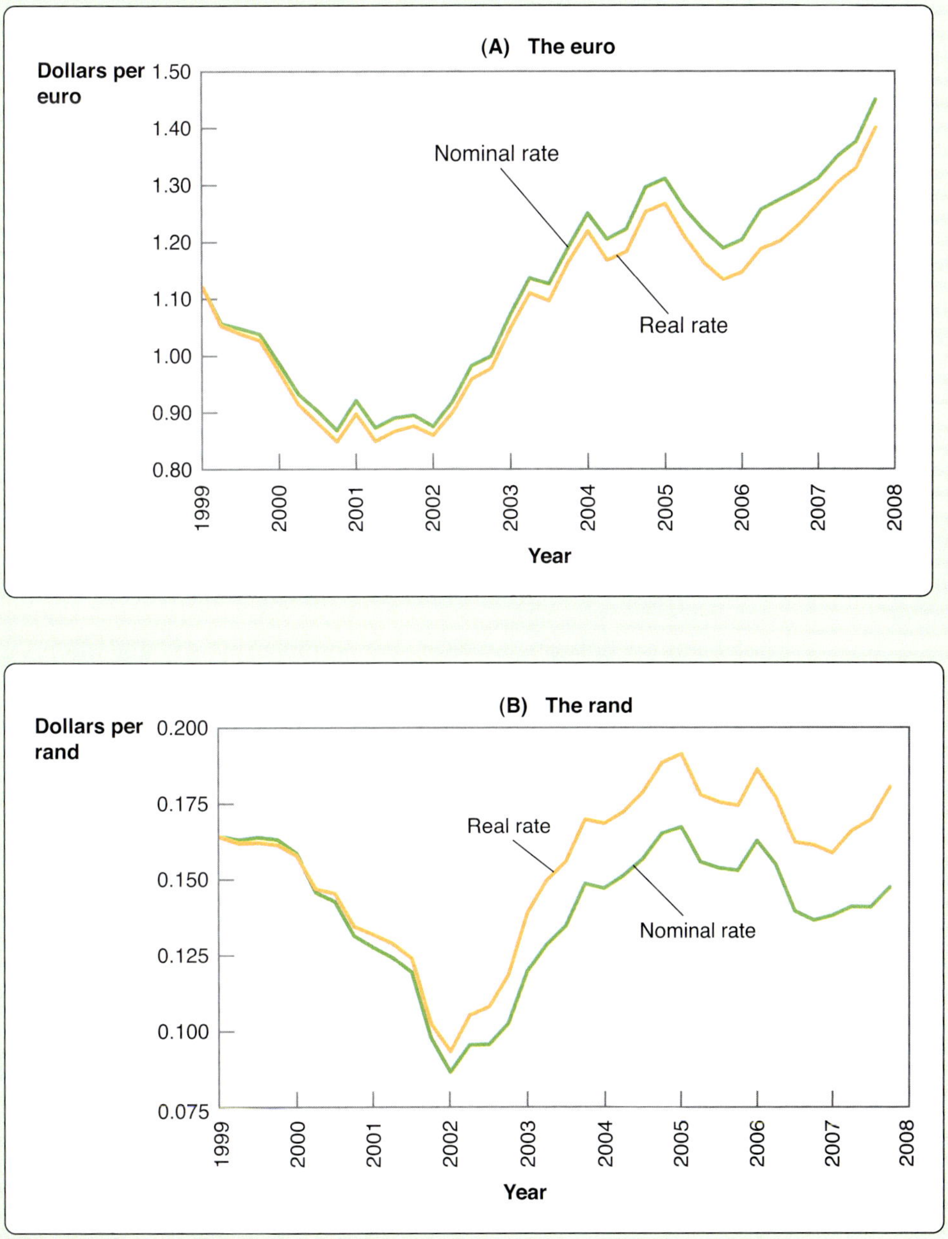

(A) Real and nominal exchange rates between the euro and the dollar have followed similar paths, because the European and U.S. price levels have been fairly stable. (B) Real and nominal exchange rates have diverged a bit more for South Africa. South Africa's inflation rate has exceeded the U.S. inflation rate, pushing South Africa's real exchange rate above its nominal rate.

Sources: Federal Reserve Bank of St. Louis; OECD; Statistics South Africa

Speculators do not fully believe the EMH. They think they can forecast exchange rates well enough to earn profits. Banks and hedge funds stake large amounts of money on this belief. Observers estimate that speculation accounts for more than half of all currency trades.

Much speculation occurs over short time periods. Speculators buy a currency and then resell it in a few days, or even within the same day. They use this approach because they think they can forecast daily exchange-rate movements better than longer-term changes. In addition, short-term speculation can produce profits quickly.

Forecasting Methods

How do speculators forecast exchange rates? Typically they use a blend of several methods. Widely used approaches include economic analysis, monitoring of order flows, and technical analysis.[1]

Economic Analysis Major speculators such as banks employ economists who forecast exchange rates using theories like the ones we've studied in this chapter. The economists try to predict the variables in these theories, such as interest rates and net exports, and to derive the implications for exchange rates.

For many speculators, however, economic analysis is not the primary forecasting tool. The reason is speculators' focus on very short time periods. Economic theories, even theories of the "short run," try to explain exchange-rate movements over months or years. Usually the theories don't explain the wiggles in rates that occur from day to day or hour to hour.

Order flow In a dealer market, the difference between total buy orders and sell orders over some period

Order Flow Many currency speculators examine **order flows.** Order flow is a concept that arises in dealer markets, which include currency markets as well as some stock and bond markets. Dealers hold inventories of currencies and accept both "buy" and "sell" orders from other traders. A currency's order flow is the difference between total buy orders and sell orders over some period.

A positive order flow means that buy orders exceed sell orders. Traders are purchasing more of a currency from dealers than they are selling to dealers, so dealers' inventories of the currency are falling. A negative order flow means sales to dealers exceed purchases, so inventories are rising.

When some circumstance causes exchange rates to change, order flows are part of the process. For example, suppose confidence in South Africa's economy increases. The demand for South African assets rises, so people want more rand. Dealers start receiving more buy orders for rand than sell orders; that is, order flow is positive. Dealers see their inventories of rand fall, and they respond by raising the price of rand. This means the rand appreciates.

[1] For more on these methods, see Callum Henderson, *Currency Strategy: A Practitioner's Guide to Currency Trading, Hedging and Forecasting*, Wiley, 2002. Henderson is a former analyst for Citigroup.

Because of this chain of effects, speculators can use order flow to predict exchange-rate movements. If they see a rising order flow, they know this is part of a process that will soon cause a currency to appreciate.

Large banks have an advantage here, because they act as currency dealers as well as speculators. They are the first to see buy and sell orders from their customers. They can identify shifts in order flow before other traders do and before exchange rates adjust.

Technical Analysis **Technical analysis** encompasses a variety of techniques for predicting prices in financial markets, including exchange rates. The common feature is that past movements in prices are used to predict future prices. The underlying idea is that financial prices repeatedly follow certain patterns. Technical analysts try to recognize a pattern while it is occurring. If they succeed, they can predict where prices will go as the pattern continues.

Technical analysis Set of methods for forecasting prices in financial markets based on the past behavior of prices

Many currency speculators use technical analysis: they forecast exchange rates based on the past behavior of rates. Yet technical analysis is controversial, with many economists saying it doesn't work. The next case study explores this issue.

CASE STUDY

More on Technical Analysis

The first methods of technical analysis were developed by stock traders a century ago. These traders used graphs of past stock prices to predict future prices. Today, however, technical analysis is not very popular in the stock market. Most analysts pick stocks by studying companies and forecasting their earnings (review Section 5.5).

In contrast, currency speculators rely heavily on technical analysis. For example, in 1988 the Bank of England surveyed commercial banks and investment banks in Britain about how they forecast exchange rates. 90% of the respondents said technical analysis was one of their tools. (The survey has not been repeated, but it's likely the results would be similar today.)

Technical analysis comes in many flavors. Some methods are complex, but we'll discuss two that are relatively simple.

Comparing Averages In one approach, technical analysts compute averages of an exchange rate over different periods. They compare an average over the recent past to an average over a longer period. If the recent average is higher, this signals that the exchange rate is following an upward trend. This trend is likely to continue, so the exchange rate should rise in the near future.

Specifically, many traders compare the average exchange rate over the past 12 days and the past 26 days. If the 12-day average is higher, the exchange rate is trending up. (The difference between the two averages has a fancy name: the 12/26-day moving average convergence divergence indicator.)

Support and Resistance Levels Another idea is that an exchange rate is likely to stay in a certain range above and below its current level. The bottom of this range is the exchange rate's *support level* and the top is the *resistance level*. If the rate falls to the support level, it is likely to bounce back up rather than fall farther. If it rises to the resistance level, it is likely to bounce back down.

To exploit this behavior, speculators wait until an exchange rate moves near a support or resistance level. At that point they know which way the rate is likely to bounce, so they can make profitable trades. The trick, of course, is to identify support and resistance levels. Again, speculators use a variety of methods. One view is that support and resistance are tied to an exchange rate's previous highs and lows. For example, if the highest value of the dollar over the last 3 months was 0.9 euros, then 0.9 may be a resistance level.

It's not obvious why support and resistance levels exist, but explanations have been suggested. Resistance might result from speculators' "profit-taking" strategies, for example. Traders often plan to sell a currency if it rises to a certain level, to lock in their gains. A trader may choose an exchange rate's past high as the level for profit taking. If many traders make this choice, the past high becomes a resistance level. When the exchange rate reaches the past high, a large number of sell orders are triggered, pushing the rate down.

Does It Work? Many economists don't believe in technical analysis. Indeed, some supporters of the efficient-markets hypothesis ridicule the approach. Burton Malkiel of Princeton University says that "technical analysis is about as useful as going to a fortune teller."

▶ Malkiel is famous for a 1973 book promoting the EMH, *A Random Walk Down Wall Street*.

As we discussed in Section 5.5, economists have compared the performance of stock mutual funds with different strategies. Some studies examine funds that use technical analysis, and they support the view that this approach doesn't work. These findings are one reason that most stock pickers eschew technical analysis.

It is not clear, however, that technical analysis is ineffective in currency markets. There is less research on this topic. And the studies that exist suggest that technical analysis *can* predict exchange rates. One example is a 2000 study by Carol Osler of the Federal Reserve Bank of New York, who examined support and resistance levels estimated by several large banks.* The banks publish these levels each day for the benefit of traders who use the banks as brokers. Osler examined exchange rates between the dollar and three currencies, the pound, the yen, and the deutschmark (Germany's currency before the euro).

Osler's results suggest that support and resistance are useful concepts. She found that exchange rates often bounce as predicted by technical analysis when they hit published support or resistance levels. This doesn't always happen, but it happens more often than it would by chance if the published levels were meaningless.

* See Carol Osler, "Support for Resistance: Technical Analysis and Intraday Exchange Rates," Federal Reserve Bank of New York *Economic Policy Review*, July 2000.

Summary

- The nominal exchange rate, e, is the price of one unit of a currency in terms of another currency.

6.1 Currency Markets and Exchange Rates

- People and firms buy foreign currency so they can purchase foreign goods and services and foreign assets.
- Financial institutions trade currencies on the interbank market, which consists of electronic networks. Large banks are dealers in this market. Banks also serve as brokers for firms and individuals that trade currencies.
- A rise in a currency's price in terms of foreign currency is an appreciation, and a fall in a currency's price is a depreciation.

6.2 Why Exchange Rates Matter

- An appreciation of the dollar helps U.S. consumers by making imports less expensive. It hurts U.S. firms by making their products more expensive compared with foreign goods. It hurts holders of foreign assets by reducing the dollar value of the assets.
- Overall, the U.S. economy sometimes benefits from a depreciation of the dollar. But politicians usually advocate a strong dollar because "strong" sounds better than "weak."
- Firms and asset holders can hedge part of their exchange-rate risk by trading futures contracts for currencies. They can't protect against persistent changes in exchange rates, because contract delivery dates are for 6 months or less.
- A country's real exchange rate, ε, is the relative price of domestic and foreign goods. This variable is eP/P^*, where e is the nominal exchange rate, P is the domestic price level, and P^* is the foreign price level.
- A country's trade-weighted real exchange rate is an average of its exchange rates against different countries' currencies, with weights proportional to its levels of trade with those countries.
- The ups and downs of the U.S. steel industry are largely explained by exchange rates. In both the 1980s and the early 2000s, a strong dollar reduced steel output and spurred protectionist trade policies.

6.3 The Long-Run Behavior of Exchange Rates

- Purchasing power parity (PPP) is a theory based on the assumption that goods and services have the same prices in all locations. It implies that the real exchange rate is constant. The nominal exchange rate is P^*/P, the ratio of the foreign and domestic price levels.
- PPP explains the long-run behavior of exchange rates. As the theory predicts, long-run changes in nominal rates are closely related to countries' inflation rates.

6.4 Real Exchange Rates in the Short Run

- In the short run, a country's real exchange rate is determined by the supply and demand for its currency. For supply and demand to balance, net exports must equal net capital outflows: $NX = NCO$.
- Net exports depend negatively on the real exchange rate: as ε rises, NX falls. The equilibrium exchange rate, ε^*, is the level at which net exports equal net capital outflows.

6.5 Fluctuations in Exchange Rates

- A rise in net capital outflows reduces the real exchange rate. NCO can shift because of changes in interest rates, confidence, or expectations about future exchange rates.
- Since the euro was created in 1999, its exchange rate against the dollar has fluctuated because of statements by the European Central Bank, shifts in confidence about the U. S. economy, and changes in U. S. and European interest rates.
- A rise in net exports at a given real exchange rate raises the equilibrium exchange rate. NX can shift because of foreign recessions or changes in commodity prices.
- In the short run, nominal and real exchange rates move together if price levels are stable.

6.6 Currency Speculation

- Speculators, including banks and hedge funds, account for more than half of currency trading. Speculators forecast exchange rates over the near future and buy currencies they think will appreciate. Their forecasting methods include economic analysis, monitoring of order flows, and technical analysis.
- Technical analysts compare averages of exchange rates over different periods and estimate support and resistance levels.
- Many economists argue these methods don't work, but most speculators use them, and some research suggests they have merit.

Key Terms

appreciation, p. 158
depreciation, p. 158
law of one price, p. 169
net capital outflows (*NCO*), p. 173
net exports (*NX*), p. 173
nominal exchange rate (*e*), p. 155
order flow, p. 182
purchasing power parity (PPP), p. 169
real exchange rate (ε), p. 164
technical analysis, p. 183
trade-weighted real exchange rate, p. 166

Questions and Problems

1. Suppose it takes $1.05 to buy 1 euro. What is the U.S. nominal exchange rate against the euro? What is the European nominal exchange rate against the U.S. dollar?

2. Recall from Section 6.1 that most currency trades involve the U.S. dollar. How would William Stanley Jevons explain this fact? (*Hint:* We met Jevons in Section 2.1)

3. Suppose the U.S. dollar appreciates for a period of time and then returns to its initial level. Compare a 10 percent appreciation that lasts for 2 years and a 50 percent appreciation that lasts 6 months.
   a. Which of these events hurts U.S. exporters more? Explain.
   b. How would the answer be different if currency futures did not exist?

4. On July 15, 2002, a CNN headline reported that "Euro tops dollar." This meant that the value of a euro rose from slightly below $1.00 to slightly above $1.00. Discuss the importance of this event.

5. Suppose it takes $1.05 to buy 1 euro, the U.S. price level is 120, and the European price level is 125.
   a. Calculate the U.S. real exchange rate against the euro.
   b. Suppose the U.S. price level rises to 130. Calculate the real exchange rate again and explain why it has risen or fallen.

6. Section 6.2 defined the U.S. real exchange rate against the euro as the price of American goods divided by the price of European goods. We measured both prices in euros. Suppose we measured both prices in dollars instead of euros. Would this change the definition of the real exchange rate? Explain.

7. For decades, 1 British pound has been worth more than 1 U.S. dollar. One Japanese yen has been worth less than 0.01 U.S. dollars (1 cent). So a pound is more than 100 times as valuable as a yen. Does this difference matter for the British and Japanese economies? Explain.

8. Suppose that, at a certain real exchange rate, a country's net exports exceed its net capital outflows. Is the equilibrium exchange rate higher or lower than this level? Explain both in words and with a graph.

9. Suppose country A sends most of its exports to country B. It gets most of its imports from country C. If A's currency appreciates against B's currency and depreciates against C's, what happens to A's imports, exports, and net exports?

10. Using graphs, show how each of the following events affects a country's net capital outflows, net exports, and equilibrium real exchange rate.
    a. A rise in foreign interest rates
    b. A fad for buying foreign goods

c. An announcement that a tax cut will occur in the future
d. Rising ethnic tensions that threaten to cause a civil war

11. Suppose a country's central bank wants to keep the real exchange rate constant. What should it do to the real interest rate if foreign economies enter recessions? Explain your answer with a graph.
12. Suppose the U.S. real exchange rate against the British pound rises by 6 percent from one year to the next. The U.S. inflation rate is 2 percent and the British inflation rate is 3 percent. What is the change in the nominal exchange rate?
13. We discussed three techniques for speculating on exchange rates: economic analysis, monitoring of order flows, and technical analysis. Assume a key part of the efficient-markets hypothesis: it is impossible to predict exchange-rate movements based on any publicly available information. Under this assumption, could any of the three techniques succeed? Explain.
14. [Advanced] Suppose there is a stable long-run level of the real exchange rate. If the exchange rate is below this level, it is expected to rise; if above, it is expected to fall.
    a. How does the *NCO* curve change if we incorporate this effect?
    b. Does this modification of our theory change the effects of various events on exchange rates (e.g., the effects of shifts in confidence or of foreign recessions)?

Online and Data Questions

www.worthpublishers.com/ball

15. Compute the changes in the U.S. trade-weighted real exchange rate from 2006 to 2007 and from 2007 to 2008. Use data on exchange rates, price levels, and trade shares from the text Web site. What economic forces might explain the changes in the exchange rate?
16. For 29 countries, Figure 6.5 plots the difference between a country's inflation rate and the U.S. inflation rate, and the percentage change in the U.S. exchange rate against the country's currency. The inflation rates and exchange-rate changes are averages over 1980–2006. Redo the figure using inflation rates and exchange rate changes in a single year, 2007. (Data are available at the text Web site.) How does the figure change when it is based on a single year rather than 27 years? What explains the differences?
17. Using data from the text Web site, compute the real exchange rate for the Russian ruble against the U.S. dollar for each year from 1992 through 2007.
    a. Do a bit of Internet research on Russia and try to explain the movements in the real exchange rate.
    b. Do movements in Russia's real exchange rate explain most of the movements in its nominal exchange rate? Explain.

chapter seven

Asymmetric Information in the Financial System

- 7.1 ADVERSE SELECTION
- 7.2 MORAL HAZARD
- 7.3 REDUCING INFORMATION ASYMMETRIES
- 7.4 REGULATION OF FINANCIAL MARKETS
- 7.5 BANKS AND ASYMMETRIC INFORMATION
- 7.6 BANKS AND TRANSACTION COSTS

AP Photo/Lawrence Jackson

Christopher Cox, Chairman of the U.S. Securities and Exchange Commission, testifies before a Congressional committee in 2006. Cox is discussing the Sarbanes-Oxley Act of 2002, which strengthened regulations governing accounting at corporations. Critics say the requirements of the Act are overly complex.

We are in the midst of studying the financial system and how it channels funds from savers to investors. Let's step back for a moment and review the big picture, which is summarized in **Figure 7.1** on page 190. We see that funds can flow from savers to investors either directly in financial markets or indirectly, through banks. Part II of this book analyzed financial markets. Part III, which covers Chapters 7–10, focuses on banks.

This chapter discusses the primary function of banks: to reduce the problem of asymmetric information in the financial system. Then Chapter 8 surveys the banking industry, discussing the different types of banks and how the industry is changing over time. Chapter 9 discusses the business of banking: how bank managers seek to earn profits and contain risk. Finally, Chapter 10 discusses government regulation of banks.

This chapter bridges the topics of financial markets and banking. The need for banks stems from problems in financial markets, especially problems caused by asymmetric information. Investors who sell securities know more than savers who buy securities, creating adverse selection and moral hazard. We introduced these ideas in Chapter 1.

FIGURE 7.1 The Flow of Funds from Savers to Investors

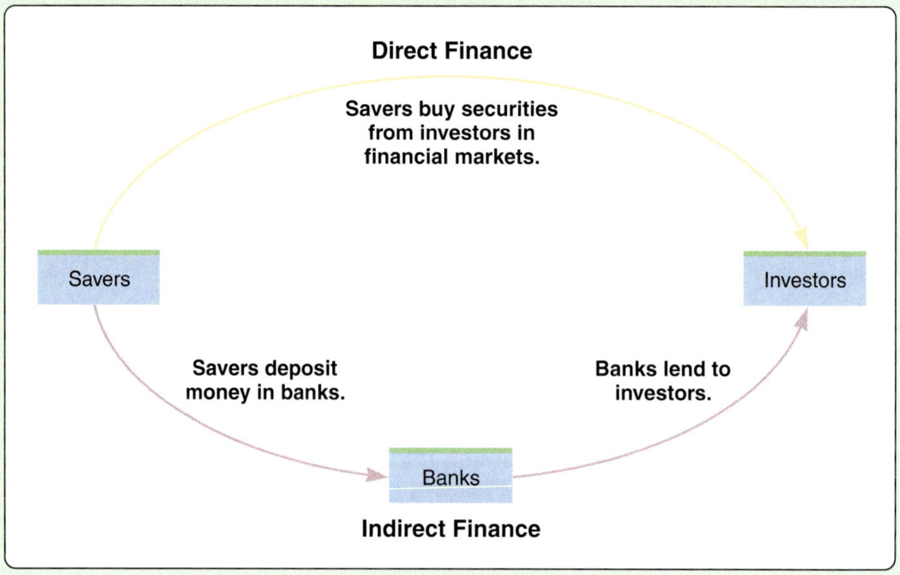

This chapter looks more closely at the harmful effects of information asymmetries in financial markets.

We also discuss efforts to reduce information asymmetries, both actions by private firms and government regulations. These efforts help financial markets work better, but they don't fix the markets' problems entirely. As a result, some investors can't raise funds in financial markets.

We then discuss how banks deal with asymmetric information. Banks attack this problem by gathering information about borrowers and by adding provisions to loan contracts that reduce moral hazard and adverse selection. Because of these measures, banks can provide funds to investors who can't sell securities in financial markets.

Finally, we discuss another function of banks: reducing transaction costs. Bank accounts make it easy for people to save and to purchase goods and services. When investors need funds, borrowing from a bank can be less expensive than issuing securities. Along with asymmetric information, transaction costs help explain the existence of indirect finance.

7.1 ADVERSE SELECTION

Often the people or firms on one side of an economic transaction know more than those on the other side. This asymmetry leads to adverse selection: among the informed parties, those who are most eager to make a deal are the least desirable to parties on the other side. Adverse selection is a big idea in economic theory, as the problem arises in many types of markets.

We'll first discuss the general concept of adverse selection and then examine the specific case of securities markets.

The Lemons Problem

In 1970, George Akerlof of the University of California, Berkeley, published the classic paper on adverse selection; he won the Nobel Prize in Economics in 2002. Akerlof presented a folksy example about used cars to show how adverse selection causes markets to malfunction.

Consider the market for 2008 Honda Accords. These cars vary in quality: some are good, and some are "lemons" that are constantly in the repair shop. If everyone knew the quality of each Accord, the used-car market would work well. The price of each car would reflect its quality. Good cars would sell for more than lemons, so every seller would get what his car is worth.

The market would also function all right if *nobody* knew the quality of each Accord. All cars would look alike, so there would be a single price for any Accord. This price would reflect the *average* quality of Accords. It would be below the price of a car that people knew to be good, but above the price of a known lemon.

Akerlof, however, considers an intermediate case in which information is asymmetric. The seller of a car knows its quality because she has experience driving it. But the buyer does not know the quality: to him, all Accords look alike.

Buyers' ignorance means there will be a single price for all Accords, as in the case when nobody observes quality. One might guess that this price will reflect the average quality of all Accords. But now there is a problem. If owners of good cars see a price based on average quality, they will realize that this price is less than their top-notch cars are worth. They will hold onto the cars rather than sell them. In contrast, owners of lemons will eagerly dump their cars for a price based on average quality. At this price, the market will be flooded with lemons.

The story gets worse from there. Buyers would pay a price based on average quality if both good and bad cars were sold. But when only lemons are available, buyers realize they will end up with one, and so the price falls. Indeed, the market can unravel.

To see this, suppose some lemons are mediocre cars and some are really terrible. A low price leads the owners of so-so cars as well as good cars to refuse to sell. With only terrible cars on the market, the price falls farther. It becomes a vicious circle: a lower price reduces the average quality of cars for sale, and lower quality reduces the price. In the end, we may find that no cars are sold, or only the very worst. Most owners can't sell their cars for what they're worth, and buyers can't find a decent car.

The problem of adverse selection affects many markets besides used cars—the market for health insurance, for example. People know more about their own health than insurance companies do. Relatively sick people are likely to buy the most health insurance, because it is a good deal for them. This fact discourages companies from selling insurance and pushes up the price.

Lemons in Securities Markets

Asymmetric information is a big problem in securities markets. When a firm sells a security, it knows more than buyers do about the security's likely returns, because it knows its business. This asymmetry leads to adverse selection, just as in the used-car market. This problem plagues both stock and bond markets.

Lemons in Stock Markets

Suppose a firm wants to raise funds by issuing stock. According to the classical theory of asset prices, the value of the stock depends on the firm's future earnings (review Section 3.2). Savers can forecast these earnings based on the firm's past performance and its announcements about future plans.

But the firm has more information. The firm's managers can predict future sales by talking to the salesforce. They learn from the research department whether new products are on the way. Engineers tell them whether factories are working smoothly.

This asymmetry causes the same problem as in the used-car market. Suppose the price of each firm's stock is based on the public's forecast of its earnings. Some firms will know their stock is undervalued: it is worth more than the selling price, because earnings are likely to be higher than the public expects. Others will know their stock is overvalued. Firms with overvalued stock will issue lots of it: like the owners of crummy cars, they are eager to sell something for more than it's worth. Firms with undervalued stock will hold back.

Savers understand this behavior. They realize that the stocks offered for sale are likely to be lemons. This belief pushes down stock prices. Lower prices mean that more firms stop issuing stock, so prices fall farther. As with used cars, a vicious cycle can cause the market to break down.

Lemons in Bond Markets

Adverse selection is not *always* a problem when firms issue bonds. The buyer of a bond knows exactly what income he will receive as long as the issuer doesn't default—and default risk is low for some issuers, such as highly successful corporations. When someone buys a safe bond, he need not worry that it's a lemon. As discussed in Section 5.3, an absence of adverse selection helps explain why corporations sometimes issue bonds rather than stock when they need funds.

Adverse selection *is* a problem in bond markets when default risk is significant. In this case, the "quality" of a bond is the probability of default. As discussed in Section 4.5, the interest rate on a bond reflects the public's assessment of this risk. A firm may know that its true default risk is higher or lower than the public thinks. If it is higher, then issuing bonds is a good deal, because the firm pays an interest rate below what it should pay given the true risk. Once again, low-quality securities can flood the market, causing it to break down.

This problem is exacerbated by a fact about investment projects: those with a high risk of failure often have high returns if they succeed. This fact increases the eagerness of risky firms to issue bonds, worsening adverse selection.

Suppose, for example, that a drug company decides to make a big, risky investment. It will spend lots of money to develop a drug that cures cancer. This project might well fail, in which case the company will go out of business. But if the project succeeds, it will produce huge profits. This company will be eager to sell bonds, even if it must pay a high interest rate. It can easily cover the interest payments if the project succeeds. If the project fails, the company defaults, making the interest rate irrelevant. Because of such scenarios, firms will try to issue lots of low-quality bonds.

A Numerical Example

To clarify the concept of adverse selection, let's consider a numerical example, summarized in **Figure 7.2.**

Assumptions Figure 7.2A sets up the example. Two firms have potential investment projects. Each project costs \$100 to undertake. One firm's project is safe. In a year, it produces \$125 in revenue for sure.

The other firm's project is risky. With probability 2/3, it produces \$150 in a year, but with probability 1/3, it produces nothing. The expected earnings from the risky project are $(2/3) \times (\$150) = \$100$, which is less than the earnings from the safe project. However, the risky project earns more than the safe project if it succeeds.

Initially, neither firm has any funds. Therefore, each must sell a bond for \$100 to finance its project. A bond promises a payment in a year, when the firm's project is complete. However, this payment is made only if the project produces revenue; if the project fails, the firm defaults. Will savers buy the firms' bonds?

The answer depends on what other options savers have. Let's assume savers can buy some other asset that yields a certain return of 10 percent. If they put \$100 into this asset, they receive \$110 in a year. Let's also assume savers buy the assets with the highest expected income. This means they will buy a firm's bond if the expected payment is at least \$110, the payment from the alternative asset. A bond's expected payment is the payment it promises times the probability that the payment is actually made—which happens if the project succeeds. That is,

$$\text{expected payment from bond} = (\text{promised payment}) \times (\text{probability of project success})$$

Symmetric Information What happens in the bond market? Suppose first that information is symmetric. This means that savers know which firm's project is safe and which is risky. As a result, they know the quality of each firm's bond. Figure 7.2B explores this case.

With symmetric information, the safe firm can sell a bond that promises to pay \$110. Savers know the firm's project will succeed, so the expected payment equals the promised payment. And a payment of \$110 is enough to compete with the alternative asset. After selling the bond, the firm carries out its project and earns \$125. It makes a profit of \$15 after paying off the bond.

FIGURE 7.2 Adverse Selection: An Example

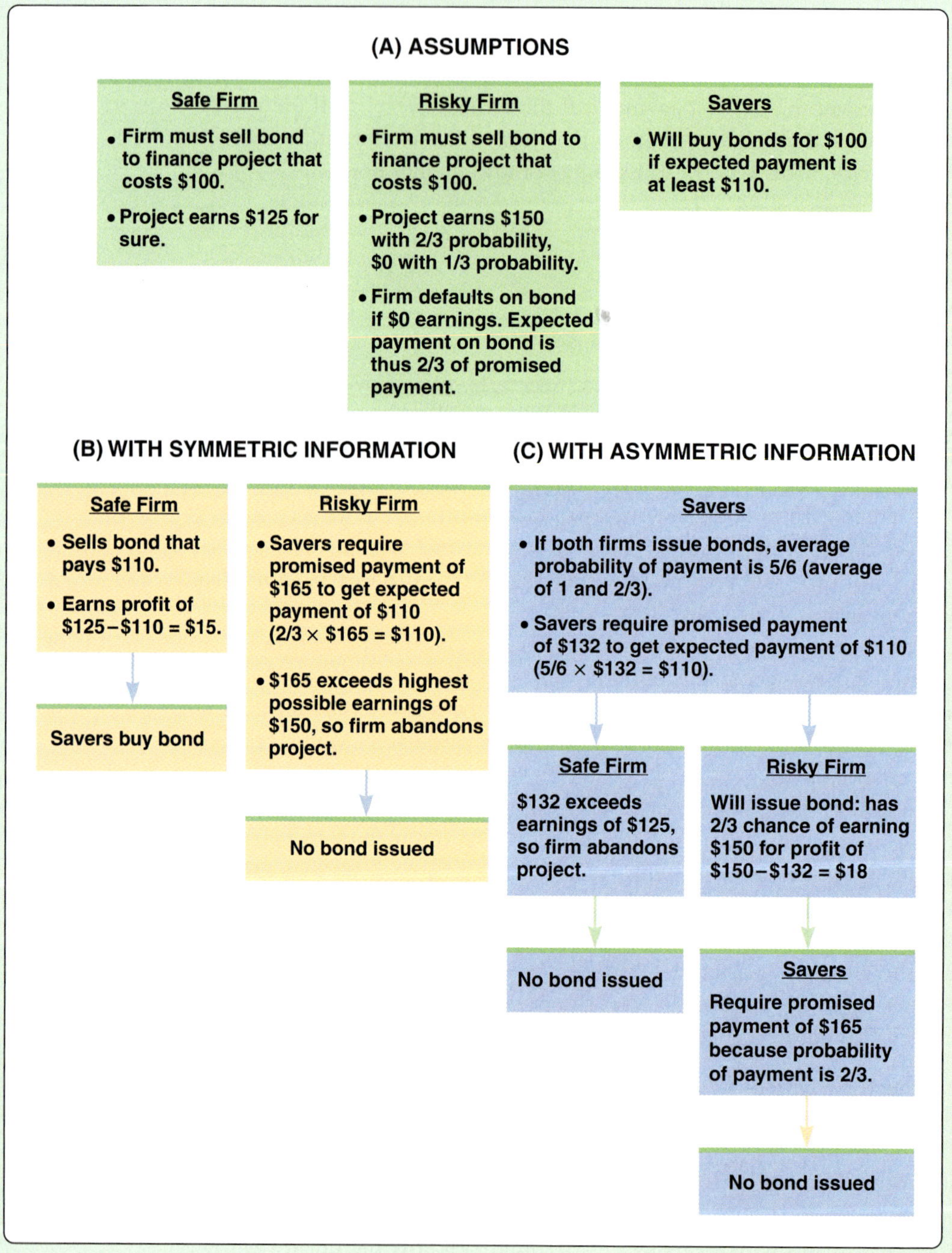

Under symmetric information, the risky firm is out of luck. Savers know that 1/3 of the time the firm will earn nothing and default on its bond; they get the promised payment only 2/3 of the time. Therefore, savers buy the bond only if 2/3 times the promised payment is at least $110. The promised payment must be at least $165, because $(2/3) \times (\$165) = \$110$.

However, \$165 exceeds \$150, the highest possible earnings from the risky project. If the risky firm promises \$165, it cannot make a profit after paying off the bond, even if its project succeeds. Therefore, it does not issue a bond or undertake the project.

Asymmetric Information Now suppose that information is asymmetric. If both firms issue bonds, savers can't tell which is safe and which is risky. So bonds from the two firms must offer the same payment. Who will issue bonds in this case? Figure 7.2C examines the possibilities.

Suppose both firms issue bonds. If a saver buys a bond, it might be from the risky firm, with a success probability of 2/3, or the safe firm, with a probability of 1. Averaging these two numbers, the overall probability of success is 5/6.

Once again, savers will buy bonds if the expected payment is at least \$110. This requires a promised payment of \$132, because then the expected payment is $(5/6) \times (\$132) = \$110$.

But now adverse selection rears its ugly head. If bonds must promise \$132, the safe firm won't issue one. It would earn only \$125, so it can't make a profit after paying off the bond. In contrast, the risky firm will be delighted to sell a bond promising \$132. If its project works, the firm earns \$150 and keeps $\$150 - \$132 = \$18$. If the project fails, the firm defaults and loses nothing.

You may see how the story ends. Savers realize that only the risky firm will sell a bond with a promised payment of \$132. Thus the probability of repayment is really 2/3, the probability for the risky firm, not 5/6. With this probability, savers won't accept a promised payment of \$132; they will require \$165, as in the symmetric-information case. But that drives the risky firm out of the market. In the end, neither firm issues bonds.

7.2 MORAL HAZARD

Like adverse selection, moral hazard arises in many areas of economics. Once again, the underlying problem is an information asymmetry: one party in an economic relationship can't observe the actions of others. Therefore, it's impossible to ensure that everyone behaves in a desirable way. There is a "hazard" of harmful behavior.

The classic example comes from the insurance industry. (The term *moral hazard* was invented by insurers before it was adopted by economists.) Suppose I buy auto insurance. The insurance company would like me to behave in a way that minimizes the claims it must pay. I should drive carefully, never talking on my cell phone, and park only in safe neighborhoods. However, once I have insurance, I may become careless. I don't worry much about fender benders or theft, because insurance will pay most of the costs.

This moral hazard hurts both insurance companies and drivers. Frequent accidents lead to higher insurance premiums. Drivers would be better off if they could promise to be careful in return for lower premiums. Unfortunately, asymmetric information makes such an agreement impossible. I know whether I talk on my cell phone while driving, but the insurance

Principal–agent problem Moral hazard that arises when the action of one party (the agent) affects another party (the principal) that does not observe the action

company does not. If I have an accident, I can blame it on bad luck. There is no way to enforce a promise to drive safely.

This kind of moral hazard is also called the **principal–agent problem.** One person or company, the agent, does something that affects another, the principal. Both parties would benefit if they could agree that the agent behave a certain way. But such an agreement is impossible, because the principal does not observe what the agent does. In the insurance example, the company is the principal, the driver is the agent, and his care in driving is the unobserved action.

Another example of moral hazard concerns workers' effort at their jobs. My boss (the principal) would like me (the agent) to work hard. If I do, my firm will be profitable and wages will rise. However, once I close my office door, I would rather peruse the ESPN Web site than tire myself out with work. Moral hazard arises because my boss is busy in his office and does not see what I'm doing.

Moral hazard arises in financial markets because savers who buy securities do not observe the actions of firms that issue securities. Here, savers are the principals and firms are the agents. Let's examine the moral hazard problem in stock markets and in bond markets.

Moral Hazard in Stock Markets

The moral hazard problem can be severe when firms issue stock. The ownership of a corporation may be spread across many shareholders. Often the managers who run a firm own only a small part of it. Yet their actions determine the profits that go to all shareholders.

In theory, a firm's managers work for its shareholders. Their job is to maximize profits. However, managers may be tempted to do things that benefit themselves but reduce profits. They may pay themselves huge salaries and decorate their offices with expensive art. They may head for the golf course at 3 PM rather than stay late to build up the business.

Moral hazard can make it difficult for firms to sell stock. If savers fear that managers will misuse their funds, they won't provide the funds in the first place. Because of this mistrust, even firms with good investment projects may have trouble financing the projects through the stock market.

Moral hazard often involves behavior that is perfectly legal. It's not against the law to earn $20 million a year or to skip work for golf, even if shareholders suffer. However, egregious cases of moral hazard may include crimes such as embezzlement, as the next case study illustrates.

CASE STUDY

Dennis Kozlowski

The case of Dennis Kozlowski is a colorful example of moral hazard. Kozlowski is the former president of Tyco, a manufacturing conglomerate. In 2005, he was convicted of larceny and fraud for appropriating Tyco's funds for his own use and sentenced to 8 to 25 years in prison. In 2006, he

Moral hazard in Sardinia, 2001. Tyco CEO Dennis Kozlowski with two of the models hired for his wife's birthday party.

AP Photo/HO/New York district attorney

entered the Mid-State Correctional Facility in Marcy, NY, a maximum-security prison. At this writing, Kozlowski also faces a lawsuit from Tyco, whose current managers want to recover the company's money.

According to prosecutors, Kozlowski and another Tyco executive received $600 million in improper payments from the company. This amounted to theft from the company's shareholders. The payments included bonuses that were kept secret and loans from the company that were later forgiven.

Prosecutors also alleged that Kozlowski charged Tyco for personal expenses. These included the cost of decorating his apartment on Fifth Avenue in New York. The work cost $5.7 million, which included a shower curtain that cost $6,000, a $2,200 wastebasket, and $2,900 worth of coat hangers. Kozlowski said he charged Tyco because he used the apartment for business-related entertainment. However, Tyco's current managers disagree. Their suit argues that Kozlowski "purchased and decorated the apartment with appointments and furnishings lacking any legitimate business justification."

▶ Some experts have expressed surprise that anyone could create a $6,000 shower curtain. According to one celebrity decorator, "you could buy $200-a-yard fabric, line it, maybe include a valance and some expensive trim—but even then, you'd probably max out at $3,500."

In 2001, Kozlowski charged Tyco for half of his then-wife Karen's 40th birthday party, which cost $2.1 million. It was a toga party on the Mediterranean island of Sardinia that featured an ice sculpture of Michelangelo's *David* that dispensed vodka in a manner of questionable taste. It's doubtful that such expenditures were the best way to maximize profits for Tyco shareholders.

Moral Hazard in Bond Markets

Like adverse selection, the moral hazard problem is less severe in bond markets than in stock markets. Bondholders don't care if a firm's managers waste money on salaries and parties, as long as the firm makes the promised payments on its bonds. But moral hazard arises when firms issue bonds with significant default risk. Managers may increase this risk by misusing funds, so savers are wary of buying the bonds.

Recall that some investment projects combine a high risk of failure with large returns if they succeed. We have seen that this fact worsens the adverse selection problem in bond markets. It also worsens moral hazard. Once a firm obtains funds, it has different options for how to use them, including some with high risk and high return. A drug company, for example, can divert funds from its normal investments to gamble everything on a cancer drug. Such a gamble is attractive if financed with borrowed money.

Savers understand the drug company's incentive to gamble and therefore ascribe a high default risk to its bonds. They may refuse to buy the bonds, preventing the company from financing any investment. The company would be better off if it could promise to invest in safe projects. Unfortunately, such a promise is unenforceable, because bondholders don't see what the company does.

The Numerical Example Again

We can illustrate the moral hazard problem in bond markets by varying our example of adverse selection (see Figure 7.2). Assume again that two investment projects cost \$100 each; one produces \$125 for sure and one produces \$150 with probability 2/3. However, let's no longer assume the two projects belong to different firms. Instead, a single firm has the option of pursuing either the safe project or the risky project.

Once again, assume the firm can sell a bond for \$100 if the expected payment is at least \$110. If the firm could guarantee that it will pursue the safe project, then the expected payment would equal the promised payment. In that case, the firm could sell a bond promising \$110. It would undertake the project, earn \$125, and make a profit of $\$125 - \$110 = \$15$.

Unfortunately, this won't happen if information is asymmetric. Suppose the firm sells a bond that promises \$110. At that point, whatever the firm has promised, it can pursue either project. Bondholders can't control the firm's decision because they don't see what it does. The firm will consider its options.

As we have seen, the safe project yields a certain profit of \$15. The risky project produces \$150 if it succeeds. In this case, the firm pays off the bond and its profit is $\$150 - \$110 = \$40$. If the risky project fails, the firm defaults on the bond and earns nothing. Since the risky project succeeds 2/3 of the time, the expected profit is $(2/3) \times (\$40) = \$26.67$. This exceeds the profit from the safe project, so the firm chooses the risky project.

Once again, the bond market unravels. Savers know the firm will choose the risky project, so they won't buy bonds promising \$110. With a 2/3 chance of success, they need a promised payment of \$165 to get an expected payment of \$110. But the firm can't profit from either project if it promises \$165. So no bond is sold and neither project is funded.

7.3 REDUCING INFORMATION ASYMMETRIES

We have painted a bleak picture of how asymmetric information causes securities markets to break down. Can this problem be solved? Participants in securities markets work in various ways to reduce adverse selection and moral hazard, making it possible for some firms to issue securities. The solutions to information problems are imperfect, however, so other firms are shut out of securities markets.

Information Gathering

Adverse selection arises because savers lack information about firms. At a broad level, it is obvious how to reduce this problem: savers should get more information. They should examine firms' past earnings and financial condition. They should learn the details of firms' projects and estimate the chances of success. They should find out which managers have reputations for skill and honesty. Such research can help savers determine which firms' securities are valuable and which are lemons.

Moral hazard can also be reduced if savers gather information—in this case, information about firms' uses of funds. Before buying securities, savers should make firms promise to undertake safe projects and not to waste money. Then they should visit the firms' offices frequently to check that the promises are kept. They should monitor firms' expenditures and raise questions about fancy shower curtains.

The Free-Rider Problem

Unfortunately, this information gathering often doesn't happen. It takes time and effort to learn about firms. And many securities are held by small savers, who lack sufficient incentives to incur these costs. If I have $1000 to save, I would like to learn about the firms offering securities so I can avoid lemons. But I can't afford to quit my job and spend my time studying firms. Similarly, once I buy a firm's security, I don't have time to visit the firm frequently, and I can't afford an accountant to monitor its finances.

Suppose a thousand savers have $1000 each, for a total of $1 million. With that much money at stake, it's worth having someone gather information about firms. One might think that savers would band together to study firms, sharing the trouble and expense. Each saver could donate a few hours of time or pay a fee to help hire an accountant. Together, savers could learn which securities are lemons and which firms are misusing their funds.

However, this may not occur because of the **free-rider problem,** a concept you may recall from your first economics course. This problem arises when people can benefit from a good without paying for it; as a result, nobody pays and the good isn't produced. In financial markets, the free-rider problem arises in the production of information.

Free-rider problem People can benefit from a good without paying for it, leading to underproduction of the good; in financial markets, savers are free riders when information is gathered

To see the problem, suppose someone started a group to study firms. A saver would have an incentive *not* to join this group. If he doesn't join, he can simply watch what securities the group buys and buy the same ones. This strategy provides the benefits of information gathering without the costs of joining the group. Similarly, a smart saver will let others do the work of monitoring firms' uses of funds. If everyone thinks this way, the savers' group never gets off the ground.

This situation is similar to free-rider problems in other contexts. The residents of a town would benefit if they got together Saturday mornings to clean up the public park. However, each individual would rather sleep in and let others do the work. So the park stays dirty. In the same way, all savers would benefit if they gathered information, but free riding prevents this from happening.

Information-Gathering Firms

The free-rider problem limits information gathering in financial markets. However, some types of firms do gather information on the value of securities. Two examples are investment banks (introduced in Section 5.1) and bond-rating agencies (introduced in Section 4.4). These firms overcome the free-rider problem by charging fees to savers and investors who benefit from their work.

Investment Banks These institutions reduce the problem of adverse selection in primary securities markets, especially by underwriting initial public offerings of stock. Investment banks assuage fears that shares in a company are lemons by researching the company and providing information to buyers of the stock. They build reputations that lead people to trust their assessments of companies. As we've seen, investment banks earn high fees because most companies need their help to issue securities.

Bond-Rating Agencies These firms, such as Moody's and Standard & Poor's, research companies and rate the default risk on their bonds. These ratings reduce adverse selection in the bond market. Savers learn which bonds are safe and which are lemons, and interest rates adjust accordingly. Safe firms can issue bonds at low cost.

Bond ratings are available for free on the Web sites of rating agencies. To earn money, the agencies sell detailed reports on companies to financial institutions such as mutual funds. In addition, most rated companies request the ratings and pay a fee. Companies know that ratings reduce adverse selection, making it easier to sell bonds for what they're worth.

Boards of Directors

Every corporation that issues securities has a board of directors that oversees it. Members are elected by the corporation's shareholders at annual meetings. Part of the board's job is to reduce problems caused by asymmetric information—specifically, to reduce moral hazard. The board monitors managers and tries to prevent them from misusing shareholders' funds.

A board of directors has a lot of power. It hires the CEO of its firm and sets her salary. The CEO and other managers must report major decisions to the board and submit statements detailing the corporation's finances. The board can fire the CEO if she doesn't act in the best interests of shareholders.

Directors receive fees for their services. A large corporation might have around 15 directors, each of whom receives $50,000 a year for participating in five or ten meetings. These fees come out of the corporation's profits. In effect, each shareholder pays part of the fees, so no one can be a free rider.

Captive Boards Unfortunately, boards of directors don't always do their jobs. Critics suggest that boards can be "captured" by the managers they are supposed to monitor. The boards end up serving the interests of managers rather than the shareholders who pay them.

One reason for this problem is that, at most corporations, some of the firm's managers are also members of the board of directors. The CEO is often the board's chair. Dennis Kozlowski, for example, was chairman of the Tyco board. He was responsible for monitoring his own behavior. Boards also include "outside" directors who are not managers of the firm. But these directors may have business dealings with the company. The Tyco board included two men whose companies leased planes to Tyco, and one who received large consulting fees. Directors with such involvements may be reluctant to question managers' actions, as they benefit from the status quo.

Elections In principle, a firm's shareholders can replace ineffective directors through elections. But this doesn't happen often. Elections take place at firms' annual meetings, which most shareholders don't attend. Typically, a firm's management mails a "proxy statement" to shareholders, asking for the right to vote on their behalf. Most shareholders agree, so managers end up controlling the election. They pick the directors who are supposed to supervise them.

If shareholders object, they can contest the election. Dissident shareholders send out their own proxy statements and collect votes. With enough votes, they can defeat management's candidates and elect other directors. However, this process is time-consuming and expensive. Dissidents must advertise for votes, like political candidates. In most elections, no shareholders are willing to pay the costs of a campaign.

Notice that the free-rider problem arises here. If directors are ineffective, all shareholders would benefit by replacing them. The total gains might exceed the costs of an election campaign. But no individual has enough incentive to launch the campaign and pay for it.

Shareholder Revolts Despite the difficulties, shareholders sometimes take control of boards of directors. They may oust directors through an election or use the threat of an election to force directors to discipline managers. These revolts are often led by large shareholders, who have enough money at stake to make the effort worthwhile.

A famous shareholder revolt occurred in 2007 at Home Depot. The firm's stock price had stagnated for several years, while the stock prices of other retailers rose. Many shareholders blamed questionable business decisions by Home Depot's CEO, Robert Nardelli. They also felt that Nardelli treated them disrespectfully. At the company's 2006 annual meeting, shareholders tried to question Nardelli about his performance, but he cut them off and ended the meeting after 30 minutes. The *New York Times* reported that Nardelli ran the meeting "like a lord over his fief." Yet Home Depot's board of directors supported Nardelli. From 2000 to 2006, his compensation averaged $40 million per year.

Among the shareholders critical of Nardelli was Relational Investors, a firm that buys stock on behalf of large pension funds. It owned about 1 percent of Home Depot's stock, worth $1 billion. The head of Relational Investors, Ralph Whitworth, argued that the stock would be worth much more if Home Depot were better managed. Whitworth announced that he would lead a revolt against Nardelli and Home Depot's board of directors at the 2007 annual meeting. Facing this threat, the board dropped its support for Nardelli. He resigned under pressure in January 2007.

We've discussed shareholders' conflicts with managers in the United States. The next case study discusses differences across countries in the shareholder–manager relationship.

CASE STUDY

International Differences in Shareholder Rights

Shareholders' ability to control managers depends on their rights under the laws governing corporations. These laws vary across countries. In several well-known studies, economists at Harvard and the University of Chicago have examined differences in shareholder rights and how these differences affect stock markets.

Shareholder rights vary in many ways. In some countries, it is even harder to replace directors than it is in the United States. In some cases, shareholders must appear in person to vote at annual meetings. They may have to deposit their shares with the company before the meeting, which is inconvenient.

Other countries have laws that strengthen shareholder rights. In some, companies are required to buy back stock from dissident shareholders. In others, shareholders can demand special meetings to vote out directors or can sue directors if they don't monitor managers effectively.

The Harvard and Chicago researchers found that countries fall into several groups in their treatment of shareholders. These groups have legal systems with different origins. For example, one set of countries, including the United States, has systems based on English common law. Shareholder rights are relatively strong in these countries. Another group has laws descended from France's Napoleonic Code; in these countries, shareholder rights are weak.

The researchers found large effects due to shareholder rights. In countries with stronger rights, firms issue more stock. In addition, a higher proportion of stock is bought by small savers. The researchers conclude that shareholder rights reduce moral hazard. Savers buy more stock if they are protected against misuse of their funds.

Figure 7.3 presents a sample of this research. It shows average data for countries with four types of legal systems, those with English, French, German, and Scandinavian roots. For each group of countries, the figure shows an

FIGURE 7.3 Shareholder Rights and Stock Market Activity

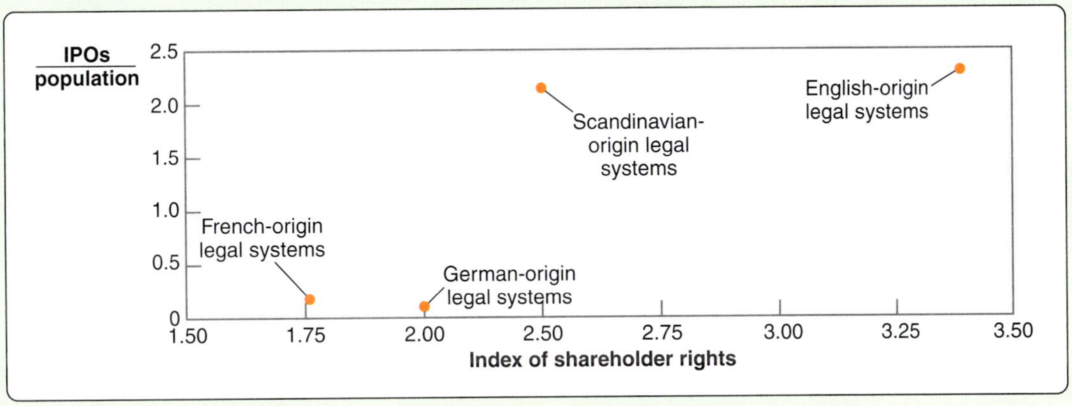

In this graph, the horizontal axis is an index of shareholder rights constructed by economists at Harvard and the University of Chicago. The vertical axis is a measure of stock-market activity, the ratio of initial public offerings during 1995–96 to population in millions. Each point shows the averages of the two variables for a group of countries with similar legal systems. The data support the view that stronger shareholder rights lead to more active stock markets.

Source: Rafael La Porta et al., "Legal Determinants of External Finance," *Journal of Finance,* July 1997

index of overall shareholder rights. The researchers constructed this index by awarding points for various laws favoring shareholders. The figure also shows a measure of stock market activity based on the frequency of initial public offerings (IPOs). It shows a positive relationship between the two variables.

Recall our discussion of economic growth in Section 1.5. We saw evidence that strong financial systems, including large stock markets, raise growth. Combining that evidence with the research discussed in this case study produces an argument for shareholder rights. Stronger rights lead to larger stock markets, which promote economic growth by channeling funds to investors.*

* The research discussed in this case study is presented in Rafael La Porta et al., "Legal Determinants of External Finance," *Journal of Finance,* July 1997, and Rafael La Porta et al., "Law and Finance," *Journal of Political Economy*, December 1998.

Private Equity Firms

We've discussed how information-gathering firms and boards of directors reduce problems in the financial system caused by asymmetric information. **Private equity firms** also perform this function. These institutions own large shares in private companies, that is, companies whose shares are not traded in stock markets.

Several types of private equity firms exist. The most important for reducing information problems are *takeover firms* and *venture capital firms.*

Private equity firm Financial institution that owns large shares in private companies; includes takeover firms and venture capital firms

Takeover firm Private equity firm that buys entire companies and tries to increase the companies' profits

Takeover Firms **Takeover firms** buy entire companies. Some of the companies are already private, and some are public companies that the takeover firms "take private." A takeover firm buys a company if it thinks it can change the company's business practices and increase profits. Leading takeover firms include The Carlyle Group, The Blackstone Group, and Kohlberg, Kravis, Roberts (KKR).

When a takeover firm buys a company, it plans to run the company temporarily, improve profitability, and then resell it. Typically, the resale takes place 3 to 10 years after the takeover. The takeover firm may sell the company to another company seeking to acquire a new business. Or the takeover firm can take the company public again through an offering of stock. Either way, if the takeover firm has succeeded in raising profits, it can sell the company for more than it paid during the takeover.

A takeover firm can buy a public company in two ways. In a *friendly takeover,* it makes a deal with the company's managers and board of directors. Everyone agrees that stockholders will relinquish their shares in the company for a certain price. The company's managers usually keep their jobs, but now they are working for the takeover firm.

A *hostile takeover* is one opposed by a company's management. In this case, a takeover firm approaches the company's shareholders, offering a price for their stock. If a majority of shareholders agree to sell, the takeover firm gains control of the company. It can replace the managers and board of directors with people who agree to the takeover.

Hostile takeovers reduce the moral hazard problem involving shareholders and managers. If a company's managers are not doing their best to maximize profits, a takeover firm has an incentive to change things. The company will be worth more if the takeover firm buys it, fires the managers, and increases profits. Therefore, the takeover firm can offer a price for company stock that is *more* than the stock is currently worth but *less* than its value if management improves. Shareholders gain from selling stock at this price, and the takeover firm gains after it reforms the company and resells it.

Venture capital (VC) firm Private equity firm that buys shares in new companies that plan to grow

Venture Capital Firms A **venture capital (VC) firm** buys ownership shares in new companies. The companies are typically small, private ones that plan to grow and need funds for investment. A venture capital firm doesn't buy a whole company, but it buys a substantial share. The company uses the payment from the VC firm to help finance its expansion.

VC firms mainly finance companies that are developing new technologies, such as Internet applications or biotechnology. For example, Google received $25 million from two VC firms, Sequoia Capital and Kleiner Perkins, in 1999, shortly after it was founded. The VC firms received a 10 percent share in Google; this share was worth $2 billion when Google went public in 2004.

The adverse selection problem makes it difficult for new, little-known companies to raise funds. VC firms reduce adverse selection by gathering information. They study companies to determine which are likely to succeed and fund those companies. VC firms employ experts in various industries to help them pick companies. For example, some VC firms hire doctors and scientists to evaluate biotech companies.

VC firms also face moral hazard problems. Often the managers of new companies have little experience running businesses (think of the graduate students who started Google). In the absence of track records, it's hard to judge whether the managers will do a good job or waste the funds they receive. To address this problem, a VC firm requires that companies it funds put officers of the firm on the companies' boards of directors. With seats on these boards, the VC firm can monitor companies' managers, reducing moral hazard.

7.4 REGULATION OF FINANCIAL MARKETS

We have seen that asymmetric information causes financial markets to malfunction. Because of the free-rider problem, individual savers do not have strong incentives to gather information. Institutions ranging from bond-rating agencies to corporate boards of directors reduce information asymmetries, but they do not eliminate the problem entirely. This situation exemplifies the basic economic phenomenon of market failure.

Government policies can sometimes fix market failures. Recall the problem of the dirty public park. Because of the free-rider problem, nobody volunteers to pick up the trash. The government can solve this problem by hiring park cleaners. Through taxes, it can force everyone to share in the costs. Similarly, the failures of financial markets create a role for government regulation. Most economists agree on this basic principle. However, like many parts of economic policy, the regulation of financial markets can be controversial. Economists disagree about which regulations help the economy and which are counterproductive.

In the United States, financial markets are regulated primarily by the **Securities and Exchange Commission (SEC),** which Congress established in 1934. The SEC creates rules designed to reduce information asymmetries, and it monitors compliance with the rules by firms and individuals. The SEC is often in the news as it modifies its regulations and responds to violations that it uncovers.

Securities and Exchange Commission (SEC) U.S. government agency that regulates financial markets

Many SEC regulations fall into two broad categories: requirements that firms disclose information to savers, and restrictions on security trades by "insiders."

Information Disclosure

The SEC requires public companies to publish information about their businesses. The rationale is simple: the more savers know about companies, the smaller the information asymmetry between the buyers and sellers of securities. Savers are less fearful of buying lemons, so the adverse selection problem is smaller.

Most required information is presented in firms' annual reports. A firm's report summarizes its operations over the past year. It also includes detailed data on the firm's finances—its revenues, costs, assets, and debts. This information helps savers determine the value of the firm's securities.

To ensure that financial data are accurate, a firm must hire outside accountants to audit it. An annual report must include a statement from the auditors saying they have checked the firm's numbers.

Scandals Unfortunately, firms sometimes lie about their finances. A rash of such cases occurred in the early 2000s; the most famous involved two companies profiled in Section 1.2, Enron and WorldCom.

Enron, the energy company, was highly profitable in the 1990s, and its stock price soared. However, it expanded into other businesses, such as broadband communications, that produced losses. If the public had learned of this, Enron's stock would have fallen. The company's managers were eager to keep the stock price high; one motive was that stock options were a large part of their pay. So managers used dishonest accounting tricks to hide the company's losses.

The details of Enron's scheme are complicated; you need to be a top-notch accountant to understand it fully. One feature was the creation of "special purpose entities" (SPEs) that were theoretically separate from Enron. The company moved debts from its accounts to those of the SPEs, making its finances look better than they were.

Enron's losses mounted and eventually couldn't be hidden. The company declared bankruptcy in 2001. As you may recall, this created hardship for the company's employees, especially those with retirement savings in company stock. Several Enron executives were convicted of fraud, including Kenneth Lay, the company's founder, and Jeffrey Skilling, the former CEO. Lay died in 2006, shortly after he and Skilling were convicted; Skilling was sentenced to 24 years in federal prison.

The case of WorldCom, the telecommunications firm, has many similarities to Enron. The central figure was Bernhard Ebbers, WorldCom's founder and CEO. Ebbers held most of his personal wealth in WorldCom stock, giving him a strong incentive to manipulate the price. Starting in 2000, WorldCom hid losses by understating some of its operating costs. The company went bankrupt in 2002; in 2005, Ebbers was convicted of fraud and sentenced to 25 years in prison.

Recall that outside accountants are supposed to ensure that firms' financial statements are accurate. In the Enron and WorldCom scandals, accountants didn't do their jobs. Both firms used Arthur Andersen, one of the country's best-known accounting firms. According to prosecutors, Andersen knowingly approved false statements by Enron. Andersen wanted to keep Enron happy because it did lots of business with the company, both auditing and consulting. Questioning Enron's accounts would have endangered an important source of revenue.

In 2002, Andersen was convicted of obstruction of justice, because employees shredded documents related to Enron. This conviction was overturned in 2005. Nonetheless, the scandal drove away most of Andersen's clients, forcing the firm out of business.

The Sarbanes-Oxley Act Outrage over accounting scandals led Congress to pass the **Sarbanes-Oxley Act,** widely known as SOX, in 2002. The act includes a long list of provisions aimed at preventing future abuses.

Sarbanes-Oxley Act
Federal legislation that strengthens the requirements for information disclosure by corporations

Parts of the act concern firms' internal accounting. Corporations must establish audit committees to collect financial data and check its accuracy.

The firm's CEO must review this work and certify the accounts. Outside auditors must review the firm's accounting procedures, as well as the numbers in the accounts. The act also increases the criminal penalties for falsehoods.

Other parts of the act concern accounting firms. To curb conflicts of interest, it limits the other services accountants can sell to companies they audit. It requires that accounting firms rotate personnel between audits of different companies, so relationships don't get cozy. The act also established a new government agency, the Accounting Oversight Board, to monitor auditors' performance.

The Sarbanes-Oxley Act is controversial. Critics argue that it increases bureaucracy and costs. Managers spend valuable time complying with the act, and companies pay higher fees for more intensive audits. The act is particularly burdensome for small companies, where the costs are large relative to revenues. A 2004 SEC study estimated that the average company with revenue below $100 million spent 2.6 percent of the revenue complying with SOX.

In 2007, the SEC issued regulations aimed at reducing the costs of SOX. The new rules scale back the level of detail required in outside audits of firms' financial statements. However, many business people think the changes don't go far enough in reducing costs.

Online Case Study: An Update on Financial-Markets Regulation

Insider Trading

Firms that issue securities know more than savers who buy securities. Disclosure requirements, which we've just discussed, reduce this asymmetry by increasing savers' information. The asymmetry can also be reduced by *decreasing* the information of firms' managers. Of course, regulators can't make people forget things. But they can require people to *act* as though they have less information than they do. That idea leads the SEC to prohibit **insider trading,** buying or selling securities based on information that is not public.

Insider trading Buying or selling securities based on information that is not public

An "insider" is someone who knows more about a firm than the average saver. Insiders include the firms' employees and people who work with the firm, such as lawyers and accountants. These people often buy and sell the firm's securities. For example, executives receive company stock as part of their compensation and then sell some of it to diversify their assets. Generally, these trades are legal.

However, insiders must choose whether to trade based only on public information. They may *not* buy or sell securities because of something they have learned from their positions—something the average saver doesn't know. And insiders may not pass such information to someone else who will use it.

To understand why insider trading is prohibited, notice first that the temptations for insider trading are strong. Suppose you work for a company that is developing a new product. You learn that a test of the product has succeeded and that the company will announce this result the next day. When that happens, the company's stock is likely to rise as savers raise their estimates of future earnings. If you buy the stock today, when most people don't know the test result, you can make a large profit overnight.

The law forbids such behavior because it worsens adverse selection. If allowed, insiders will buy securities they know are valuable and sell lemons. This hurts uninformed savers on the other sides of the trades. If you, the insider, buy stock the day before the test announcement, your gain is a loss for the person who sells the stock. He loses the profits he would earn if he kept the stock.

If insider trading occurs frequently, then savers become wary of buying securities. They fear they will be ripped off by insiders. The end result is that firms find it harder to issue securities. Insider trading impedes the flow of funds from savers to investors. Unfortunately, as the next case study details, insider trading can prove hard to resist.

CASE STUDY

Some Inside Traders

A classic example of insider trading involves Manugistics Group, a company that produces supply-management software. Barry Saffer was an employee who prepared the company's financial analyses and news releases. In that job, he learned lots of news about the company before it was announced publicly.

▶ Section 5.6 discusses how someone who can predict stock price movements can profit from purchases of options.

Saffer used his inside information to trade options on Manugistics stock. He bought call options when there was good news, meaning the stock was likely to rise. He bought put options when there was bad news. To avoid detection, Saffer lied about his employer when setting up brokerage accounts. He earned $200,000 from trades between 1999 and 2002 but eventually pled guilty to securities fraud.

Another case involves ImClone Systems, a biotechnology firm. On December 27, 2001, the firm learned some bad news: the Food and Drug Administration had rejected its application for a cancer drug. This decision was announced publicly on December 28, causing the firm's stock to fall sharply.

On December 27, Sam Waksal, the chief executive of ImClone, sold $19 million of the company's stock. By selling that day, Waksal avoided a large loss on the 28th. In 2003, he was convicted of insider trading and sentenced to 7 years in prison. The jury found that Waksal sold his stock because he knew about the FDA decision.

This case is well known because it involved a celebrity, Martha Stewart. Stewart and Waksal were close friends and used the same stockbroker, Peter Bacanovic of Merrill Lynch. Like Waksal, Stewart sold shares of Imclone on December 27. The government accused Stewart of selling because Bacanovic told her Waksal was selling—another type of inside information. In 2004, Stewart was convicted of lying about her actions to investigators. She served 5 months in prison plus 5 months of home confinement with an electronic monitoring bracelet on her ankle.

A 2007 case involved inside information about stock ratings. Large securities firms publish ratings for companies' stock and adjust the ratings when news arrives. Often an upgrade raises demand for a stock, pushing up the price. Michael Guttenberg worked for UBS, a large securities firm whose ratings are influential. From 2001 to 2006, he tipped off two stock traders, one at a hedge fund and one at a broker-dealer, about ratings changes that had not yet been made public. With these tips, the traders knew that certain stock prices were likely to rise when the new ratings were announced. They earned millions of dollars by purchasing these stocks and shared their profits with Guttenberg. The SEC uncovered the scheme in 2007 and federal prosecutors filed charges against the participants. Michael Guttenberg pled guilty to insider trading in February 2008.

7.5 BANKS AND ASYMMETRIC INFORMATION

Asymmetric information makes it hard for investors to sell securities. Government regulators and information-gathering firms reduce this problem, but they cannot eliminate it. Many companies can't raise funds in securities markets because savers don't know enough about them. These companies are generally smaller and newer ones.

This is where banks come in. Banks specialize in reducing the problem of asymmetric information. As a result, firms and individuals can borrow from banks even if they are not well known to savers. They get funds from savers indirectly, because bank loans are funded by savers' deposits.

Banks have several methods of reducing information asymmetries and the problems of adverse selection and moral hazard. Let's examine these methods.

Screening Borrowers

Adverse selection is reduced if someone gathers information about borrowers. Banks perform this function. When a firm applies for a loan, it must provide information about its finances: its assets, existing debts, profit history, and so on. The firm also submits a business plan detailing the project to be funded. Individuals seeking loans must provide information on their personal finances and plans.

Successful bankers are good at interpreting such information. They study past lending to learn what types of borrowers are likely to default. Loan officers are trained to screen borrowers and gain expertise by doing so repeatedly. As a result, banks can do better than the average saver at determining whom it's safe to lend to.

Recall the free-rider problem in securities markets: if many savers buy a company's securities, no individual has sufficient incentive to gather information. Banks reduce this problem, because a firm typically borrows from a single bank. The bank has an incentive to gather information because, as the sole lender, it gets all the benefits.

Banks enhance their information gathering by developing long-term relationships—by lending repeatedly to the same borrowers. Experience with

Line of credit A bank's commitment to lend up to a certain amount whenever a borrower asks

a firm is often the best guide to its default risk. Banks encourage long-term relationships by offering **lines of credit.** These are commitments to lend up to a certain amount whenever the borrower asks. Lines of credit provide liquidity to borrowers: when needed, they can get funds quickly and easily. At the same time, banks benefit because credit lines create ongoing relationships.

Collateral and Net Worth

In addition to gathering information, banks reduce default risk through provisions in loan contracts. One type of provision concerns collateral and borrowers' net worth.

Collateral An asset of a borrower that a bank can seize if the borrower defaults

Collateral **Collateral** is an asset of a borrower, such as a building or a firm's inventory. When a borrower takes out a loan, it pledges the collateral to the bank. This means the bank can seize the asset if the borrower defaults.

Collateral benefits a lender in two ways:

1. It reduces the loss when a borrower defaults. By seizing collateral and selling it, the bank can recover some or all the money it is owed.
2. It reduces the probability of default. With no collateral at stake, borrowers have incentives to try risky projects: they may win big, and they lose nothing if the project fails and they default. But default hurts borrowers if banks seize collateral. Thus collateral makes risky firms less eager to borrow, reducing adverse selection. It makes borrowers seek safety when choosing projects, reducing moral hazard.

A Final Example We can illustrate this point by varying our numerical example of moral hazard from Section 7.2. Once again, a firm has two possible projects, one that produces \$125 for sure and one that produces \$150 with probability 2/3. A bank lends enough money for one project, and the firm promises to pay back \$110. If there is no collateral, our earlier analysis applies again: the firm will choose the risky project, because it produces a higher expected profit.

But suppose the bank requires an asset as collateral—one worth \$50. This changes the firm's calculations. If it chooses the safe project, it succeeds for sure, pays the bank, and keeps its collateral. It earns $\$125 - \$110 = \$15$.

If the firm chooses the risky project, then with probability 2/3 it earns \$150 and pays \$110, for a profit of \$40. With probability 1/3, it defaults. In this case, the firm loses its collateral, so its profit is $-\$50$. The expected profit is $(2/3) \times (\$40) + (1/3) \times (-\$50) = \$10$. This is less than the \$15 guaranteed by the safe project.

So the story has a happy ending. The firm chooses the safe project and earns a profit, and the bank's loan is repaid for sure.

Net worth (capital) Difference between assets and liabilities

Net Worth A loan contract may also set a minimum for the borrower's **net worth,** also known as its **capital.** This is the difference between the borrower's total assets and its debts. A net-worth requirement restricts the borrower's actions; for example, it can't take out another loan if that would push net worth below the minimum.

Net-worth requirements serve the same purposes as collateral. They discourage borrowers from taking risks, because borrowers have something to lose if projects fail. They also protect lenders against default. If a borrower goes bankrupt, its assets are sold and lenders can claim some of the proceeds.

Covenants and Monitoring

Banks also address moral hazard by including **covenants** in loan contracts. Covenants are restrictions on the actions of borrowers that reduce default risk. A covenant may require that a loan be used for a specific purpose, such as buying equipment. A "negative" covenant may forbid certain risky activities on the part of the borrower. Some covenants protect the collateral for a loan. For example, if an individual uses his house as collateral, he must purchase fire insurance. Net-worth requirements, which we already discussed, are another type of covenant.

Covenant Provision in a loan contract that restricts the actions of the borrower

To enforce covenants, banks monitor firms. Under many loan agreements, the borrower must report periodically to the lender on its activities and financial situation. Financial data are audited by an independent accountant to keep the firm honest. If the firm violates a covenant, the bank has the right to demand immediate repayment of the loan.

A bank can improve its monitoring by requiring **compensating balances.** This means a borrower must maintain a checking account at the bank with a certain minimum balance. The bank learns a lot about the firm's activities by observing the funds flowing in and out of the account. Compensating balances are also collateral that the bank can seize easily.

Compensating balance Minimum checking deposit that a borrower must maintain at the bank that has lent it money

Interest Rates and Credit Rationing

Banks try to minimize default risk through screening, collateral, and covenants. Most loans still carry some risk, however. Banks cope with this risk by adjusting interest rates. Riskier borrowers must pay higher rates to compensate for banks' losses from defaults.

The interest rate charged to banks' safest customers is called the **prime rate.** These customers are usually large, well-established firms. Most small businesses pay interest rates 2 to 4 percentage points above the prime rate, depending on how risky they look. An upcoming case study discusses how banks evaluate business loans.

Prime rate Interest rate banks charge on business loans with the lowest default risk

One might guess that banks will lend to any borrower if the interest rate is high enough. In fact, they won't. Some borrowers are offered loans at interest rates reflecting their risk, but those who look very risky can't borrow at all. A bank's refusal to lend at any interest rate is called **credit rationing.** Credit rationing occurs because high interest rates worsen adverse selection.

Credit rationing Refusal of a bank to lend to a borrower at any interest rate

To see this, suppose a bank's highest interest rate is 10 percent. For some borrowers, default risk looks high enough that the bank will lose money if it lends at 10 percent. The bank could raise the rate to 20 percent to compensate for defaults, but this strategy might backfire. A 20 percent rate will drive away many loan applicants, leaving only the riskiest borrowers. The only way to earn a profit while paying 20 percent is to gamble on a project that could yield big returns. Raising the interest rate can increase default rates by enough to reduce the bank's profits. The bank does better by refusing to lend.

Credit rationing means that some people and firms who want to borrow can't get loans from banks. As we'll detail in Chapter 8, this fact creates a role for other types of lenders, such as finance companies. Credit rationing may also justify government policies that encourage bank lending.

CASE STUDY

The Five C's of Business Lending

Loan officers at banks decide whether to grant loans to applicants. They are trained to examine individuals and firms and judge their creditworthiness. For business loans, loan officers sometimes summarize their criteria as the "five Cs." These concepts are closely related to ideas that we have discussed.

▶ These five Cs come from the government's Small Business Administration. Other sources give slightly different lists of five or six Cs. Some mention "control" (meaning the ease of seizing capital) or "cash flow" (future earnings, which are included under "capacity" here).

- *Capacity* This means the financial capacity of the firm to repay the loan. Loan officers determine capacity by forecasting the firm's earnings. Typically, they take past earnings as a baseline and make adjustments for the impact of new projects. They make sure that forecasted earnings are high enough to support the payments promised under the loan.
- *Conditions* This refers to conditions outside the firm that affect its earnings and default risk. Is the firm's industry growing or shrinking? How strong are the firm's competitors? Will suppliers provide the firm's inputs at good prices? How healthy are the national and local economies?
- *Character* Firms are most likely to repay loans if their owners and managers are honest and responsible. So loan officers check the personal credit histories of applicants and look for criminal records. They check references and try to learn applicants' reputations in their industries. They often rely heavily on personal interviews.
- *Collateral* Loan officers estimate the value of collateral. For example, they get appraisals for buildings. They also consider the collateral's liquidity. If a bank seizes a firm's machinery, can it sell the machinery to anyone?
- *Capital* As we've discussed, this is another name for net worth, the difference between a borrower's assets and liabilities. Net worth gives borrowers something to lose if they take on risky projects. Loan officers are more likely to approve applicants with significant net worth.

CASE STUDY

Traditional Home Mortgages

For many people, the most important role of a bank is to provide money to buy a home. Home loans illustrate many of the ideas we have discussed. We'll focus here on traditional mortgage loans, which have fixed interest rates and are made to "prime" borrowers, people with good credit histories. Chapters 8 and 9 discuss the development of subprime mortgages and adjustable interest rates.

A traditional mortgage loan covers 80–90 percent of the price of a house. The borrower makes a constant monthly payment for 15 or 30 years. The bank calculates the payment based on the size of the loan and the interest rate. For example, a 30-year loan of $200,000 at an 8 percent interest rate requires monthly payments of $1428.80.

▶ This calculation uses the techniques for measuring interest rates discussed in Section 3.6.

Screening Borrowers What are banks' criteria for approving mortgage loans? Applicants are asked lots of questions about their employment, earnings history, assets, and so on. However, loan approval depends primarily on two things:

1. *Debt–income ratios* These are ratios of monthly debt payments to the borrower's monthly income. Currently, for prime mortgages many banks require that mortgage payments be less than 28 percent of income. In addition, total debt payments—the mortgage plus credit cards, auto loans, etc.—must be less than 36 percent of income. Banks want to ensure that borrowers can afford their promised payments.
2. *Credit scores* Credit bureaus, such as Equifax and Experian, collect information on people's use of credit. Each person's history is summarized with a numerical rating called a **credit score.** A high score means a person is likely to repay loans that she receives; a low score means a high risk of default.

Credit score Numerical rating capturing a person's likelihood to repay loans based on her credit history

A person's score changes over time depending on how she uses credit. Borrowing money and repaying it on time raises the score. Points are lost for late payments; the more recent the delinquencies, the heavier the penalties. Of course lots of points are lost if a borrower defaults permanently. Points are deducted for credit card balances near the card limit, as these suggest financial problems. Credit scores range from about 350 to the 800s. Banks set minimum scores, typically in the 600s, for prime mortgages.

Collateral and Down Payments The hallmark of a home loan is that the home serves as collateral. In addition, banks ensure that borrowers have significant net worth by requiring down payments. The bank lends less than 100 percent of the house price, so the borrower ends up owning a house worth more than his mortgage debt (unless the price of the house falls by a lot). For the best interest rates, banks usually require a down payment of 20 percent. Borrowers can put down less if they pay higher rates.

Covenants These focus on protecting the collateral. As mentioned before, borrowers must maintain homeowner's insurance. Often the bank monitors this by collecting monthly insurance payments along with the mortgage, then passing them on to the insurance company. Another common covenant requires the borrower to use the house as her primary residence. Lenders believe a house is more likely to be trashed if it is rented out. And an owner is more careful not to default if her home is at stake.

7.6 BANKS AND TRANSACTION COSTS

Transaction costs Costs in time and money of exchanging goods, services, or assets

This chapter emphasizes a central function of banks—reducing information problems. Another function is also important—reducing **transaction costs,** the costs in time and money of exchanging goods, services, or assets. Banks reduce transaction costs for both savers and investors, creating another reason for indirect finance.

Reducing Costs to Savers

Banks reduce transaction costs for savers in two ways: they reduce the costs of acquiring assets, and they provide liquidity.

Costs of Acquiring Assets It is costly for a saver to purchase securities. If she buys a stock or bond, she must contact a broker and pay a fee. If she buys many securities to diversify, she must pay many fees. It is easier and less expensive to set up a bank account and make deposits. Traditionally, this difference in transaction costs led most people to put their savings in banks. Only the wealthy bought securities.

Over the last several decades, the transaction-cost advantage of banks has been eroded by the growth of mutual funds. Mutual funds make it easy to hold a diversified set of securities, and many funds have low fees. For most people today, banks aren't the only way to save. However, most mutual funds have substantial minimum balances—often $2500—making them inaccessible to the smallest savers. In contrast, some bank accounts have minimum balances of $1.

Liquidity We discussed the concept of liquidity in Section 2.4: an asset's liquidity is the ease of exchanging it for money. Bank deposits are highly liquid. Checking deposits *are* money, as they can be spent directly on goods and services; savings deposits can be exchanged for money in a few minutes at an ATM. In contrast, it usually takes a day or more to sell securities or mutual fund shares and receive money.

The liquidity of bank deposits reduces transaction costs when people buy goods and services. If you see something appealing in a store, you can buy it easily with the funds in your bank account. Life would be less convenient if you had to sell mutual fund shares before making the purchase.

The benefit of liquidity reduces the interest that banks must pay to attract deposits. For example, in June 2008 the interest rates on many savings accounts were below 1 percent. The rate on 3-month Treasury bills, which are less liquid, was about 2 percent.

Reducing Costs to Investors

It is expensive for a firm to issue stocks or bonds. The firm usually hires an investment bank to underwrite the securities. It must also pay accountants to prepare financial statements and lawyers to draw up contracts, services that cost hundreds of thousands of dollars.

Many of these costs are "fixed"—they do not depend on the size of the security offering. When a large company issues $50 million of securities, the costs are moderate compared to the funds that are raised. But a restaurant seeking $50,000 for renovations can't afford to pay $200,000 to securities lawyers. Transaction costs are another reason, in addition to information problems, that small firms don't issue securities.

Transaction costs are lower when firms borrow from banks. This fact reflects *economies of scale:* a bank lends to many firms, reducing the cost of each loan. A bank's lawyers draw up one standard loan contract and use it for many borrowers. The bank develops standard criteria for evaluating loan applicants, allowing it to process loans quickly.

Transaction costs are especially low when firms establish lines of credit with banks. These arrangements allow a firm to get funds quickly without submitting a new loan application. This benefit of credit lines complements their role in reducing information problems (see Section 7.5).

Summary

- The primary function of banks is to reduce the problems of adverse selection and moral hazard caused by asymmetric information in the financial system.

7.1 Adverse Selection

- Adverse selection arises in many markets, including financial markets. Issuers of securities know the securities' quality, but buyers do not. Markets can break down because only low-quality securities are offered for sale. This problem is severe for unknown firms, so they can't issue securities.
- Adverse selection is exacerbated by the fact that risky projects may have high returns if they succeed. Risky firms would like to sell bonds to finance gambles.

7.2 Moral Hazard

- Moral hazard arises in many contexts, including financial markets. Savers can't observe what firms do with their funds, so firms may take actions that harm savers. Such actions include excessive risk-taking and using funds for the personal benefit of managers.

7.3 Reducing Information Asymmetries

- Savers can reduce adverse selection and moral hazard by gathering information about firms. However, the free-rider problem reduces information gathering.
- Several types of firms gather information on companies, reducing moral hazard and adverse selection. These include investment banks and bond rating agencies.
- A company's board of directors monitors managers to reduce moral hazard. However, a board may not do its job if it is captured by managers. Shareholders can replace directors through elections, but this is difficult.
- Shareholder rights vary across countries. Researchers have found that greater rights produce larger stock markets and more stockholding by small savers.
- Private equity firms include takeover firms and venture capital firms. Takeover firms reduce moral hazard by purchasing underperforming companies and replacing the management. Venture capital firms provide funds to new companies. They gather information on the companies, reducing adverse selection, and they help manage the companies, reducing moral hazard.

7.4 Regulation of Financial Markets

- U.S. financial markets are regulated by the Securities and Exchange Commission (SEC).
- The SEC requires companies to disclose information about their finances, with checks by outside accountants. These requirements were strengthened by the Sarbanes-Oxley Act, a response to the Enron and WorldCom scandals.
- Other SEC regulations forbid insider trading. Numerous people have been convicted of insider trading in recent years.

7.5 Banks and Asymmetric Information

- Because banks reduce the problem of asymmetric information, they can provide funds to borrowers who cannot issue securities.
- Banks address asymmetric information by screening and monitoring borrowers, establishing long-term relationships, requiring collateral or net worth, specifying loan covenants, adjusting interest rates for risk, and rationing credit.
- In evaluating applicants for business loans, banks consider the five Cs: capacity, conditions, character, collateral, and capital.
- When banks make traditional home mortgages, they evaluate borrowers based on debt-income ratios and credit scores. A home serves as collateral for a loan. Banks require down payments and impose covenants to protect the collateral.

7.6 Banks and Transaction Costs

- Banks reduce the costs to savers of acquiring assets, and they provide liquidity. Banks also allow investors to avoid the costs of issuing securities.

Key Terms

collateral, p. 210
compensating balance, p. 211
covenant, p. 211
credit rationing, p. 211
credit score, p. 213
free-rider problem, p. 199
insider trading, p. 207
line of credit, p. 210
net worth (capital), p. 210
prime rate, p. 211
principal–agent problem, p. 196
private equity firm, p. 203
Sarbanes-Oxley Act, p. 206
Securities and Exchange Commission (SEC), p. 205
takeover firm, p. 203
transaction costs, p. 214
venture capital (VC) firm, p. 204

Questions and Problems

1. Would each of the following events increase or decrease the volume of bank loans? Explain.
   a. New regulations make it easier for shareholders to replace company directors.
   b. A new law makes it a felony to default on a bank loan.
   c. All the economy's small firms are bought by large firms.
   d. Mutual funds reduce their minimum balances for shareholders.
2. a. Suppose you are hiring a worker for your firm. You advertise a position for $50,000, but an applicant offers to work for $40,000. Should you jump at this offer?
   b. Suppose you have $1000 to lend and offer it for 10 percent interest. Someone promises to pay 20 percent if you lend to him. Should you jump at this offer?
3. Some U.S. companies have 1-year terms for directors. The entire corporate board must run for election at each annual meeting. Other companies have 3-year terms; only a third of directors face votes at each meeting. A 2004 study found that the companies with 3-year terms have lower stock prices, controlling for other factors. What might explain this finding?
4. Why do people commit each of the following crimes? Who is hurt by the crimes? Discuss

who is hurt directly and also the broader effects on the financial system. (As an analogy, shoplifting hurts store owners directly; its broader effects include higher prices for goods.)

a. False accounting

b. Insider trading

5. Some people have criticized the long prison sentences imposed in recent corporate scandals. In commenting on Dennis Kozlowski's sentence of 8–25 years, one lawyer who was not involved in the case said, "Certainly the judge had to strike a balance by sending a message that these were serious crimes. But it is arguable that you shouldn't be going away for as long as someone who commits manslaughter or homicide." In your opinion, are recent sentences reasonable? Explain.

6. Edward C. Johnson, 3rd, was the CEO of Fidelity mutual funds and also the chair of the Fidelity board. In 2004, the SEC issued a regulation requiring chairs at mutual funds to be independent of management, forcing Johnson to resign as chair. Johnson opposed the SEC action. Here are two arguments he made:

   (1) "Mandating an independent chairperson is akin to requiring that every ship have two captains.... If a ship I was sailing on were headed for an iceberg, I'd want one—and only one—captain giving orders. I'd like to know that he'd spent some time at sea and knew what he was doing."

   (2) "If a wrong-doer is tempted to try some abuse against fund shareholders, which board chairman would they rather try sneaking it past—an industry veteran with a direct and personal interest in the fund—or a chairman with 40 years experience making carbonated beverages, and who has just flown in for a two-day board meeting?"

   Summarize Johnson's arguments against independent chairs in your own words. Also suggest responses that might be made by a supporter of the SEC regulation.

7. Consider the example in Figure 7.2. Assume that neither firm knows whether its project is safe or risky. For each firm, there is a 1/2 chance that the project is safe, producing \$125 for sure. There is a 1/2 chance the project is risky, producing \$150 with probability 2/3 and 0 with probability 1/3. This means that, overall, each firm has a 1/2 chance of earning \$125, a 1/3 chance of earning \$150, and a 1/6 chance of earning zero. Otherwise, make the same assumptions as before. Will the firms be able to sell bonds? Show your reasoning.

8. Consider the example in Figure 7.2 with asymmetric information: the two firms know which one is risky and which is safe, but savers do not. Keep the example the same as in the figure, except for the earnings of the risky firm. For the following cases, say whether the safe firm can sell a bond, and whether the risky firm can sell a bond.

   a. The risky firm's project earns \$150 with probability 3/4 and 0 with probability 1/4.

   b. The risky firm's project earns \$150 with probability 4/5 and 0 with probability 1/5.

9. Consider the example of collateral in Section 7.5. The example assumes that collateral is \$50. Determine the smallest level of collateral that causes the firm to choose the safe project. Assume the firm maximizes its expected profit.

10. Suppose you take out a 30-year mortgage of \$100,000 with a fixed interest rate of 7 percent. You must make 360 equal monthly payments. Write an equation that defines what the payment is. (*Hint:* Use the approach to measuring interest rates in Section 3.6. The equation is hard to solve without a computer.)

Online and Data Questions

www.worthpublishers.com/ball

11. Figure 7.3 presents data on IPOs and shareholder rights. The figure gives averages for four groups of countries. On the text Web site,

get data for the 49 individual countries in the groups. Make a version of the figure that shows the data for each country. How strong is the relation between IPOs and shareholder rights? Are there exceptions to the usual relation? What might explain these exceptions?

12. Find out what it means for a company to create a "poison pill." (You can put this term in an online search engine.) Who does this, and why? Some economists think poison pills should be illegal. Why is that?

chapter eight

The Banking Industry

- 8.1 TYPES OF BANKS
- 8.2 DISPERSION AND CONSOLIDATION
- 8.3 SECURITIZATION
- 8.4 SUBPRIME LENDERS
- 8.5 GOVERNMENT'S ROLE IN LENDING

AP Photo/Mark Lennihan; © Rab Harling/Alamy

Two places to get a loan.

Figure 8.1 on p. 220 shows the number of U.S. commercial banks operating in each year from 1960 to 2007. The number grew slowly over the first part of this period, peaking at about 15,000 in 1984. Then a sharp decline began. The main cause was mergers of two or more banks into one larger bank. In 2007, there were fewer than 7500 commercial banks, and the number was still falling.

Yet by worldwide standards, the United States still has a large number of banks. As of 2007, the United Kingdom had only 170 commercial banks, and Japan had 161. Canada had 71, less than 1 percent of the U.S. number, despite a population 10 percent of the U.S. size.

This chapter examines the banking industry. We discuss why the United States has so many banks, and why the number is declining. We also discuss the diverse types of banks and the roles they serve. The banking industry includes giants such as Citigroup and JP Morgan Chase, which operate around the globe, and small banks that operate in a single town.

Another key trend in the banking industry is a rise in **securitization.** In this process, a financial institution buys a large number of loans from banks, then issues securities entitling the holders to shares of payments

Securitization Process in which a financial institution buys a large number of bank loans, then issues securities entitling the holders to shares of payments on the loans

FIGURE 8.1 U.S. Commercial Banks, 1960–2007

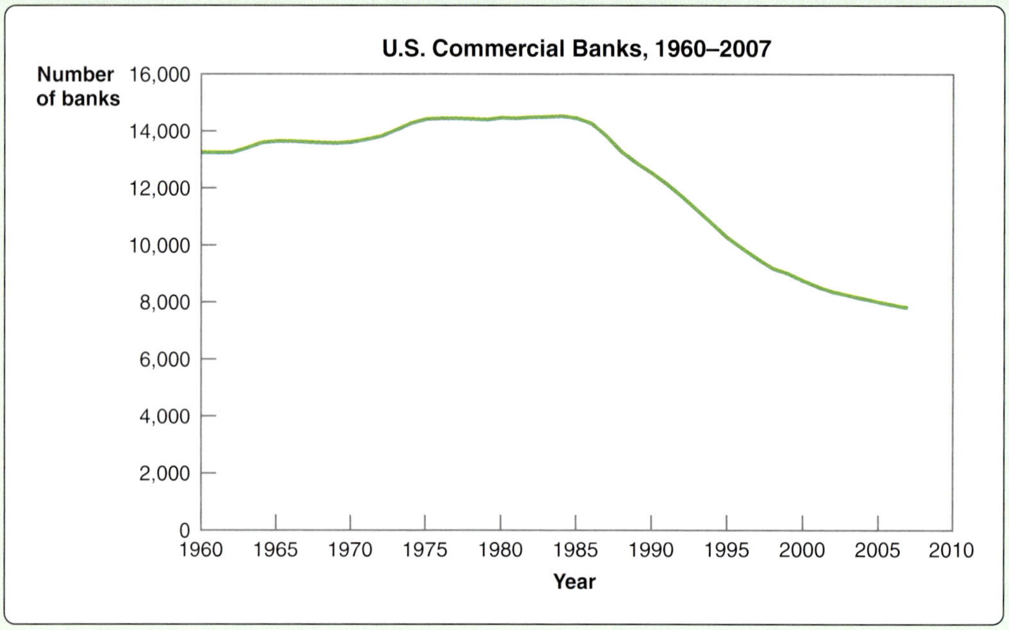

on the loans. Securitization is especially common for home mortgages. We examine the reasons for securitization and its effects on banks, their borrowers, and buyers of the securities.

This chapter also examines a fringe of the banking industry called **subprime lenders.** These companies make loans to people with weak credit histories, who can't borrow from mainstream banks. Subprime lenders include a variety of institutions, ranging from finance companies to pawnbrokers. They have gained notoriety in recent years, largely because of defaults on subprime mortgage loans.

Subprime lenders Companies that lend to people with weak credit histories

Finally, we'll discuss governments' involvement in bank lending. In many countries, the government owns banks, so it determines who gets loans. In the United States, banks are private, but the government encourages lending to certain groups. We'll discuss policies that promote lending to home buyers, students, and people in low-income areas.

8.1 TYPES OF BANKS

Chapter 1 defined a *bank* as a financial institution that accepts deposits and makes loans. This definition covers several types of banks, which are listed in **Table 8.1.** The two main categories are commercial banks and thrifts, each of which has subgroups.

Commercial Banks

Commercial banks are the largest part of the banking system. In 2007, U.S. commercial banks had about $7 trillion in deposits and $6 trillion in outstanding loans. Two million people worked for these banks.

Commercial banks are split into three groups, based partly on size. A bank's size is measured by its total assets, which include outstanding loans and other assets, such as securities.

TABLE 8.1 Types of Banks

Commercial Banks

- Money-center banks
- Regional and superregional banks
- Community banks

Thrift Institutions

- Savings institutions
- Credit unions

Finance Companies*

* Finance companies perform only one of the two functions that define a bank. They make loans but do not accept deposits.

Money-Center Banks

Five or six of the largest banks comprise this category. Two features define a **money-center bank.** First, its headquarters are located in a major financial center (New York, Chicago, or San Francisco). Second, it finances its lending primarily by borrowing from other banks or by issuing bonds. A money-center bank accepts deposits, but deposits are *not* its main source of funds. The money-center category includes Citibank and JP Morgan Chase, two of the three largest banks in the United States. In 2007, each of these banks had assets of about $1.2 trillion.

Money-center bank Commercial bank located in a major financial center that raises funds primarily by borrowing from other banks or by issuing bonds

Money-center banks make many types of loans, including business loans and mortgages. They lend to consumers through the credit cards that they issue. Their largest loans go to private equity firms taking over companies and to foreign governments.

Money-center banks also engage in many businesses besides lending. They trade currencies and derivative securities, for example. In the late 1990s, money-center banks started providing investment-banking services, such as underwriting securities. Investment banking is a growing source of profits for money-center banks.

Regional and Superregional Banks

This category includes all non-money-center banks with assets above $1 billion. In 2007, they numbered about 400. A **regional bank** operates in a broad geographic area, such as the mid-Atlantic region. A **superregional bank** operates across most of the country.

Regional bank Commercial bank with assets above $1 billion that operates in one geographic region

Superregional bank Commercial bank with assets above $1 billion that operates across most of the United States

These banks make many types of loans to firms and consumers, but their businesses are narrower than those of money-center banks. Regional and superregional banks concentrate on the core functions of deposit-taking and lending. They raise relatively little of their funds by borrowing from other banks or issuing bonds, and they usually don't trade currencies or underwrite securities.

The largest superregional bank is Bank of America (BoA), with headquarters in Charlotte, NC. As of 2007, BoA had roughly 6000 branches in 33 states. Its $1.3 trillion in assets made it the nation's largest bank, just ahead of Citibank and JP Morgan Chase. Unlike most regional and superregional banks, BoA has started expanding into investment banking.

I have a checking account at M&T Bank, a regional bank based in Buffalo, NY. In 2007, M&T had 650 branches in an area from New York to Virginia, including one next to the Baltimore campus of Johns Hopkins University. M&T's assets were $59 billion, making it the twenty-fourth largest U.S. bank. The Baltimore Ravens play football in M&T Bank Stadium.

Community bank Commercial bank with less than $1 billion in assets that operates in a small geographic area

Community Banks A **community bank** has less than $1 billion in assets. It operates in a small geographic area, raising funds from local depositors and lending them to consumers and small businesses. An example is Harford Bank, based in Aberdeen, MD, 40 miles north of Baltimore. In 2007, Harford Bank had $200 million in assets and seven branches in Aberdeen and neighboring towns.

Of the 7000+ commercial banks in the United States, more than 90 percent are community banks. However, the total assets of these banks are barely above $1 trillion. Bank of America is larger than all the community banks combined.

Thrift Institutions

Thrift institutions *(thrifts)* Savings institutions and credit unions

The core functions of **thrift institutions** (thrifts), like those of commercial banks, are deposit-taking and lending. There are two types of thrifts, savings institutions and credit unions.

Savings institution Type of bank created to accept savings deposits and make loans for home mortgages; also known as *savings banks* or *savings and loan associations (S&Ls)*

▶ Savings banks and S&Ls are slightly different institutions, with minor differences in the regulations that govern them. These differences are not important for our purposes.

Savings Institutions These thrifts are also known as *savings banks* or *savings and loan associations (S&Ls)*. The original purpose of **savings institutions** was to serve households by accepting savings deposits and by lending for home mortgages. Savings institutions were created in the nineteenth century, when commercial banks focused on business lending. Most savings institutions were established as *mutual banks,* meaning they were owned by their depositors and did not issue stock.

Over time, most savings institutions issued stock and ceased being mutual banks. They also expanded their businesses; today, savings institutions offer checking as well as savings accounts, and they make many types of loans. These changes have blurred the distinction between savings institutions and commercial banks, although the former still focus more on mortgages. As Chapter 10 explains, different government agencies regulate commercial banks and savings institutions.

In 2007, the United States had about 1200 savings institutions with $2 trillion in assets. The largest was Washington Mutual, with over $300 billion in assets—but it failed in September 2008, a victim of the subprime mortgage crisis that we discuss in Section 8.4. WaMu's demise left Sovereign Bank as the nation's largest savings institution. Sovereign has 750 branches in the Northeast and about $80 billion in assets.

Credit union Nonprofit bank owned by its depositor members, who are drawn from a group of people with something in common

Credit Unions A **credit union** is a nonprofit bank. Like a mutual bank, it is owned by its depositors, who are called "members." Only members can borrow from the credit union. Credit unions make several types of loans, including home mortgages, auto loans, and small personal loans.

Membership in a credit union is restricted to a group of people who all have something in common. They might be employees of a company, members of a labor union, or veterans of a military service. Restricted membership reduces the problem of asymmetric information in lending. The fact that a borrower qualifies for membership provides information about his default risk. So does the history of his account at the credit union. This information helps loan officers screen out risky borrowers.

Sizable credit unions include those serving the U.S. Navy and the employees of various state governments. Most credit unions are small, however, with assets below $10 million. There are roughly 10,000 credit unions in the United States (more than the number of commercial banks), but their total assets are only $800 billion (well below Bank of America's assets).

Finance Companies

Table 8.1, which lists types of banks, includes **finance companies** with an asterisk. Like banks, finance companies make loans; for example, they compete with banks in issuing mortgages and auto loans. However, finance companies do *not* accept deposits, so they meet only half the definition of a bank. Finance companies raise funds exclusively by issuing bonds and borrowing from banks.

Finance company Nonbank financial institution that makes loans but does not accept deposits

Many finance companies specialize in a certain kind of loan. For example, some lend to businesses for new equipment. Others are owned by manufacturing companies and lend to their customers. This group includes General Motors Acceptance Corporation (GMAC) and Ford Motor Credit Company, which make auto loans. Another market niche that finance companies operate in is subprime lending, as we discuss in Section 8.4.

8.2 DISPERSION AND CONSOLIDATION

So far we've described the banking industry as it exists today. This description is just a snapshot of an industry that is changing rapidly. Mergers are reducing the number of banks and increasing their average size. Banks are also expanding into new businesses. Let's discuss this process and where the industry might be heading.

Why So Many Banks?

Let's start with a fact we discussed earlier: the United States has far more banks than other countries. This fact remains despite the mergers of recent years. The large number of banks reflects the history of government regulation. In 1927, Congress passed the McFadden Act, which forbade banks to operate in more than one state. This law meant that each state had a separate banking industry. In addition, states limited the number of branches a bank could operate. In many states each bank was allowed only one branch (the "unit banking" rule discussed in Section 1.5). Because of these policies, a bank served only a small geographic area. Many banks were needed to cover a whole state.

Over time, these restrictions on banks were relaxed. Most states removed their limits on branches in the 1970s and 1980s. In 1994, Congress passed the Riegle-Neal Act, which repealed the McFadden Act's ban on interstate banking. Today, banks can expand around the country.

Yet past regulations still influence the banking industry. Many banks from the old days have disappeared through mergers, but thousands are still around. Other countries have fewer banks because they never restricted branching or the areas that banks could serve.

What motivated the restrictions on U.S. banks? The answers lie in the country's history. Bank regulations have evolved through a series of political battles, which we discuss in the next case study.

CASE STUDY

The Politics of Banking in U.S. History

Throughout U.S. history, debates over banking have been tied to broader political battles. One recurring theme is efforts by "populists" to limit the power of corporations and the wealthy. The targets of populists have often included banks.

Another theme is the struggle for power between the federal government and the states. In banking, the two levels of government have competed to set regulations and to issue **bank charters** allowing banks to open.

Bank charter Government license to operate a bank

The First and Second Banks Starting in George Washington's administration, America's leaders split into Federalists, led by Alexander Hamilton, and Democratic-Republicans, led by Thomas Jefferson. Federalists wanted more power for the national government and Democratic-Republicans wanted less.

Initially, banks were chartered by the states. Hamilton, as Washington's secretary of the treasury, proposed that the federal government create the First Bank of the United States. A charter was granted in 1791. The First Bank was a privately owned commercial bank, but it also served some functions of a central bank. It issued a national currency (see Section 2.2), lent money to the government, and served as a lender of last resort.

Democratic-Republicans opposed the creation of the First Bank, starting a struggle that lasted several decades. The bank's 20-year charter expired in 1811, and Congress refused to renew it. In 1816, however, it chartered a replacement, the Second Bank of the United States, for another 20 years. The Second Bank, located in Philadelphia, is pictured on the cover of this book.

Andrew Jackson was elected president in 1828. He was a believer in states' rights, a champion of the common man, and an opponent of "moneyed interests" such as bankers. One of his primary goals was to eliminate the Second Bank of the United States.

Jackson criticized the profits earned by the bank's stockholders, a small group of wealthy people. He was also angered by a case of embezzlement at the bank's Baltimore branch. Jackson argued that the bank's profits "must come directly or indirectly out of the earnings of the American people." The establishment of the bank, he declared, was "a prostitution of our government to the advancement of the few at the expense of the many."

In 1832, Congress passed legislation to renew the Second Bank's charter, but Jackson vetoed it. The bank went out of business in 1836, leaving only state-chartered banks.

The National Bank Act Abraham Lincoln believed in a strong federal government, one that worked to build the national economy. Early in his political career, he was a strong supporter of the Second Bank.

As president, Lincoln proposed the National Bank Act, which Congress passed in 1863. The act established a federal agency, the Comptroller of the Currency, to charter banks. Since then, the United States has had both **national banks** chartered by the comptroller and **state banks** chartered by state agencies.

National bank Bank chartered by the federal government

State bank Bank chartered by a state government

Lincoln was motivated partly by episodes of fraud at state banks. In addition, like Alexander Hamilton, he hoped to unify the nation's currency. Each national bank was required to accept currency issued by the others. Finally, national banks helped finance Union spending on the Civil War, as they were required to purchase Treasury bonds.

Battles over Branching The late nineteenth century saw the rise of large corporations, such as Standard Oil and U.S. Steel. Populists vilified the leaders of these companies as "robber barons" who exploited workers and consumers. In 1890, Congress passed the Sherman Antitrust Act, aimed at curbing firms' power to set monopoly prices.

In banking, the battle between big business and the populists focused on branching restrictions. Most banks were too small to provide the loans needed by large corporations. Banks wanted to merge, but branching restrictions prevented mergers in most states. Bankers proposed legislation to relax these restrictions, and the issue was debated from the 1890s to the 1920s.

Some states did relax branching restrictions, but many refused, especially in the Midwest. The populist movement was strong there, and banks were unpopular because they sometimes seized farms. In addition, while some bankers supported branching, others opposed it. Many unit banks were happy with the status quo, which gave them local monopolies. The American Bankers Association lobbied against branching.

Initially, branching restrictions applied only to state banks. Starting in 1927, however, the McFadden Act required national banks to obey the branching laws of the states where they operated. The McFadden Act also forbade branching across state lines, as noted earlier.

The Glass-Steagall Act Many banks failed in the 1930s, helping to cause the Great Depression. Populists blamed these events on risky and unethical behavior by bankers. Banks speculated in the stock market and lost money in the 1929 crash. They were also accused of making unsound loans to companies whose stocks they owned. Today, historians don't think such practices were a major cause of bank failures, but at the time there was a movement to discipline banks.

The result was the Glass-Steagall Act of 1933, which restricted the scope of banks' activities. Commercial banks were forbidden to engage in the businesses of securities firms. They couldn't own stocks, and they couldn't serve as underwriters. The goal was to keep banks out of risky businesses that could lead to failures.

The Decline of Restrictions After World War II, the tide turned toward deregulation of banks. Improved communications increased the incentives for geographic expansion. Populist fears of large banks waned. And experience showed that bank regulation could be a drag on the economy (recall the case study on branching in Section 1.5).

As noted earlier, most states eliminated branching restrictions in the 1970s and 1980s. Some interstate banking arose through "reciprocity" agreements, in which states agreed to let in branches of one another's banks. Finally, in 1994 the Riegle-Neal Act allowed branching throughout the country.

The Glass-Steagall restrictions on banks' activities were also eroded over time. Starting in the 1960s, court rulings allowed commercial banks to underwrite safe securities, such as commercial paper. In 1987, the Federal Reserve allowed commercial banks to provide investment banking services as long as this work produced less than 5 percent of total revenue. This limit was later raised to 10 percent and then 25 percent. Finally, in 1999 Congress passed the Gramm-Leach-Bliley Act, which fully repealed the separation of commercial banks and securities firms.

Consolidation in Commercial Banking

We've seen in Figure 8.1 that the number of U.S. commercial banks fell from 15,000 in 1984 to fewer than 7500 in 2007. Over the same period, the number of savings institutions fell from 3400 to 1200. Bank failures are one factor behind this decline. Loan defaults and other problems forced some banks to shut down in the late 1980s and early 1990s, as we detail in Chapters 9 and 10.

The primary factor, however, is bank consolidation: mergers of healthy banks. In a merger, two banks agree to combine their businesses, or one bank buys the other. The end of branching restrictions allowed mergers between banks in the same state, and the Riegle-Neal Act prompted a surge of interstate mergers.

Mergers have increased the concentration of the banking industry: assets have shifted from small banks to larger ones. Community banks held 22 percent of all commercial-bank assets in 1990, but only 11 percent in 2007. At the other end of the scale, in 1990 the 10 largest banks held 17 percent of total assets. In 2007, this figure was 40 percent.

Many of today's banks were created by a series of mergers. For example, Chemical Bank bought Manufacturers Hanover in 1991. Then, in 1996, Chase Manhattan Bank bought Chemical. In 2000, Chase Manhattan merged with JP Morgan to form JP Morgan Chase. Meanwhile, Banc One bought First Chicago Bank in 1998; JP Morgan Chase purchased Banc One in 2004.

A number of commercial banks responded quickly to the Gramm-Leach-Bliley Act. Some turned themselves into FHCs by creating subsidiaries that offer the services of securities firms. Others merged with existing securities firms and insurance companies. In 2007, there were 655 FHCs. Often their names are similar to those of the commercial banks they own. Citigroup, for example, is an FHC that owns Citibank and other financial institutions (see the upcoming case). JP Morgan Chase and Co. is an FHC whose holdings include JP Morgan Chase Bank.

The reasons for this consolidation are similar to those for geographic expansion. Empire building is a possible motive. So is diversification. With a mix of businesses, FHCs don't lose too much if one business does badly.

A financial holding company also benefits from **economies of scope**: it reduces costs by combining different activities. For example, a commercial bank must gather information about a firm to lend it money, and an investment bank must gather information to sell the firm's securities. If one institution provides both services, it gathers the information only once. Similarly, an FHC can combine the marketing of several products. The company can offer a customer bank accounts, mutual funds, and insurance at the same time.

Economies of scope Cost reductions from combining different activities

CASE STUDY

Citigroup

Citigroup (often shortened to "Citi" in its marketing) is the world's largest financial institution. In March 2008, it had assets of $2.2 trillion, $1.3 trillion held by Citibank and the rest by other units of the FHC. Citigroup has 200 million customer accounts in over 100 countries. It provides all the major services of securities firms, commercial banks, and finance companies, and it sells insurance.

History Citigroup was built through a series of mergers. Most were the work of one man, Sanford Weill, who had a vision of melding disparate businesses into a "financial supermarket." One biography of Weill is called *Tearing Down the Walls.*

In 1986, Weill became CEO of Commercial Credit, a failing finance company in Baltimore. He turned the company around and started buying other companies. In 1988, Commercial Credit bought the brokerage firm Smith Barney. In 1993, it bought Shearson, another brokerage, and Travelers Insurance. The conglomerate took the Travelers name. In 1997, Travelers bought Salomon Brothers, one of the largest investment banks.

At that point, Weill wanted to acquire a commercial bank. After unsuccessful talks with JP Morgan, he struck a deal to merge Travelers with Citicorp, a holding company that owned Citibank. The new conglomerate, established in 1998, was named Citigroup. At the time, the deal was the largest corporate merger in history. Initially, Weill and John Reed, the head of Citicorp, agreed to run Citigroup together. In 2000, however, the board of directors forced Reed out and made Weill the sole chairman and CEO.

The Travelers-Citicorp merger was surprising because it appeared to violate the Glass-Steagall Act. Lawyers for Travelers found a loophole: the act allowed the companies to merge as long as they separated again within a few years. Weill and Reed knew that Congress was considering proposals to repeal Glass-Steagall. They agreed on a temporary merger, gambling that the law would change so they could make the merger permanent. This strategy succeeded when Congress passed the Gramm-Leach-Bliley Act in 1999.

In the early 2000s, Citigroup grew through a series of acquisitions. One large purchase was Associates First Capital, a finance company specializing in subprime lending, which became CitiFinancial. Citigroup also bought commercial banks in California, Mexico, and Poland.

Why Was Citigroup Created? We've discussed several motives for consolidation of financial institutions: economies of scale and scope, diversification, and empire building. All appear relevant to the development of Citigroup.

In explaining his business strategy, Weill emphasized economies of scope. Citigroup is designed for "cross-selling," in which agents in one division sell the services of other divisions. Stockbrokers offer insurance policies to their customers, and insurance agents offer mutual funds.

Citigroup is diversified across industries and continents, which insulates it from setbacks in individual divisions. For example, Citigroup lost $2 billion in Argentina during the country's financial crisis of 2001–2002. Around the same time, Enron and WorldCom defaulted on large loans. Citigroup prospered in other areas, however, and its total profits remained high. In 2007, Citigroup lost $18 billion on securities tied to subprime mortgages (see Section 8.4). This debacle reduced profits significantly, but it didn't threaten the firm's survival.

When Sanford Weill's biographers discuss the creation of Citigroup, they emphasize his personal ambition. Weill's roots were modest—he was the son of immigrants in Brooklyn, NY—and he is proud of his rise to become *King of Capital* (another biography title). Weill earned more than $1 billion from 1993 to 2006, but reportedly money wasn't his main motivation: "It's just a way of keeping score," says one associate. Weill's drive to be number one was exemplified by his efforts to oust John Reed from Citigroup.*

The Prince Era Weill retired as CEO of Citigroup in 2003 and as chairman in 2006. He was replaced in both jobs by Charles Prince, a close associate since Weill began at Commercial Credit. Under Prince, Citigroup experienced a difficult period.

When Prince became CEO, he shifted Citigroup's strategy for growth. In Prince's view, Weill had pushed as far as possible in broadening the firm's scope through acquisitions. Prince said in 2004, "The only way we could do a transformational acquisition would be to buy Canada." He decided to seek "organic" growth: Citigroup would focus on expanding its existing businesses rather than buying new ones.

As part of this strategy, Prince opened hundreds of new branches of Citibank, many in places such as Boston where Citibank hadn't operated previously. Prince hoped to take deposits and loan business away from rivals such as Bank of America. Prince also expanded the presence of Citibank and CitiFinancial in foreign countries, including Brazil, India, Russia, and Korea.

This strategy did not prove very successful. Under Prince, Citigroup often reported disappointing levels of profits. Its stock price hovered around $50 from 2004 to early 2007, a period of rising stock prices at most banks. Analysts blamed Citigroup's problems on high costs, including the costs of building new branches. They also suggested that Citigroup was spreading itself too thin in expanding around the world. In many countries, the firm's operations were too small to benefit from economies of scale.

These problems caused many of Citigroup's shareholders to lose confidence in Prince. The last straw came in 2007, when Citigroup suffered its $18 billion loss on subprime mortgages and its stock fell below $30. The firm's board of directors forced Prince to resign in November 2007. The board appointed Vikram Pandit as the new CEO.

The text Web site links to Citigroup's annual reports, which provide updates on the firm's strategy.

* For more on Sanford Weill and the building of Citigroup, see *Tearing Down the Walls,* by Monica Langley, Free Press, 2003; *King of Capital,* by Amey Stone and Mike Brewster, Wiley, 2004; and Weill's autobiography, Sanford Weill and Judah S. Kraushaar, *The Real Deal: My Life in Business and Philanthropy,* Warner Books 2006.

8.3 SECURITIZATION

A bank is an institution that takes deposits and makes loans. Traditionally, banks have held the loans they make as assets, receiving a flow of income as the loans are repaid. Today, however, many loans are sold by banks and securitized; that is, the loans are transformed into securities that are traded in financial markets.

Figure 8.2 illustrates the securitization process. Banks and finance companies make loans and then sell them to a large financial institution. This institution gathers a pool of loans with similar characteristics; for example, a pool might be $100 million worth of mortgage loans to people with certain credit scores. The institution issues securities that entitle an owner to a share of the payments on the loan pool. Other financial institutions buy these securities, then trade them in secondary markets.

The Securitization Industry

Home mortgages are the type of loan most often securitized. The two largest issuers of these *mortgage-backed securities* are the Federal National Mortgage Association, commonly known as Fannie Mae, and the Federal Home Loan Corporation, or Freddie Mac. Fannie Mae and Freddie Mac are a type of institution called a **government-sponsored enterprise (GSE),** meaning they are private corporations with links to the government (we discuss GSEs in Section 8.5). Mortgage-backed securities are also issued by large investment banks such as Morgan Stanley.

Government-sponsored enterprise (GSE) Private corporation with links to the government

Fannie Mae issued the first mortgage-backed security in 1970. Securitization grew rapidly, and in 2007 over half of outstanding mortgage debt was securitized. Generally, Fannie Mae and Freddie Mac securitize only prime mortgages, the mortgages of people with good credit ratings. Securities issued by Fannie and Freddie are highly liquid: like stocks and bonds,

FIGURE 8.2 Securitization of Loans

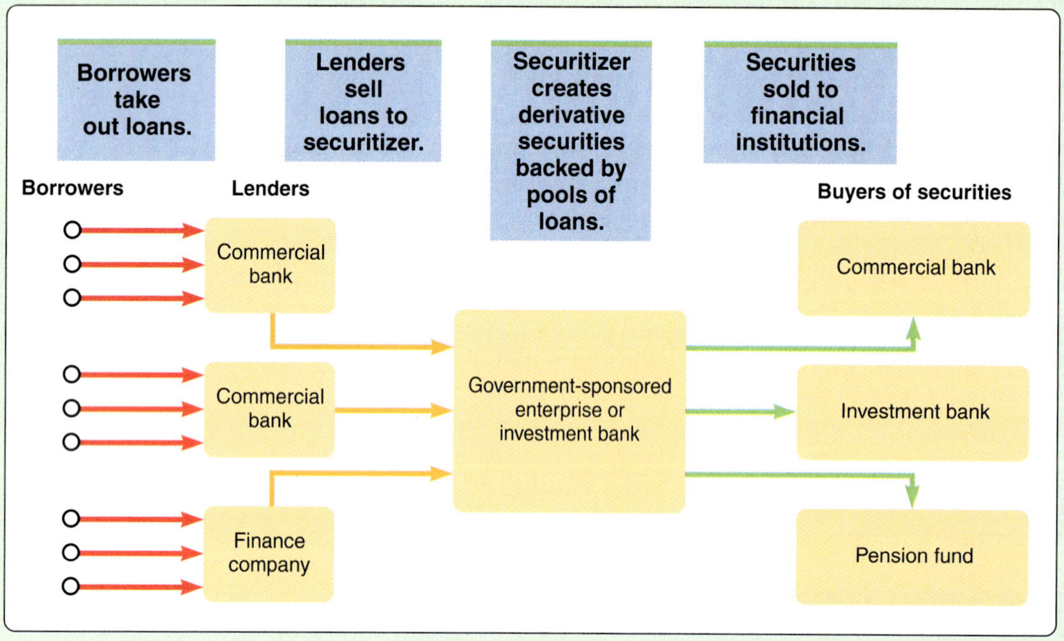

they are traded continuously on electronic exchanges. Investment banks issue securities backed by subprime mortgages; these securities are relatively risky and illiquid.

Since the 1990s, securitization has spread from mortgages to other types of loans, such as auto loans and credit card debt. Student loans are also securitized. Large providers of student loans, such as Citigroup, hold on to some of their loans and securitize others.

Why Securitization Occurs

Securitization occurs because banks want to sell loans, and because securities backed by bank loans are attractive to many institutions. Let's discuss the incentives for securitization, focusing on mortgage-backed securities.

Benefits for Banks Banks sell mortgages because it is risky to hold them. All mortgage loans carry some default risk. And the loans made by a particular bank may be poorly diversified, increasing risk. If the bank lends in one geographic area, for example, a downturn in the local economy can cause a large number of defaults. By selling loans, the bank shifts default risk to the ultimate holders of the loans.

From one point of view, selling loans might seem an odd practice. Why should a bank lend money in the first place if it plans to get rid of the loan? The answer is that the bank still performs its basic function of reducing asymmetric information. It uses its expertise to screen borrowers, design covenants, and set collateral (review Section 7.5). Because it does this work, a bank can sell a loan for more than the original amount it gave the borrower. In effect, the institution buying the loan pays the bank for reducing information problems. The bank earns a profit, while avoiding the default risk it would face if it held onto the loan.

Many banks both *sell* mortgage loans and *buy* mortgage-backed securities. In effect, they trade the relatively few loans they make for small pieces of many loans. They gain diversification, reducing risk. They also gain liquidity, as mortgage-backed securities can be sold more quickly than individual mortgages.

Demand for Mortgage-Backed Securities Many financial institutions buy the securities issued by Fannie Mae and Freddie Mac. Large purchasers include mutual funds and pension funds as well as banks. For these institutions, Fannie and Freddie's securities are attractive alternatives to bonds. The securities are highly liquid. They are also considered safe, because they are backed by loans to low-risk borrowers and because of Fannie and Freddie's links to the government. At the same time, the securities pay a bit more interest than other safe assets, such as Treasury bonds.

Securities backed by subprime mortgages are risky. They appeal to risk-taking financial institutions such as investment banks and hedge funds. As we discuss in an upcoming case study, many institutions have suffered losses on subprime mortgage-backed securities.

8.4 SUBPRIME LENDERS

Banks lend to millions of firms and individuals. Yet not everyone can borrow from a bank. Banks ration credit: they deny loans to people whose default risk appears high. This group includes people with low incomes or poor credit histories.

Government regulation increases this credit rationing. As we detail in Chapter 10, regulators seek to keep bank deposits safe. To that end, they discourage banks from lending to people with high default risk.

Such people often turn to subprime lenders, companies that specialize in high-risk loans. Subprime lenders include finance companies, payday lenders, pawnshops, and illegal loan sharks. Each type of lender has methods for coping with default risk, which are summarized in **Table 8.2.**

TABLE 8.2 Subprime Lenders

Type of Lender	How Lender Copes with Default Risk
Finance company	Credit scoring; high interest rates
Payday lender	Postdated checks; very high interest rates
Pawnshop	Very high collateral
Illegal loan shark	Very high interest rates; threats to defaulters

Finance Companies

As mentioned in Section 8.2, some finance companies specialize in subprime lending. Their loans include mortgages, auto loans, and personal loans. Examples of subprime lenders are Household Finance Corporation (HFC), Countrywide Financial, and CitiFinancial. Many of these companies are subsidiaries of financial holding companies that also own commercial banks. CitiFinancial, for example, is part of Citigroup, and HFC is part of the HSBC Group.

Subprime lending has grown rapidly since the 1990s, a trend that reflects the development of credit scoring. Asymmetric information is the reason that people with weak credit histories have trouble borrowing. Lenders fear that default risk is high, and they can't compensate by raising interest rates. High rates can backfire by worsening the problem of adverse selection. Credit scoring makes information more symmetric, reducing adverse selection. Lenders believe that credit scores are accurate measures of default risk. They adjust interest rates accordingly, charging higher rates to people with lower scores. With this approach, less credit rationing is needed.

The largest part of subprime lending is home mortgages. Finance companies provide mortgages to people with credit scores below the levels required by banks. They compensate for default risk with high interest rates, typically between two and five percentage points above the best mortgage rate. Often subprime lenders add fees when a mortgage is made.

Subprime mortgages grew from almost nothing in 1990 to 14 percent of all outstanding mortgages in 2007. These mortgages allowed people who previously couldn't get credit to buy homes. Partly because of subprime lending, the fraction of U.S. households owning homes rose from 64 percent in 1994 to a peak of 69 percent in 2004. Over the same period, many subprime lenders earned high profits. But then the story of subprime mortgages took a bad turn, as the next case study discusses.

CASE STUDY

The Subprime Mortgage Fiasco

Throughout 2007 and into 2008, the subprime mortgage crisis dominated the financial news. The crisis touched many people, from Wall Street executives who lost their jobs to low-income people who lost their homes. Let's examine the causes and effects of this episode.

Risky Lending In retrospect, the basic cause of the crisis is clear. Eager to increase business, finance companies made mortgage loans to people who were likely to have trouble paying them back. As we've discussed, lenders believed they could measure default risk with credit scores and adjust interest rates to compensate for this risk. A reliance on credit scores led lenders to neglect traditional safeguards against defaults.

As discussed in Section 7.5, traditional mortgages require substantial down payments. Subprime lenders reduced down payments and even offered mortgages with zero down. Lenders also loosened limits on the ratio of mortgage payments to borrowers' incomes. Formally, they kept these limits, but often with a "no documentation" policy: borrowers stated their incomes but weren't asked for proof such as pay stubs. Some people obtained mortgages by exaggerating their incomes.

Lenders also tempted borrowers with low introductory interest rates, often called *teaser rates.* In many mortgage contracts, the interest rate was

4 percent or less for the first two years. Then the interest rate jumped sharply, raising monthly payments on the mortgage. Many people took out loans they could afford initially but got in trouble when their payments rose.

In taking risks on subprime mortgages, borrowers and lenders were joined by investment banks. These institutions securitized subprime mortgages and bought many of the securities, as did hedge funds. Because the mortgages carried high interest rates, the securities they backed promised high returns—as long as default rates were moderate. Like the finance companies that made subprime loans, investment banks and hedge funds didn't foresee the crisis of 2007.

The Boom Period Risky mortgage lending didn't produce a crisis immediately. Subprime lending was profitable in the late 1990s and early 2000s, because default rates were moderate. As shown in **Figure 8.3,** the percentage of subprime borrowers who were behind on their mortgage payments was about 10 percent in 2000. This delinquency rate rose during the recession of 2001, but it was back down to 10 percent in 2004. In 2005, only 3 percent of subprime mortgages were in foreclosure, meaning the lender had given up on repayment and moved to seize the borrower's house. This was well above the 0.4 percent foreclosure rate for prime mortgages, but subprime interest rates were high enough to compensate.

FIGURE 8.3 The Subprime Mortgage Crisis

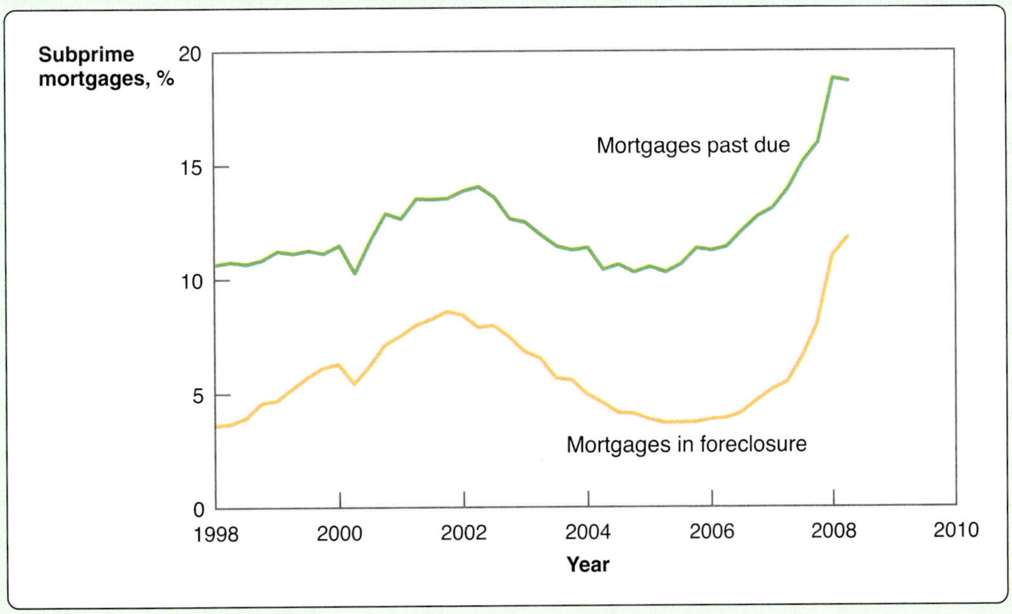

Starting in 2006, a rising fraction of subprime mortgage borrowers fell behind on their payments. Foreclosures on subprime mortgages also rose.

Source: Mortgage Bankers Association

Two factors held down defaults, one being interest rates. The recession of 2001 prompted the Federal Reserve to cut short-term rates and keep them low for several years. This policy reduced interest rates throughout the economy, including mortgage rates. As a result, people's mortgage payments didn't jump too sharply when teaser rates ended.

The other factor was rising house prices. The average U.S. house price more than doubled from 1997 to 2006. Arguably this increase was an asset-price bubble (review Section 3.4). In any case, rising prices made it easier for homeowners to cope with high mortgage payments. Someone short on cash could take out a second mortgage, as the higher value of his home gave him more collateral. Or he could sell the home for more than he paid for it, pay off his mortgage, and earn a capital gain.

The Crash The conditions sustaining the subprime boom eventually changed. The Fed raised interest rates over 2004 and 2005. House prices peaked in mid-2006 and started falling. At that point, many people found themselves with payments they couldn't afford and no way out. The delinquency rate on subprime mortgages started rising, reaching 19 percent in mid-2008 (Figure 8.3). The foreclosure rate was 12 percent, more than three times the level two years before, and appeared to be headed higher.

At the end of 2007, studies predicted that the subprime crisis would ultimately cost a million mortgage holders their homes. It was also costly for mortgage lenders. Foreclosure is a lengthy and expensive legal process, and by the time houses are seized they are often worth less than the amounts owed on them. In 2007, the subprime crisis forced two large finance companies, Ameriquest and New Century Financial, into bankruptcy.

As subprime defaults rose, the prices of securities backed by subprime mortgages plummeted. By the end of 2007, losses on these securities exceeded $1 billion at 14 financial institutions. Citigroup's losses of $18 billion were the largest, and Merrill Lynch lost $8 billion. Citigroup's CEO, Charles Prince, and Merrill's CEO, Stanley O'Neal, were both fired.

▶ Prince and O'Neal suffered career setbacks when they lost their jobs, but not financial hardship. O'Neal received a severance package of about $160 million. Prince received a relatively paltry $40 million, but Citigroup threw in an office, administrative assistant, car, and driver for as long as he remained unemployed.

The investment bank Bear Stearns lost $3 billion on securities backed by subprime mortgages and almost went bankrupt. In March 2008, the Federal Reserve intervened to prevent this outcome, arranging a takeover of Bear by JP Morgan Chase. Chapter 18 discusses this action and other responses of the Fed to the subprime crisis.

Online Case Study: An Update on the Mortgage Crisis

Payday Lenders

Payday lender Company that provides cash in return for a postdated check

Payday lenders are companies that make small loans to people who need cash urgently. A typical loan is a few hundred dollars for a few weeks. Some payday lenders are local businesses with a single office; others, such as Advance America and ACE Cash Express, have outlets around the country.

To borrow from a payday lender, a customer writes a check with some future date on it—often the next payday. The check covers the amount of the loan plus a fee. The lender gets repaid by cashing the check on the designated day, unless the borrower repays the loan with cash or pays another fee to extend the loan.

Unlike banks, payday lenders gather little information about borrowers. They lend to anyone with a checking account and a pay stub to prove employment. Instead of screening borrowers, payday lenders rely on the post-dated checks to reduce defaults. A check is written for a day when funds are likely to be available. In addition, bounced-check fees at a borrower's bank encourage her to make sure the check clears.

Payday lenders also compensate for default risk with *very* high interest rates. A common fee is 15 percent of the loan amount: for $200 in cash, you write a check for $230. For a four-week loan, this fee is equivalent to an annual interest rate of 515 percent. Surveys suggest that the average annual rate on payday loans is around 400 percent.

Like subprime mortgages, payday lending began in the 1990s and grew rapidly. As of 2005, payday lenders had 23,000 offices in the United States, most located in low-income areas. Studies estimate that about 15 percent of U.S. households have borrowed from payday lenders.

Legal changes have spurred this type of lending. Most states have **usury laws** that set maximum interest rates, often around 40 percent per year. In the 1990s, however, payday lenders lobbied state legislatures to exempt them from usury laws. They argued that their loans help people in emergencies and that high interest rates are needed to offset default risk. Many legislatures agreed to legalize very high rates.

Usury law Legal limit on interest rates

CASE STUDY

Is Payday Lending Predatory?

Payday lenders say their industry benefits consumers. While expensive, payday loans can stave off disaster when people are short of cash. They can be used, for example, to pay rent and avoid eviction. The Community Financial Services Association, an organization of payday lenders, says their loans are a "convenient and practical short-term credit option." On its Web site, Advance America says "when your wallet's coming up short, we're here for you."

Yet payday lenders are criticized by advocates for consumers and the poor, and they frequently receive negative attention in the media. Critics allege that payday lenders practice **predatory lending**: they take unfair advantage of borrowers who are poor and uninformed about financial matters. According to this view, default rates are not high enough to justify the three-digit interest rates on payday loans. And people who take out the loans often get into financial trouble.

Predatory lending Unfair lending practices aimed at poor and uninformed borrowers

Payday loans are dangerous because a borrower may still be short on cash when his loan is due. In this situation, some people make an interest payment but take out a new loan to cover their initial borrowing. Others take out a larger loan to "roll over" both the initial loan and the interest.

Sometimes a loan is rolled over again and again. With high interest rates, the borrower quickly runs up a large debt.

Bloomberg News published an article in 2004 highlighting the case of Jason Withrow, a Navy petty officer in Georgia.* In July 2003, at age 25, Withrow was struck by a car while on sentry duty. His back injured, he had to quit a part-time job unloading beer kegs at the base liquor store. He ran short of cash to support his wife, a nursing student, and their daughter.

Withrow turned to a payday lender near his base that lent him $300 for a $90 fee. Two weeks later he rolled over the loan. Over time Withrow paid back part of his debt, but kept borrowing to cover the rest. By February 2004, he had borrowed from four payday lenders and paid about $5000 in interest—and still owed $1800. At that point he found help at a charity, the Navy-Marine Relief Society, which gave him an interest-free loan to settle his accounts.

The *New York Times* reported in 2006 on payday lending in Gallup, New Mexico.† Gallup, a poor town near a Navajo reservation, has 22,000 residents and 40 payday lenders. Many people are caught in "debt traps" like Jason Withrow was. The owner of a Gallup restaurant told the *Times* that he typically is under court order to garnish the wages of around a dozen employees with debts to payday lenders.

In addition to high interest rates, critics of payday lending complain about aggressive debt-collection techniques. Some lenders have threatened defaulters with criminal prosecution for writing bad checks. In one egregious case, in Tacoma, WA in the early 2000s, this message was delivered by collectors posing as agents of a fictitious law-enforcement agency. The collectors also called borrowers' children, telling them "your Mommy and Daddy are going to jail."

Stories such as these have led some states to reconsider their lending laws. In 1997, North Carolina allowed payday lending for four years, but the legislature rejected an extension in 2001. In 2004, Georgia limited annual interest rates to 60 percent, driving payday lenders out of the state. Payday lending is also absent in 12 states, mostly in the Northeast, that never created exceptions to usury laws.

The U.S. Congress has also addressed payday lending—specifically, lending to military personnel. In the past, many customers of payday lenders were young service members like Petty Officer Withrow, people with modest incomes and limited financial experience. The Defense Department complained that debts distracted soldiers and sailors from their duties and jeopardized security clearances. In 2006 Congress responded with a 36 percent interest-rate cap on loans to service members. President Bush signed this legislation, ending payday lending to the military.

For a harsh critique of payday lending, link through the text Web site to the site of the Center for Responsible Lending. For the other side of the story, see the site of the Community Financial Services Association, the lenders' organization.

* The Bloomberg article discussed in this case is "JP Morgan, Banks Back Lenders Luring Poor with 780 Percent Rates," November 23, 2004, www.bloomberg.com. The article highlights the fact that prestigious banks provide funds to payday lenders.

† The *New York Times* article is Erick Eckholm, "Seductively Easy, Payday Loans Often Snowball," *New York Times*, December 23, 2006.

Pawnshops

Pawnshop Small lender that holds an item of value as collateral

Like a payday lender, a **pawnshop** is a source of small, short-term loans. It protects against default with very high collateral. A borrower deposits an item he owns and receives a loan for 30–50 percent of the resale value. The pawnshop has the right to sell the collateral if the loan is not repaid.

Among the roughly 13,000 pawnshops in the United States, some are independent businesses and others belong to national chains such as Cash America (which also offers payday loans). A pawnshop's typical loan is $75–$100 for 60 or 90 days. Common collateral includes jewelry, televisions, and—in some states—guns. About 80 percent of borrowers repay their loans and get back the collateral.

Pawnshops appeared in Europe in the fifteenth century, and they have existed in the United States since colonial times. The industry grew rapidly from the 1970s to the 1990s. Since then business has leveled off, as pawnbrokers compete with payday lenders.

A variation on pawnshop lending is an *auto title loan*. A borrower pledges her car as collateral and turns over the title. She can keep using the car as long as she makes her loan payments. However, she must give the lender a car key so the collateral can be seized if she defaults.

Illegal Loan Sharks

Loan shark Lender that violates usury laws and collects debts through illegal means

Another source of subprime loans is illegal **loan sharks.** These lenders charge interest rates that violate usury laws. Loan-sharking is a traditional business of organized crime.

Loan sharks' disregard for the law helps them cope with default risk. They can encourage repayment with threats of violence. They can seize defaulters' property without the trouble of getting a court judgment.

Yet loan-sharking is a declining industry. Many customers have switched to legal payday lenders or pawnshops. Today loan sharks operate mainly in immigrant communities. They sometimes require immigration papers as collateral for loans.

The last organized-crime figure convicted of loan-sharking was Nicodemo Scarfo, Jr., of Philadelphia. In 2002, he was sentenced to 33 months in prison for charging an interest rate of 152 percent. Scarfo's defenders point out that he charged less than most payday lenders.

8.5 GOVERNMENT'S ROLE IN LENDING

Throughout this book, we've seen that asymmetric information impedes lending. People and firms may have productive uses for funds but be unable to borrow because lenders lack information about them. Banks reduce this problem by screening and monitoring borrowers, and subprime lenders address the problem in a variety of ways. Yet no lender has a perfect solution to the asymmetric-information problem. The financial system may fail to channel funds to good borrowers.

This market failure may justify government intervention in the financial system. Section 7.4 discussed the regulation of securities markets.

Governments also intervene in banking to help people and firms who might have trouble getting loans. In the United States, policies focus on several kinds of borrowers: home buyers, small businesses, students, and residents of low-income neighborhoods.

In most cases the government doesn't lend its own money. Instead, its policies encourage lending by private banks. We'll discuss the main U.S. policies and then examine those of other countries. Many foreign governments own banks and therefore control lending directly.

Mortgage Agencies

Owning a home is often called "the American Dream," and the U.S. government has long sought to encourage home ownership. As part of this policy, the government created Fannie Mae and Freddie Mac, the mortgage agencies we introduced in Section 8.3. Fannie Mae was established in 1938 as part of President Franklin Roosevelt's New Deal, and Freddie Mac was established in 1970.

Fannie and Freddie raise funds by issuing bonds and use the funds to purchase mortgages. In the days before securitization, these agencies held onto all the mortgages they bought. Now they securitize and sell around half of the mortgages and hold the rest (either by holding the original mortgages or by creating mortgage-backed securities and holding those).

Fannie and Freddie's activities raise the supply of mortgage loans. Banks are more willing to lend because they can sell their loans, eliminating default risk. And when banks sell mortgages, they receive funds they can use for new mortgages. With more mortgages available, more people can buy homes.

As mentioned earlier, Fannie Mae and Freddie Mac are an unusual kind of institution called a *government-sponsored enterprise* (GSE). They are private, profit-making corporations, with stocks traded on the New York Stock Exchange. Yet they have links to the government. The U.S. president appoints some of the directors of Fannie and Freddie. In addition, these institutions are allowed to borrow from the Treasury, which most companies can't do.

Fannie and Freddie have grown rapidly over time and now buy more than half of all U.S. mortgages. In 2007, the total debt of the two institutions was $1.5 trillion (for comparison, the debt of the U.S. government was $5 trillion). For many years, Fannie and Freddie produced high profits for their stockholders.

This success reflected Fannie and Freddie's status as GSEs. In theory, a GSE can go bankrupt and default on its bonds, like any private company. In practice, people in financial markets have long believed that the government stands behind GSEs and will pay off their debts if necessary. This means that GSE bonds carry little or no default risk, and therefore pay lower interest rates than bonds from other financial institutions. Fannie and Freddie prospered for a long time because they could raise funds cheaply.

In 2008, the fortunes of the GSEs changed dramatically. While Fannie and Freddie securitize only prime mortgages, they purchase subprime mortgages and subprime mortgage-backed securities issued by investment banks. The subprime crisis that started in 2007 caused mounting losses at the GSEs, and people began to question their survival.

In September 2008, as this book was going to press, the government took dramatic action: it placed Fannie Mae and Freddie Mac under *conservatorship.* Technically the companies remained private, but government regulators took control of their operations. This arrangement was meant to be temporary, and a debate began about Fannie and Freddie's future—whether they should be private firms, part of the government, or something in between.

Online Case Study: An Update on the Mortgage Crisis

Loan Guarantees

The government encourages certain types of lending through **loan guarantees.** In this arrangement, a bank makes a loan and the government agrees to pay it off if the borrower defaults. Essentially, the government provides insurance to the bank, making the bank more willing to lend. The bank pays a fee for this guarantee, typically one-half or one percent of the loan amount. However, guarantee programs usually cost the government money. It pays out more to cover defaults than it receives in fees.

Loan guarantee Government promise to pay off a loan if the borrower defaults

Once again, housing is a focus of policy. The Veteran's Administration guarantees mortgages for people who have served in the military. The Federal Home Administration (FHA) guarantees mortgages for low-income people. (In this case, borrowers must pay substantial fees.) Overall, about ten percent of U.S. mortgages were guaranteed by the government in 2007.

The government also guarantees business loans through the Small Business Administration (SBA). A company qualifies for this program if it is "small," which the SBA defines for each industry. For example, a furniture manufacturer qualifies if it has fewer than 500 employees. The rationale for the SBA program rests on the problem of asymmetric information. As noted in Section 7.5, this problem is more severe for small firms than for large firms. Lenders may shy away from small businesses because they can't judge default risk. SBA loan guarantees reduce this problem.

However, some economists criticize the SBA. They point out that banks reduce the asymmetric-information problem through screening and monitoring. In their view, banks do well enough that promising businesses can get loans without government help. According to the American Enterprise Institute, a conservative think tank, spending by the SBA is simply a "wasteful, politically-motivated subsidy."

The government also guarantees student loans. These guarantees, too, have caused controversy. As a student, you may have a special interest in this topic, so let's discuss it in detail.

CASE STUDY

Student Loans

Most college students must borrow to finance their education. Borrowing can be difficult, as students typically have low incomes and short credit histories. The U.S. government addresses this problem with student loan programs.

Student loans are administered by the U.S. Department of Education. As of 2007, the department oversaw about $400 billion in outstanding loans. The majority of these loans were *Stafford Loans* to undergraduate and graduate students. Other loans included *PLUS Loans* to the parents of undergraduates.

▶These figures apply to students who are dependents of their parents. Financially independent students can borrow larger amounts.

As of the 2008–09 academic year, most college freshmen could borrow up to $5500 under the Stafford program. Sophomores could borrow $6500 and juniors and seniors could borrow $7500. Repayment of a loan is usually spread over 10 years, starting 6 months after the borrower leaves school.

A student who demonstrates financial need receives "subsidized" Stafford Loans. The interest rate is 6.0 percent and the government pays the interest for the period before the student starts payments. A student who does not demonstrate need receives unsubsidized loans. In this case, the interest rate is 6.8 percent and interest for the prepayment period is added to the student's debt.

Who Lends? Students receive Stafford Loans through two different programs. In one, the Ford Direct Loan Program, the government plays the role of a bank. It lends its funds to students and receives their loan payments.

The other loan program is the Federal Family Education Loan (FFEL) Program. FFEL loans are made by private banks and finance companies. The government guarantees these loans against default, and it sometimes pays part of the interest. Borrowers pay the same rate as in the Direct Loan program, while lenders are promised a minimum rate tied to the commercial paper rate. If the borrowers' rate is below the lenders' minimum, the government pays the difference.

The largest provider of FFEL loans is the Student Loan Marketing Association, or Sallie Mae. This company was originally a government-sponsored enterprise, but it cut all ties to the government in 2004. In 2007, Sallie Mae had $163 billion in outstanding student loans. Citibank is the second-largest provider, with loans of $37 billion in 2007.

Each college chooses whether its students receive funds through the Direct Loan program or the FFEL program. Currently about 3/4 choose FFEL. Students get the same deal either way, but the government bears different costs. People disagree about which program is better. Some members of Congress advocate expanding Direct Loans and eliminating FFEL, and others advocate the reverse. Economic conservatives favor the FFEL program because it involves private lenders. They believe private firms are better than the government at most economic activities, including lending. They cite the poor performance of government-owned banks in other countries. Economic liberals dislike the FFEL program because lenders receive payments from the government. If all loans were direct, these subsidies would disappear. The savings could be used to reduce the interest rates charged to students.

Politics and Interest Rates Interest rates on student loans have fluctuated in recent years. These changes reflect political battles over the loan program.

In 2005, the interest rate on all Stafford Loans was 4.7 percent. In that year, however, Congress passed the Deficit Reduction Act. The act reduced government spending in several areas, but the largest cuts were in student loan programs. Under the act, the interest rate on Stafford Loans rose to 6.8 percent in 2006. With students paying more, the loan program became less expensive for the government.

The Deficit Reduction Act was controversial, with most Democrats opposed. It passed the House of Representatives by two votes and passed the Senate when Vice President Cheney broke a tie. In 2007, the Democrats gained control of Congress and partly reversed the Deficit Reduction Act. They did so with the College Cost Reduction and Access Act (CCRAA), which President Bush signed in September 2007.

A senior nursing student and her mother review loan options in the financial aid office of Clemson University.

AP Photo/Mary Ann Chastain

The CCRAA cuts interest rates on some but not all Stafford Loans—the subsidized loans for students with financial need. Rates on these loans are falling in several steps and will end up at 3.4 percent in 2011. The interest rate on unsubsidized loans will stay at the current level of 6.8 percent. Another provision of the CCRAA ties payments on student loans to borrowers' incomes. Starting in July 2009, no one will be required to pay more than 15 percent of after-tax income for Stafford Loans. When payments are reduced under this rule, the unpaid amount will be added to the loan balance—but any balance remaining after 25 years will be forgiven.

The CCRAA will *not* increase the cost of student loans to the government. Instead, lower interest payments from students will be offset by smaller subsidies to lenders. Subsidies will fall because the CCRAA reduces the interest rates guaranteed to lenders under the FFEL program.

Lenders have complained vigorously about the reduced subsidies. They argue that some institutions will be forced out of the student loan business, reducing the availability of loans. The president of the Consumer Bankers Association predicts the CCRAA will "come to be viewed as irresponsible legislation that undermined rather than expanded college opportunity."

Others scoff at this concern. In arguing for the CCRAA, an official of the American Association of Collegiate Registrars said student loans are "a mundane business that has been turned into a gold mine by a handful of companies." Senator Edward Kennedy, the chair of the Senate Education Committee, says the CCRAA "restores the balance to this grossly unfair student loan system by directing funds to the students, not to the banks."

The Community Reinvestment Act

People in low-income areas can have trouble getting bank loans. Until the 1970s, some banks practiced *redlining:* they marked areas on a map (usually outlined in red ink) where they wouldn't lend. People in these areas were denied credit regardless of their individual characteristics.

The reasons for redlining are debatable. It might be rational to think that loans in low-income areas are risky. On the other hand, lenders could be unfairly prejudiced against certain neighborhoods. Many redlined areas were predominantly African-American, so racial discrimination could be a factor.

Community Reinvestment Act (CRA) 1977 law requiring banks to lend in low-income areas

Either way, a scarcity of bank loans held back communities' economic development. In 1977, Congress addressed this problem with the **Community Reinvestment Act (CRA),** which requires banks to lend in poor areas. The CRA encourages loans for mortgages, small businesses, and "community development" projects such as job training and health care.

The government monitors banks to enforce the CRA. Each bank is examined every 3–5 years. Regulators determine the broad geographic area where a bank should lend, based on branch locations and where depositors live. Then they examine lending in the low-income parts of the area.

A standard CRA exam is a big project. The bank must write a report on its efforts to comply with the act. It must show that its advertising and loan screening don't favor one neighborhood over another. The bank must also submit data on individual loans, showing borrowers' incomes and residences. Examiners then visit the bank to interview the staff and study records. They also seek comments on the bank from local governments and community organizations. At the end of this process, the bank receives a grade on its CRA lending. Grades range from "outstanding" to "substantially not in compliance." A low grade creates bad publicity. In addition, regulators may forbid the bank to open new branches or merge with another bank.

Opinions vary on the CRA's effects. In recent years more than 95 percent of banks have received grades of "outstanding" or "satisfactory." Banks say they are meeting the goals of the act. But some community groups allege grade inflation. They say banks still don't do enough lending in low-income areas.

Banks complain that CRA exams take too much of their managers' time. In response, the government modified the exams in 2005. Community banks (those with assets below $1 billion) are eligible for "streamlined" exams with less paperwork. Banks welcomed this change, but critics say it weakens enforcement of the CRA.

Government-Owned Banks

▶ The United States has one bank that is fully government-owned: the Bank of North Dakota, in Bismarck, is owned by the state government.

In the United States, banks are private, profit-making corporations. In many other countries, the government owns banks. Government officials decide who gets loans and what interest rates they pay. In most European countries, the government owns some banks but the majority are private. In many developing countries, most or all banks are government-owned. Examples include China, India, Brazil, and most African countries.

Most economists oppose government ownership of banks. They believe that private banks are best at channeling funds to productive uses. Government bankers make wasteful loans to people with political connections. Sometimes they take bribes.

Several studies have compared countries with different levels of government bank ownership. They find that government ownership reduces lending to the most productive firms. The quality of investment suffers, leading to lower economic growth.

▶These findings come largely from studies at the World Bank. See Section 1.5 for more on World Bank research on banking and economic growth.

China exemplifies the problems with government-owned banks. Four such institutions dominate Chinese banking. These banks report high default rates on loans, which suggest that their lending is imprudent. And critics allege that the banks underreport defaults, meaning the true problem is worse. Since 2000, China's banks have also suffered a series of corruption scandals, with numerous officials jailed for embezzlement or bribery. China's economic growth has been high since the 1990s, but its banking problems could threaten future growth.

Summary

8.1 Types of Banks

- Commercial banks take deposits and make loans. U.S. commercial banks include a handful of money-center banks, hundreds of regional and super-regional banks, and thousands of community banks that operate in small geographic areas.
- Thrift institutions also take deposits and make loans. Thrifts include savings institutions, which lend largely for home mortgages, and credit unions, which are nonprofit banks owned by their depositors.
- Finance companies make loans but do *not* take deposits. They raise funds by issuing bonds and borrowing from banks.

8.2 Dispersion and Consolidation

- The United States has far more banks than other countries, a legacy of political battles in the nineteenth and early twentieth centuries. Populist opposition to large banks produced branching restrictions and a ban on interstate banking.
- States eliminated branching restrictions in the 1970s and 1980s, and Congress allowed interstate banking in 1994. These changes produced a merger wave that halved the number of commercial banks between 1984 and 2007. Possible motives for mergers include economies of scale, diversification, and empire building.
- U.S. banks have expanded their operations to countries around the world. Foreign branches of U.S. banks accept both deposits of local currency and deposits of dollars.
- The Glass-Steagall Act of 1933 forbade commercial banks to merge with other kinds of financial institutions. Glass-Steagall was repealed in 1999, allowing the creation of financial holding companies that combine banks, securities firms, and insurance companies. The largest FHC is Citigroup, built by Sanford Weill through a series of mergers.

8.3 Securitization

- Many bank loans are securitized. A financial institution buys loans, pools them together, and issues securities entitling owners to shares of the payments on the loan pool.
- Securitization is most common for home mortgages. The largest issuers of mortgage-backed securities are Fannie Mae and Freddie Mac, which securitize prime mortgages. Investment banks securitize subprime mortgages.
- Securitization allows banks to eliminate default risk on their loans. Many financial institutions buy securities issued by Fannie Mae and Freddie Mac, which are liquid and considered safe. Securities backed by subprime mortgages are bought by risk-taking institutions such as hedge funds and investment banks.

8.4 Subprime Lenders

- People with low incomes or poor credit histories have trouble getting bank loans. They borrow from subprime lenders of various types.

- Many finance companies specialize in subprime lending. They use credit scores to measure borrowers' default risk and adjust interest rates to offset this risk.
- In the 1990s and early 2000s, subprime lenders loosened their standards for approving mortgages. The ultimate result was a sharp rise in mortgage defaults beginning in 2006. Many people lost their homes, finance companies went bankrupt, and holders of subprime-mortgage-backed securities suffered large losses.
- Payday lenders make small, short-term loans at very high interest rates. Advocates for consumers and the poor accuse these companies of predatory lending, arguing that customers get into financial trouble through repeated borrowing.
- Pawnshops also make small, short-term loans. They address default risk by requiring an item of value, such as jewelry, as collateral.
- Loan sharks charge very high interest rates and use illegal means, such as threats of violence, to ensure repayment. Loan sharking has declined since the 1990s because of competition from legal payday lenders.

8.5 Government's Role in Lending

- The U.S. government created Fannie Mae and Freddie Mac to increase the supply of mortgage loans. These institutions are government-sponsored enterprises, private corporations with links to the government. They issue bonds, purchase mortgages, and securitize and sell some of the mortgages.
- The government uses loan guarantees to encourage lending to certain types of borrowers, including small businesses and students.
- Most student loans are Stafford Loans. Some Stafford Loans are made directly by the government. Others are made by banks and finance companies, with the government providing subsidies and loan guarantees. Interest rates on Stafford Loans have fluctuated as Congress changes funding for the program and the subsidies to lenders.
- The Community Reinvestment Act requires banks to lend in low-income neighborhoods.
- In many countries, the government owns some or all banks. Most economists think that government-owned banks do a poor job of allocating funds, harming economic growth.

Key Terms

bank charter, p. 224
community bank, p. 222
Community Reinvestment Act (CRA), p. 244
credit union, p. 222
economies of scope, p. 229
Eurodollars, p. 228
finance company, p. 223
financial holding company (FHC), p. 228
government-sponsored enterprise (GSE), p. 231
loan guarantee, p. 241
loan shark, p. 239
money-center bank, p. 221
national bank, p. 225
pawnshop, p. 239
payday lender, p. 236
predatory lending, p. 237
regional bank, p. 221
savings institution, p. 222
securitization, p. 219
state bank, p. 225
subprime lender, p. 220
superregional bank, p. 221
thrift institutions, p. 222
usury law, p. 237

Questions and Problems

1. HSBC has $1 trillion in assets and operates in about 100 countries. It calls itself "the world's local bank." What business strategies does this phrase suggest? Why might these strategies be successful?

2. Suppose that Melvin's Bank purchases Gertrude's Bank, making Gertrude a subsidiary of Melvin. Does this acquisition benefit the stockholders of Melvin's Bank? Does the answer depend on the motives for the purchase? Explain. (*Hint:* Review the motives for bank consolidation discussed in Section 8.2.)

3. Securitization has spread from mortgages to student loans and credit card debt. However, few loans to businesses have been securitized. Explain why.

4. Finance companies can make riskier loans than banks because they face fewer government regulations. Why does the government regulate finance companies more lightly than banks? (*Hint:* How does each type of institution raise funds?)

5. Suppose that loan sharks propose legislation to promote their industry. They want a legal right to break the kneecaps of loan defaulters.
   a. Suppose you were hired as a lobbyist for the loan sharks. What arguments could you make to support their proposal?
   b. How would you respond to these arguments if you oppose kneecap breaking?

6. Consider the example in Chapter 7 of two firms that want to issue bonds (see Figure 7.2). Assume as before that a firm makes the promised payment on a bond only if its project succeeds.
   a. Suppose the government guarantees the firms' bonds: it makes the promised payment if either firm defaults. Can both firms sell bonds? What payments must they promise?
   b. What is the average cost to the government of guaranteeing a bond, assuming it does so for each firm?
   c. What is the average profit on an investment project, assuming both firms finance their projects with government-guaranteed bonds?
   d. Which is higher, the average cost of a bond guarantee (part (b)) or the average profit on a project (part (c))? In light of this comparison, do the guarantees promote economic efficiency? Explain why or why not. (*Hint:* How do the guarantees affect the adverse selection problem?)

Online and Data Questions

www.worthpublishers.com/ball

7. The text Web site provides data on 82 countries from a 2002 study on government bank ownership. For each country, the data include (a) the percentage of bank assets at government-owned banks in 1970, (b) the average growth rate of bank loans as a percentage of GDP from 1960 to 1995, and (c) the average growth rate of real GDP per person from 1960 to 1995.
   a. Make a graph with variable (a) on the horizontal axis and variable (b) on the vertical axis and plot each country. What might explain the relationship between these variables?
   b. Make a graph with (a) on the horizontal axis and (c) on the vertical axis. What might explain the relationship between these variables?

8. Many states allow payday lending but impose restrictions on the practice. For example, a state may limit the amount someone can borrow or the number of times a loan can be rolled over. Find out whether payday lending is legal in your state, and if so, what restrictions exist. How stringent are these restrictions compared to those in other states?

9. The Web site of the Community Financial Services Association, the payday lenders' organization, has a page on "Myths and Realities" about payday lending. Do you agree with the CFSA about what's a myth and what's reality? Do some research to answer this question, starting with the CFSA site and that of the Center for Responsible Lending (both linked to the text Web site).

10. What are the current interest rates on 1-year certificates of deposit at a commercial bank and a credit union located near you? Is one institution's rate higher than the other's? What might explain the difference?

11. Find out whether your college offers Stafford Loans through the Direct Loan Program or the FFEL Program. Ask a financial aid officer to explain the college's choice.

The Business of Banking

- 9.1 BANKS' BALANCE SHEETS
- 9.2 OFF-BALANCE-SHEET ACTIVITIES
- 9.3 HOW BANKS MAKE PROFITS
- 9.4 THE EVOLVING PURSUIT OF PROFITS
- 9.5 MANAGING RISK
- 9.6 INSOLVENCY

April 6, 1998: Sanford Weill, CEO of Travelers Group, on his way to the press conference announcing the merger of his firm with Citicorp. The merger created Citigroup, the world's largest financial institution. In 2000, Weill became chairman and CEO of Citigroup.

Perhaps one day you will be president of a commercial bank. You probably have some idea what this job will be like. You'll dress well and have a nice office. Your salary will be high. But what exactly will you do to earn this salary?

Like the head of any business, you will try to make profits. As a banker, you earn profits by accepting deposits and lending them out at higher interest rates than you pay. You can add to these profits through other activities, such as currency dealing or speculating on derivatives.

Your job will be challenging, because banking is a risky business. If things go wrong, your bank will lose money. Losses can arise for many reasons, including defaults on loans, large withdrawals by depositors, changes in interest rates, and slowdowns in the general economy. Your bank might lose so much that it is forced out of business, costing you your job.

This chapter discusses the business of banking. It analyzes banks' strategies for raising funds and using them to make profits. We also discuss banks' efforts to contain risk. We will see examples of both successes and failures.

Banking is a rapidly changing business. In recent decades, banks have lost some traditional sources of profits while gaining new opportunities. These changes have arisen from new technologies, changes in government regulations, and the growth of financial markets. We will see how banks have responded to these developments and the state of the business today.

9.1 BANKS' BALANCE SHEETS

Liabilities Amounts of money owed to others

Balance sheet Financial statement that summarizes an entity's assets, liabilities, and net worth at a given date

Net worth (*equity* or *capital*) Difference between assets and liabilities

Remember the definition of a bank: it is a financial institution that accepts deposits and makes loans. Loans are assets of the bank and one of the uses it makes of its funds. They produce a flow of income in the form of interest payments. Deposits are **liabilities** of the bank—amounts the bank owes to others—and one source of its funds. If you have $100 in a checking account, the bank owes you $100.

Banks have other assets besides loans, and other liabilities besides deposits. A bank's assets and liabilities are summarized in a statement called a **balance sheet,** which captures the bank's financial condition at a given date. The balance sheet lists the bank's assets on the left side and its liabilities on the right.

The right side of the balance sheet also includes the bank's **net worth,** defined as

$$\text{net worth} = \text{assets} - \text{liabilities}$$

A bank's net worth is also called *equity* or *capital.* It is the level of assets the bank would have if it paid off all its liabilities.

Each individual bank maintains a balance sheet. The combined assets and liabilities for a group of banks can be shown in a *consolidated balance sheet.* **Table 9.1** is a consolidated balance sheet for all U.S. commercial banks on March 31, 2008. The total assets of these banks were $11.2 tril-

TABLE 9.1 Consolidated Balance Sheet, U.S. Commercial Banks

On March 31, 2008
(Billions of Dollars)

Assets		Liabilities and Net Worth	
Cash Items	$302.9	Checking Deposits	$612.8
Reserves (Vault Cash + Deposits at Fed)		Nontransaction Deposits	6,260.6
Deposits at Other Banks		Savings Deposits	
In Process of Collection		Small Time Deposits	
		Large Time Deposits	
Securities	2,576.8	Borrowings	2,305.6
Loans	7,282.5	Other Liabilities†	848.4
Other Assets*	1,019.6	Net worth	1,154.4
Total	$11,181.8	Total	$11,181.8

* Category includes miscellaneous items such as collateral seized from loan defaulters and the value of banks' buildings and equipment.

† Category includes miscellaneous items such as taxes due to the government and dividends due to stockholders.

lion, and total liabilities were \$10.0 trillion. Net worth was \$1.2 trillion (= \$11.2 trillion − \$10.0 trillion).

The balance sheet splits banks' assets and liabilities into several categories. A central part of bankers' jobs is determining the levels of these different items.

Liabilities and Net Worth

We begin with the liabilities side of the balance sheet (the right side of Table 9.1). When banks raise funds, they incur liabilities of several types to the people or firms that provide the funds. The major items are checking deposits, nontransaction deposits, and borrowings.

Checking Deposits This category covers deposits that customers use to purchase goods and services. People spend these deposits by writing checks, swiping debit cards, and authorizing electronic payments. Checking deposits are part of the narrow measure of the money supply, M1 (review Section 2.3).

Some checking accounts pay no interest. Others, called *NOW accounts,* pay low interest rates. (NOW stands for negotiable order of withdrawal.) NOW accounts usually have higher fees or minimum balances than zero-interest accounts.

In March 2008, checking deposits comprised only 6 percent of total bank liabilities. Because of low interest rates, few people hold large amounts of wealth in checking accounts.

Nontransaction Deposits These deposits *cannot* be spent directly with checks or debit cards. However, they pay higher interest rates than checking deposits. Nontransaction deposits include both savings deposits and time deposits, which we introduced in Section 2.4. Savings deposits can be withdrawn from a bank at any moment; time deposits are committed for a fixed period of time. Time deposits are commonly called *CDs,* for certificates of deposit.

Small CDs, those less than \$100,000, are held mainly by individual savers. Most large CDs, those over \$100,000, are held by corporations and financial institutions. After large CDs are issued by banks, their holders can resell them in secondary financial markets. This fact makes large CDs highly liquid: they can easily be traded for cash.

Together, savings and time deposits made up 62 percent of commercial-bank liabilities as of March 2008. They are the major sources of funds for commercial banks.

▶The term *federal funds* may be confusing. These are loans from one bank to another, *not* loans from the Federal Reserve. The terminology reflects the fact that, in the past, banks often borrowed federal funds to satisfy reserve requirements set by the Fed.

Borrowings A bank may want more funds than it raises from deposits. This can occur, for example, if the bank wants to increase its lending. In this case, the bank borrows money. In 2008, borrowings were 23 percent of commercial-bank liabilities. A bank can borrow in several ways:

- *Federal funds* First, a bank can borrow from another bank, one that has more funds than it needs for other purposes. Loans from one bank to another are called **federal funds.** They are usually *overnight loans,* meaning they have a term of one day.

Federal funds Loans from one bank to another, usually for one day

Repurchase agreement (*repo*) Sale of a security with a promise to buy it back at a higher price on a future date

- *Repos* A bank can also borrow from a corporation or financial institution that has spare cash. This borrowing occurs through a **repurchase agreement,** or *repo.* To see how repos work, suppose a bank makes a repo agreement with a pension fund. The bank sells the pension fund a security, such as a Treasury bill, and agrees to buy it back later at a higher price. This deal is equivalent to a loan, since the bank receives cash temporarily. The security is collateral for the loan, and the increase in the security's price is interest.
- *Bonds* Bonds are another means of borrowing. Technically, it is not legal for commercial banks to issue bonds. But financial holding companies issue bonds, and they pass on the funds they raise to banks that they own. Bonds are an important source of funds for large banks.
- *Loans from the Fed* Finally, banks can borrow from the Federal Reserve. They can approach the Fed to request a *discount loan,* or they can bid in loan auctions that the Fed holds periodically.

▶Chapter 11 details the ways that banks borrow from the Fed.

Net Worth The final item on the right side of the balance sheet is net worth, or capital. Recall that this variable is defined as assets minus liabilities, ensuring that the two sides of the balance sheet add up to the same amount. In March 2008, U.S. commercial banks had net worth equal to 12 percent of their liabilities, or 10 percent of assets.

A bank acquires capital by issuing stock. Savers buy the stock, providing funds to the bank in return for ownership shares. A bank's capital is available to buy assets, along with the funds from deposits and borrowing. The bank's profits are added to its capital. Losses reduce capital. Capital also falls when a bank pays dividends to its stockholders.

Assets

We now turn to the asset side of the balance sheet, which shows how banks use the funds they raise. Banks hold several types of assets, which are listed on the left side of Table 9.1. The major categories are cash items, securities, and loans.

Vault cash Currency in banks' branches and ATMs

Reserves Vault cash plus banks' deposits at the Federal Reserve

Cash Items This category includes several components, which together comprised 3 percent of bank assets in 2008. One component is **vault cash,** the currency sitting in banks' branches and ATMs. Another is deposits in banks' accounts at the Federal Reserve. The sum of these two components is called **reserves.**

Reserves are a bank's most liquid asset. Banks need reserves so they can provide money when depositors want it. If a depositor wants cash, she gets it from a bank branch or ATM. When she buys something with a check or debit card, the funds come from her bank's account at the Fed.

▶Figure 2.2 charts the steps by which payments occur when a depositor writes a check.

Reserves produce little income. A bank earns nothing on its vault cash. In October 2008, banks started receiving interest on their deposits at the Fed, but the interest rates are low. As a result, banks hold only a small part of total assets as reserves. In the past, Fed regulations required banks to hold more reserves, but these regulations have become ineffective.

In addition to reserves, a bank's cash items include deposits at other banks. Often a small bank holds deposits at a larger bank that provides it with services. For example, as discussed in Section 6.1, large banks trade foreign currencies on behalf of small banks.

A final component of cash assets is *cash items in process of collection*. These are checks that have been deposited in a bank but have not yet cleared. The bank is waiting for the funds promised by the check.

Securities Securities are 23 percent of bank assets listed in Table 9.1. By law, banks are restricted to securities with low risk. These include Treasury bonds, municipal bonds, highly rated corporate bonds, and securities issued by government-sponsored enterprises (such as Fannie Mae's mortgage-backed securities). Banks are not allowed to hold stocks or junk bonds.

Securities pay interest. The interest rates are lower than rates on bank loans, but banks hold securities because they pay more than reserves while also providing liquidity. If depositors make large withdrawals, a bank may run low on reserves, but it can easily get more by selling securities. For this reason, securities held by banks are often called *secondary reserves*.

Loans Loans are banks' most important asset class, accounting for 65 percent of total assets in Table 9.1. Banks make loans to several types of borrowers: consumers, businesses, governments, and other banks. We detail these different types of loans in Section 9.3.

Loans are less liquid than securities: it is hard to turn them into cash quickly. In addition, borrowers sometimes default on loans. Nonetheless, loans can be profitable because they pay higher interest rates than safe securities.

9.2 OFF-BALANCE-SHEET ACTIVITIES

Banks earn income from the loans and securities listed on their balance sheets. They also receive income from **off-balance-sheet (OBS) activities.** These activities are not revealed on bank balance sheets, because they don't affect the current levels of the assets and liabilities reported there.

Off-balance-sheet (OBS) activities Bank activities that produce income but are not reflected in the assets and liabilities reported on the balance sheet

OBS activities are a growing part of the banking business. Of the many kinds of activities, we discuss five important examples. You will recognize several from earlier chapters.

Lines of Credit

We mentioned lines of credit (also called *loan commitments*) in Section 7.5. A line of credit gives an individual or firm the right to borrow a certain amount of money at any time. Banks grant lines of credit to build long-term relationships with borrowers.

Lines of credit also produce income for banks, as firms pay fees to keep them open. Firms are willing to pay for the guarantee of a quick loan when it is needed. A line of credit does not affect a bank's balance sheet until an actual loan is made. At that point, the loan category of assets rises by the amount of money lent out, and cash assets fall by the same amount.

Letters of Credit

Letter of credit A bank's guarantee, in return for a fee, of a payment promised by a firm

When a bank issues a **letter of credit,** it guarantees some payment promised by a firm. In return for a fee, the bank agrees to make the payment if the firm does not. In effect, the bank sells insurance against default. There are two kinds of letters of credit:

- A *commercial letter of credit* guarantees a payment for goods or services. To see its purpose, suppose an importer has ordered goods from a foreign company, promising to pay when the goods arrive. The foreign company may be wary of shipping the goods, because the importer might not pay the bill. The importer solves this problem by purchasing a letter of credit from a bank. The foreign company is willing to ship because payment is guaranteed.
- A *standby letter of credit* guarantees payments on a security. A company might buy a standby letter when it issues commercial paper. The bank that provides the letter agrees to pay off the paper if the company defaults. As a result of this guarantee, the commercial paper gets higher grades from bond-rating agencies. Higher ratings reduce the interest rate that the company must pay on the paper.

Asset Management

In addition to holding their own assets, banks manage assets for others. A small pension fund, for example, might want to buy securities but lack the expertise to choose the right mix. The pension fund gives its money to a bank that purchases securities on the fund's behalf. The bank receives fees for this service. Wealthy individuals also hire banks to manage assets, an activity called *private banking.*

Derivatives

We discussed derivative securities, such as futures and options, in Sections 5.6 and 6.2. Large banks trade derivatives on stocks, bonds, and currencies. Derivatives do not appear on bank balance sheets, because they are not currently assets or liabilities. Rather, they are agreements about future transactions.

Banks use derivatives to hedge against risks they face, such as changes in interest rates. Section 9.5 discusses this practice. Some banks also seek income by speculating with derivatives.

Investment Banking

Some commercial banks provide investment-banking services, such as underwriting securities and advising on mergers and acquisitions. Commercial banks were allowed to enter these businesses in 1999, when the Glass-Steagall Act was repealed (review Section 8.2). Investment-banking activities are important sources of income for the largest banks.

9.3 HOW BANKS MAKE PROFITS

So far we've outlined commercial banks' main business activities, both on and off the balance sheet. Let's now discuss how banks combine these activities to earn profits. We start with a fictional example that introduces some key ideas.

Melvin Opens a Bank

One day a man named Melvin opens a bank in Baltimore. He calls it Melvin's Bank. Melvin raises $20 by selling shares of the bank's stock to his friends. This $20 is the bank's initial capital, or net worth.

At first, Melvin's Bank deposits part of its $20 at the Federal Reserve Bank of Richmond and holds the rest as vault cash. The entire $20 counts as reserves. These reserves are the bank's only asset, and it has no liabilities. So the bank's balance sheet has only two items:

Assets		Liabilities and Net Worth	
Reserves	20	Net Worth	20

To raise more funds, Melvin seeks deposits. He puts a sign outside his bank saying "Deposit Your Money Here!" Britt, the star pitcher you met in Chapter 1, passes by the bank and notices the sign. He has just been traded to the Orioles and needs a bank in Baltimore. He deposits $50 in cash in a Melvin's checking account. He also deposits $50 in a savings account so he can earn interest.

Britt's two deposits change Melvin's balance sheet. They add $100 to the bank's reserves, and they also create liabilities. Now the balance sheet looks like this:

Assets		Liabilities and Net Worth	
Reserves	120	Checking Deposits	50
		Nontransaction Deposits	50
		Net Worth	20
TOTALS	120		120

This situation does not last long. The bank does not want to keep reserves as its only asset, because they pay little interest. Out of $120, Melvin's Bank keeps $10 in reserves, in case Britt wants to make a withdrawal. It buys $30 in Treasury bills to provide secondary reserves. This leaves $80, which it lends to Harriet for her eSmells business.

Let's say that all these transactions occur in 2014. Reflecting this activity, the balance sheet at the end of the year is:

MELVIN'S BANK BALANCE SHEET
December 31, 2014

Assets		Liabilities and Net Worth	
Reserves	10	Checking Deposits	50
Securities	30	Nontransaction Deposits	50
Loans	80	Net Worth	20
TOTALS	120		120

At this point, Melvin's banking business is in full swing. The bank has raised funds and used them to acquire assets. If the income from assets exceeds the interest paid on deposits, the bank can make a profit.

As this example illustrates, actions by a bank and its customers shift the bank's balance sheet. Sometimes assets and liabilities change together, as when Melvin's Bank gains $100 in deposits and $100 in reserves. Other times only one side of the balance sheet changes, as when the bank shifts assets from reserves to loans and securities. Whatever happens, total assets always equal total liabilities plus net worth.

In addition to holding assets, Melvin's Bank engages in off-balance-sheet activities. For example, it issues letters of credit to Harriet's company when Harriet orders computers from other companies. Fees for letters of credit add to the bank's income.

The Income Statement

Income statement Financial statement summarizing income, expenses, and profits over some time period

How profitable is Melvin's Bank? We can address this question by analyzing the bank's **income statement,** the financial statement that summarizes its income and expenses. Let's construct Melvin's income statement for the year 2015.

This exercise requires several assumptions. First, for simplicity, let's say that Melvin's balance sheet does not change during 2015. Throughout the year, Melvin maintains the balance sheet for December 31, 2014 that we examined above.

We also assume the interest rate on loans is 8 percent and the rates on both Treasury bills and savings deposits are 4 percent. In this example, checking accounts pay no interest, and the bank earns no interest on reserves. During 2015, Melvin's Bank earns $5 from OBS activities, such as letters of credit. Finally, the bank has $6 in costs, such as salaries for its employees.

Based on these assumptions, **Table 9.2** presents Melvin's income statement. The statement divides Melvin's revenue into two parts, interest income and non-interest income. As interest income, the bank earns 4 percent on its $30 in securities, yielding 4%($30) = $1.20. It also earns 8 percent on $80 in loans, yielding 8%($80) = $6.40. Adding these numbers, total interest income is $7.60. Non-interest income is $5.00, the bank's earnings from OBS activities. Total income is $12.60, the sum of interest and non-interest income.

TABLE 9.2 Income Statement for Melvin's Bank

For the year ended December 31, 2015			
Interest Income			
Securities	4%($30) = $1.20		
Loans	8%($80) = $6.40		
Total		$7.60	
Non-Interest Income (letters of credit)		$5.00	
TOTAL INCOME			$12.60
Interest Expense (savings accounts)		4%($50) = $2.00	
Non-Interest Expense (salaries, etc.)		$6.00	
TOTAL EXPENSE			$8.00
PROFITS (Income − Expense)			$4.60

$$\text{ROA} = \frac{\text{profits}}{\text{assets}} = \frac{\$4.60}{\$120} = 3.8\%$$

$$\text{ROE} = \frac{\text{profits}}{\text{net worth}} = \frac{\$4.60}{\$20} = 23\%$$

The income statement also divides the bank's expenses into interest and non-interest components. The bank pays 4 percent interest on $50 in savings accounts: 4%($50) = $2.00. This is the only interest expense, since checking accounts don't pay interest. The bank's non-interest expenses are $6.00 in salaries and other costs. Total expenses are $8.00.

Finally, Melvin's profits are total income minus total expenses. Profits are $12.60 − $8.00 = $4.60.

Profit Rates

Is $4.60 a high level of profits? Banks evaluate their profitability with two variables. One is the **return on assets** (ROA). This is the ratio of a bank's profits to its assets:

Return on assets (ROA) Ratio of a bank's profits to its assets; ROA = profits/assets

$$\text{ROA} = \frac{\text{profits}}{\text{assets}}$$

Recall that Melvin's Bank has $120 in assets. Its ROA is $4.60/$120 = 3.8%.

The second measure of profitability is more important. The **return on equity** (ROE) is the ratio of a bank's profits to its capital:

Return on equity (ROE) Ratio of a bank's profits to its capital; ROE = profits/capital

$$\text{ROE} = \frac{\text{profits}}{\text{capital}}$$

The ROE for Melvin's bank is $4.60/$20 = 23%.

The ROE shows how much the bank earns for each dollar its stockholders put in the business. Bank managers try to produce high ROEs, just as managers in other businesses try to produce high returns for stockholders.

9.4 THE EVOLVING PURSUIT OF PROFITS

Let's now turn from Melvin's Bank to the real world. Like Melvin, real banks make profits if their income exceeds their expenses. So they try to raise funds cheaply and find good sources of income.

How can banks achieve these goals? The answers to this question change over time. Over the last few decades, banks have transformed both their balance sheets and their OBS activities. The evolution of banking has been complex, but many changes have occurred for three basic reasons: competition from securities markets, deregulation, and financial innovation. **Table 9.3** summarizes the effects of these three forces on banks' assets, liabilities, and OBS activities. Some traditional sources of bank profits have disappeared, and new opportunities have arisen. Banks have had to adjust rapidly to remain profitable.

Before discussing the details, let's examine the bottom line. Despite challenges, banks in the United States have generally produced healthy profits in recent decades. **Figure 9.1** shows the average return on equity for commercial banks in each year from 1960 through 2007. Over the 1960s and 1970s, ROE averaged 12 percent. In the 1980s, a banking crisis pushed ROE down sharply, but it recovered in the early 1990s. ROE averaged 14 percent from 1992 through 2007.

Online Case Study: An Update on Bank Profits

Sources of Funds

From the liability side of the balance sheet, we see that banks raise funds in a variety of ways. Some liabilities are more costly than others because of differences in interest rates. Banks try to maximize their funding from low-cost sources.

TABLE 9.3 Changes in Commercial Banking: Causes and Effects

Competition from Securities Markets
Growth of mutual funds → banks lose deposits
Development of junk bonds and commercial paper → fewer C&I loans

Deregulation
Elimination of interest-rate caps → banks compete with mutual funds, retain savings and time deposits
Repeal of Glass-Steagall → banks offer investment banking services

Financial Innovation
Credit scoring and securitization → more real estate loans
Development of derivatives → opportunities for speculation

FIGURE 9.1 Average Return on Equity, U.S. Commercial Banks, 1960–2007

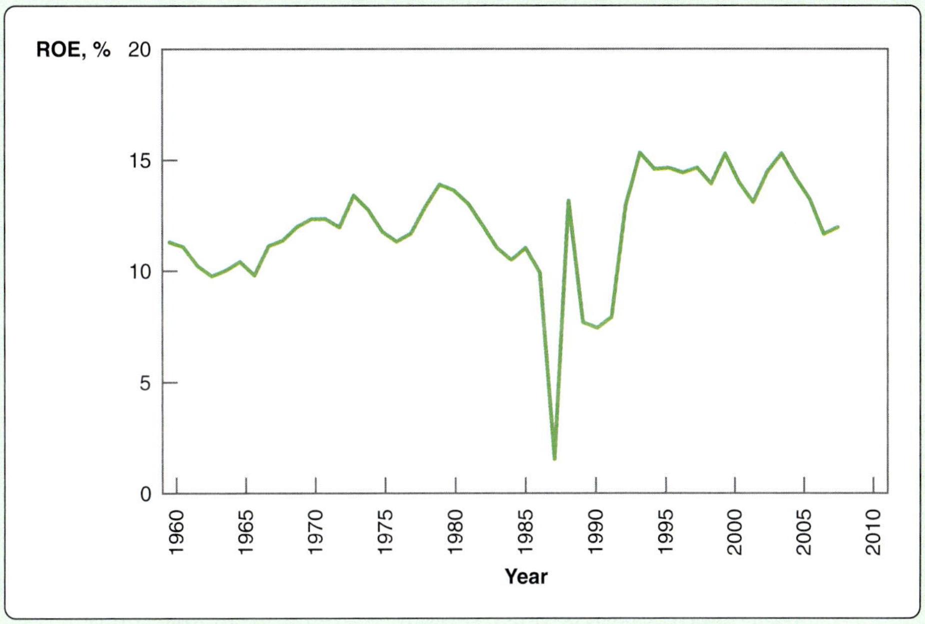

U.S. banks earned healthy profits over the period 1960–2007, except during the banking crisis of the 1980s.
Source: Federal Reserve Board

Cheap and Expensive Funds The cheapest source of funds is checking deposits, which pay little or no interest. These deposits create non-interest expenses for processing checks and debit payments, but they are still inexpensive overall. Other low-cost funds include savings deposits and small time deposits. These deposits, held by small savers, typically pay interest rates from 1 percent to 3 percent lower than Treasury securities with the same maturity. Savers accept low interest rates because they value the liquidity of bank deposits. In addition, some people simply don't know that higher interest rates are available from securities.

Banks' other funds come from large time deposits and borrowings, such as federal funds and repurchase agreements. These funds are relatively expensive, because they are provided by large, sophisticated institutions that shop for the highest interest rate. To borrow from these institutions, banks must offer interest rates close to Treasury rates.

Bankers call their inexpensive sources of funds **core deposits.** Core deposits are the sum of checking deposits, savings deposits, and small time deposits. Borrowings and large time deposits are called **purchased funds.**

Core deposits Banks' inexpensive sources of funds (checking deposits, savings deposits, and small time deposits)

Purchased funds Banks' expensive sources of funds (borrowings and large time deposits)

A Two-Step Process Because of the varying costs, many banks raise funds in two steps. First, they try to maximize core deposits. They attract these deposits by establishing convenient branches, providing good service, and advertising. Second, banks choose their levels of purchased funds. They can choose these levels because the supply of purchased funds is essentially unlimited. Many institutions are happy to buy large CDs or lend to banks if the interest rates match Treasury rates.

Banks' choices of purchased funds depend on their opportunities for using these funds. For example, a bank might have a large number of attractive loan applications but lack enough core deposits to make all the loans. In this situation, the bank uses purchased funds to increase its lending.

Some History Banks' sources of funds have changed over time. **Figure 9.2** splits commercial-bank liabilities into three categories: checking deposits; other core deposits, meaning savings deposits and small CDs; and purchased funds, meaning large CDs and borrowings. The figure shows the share of each category in total liabilities for the period 1973–2007.

In 1973, checking deposits and other core deposits were banks' primary sources of funds. Purchased funds were only 25 percent of liabilities. Core deposits were plentiful, because small savers had few alternatives to putting their money in banks. High brokerage fees prevented them from buying securities.

This situation changed with the growth of mutual funds, especially money-market funds that hold Treasury bills and commercial paper. These funds are safe, and they paid high interest rates in the 1970s and 1980s. Bank deposits started to fall as money flowed into mutual funds.

Banks responded by raising interest rates on savings and time deposits. This response was made possible by deregulation: the Federal Reserve had set caps on deposit rates, but eliminated most of them during the 1980s.

FIGURE 9.2 U.S. Commercial Bank Liabilities, 1973–2007

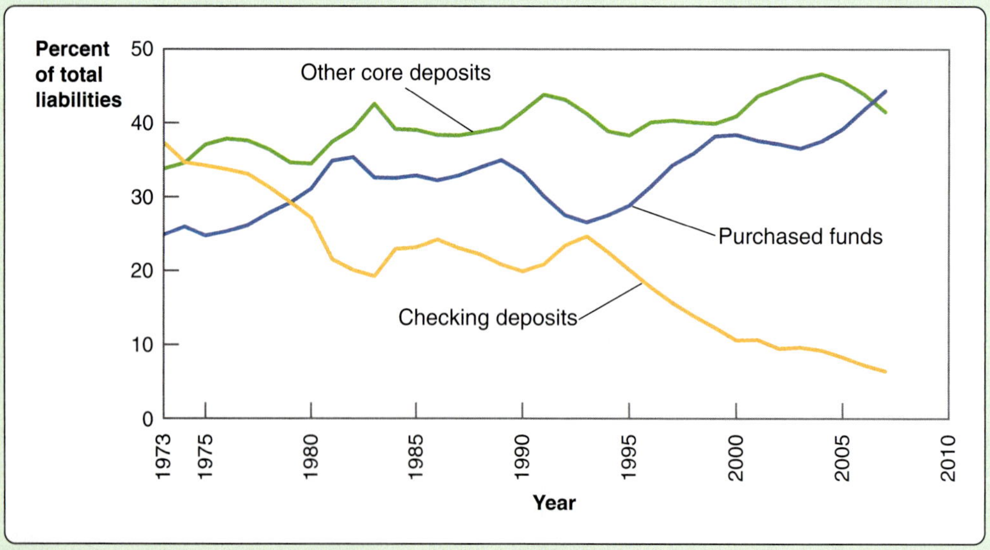

Since 1973, checking deposits have fallen dramatically as a percentage of commercial bank liabilities. They have been replaced by other core deposits (savings deposits and small time deposits) and by purchased funds (large time deposits and borrowings).

Source: Federal Reserve Board

Since then, interest rates for the "other core deposits" category have been high enough to attract small savers.

However, money has continued to flow out of checking accounts, which still pay little or no interest. Checking deposits fell from 37 percent of liabilities in 1973 to 6 percent in 2007. These losses have been partly replaced by other core deposits, but banks have also turned increasingly to purchased funds. This category was 44 percent of liabilities in 2007.

To summarize, banks have seen a fall in their least expensive source of funds (checking deposits) and a rise in their most expensive source (purchased funds). So interest expenses have risen. To offset this trend, banks have sought higher income from loans and off-balance-sheet activities. But one bank has relied on a different strategy: boosting its core deposits.

CASE STUDY

Commerce Bank

Commerce Bank is one of America's fastest-growing banks. It started in 1973 with a single branch in Marlton, New Jersey, and now operates throughout the mid-Atlantic region and in Florida. In 2007, it had 450 branches and assets of $50 billion, placing it among the 30 largest commercial banks in the United States. Commerce has announced goals of 800 branches and $100 billion in assets by 2011.

You can also "have it your way" at Burger King. The identical slogans are not a coincidence: Virgil Hill, the founder of Commerce Bank, had previously owned 40 Burger King franchises. You can link through the text Web site to Commerce Bank's Web site.

The central idea of Commerce's business strategy is to maximize core deposits. The bank seeks to raise lots of inexpensive funds to finance loans. Commerce pursues this goal by stressing customer service. Its registered trademark is "America's most convenient bank," and it advertises a "have it your way" approach to customers.

Commerce backs up its mottos with branches that are open 7 days a week. Posted weekday hours typically run from 7:30 AM to 8:00 PM—and employees are trained to open 10 minutes early and close 10 minutes late. Commerce's bank-by-phone system has live operators 24 hours a day. For customers with deposits over $2500, Commerce offers free access to ATMs around the world. If another bank charges a fee for using its ATM, Commerce refunds the fee.

A customer enjoys one of the amenities of Commerce Bank.

MATT GREENSLADE/PHOTO-NYC.COM

Commerce also tries to make its branches pleasant for customers. It calls the branches "stores." The interiors are designed to be welcoming, with no screens between tellers and customers. Staff members greet customers at the door. In 2006, customers received 21 million free pens, 12 million lollipops, and 2 million dog biscuits. You may win a prize if you wear red, the color of the Commerce logo, on a Friday.

Commerce's Web site displays "fan mail" from satisfied customers. Many letters tell of employees spending long hours to sort out customers' problems. Teresa of Staten Island, New York says:

> *I had a wonderful experience in your branch location yesterday and feel the need to compliment you. A young man named [deleted] helped my husband and myself to count coins yesterday . . . lots and lots of coins! [Deleted] worked so hard for us that he literally worked up a sweat! but never stopped smiling. He was extremely knowledgeable & was sure to inform us what Commerce had to offer, prompting us to open a savings account.*

William from New Jersey reports that his car broke down in the parking lot of a Commerce branch. The branch manager left a meeting to come outside and look under the hood. (He and William concluded that the starter was broken.)

Apparently many people like Commerce Bank. The bank's deposits rose from $7 billion in 2000 to $46 billion in 2008. The growing supply of inexpensive funds produced high profits, and Commerce's stock price rose from $10 to $35.

Seeking Income

Just as different liabilities have different costs, different assets produce different levels of income. The search for profits has led banks to shift their asset holdings over time. They have also expanded their off-balance-sheet activities.

Banks' primary assets are loans. For commercial banks, loans have been a steady 60–70 percent of assets since the 1960s. But banks have shifted their funds among different types of loans. For the period 1973–2007, **Figure 9.3** shows how three major types of lending—commercial, real estate, and consumer—have changed as percentages of total loans. Let's examine each category.

C&I Loans Before the 1980s, the largest component of bank lending was *commercial and industrial loans.* These are loans to firms: long-term loans for investment and short-term loans for working capital. Figure 9.3 shows that C&I loans have declined in importance, going from 35 percent of total loans in 1973 to 21 percent in 2007.

A major reason is the growth of bond markets. Junk bonds, discussed in Section 4.5, were created in the late 1970s. The junk-bond market allows more firms to bypass banks in raising funds. Commercial paper has also become common, allowing firms short-term as well as long-term borrowing in securities markets.

The C&I lending that remains has become a relatively unprofitable part of banking. Interest rates have been driven down by competition, both among banks and with securities markets. Companies that receive C&I loans are good at shopping around for low rates.

Real Estate Loans This category includes both home mortgages and commercial real estate loans for the construction of offices, factories, and stores.

FIGURE 9.3 Composition of U.S. Commercial Bank Loans, 1973–2007

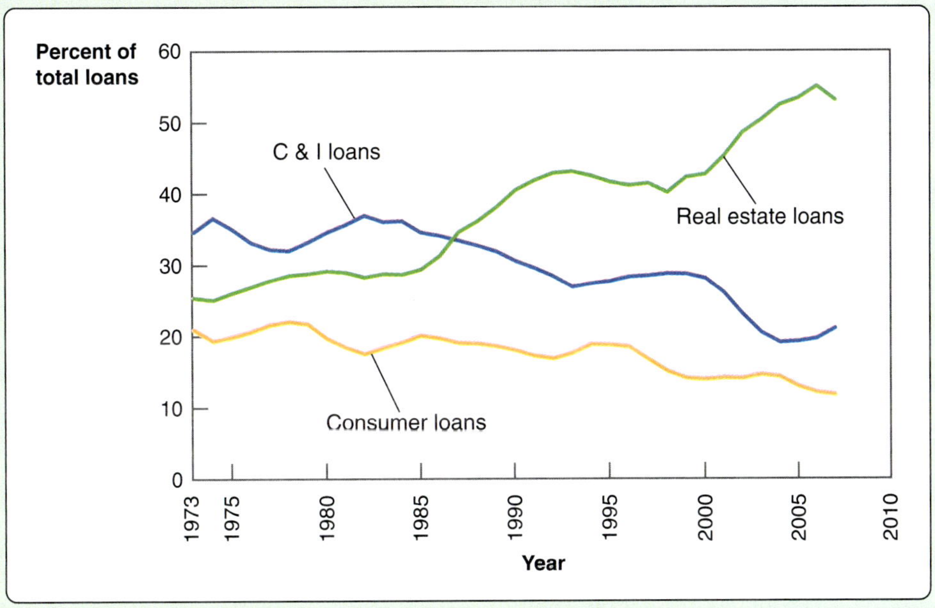

Since 1973, C&I loans and consumer loans have fallen as percentages of total loans by commercial banks. Real estate loans have risen.

Source: Federal Reserve Board

Real estate grew from 25 percent of total lending in 1973 to 53 percent in 2007.

Real estate loans generally pay higher interest rates than C&I loans. The downside is that default risk is also higher. Commercial real estate is a volatile industry, and a bad period can cause many developers to fail. Home mortgages can also be risky. Nonetheless, banks have expanded real estate lending to replace lost C&I lending and because they need higher interest income to offset rising interest expenses.

Real estate lending has also been spurred by financial innovations that reduce banks' risk. One tool is securitization, which shifts risk from banks to the holders of mortgage-backed securities (see Section 8.3). Another is credit scoring, which helps banks screen out the riskiest mortgage applicants. (These borrowers often turn to finance companies for mortgages, as discussed in Section 8.4.)

Consumer Loans Overall, consumer lending fell from 21 percent of loans in 1973 to 12 percent in 2007. Within this category, traditional personal loans declined rapidly, but credit card lending rose. You take out a bank loan any time you carry a balance on a credit card issued by a bank.

Banks earn high profits from issuing credit cards. The cards produce high interest income, plus fees from both cardholders and merchants who accept the cards. Profitability explains why you see so many credit card ads and why you get free T-shirts for acquiring new cards.

Off-Balance-Sheet Activities OBS activities are a growing part of the banking business, producing higher non-interest income. Once again, as summarized in Table 9.3, the sources of change include deregulation and financial innovation. The repeal of the Glass-Steagall Act allowed commercial banks to offer investment-banking services. Growing markets for derivatives have created opportunities for banks to speculate on these securities.

Like most businesses, banks search constantly for new ways to earn profits. The next two case studies discuss recent strategies. In each case, banks' actions have caused controversy.

CASE STUDY

Tying

As we have discussed, commercial and industrial loans are a relatively unprofitable part of banking today. Nonetheless, many large banks are eager to make C&I loans. What motivates these banks?

One answer is that banks want to establish relationships with the firms that receive C&I loans. Banks hope these firms will turn to them for more profitable services in the future—especially securities underwriting. As the *Wall Street Journal* put it, banks act "like a bar that sets out free chips and then charges $8 a beer." C&I loans are the chips and underwriting is the beer.

One example is lending during the boom in the telecommunications industry. In 2000 and 2001, companies such as Nortel Networks and WorldCom received lines of credit for billions of dollars from JP Morgan Chase, Citigroup, and other large banks. Within months, the same banks were hired to underwrite bond issues for the companies.

Many economists argue that it's efficient for a single bank to provide both loans and underwriting. A bank gathers information about its loan customers and can use the same information to help issue securities. One-stop shopping is also convenient for the customers.

However, there are tricky legal issues. A 1970 law forbids *tying:* a bank can't demand that a firm purchase its underwriting services as a condition for a loan. The rationale is that tying gives commercial banks an unfair advantage over investment banks in competing for underwriting business. This could diminish competition and raise the cost of underwriting.

On the other hand, it is legal for banks to use loans to promote underwriting if they don't connect the two activities explicitly. In 2003, the Federal Reserve clarified this point by issuing an interpretation of the antitying law. The Fed said that banks can make loans based on "a desire or a hope (but not a requirement) that the customer will obtain additional products from the bank."

Controversy has arisen over the gray area between legal product promotion and illegal tying. Some companies complain that banks pressure them to buy investment-banking services and cut off loans if they don't. This behavior violates the spirit of the law even if nothing illegal is written in loan contracts. Banks deny this charge.

The Federal Reserve is responsible for enforcing the antitying law. Some members of Congress have urged the Fed to pursue violators more vigorously. In contrast, the Bush Administration advocated a loose interpretation of the law, arguing that the dangers of tying are exaggerated. For now, the Fed's policy is based on its 2003 statement.*

* For more on tying, see Jathon Sapsford and Paul Beckett, "Loss Leader: Linking of Loans to Other Businesses Has Peril for Banks," *Wall Street Journal*, September 19, 2002; and "Finance Execs Report Illegal Bank Tying," by Tim Reason, CFO.com, June 11, 2004.

CASE STUDY

Fees

We've seen that non-interest income is a rising share of bank profits. This trend is partly the result of OBS activities such as underwriting. But it also reflects a new twist on the traditional activities of deposit-taking and lending. Banks have boosted their income by raising a variety of fees charged to depositors and borrowers. Examples include fees for using ATMs, monthly service fees on checking accounts, and fees for stopping payment on a check. Two types of fees have produced especially large revenues: overdraft fees and credit card fees. Each has generated controversy.

Overdraft Programs In the late 1990s, many banks started granting "courtesy overdrafts." Under this policy, a bank honors a customer's check even if his account has insufficient funds; the account balance is allowed to become negative. The bank charges a fee, which averaged $34 per overdraft in 2007. Then the customer has a grace period, typically a week or two, to bring his balance above zero. If he doesn't, the bank adds more fees.

Around 2004, many banks extended courtesy overdrafts to debit card purchases and ATM withdrawals. Before 2004, someone who swiped her card at a store had her purchase denied if her account balance didn't cover it. Now the purchase may be approved, with the bank charging the same overdraft fee as for a check.

Consumer groups criticize courtesy overdrafts. They argue that overdrafts amount to short-term loans with exorbitant interest rates, since the amounts overdrawn are often small compared to fees. A 2007 study by the Center for Responsible Lending (CRL) estimates that the average person pays $0.86 in fees for every dollar overdrawn with a check and $2.17 for every dollar overdrawn with a debit card.

▶We met the Center for Responsible Lending when we discussed payday lending in Section 8.3.

The CRL reports a horror story about a college student identified only as G.C. On March 30, 2007, G.C. had $3.49 in his bank account and used his debit card for a $4.58 purchase. The bank covered the difference of $1.09 but charged a $35 fee. Over the next two days, G.C. used his card six more times to buy coffee and school supplies. These purchases ranged from $1.70 to $3.01, and the bank charged $35 each time. Overall, between March 30 and April 2, G.C. spent $13.06 with his debit card and ran up $245 in fees.

Banks must disclose their overdraft policies and fees when customers open accounts. Critics complain, however, that this information is buried in the fine print of brochures. People may not know about overdraft fees until they see the fees charged to their accounts.

Credit Card Fees Since the 1990s, banks have steadily raised several types of credit card fees. The average fee for a late payment rose from $13 in 1994 to $39 in 2007. Over the same period, the average fee for exceeding a credit limit rose from $13 to $35. Fees have risen for cash advances, balance transfers, and overseas purchases as well.

For current information on bank fees, link through the text Web site to Bankrate.com, which reports overdraft fees, and Cardweb.com, which reports credit card fees and interest rates.

In addition to flat fees, late payments and high balances can trigger increases in interest rates. At some banks, *penalty rates* have risen to 30 percent or more. Some credit card agreements allow a bank to raise a borrower's interest rate even if he pays his bills on time and stays under his credit limit. The rate rises if the borrower makes a late payment on some *other* debt, such as another credit card, or if his total debts rise. This rule, called a *universal default clause,* appeared in 40 percent of card agreements in 2007.

Like overdraft programs, credit card fees have drawn widespread criticism. In 2007, Senator Carl Levin (D-MI) proposed the "Stop Unfair Credit Card Practices Act." Senate hearings on this bill featured testimony from Wesley Wannemacher, an Ohio man who used a Chase credit card for $3200 in purchases (most related to his wedding) in 2001 and 2002. These purchases exceeded Wannemacher's credit limit of $3000, so Chase raised his interest rate to 32 percent. It also charged him 47 overlimit fees between 2002 and 2007. During that period, Wannemacher made card payments totaling $6300, almost twice his original debt, but was still left with a $4400 balance.

Senator Levin's proposal would restrict credit card issuers in a variety of ways. Penalty interest rates would be limited to the previous rate plus 7 percent. In addition, these rates would apply only to new purchases, not to the balance when the rate was raised. The act would also limit the number of times a bank can charge overlimit fees. As of 2008, the Senate was considering this legislation.

The threat of congressional action has led some banks to change their credit card policies. In 2007, both Citibank and Chase removed universal default clauses from their card agreements. Chase also said it would charge fewer overlimit fees. Three days before Wesley Wannemacher's Senate testimony, Chase waived his $4400 card balance.

Other card issuers have resisted the pressure for change. At the Senate hearing where Wannemacher testified, Roger Hochschild, the president of Discover Bank, defended universal default clauses. He argued that borrowers' overall credit records are "important criteria for how to manage risk and pricing."

9.5 MANAGING RISK

Banking is a risky business. Banks' loans and OBS activities usually produce profits, but they can produce large losses if things go wrong. A key task for bankers is to identify risks and take steps to reduce them. This job is complicated, because banks face many kinds of risk. Major categories include liquidity risk, credit risk, interest-rate risk, market risk, and economic risk. Let's discuss each of these risks and how banks address them.

Liquidity Risk

Banks hold reserves to be ready for withdrawals. They also hold liquid securities that they can turn quickly into reserves. However, a bank's liquid assets usually total to much less than deposits in the bank. If depositors want to withdraw large amounts, the bank may not have enough reserves and securities to meet this demand. This is **liquidity risk.**

Liquidity risk The risk that withdrawals from a bank will exceed its liquid assets

If withdrawals exceed a bank's liquid assets, it can fall back on illiquid assets—its loans. It can sell loans to other financial institutions, giving up future payments on the loans in return for reserves. These extra reserves allow the bank to satisfy its customers' demand for withdrawals.

However, by definition an illiquid asset is hard to sell quickly. We've seen that banks sometimes sell loans profitably; for example, they sell mortgages to Fannie Mae and Freddie Mac. However, many types of loans are difficult to sell. To find buyers quickly, a bank may have to accept low prices—less than the loans are really worth. The bank loses money on the deals. Bankers say the loans are sold at *fire-sale prices.*

▶The metaphor behind the term *fire sale* is a company whose warehouse has burned down. If the company doesn't sell its goods quickly, they will be stolen or damaged by the elements. The company must unload the goods for whatever prices it can get.

The illiquidity of loans reflects the basic problem of asymmetric information. As we discussed in Section 7.7, a bank gathers information about its borrowers, so it has a good idea of the default risk for its loans. Other banks, which have not screened the borrowers, may be uncertain of this risk. Because of this uncertainty, they will not pay much for the loans. The seller must accept fire-sale prices, even if it knows that default risk is low.

An Example To illustrate liquidity risk, let's return to Melvin's Bank. We assume the bank starts with the balance sheet shown in **Table 9.4A.** Notice that total deposits are \$100 and liquid assets (reserves plus securities) are only \$40.

Suppose that Britt, the bank's depositor, decides to get married. He withdraws the entire \$50 in his savings account to buy a ring. This withdrawal causes a crisis. The bank uses its \$40 in liquid assets to pay Britt, but it is still \$10 short. To raise this amount, it must sell loans. A competitor, Gertrude's Bank, agrees to buy loans, but only at a fire-sale price: Gertrude

TABLE 9.4 Liquidity Risk at Melvin's Bank

(A) Initial Balance Sheet				(B) Balance Sheet After \$50 Withdrawal			
Assets		**Liabilities and Net Worth**		**Assets**		**Liabilities and Net Worth**	
Reserves	10	Checking Deposits	50	Reserves	0	Checking Deposits	50
Securities	30	Nontransaction Deposits	50	Securities	0	Nontransaction Deposits	0
Loans	80	Net Worth	20	Loans	60	Net Worth	10
TOTAL	120	TOTAL	120	TOTAL	60	TOTAL	60

will pay 50 cents for each dollar of loans. So Melvin's Bank must sell $20 of loans to raise $10.

Table 9.4B shows Melvin's balance sheet after these transactions. Liabilities fall by $50, the amount of Britt's withdrawal. On the asset side, liquid assets fall by $40 and loans fall by $20, the amount sold to Gertrude. So total assets fall by $60. The bank's capital—assets minus liabilities—falls from $20 to $10. Because of its liquidity crisis, Melvin's Bank has lost half the money that its stockholders put in.

The Liquidity-Profit Trade-off There is a simple way to reduce liquidity risk: hold more liquid assets. The more a bank holds, the less likely it will be to run out when depositors make withdrawals.

Table 9.5 illustrates this point. In this example, Melvin's Bank starts with a high level of liquidity. On its initial balance sheet, shown in Table 9.5A, the bank holds $20 more in securities than in Table 9.4A, and $20 less in loans. Once again Britt withdraws $50, but this time the bank has enough liquid assets to cover the withdrawal. Let's say it uses $45 of securities and $5 of reserves, producing the balance sheet in Table 9.5B. The bank avoids a fire sale of loans, so its capital does not fall.

We've previously seen a disadvantage to liquid assets: they pay less interest than loans. Therefore, if high liquidity is not needed, it reduces profits. This happens if depositors do *not* make large withdrawals.

In our example, Melvin's Bank increases liquidity by replacing $20 in loans with securities. This shift reduces the bank's income by $20 times the difference in interest rates. If loans pay 8 percent and securities pay 4 percent, the bank loses $20 × (8% − 4%) = $0.80.

So a bank faces a balancing act when it chooses its level of liquidity. It wants to hold enough liquid assets to avoid running out. But it doesn't want to hold too many, because profits would suffer.

Short-term Borrowing Banks try to ease the trade-off we've discussed. They want to minimize liquid assets but still avoid running out. One tool for reconciling these goals is borrowing. When a bank needs funds to meet withdrawals, it can borrow rather than sell loans at fire-sale prices.

As we've discussed, banks can borrow from a variety of sources, including corporations and the Federal Reserve. But most short-term borrowing

TABLE 9.5 The Benefit of Liquidity

(A) Melvin's Initial Balance Sheet				(B) Melvin's Balance Sheet After $50 Withdrawal			
Assets		**Liabilities and Net Worth**		**Assets**		**Liabilities and Net Worth**	
Reserves	10	Checking Deposits	50	Reserves	5	Checking Deposits	50
Securities	50	Nontransaction Deposits	50	Securities	5	Nontransaction Deposits	0
Loans	60	Net Worth	20	Loans	60	Net Worth	20
TOTAL	120	TOTAL	120	TOTAL	70	TOTAL	70

is from other banks. If one bank is low on liquidity, it borrows federal funds from another bank with more liquidity than it needs.

This process is quick and easy. Two banks agree on a loan and the lender contacts its district Federal Reserve Bank electronically. It tells the Fed to debit its account there and move the funds to the borrower's account. Some loans are made for a single day: the transfer of funds is reversed the next day, with a small amount of interest added on. Other loans are "continuing," meaning the borrower bank keeps the funds until it or the lender bank chooses to end the loan.

Table 9.6 shows how Melvin's Bank can use the federal funds market. The bank starts with a low level of liquidity in Table 9.6A: it has only $40 in reserves and securities. Once again Britt withdraws $50, and a liquidity crisis looms.

Fortunately, Gertrude's Bank has just received a large deposit, raising its reserves. This bank has more reserves than it needs, so it is happy to lend some out and earn interest. Melvin borrows $50 of federal funds from Gertrude and uses the money to pay Britt.

On Melvin's balance sheet, deposits fall by $50 and borrowings rise by $50 in Table 9.6B. The bank replaces one liability with another. Its assets and capital don't change.

Because of the federal funds market, banks can usually get liquidity when they need it. The system is not foolproof, however. It can break down if the economy experiences a banking panic, with withdrawals from many banks at once. We discuss this scenario in Chapter 10.

Credit Risk

Credit risk *(default risk)*
The risk that loans will not be repaid

Credit risk is another name for default risk, the risk that borrowers won't repay their loans. As we discussed in Section 7.5, banks reduce this risk by, for example, screening borrowers and putting covenants in loan contracts. Nonetheless, borrowers sometimes default.

If a borrower defaults on a bank loan, the loan ceases to be an asset for the bank. A loan is worthless if it is not going to produce payments. The bank must *write off* the loan: it removes the loan from its balance sheet. This action reduces the bank's total assets, so its net worth falls. The bank's stockholders have lost money.

TABLE 9.6 Using the Federal Funds Market

(A) Melvin's Initial Balance Sheet

Assets		Liabilities and Net Worth	
Reserves	10	Checking Deposits	50
Securities	30	Nontransaction Deposits	50
Loans	80	Net Worth	20
TOTAL	120	TOTAL	120

(B) Melvin's Balance Sheet After $50 Withdrawal

Assets		Liabilities and Net Worth	
Reserves	10	Checking Deposits	50
Securities	30	Nontransaction Deposits	0
Loans	80	Borrowings	50
		Net Worth	20
TOTAL	120	TOTAL	120

TABLE 9.7 Credit Risk at Melvin's Bank

(A) Initial Balance Sheet				(B) Balance Sheet After Loan Defaults			
Assets		**Liabilities and Net Worth**		**Assets**		**Liabilities and Net Worth**	
Reserves	10	Checking Deposits	50	Reserves	10	Checking Deposits	50
Securities	30	Nontransaction Deposits	50	Securities	30	Nontransaction Deposits	50
Loans	80	Net Worth	20	Loans	75	Net Worth	15
TOTAL	120	TOTAL	120	TOTAL	115	TOTAL	115

Table 9.7 gives an example. Initially, Melvin's Bank has $80 in loans (Table 9.7A), but one of its borrowers defaults on a loan of $5. The bank writes off this loan, reducing its loans to $75. As shown in Table 9.7B, total assets on the bank's balance sheet fall by $5. Liabilities don't change, so the $5 fall in assets causes a $5 fall in net worth.

Banks seek to reduce their credit risk. One way is to shift this risk to other institutions through loan sales. When a bank sells a loan, the loan is removed from its balance sheet. If the borrower defaults, the loss falls on the buyer of the loan.

If a bank must sell loans quickly, it may have to accept fire-sale prices. However, in nonemergency situations, banks can get attractive prices for some kinds of loans. This happens when loan buyers are relatively well informed about default risk. For example, banks can sell mortgages because default risk is predictable based on borrowers' incomes and credit scores (see Sections 8.3 and 8.4). Banks earn profits by making mortgage loans and selling them, and they avoid credit risk.

One version of a loan sale is *syndication*. Before making a loan, a bank agrees to sell parts of the loan to a group of other financial institutions, called a syndicate. These institutions may include pension funds and investment banks as well as other commercial banks. The original lender keeps only a fraction of the loan on its balance sheet. Syndication is common for very large loans, because no single bank wants to take on all the credit risk. For example, companies often use syndicated loans to finance acquisitions of other companies.

Interest-Rate Risk

Banks' profits are affected by short-term interest rates in financial markets, such as the Treasury bill rate. Increases in interest rates tend to reduce profits, and decreases raise profits. The resulting instability in profits is called **interest-rate risk.**

Interest-rate risk Instability in bank profits caused by fluctuations in short-term interest rates

The explanation for interest-rate risk involves the maturities of banks' assets and liabilities. Most liabilities have short maturities, meaning funds are not committed to the bank for long. Checking and savings deposits have zero maturities: they can be withdrawn at any moment. Time deposits typically mature after a year or two. Most borrowing by banks is short-term; for example, federal funds are usually borrowed for one day at a time.

Because of these short maturities, interest rates on bank liabilities must compete with rates on securities. Suppose the Treasury bill rate rises. Rates on banks' purchased funds (borrowings and large CDs) adjust immediately. Rates on core deposits move more slowly, but they must rise before long or depositors will take their money elsewhere. Bankers say their liabilities are *rate sensitive.*

In contrast, bank assets typically have long maturities. Many business loans have terms of 10 years. Traditional home mortgages have 30-year terms. If the T-bill rate rises, banks can charge higher rates on future loans. But the loans they hold currently have lower rates locked in for long periods. These loans are *not* rate sensitive.

To summarize, higher short-term interest rates raise the rates that banks pay on liabilities and have less effect on rates received on assets. So interest expense rises by more than interest income. Bank profits fall.

An Example **Table 9.8** illustrates interest-rate risk at Melvin's Bank. The column headed "Initial Statement" repeats Table 9.2 on page 257, which assumes interest rates of 4 percent on T-bills, 4 percent on savings deposits, and 8 percent on loans. These interest rates imply profits of $4.60 and a return on equity of 23 percent.

The right-hand column shows how the income statement changes if the T-bill rate rises to 7 percent. We assume that savings deposits are rate

TABLE 9.8 Interest-Rate Risk

Income Statement for Melvin's Bank

	Initial Statement		Statement After a Rise in Short-Term Interest Rates	
Interest Income				
Securities	4%($30) = $1.20		7%($30) = $2.10	
Loans	8%($80) = $6.40		8%($80) = $6.40	
Total	$7.60		$8.50	
Non-Interest Income (letters of credit)	$5.00		$5.00	
TOTAL INCOME		$12.60		$13.50
Interest Expense (savings accounts)	4%($50) = $2.00		7%($50) = $3.50	
Non-Interest Expense (salaries, etc.)	$6.00		$6.00	
TOTAL EXPENSE		$8.00		$9.50
PROFITS (Income − Expense)		$4.60		$4.00
$\text{ROA} = \frac{\text{profits}}{\text{assets}}$	$\frac{\$4.60}{\$120} = 3.8\%$		$\frac{\$4.00}{\$120} = 3.3\%$	
$\text{ROE} = \frac{\text{profits}}{\text{net worth}}$	$\frac{\$4.60}{\$20} = 23\%$		$\frac{\$4.00}{\$20} = 20\%$	

Note: Highlighted items are affected by the rise in short-term interest rates.

sensitive: their rate also rises to 7 percent. In contrast, the interest rate on loans stays at its previous level of 8 percent.

To see how profits change, notice first that the bank owns \$30 in T-bills. With a 4 percent interest rate, total earnings on T-bills were 4% (\$30) = \$1.20. With an interest rate of 7 percent, these earnings are 7% (\$30) = \$2.10. The bank's earnings on loans do not change. Total interest income rises by the increase in earnings on T-bills: \$2.10 − \$1.20 = \$0.90.

The bank has \$50 in savings deposits, with interest rates that also rise from 4 percent to 7 percent. At 4 percent, total payments on savings deposits were 4% (\$50) = \$2.00; at 7 percent, these payments are 7% (\$50) = \$3.50. The bank's interest expense rises by \$3.50 − \$2.00 = \$1.50.

To summarize, the bank's interest income rises by \$0.90 but its interest expense rises by \$1.50, for a net loss of \$0.60. The bank's total profits fall from \$4.60 to \$4.00 and its ROE falls from 23 percent to 20 percent.

Measuring Interest-Rate Risk Banks want stable profits, so they try to contain interest-rate risk. The first step is to measure this risk. One measure is the **rate-sensitivity gap.** This variable captures the mismatch between a bank's assets and liabilities:

Rate-sensitivity gap
Difference between rate-sensitive assets and rate-sensitive liabilities

$$\text{rate-sensitivity gap} = \text{rate-sensitive assets} - \text{rate-sensitive liabilities}$$

The rate-sensitivity gap is usually negative. In Table 9.8, rate-sensitive assets (T-bills) are \$30 and rate-sensitive liabilities (savings deposits) are \$50. The rate-sensitivity gap is −\$20.

When interest rates change, the effect on a bank's profits is proportional to its rate-sensitivity gap. The more negative the gap, the more the bank loses if rates rise. Specifically,

$$\text{change in profits} = (\text{change in short-term interest rate}) \times (\text{rate-sensitivity gap}) \quad \textbf{(9.1)}$$

In our example, the short-term interest rate rises from 4 percent to 7 percent, so the change in the rate is 3 percent. With a rate-sensitivity gap of −\$20, the change in profits is 3% (−\$20) = −\$0.60. This calculation confirms Table 9.8, which shows the same decrease in profits, from \$4.60 to \$4.00.

Reducing Risk Banks use several techniques to reduce interest-rate risk: loan sales, floating interest rates, and derivatives.

Loan sales We saw earlier that loan sales reduce credit risk. They can also reduce interest-rate risk. If a bank sells long-term loans, it has fewer assets with fixed interest rates, so it can acquire more rate-sensitive assets. The rate-sensitivity gap moves closer to zero, making profits more stable.

Floating interest rate
Interest rate on a long-term loan that is tied to a short-term rate

Floating rates A bank can also use **floating interest rates** for its long-term loans. A floating rate is an interest rate tied to a short-term rate. For example, the rate on a 10-year business loan might be the T-bill rate plus 2 percent. If T-bills pay 4 percent, the bank receives 6 percent on the loan. If the T-bill rate rises to 7 percent, the loan rate rises to 9 percent.

Floating rates turn long-term loans into interest-sensitive assets. The loans themselves are committed for long periods, but the interest rates respond to short-term rates. Like loan sales, floating rates push a bank's rate-sensitivity gap toward zero.

Today, most C&I loans in the United States have floating rates. A significant fraction of mortgages also have floating rates, as we discuss in the next case study.

Derivatives Finally, banks can hedge interest-rate risk with derivatives. For example, a bank can sell futures contracts for Treasury bonds, a transaction that yields profits if bond prices fall (review Section 5.6). Bond prices fall when interest rates rise, so higher rates produce profits for the bank. These profits offset the loss arising from the rate-sensitivity gap.

CASE STUDY

Fixed- versus Floating-Rate Mortgages

Some home mortgages have interest rates that are fixed for the term of the loan, typically 30 years, while others have floating rates. In the United States, banks offer both types of mortgages to prime borrowers (those with good credit ratings). In 2007, about a fifth of all prime mortgages had floating rates.

Floating-rate mortgages are commonly called *ARMs,* for adjustable-rate mortgage. In most cases, the interest rate is fixed for an initial period and then floats for the rest of the loan term. For example, the interest rate on a "3/1 ARM" is fixed for 3 years and then adjusts annually. As with other floating-rate loans, adjustments are tied to short-term interest rates.

Usually the initial interest rate on an ARM is less than the rate on a fixed-rate mortgage. A borrower who chooses a 3/1 ARM saves money for at least 3 years. And there's a good chance the ARM rate will stay relatively low. Over their history, ARMs have been less expensive than fixed-rate mortgages in most years.

On the other hand, ARMs are risky. If short-term interest rates rise, the ARM rate can rise above the fixed rate. Monthly mortgage payments are recalculated based on the new interest rate, so they jump up. This risk is the price of a low initial rate.

When you buy a house, which type of mortgage should you choose? The answer is not clear-cut. It depends both on your personal finances and on the state of the economy. Economists and financial advisors have pointed out several key factors:

- *Your tolerance for risk* Some people must stretch to pay their monthly bills, so a rise in mortgage payments would cause serious problems. These people should probably choose the safety of fixed-rate mortgages. ARMs are for people who can live with uncertainty about their mortgage payments.

- *Your likely tenure in the home* An ARM is attractive if you plan to sell your house in a few years. You benefit from the low initial interest rate, and you will pay off the mortgage before the rate has a chance to rise much. The safety of a fixed rate is more important if you plan to remain in the house for the entire term of the mortgage.
- *The yield curve* The interest rate on a fixed-rate mortgage is a long-term rate, usually a 30-year rate. The rates on ARMs depend on shorter-term rates; for example, initial rates on 3/1 ARMs depend on 3-year interest rates. So the initial savings from an ARM depend on the term structure of interest rates (review Section 4.4). ARMs are most attractive when the yield curve is steep, meaning long rates are far above short rates.
- *The price of your dream house* Approval for a mortgage depends on the ratio of the initial payment to monthly income. Since ARMs reduce initial payments, they help people qualify to buy more expensive homes. Of course, this is a good thing only if you can tolerate risk. The combination of an ARM *and* an expensive house can produce high future payments.

Market and Economic Risk

Market risk Risk arising from fluctuations in asset prices

Economic risk Risk arising from fluctuations in the economy's aggregate output

Banks face two more types of risk. **Market risk** arises from fluctuations in asset prices. As we discussed in Sections 5.6 and 6.6, large banks use derivatives to bet on the prices of stocks, bonds, and currencies. This speculation can produce large profits, but also large losses if asset prices move the wrong way. Recall the case of Societé Generale, which lost 7 billion dollars when Jerome Kerviel bet on European stock markets.

Economic risk arises from fluctuations in the economy's aggregate output. A temporary fall in output—a recession—reduces banks' profits for various reasons. For example, in a recession firms cut investment, so they borrow less. This reduces banks' opportunities for profitable loans. A recession also hurts banks' off-balance-sheet activities. It reduces the number of transactions among companies, so banks sell fewer letters of credit. Fewer companies issue securities during recessions, so large banks earn less from underwriting.

Interactions Among Risks

Managing risk is a complex task. Banks face many risks, and different risks interact with one another. For example, a rise in interest rates is likely to reduce asset prices, so banks are hurt by interest-rate risk and market risk at the same time. A recession can push down asset prices and increase loan defaults, causing losses from economic risk, market risk, and credit risk.

Complicating matters further, strategies for reducing one kind of risk may increase another kind. For example, we've seen that loan sales reduce interest-rate risk and credit risk. But this practice also reduces interest income, forcing banks to rely more heavily on income from OBS activities. These activities carry market risk and economic risk.

The interactions among risks mean that banks need to manage all of them together. Analysts at a bank examine the bank's entire business and look for excessive risk. They do so largely by examining scenarios for the economy, such as a recession, a rise in interest rates, or a fall in real estate prices. The analysts judge the likelihood that these events will occur and estimate the bank's losses given its current balance sheet and OBS activities. If plausible scenarios produce large losses, the bank tries to adjust its business to reduce risk.

9.6 INSOLVENCY

We've seen that banks face many risks, from loan defaults to rising interest rates to recessions. A bank loses money when events like these occur. If the losses are large enough, the bank can face **insolvency.** This means its total assets fall below its liabilities. Its net worth becomes negative.

Insolvency Liabilities exceed assets, producing negative net worth

An insolvent bank cannot stay in business. With negative net worth, it cannot pay off all its deposits and borrowings. In this situation, government regulators step in and force the bank to close.

▶Chapter 10 discusses the process of closing insolvent banks.

Insolvency hurts a bank's stockholders. Their stock becomes worthless, as the bank will have no future earnings. Bank managers also suffer because they lose their jobs. So managers seek to avoid insolvency.

An Example

Insolvency can occur if a bank suffers large losses for any reason. Let's consider an example in which insolvency is caused by loan defaults.

In **Table 9.9A,** Melvin's Bank starts with net worth of \$20. It has \$80 in loans. Then disaster strikes: borrowers default on \$30 of the loans (not just \$5, as in our earlier example of credit risk). When the bank writes off the bad loans, its net worth falls to −\$10, as shown in **Table 9.9B.** Melvin's Bank is now insolvent. It owes depositors \$100, and it has only \$90 in assets to pay them back. Melvin's story ends sadly as the government shuts down his bank.

The Equity Ratio

Banks strive to reduce the risk of insolvency. They can do so by holding more capital. Suppose Melvin's Bank had started with \$50 in capital rather than \$20. Then its capital would have stayed positive even after it lost \$30 to bad loans. Higher capital means a deeper cushion against losses.

TABLE 9.9 Insolvency

(A) Melvin's Initial Balance Sheet

Assets		Liabilities and Net Worth	
Reserves	10	Checking Deposits	50
Securities	30	Nontransaction Deposits	50
Loans	80	Net Worth	20
TOTAL	120	TOTAL	120

(B) Melvin's Balance Sheet after Loan Defaults

Assets		Liabilities and Net Worth	
Reserves	10	Checking Deposits	50
Securities	30	Nontransaction Deposits	50
Loans	50	Net Worth	−10
TOTAL	90	TOTAL	90

Equity ratio (ER) Ratio of a bank's capital to its assets; ER = capital/assets

To be more precise, a bank's insolvency risk depends on its level of capital relative to its assets. This is measured by its **equity ratio** (ER):

$$\text{equity ratio} = \frac{\text{capital}}{\text{assets}}$$

The equity ratio shows what percentage of assets a bank would have to lose to become insolvent. In Table 9.9, the initial equity ratio for Melvin's Bank is $20/$120 = 16.7%. The bank becomes insolvent because it loses 25 percent of its assets ($30/$120). The bank would have survived if its equity ratio were greater than 25 percent.

Holding capital constant, a higher level of assets reduces the equity ratio. The greater a bank's assets, the more it has to lose if things go wrong. It therefore faces greater insolvency risk.

A bank can raise its equity ratio either by raising capital (the numerator) or by reducing assets (the denominator). The bank can raise capital by issuing new stock or by reducing dividends to stockholders. It can reduce assets by making fewer loans or purchasing fewer securities. Any of these actions reduces insolvency risk.

The Equity Ratio and the Return on Equity

Raising the equity ratio also has a big disadvantage: it makes a bank less profitable. Recall that profitability is measured by the return on equity (ROE), which is the ratio of profits to capital. This variable falls when the equity ratio rises.

We can see this effect with a little algebra. We take the formula for ROE and divide both the numerator and denominator by assets:

$$\text{ROE} = \frac{\text{profits}}{\text{capital}} = \frac{\dfrac{\text{profits}}{\text{assets}}}{\dfrac{\text{capital}}{\text{assets}}}$$

In this formula, profits/assets is the return on assets (ROA). Capital/assets is the equity ratio. So we can simplify to

$$\text{ROE} = \frac{\text{ROA}}{\text{ER}} \qquad (9.2)$$

The return on equity depends on the return on assets and the equity ratio. For a given ROA, raising the equity ratio reduces the ROE.

To understand this effect, suppose a bank raises its equity ratio by issuing new stock. It keeps its assets the same. With the same assets, the bank gets the same flow of profits—but now these profits are split among more stockholders. Each share of stock earns less.

To summarize, a bank faces a trade-off when it chooses its equity ratio. A higher ratio reduces insolvency risk but also reduces the return on equity. A bank would like a ratio that is high enough to make insolvency unlikely but low enough to produce good returns for its stockholders.

CASE STUDY

The Banking Crisis of the 1980s

Figure 9.4 shows the number of U.S. bank failures in each year from 1960 through 2007. In most of these years, fewer than 10 banks failed. The big exception is the 1980s, when failures grew rapidly, peaking at 534 in 1989. Some of the failed institutions were commercial banks, but the majority were Savings and Loan Associations. The episode is often called the *S&L crisis.*

Two causes of the crisis were rising interest rates and loan defaults. Examining the episode yields a deeper understanding of interest-rate risk and credit risk.

Rising Interest Rates Banks' rate-sensitivity gaps were highly negative in the 1980s, especially at S&Ls. Most liabilities of S&Ls were deposits with zero maturities, and most assets were long-term, fixed-rate mortgages. Many of these loans had been made in the 1960s, when interest rates were low. In 1965, the Treasury bill rate was about 4% and the 30-year mortgage rate was 6%.

Interest rates rose rapidly in the 1970s and early 1980s. Recall that the nominal interest rate is the sum of the real rate and inflation ($i = \pi + r$). In the 1970s real rates were low, but inflation pushed up nominal rates (see Figure 3.5). At the end of the decade, the Fed raised real rates to fight inflation. It took time for inflation to respond, so both real rates *and* inflation were high in the early 80s. The nominal rate on T-bills peaked at 14 percent in 1981.

FIGURE 9.4 Failures of U.S. Commercial Banks and Savings Institutions, 1960–2007

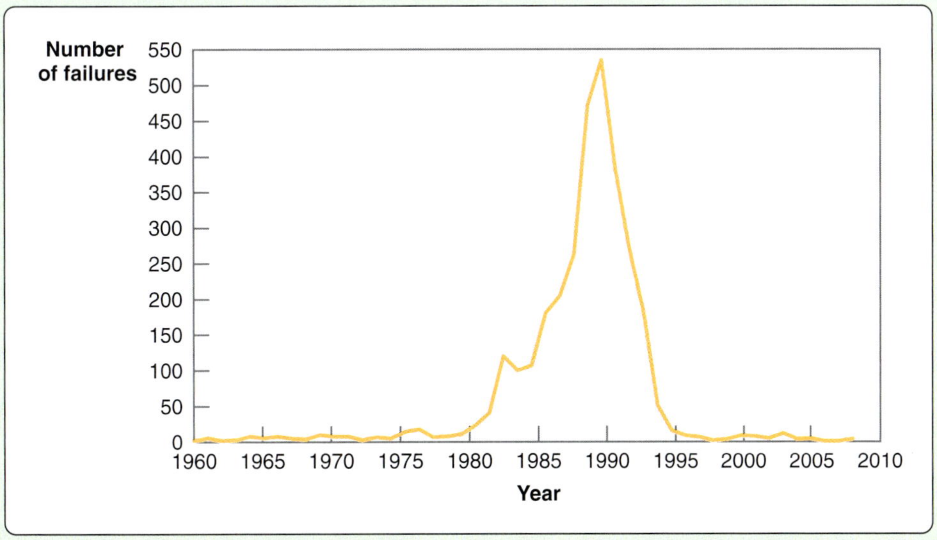

Bank failures were rare from 1960 through 2007, except during the banking crisis of the 1980s.
Source: Federal Deposit Insurance Corporation

You can guess what happened from our earlier discussion of interest-rate risk. Banks were forced to raise interest rates on deposits along with the T-bill rate. In the early 1980s, they paid higher rates on deposits than they received on many mortgages. So they suffered large losses.

The Commercial Real Estate Bust In the early 1980s, banks sharply raised their lending for commercial real estate projects, such as office buildings and shopping centers. This lending rose for several reasons:

- Real estate prices were high, spurring new construction. So there was a large demand for real estate loans.
- Banks were looking for new loan opportunities. They sought to replace the C&I loans they were losing as borrowers turned to bonds and commercial paper.
- Regulations changed. Traditionally, S&L's specialized in home mortgages and were forbidden to lend for commercial real estate. Congress lifted this ban in 1980, so S&L's joined commercial banks in lending to commercial real estate developers.

In retrospect, this lending was imprudent. Banks made the same basic mistake as subprime mortgage lenders two decades later: eager for business, they relaxed their loan standards. Banks approved loans for risky projects with low collateral. When the real estate industry experienced problems, many developers went bankrupt and defaulted on loans.

Several events triggered these defaults. Many defaults occurred during the recession of 1981–82, which decreased the demand for real estate. More defaults occurred in 1986, when world oil prices fell, hurting the oil-producing economies of Texas and neighboring states.

The final blow came at the end of the 1980s. Rapid building in the first part of the decade created an oversupply of commercial real estate. Developers had a hard time renting space, and property prices plummeted. Loan defaults mounted, pushing many banks into insolvency.

This analysis blames the S&L crisis on loan defaults and rising interest rates. Many economists cite a third cause: poor government regulation. We revisit the S&L crisis in Chapter 10, where we discuss bank regulation.

Summary

9.1 Banks' Balance Sheets

- A bank's balance sheet shows its assets on the left side and its liabilities and net worth (equity or capital) on the right.
- The major liabilities (sources of funds) of commercial banks are checking deposits, nontransaction deposits, and borrowings. The major assets (uses of funds) are cash items (including reserves), securities, and loans.

9.2 Off-Balance-Sheet Activities

- In addition to holding assets and liabilities, banks engage in off-balance-sheet activities. OBS activities include lines of credit, letters of credit, asset management, derivatives trading, and investment banking services.

9.3 How Banks Make Profits

- A bank starts with capital from its owners and raises additional funds from deposits and borrowings. It uses these funds to acquire assets that produce interest income. It also earns non-interest income from OBS activities.
- A bank's income statement shows its interest and non-interest income, its interest and non-interest expenses, and its profits over some period, such as a year.
- Banks' profitability is measured by the return on assets (profits/assets) and the return on equity (profits/capital).

9.4 The Evolving Pursuit of Profits

- Core deposits include checking deposits, savings deposits, and small time deposits, all relatively inexpensive sources of funds. Purchased funds, which include large time deposits and borrowings, are more expensive.
- Banks seek to maximize core deposits through advertising and customer service. They choose their levels of purchased funds based on loan opportunities.
- Over time, banks' sources of funds have shifted away from checking deposits and toward purchased funds. These trends have raised banks' interest expenses.
- Commercial and industrial loans have fallen over time, while real estate loans and credit card loans have risen.
- Banks' off-balance-sheet activities have grown over time, raising the importance of non-interest income to profitability.
- Large banks often make C&I loans in the hope that borrowers will hire them to underwrite securities. This practice is generally legal, unless lending and underwriting are tied together explicitly.
- Fees are a rising share of bank income. Consumer groups have criticized overdraft fees and fees on credit cards.

9.5 Managing Risk

- Liquidity risk is the risk that withdrawals will exhaust a bank's liquid assets, forcing a fire sale of loans. In choosing assets, banks face a trade-off between liquidity risk and profits. The federal funds market reduces liquidity risk.
- Credit risk is the risk of loan defaults. Banks reduce this risk through loan sales.
- Interest-rate risk arises from the maturity mismatch between bank liabilities, which are mainly short-term, and assets, which are mainly long-term. A rise in interest rates reduces bank profits. Banks reduce interest-rate risk through loan sales, floating interest rates, and trades of derivatives.
- Choosing a floating-rate mortgage reduces a borrower's initial payments but increases his risk. The desirability of a floating-rate mortgage depends on risk tolerance, expected tenure in the home, the price of the home, and the yield curve.
- Market risk is banks' risk from changes in asset prices. Economic risk is risk from fluctuations in the economy's aggregate output.

9.6 Insolvency

- If a bank suffers large losses, its capital can become negative. The bank is insolvent and must shut down.
- The risk of insolvency depends on the equity ratio (capital/assets). A higher ER reduces risk but also reduces the return on equity.
- The S&L crisis of the 1980s drove many banks into insolvency. The crisis was triggered by rising interest rates and defaults on commercial real estate loans.

Key Terms

balance sheet, p. 250
core deposits, p. 259
credit risk, p. 269
economic risk, p. 274
equity ratio (ER), p. 276
federal funds, p. 251
floating interest rate, p. 272
income statement, p. 256
insolvency, p. 275
interest-rate risk, p. 270
letter of credit, p. 254
liabilities, p. 250
liquidity risk, p. 267
market risk, p. 274
net worth, p. 250
off-balance-sheet (OBS) activities, p. 253
purchased funds, p. 259
rate-sensitivity gap, p. 272
repurchase agreements (repos), p. 252
reserves, p. 252
return on assets (ROA), p. 257
return on equity (ROE), p. 257
vault cash, p. 252

Questions and Problems

1. Suppose Melvin's Bank starts with the balance sheet in Table 9.4A and the income statement in Table 9.2. Show how the balance sheet and income statement change in each of the following scenarios. Also calculate the new ROA, ROE, and rate-sensitivity gap.
   a. The bank issues $20 of new stock and uses the proceeds to make loans.
   b. Britt moves $25 from his savings account to his checking account.
   c. The bank is hired to manage the assets of a wealthy person, for which it is paid $10 a year.
   d. The bank lends $5 of reserves to another bank in the federal funds market. (Assume the federal funds rate is the same as the Treasury bill rate.)
   e. The bank replaces $10 of its loans with floating-rate loans, which pay the Treasury bill rate plus 2 percent.
2. Suppose again that Melvin's Bank starts with the balance sheet in Table 9.4A. Then the bank sells $10 of loans for $10 of cash.
   a. What is the immediate effect on the balance sheet?
   b. After the loan sale, what additional transactions is the bank likely to make? What will the balance sheet look like after these transactions?
3. Suppose Ashley's Finance Company raises most of its funds by issuing long-term bonds. It uses these funds for floating-rate loans.
   a. How does the company's rate-sensitivity gap differ from those of most banks?
   b. What deal could Ashley and Melvin make to reduce risk for both of their institutions?
4. Canada does not have an institution like Fannie Mae that securitizes mortgages. How do you think this fact affects the types of mortgages

offered by Canadian banks? (*Hint:* Think about interest-rate risk.)

5. Robert Shiller of Yale University has suggested a variation on ARMs in which mortgage interest rates are tied to inflation, not to short-term interest rates. Discuss the pros and cons of this idea for banks and for borrowers.

6. Suppose the Federal Reserve raises short-term interest rates, an action that is likely to reduce aggregate output temporarily. Describe the various effects on the profits of commercial banks.

7. How does each of the following developments affect banks' desired equity ratios? Explain.
   a. An increase in OBS activities
   b. A shift from C&I lending to real estate lending
   c. A shift from fixed-rate to floating-rate loans
   d. An increase in securitization

Online and Data Questions

www.worthpublishers.com/ball

8. The text Web site provides data on the percentage of new prime mortgages with adjustable rates in each year since 1990. Link from there to the St. Louis Fed site for data on interest rates over the same period. How do the rates on 10-year Treasury bonds and 90-day Treasury bills affect the popularity of ARMs? Can you explain the effects?

9. The text Web site provides data on the percentage of prime mortgages with adjustable rates in each U.S. state. In which states are ARMs most common and least common? What might explain these facts?

10. Examine a recent annual report for the bank where you have a checking account. (The bank's Web site should have a link to its annual report.) Also examine the updated Table 9.1 and Figure 9.1 at the text Web site.
    a. How does your bank's composition of assets and liabilities differ from averages for U.S. commercial banks? What explains these differences?
    b. In recent years, how has your bank's return on equity differed from the U.S. average? What factors might explain the above- or below-average performance?

11. Examine the cardmember agreement for a credit card you hold (or one held by a friend or family member). Determine the total amount you would pay in fees if you (a) exceed your credit limit, (b) send a payment in late, and (c) take a $100 cash advance. What would your interest rate be after all these events?

chapter ten 10

Bank Regulation

- 10.1 BANK RUNS
- 10.2 DEPOSIT INSURANCE
- 10.3 MORAL HAZARD AGAIN
- 10.4 WHO CAN OPEN A BANK?
- 10.5 RESTRICTIONS ON BALANCE SHEETS
- 10.6 SUPERVISION
- 10.7 CLOSING INSOLVENT BANKS

The government has eliminated many past restrictions on banks. Today, commercial banks are free to expand geographically, and they can enter new businesses such as investment banking. Yet U.S. banking remains a heavily regulated industry.

Federal and state governments restrict banks in many ways. Regulators decide who can open a bank. They limit the types of assets that banks can hold and set minimum levels of capital that banks must maintain. Government examiners visit banks regularly to review their activities. If examiners disapprove of a bank's practices, they can order changes or even force the bank to close.

Most of this regulation exists to prevent bank failures. Over history, failures have caused devastating losses to the owners of banks and their depositors. Bank failures have also been costly to the government and the overall economy. Because of these experiences, regulators try to limit the problems that produce failures.

Regulators are especially concerned with two causes of bank failures. One is a **bank run,** in which depositors lose confidence in a bank and make sudden, large withdrawals. The other is a problem of moral hazard: owners and managers of banks may misuse the funds they are given by depositors. This chapter examines both problems and how bank regulators address them.

AP/Wide World Photos

September 17, 2007: Customers of Northern Rock Bank line up to withdraw money from a branch in York, England during a run on the bank.

Bank run Sudden, large withdrawals by depositors who lose confidence in a bank

10.1 BANK RUNS

In any industry, a firm can fail. It can lose money, run out of funds, and be forced out of business. Often, economists think this outcome is efficient. If a firm is not profitable, its resources should be freed up for more productive uses.

When it comes to banks, however, economists have a less benign view of failure. One reason is the occurrence of bank runs. A run can push a healthy bank into insolvency, causing it to fail for no good reason. Both the bank's owners and its depositors suffer needless losses.

How Bank Runs Happen

The risk of a bank run is an extreme form of liquidity risk, the risk that a bank will have trouble meeting demands for withdrawals. As discussed in Section 9.5, banks manage this risk by holding reserves and secondary reserves, such as Treasury bills. If they are short on reserves, they borrow federal funds from other banks. Normally these methods are sufficient to contain liquidity risk.

However, things are different when a bank experiences a run. A sudden surge in withdrawals overwhelms the bank. It runs out of liquid assets and cannot borrow enough to cover all the withdrawals. The bank is forced to sell its loans at fire-sale prices, reducing its capital. If the bank loses enough, capital falls below zero: the run causes insolvency.

What causes runs? Some occur because a bank is insolvent, even before the run: the bank does not have enough assets to pay off its liabilities and will likely close. In this situation, depositors fear they will lose their money. These fears are compounded by the first-come, first-served nature of deposit withdrawals. The first people to withdraw get their money back, while those who act slowly may find that no funds are left. So depositors rush to withdraw before it's too late, and a run occurs.

A run can also occur at a bank that is initially solvent. This happens if depositors lose confidence in the bank, which can happen suddenly and without good reason. Suppose someone starts a rumor that a bank has lost money and become insolvent. This rumor is totally false. However, depositors hear the rumor and worry that it might be true. Some decide to play it safe and withdraw their funds.

Seeing these withdrawals, other depositors begin to fear that a run is starting. They decide to get their money out before everyone else does and the bank fails. Suddenly, there are lots of withdrawals: a run *does* occur. Ultimately, the bank is forced into a fire sale of assets, and its capital is driven below zero.

Section 3.5 discussed the phenomenon of self-fulfilling expectations. We saw there how expectations can influence asset prices. If people expect stock prices to fall, then they sell stocks, causing prices to fall. Bank runs are the same kind of event: if people expect a run, then a run occurs. This can happen even if nothing is wrong at the bank before the run.

TABLE 10.1 A Run on Melvin's Bank

(A) Initial Balance Sheet				(B) Balance Sheet After Run			
Assets		**Liabilities and Net Worth**		**Assets**		**Liabilities and Net Worth**	
Reserves	10	Checking deposits	50	Reserves	0	Checking deposits	10
Securities	30	Savings deposits	50	Securities	0	Savings deposits	10
Loans	80	Net worth	20	Loans	0	Net worth	−20
TOTAL	120	TOTAL	120	TOTAL	0	TOTAL	0

An Example

Suppose Melvin's Bank has the balance sheet shown in **Table 10.1A.** The bank has a positive level of capital, or net worth. It also has enough reserves and Treasury bills to meet normal demands for withdrawals. There is no good reason for Melvin's Bank to go out of business.

Then a negative rumor about the bank starts circulating. Worried depositors decide to withdraw their funds. We'll assume they want to withdraw all the money in savings and checking accounts, a total of $100.

To pay depositors, Melvin's Bank first uses its reserves and Treasury bills, a total of $40. Then, with its liquid assets exhausted, the bank must quickly sell its loans. We'll assume this fire sale produces only 50 cents per dollar of loans. The bank sells its $80 in loans, receives $40, and gives this money to depositors. At this point, the bank has paid off a total of $80 in deposits.

The bank's new balance sheet is shown in **Table 10.1B.** The bank now has no assets. It still has $20 in liabilities, as it paid off only $80 out of the $100 in deposits. (The table assumes the remaining deposits are split evenly between checking and savings accounts.) The bank is insolvent. It cannot pay the last $20 demanded by depositors, so it goes out of business.

This example assumes that Melvin's Bank *cannot* borrow federal funds to pay depositors. This is a plausible assumption in this case. Other banks see the run on Melvin's Bank and recognize that it threatens Melvin's solvency. They won't lend federal funds because the loan won't be repaid if Melvin is forced to close.

The run on Melvin's Bank hurts two groups of people. The first are the owners of the bank: they lose the $20 in capital that they had before the run. The second are the holders of the last $20 in deposits. When the bank closes, these deposits become worthless.

Suspension of Payments

A bank run often leads to a **suspension of payments.** Overwhelmed by the demand for withdrawals, a bank announces that it will not allow them. A depositor who shows up at the bank finds the doors closed.

Suspension of payments Refusal by a bank to allow withdrawals by depositors

Sometimes suspension of payments is a prelude to permanent closure of a bank. But often it is meant to be temporary. The bank hopes that suspension will stop the run that threatens its solvency. If this happens, the bank can reopen. Depositors leave their money in the bank and it carries on business as before.

Suspension of payments can end a run in two ways. First, it can help change the self-fulfilling psychology of the run. While the bank is closed, depositors have a chance to calm down. They can check that the bank is solvent and realize there's no good reason to withdraw their money.

Second, suspension gives the bank a chance to increase its liquid assets. It may be able to borrow from other banks. With a little time, it may find buyers for its loans that pay what the loans are worth, not fire-sale prices. With a high level of liquid assets, the bank can meet demands for withdrawals when it reopens.

In the United States, suspensions of payments were common in the nineteenth and early twentieth centuries. Banks facing runs suspended payments for periods of a few days to a few months and then reopened. Often these actions were not strictly legal, as depositors had the right to immediate withdrawals. However, bank regulators granted exceptions or simply ignored suspensions because they wanted banks to survive.

CASE STUDY

Bank Runs in Fiction and Fact

Bank runs have produced many colorful stories. Let's discuss three examples, one fictional and two real.

A Disney Bank Run A run occurs in the classic Walt Disney movie *Mary Poppins*. It is caused by a family argument. The story begins when Mr. Banks takes his young son Michael to the bank where he works to deposit Michael's savings of tuppence (two pence).

Outside the bank is a woman selling birdseed for tuppence a bag. Seeing her, Michael decides he would rather feed the birds than deposit his money. Mr. Banks rejects this foolish idea and gives Michael's tuppence to Mr. Dawes, the head of the bank. Michael becomes angry and starts struggling with Mr. Dawes, shouting "give me back my money!"

Bank customers see the commotion and fear the bank has become insolvent. They rush to withdraw their money, and a run is underway. The bank runs out of liquid assets and is forced to suspend payments.

Hollywood gives us a happy ending. The bank clears up the misunderstanding about Michael's tantrum and convinces depositors it is solvent. It reopens and depositors leave their money in their accounts. Mr. Banks is initially fired for his role in the run, but he is soon rehired and promoted.

Guta Bank In the real world, bank runs often end less happily than in the movies. One example comes from Russia in 2004. A financial crisis in the late 1990s had caused many bank failures, leaving depositors nervous. They became more nervous in May 2004, when the Central Bank of Russia closed a small bank for financing criminal activities.

In announcing this closure, an official mentioned that other banks were under investigation. This prompted rumors about which banks might be closed, with lists circulating on the Internet.

Many rumors involved Guta Bank, Russia's twentieth largest with $1 billion in assets. In retrospect, there is no evidence that Guta did anything wrong, and it was solvent. But the rumors spooked depositors. They withdrew $345 million in June, and Guta ran out of liquid assets. On July 5, customers couldn't get cash from Guta's ATMs. On July 6, the bank closed its doors, posting a notice that payments were suspended.

Initially, Guta hoped to reopen, like the bank in *Mary Poppins*, but it wasn't able to regain depositors' confidence. On July 9, Guta's owners sold it to a government-owned bank, Vneshtorbank, for the token sum of 1 million rubles ($34,000). At that point, Guta's branches reopened, but as branches of Vneshtorbank.

It's not known who started the rumors about Guta Bank. Journalists have speculated that the culprits were rival banks or government officials. They suggest the Russian government wanted to help the banks it owned, including Vneshtorbank, take business from private banks like Guta. One piece of evidence: the Central Bank refused a plea from Guta for an emergency loan but approved a loan to Vneshtorbank after it took over Guta.

Northern Rock Before September 2007, the United Kingdom had not experienced a bank run for 140 years (if we don't count *Mary Poppins*). Then suddenly, on September 14, long lines of worried depositors formed at branches of Northern Rock Bank (see the photo on p. 283). Depositors also jammed the banks' phone lines and crashed its Web site. Between September 14 and September 17, depositors managed to withdraw 2 billion pounds (roughly $4 billion) from Northern Rock.

Northern Rock Bank is headquartered in Northern England (hence the name), and it lends primarily for home mortgages. Before the run, Northern Rock was the fifth-largest mortgage lender in the U.K., and growing rapidly. The bank's lending far exceeded its core deposits, so it used purchased funds to finance much of the lending. A major source of funds was short-term loans from other banks (the equivalent of federal funds in the United States).

▶ See Section 9.4 for a review of core deposits and purchased funds.

Northern Rock's problems began across the Atlantic, with the subprime mortgage crisis in the United States. In the summer of 2007, people worried that the U.S. crisis might spread, threatening the solvency of other countries' financial institutions. With this idea in the air, banks became wary of lending to each other—and especially wary of lending to banks that specialized in mortgages. As a result, Northern Rock had trouble raising purchased funds. Other banks either refused to lend to Northern Rock or demanded high interest rates.

In a bind, Northern Rock turned to the U.K.'s central bank, the Bank of England, asking it to perform its role as lender of last resort (see Section 2.5). The Bank of England approved a loan to Northern Rock and planned an announcement, but the news leaked out prematurely. On September 13, a well-known business reporter said on television that Northern Rock "has had to go cap in hand" to the Bank of England. Hearing that their bank had a problem, Northern Rock's depositors had the typical reaction: on September 14, they rushed to withdraw their funds.

Deposits flowed out of Northern Rock for three days, until the British government intervened. On September 17, the government announced it would guarantee the bank's deposits: if the bank failed, the government would compensate depositors. This action restored confidence enough to end the run.

Yet Northern Rock's problems were not over. The run damaged the bank's reputation, and it continued to have trouble raising funds. It borrowed more and more from the Bank of England, and fears grew about its solvency. In February 2008, the government responded by nationalizing Northern Rock—by taking ownership of it. The government compensated the bank's shareholders. It also said it will sell Northern Rock back to private interests in the future, but it's not clear when.

Bank Panics

Sometimes runs occur simultaneously at many individual banks. People lose confidence in the whole banking system, and depositors everywhere try to withdraw their money. This event is called a **bank panic.**

Bank panic Simultaneous runs at many individual banks

Nationwide bank panics were once common in the United States. Between 1873 and 1933, the country experienced an average of three panics per decade. Bank panics occur because a loss of confidence is contagious. A run at one bank triggers runs at others, which trigger runs at others, and so on.

Suppose a run occurs at Melvin's Bank. Gertrude's Bank is next door to Melvin's, and Gertrude's depositors notice the run. It occurs to these depositors that the same thing might happen at their bank. To be safe, they withdraw their money, and Gertrude's experiences a run. Now runs have hit two banks. Seeing this, depositors at other banks get nervous. More runs occur, and the panic spreads through the economy.

In the United States, a typical bank panic started with runs on New York banks. These triggered runs in other parts of the East, and then the panic spread westward. The next case discusses the last and most severe bank panics in U.S. history.

CASE STUDY

Bank Panics in the 1930s

Figure 10.1 shows the percentage of all banks that failed each year in the United States from 1876 to 1935. Before 1920, the failure rate was low despite periodic panics. Banks suspended payments but most eventually reopened.

Bank failures rose moderately in the 1920s. Most failures occurred at small, rural banks. These banks made loans to farmers, and falling agricultural prices during the 1920s led to defaults. These failures were isolated, however; most banks appeared healthy.

FIGURE 10.1 U.S. Bank Failure Rate, 1876–1935

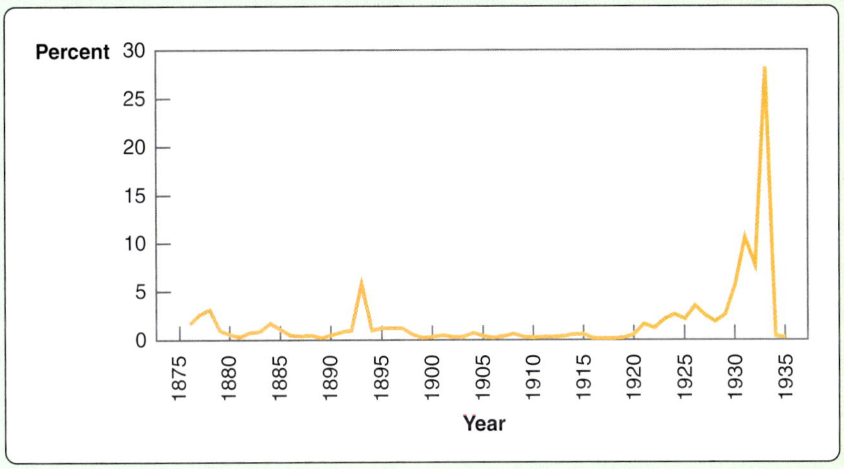

The bank failure rate is failures during a year as a percentage of the total number of banks. The failure rate rose moderately during the 1920s and skyrocketed during the banking panics of the early 1930s.

Source: George J. Benston et al., *Perspectives on Safe and Sound Banking: Past, Present and Future*, Cambridge, MA: MIT Press, 1986

Major trouble began in 1930. Failures rose at rural banks in the Midwest, and this made depositors nervous about other banks in the region. These worries were exacerbated by general unease about the economy, a result of the 1929 stock market crash. Bank runs started in the Midwest, and this time they spread eastward.

A psychological milestone was the failure of the Bank of the United States, located in New York, in December 1930. It was one of the country's largest banks, and the largest ever to fail. In addition, although it was an ordinary commercial bank, its name suggested some link to the government. Its failure shook confidence in the whole banking system.

Other events eroded confidence further. Some well-known European banks failed in 1931. In the 1932 election campaign, Democrats publicized banking problems to criticize the Republican government. The stream of worrisome news produced a nationwide panic.

The bank panics of the 1930s were the most severe in U.S. history. One reason, say economic historians, was that banks were slow to suspend payments. Suspensions had helped end the panics of the late nineteenth and early twentieth centuries. In the 1930s, however, banks were influenced by the Federal Reserve, which was founded in 1913. The Fed discouraged suspensions, which in retrospect was a mistake.

Democrat Franklin Roosevelt became president on March 4, 1933, and he quickly took charge of the banking crisis. On March 6, Roosevelt announced a *bank holiday*: across the country, all banks were required to suspend payments. Starting on March 13, banks were allowed to reopen, but only if the Secretary of the Treasury certified they were solvent.

A quarter of all U.S. banks failed in 1933, but Roosevelt's policies ended the panic.

President Roosevelt understood the psychology of panics. His famous statement that "we have nothing to fear but fear itself" referred partly to banking. It captures the fact that panics result from self-fulfilling expectations.*

* For more on the bank panics of the 1930s, see Chapter 7 of Milton Friedman and Anna Schwartz, *A Monetary History of the United States*, 1867–1960, Princeton University Press, 1963.

10.2 DEPOSIT INSURANCE

No bank panics have occurred in the United States since 1933. Runs have occurred at individual banks, but they are rare. That's because the government has found a solution to the problem: **deposit insurance.**

Deposit insurance Government guarantee to compensate depositors for their losses when a bank fails

How Deposit Insurance Works

Deposit insurance is a government's promise to compensate depositors for their losses when a bank fails. In our example of Melvin's Bank, insurance would pay off the last $20 in deposits after Melvin runs out of assets in Table 10.1B. In addition to protecting depositors when bank failures occur, insurance makes failures less likely. This effect arises because insurance eliminates bank runs, a major cause of failures.

The reason is simple. A run occurs when depositors start worrying about the safety of their deposits and try to withdraw them. Deposit insurance eliminates the worry, as depositors know they will be paid back if their bank fails. They have no reason to start a run, even if they hear bad rumors about the bank. A solvent bank keeps its deposits and remains solvent.

Deposit Insurance in the United States

Deposit insurance is provided primarily by the **Federal Deposit Insurance Corporation (FDIC),** a U.S. government agency. Congress created the FDIC in 1933 in response to the bank panics of the early 1930s. Today, the FDIC insures all deposits at commercial banks and savings institutions. Credit unions have a separate insurance fund.

Federal Deposit Insurance Corporation (FDIC) Government agency that insures deposits at U.S. commercial banks and savings institutions

If a bank fails and depositors lose money, the FDIC compensates them up to some limit. Usually, this limit is $100,000 per bank account. Anyone with a deposit below $100,000 is compensated fully when a bank fails. The limit is $250,000 for some kinds of retirement accounts.

▶ In October 2008, the FDIC temporarily raised the limit on insurance coverage to $250,000 for all accounts. The goal was to bolster the public's confidence in banks, which was shaken by the financial crisis of 2007–2008. The FDIC announced that coverage limits would return to their previous levels at the end of 2009.

The FDIC's large insurance fund holds U.S. government bonds. In principle, this fund is financed by premiums charged to banks. For most banks, however, the premiums have been near zero since 1996. Premiums have not been needed, because the insurance fund earns interest on its bond holdings. In addition, costs have been low because few banks have failed. Under current law, premiums will rise if the fund falls below a certain level.

While large, the FDIC insurance fund is far less than the total insured deposits in banks. If there were widespread bank failures, the fund could run out of money before it paid all claims. In this event, it is likely the government would step in and provide additional funds.

Government help was needed during the S&L crisis of the 1980s. This episode, described in Section 9.6, depleted the funds of the Federal Savings and Loan Insurance Company, which insured S&Ls at the time. In 1989, Congress abolished this agency, and the FDIC started insuring savings institutions as well as commercial banks. Meanwhile, the government paid off depositors at failed S&Ls. The cost of this bailout, about $150 billion, was ultimately borne by U.S. taxpayers.

Not all countries have deposit insurance. In Russia, insurance was created only in 2005—too late for Guta Bank. The U.K. had deposit insurance in 2007, but it paid only 90 percent of losses. Northern Rock's customers ran to the bank because they stood to lose 10 percent of their deposits if the bank failed (until the fourth day of the run, when the government guaranteed deposits fully). Later we'll compare the use of deposit insurance in different parts of the world.

10.3 MORAL HAZARD AGAIN

Deposit insurance fixes the problem of bank runs. Unfortunately, it makes another problem worse. This problem is one of moral hazard: bankers have incentives to misuse deposits. Let's discuss the problem and how it interacts with deposit insurance.

Misuses of Deposits

One of banking's central functions is to reduce moral hazard in loan markets. Recall that moral hazard is also called the principal–agent problem. Borrowers (the agents) have incentives to misuse the funds they receive from savers (the principals). Banks reduce this problem through monitoring, loan covenants, and collateral (see Section 7.7).

Unfortunately, banking creates new moral hazard problems. Here, bankers are the agents and their depositors are the principals. Bankers have incentives to use deposits in ways that benefit themselves but hurt depositors. The misuse of deposits takes two basic forms: excessive risk-taking and looting.

Excessive Risk Bankers can exploit depositors through risky activities. Suppose a bank lends to borrowers with risky projects who are willing to pay high interest rates. If the projects succeed, the interest income produces high profits for the bank's owners. If the projects fail, the borrowers default and the bank may become insolvent.

However, not all the losses from insolvency fall on the bank. Depositors also lose when the bank can't pay them back. Bankers have incentives to gamble because someone else pays part of the costs if their gambles fail.

Similarly, bankers have incentives for risky off-balance-sheet activities. Suppose a bank speculates with derivatives—it makes a bet on future interest rates or asset prices. The bank earns large profits if the gamble pays off, and depositors share the costs if it doesn't. The gamble is "heads I win, tails you lose."

Suppose a bank's net worth, or capital, is \$20. The bank uses derivatives to make a gamble, one that has a 50 percent chance of earning \$50 and a 50 percent chance of losing \$50. If the bank wins this gamble, its net worth rises by \$50, to \$70. If it loses, its net worth falls to –\$30, and the bank fails.

If the bank fails, its owners lose only \$20, their initial capital. Depositors lose \$30, because the insolvent bank can't pay off all its deposits. The gamble is a good deal for the bank, as it risks only \$20 to gain \$50. It is a bad deal for depositors, who gain nothing if the gamble succeeds but lose \$30 if it fails.

Looting Bankers can also exploit depositors in a less subtle way: by stealing their money. The famous robber Willie Sutton was once asked why he chose to hold up banks. His response was, "That's where the money is."

The same reasoning applies to white-collar crime when a bank's management is unscrupulous. Large amounts of money flow in and out of banks, creating opportunities for fraud and embezzlement. History provides many examples of bank failures caused by dishonesty.

As usual, the root of moral hazard is asymmetric information. If depositors could see what bankers do with their money, they could forbid gambling and stealing. But it isn't easy to observe what happens inside banks, as the next case study illustrates.

CASE STUDY

The Keystone Scandal

The town of Keystone, West Virginia, has only about 400 residents. But it was the scene of one of the costliest bank failures in U.S. history, an episode that vividly illustrates the problem of moral hazard in banking.

The First National Bank of Keystone was a community bank founded in 1904. In 1977, when it had only \$17 million in assets, the bank was bought by an ambitious entrepreneur, J. Knox McConnell, and started growing quickly. It expanded its business beyond the Keystone area, making mortgage loans throughout West Virginia and western Pennsylvania.

The bank's assets rose to \$90 million in 1992. At that point, it started purchasing loans from banks around the country. It bought risky loans with high interest rates, including subprime loans for home improvements and loans for debt consolidation (loans used to pay off other debt). In buying these loans, First National took on more risk than commercial banks usually tolerate. It securitized and sold some of the loans and kept others on its balance sheet. First National's assets reached \$1.1 billion in 1999.

The bank needed large deposits to fund its growing assets. It got these by offering interest rates on CDs that were two percentage points above the industry norm. It advertised these rates on the Internet, attracting deposits from around the country.

First National appeared very profitable. It earned high interest income on its risky assets, so it easily covered its interest expense. In 1995, it reported a return on equity of 81 percent. The newspaper *The American Banker* named First National Bank of Keystone the most successful small bank in the country.

But two related problems did Keystone Bank in. First, over the decade of the 1990s, defaults rose on the types of loans the bank purchased. The bank suffered losses on the loans it held on its balance sheet, and it started receiving lower prices for the securitized loans that it sold. In retrospect, Keystone's losses on risky loans look similar to the losses of subprime mortgage lenders in 2007 (see Section 8.4).

Second, top bank managers embezzled tens of millions of dollars. They paid fees to themselves and companies they owned for phony work on their loan securitization business. Some commentators suggest that Keystone's managers knew this business was unprofitable and pursued it only because it facilitated their theft.

For years, the managers of First National Bank of Keystone deceived government regulators about their behavior. They kept loans on the bank's balance sheet after the loans were sold, inflating the bank's assets and net worth. They forged documents in which the bank's board of directors approved payments. When regulators investigated the bank, desperate executives buried two truckloads of documents on the ranch of Senior Vice President Terry Church.

Eventually, regulators found out the truth. In 1999 they determined that 70 percent of First National's assets were fictitious, which implied that its true net worth was deeply negative. They closed the bank, and federal prosecutors brought criminal charges against managers. Several were convicted and sentenced to prison; Vice President Church got 27 years. (J. Knox McConnell, founder and longtime bank president, had died in 1997 before the scandal broke.)

Many people were hurt by the Keystone fiasco. It cost the FDIC $70 million in insurance payments. About 500 people lost deposits that exceeded the FDIC limit. One was the retired owner of a hardware store in the town of Keystone, who saw his life savings fall from $220,000 to $100,000.

Innocent bank employees lost their jobs when the bank closed. Many also lost their wealth, as, like the Enron employees discussed in Section 1.2, they held company stock. The town of Keystone lost the taxes paid by First National, which were two-thirds of its revenue. The town laid off seven of its fifteen employees, including two of four police officers.

The Problem with Deposit Insurance

We can now see a drawback of deposit insurance: it exacerbates the problem of moral hazard. Without insurance, depositors worry that banks may fail, giving them an incentive to monitor banks. Before depositing money, prudent people will investigate a bank's safety. For example, they might check balance sheets and income statements to be sure that insolvency risk is low. After making deposits, people will watch the bank and withdraw their money if there are signs of trouble.

We saw that nervous depositors can cause bank runs. But they also have a positive effect: they discourage banks from misusing deposits. If a bank takes excessive risks or money disappears mysteriously, depositors are likely to notice and withdraw their funds. And the bank will have trouble attracting new deposits. This threat gives banks a reason to keep deposits safe.

Insurance eliminates depositors' incentives to monitor banks. Depositors know they will be compensated if banks fail, so they don't care much if bankers take risks or embezzle their money. They don't bother to check balance sheets for danger signs. This inattention gives bankers greater freedom to misuse deposits: they don't fear that bad behavior will be punished by withdrawals.

With deposit insurance, bank failures aren't costly for depositors but they *are* costly for the insurance fund. If moral hazard produces a large number of failures, the fund is depleted. The government may need to provide new funds, as in the S&L crisis. Moral hazard and the absence of monitoring can end up hurting taxpayers.

Limits on Insurance

Governments recognize the problem with deposit insurance and have tried to reduce it by limiting the protection they provide. Recall that the FDIC usually limits its payments to $100,000 per account. Some deposits, such as large CDs held by corporations, exceed this level. So large depositors have incentives to monitor banks and withdraw their funds if banks misuse them.

Many countries have stronger limits on deposit insurance than the United States does. We've seen that, in 2007, the U.K. replaced only 90 percent of lost deposits. After the Northern Rock run, the U.K. instituted 100 percent insurance up to 35,000 pounds (about $70,000). However, many European countries still pay only 90 percent, and cap payments at 20,000 euros ($25,000). With less than 100 percent coverage, bank failures hurt all depositors, so all have incentives for monitoring.

Many countries offer even less deposit insurance. Indeed, about half the countries in the world, including most of the poorer ones, have no deposit insurance at all.

What's the best level of deposit insurance? The answer isn't clear. More insurance reduces bank runs but increases moral hazard. The first effect reduces the risk of bank failure, but the second increases this risk. Economists disagree about which effect is larger.

CASE STUDY

Deposit Insurance and Banking Crises

The debate over deposit insurance has stimulated much research. Economists have tried to measure the effects of insurance by comparing different countries and time periods. One well-known study was published in

2002 by economists at the World Bank and the International Monetary Fund (IMF).*

This study examined 61 countries over the period 1980–1997. Deposit insurance became more common over this period: 12 of the 61 countries had insurance in 1980, and 33 in 1997. Where insurance existed, its generosity varied widely. Limits on coverage ranged from the equivalent of $20,000 in Switzerland to $260,000 in Norway.

The study examined the effects of deposit insurance on national banking crises. A "crisis" was defined as a year with a high level of bank failures, as measured by several criteria. For example, the researchers counted a year as a crisis if at least 2 percent of GDP was lost through bank failures, or if the government declared a lengthy bank holiday. A total of 40 bank crises occurred in the countries and years covered by the study.

Overall, the World Bank/IMF study found that the negative effects of deposit insurance outweigh the positive effects. Banking crises occurred more often in countries with insurance than in countries without it. In addition, raising the limit on insurance coverage made crises more likely.

However, there is an important qualification: the effects of insurance depend on other bank regulations. Some of the countries in the study—generally the richer ones—enforced strict supervision of banks, monitoring them to prevent theft and excessive risk taking. Other countries, including most of the poorer ones, lacked effective supervision.

The study found that deposit insurance makes crises more likely in countries with weak supervision but *less* likely in countries with strong supervision. This finding makes sense. Supervision reduces moral hazard: with regulators watching, it is harder for banks to misuse deposits. Thus, supervision dampens the adverse effect of deposit insurance while preserving the beneficial effect of fewer bank runs.

* See Asli Demirguc-Kunt and Enrica Detragiache, "Does Deposit Insurance Increase Banking System Stability?" *Journal of Monetary Economics*, October, 2002.

10.4 WHO CAN OPEN A BANK?

Governments are keenly aware of the moral hazard problem in banking. They can reduce this problem by eliminating deposit insurance, but that can lead to bank runs. So many governments maintain insurance and combat moral hazard through bank regulation. Regulators monitor banks' activities and try to prevent them from misusing depositors' funds. Regulators do the job that depositors neglect when they are insured.

The rest of this chapter discusses the major facets of bank regulation. Regulators' involvement with a bank starts when it opens. Melvin cannot decide on his own when to open his bank. Instead, he needs a bank charter—a license from the government to operate a bank. Regulators grant a charter only if they think the new bank will keep its deposits safe.

Chartering Agencies

As discussed in Section 8.2, a commercial bank may be chartered either by the federal government or by a state. Federal charters are granted by the Office of the Comptroller of the Currency (OCC), which is part of the Treasury Department. Each state government has its own chartering agency, such as Maryland's Office of Financial Regulation. Banks chartered by the OCC are called national banks, and banks chartered by states are called state banks.

In the past, the regulations imposed on state and national banks have sometimes differed, leading banks to prefer national over state charters, or vice versa. Today there isn't much difference in regulations, so state and national banks coexist. About three quarters of commercial banks are state banks, but they are generally smaller than national banks.

Like commercial banks, savings institutions and credit unions can be chartered by either federal or state agencies. Federal charters are granted by the Office of Thrift Supervision and the National Credit Union Administration.

Obtaining a Charter

To obtain a charter, a prospective bank completes a lengthy application and submits it to the chartering agency. The application describes the bank's business plan, its expected earnings, its initial level of capital, and its top management. Regulators review the application and judge the soundness of the bank's plans. If the risk of failure appears too high, the application is denied. This process is analogous to a bank's evaluation of loan applications (see Section 7.7). Banks study applicants' business plans to screen out borrowers who will misuse loans. Similarly, regulators try to screen out banks that will misuse deposits.

Much of the chartering process centers on a review of key personnel. Regulators gather information on the proposed bank's owners and top managers to be sure they have the experience to run a bank. Most important, regulators try to weed out crooks and gamblers who might be attracted to banks because "that's where the money is." To that end, regulators examine applicants' careers and interview past employers. They check credit histories and tax records, and send fingerprints to the FBI. If a proposed banker has a questionable past, regulators may demand that he be replaced before granting a charter.

In addition to chartering new banks, regulators must approve changes in ownership. They check the background of anyone buying a large share of a bank to prevent untrustworthy people from entering the business.

The Separation of Banking and Commerce

A perennial controversy is whether firms outside banking should be allowed to establish or merge with banks. Section 8.2 discussed the repeal of the Glass-Steagall Act in 1999. Because of this action, commercial banks can now merge with other types of financial institutions, such as investment banks and brokerage firms.

However, there is still a wall between banks and nonfinancial firms. The Bank Holding Company Act of 1956 prohibits a nonfinancial company from owning a bank, or vice versa. Citigroup can acquire other financial institutions, but it can't merge with General Motors or Microsoft. This restriction is called the *separation of banking and commerce*.

Supporters of this policy cite a number of dangers from mixing banking and commerce. One is the potential for conflicts of interest. Suppose, for example, that a bank and an auto firm are owned by the same conglomerate. The bank may feel pressure to lend to the auto firm, even for unsound investment projects. The bank may deny loans to competing auto companies with good projects. This bias in lending prevents funds from flowing to the most productive uses. Therefore, it reduces the efficiency of the economy. Unsound lending also increases a bank's default risk, potentially threatening its solvency.

Despite these arguments, some economists think the separation of banking and commerce should be relaxed. They argue that links between financial and nonfinancial firms can create economies of scope (see Section 8.2). They also point out that European countries allow banks and nonfinancial firms to own each other, without disastrous consequences. In recent years, much of the debate about banking and commerce has revolved around a single company, as the next case study discusses.

CASE STUDY

Wal-Mart Bank?

The separation of banking and commerce has a loophole: **industrial loan companies (ILCs).** An ILC is a type of financial institution that exists in seven states, with the largest number in Utah. ILCs were first established in the early twentieth century to lend to industrial workers who couldn't get other credit; they were the subprime lenders of the day. However, ILCs have evolved over time and now engage in most activities of commercial banks.

Industrial loan company (ILC) Financial institution that performs many functions of a commercial bank; may be owned by a nonfinancial firm

ILCs are regulated by state banking authorities and the FDIC, agencies that also regulate some commercial banks. However, ILCs are *not* counted as banks when it comes to the separation of banking and commerce. A number of nonfinancial firms own ILCs, including General Motors, General Electric, and Target.

ILCs occupy a small niche in the financial system, and they haven't attracted much attention—until Wal-Mart became interested in owning one. In 2002, Wal-Mart tried to buy an ILC in California, but the state legislature passed a law to prevent it. In 2005, Wal-Mart applied for an ILC charter in Utah, but the application was criticized by groups ranging from labor unions to banks. Several members of Congress proposed legislation to block Wal-Mart's plan.

Some groups opposed Wal-Mart for reasons unrelated to banking, such as the company's policies on employee benefits. But the strongest opposition came from community banks, small banks that serve a single locality. These banks feared that Wal-Mart's ability to cut costs could drive them

At a 2006 rally in Washington, D.C., members of the National Community Reinvestment Coalition protest Wal-Mart's plan to establish an industrial loan company.

Mark Wilson/Getty Images

out of business. Ronald Ence, vice president of Independent Community Bankers of America, said of Wal-Mart, "There's no doubt in my mind they'll be able to do to community banks what they've done to the local grocery store and the local hardware store and the local clothing store."

In its application for an ILC charter, Wal-Mart denied that it would compete with community banks. It proposed to use its ILC for a narrow purpose: to process credit and debit card payments at its stores. Currently, Wal-Mart pays outside banks to process these transactions, and the company estimates it would save $5 million a year by doing the work internally. Wal-Mart officials promised repeatedly that its ILC would not accept deposits from consumers or make loans.

"Don't believe it," said Congresswoman Stephanie Tubbs Jones, Democrat of Ohio. Wal-Mart critics, such as Congresswoman Jones, insisted that Wal-Mart had plans to expand its banking operations. The president of a North Dakota bank said, "I cannot believe they are doing all of this to save $5 million a year" ($5 million may sound like a lot, but for Wal-Mart it represents nine minutes of sales).

For now, Wal-Mart's plans (whatever they were) have been stymied. Before granting an ILC charter, Utah regulators require the ILC to arrange deposit insurance from the FDIC. Because of the opposition to Wal-Mart, the FDIC decided to postpone approval of insurance until at least 2008. Facing uncertainty about the FDIC's decision, plus hostile legislation in Congress, Wal-Mart threw in the towel. It withdrew its ILC application in 2007.

▶ Wal-Mart stores have "Money Centers" that provide some financial services, such as check cashing and international money transfers. Nonfinancial firms have always been allowed to provide these services.

Five hundred miles south of Utah, Wal-Mart has had better luck entering the banking business. In 2007, just as Wal-Mart was giving up on its ILC, its subsidiary Wal-Mart de Mexico announced the creation of

Adelante (Spanish for "Get Ahead"), a full-fledged commercial bank offering a range of deposits and loans. Now a Mexican who visits Wal-Mart can talk to a loan officer after buying a pair of socks. This is clearly legal under Mexican law, which does not require the separation of banking and commerce.

Few Mexicans criticized Wal-Mart's move into banking. Indeed, bank regulators expressed support, suggesting that Wal-Mart will provide needed competition for other banks. An official at the Mexican Finance Ministry said, "The interest rates that banks charge in Mexico are too high, especially in credit cards [around 40 percent]. We hope the newcomers introduce new products and prompt the banks to lower them."

10.5 RESTRICTIONS ON BALANCE SHEETS

After a bank receives a charter, regulators restrict its activities in many ways. One set of regulations concerns the assets that banks are allowed to hold on their balance sheets. Other regulations mandate minimum levels of capital that banks must hold. All these rules are meant to reduce moral hazard and the risk of insolvency.

The United States has a complex system in which different agencies regulate different groups of banks. Before describing regulations in detail, let's discuss who the regulators are.

Who Sets Regulations?

The agency that regulates a commercial bank is determined by two factors: whether the bank is a national or state bank, and whether it's a member of the Federal Reserve System. All national banks are required to join the Fed System, but membership is optional for state banks.

Table 10.2 lists the regulators of commercial banks. All national banks are regulated by the OCC, the agency that chartered them. A state bank that belongs to the Fed System has two regulators: the state agency that chartered it and the Federal Reserve Bank for its region. A state bank that does *not* belong to the Fed System is regulated by a state agency and the FDIC. The FDIC regulates this group of banks as well as providing insurance for all commercial banks and savings institutions.

For example, M&T Bank is a state bank chartered in New York and a member of the Federal Reserve System. So it is regulated by the State of New York Banking Department and the Federal Reserve Bank of New York. These regulators oversee all of M&T's operations, which stretch from New York to Virginia.

TABLE 10.2 Who Regulates Commercial Banks?

National Banks	Office of the Comptroller of the Currency (OCC)
State Banks	
Members of Federal Reserve System	Federal Reserve and state agencies
Non-members of Federal Reserve System	FDIC and state agencies

The story gets more complex when we look beyond commercial banks. Savings institutions are regulated partly by a

▶Yet another wrinkle concerns bank holding companies and financial holding companies, conglomerates that own commercial banks and other financial institutions (review Section 8.2). BHCs and FHCs are regulated by the Federal Reserve; for example, they need the Fed's approval to acquire new subsidiaries. This regulation occurs separately from regulation of the individual banks owned by BHCs and FHCs.

federal agency, the Office of Thrift Supervision, and partly by state agencies. Credit unions are regulated by another mix of federal and state agencies.

The government has considered proposals to streamline bank regulation. For example, in 1993 the Clinton administration proposed legislation to create a Federal Banking Commission. This commission would have replaced the OCC and the Office of Thrift Supervision and taken over the regulatory functions of the Fed and FDIC. However, such proposals have not been enacted. One reason is opposition from the Fed, which does not want to relinquish its role in regulation.

In any case, the different agencies that regulate banks generally set similar rules. Therefore, we will discuss most regulations without distinguishing among different regulators or groups of banks.

Restrictions on Assets

Banks can choose among a variety of assets, including safe assets with relatively low returns and riskier assets with high returns. As we've discussed, moral hazard distorts this choice. Banks have incentives to take on too much risk because the costs that might result are paid partly by depositors or the deposit insurance fund.

To address this problem, regulators restrict the assets that banks can hold. In the United States, there are strict limits on securities holdings. Banks can hold only the safest securities, such as government bonds and high-rated corporate bonds. They can't hold junk bonds or stock in any company.

In some countries, regulators are less restrictive. For example, banks in Germany and Japan can own stocks as well as bonds. In Japan's case, this policy proved costly when stock prices crashed during the 1990s. Losses on stocks helped push many banks into insolvency there.

U.S. regulators also restrict the loans that banks make. Again, the goal is to reduce the risk of large losses. To this end, lending must be diversified: no single loan can be too large. At national banks, loans to one borrower cannot exceed 25 percent of the bank's capital. Loan limits at state banks vary by state.

After the S&L crisis of the 1980s, regulators introduced special limits on real estate loans. For example, a loan for commercial real estate cannot exceed 80 percent of the property's value.

Capital Requirements

Recall the discussion of capital in Section 9.6. When a bank chooses its level of capital, it faces a trade-off. Lower capital raises the return on equity but it also raises the bank's insolvency risk. This trade-off creates moral hazard. Bank owners benefit from the higher return on equity, but, as we've stressed throughout this chapter, they don't bear the full cost of insolvency. As a result, banks have incentives to choose low levels of capital, creating excessive risk.

Capital requirements Regulations setting minimum levels of capital that banks must hold

Regulators address this problem by imposing **capital requirements.** These rules mandate minimum levels of capital that banks must hold. Required capital is set high enough to keep insolvency risk low.

The Basel Accord Most bank regulations—like most laws of all types—are set separately for each country by national governments. Capital requirements are an exception. These rules are determined largely by international agreements.

Specifically, current capital requirements are based on the **Basel Accord.** This agreement was signed by bank regulators from around the world in 1988, in the Swiss city of Basel. The accord is a set of recommendations, not a binding treaty, but over 100 countries have adopted its provisions.

Basel Accord 1988 agreement that sets international standards for bank capital requirements

The accord was motivated by the internationalization of banking (review Section 8.2). Regulators believe that when banks compete internationally, those based in countries with low capital requirements have an advantage over those facing stricter requirements. Consequently, each country has an unhealthy incentive to weaken capital requirements to help its banks. The Basel Accord ensures a level playing field with strong requirements everywhere.

Current U.S. Requirements In the United States, capital requirements have two parts. The first is a simple rule that predates the Basel Accord. This rule sets a minimum equity ratio, or ratio of capital to assets. Currently, the minimum is 5 percent: a bank's capital must equal at least 5 percent of its assets.

The second requirement is part of the Basel Accord. This rule accounts for the riskiness of different kinds of assets. Among the assets that banks hold, some are very safe and others are relatively risky. The riskier a bank's assets, the more capital it is required to hold. Higher capital protects banks from insolvency if risky assets lose value.

Specifically, the Basel Accord requires banks to hold capital of at least 8 percent of *risk-adjusted assets*. This variable is a weighted sum of different groups of assets, with higher weights for higher risk. The safest assets, such as reserves and Treasury bonds, have weights of zero. Loans to other banks have weights of 20 percent. A number of assets have 50 percent weights, including municipal bonds and residential mortgages. The weights on most other loans are 100 percent.

An Example To understand these rules, let's return to our favorite financial institution, Melvin's Bank. **Table 10.3A** shows the asset side of Melvin's balance sheet, with the usual asset classes (reserves, securities, and loans) broken into subcategories. **Table 10.3B** calculates Melvin's required level of capital based on the two rules that he faces, the minimum equity ratio and the risk-based Basel requirement.

Recall that the minimum equity ratio is 5 percent. Melvin's total assets in this example are $150, so his capital must be at least 5 percent of $150, or $7.50.

To calculate the Basel requirement, we apply the appropriate weights to different assets in Table 10.3A. For example, Melvin's Bank owns $10 in municipal bonds. The Basel rules give municipal bonds a weight of 0.5, so this item contributes $5 to the weighted sum of assets. The bank has $90 in commercial and industrial loans; with a weight of 1.0, this item contributes the full $90 to the weighted sum. Adding up the weighted assets, we get a total of $107. Melvin's capital must be at least 8 percent of $107, which is $8.56.

TABLE 10.3 Capital Requirements for Melvin's Bank

(A) Computing Weighted Assets

	Assets	Weights	Weighted Assets
Reserves	10	0.0	0
Securities			
Treasury bonds	10	0.0	0
Municipal bonds	10	0.5	5
Loans			
Interbank	10	0.2	2
Home mortgages	20	0.5	10
C&I	90	1.0	90
TOTAL	150		107

(B) Minimum Levels of Capital

Based on minimum equity ratio:

$$\text{Minimum capital} = (0.05)(\text{total assets})$$
$$= (0.05)(\$150)$$
$$= \$7.50$$

Based on Basel requirement:

$$\text{Minimum capital} = (0.08)(\text{weighted assets})$$
$$= (0.08)(\$107)$$
$$= \$8.56$$

▶This example ignores off-balance-sheet activities, which are addressed in a 1996 amendment to the Basel Accord. A bank must hold extra capital, beyond 8 percent of risk-weighted assets, if it engages in risky OBS activities such as speculating with derivatives. The OBS activities of Melvin's Bank could push its required capital above $8.56.

To conclude, the minimum equity ratio requires Melvin's Bank to hold at least $7.50 in capital, and the Basel rule requires at least $8.56. In this example, the second requirement is the more stringent one. This is not always the case, however; which requirement is stricter depends on the bank's mix of assets. (Problem 7 explores this point.)

Basel 2 Capital requirements are in a state of flux. Economists and bank regulators have argued that the Basel requirements don't always account accurately for risk. Prompted by this criticism, the committee of regulators that wrote the original Basel Accord has proposed a new set of rules, called "Basel 2." These recommendations were published in 2004.

Part of Basel 2 is an increase in the number of categories used to compute risk-weighted assets. The original accord lumps together assets with different levels of risk. For example, all corporate bonds have the same weight, regardless of their default risk. Basel 2 assigns weights ranging from 20 percent for AAA rated bonds to 150 percent for junk bonds. (U.S. regulators forbid banks to own junk bonds, but some countries allow it.)

Basel 2 also aims to make capital requirements more flexible. It allows regulators in different countries to adjust requirements based on local conditions. It allows some large banks to develop their own formulas for risk-weighted assets, subject to regulators' approval.

Like the original Basel Accord, Basel 2 is a set of nonbinding recommendations. European countries have begun to adopt the recommendations, but U.S. regulators are hesitant. They fear that the new rules will let many banks reduce their capital, increasing insolvency risk. The U.S. has proposed changes in Basel 2, and it's not clear what will ultimately happen.

Online Case Study: An Update on Capital Requirements

10.6 SUPERVISION

Another element of government regulation is **bank supervision,** or monitoring of banks' activities. The agency that regulates a bank checks that the bank is meeting capital requirements and obeying restrictions on asset holdings. Regulators also make more subjective assessments of the bank's insolvency risk. If they perceive too much risk, they demand changes in the bank's operations.

Bank supervision Monitoring of banks' activities by government regulators

Supervision is a big job, as regulators must keep abreast of what's happening at thousands of banks. Let's discuss the main parts of the supervision process: information gathering, bank ratings, and enforcement actions.

Information Gathering

A bank's supervisors gather information in two ways. First, they require the bank to report on its activities. Most important are **call reports,** which a bank must submit every quarter. A call report contains detailed information on the banks' finances, including a balance sheet and income statement. Regulators examine call reports for signs of trouble, such as declining capital, increases in risky assets, or rising loan delinquencies.

Call report Quarterly financial statement, including a balance sheet and income statement, that banks must submit to regulators as part of bank supervision

Second, regulators gather information through **bank examinations,** in which a team of regulators visits a bank's headquarters. Every bank is visited at least once a year, more often if regulators suspect problems based on call reports or past exams. Examiners sometimes arrive without warning, making it harder for banks to hide questionable activities.

Bank examination Visit by regulators to a bank's headquarters to gather information on the bank's activities; part of bank supervision

Examiners review a bank's detailed financial records. They study internal memos and minutes of meetings to better understand the bank's business. They interview managers about various policies, such as the criteria for approving loans. Examiners also check outside sources to verify information provided by the bank. For example, they contact some of the bank's loan customers to ensure that the loans really exist and that borrowers have the collateral reported by the bank.

CAMELS Ratings

After examiners visit, banks have an experience familiar to college students: they get grades. The grades are evaluations of risks to solvency. Regulators give each bank a rating for six different kinds of risk, plus an overall rating.

The ratings range from 1 to 5, with 1 the best. A rating of 1 means a bank is "fundamentally sound"; a 5 means "imminent risk of failure."

CAMELS ratings Evaluations by regulators of a bank's insolvency risk based on its **c**apital, **a**sset quality, **m**anagement, **e**arnings, **l**iquidity, and **s**ensitivity

These scores are called **CAMELS ratings.** CAMELS is an acronym, with each letter standing for a risk that regulators evaluate: **c**apital, **a**sset quality, **m**anagement, **e**arnings, **l**iquidity, and **s**ensitivity.

- *Capital* A bank's examiners check that it is meeting the capital requirements outlined in Section 10.5. They also make a more subjective assessment of whether the bank has enough capital given the risks it faces. They look for signs that the bank will lose capital in the future. A bank's rating can fall, for example, if it is paying large dividends to shareholders, as these deplete capital.
- *Asset quality* Examiners gauge the riskiness of a bank's assets, especially default risk on loans. They select a sample of loans and gather information on the borrowers, such as their credit histories and current financial situation, to judge the likelihood of default. Examiners also check whether any borrowers have already stopped making payments, so loans should be written off; banks may be slow to write off bad loans because this reduces their capital. In addition to reviewing specific loans, examiners consider a bank's general policies for loan approval. They evaluate whether these policies are effective at screening out risky borrowers. They also check whether the bank follows its stated policies or makes exceptions.
- *Management* Examiners try to evaluate the competence and honesty of bank managers. This is important because many bank failures result from flawed management, as you'll recall from the Keystone case. Examiners also check whether a bank's board of directors is monitoring managers effectively. And they check how well managers control lower-level employees. For example, they look for safeguards against rogue traders who gamble the bank's money, like Nick Leeson and Jerome Kerviel (see Section 5.6).
- *Earnings* Examiners look at a bank's current earnings and try to project future earnings. High earnings raise the bank's capital over time, reducing insolvency risk.
- *Liquidity* Examiners evaluate a bank's liquidity risk—the risk that it will have difficulty meeting demands for withdrawals. As discussed in Section 9.5, liquidity risk depends on the bank's level of reserves (vault cash plus deposits at the Fed) and its holdings of liquid securities, or secondary reserves.
- *Sensitivity* This means sensitivity to interest rates and asset prices—in other words, interest-rate risk and market risk. Examiners look for activities that could produce large losses if asset prices move in an unexpected direction. One example is excessive speculation with derivatives.

Enforcement Actions

If a bank's overall CAMELS rating is 1 or 2, regulators leave it alone until its next examination. If the rating is 3 or worse, regulators require the bank to take action to reduce risk and improve its score. Regulators can either negotiate an agreement with the bank or issue a unilateral order.

Banks are required to fix whatever problems are creating excessive risk. This could mean tightening the loan approval process. It could mean slowing the growth of assets or cutting dividends to shareholders or firing bad managers.

Regulators also have the power to impose fines on banks. They do so when a bank's problems are severe or the bank is slow to fix them. If regulators find evidence of criminal activity, such as embezzlement, they turn the case over to the FBI.

10.7 CLOSING INSOLVENT BANKS

Regulators try to prevent banks from becoming insolvent, but sometimes it happens. Consequently, another task of regulators is to deal with insolvent banks. Today, U.S. regulators force these banks to close quickly. This policy reflects past experiences, such as the S&L crisis of the 1980s, in which delays in closing banks proved costly.

The Need for Government Action

In most industries, an unprofitable firm cannot survive for long. If it loses enough money, it becomes insolvent: its debts to banks and bondholders exceed its assets. In this situation, the firm has trouble making debt payments, and lenders won't provide additional funds. The firm is forced into bankruptcy.

However, this process may *not* occur for an insolvent bank. The reason is that the bulk of bank liabilities are insured deposits. As discussed in Section 10.3, insurance makes depositors indifferent to their banks' fates. An insolvent bank is likely to fail eventually, but depositors don't suffer. So the bank may be able to attract deposits and stay in business for a long time.

This is dangerous for two reasons. First, the bank may continue practices that led it to insolvency, such as lax procedures for approving loans. This behavior is likely to produce further losses, so the bank's net worth becomes more and more negative. Eventually the bank collapses at a high cost to the insurance fund.

Second, the bank may do risky things that it *didn't* do in the past. The reason is that the moral hazard problem, which exists for all banks, is particularly severe for insolvent ones. When a bank has a positive level of capital, its owners have something to lose if they take excessive risks. By contrast, if the owners' capital has already fallen below zero, *all* the losses from failed gambles fall on others.

At the same time, risk-taking can have large benefits for owners of an insolvent bank. If their gambles succeed, the bank may earn enough to push its capital above zero. The owners gain wealth, and the bank is in a good position to continue in business. So insolvent banks are likely to take big risks. This behavior is called *gambling for resurrection.*

Because of these problems, most economists think regulators should force an insolvent bank to shut down. And it's important to act quickly, before the bank has a chance to incur further losses.

Forbearance

Despite the dangers posed by insolvent banks, regulators have sometimes chosen *not* to shut them down. Banks have continued to operate with negative capital. A regulator's decision not to close an insolvent bank is called **forbearance.**

Forbearance Regulator's decision to allow an insolvent bank to remain open

Forbearance occurs because bank closures are painful. Bank owners lose any chance for future profits, managers lose their jobs, and depositors lose their uninsured funds. Closures are costly for the FDIC, which must compensate insured depositors. Closures can also be embarrassing for regulators, because they suggest that bank supervision has been inadequate. For all these reasons, regulators are tempted to let insolvent banks stay open.

Forbearance is a gamble on the part of regulators. As we've discussed, an insolvent bank may start earning profits and become solvent. If that happens, everyone avoids the pain of closure. On the other hand, if the bank continues to lose money, closure is more costly when it finally occurs.

Forbearance requires regulators to bend their usual rules. Obviously, a bank can't satisfy capital requirements when its capital is negative. So regulators must allow accounting tricks that raise the bank's measured capital. Gimmicky accounting allows the bank to *appear* solvent even though it isn't.

One example is the treatment of bad loans. If a borrower stops making payments on a loan, the bank is supposed to write it off—to remove the loan from its balance sheet. This action reduces the bank's assets and capital (see Table 9.7). However, as part of forbearance, regulators may not enforce the requirement to write off bad loans. They let the bank keep the loans on its balance sheet, artificially raising its assets.

A prime example of forbearance comes from Japan. In the 1990s, many Japanese banks became insolvent because of a deep recession and crashes in real estate and stock prices. Desperate to avoid bank failures, regulators allowed large overstatements of bank assets. For example, banks could value stocks at the prices they paid for them, which were far above then-current prices. They were allowed to keep large quantities of bad loans on their balance sheets. In some cases, Japan's central bank went a step further and simply gave money to banks to increase their capital.

We'll return to this episode in Chapter 13, where we discuss how banking problems hurt the overall Japanese economy. Here, we detail an infamous case of forbearance in the United States.

CASE STUDY

Regulatory Failure in the S&L Crisis

We introduced the S&L crisis of the 1980s in Section 9.6. Many S&Ls became insolvent when interest rates rose and when real estate developers defaulted on loans. The crisis was partly the result of bad luck and partly caused by excessive risk-taking by banks. However, most economists also blame bank regulators—specifically, the Federal Home Loan Bank Board (FHLBB), which regulated S&Ls at the time. Poor decisions by regulators made a bad situation worse.

Many S&Ls were insolvent by the early 1980s, when interest rates peaked. In retrospect, the FHLBB should have closed these institutions, but regulators were reluctant to act. They chose a policy of forbearance. They hoped that S&Ls would return to solvency when interest rates fell.

The FHLBB loosened regulations to help S&Ls stay open. It reduced capital requirements in 1980 and 1982. It also changed accounting rules to allow S&Ls to report higher levels of assets, and hence higher capital. For example, it allowed banks to write off bad loans over a 10-year period rather than all at once.

The FHLBB also allowed increases in banks' "supervisory goodwill." These are credits for actions taken at the request of regulators, such as takeovers of failed banks. Regulators count these credits as bank assets, even though they don't have much economic meaning.

As we have discussed, the moral hazard problem is severe at insolvent banks. In the 1980s, many S&Ls gambled for resurrection with high-interest, high-risk loans to real estate developers. Regulators failed to prevent this risk-taking, for several related reasons. The Reagan administration generally believed that government regulators should interfere less in the economy. The budget of the FHLBB was reduced, leading to less frequent bank exams. And regulators lacked the expertise to evaluate commercial real estate loans, as S&Ls were restricted to home mortgages before 1980.

Another factor was politics. Members of Congress pressed regulators to be lenient with S&Ls that were run by their supporters. The most famous example was a meeting at which five U.S. Senators urged the head of the FHLBB to end an investigation of Lincoln Savings and Loan, of Irvine, California. It later came out that these senators had received a total of $1.3 million in campaign contributions from Charles Keating, the chairman of Lincoln. The senators became known as the "Keating Five." In 1991, the Senate Ethics Committee recommended a formal censure for one of them, Alan Cranston of California, and criticized the others for "questionable conduct."

In 1989, the government finally addressed the S&L crisis. At the urging of the Bush administration, Congress established the Resolution Trust Corporation to take over insolvent S&Ls, close them quickly, and compensate depositors. The ultimate cost was $153 billion (about 3 percent of U.S. GDP in 1989), paid by the government from tax revenue. The number of S&Ls fell by half between 1986 and 1995.

Congress also changed the regulation of S&Ls. It abolished the FHLBB and created the Office of Thrift Supervision. It abolished the insurance fund for S&Ls and gave them coverage by the FDIC. In 1991, Congress passed the FDIC Improvement Act, which established today's stringent rules for closing banks.

Deciding on Closure

Regulators monitor banks' capital as part of the supervision process. Under the rules established in 1991, regulators can close a bank immediately if its capital falls below 2 percent of its assets. Note that closure can occur while the bank is still barely solvent—capital can be low but positive. Regulators try to act before capital becomes negative, which would create severe moral hazard.

Regulators have a second option when capital falls below 2 percent of assets: they can give the bank a final chance to increase its capital. The bank can try to add capital by issuing new stock, which people will buy if they think the bank will be profitable in the future. Usually the bank is given 3 to 9 months to increase capital substantially. If it can't, then it must close.

The Closure Process

The decision to close a bank is made by the agency that granted the bank a charter (either the OCC or a state agency). This agency calls in the FDIC, which becomes a *receiver* for the bank. This means the FDIC takes over the bank's assets and liabilities. It then disposes of these items using one of two methods:

1. Under the *payoff method*, the FDIC pays insured depositors what they are owed by the closed bank. Then the FDIC sells the bank's assets for as much as it can get. The proceeds offset part of the cost of paying depositors. The bank ceases to exist and depositors must find a new place to put their funds.
2. Under the *purchase and assumption* method, the FDIC sells all the assets and liabilities of the closed bank to another, healthier bank. This new bank takes over the business of the closed bank. Usually the FDIC must accept a negative price for the closed bank—it pays the bank that acquires it—because the liabilities that are sold exceed the assets. Under the purchase and assumption method, depositors keep their deposits and bank branches stay open under new ownership.

In every bank closure, the FDIC is required to choose the method that is least expensive to the insurance fund. Usually this is the purchase and assumption method. When a healthy bank takes over a closed bank, it gains relationships with new customers, which produce deposits and loan opportunities. The value of customer relationships reduces the amount the FDIC must pay to sell the closed bank.

Summary

- U.S. banks are heavily regulated by the government. Most regulations are intended to reduce the risk of bank failure.

10.1 Bank Runs

- A bank run occurs when depositors lose confidence in a bank and make sudden, large withdrawals. A run can drain a bank's liquid assets, force a fire sale of loans, and cause the bank to fail.
- A run can result from self-fulfilling expectations: people withdraw money because they expect withdrawals by others.
- Sometimes a bank facing a run can suspend payments temporarily and then reopen. Suspension gives the bank time to reassure depositors and to increase its liquid assets.
- A bank panic is a wave of runs at many banks. The United States experienced severe bank panics in the early 1930s.

10.2 Deposit Insurance

- Deposit insurance is a promise by the government to compensate depositors if a bank fails. In the United States, deposits are insured up to $100,000 per account by the Federal Deposit Insurance Corporation (FDIC).
- Deposit insurance prevents bank runs because it makes depositors confident that their money is safe.

10.3 Moral Hazard Again

- Banking creates a problem of moral hazard: bankers have incentives to misuse deposits. Bankers may take excessive risks, or they may simply steal money, as happened at the First National Bank of Keystone.
- Deposit insurance exacerbates moral hazard because it reduces depositors' incentives to monitor banks. Because of this effect, governments limit the coverage of deposit insurance.
- Some research suggests that deposit insurance makes banking crises more likely, at least in countries with weak bank supervision.

10.4 Who Can Open a Bank?

- A new bank must obtain a charter from either a federal or state agency. The prospective bank must convince officials that its risk of failure is low.
- U.S. law requires the separation of banking and commerce. Banks can't own commercial firms, and vice versa.
- Wal-Mart has tried to establish an industrial loan company, which could perform some banking functions, but has been stymied by political opposition.

10.5 Restrictions on Balance Sheets

- In the United States, banks are regulated by a variety of federal and state agencies. However, the different regulators usually set similar rules.
- Regulators restrict the riskiness of banks' assets. For example, banks can hold only the safest securities, and their loans must be diversified.
- U.S. banks must hold capital of at least 5 percent of their total assets. Under the Basel Accord, they must also satisfy capital requirements based on risk-adjusted assets.

10.6 Supervision

- One part of bank regulation is supervision, or monitoring of banks' activities. Banks must submit quarterly call reports on their finances. In addition, regulators perform on-site examinations of every bank at least once a year.
- After an examination, a bank is given a set of CAMELS ratings that summarize various types of insolvency risk. If a bank's CAMELS ratings are poor, regulators require changes in the bank's practices to reduce risk.

10.7 Closing Insolvent Banks

- Insolvent banks may stay in business because insured depositors continue to provide them with funds. Regulators must close these banks quickly to prevent them from losing more money.
- Regulators sometimes allow insolvent banks to stay open, hoping to avoid the pain of closure. Such forbearance can ultimately lead to expensive, taxpayer-funded bailouts, as occurred during the S&L crisis of the 1980s.
- Under current law, regulators can close a bank when its capital falls below 2 percent of its assets. The FDIC either closes the bank and compensates depositors (the payoff method) or arranges a takeover by a healthier bank (the purchase and assumption method).

Key Terms

bank examination, p. 303

bank panic, p. 288

bank run, p. 283

bank supervision, p. 303

Basel Accord, p. 301

call report, p. 303

CAMELS ratings, p. 304

capital requirements, p. 300

deposit insurance, p. 290

Federal Deposit Insurance Corporation (FDIC), p. 290

forbearance, p. 306

industrial loan company (ILC), p. 297

suspension of payments, p. 285

Questions and Problems

1. Suppose you are a depositor at Melvin's Bank, which has the balance sheet shown in Table 10.1A. Deposit insurance does not exist. You originally deposited your money in Melvin's Bank because its branch locations are more convenient than those of other banks.
   a. Suppose you know that Melvin's other depositors plan to keep their money there. Should you do the same or withdraw your money and deposit it elsewhere?
   b. Suppose you know that other depositors plan to make large withdrawals from Melvin's Bank. What should you do?
   c. What do your answers to parts (a) and (b) tell you about the likelihood and causes of bank runs?

2. Suppose an economy has a high level of loans from one bank to another. How might this fact affect the likelihood of a bank panic?

3. Some economists suggest that banks should be charged premiums for deposit insurance based on their levels of capital. Premiums should be higher if capital is lower. What is the rationale for this proposal? Are there any drawbacks to the idea?

4. Suppose Wal-Mart is allowed to open a bank that accepts deposits and makes loans at its U.S. stores.
   a. How might this affect existing banks, especially community banks? (See Section 8.2 for a review of community banks.)
   b. In general, who might gain and who might lose if Wal-Mart opens a bank?

5. Consider an analogy (the type on the SATs): "A bank regulator is to a bank as a bank is to a borrower." In what ways is this analogy true? (See Section 7.7 for a review of the bank–borrower relationship.)

6. Suppose Melvin's Bank can make a bet on derivatives that has a 2/3 probability of earning \$20 and a 1/3 probability of losing \$40.
   a. Assume Melvin has \$20 in capital. What are the possible costs and benefits of the bet for Melvin and the deposit insurance fund? Is Melvin likely to make the bet?
   b. How are the answers in part (a) different if Melvin's Bank has \$50 in capital? What if it has \$0 in capital?
   c. In light of these examples, discuss the benefits of (i) capital requirements (ii) bank supervision, and (iii) quick closure of insolvent banks.

7. Let's change the example of capital requirements in Table 10.3. Assume that Melvin's Bank holds \$40 in Treasury bonds (rather than \$10) and \$30 in loans to other banks (rather

than \$10). Otherwise, Melvin's assets are the same as in the table.

a. Calculate the level of capital that Melvin must hold to satisfy (i) the minimum equity ratio and (ii) the risk-based Basel requirement.

b. Which of the two requirements is more stringent in this case? Is the answer different than it was for the original Table 10.3? If so, why?

8. Consider two possibilities: (i) A bank is forced to close even though there is no good reason for it to close; (ii) A bank remains open even though there *are* good reasons for it to close.

   a. Explain why (i) and (ii) are possible and what regulations affect the likelihood of these outcomes.

   b. Can some combination of regulations make both (i) and (ii) unlikely?

Online and Data Questions

www.worthpublishers.com/ball

9. Link through the text Web site to the site of the Office of the Comptroller of the Currency and look up "Enforcement Actions." Find an example of a specific enforcement action against a bank. Explain what the OCC did and what problem it was trying to rectify.

10. The text Web site has a link to a paper by Christine Blair, an economist at the FDIC, called "The Mixing of Banking and Commerce." Read this paper and briefly summarize the arguments for and against the "mixing" in the title. Which side do you agree with?

chapter eleven

The Money Supply and Interest Rates

- 11.1 THE FEDERAL RESERVE SYSTEM
- 11.2 THE FED AND THE MONETARY BASE
- 11.3 COMMERCIAL BANKS AND THE MONEY SUPPLY
- 11.4 A FORMULA FOR THE MONEY SUPPLY
- 11.5 THE FED'S MONETARY TOOLS
- 11.6 MONEY TARGETS VERSUS INTEREST-RATE TARGETS
- 11.7 INTEREST-RATE POLICY

REUTERS/HO/Landov

March 28, 2006: Ben Bernanke (fourth from top at left) chairs his first meeting of the Federal Open Market Committee, which sets the Fed's interest-rate target. The committee voted to raise the target by a quarter of a percentage point.

We began Chapter 2 by discussing the attention that Ben Bernanke received when he was appointed Chairman of the Federal Reserve. This attention has continued. Almost every day, the media discuss Bernanke and other Fed officials—what they are saying and what policies they are likely to pursue. Even a brief, off-the-cuff remark can be big news.

An example occurred in April 2006. On a Saturday night, Bernanke attended the annual White House Correspondents Dinner, where he chatted with CNBC anchor Maria Bartiromo. The next Monday, Bartiromo reported that she asked Bernanke whether he was sure the Fed would keep interest rates constant in the near future. According to Bartiromo, Bernanke's answer was "no." This news caused stock prices to drop sharply over the next hour. Bernanke later called his loose talk "a lapse in judgment" and promised to keep quiet at future dinners.

The media's interest in Ben Bernanke reflects the Fed's influence on the national economy. The Fed's power arises primarily from its control of monetary policy. Earlier chapters have sketched how monetary policy works. The Fed adjusts the money supply, which affects interest rates, which in turn affect the levels of output, unemployment, and inflation.

The next four chapters of this book flesh out the story of how the Fed affects the economy. In this chapter, we begin by describing the Federal Reserve System and how it determines the money supply. Previously we've simply assumed that the Fed picks a level for the money supply. Here we'll study the process through which money is created, one that involves commercial banks and the public as well as the Fed. We'll examine the Fed's tools for pushing the money supply to the level it chooses.

This chapter also examines the relation between the money supply and interest rates. We'll see that the Fed sets targets for one particular interest rate, the rate on federal funds, and adjusts the money supply to hit these targets.

11.1 THE FEDERAL RESERVE SYSTEM

The United States had a central bank for brief periods in the early 1800s—the First Bank of the United States and then the Second Bank. Andrew Jackson put the Second Bank out of business in 1836 because he and fellow populists feared the bank's power (see Section 8.2). However, the bank panics of the late nineteenth and early twentieth centuries, discussed in Section 10.1, strengthened support for a central bank. Political leaders became convinced that the country needed a central bank to serve as lender of last resort during panics. In 1913, Congress passed the Federal Reserve Act, which established the Fed System.

Under the Federal Reserve Act, the U.S. is divided into twelve Federal Reserve Districts, each with a Federal Reserve Bank. For example, the First District includes most of New England and is served by the Federal Reserve Bank of Boston; the Twelfth District covers Western states and is served by the Federal Reserve Bank of San Francisco. The Board of Governors, located in Washington, D.C., oversees the system. The board has seven members, including the chair (currently Ben Bernanke) and vice chair (currently Donald Kohn).

Visit the text Web site to view a map showing the twelve Federal Reserve Districts and the locations of their banks.

Formally, a Federal Reserve Bank is not part of the government. It is owned by commercial banks in its district, which buy shares in the bank and receive dividends of 6 percent per year. Each Federal Reserve Bank has a board of directors with nine members, six elected by the commercial banks and three appointed by the Board of Governors in Washington. The directors appoint a president to run the bank, with the approval of the Board of Governors. Under this system, commercial banks and the board in Washington share control over Federal Reserve Banks.

Members of the Board of Governors are appointed by the president of the United States and confirmed by Congress. Once appointed, governors are independent of elected officials and often serve for a long time. A governor's term lasts 14 years and cannot be ended involuntarily (although many governors leave early for high-paying jobs in the private sector). The term of the Fed chair is only 4 years, but some chairs have been reappointed many times. Before Ben Bernanke took office in 2006, Alan Greenspan was chair for over 18 years.

▶Chapter 16 discusses the rationale for the Fed's independence from elected officials.

11.2 THE FED AND THE MONETARY BASE

How does the Fed control the money supply? In answering this question, we will focus on the primary definition of the money supply, M1. This aggregate is the sum of currency in circulation, checking deposits, and traveler's checks (review Section 2.3). We'll ignore traveler's checks here, because this component is small. We use M to stand for the money supply, C for currency in circulation, and D for checking deposits, giving us

$$M = C + D$$

The Federal Reserve does *not* directly create the money supply. The Fed issues currency, but checking deposits are created by banks and their customers. What the Fed *does* create is the monetary base. Our first task is to discuss this concept. Then we'll see how the Fed can manipulate the money supply by adjusting the base.

The Monetary Base

The **monetary base,** B, is the sum of two quantities, currency in circulation, C, and bank reserves, R. Currency in circulation is also part of the money supply. Bank reserves are vault cash plus banks' deposits at the Fed (see Section 9.1). In symbols,

$$B = C + R$$

Monetary base (B) Sum of currency in circulation and bank reserves ($B = C + R$); the Federal Reserve's liabilities to the private sector of the economy

A fine point: All currency created by the Fed is included in the monetary base, but it is split between the C and R components. Currency outside banks—cash held by people and nonbank firms—counts as currency in circulation. Currency does *not* fall in this category if it is sitting in a bank or ATM. In this case, it counts as vault cash, which is part of bank reserves.

What is the meaning of the monetary base? Economists interpret it as the liabilities of the Federal Reserve to the private sector of the economy. Currency in circulation is a liability of the Fed to the people and firms that hold the currency. Formally, if you own a \$20 bill, that means the Fed owes you \$20.

Reserves are a liability of the Fed to banks. If a bank holds \$100 of vault cash, the Fed owes it \$100. The same is true if the bank has \$100 of deposits in its account at the Fed.

Creating the Base

Suppose that a central bank is established and wants to create a monetary base of \$100. Or that an existing central bank wants to raise or lower the base by \$100. Central banks have two methods for changing the base, open-market operations and loans.

Open-market operations Purchases or sales of bonds by a central bank

Open-Market Operations Purchases or sales of bonds by a central bank are **open-market operations.** When the Federal Reserve performs open-market operations, it usually trades U.S. Treasury bonds. A purchase of bonds (an *expansionary open-market operation*) raises the monetary base. A sale of bonds (a *contractionary open-market operation*) reduces the base.

▶ In addition to Treasury bonds, the Fed trades securities issued by government-sponsored enterprises such as Fannie Mae and Freddie Mac. Section 8.5 describes these GSEs.

To see how this works, consider an expansionary open-market operation: the Fed purchases \$100 of bonds. It buys them from a government bond dealer. The Fed pays the dealer either by giving it \$100 in cash or (more realistically) by depositing \$100 in a bank account held by the dealer. In either case, the monetary base rises:

- If the Fed gives the dealer cash, then currency in circulation (C) rises by \$100. Currency in circulation is part of the monetary base, so the base rises by \$100.
- If the Fed deposits \$100 in the dealer's bank account, it changes the balance sheet of the dealer's bank. On the liability side, deposits rise by \$100; on the asset side, the bank gains \$100 in reserves (R). Reserves are part of the monetary base, so the base rises by \$100.

To summarize, however the Fed pays the bond dealer,

$$\$100 \text{ purchase of bonds by Fed} \rightarrow B \uparrow \$100$$

A contractionary open-market operation reverses this process. Say the Fed sells \$100 of government bonds to a dealer. To pay for the bonds, the dealer either hands over cash, reducing currency in circulation, or withdraws funds from a bank, reducing reserves. Either way the base falls by \$100:

$$\$100 \text{ sale of bonds by Fed} \rightarrow B \downarrow \$100$$

Loans The Fed can also change the monetary base by lending money to a bank. When the Fed makes such a loan, it credits the bank's account at the Fed, which is part of the bank's reserves. A \$100 loan raises reserves by \$100, so the base rises by that amount:

$$\$100 \text{ loan from Fed to bank} \rightarrow B \uparrow \$100$$

A bank that receives a loan from the Fed eventually repays the loan. When that happens, the Fed debits the bank's account and the bank loses reserves. Therefore,

$$\text{Repayment of } \$100 \text{ loan from Fed} \rightarrow B \downarrow \$100$$

Discount loan Loan from the Federal Reserve to a bank made at the bank's request

Discount rate Interest rate on discount loans

Term Auction Facility (TAF) Program in which the Fed chooses a quantity of loans to make and allocates them to banks that submit the highest interest-rate bids

The Fed lends to banks in two different ways:

1. At any time, a bank can approach the Fed and request a **discount loan.** The Fed sets an interest rate for discount loans called the **discount rate.**
2. Periodically, the Fed makes loans through its **Term Auction Facility (TAF).** The Fed commits to lending a certain amount of money and banks submit interest-rate bids. The highest bidders are awarded loans.

Discount loans have existed since the Fed was founded. In contrast, the Term Auction Facility was created only in December 2007. Later we'll discuss why the Fed introduced a new method of lending. For now, the point is that any loan from the Fed increases the monetary base.

The Fed's Balance Sheet

In Chapter 9, we summarized the operations of commercial banks by examining their balance sheets. We can do the same for the Federal Reserve. We've already discussed the key items on the Fed's balance sheet; pulling them together, we get

THE FED'S BALANCE SHEET

Assets	Liabilities
Government bonds	Currency in circulation
Loans to banks	Bank reserves

The Fed's assets are the government bonds it has purchased and the loans it has made to banks. Its liabilities are the two components of the monetary base, currency and reserves.

When the Fed adjusts the monetary base, its actions are reflected on its balance sheet. For example, suppose the Fed purchases \$100 of government bonds (an expansionary open-market operation). It sends \$100 to the bank account of a security dealer, raising the bank's reserves. On the Fed's balance sheet, there is a \$100 rise in a liability, reserves, and a \$100 rise in an asset, government bonds.

Now suppose the Fed lends \$100 to a bank, adding to the bank's reserves. On the Fed's balance sheet, there is a \$100 rise in reserves and a \$100 rise in an asset, loans to banks.

The Fed's balance sheet is also influenced by a factor beyond its control: the public's decisions about how much currency to hold. Suppose you take \$100 from your bank's ATM machine and put it in your wallet. Your action reduces your bank's vault cash, which is part of reserves. So, on the liability side of the Fed's balance sheet, reserves fall by \$100. The other liability, currency in circulation, rises by \$100.

Notice that your action does *not* affect the monetary base, which is the sum of currency in circulation and reserves. One component of the base falls by \$100 and the other rises by \$100, leaving the base unchanged.

▶ The Fed's balance sheet also includes items that we ignore here:

- Liabilities include deposits by the U.S. Treasury. (These deposits are liabilities of the Fed to the government, not to the private sector, and so are not part of the monetary base).
- Assets include reserves of foreign currency, which the Fed uses to intervene in foreign-exchange markets.
- The balance sheet also includes capital provided by commercial banks, the formal owners of the Federal Reserve Banks.

11.3 COMMERCIAL BANKS AND THE MONEY SUPPLY

So far we've focused on the monetary base (B), which is currency plus reserves ($C + R$). Our goal is to understand the money supply (M), or currency plus checking deposits ($C + D$). The money supply is larger than the base, because banks' checking deposits exceed their reserves.

The monetary base is one factor that affects the money supply. The Fed can influence the money supply by adjusting the base. However, the money supply also depends on the behavior of banks and their customers, which the Fed does not control. Let's examine the process that determines the money supply.

An Economy Without Banks

To understand the role of banks, first imagine an economy where banks don't exist. In this case, there are no bank reserves and no checking deposits. Cash is used for all transactions.

In this economy, the monetary base and the money supply are the same thing. Each equals currency in circulation. In algebraic terms, $C + R$ (the base) and $C + D$ (money) are the same thing if R and D are zero. For example, suppose currency in circulation is $1000. Then the components of the base and the money supply are

C	1000
R	0
D	0
$B = C + R$	1000
$M = C + D$	1000

A Bank Creates Money. . .

Suppose we start with the bankless economy we've just described. One day, an enterprising person opens a commercial bank, called The Friendly Bank. Let's examine how this bank's behavior influences the money supply. We will use the bank's balance sheet to summarize its actions.

▶Problem 11.3 examines how the money-creation process changes when we include more items on The Friendly Bank's balance sheet.

Let's keep the example simple to focus on key ideas. Assume The Friendly Bank raises funds entirely through checking deposits. It holds some of these funds as reserves and uses the rest for loans. We'll ignore the other items on the balance sheets of real-world banks, such as securities, savings deposits, and net worth (see Section 9.1).

Currency–deposit ratio (*C/D*) Ratio of currency in circulation to checking deposits

The Bank Takes Deposits

When The Friendly Bank opens, people have a place to deposit their money. Recall that people initially have $1000 in cash. For our example, assume that $800 is deposited in checking accounts at The Friendly Bank, leaving $200 in cash. This implies that the ratio of currency in circulation (C) to checking deposits (D) is 200/800, or 0.25. This term is called the **currency–deposit ratio.**

These deposits occur on a Monday. Initially, The Friendly Bank either holds the $800 as vault cash or deposits it at the Fed. Either way, the $800 counts as reserves. So the bank's balance sheet is

THE FRIENDLY BANK'S BALANCE SHEET AS OF MONDAY

Assets		Liabilities	
R	800	D	800

Remember, we're interested in the monetary base and the money supply. Let's tally up these aggregates:

MONDAY

C	200
R	800
D	800
$B = C + R$	1000
$M = C + D$	1000

The base is still \$1000, its level in the bankless economy. At this point, the money supply is also stuck at \$1000. Money has shifted from currency to deposits, but the total of the two is unchanged.

The Bank Makes Loans The Friendly Bank doesn't want to keep reserves as its only asset; it wants to make loans that pay more interest. Of its \$800 in checking deposits, assume the bank lends \$600 and keeps \$200 as reserves. This implies that the bank's **reserve–deposit ratio** is $200/800 = 0.25$.

Reserve–deposit ratio (*R*/*D*) Ratio of bank reserves to checking deposits

The bank makes its loans (L) on Tuesday. On its balance sheet, assets shift from reserves to loans:

THE FRIENDLY BANK'S BALANCE SHEET AS OF TUESDAY

Assets		Liabilities	
R	200	D	800
L	600		

Assume the loans are made in cash. When people receive the loans, currency in circulation rises by \$600. Now the monetary aggregates are

TUESDAY

C	800
R	200
D	800
$B = C + R$	1000
$M = C + D$	1600

At this point, the base is still \$1000. But the money supply is \$1600, higher than its level before The Friendly Bank opened.

This example shows how a bank can create money. The bank gives people deposits in return for currency, and then lends out part of the currency. The sum of currency in circulation and deposits—the money supply—ends up higher than it started.

. . . and More Money

The story continues. The loans made by The Friendly Bank on Tuesday trigger further transactions, which cause further increases in the money supply. Let's see the next steps in this process.

More Deposits In the last transaction, borrowers received \$600 in cash from The Friendly Bank. They may spend some or all of this money, so other people receive it. Regardless, whoever ends up with the \$600 doesn't want to keep all of it in cash. Let's assume again that people choose a currency–deposit ratio of 0.25. Out of \$600, they keep \$120 in cash and deposit \$480, because $120/480 = 0.25$.

The deposits occur on Wednesday, raising The Friendly Bank's total deposits and reserves. The bank's balance sheet becomes

THE FRIENDLY BANK'S BALANCE SHEET AS OF WEDNESDAY

Assets		Liabilities	
R	680	*D*	1280
L	600		

The monetary aggregates are

WEDNESDAY

C	320
R	680
D	1280
$B = C + R$	1000
$M = C + D$	1600

More Loans You can probably guess the next step: after Wednesday's increase in reserves, the bank makes more loans. Assume the bank still chooses a reserve–deposit ratio of 0.25. Since total deposits are \$1280, the bank wants reserves of (0.25)(\$1280) = \$320. To reduce reserves to this level, the bank lends \$360.

These loans occur on Thursday. The bank's balance sheet becomes

THE FRIENDLY BANK'S BALANCE SHEET AS OF THURSDAY

Assets		Liabilities	
R	320	*D*	1280
L	960		

The monetary aggregates are

	THURSDAY
C	680
R	320
D	1280
$B = C + R$	1000
$M = C + D$	1960

At this point, the money supply has risen again, as the new loans add to currency in circulation. The monetary base is still \$1000, its level before the bank opened.

And So On. . . You should see that we can continue this story indefinitely. Of the \$360 lent out on Thursday, people keep \$72 in cash and deposit \$288 on Friday (because $72/288 = 0.25$, the currency–deposit ratio in this example). The bank's reserves rise. The bank closes for the weekend, but the following Monday it makes new loans to push its reserve–deposit ratio back to 0.25. The loans on Monday lead to new deposits on Tuesday, which produce new loans on Wednesday, and on it goes.

None of these transactions affects the monetary base. In each one, currency and reserves change by offsetting amounts. In contrast, the money supply rises over time. Money is created each time the bank makes new loans.

Limits to Money Creation

Let's step back from our calculations and see where we're heading. Although The Friendly Bank creates more and more money, the money supply does not become infinite. In the process we've examined, the increases in money get smaller at each stage. Eventually, the increases die out and the money supply settles at a stable level.

Figure 11.1 summarizes the process of money creation. Of \$1000 in cash, \$800 is deposited in The Friendly Bank when it opens; \$600 of the deposits are lent out, increasing the money supply by that amount; \$480 is redeposited; and \$360 is lent out again. This process continues, but each deposit or loan is less than the one before.

Money creation dies out because of "leakage" from the deposit–loan process. Two types of leakage occur. First, not all of the bank's loans are redeposited, because the public holds some as cash. Second, not all deposits are lent out again, because the bank keeps some as reserves.

What is the final level of the money supply? We will answer this question by deriving a general formula for the money supply, which we can then apply to our example.

FIGURE 11.1 The Money Creation Process

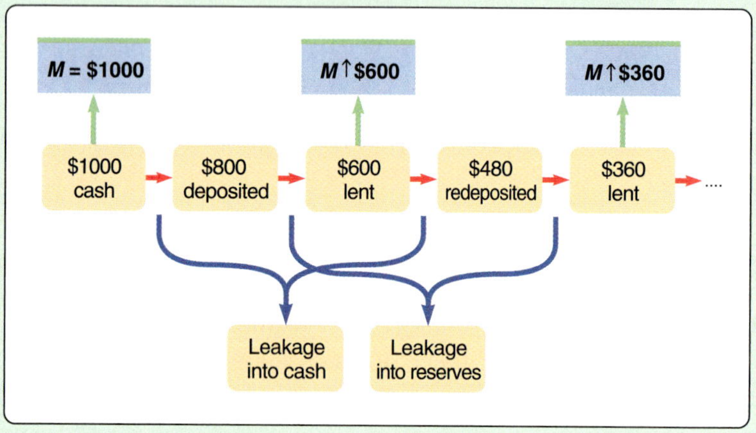

Banks create money. Money is deposited in a bank, lent out, redeposited, and lent out again, causing the money supply to rise repeatedly. The increases in money die out eventually because of leakages into currency and bank reserves. (Here, the currency–deposit ratio is 0.25 and the reserve–deposit ratio is 0.25.)

11.4 A FORMULA FOR THE MONEY SUPPLY

We've seen that the Fed creates the monetary base and banks expand the money supply beyond the base. A little algebra will show us the exact relationship between the two variables.

Deriving the Formula

The money supply, M, is $C + D$, and the base, B, is $C + R$. The ratio of these two variables, M/B, is

$$\frac{M}{B} = \frac{C + D}{C + R}$$

On the right side of this equation, divide both the numerator and the denominator by D:

$$\frac{M}{B} = \frac{(C/D) + 1}{(C/D) + (R/D)}$$

This equation shows that M/B is determined by two variables. One is C/D, the currency–deposit ratio, and the other is R/D, the reserve–deposit ratio.

To find the money supply, we bring B from the left side of the preceding equation to the right side:

$$M = \frac{(C/D) + 1}{(C/D) + (R/D)} B \qquad \textbf{(11.1)}$$

According to Equation (11.1), the money supply, M, is determined by the monetary base, B, and another term involving the currency–deposit and reserve–deposit ratios. We denote this term by m:

$$m = \frac{(C/D) + 1}{(C/D) + (R/D)} \tag{11.2}$$

With this notation, Equation (11.1) simplifies to

$$M = mB \tag{11.3}$$

Notice that the term m is greater than 1 as long as R/D is less than 1 (meaning banks' reserves are less than their deposits). For this reason, m is called the **money multiplier.** Equation (11.3) says *the money supply equals the money multiplier times the monetary base.*

Money multiplier (m) Ratio of the money supply to the monetary base; $M = mB$

Let's apply our formula for the money supply to the example of The Friendly Bank. We assume again that the currency–deposit ratio (C/D) is 0.25 and the reserve–deposit ratio (R/D) is also 0.25. Plugging these numbers into the expression for the money multiplier, Equation (11.2), we get

$$m = \frac{0.25 + 1}{0.25 + 0.25} = 2.5$$

In the example, the monetary base, B, is always \$1000. The money supply, mB, is $(2.5) \times (\$1000) = \$2500$. We saw how the Friendly Bank's loans raised the money supply from \$1000 to \$1600, and then to \$1960. If we continued our calculations, we would find that the money supply eventually reaches \$2500.

Changes in the Money Supply

We can use our formula to see why the money supply might change. First, the money supply rises if the base rises:

$$\uparrow B \rightarrow \uparrow M$$

Because of the multiplier, a rise in B has a more than 1-for-1 effect on M. If the multiplier is 2.5, then a \$100 rise in the base (say, from \$1000 to \$1100) raises the money supply by \$250 (from \$2500 to \$2750).

The money supply also changes if the money multiplier changes. This occurs if either the currency–deposit ratio or the reserve–deposit ratio changes. Specifically, a rise in either ratio reduces the multiplier, and hence the money supply:

$$\uparrow C/D \rightarrow \downarrow m \rightarrow \downarrow M$$
$$\uparrow R/D \rightarrow \downarrow m \rightarrow \downarrow M$$

For example, if C/D rises from 0.25 to 0.50 and R/D stays at 0.25, then m falls from 2.5 to 2.0. If the monetary base is \$1000, the money supply falls from \$2500 to \$2000. You can check that a rise in R/D has a similar effect.

These effects should make sense to you. Recall that the money supply is limited by leakages from the process of depositing and lending. A higher currency–deposit ratio means more leakage into cash: banks receive fewer deposits. A higher reserve–deposit ratio means more leakage into reserves: banks lend less. In each case, greater leakage means less money is created from a given monetary base.

TABLE 11.1 The Money Multiplier and the Monetary Base (as of March 2008, in billions of dollars)

The Key Quantities	The Ratios	The Base and the Money Supply
Currency (C) = \$762	$C/D = 1.262$	Base (B) = $C + R$ = \$828
Reserves (R) = \$66	$R/D = 0.109$	Money supply (M) = $C + D = mB$ = \$1366
Checking deposits (D) = \$604	$m = \dfrac{C/D + 1}{C/D + R/D} = 1.650$	

Source: Federal Reserve

The U.S. Money Multiplier

Let's now move from hypothetical examples to the U.S. economy. **Table 11.1** presents data on currency in circulation, bank reserves, and checking deposits in March 2008. These numbers imply a currency–deposit ratio of about 1.3 and a reserve–deposit ratio of about 0.1. The money multiplier is 1.65.

The monetary base for March 2008 is \$828 billion. So Equation (11.3) implies a money supply of

$$M = mB = (1.65)(\$828 \text{ billion}) = \$1366 \text{ billion}$$

▶Remember that we've ignored traveler's checks. In March 2008, there were \$6 billion in traveler's checks circulating. When these are included, the money supply is slightly higher: \$1372 billion.

You can check this calculation by adding together the two components of the money supply, currency and deposits. This confirms that the money supply is \$1366 billion.

The money multiplier has fallen substantially since the 1980s, when it was about 3. The reason is that the currency–deposit ratio has risen from 0.4 to 1.3. The ratio of 1.3 means people now hold more cash than checking deposits. The rise in cash holdings has increased leakage from the money-supply process.

Economists think that cash holdings have risen for two reasons. The first is the "underground economy," especially drug dealing. People use cash to hide illegal transactions and to evade taxes. The second is the dollarization phenomenon discussed in Section 2.2. People in foreign countries hold dollars as a store of value because they don't trust local assets.

The next case study concerns the Great Depression of the 1930s, an episode we have discussed several times. The depression comes up here because one of its causes was a change in the money multiplier.

CASE STUDY

The Money Multiplier and the Great Depression

Changes in the money supply have strong effects on the economy. No episode demonstrates this fact more clearly than the Great Depression of the 1930s. Between 1929 and 1933, the money supply fell by 33 percent. Over the same period, real GDP fell by 31 percent, and the unemployment rate rose from 3 percent to 25 percent.

What caused the money supply to fall? The story begins with the bank panics of the early 1930s, which we discussed in Section 10.1. Many banks failed, and depositors suffered large losses. Fearing additional failures, people started taking money out of banks and keeping it in cash. This behavior raised the currency–deposit ratio, C/D. As shown in **Figure 11.2A**, C/D rose from 0.17 in 1929 to a peak of 0.41 in March 1933.

FIGURE 11.2 The Money Multiplier and the Great Depression

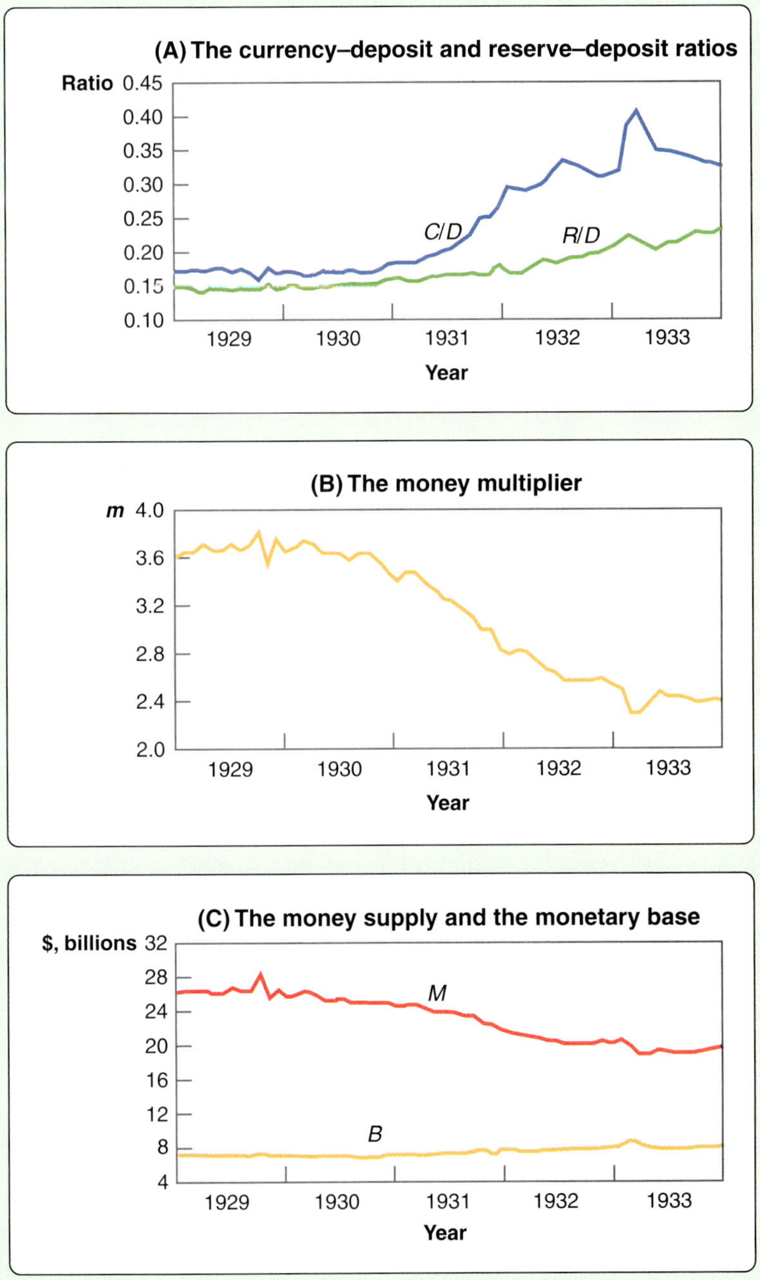

The bank panics of the early 1930s raised the currency–deposit ratio and the reserve–deposit ratio (A), reducing the money multiplier (B). The fall in the multiplier reduced the money supply despite a rise in the monetary base (C).

Source: Milton Friedman and Anna Jacobson Schwartz, *A Monetary History of the United States, 1867–1960*, Princeton University Press, 1963, pp. 703–748

The panics also changed the behavior of the banks that remained open. They, too, feared that new panics might occur, prompting large withdrawals. To guard against liquidity crises, banks started holding more reserves. In Figure 11.2A, the reserve–deposit ratio, R/D, rose from 0.14 to 0.23.

The rises in C/D and R/D both reduced the money multiplier, m. As shown in **Figure 11.2B**, the multiplier fell from 3.8 in 1929 to 2.4 in 1933. The monetary base rose, as graphed in **Figure 11.2C**, but not enough to offset the fall in the multiplier. The money supply fell, helping to precipitate the depression.

The fall in the money supply resulted from the behavior of banks and their customers, not from any deliberate policy of the Federal Reserve. Nonetheless, economic historians fault the Fed for allowing the money supply to fall. In retrospect, the Fed should have increased the monetary base more quickly. Such action could have prevented the fall in the money supply and dampened the economic downturn. At the time, however, Fed officials remained passive and blamed the deteriorating economy on forces beyond its control.*

* The classic account of this episode is in Milton Friedman and Anna Jacobson Schwartz, *A Monetary History of the United States, 1867–1960*, Princeton University Press, 1963, Chapter 7.

11.5 THE FED'S MONETARY TOOLS

Now that we've seen how the money supply is determined, let's focus on the role of the Federal Reserve. Money creation involves commercial banks and their customers, but the Fed ultimately controls the process. The Fed can choose a level for the money supply and push it there.

The Fed has several tools for controlling the money supply: open-market operations, lending policies, and reserve requirements. The first two affect the monetary base, and the third affects the money multiplier.

Open-Market Operations

We've seen that purchases and sales of government bonds by the Fed change the monetary base. For example, a \$100 purchase of bonds (an expansionary open-market operation) raises the base by \$100.

We can now see that open-market operations affect the money supply as well as the base. The effect on the money supply is larger because of the money multiplier. A \$100 purchase of bonds raises the base by \$100 and the money supply by \$100(m). If the multiplier is 1.65 (its level in 2008), the money supply rises by \$165.

The Fed can use open-market operations to change the money supply when it wants to. It can also use this tool for a different purpose: to *prevent* the money supply from changing when the multiplier changes. If m falls, for example, the Fed can use open-market operations to raise the base, B. The correct increase leaves mB, the money supply, unchanged. Such a reaction is called a *defensive open-market operation.*

Of the Fed's monetary tools, open-market operations are the most heavily used. The Fed buys and sells billions of dollars of government bonds every day. We'll discuss some details later in this chapter.

Lending Policies

Recall that the Fed affects the monetary base through lending as well as through open-market operations. It can change the money supply by changing its level of lending, which it can do by changing the discount rate or by auctioning loans.

Changing The Discount Rate Discount loans are one type of lending from the Fed to banks. Discount loans are initiated by the borrowers, so the Fed does not directly control the level of loans. However, the Fed can influence banks' borrowing by changing the interest rate it charges, the discount rate.

For example, suppose the Fed raises the discount rate. This action discourages banks from borrowing. Discount loans fall, reducing the monetary base and hence the money supply:

$$\uparrow \text{discount rate} \rightarrow \downarrow \text{discount loans} \rightarrow \downarrow B \rightarrow \downarrow M$$

A decrease in the discount rate has the opposite effects: it encourages banks to borrow, raising the base and the money supply.

In practice, however, the Fed rarely uses the discount rate to manipulate the money supply. In recent years, it has kept the rate high enough so the level of discount loans is consistently low. When the Fed wants to raise the monetary base, it uses open-market operations rather than trying to increase discount loans.

Specifically, the Fed sets the discount rate above the federal funds rate—the rate at which banks lend reserves to one another. As of 2008, the discount rate was a quarter of a percentage point above the federal funds rate. If a bank wants reserves, it can get them more cheaply from another bank than from the Fed. As a result, banks usually don't seek discount loans.

To be clear, discount lending can be important during emergencies, when banks can't borrow from their usual sources. For example, the Fed made large quantities of discount loans on September 11, 2001, when the terrorist attacks disrupted financial markets (see Section 2.5). The point here is that discount loans are *not* a major part of the normal money-supply process.

Loan Auctions As mentioned in Section 11.2, the Fed started lending to banks through the Term Auction Facility in December 2007. As of Spring 2008, the Fed was auctioning loans every two weeks. A typical auction offered $30 billion of loans with terms of 28 days. The interest rates determined in the auctions were close to the federal funds rate.

In isolation, auctions of loans raise the monetary base and the money supply. However, the Fed does *not* use auctions for this purpose, just as it doesn't use the discount rate. When it auctions loans, it offsets the effects on the monetary base with open-market operations. A $30 billion auction, which raises the base, is accompanied by a $30 billion sale of bonds, which reduces the base. The net effects on the base and the money supply are zero.

Why does the Fed auction loans? The auctions were a response to uncertainty in financial markets in 2007–08, which started with the subprime mortgage crisis (see Section 8.4). In this environment, the Fed feared that some banks would have trouble borrowing in the federal funds market. At the same time, banks were reluctant to ask the Fed for discount loans, as such requests were interpreted as signs of weakness. The auctions were intended as a new way for banks to borrow reserves, not a new tool for controlling the money supply.

▶ Chapter 18 discusses the problems of the financial system in 2007–08 and the Fed's responses.

Reserve Requirements

Reserve requirements Regulations that set a minimum level for banks' reserve–deposit ratios

The Fed's third monetary tool is **reserve requirements,** regulations that set a minimum level for banks' reserve–deposit ratios. This minimum is called the *required reserve ratio.* If the required reserve ratio is 0.1, for example, each bank's reserves must equal at least 10% of its checking deposits. If deposits are \$1000, minimum reserves are \$100.

The Fed can influence the money supply by changing the required reserve ratio. Suppose the required ratio is initially 0.1. Banks must choose a reserve–deposit ratio, R/D, that is 0.1 or higher. Let's assume that banks choose a ratio between 0.1 and 0.2.

Then the Fed raises the required reserve ratio to 0.2. To meet the new requirement, banks must raise their reserve–deposit ratios to at least 0.2. This higher reserve–deposit ratio reduces the money multiplier, which in turn reduces the money supply:

$$\uparrow \text{required reserve ratio} \rightarrow \uparrow (R/D) \rightarrow \downarrow m \rightarrow \downarrow M$$

The Banking Act of 1933 gave the Fed the power to set reserve requirements. The original purpose was to prevent liquidity crises by keeping bank reserves high. In the years that followed, the Fed sometimes used reserve requirements to influence the money supply. Yet this tool has fallen into disuse. The next two cases discuss reserve requirements in the past and in the present.

CASE STUDY

Another Mistake: The Fed in 1937

As we saw in the last case study, U.S. output and employment fell calamitously in the early 1930s. In 1933, however, a strong recovery began. Real GDP grew an average of 10 percent per year from 1934 through 1937, and the unemployment rate fell from 25 percent to 14 percent.

It appeared that unemployment was headed down farther, but then something went wrong. A sharp recession occurred, with real GDP falling 5 percent in 1938 and unemployment rising back to 19 percent. Unemployment was still 15 percent in 1940, on the eve of World War II.

As in the early 1930s, a major cause of the downturn was the behavior of the money supply. The money supply grew by 14 percent per year during 1934–1936, but fell during 1937–1938. Once again, historians blame a mistake by the Federal Reserve, this time involving reserve requirements.

The story starts with the high reserve–deposit ratios of the 1930s. Banks chose high levels of reserves to guard against bank runs, as discussed in the previous case. At many banks, reserves greatly exceeded the minimum established by reserve requirements. The gap between actual reserves and the minimum is called *excess reserves.* Banks in the 1930s held substantial excess reserves.

The Fed worried that this situation weakened its control of the money supply. Banks might decide at some point that their excess reserves were unnecessary and lend them out. If that happened, the reserve–deposit ratio would fall, raising the money multiplier and the money supply. A sharp rise in the money supply could cause inflation.

To address this risk, the Fed raised reserve requirements at three points in 1936 and 1937. Overall, the required reserve ratio for major banks rose from 0.14 to 0.25. The goal was *not* to change the current level of reserves or the money supply. Instead, the Fed wanted to turn excess reserves into required reserves. Without excess reserves, banks could not suddenly reduce the reserve–deposit ratio.

The Fed's actions backfired. Banks wanted to hold excess reserves. They wanted a cushion so they would still meet reserve requirements if large withdrawals occurred. When the Fed raised required reserves, banks raised their actual reserves to maintain a gap between the two.

The result was a sharp rise in the reserve–deposit ratio. This increase reduced the money multiplier, which in turn reduced the money supply and prolonged the depression.

CASE STUDY

The Decline of Reserve Requirements

We've seen that banks held substantial excess reserves in the 1930s. This changed after World War II, as banks became less worried about runs. They sought to reduce reserves, which paid no interest, and lend out as much money as possible.

From the 1940s through the 1980s, reserve requirements were the main determinant of reserves. At most banks, reserves were close to the bare minimum required by the Fed. In 1980, the total reserves of all banks exceeded required reserves by less than 1 percent.

This situation started changing in the 1990s. Required reserves fell, and at the same time banks started wanting to hold more reserves. Today, the reserves that most banks desire exceed the legal minimum. This fact makes reserve requirements irrelevant: if a bank chooses \$100 in reserves, it doesn't matter if the Fed tells it to hold at least \$75. In economists' language, reserve requirements are not "binding."

This trend has occurred for three reasons:

1. *The Fed has reduced reserve requirements.* In the past, banks were required to hold reserves based on time deposits as well as checking deposits. In 1990, reserve requirements for time deposits were eliminated. In addition, in 1992 the Fed reduced the required reserve ratio for checking deposits from 0.12 to 0.10.

2. *Banks have used sweep programs to reduce their required reserves.* As discussed in Section 2.4, sweep programs began in 1994. Banks move funds temporarily from checking accounts to money-market deposit accounts, reducing the average level of checking deposits. For a given required reserve ratio, lower checking deposits reduce required reserves.
3. *ATMs have increased banks' desire for reserves.* Recall that money in ATMs is counted as vault cash, and hence reserves. As the number of ATMs has risen, banks have held more and more cash. Today, many banks could satisfy reserve requirements with vault cash alone, even if they had no deposits at the Fed.

Factors (1) and (2) have reduced required reserves. Required reserves for commercial banks fell from about $60 billion in 1990 to $40 billion in 2008. Factor (3) has raised the levels of reserves that banks choose to hold. Together, the three factors have pushed reserves above required reserves at most banks.

Economists at the Federal Reserve Bank of New York estimate that reserve requirements were binding for less than 30 percent of commercial banks in 2000. Even fewer banks are bound by reserve requirements today, as sweep programs and ATMs have continued to grow.*

Since reserve requirements are largely ineffective, some economists think they should be abolished. Banks incur costs in avoiding these regulations: it takes people and computers to run sweep programs. These operations could be eliminated if there were no reserve requirements. Canada and the U.K. have eliminated reserve requirements, but so far the Fed has not.

Online Case Study: Interest on Reserves

However, the Fed has recently made a different change in policy. In October 2008, it announced that it would start paying interest on reserves. This action reduces banks' incentives to minimize reserves, which may decrease the effects of reserve requirements on banks' behavior.

* See Paul Bennett and Stavros Peristiani, "Are U.S. Reserve Requirements Still Binding?," Federal Reserve Bank of New York *Economic Policy Review,* May 2002.

11.6 MONEY TARGETS VERSUS INTEREST-RATE TARGETS

Now that we've seen how the Fed controls the money supply, let's remember why the money supply is important. According to the liquidity-preference theory, the nominal interest rate, i, is determined by money supply and money demand. The Fed can raise the interest rate by cutting the money supply or reduce it by raising the money supply (review Section 4.3). In turn, changes in the nominal interest rate affect the real interest rate, aggregate output, and inflation, as we detail in Chapter 12.

This brings us to a point that sometimes confuses people. Economics textbooks (including this one) say the Fed affects the economy by changing the money supply. However, when the news media discuss Fed policies, they rarely mention the money supply; instead, they focus on interest rates. A typical headline is "Fed raises interest rate by 1/4 percent," not "Fed reduces money supply by \$10 billion." So what is it the Fed really sets—the money supply, the interest rate, or both?

Two Approaches to Monetary Policy

This issue arises because the Fed can run monetary policy in two ways: money targeting and interest-rate targeting. We can understand these two approaches using the liquidity-preference theory of interest rates.

Money targeting
Approach to monetary policy in which the central bank chooses a level for the money supply and adjusts it when economic conditions change

A Money Target **Figure 11.3** illustrates **money targeting.** Under this approach, the Fed chooses a level for the money supply, labeled $\overline{M}$. It uses the tools discussed in this chapter, primarily open-market operations, to move the money supply to $\overline{M}$. According to the liquidity-preference theory, $\overline{M}$ and the money-demand curve determine the nominal interest rate.

The Fed adjusts $\overline{M}$ periodically as conditions change. If the economy is in a slump, for example, the Fed may increase $\overline{M}$. This action reduces the interest rate. The lower interest rate stimulates the economy.

Interest-rate targeting
Approach to monetary policy in which the central bank chooses a level for the nominal interest rate and adjusts it when economic conditions change. The central bank sets the money supply at the level needed to hit the interest-rate target.

An Interest-Rate Target **Figure 11.4** illustrates **interest-rate targeting.** In this approach, the Fed chooses a nominal interest rate, labeled $\bar{i}$. Using its monetary tools, the Fed adjusts the money supply to whatever level produces the target interest rate. As shown in the figure, this level is the one that intersects the money demand curve at $\bar{i}$.

When conditions change, the Fed adjusts $\bar{i}$. In a slump, it might reduce $\bar{i}$ to stimulate the economy. To implement this policy, the Fed adjusts the money supply so supply and demand intersect at the new $\bar{i}$.

FIGURE 11.3 Money Targeting

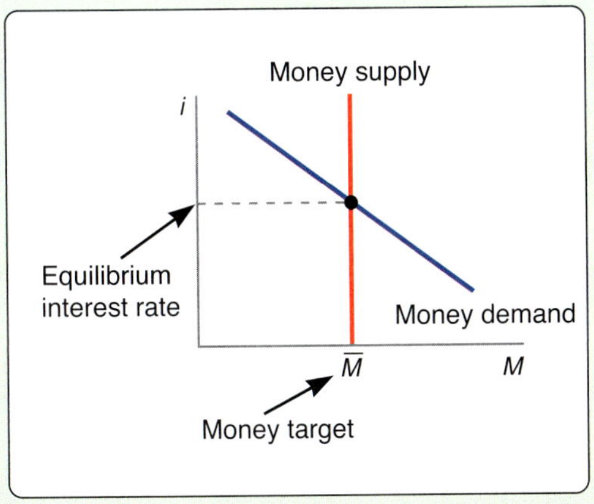

Under money targeting, the Fed chooses a level for the money supply, $\overline{M}$. The choice of $\overline{M}$ and the money-demand curve determine the nominal interest rate, i.

FIGURE 11.4 Interest-Rate Targeting

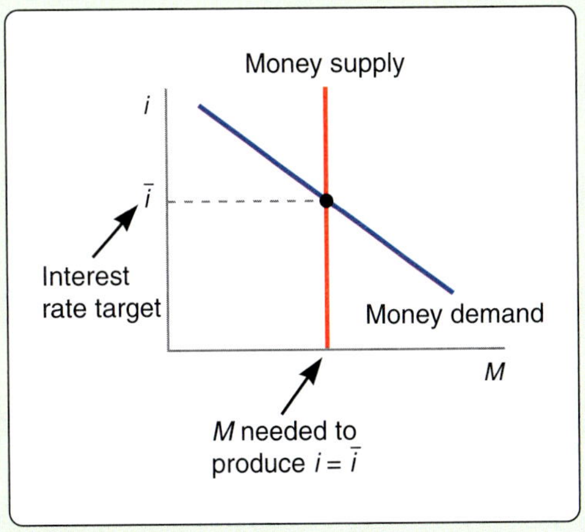

Under interest-rate targeting, the Fed chooses a level for the nominal interest rate, $\bar{i}$. It adjusts the money supply as needed to produce the target interest rate.

Does the Choice Matter?

Does it matter which variable the Fed targets? In some cases it doesn't: an interest-rate target and a money target can be different ways of describing the same policy. But the distinction does matter in some circumstances, namely, when the money-demand curve shifts.

Equivalent Policies To see this point, let's examine a specific money-demand curve—one with numbers attached. **Figure 11.5** presents such a curve. One policy the Fed might choose is a money target of \$10 billion. For the assumed money-demand curve, the figure shows that this policy produces a nominal interest rate of 4 percent.

Another possible policy is an interest-rate target of 4 percent. However, this policy is not really different from the money target. To hit a 4 percent interest rate, the Fed must set a money supply of \$10 billion. The money supply and interest rate end up the same with either one targeted.

Shifting Money Demand So far, we've assumed the money-demand curve is fixed in one position. In reality, money demand can shift due to changes in aggregate spending or in transaction technologies (see **Table 4.2**).

When money demand shifts, the Fed's response depends on its target. **Figure 11.6** illustrates this point. Initially the money-demand curve is the same as shown in Figure 11.5, so a money target of \$10 billion and an interest-rate target of 4 percent are equivalent. Then the demand curve shifts to the right: the quantity of money demanded rises at every interest rate.

FIGURE 11.5 The Two Targets with Stable Money Demand

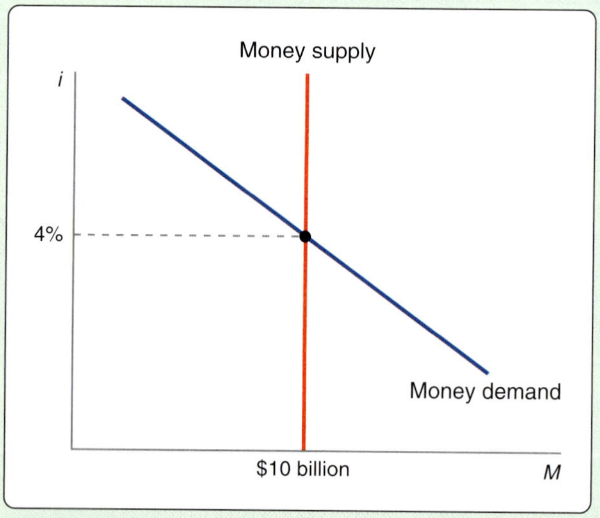

In this example, the money-demand curve is fixed. An interest-rate target of 4 percent and a money target of \$10 billion are equivalent policies.

FIGURE 11.6 The Two Targets with Shifting Money Demand

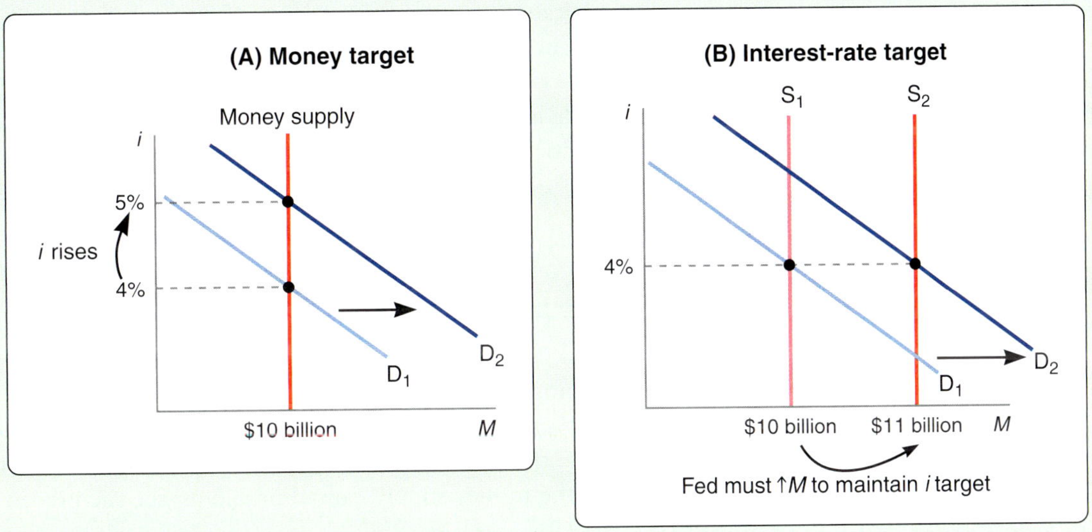

In this example, the money-demand curve shifts to the right. Under money targeting, the Fed keeps the money supply fixed and the interest rate rises (A). Under interest-rate targeting, the Fed raises the money supply to keep the interest rate fixed (B).

Figure 11.6A shows what happens if the Fed has a money target of \$10 billion. The Fed keeps the money supply at this level when money demand shifts. The equilibrium interest rate rises from 4 percent to 5 percent.

Figure 11.6B shows what happens with a 4 percent interest-rate target. Under this policy, the Fed adjusts the money supply to the level needed to keep the interest rate at the target. That money-supply level is \$10 billion before the money-demand shift but \$11 billion after the shift. So the Fed raises the money supply to \$11 billion.

To summarize, the Fed's choice of target determines what changes when money demand shifts. With a money target, the money supply stays fixed and the interest rate adjusts. With an interest-rate target, the interest rate stays fixed and the money supply adjusts.

The Fed's Choice

In practice, the Fed targets the interest rate. Fed officials meet periodically to choose a level for the interest rate and then announce their choice. The Fed adjusts the money supply constantly to hit the interest-rate target, but that occurs in the background. This approach explains why headlines say "Fed raises interest rate" rather than "Fed reduces money supply."

Why has the Fed chosen interest-rate targeting? Economists believe the money-demand curve shifts frequently because of changes in transaction technologies. Changes occur in the number of ATM machines, the use of credit cards, and other factors that affect money demand. Under money targeting, these shifts would cause interest rates to fluctuate over time. Most economists think these fluctuations would be undesirable. Changes in interest rates cause changes in aggregate output. Economic growth fluctuates. Interest-rate targeting keeps rates stable when money demand shifts, which in turn stabilizes output. The Fed prefers stability.

The Fed has tried money targeting in the past, most recently from 1979 to 1982. Most economists think money targeting was a failure. The 1979–1982 experience is a major reason the Fed uses interest-rate targeting today. The next case discusses this episode.

CASE STUDY

The Monetarist Experiment

The *monetarist* school of economics, led by Milton Friedman, advocated money targeting during the 1960s and 1970s. Monetarists said the Fed should increase the money supply at a slow, steady rate, arguing that this policy would stabilize the economy. They pointed to periods such as the 1930s when shifts in the money supply caused problems (see the preceding case studies on the 1930s).

▶Chapter 16 discusses the monetarists and their views on economic policy.

For many years the Fed ignored the monetarists' advice and targeted interest rates. In October 1979, however, Fed Chairman Paul Volcker announced a new policy, a form of money targeting. The Fed would set a target range for the growth of M1 and seek to keep actual M1 growth within this range. It would allow interest rates to fluctuate in response to money-demand shifts. Volcker's announcement began the Fed's "monetarist experiment."

Most economists think the experiment failed. Money demand fluctuated during this period, reflecting financial innovations such as money-market mutual funds and NOW accounts (checking accounts that pay interest). As one would expect with money targets, interest rates were unstable. During 1980, the 3-month Treasury bill rate rose to 15 percent, then fell to 7 percent, then rose to 15 percent again. The T-bill rate continued to fluctuate over 1981–1982.

Instability in interest rates caused instability in economic growth. A recession occurred in 1980, then the economy recovered briefly, then another recession occurred in 1981–82—this one the worst since the 1930s, with unemployment over 10 percent.

This experience did not convince everyone that money targets are unwise. According to monetarists, the Fed under Volcker did not give their policy a fair chance. As shown in **Figure 11.7,** the growth of M1 was *not* stable after 1979, when Volcker began his experiment. Money growth bounced above and below the target ranges. Critics say the Fed didn't really try to meet its targets.

Why would the Fed announce targets it didn't intend to meet? Economic historians give a political explanation. Volcker wanted to reduce inflation, which was over 10 percent per year in the late 1970s. Reducing inflation requires that the Fed raise interest rates and cause a recession, which is unpopular. Volcker feared criticism, and perhaps efforts in Congress to reduce the Fed's independence.

FIGURE 11.7 The Monetarist Experiment

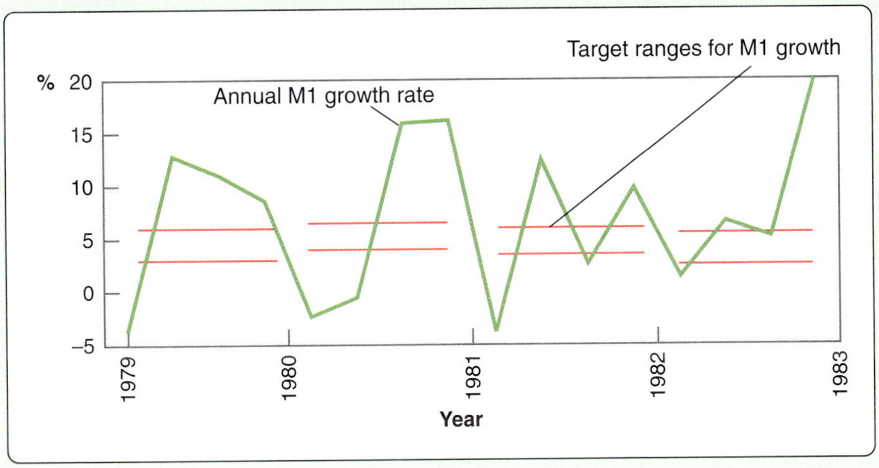

From October 1979 to October 1982, the Fed set target ranges for the growth rate of M1. Opponents of money targeting view this policy as a failure, citing the volatility of interest rates. Others argue that money targeting wasn't given a fair chance, as the Fed didn't keep M1 growth within the announced ranges.

Source: Brian Snowden and Howard R. Vane, *A Macroeconomics Reader*, Routledge, 1997

With interest-rate targets, raising rates means announcing higher targets. Volcker preferred to announce a reduction in money growth, which sounds less objectionable. Lowering money growth raises interest rates, but the public doesn't fully understand this effect. It is less obvious that the Fed is intentionally raising rates and slowing the economy.

So perhaps the 1979 policy was a just a political gimmick. Nonetheless, the post-1979 experience damaged the reputation of money targets. In October 1982, Volcker announced that the Fed was switching back to interest-rate targets, and it has stuck with that policy ever since.

Visit the text Web site to read a 1984 debate on the Monetarist Experiment between Milton Friedman and Benjamin Friedman (an antimonetarist, no relation to Milton).

11.7 INTEREST-RATE POLICY

Now that we've explored the concept of interest-rate targeting, we can describe some practical aspects of monetary policy. We'll discuss how the Fed chooses interest-rate targets and how it uses its policy tools to hit the targets.

The Federal Funds Rate

As we discussed in Chapter 4, "the" interest rate exists only in theory. In real economies, there are many interest rates on different kinds of loans and securities. To set interest-rate targets, the Fed must first choose *which* rate to target.

Currently, the Fed targets the **federal funds rate,** the rate that banks charge one another for loans of reserves. The loans are made for one day at a time, so the federal funds rate is a very short-term rate. It is sometimes called the *overnight interest rate.*

Federal funds rate Interest rate that banks charge one another for one-day loans of reserves, or federal funds; *also overnight interest rate*

Remember that, despite the name, the federal funds rate is *not* chosen directly by the Fed. It is determined in the federal funds market, where banks lend to one another. (In contrast, the discount rate *is* set directly by the Fed, because the Fed is the lender.) So what the Fed sets is not the actual federal funds rate, but a *target* for this rate. In our theoretical analysis, we assumed the Fed can adjust the money supply to hit its target exactly. In practice, the Fed's control of the federal funds rate is imperfect, so the actual rate deviates somewhat from the target. We'll return to this point after we discuss how the target is chosen.

The Federal Open Market Committee

Federal Open Market Committee (FOMC) Body that sets the Fed's targets for the federal funds rate

Within the Federal Reserve System, monetary policy is set by the **Federal Open Market Committee,** or FOMC. This committee chooses the target for the federal funds rate. It gets its name from the open-market operations that the Fed uses to implement the committee's decisions.

As we described in Section 11.1, the Federal Reserve System includes twelve Federal Reserve Banks and a Board of Governors. The FOMC has twelve members: the seven governors and the presidents of five of the banks. The twelve presidents take turns serving on the FOMC, except for the president of the New York Fed, who is a permanent member. The chair of the Board of Governors (currently Ben Bernanke) is also chair of the FOMC.

The FOMC meets every six weeks at the board headquarters in Washington, D.C. The committee members discuss the state of the economy and choose a target for the federal funds rate. The target is announced at the end of the meeting, and the news is reported immediately. That's when you see headlines like "Fed reduces rates by 1/4 percent."

Once a target is set, it usually stays in place for six weeks, until the next scheduled meeting of the FOMC. However, if conditions change rapidly between meetings, the chair can arrange a videoconference among committee members to consider an immediate response. For example, amid growing fears of a recession, Chairman Bernanke convened a videoconference on January 22, 2008. On that occasion the committee cut its federal funds rate target by 3/4 of a percent, from 4.25 percent to 3.5 percent.

Figure 11.8 shows the FOMC's target for the federal funds rate from January 2000 through March 2008. We can see that the target moves around a lot. It fell rapidly in 2001–2002, rose over 2004–2006, and started falling again late in 2007. *A central goal in the rest of this book is to understand why the Fed adjusts its federal funds rate target.*

Implementing the Targets

Once the FOMC has chosen a target for the federal funds rate, its work is done until the next meeting. The job of hitting the target, or coming as close as possible, falls to the Federal Reserve Bank of New York—specifically, to a group of bond traders at the bank's "trading desk." These traders perform the Fed's open-market operations. Let's discuss their work.

FIGURE 11.8 The Federal Funds Rate Target

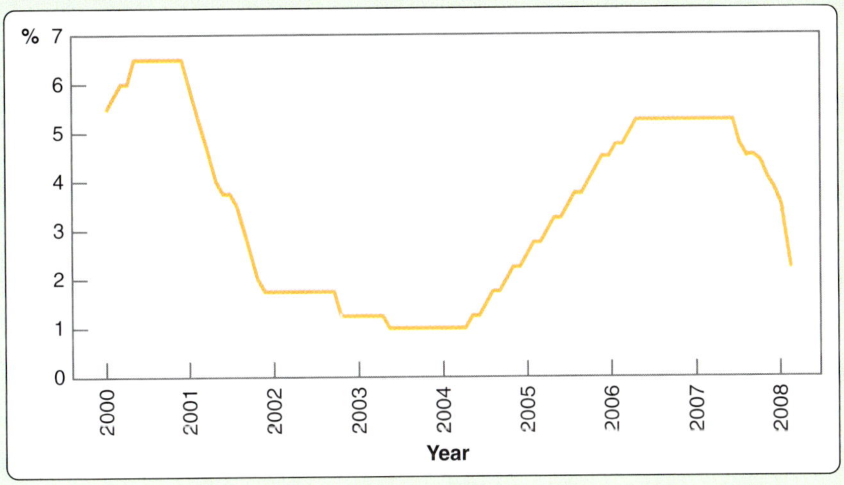

This graph shows the Federal Open Market Committee's target for the federal funds rate from January 2000 through March 2008. The target fluctuates considerably over time.

Source: Federal Reserve Board

Effects of Open-Market Operations Open-market operations change the money supply, which affects the overall level of interest rates. Rates on many types of bonds and loans respond to open-market operations. However, some rates are affected more quickly and directly than others. The federal funds rate is especially responsive to open-market operations, which is one reason the Fed targets this rate.

Recall the federal funds market, which we discussed in Section 9.5. At any point in time, some banks have more reserves than they need to meet customers' demands for withdrawals, while other banks are short on reserves. Banks with extra reserves lend to banks that need reserves. The interest rate on these loans, the federal funds rate, is determined by supply and demand. Open-market operations affect supply and demand in the federal funds market because they change banks' levels of reserves.

For example, suppose the Fed carries out a contractionary open-market operation: it sells bonds to dealers. These dealers draw on bank accounts to pay for the bonds, draining reserves from banks. Some banks run short of reserves, increasing the demand for federal funds. Other banks that had extra reserves see these reserves disappear, reducing the supply of federal funds. Higher demand and lower supply push up the federal funds rate.

The federal funds market is active throughout the business day. Banks lend to each other continuously as their reserves fluctuate with deposits and withdrawals. When the Fed performs open-market operations, the market reacts quickly. The federal funds rate usually adjusts within a few minutes.

Choosing Daily Operations The New York Fed performs open-market operations every day. Most days, its traders are trying to keep the federal funds rate constant at the FOMC's target. Their basic approach is to adjust bank reserves so the supply of overnight loans equals the demand. An imbalance between supply and demand would push the funds rate away from the target.

The central problem is to determine the right level of reserves. New York Fed economists spend the first part of each morning researching this issue. They examine the current level of reserves and the behavior of the funds rate in the day's early trading. They phone federal funds traders to get their views on what might happen in the coming hours. They also examine various factors that affect day-to-day fluctuations in reserves.

One such factor is currency holdings. When people withdraw cash from their bank accounts, reserves fall. So Fed economists must forecast the day's demand for cash. Another factor is receipts and payments by the U.S. Treasury. If Social Security checks have just been mailed, for example, bank reserves are likely to rise as the checks are deposited. The increase in reserves will lower the federal funds rate unless the Fed offsets it with open-market operations.

After the morning analysis of reserves is complete, the manager of open-market operations has a conference call with officials at the Fed Board of Governors and one of the Fed Bank presidents outside New York. This group approves a plan for the day's open-market operations. They choose the quantity of bonds to buy or sell and details such as the choice of maturities. On a typical day, the Fed trades anywhere from $1 billion to $20 billion in government bonds.

Making the Trades The Fed trades bonds with about 25 financial institutions known as *primary dealers.* These dealers are major commercial and investment banks, such as JP Morgan Chase and Goldman Sachs. When the Fed wants to make a trade, it notifies all primary dealers electronically, giving them 10 or 15 minutes to respond with bids. For example, the Fed might say it wants to sell Treasury bonds with a certain maturity, and primary dealers say what prices they are willing to pay. The Fed accepts the most favorable bids.

The Fed performs two kinds of trades. In an *outright open-market operation*, it simply buys or sells bonds. This transaction permanently changes bank reserves and the monetary base. In a *temporary open-market operation*, the Fed makes a repurchase agreement with a bond dealer. This means the Fed buys or sells bonds with an agreement to reverse the transaction in a certain number of days (see Section 9.1). This action temporarily changes bank reserves. The Fed uses this approach to offset temporary shifts in the supply and demand for federal funds.

The Results The Fed's bond traders try to keep the federal funds rate at the FOMC's target. The system doesn't work perfectly, because open-market operations are based on forecasts in the early morning. Events later in the day can change the supply and demand for federal funds, pushing the funds rate away from the target.

However, the system works pretty well. Usually, the Fed judges the market accurately enough to keep the funds rate close to the target. **Figure 11.9** compares the actual federal funds rate to the target for each day during the first three months of 2008. On most days, the difference between the two variables is small.

FIGURE 11.9 Hitting the Target

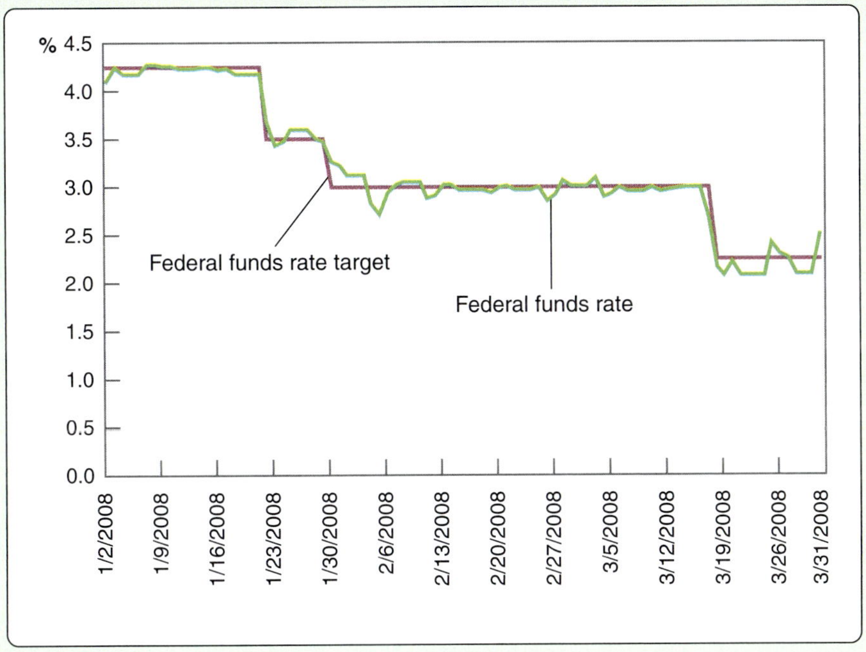

This graph compares the actual federal funds rate to the FOMC's target for every day in January through March 2008. On most days, the actual rate is close to the target.

Source: Federal Reserve Board

Summary

11.1 The Federal Reserve System

- The Federal Reserve System includes twelve regional Federal Reserve Banks and a Board of Governors in Washington, D.C. A Federal Reserve Bank is formally owned by the commercial banks in its region. Members of the Board of Governors are appointed by the president and confirmed by Congress, but once in office they are independent of elected officials.

11.2 The Fed and the Monetary Base

- The Federal Reserve controls the monetary base, the sum of currency in circulation and bank reserves ($B = C + R$). The base is the total liabilities of the Fed to the private sector.
- The Fed can change the monetary base by conducting open-market operations (purchases and sales of bonds) or by lending to banks. It makes discount loans to banks that request them, and it periodically allocates loans through auctions.
- The Fed's assets include the bonds purchased in open-market operations and the loans made to banks. Its liabilities include currency in circulation and bank reserves, the two components of the monetary base.

11.3 Commercial Banks and the Money Supply

- Ignoring traveler's checks, the money supply is currency in circulation plus checking deposits: $M = C + D$. The money supply is influenced by the behavior of commercial banks and the public as well as by the Fed.
- Money is created through a process in which funds are deposited in banks, banks lend out the deposits, the loans are redeposited, and so on.

- Money creation is limited by leakages from the deposit–loan process into cash and into bank reserves.

11.4 A Formula for the Money Supply

- The money supply is the money multiplier times the monetary base: $M = mB$. The multiplier depends on the currency–deposit ratio and the reserve–deposit ratio: $m = [(C/D) + 1]/[(C/D) + (R/D)]$.
- A rise in the monetary base raises the money supply. A rise in the currency–deposit ratio reduces the money multiplier and the money supply. A rise in the reserve–deposit ratio also reduces the multiplier and the money supply.
- The bank panics of the early 1930s led to increases in the currency–deposit ratio and the reserve–deposit ratio, which reduced the money multiplier. The fall in the multiplier reduced the money supply, helping to cause the Great Depression.

11.5 The Fed's Monetary Tools

- While money creation involves commercial banks and the public, the Federal Reserve ultimately controls the level of the money supply.
- Open-market operations are the Fed's main tool for controlling the money supply. A $100 purchase of bonds raises the money supply by $100 times the money multiplier.
- The Fed can also influence the money supply by changing the discount rate or by auctioning loans.
- The Fed can influence the money supply by changing reserve requirements, which set minimum levels for banks' reserve–deposit ratios. However, this tool has fallen into disuse because reserve requirements are not binding for most banks.

11.6 Money Targets versus Interest-Rate Targets

- A central bank can practice money targeting, in which it chooses a level for the money supply. Alternatively, it can practice interest-rate targeting, in which it chooses a level for the interest rate and adjusts the money supply to hit this target.
- Under money targeting, shifts in money demand cause the interest rate to change. Under interest-rate targeting, shifts in money demand do not affect the interest rate. Because of this difference, the Fed targets interest rates rather than money.
- The Fed tried money targeting from 1979 to 1982. Many economists think this policy caused instability in interest rates and the economy.

11.7 Interest-Rate Policy

- The Fed targets a specific interest rate, the federal funds rate. This is the interest rate on overnight loans between banks.
- Targets for the federal funds rate are chosen by the Federal Open Market Committee, which includes the seven Fed governors and five of the Federal Reserve Bank presidents. The FOMC meets every six weeks to choose a target.
- The Fed uses open-market operations to control the federal funds rate. Open-market operations change the level of bank reserves, which affects the supply and demand for overnight loans.
- Bond traders at the Federal Reserve Bank of New York conduct open-market operations every day. On most days, these actions keep the federal funds rate close to the FOMC's target.

Key Terms

currency–deposit ratio (C/D), p. 318

discount loan, p. 316

discount rate, p. 316

federal funds rate, p. 335

Federal Open Market Committee (FOMC), p. 336

interest-rate targeting, p. 331

monetary base (B), p. 315

money multiplier (m), p. 323

money targeting, p. 331

open-market operations, p. 315

reserve requirements, p. 328

reserve–deposit ratio (R/D), p. 319

Term Auction Facility (TAF), p. 316

Questions and Problems

1. Continue the story of The Friendly Bank (Section 11.2) for a few more days. Show the bank's balance sheet, the monetary base, and the money supply for Friday and the following Monday, Tuesday, and Wednesday. Continue to assume the currency–deposit ratio and reserve–deposit ratio are 0.25.

2. Start with the Wednesday balance sheet for The Friendly Bank on page 320. Suppose that, at the end of Wednesday, the Fed buys \$100 in government bonds from a dealer with an account at the bank. Otherwise, everyone behaves the same way as in the text. Show the bank's balance sheet, the monetary base, and the money supply for Thursday and Friday.

3. Let's change the story of The Friendly Bank by introducing savings deposits. Assume that when people put money in the bank, half of it goes to checking deposits (D) and half to savings deposits (S). The ratio of currency to *total* deposits, $C/(D+S)$, is 0.25. The ratio of reserves to checking deposits, R/D, is 0.25.
   a. Notice that reserves are a fraction of checking deposits and don't depend on savings deposits. Why might this be a reasonable assumption?
   b. Redo the story of The Friendly Bank, showing the bank's balance sheet and the monetary aggregates for the first four days the bank is in business.
   c. Compare your answer for part (b) to the corresponding calculations on pages 318–321, where we ignore savings deposits. In which case is the most money created? What explains this result?

4. Suppose someone keeps \$100 in cash under her pillow. One day, she takes it out and deposits it in a checking account.
   a. Does this action directly affect the monetary base or the money supply? Explain why or why not.
   b. Does the action eventually lead to a change in the monetary base or the money supply? Explain why or why not.

5. Suppose that foreigners start holding more U.S. currency. For a given interest rate, Americans don't change their holdings of either currency or checking deposits. Assume the Fed keeps the monetary base constant. Describe what happens to (a) the money supply, (b) the money-demand curve, and (c) the equilibrium interest rate. Explain your answers.

6. Redo Question 5, but do *not* assume the monetary base is constant. Instead, answer each part of the question assuming the Fed targets the money supply. Then answer each part assuming the Fed targets the interest rate. What happens to the monetary base in each of these cases?

7. Suppose the discount rate were below the federal funds rate, and banks can borrow as much as they want from the Fed. How could a bank earn easy profits? Would the federal funds rate stay above the discount rate? Explain.

8. Milton Friedman believed the Fed should control the money supply precisely. In the 1960s, he proposed that the required reserve ratio be raised to 100 percent. How would this policy improve control of the money supply? What are the drawbacks to the policy?

9. Table 11.1 gives the amount of U.S. currency in circulation. Divide this amount by the U.S. population (about 300 million) to get currency holdings per capita. Do you hold more or less than this amount of currency? What accounts for the difference?

10. In the text, we ignored traveler's checks in deriving the money multiplier. Suppose we are more careful and include traveler's checks in the money supply. Let T be the level of traveler's checks, so T/D is the ratio of traveler's checks to checking deposits. Derive the

money multiplier in terms of C/D, R/D, and T/D.

11. Suppose the Fed wants to reduce the money supply by \$100. Should it buy or sell government bonds? How much should it buy or sell?

12. Assume the monetary base, the currency–deposit ratio, and the reserve–deposit ratio are at their levels in March 2008 (see Table 11.1). Then the currency–deposit ratio rises from 1.262 to 1.5. Give numerical answers to the following questions.
    a. How does the change in the currency–deposit ratio affect the money multiplier, m?
    b. If the Fed wants to keep the money supply constant, how must it adjust the monetary base when m changes?
    c. What open-market operations are needed to adjust the base and keep the money supply constant?

13. The Fed bought an unusually large quantity of Treasury bonds at the end of December 1999. What explains this behavior? (*Hint:* Y2K.)

14. Which is more stable from day to day, the discount rate or the federal funds rate? Explain.

chapter twelve 12

Short-Run Economic Fluctuations

- **12.1** THE BUSINESS CYCLE
- **12.2** WHAT DETERMINES AGGREGATE EXPENDITURE?
- **12.3** FLUCTUATIONS IN THE INFLATION RATE
- **12.4** THE COMPLETE ECONOMY
- **12.5** LONG-RUN MONETARY NEUTRALITY
- APPENDIX: THE LOANABLE FUNDS THEORY AND THE NEUTRAL INTEREST RATE

Courtesy Cecilia Varas

The economy is always an issue at election time.

Figure 12.1 on p. 344 shows the rates of U.S. unemployment and inflation from 1960 through 2007. These variables fluctuate a lot. Since 1960, inflation has been less than 2 percent in some years and more than 10 percent in others. Unemployment has been under 4 percent and over 10 percent.

People care greatly about these economic fluctuations. One way to see this is to examine presidential elections. When an incumbent is running, many voters are influenced by unemployment and inflation.

As Figure 12.1 shows, both variables were fairly low in the 1960s and early 1970s. This experience helped Lyndon Johnson win the presidency in 1964 and Richard Nixon win reelection in 1972. Unemployment and inflation both rose after that, to the misfortune of Gerald Ford in 1976 and Jimmy Carter in 1980.

By 1984 inflation was low again and unemployment was falling; Ronald Reagan declared "morning in America" and won reelection in a landslide. George H. W. Bush ran for reelection in 1992 while unemployment was rising, and lost. Both 1996 and 2004 were years of low inflation and falling unemployment, helping Bill Clinton and George W. Bush to reelection.[1]

[1] For more on the economy and presidential elections, see Ray Fair, *Predicting Presidential Elections and Other Things*, Stanford University Press, 2002.

FIGURE 12.1 The Economy and Presidential Elections

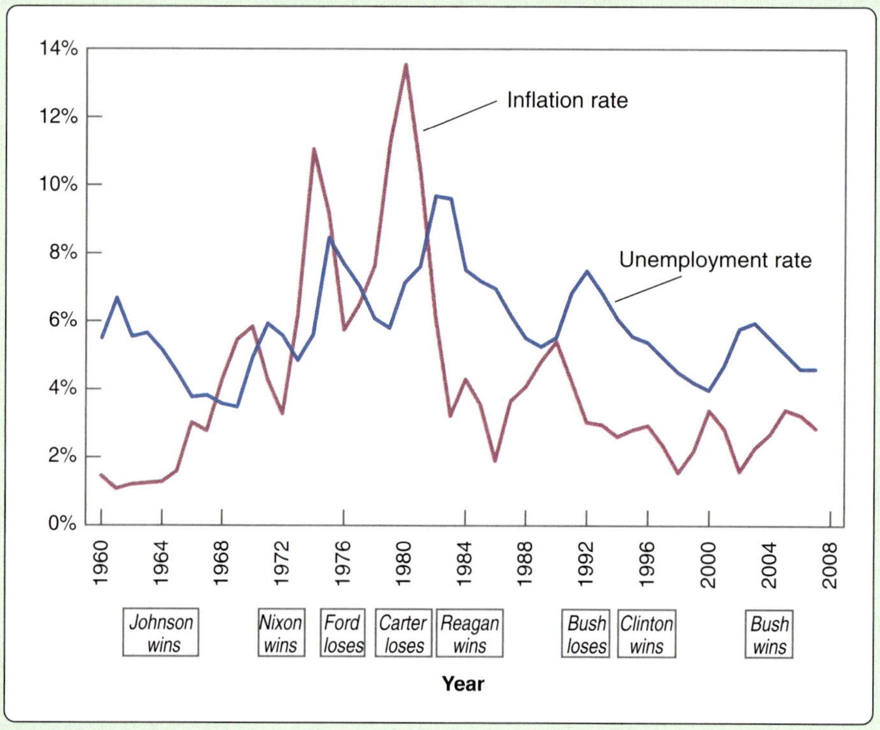

When presidents run for reelection, they are likely to win if the inflation rate is low and unemployment is low or at least falling. In the opposite circumstances, presidents are likely to lose.

Source: Bureau of Labor Statistics

Business cycle Short-run (year-to-year) fluctuations in an economy's output and unemployment

Aggregate expenditure/Phillips curve (AE/PC) model Theory of short-run economic fluctuations that assumes a negative relationship between the interest rate and output (the AE curve) and a positive relationship between output and inflation (the Phillips curve)

This chapter discusses short-run economic fluctuations. We start by describing the **business cycle,** the year-to-year movements in an economy's output. The business cycle causes the unemployment movements we see in Figure 12.1, because firms adjust their workforces as their output changes.

We then develop a theory to explain the business cycle and the fluctuations in inflation that accompany it. This theory is the **aggregate expenditure/Phillips curve (AE/PC) model.** In this model, output is determined by total spending on goods and services by people, firms, and governments. Spending and output shift over time for many reasons, but monetary policy is a major factor. The central bank can raise output in the short run by reducing interest rates or lower output by raising rates, an effect captured by the *aggregate expenditure curve.*

The model explains the short-run behavior of inflation with the *Phillips curve,* which links inflation to the business cycle. High output and low unemployment cause the inflation rate to rise; low output and high unemployment cause inflation to fall. Inflation also fluctuates for other reasons, such as changes in oil prices.

12.1 THE BUSINESS CYCLE

An economy's output and unemployment rate fluctuate over the business cycle. *Output* means the level of real gross domestic product (real GDP). The **unemployment rate (U)** is the percentage of the labor force without jobs. For example, if 100 people are available for work but 6 don't have jobs, the unemployment rate is 6 percent.

The business cycle means the *short-run* movements in output and unemployment. From year to year, these variables fluctuate around their normal or average levels. Before discussing the cycle, we need to discuss these normal levels.

In a previous economics course, you may have seen a different model of short-run fluctuations, the aggregate demand/aggregate supply (AD/AS) model. The AE/PC and AD/AS models look different, but they make similar predictions about the economy's behavior. The AE/PC model is convenient for analyzing key issues, especially the effects of interest-rate changes by the central bank. An online Appendix to this chapter presents a detailed comparison of the AE/PC and AD/AS models.

Long-Run Output and Unemployment

The normal level of output is called *potential output*, and the normal unemployment rate is the *natural rate*. These variables are also called the *long-run* levels of output and unemployment. If we take the average of output over a long time period, say 10 or 20 years, it is close to potential output. Similarly, average unemployment is close to the natural rate.

▶ To review the concept of real GDP, see the Chapter 1 Appendix.

Unemployment rate (U) Percentage of the labor force without jobs

Output **Potential output (Y^*)** is the normal level of output that an economy is able to produce. It depends on the levels of resources, such as the number of workers and the amount of physical capital (factories and machines). Potential output also depends on the technologies available for turning resources into goods and services.

Potential output (Y^*) The normal or average level of output, as determined by resources and technology

Potential output is not the *maximum* amount the economy can produce. Instead, it is the amount produced when resources are used with a normal intensity. This means that people work their usual number of hours and factories produce at their usual rates. Output can rise above potential if people work overtime and factories go on double shifts.

In most countries, potential output rises slowly over time. The economy becomes more productive as its labor force grows, capital accumulates, and new technologies are invented. This process is long-term economic growth.

In the United States, the growth of potential output has varied over time. Potential output grew 1–2 percent per year in the 1970s and 1980s, but growth increased in the mid-1990s. Since then the growth rate of potential output has been around 3 percent. Economists attribute the growth speedup to the spread of computers and related technologies.

Unemployment The **natural rate of unemployment (U^*)** is the normal or average level of unemployment. It is the unemployment rate when the economy's resources, including its labor force, are used with a normal intensity. Unemployment is at the natural rate when output equals potential output.

Natural rate of unemployment (U^*) Normal or average level of unemployment; see also *NAIRU* (p. 363)

All economies have unemployment. Some workers lose their jobs and take time to find new ones. Others are unemployed indefinitely because they lack skills or don't live where the jobs are. The extent of such problems determines the natural rate of unemployment.

The natural rate varies across countries. Economists estimate that the natural rate in the United States is currently around 5 percent. The natural rate is around 8–10 percent in some European countries, such as France and Germany.

Economists disagree on why, but some cite government policies. For example, many European countries have generous unemployment insurance: someone without a job can receive benefits indefinitely. In the United States, benefits expire after 6 months. The European system reduces workers' incentives to search for jobs, and this effect may raise unemployment.

Within a country, the natural rate of unemployment can change over time. The next case discusses changes in the United States.

CASE STUDY

The Natural Rate in the United States

We do not observe the natural rate directly, but economists estimate it. One approach is to draw a trend line through the unemployment data—a line that follows long-term movements but smooths out yearly fluctuations. **Figure 12.2** uses this technique to estimate the U.S. natural rate from 1960 through 2007.

The figure shows that the natural rate rose and then fell. The estimated natural rate is 4.9 percent in 1960, peaks at 7.0 percent in 1983, and falls to

FIGURE 12.2 The U.S. Natural Rate of Unemployment, 1960–2007

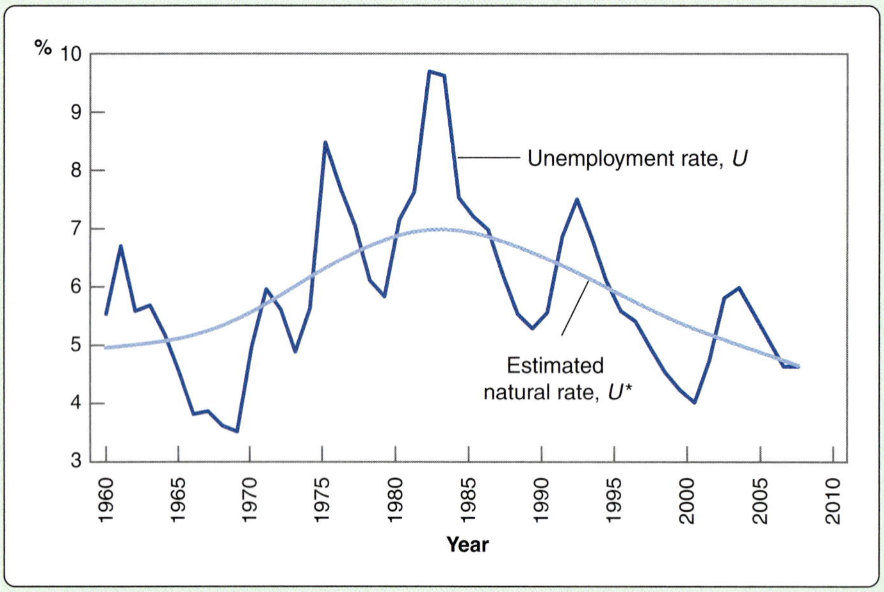

We can estimate the natural rate U^* by drawing a smooth trend line through unemployment data. The U.S. natural rate rose between 1960 and the early 1980s, and it has fallen since then.

Sources: Bureau of Labor Statistics and author's estimates of U^*

4.6 percent in 2007. The recent fall is good news: it suggests that relatively low unemployment is becoming the norm.

Why has the natural rate changed over time? There are probably several reasons. Many economists cite two factors, the changing ages of workers and productivity growth.

The Baby Boom Effect On average, young workers have less training and job security than older workers, so they are unemployed more often. Thus the unemployment rate depends partly on how much of the labor force is young, a fraction that changes over time.

The "baby boom" generation born after World War II entered the labor force in the 1960s and 1970s. As a result, the share of workers under 25 rose from 17 percent in 1960 to 24 percent in 1978. Then the boomers aged, reducing the share of workers under 25 to 16 percent in 2000. This rise and fall in young workers helps explain the rise and fall in the natural rate.

Productivity Growth Some economists believe the natural rate is influenced by the growth of worker productivity. Productivity growth was high after World War II but slowed in the 1970s. Slow productivity growth explains the slow growth of potential output in the 1970s and 1980s. With the computer revolution of the 1990s, the growth of productivity and potential output picked up again.

The productivity slowdown of the 1970s helps explain the rise in unemployment that occurs around that time in Figure 12.2. With slower productivity growth, firms could not afford to raise wages as quickly as before. But workers resisted a slowdown in wage growth. With wage demands too high relative to productivity, firms hired fewer workers.

This process was reversed in the 1990s when productivity growth accelerated. Workers' wage demands didn't rise as fast as productivity, so unemployment fell.*

* For more on the U.S. natural rate, see Laurence Ball and N. Gregory Mankiw, "The NAIRU in Theory and Practice," *Journal of Economic Perspectives*, Fall 2002.

Booms and Recessions

Potential output grows smoothly over time. It rises gradually as resources increase and technology improves, but it does not jump sharply from year to year. Similarly, the natural rate of unemployment can vary over time, but it changes gradually.

In contrast, the growth of *actual* output—of real GDP—fluctuates erratically. Sometimes actual output rises above potential and sometimes it falls below. Unemployment also fluctuates from year to year, as we saw in Figure 12.2. These fluctuations define the business cycle.

Output Fluctuations **Figure 12.3A** illustrates the behavior of output. In this graph, Y^* is potential output, which grows smoothly, and Y is actual output. Y follows the trend in Y^*, but it is volatile.

FIGURE 12.3 The Business Cycle

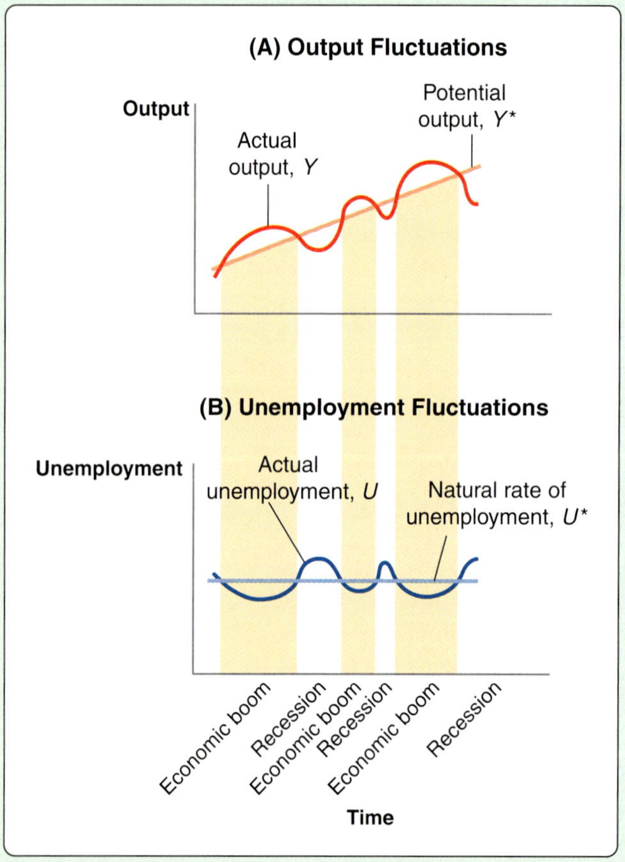

Economies alternate between economic booms and recessions. In a boom, output (A) rises above potential, and unemployment (B) falls below the natural rate. The opposite occurs in a recession.

Periods when actual output exceeds potential output are called **economic booms.** In these periods, the economy produces more than usual given its resources. Periods with output below potential are called **recessions.**

Economists measure the size of booms and recessions with the **output gap.** This variable is the percentage difference between actual and potential output. Mathematically,

$$\text{output gap} = \frac{Y - Y^*}{Y^*}$$

The output gap is positive in booms and negative in recessions. For example, a gap of −5 percent means a recession, with actual output 5 percent below potential.

Economic boom Period when actual output exceeds potential output

Recession Period when actual output falls below potential output

Output gap Percentage difference between actual and potential output; $(Y - Y^*)/Y^*$

Okun's law Relation between output and unemployment over the business cycle: the output gap falls by 2 percentage points when unemployment rises 1 point above the natural rate; $(Y - Y^*)/Y^* = -2(U - U^*)$

Unemployment Fluctuations

Figure 12.3B shows the behavior of unemployment over the business cycle. In this graph, U is actual unemployment and U^* is the natural rate. Unemployment is above the natural rate in recessions and below it in booms.

Notice the close relationship between unemployment and output. Unemployment is low when output is high (in booms), and high when output is low (in recessions). This should make sense. When output rises, firms hire more workers to produce the output. This hiring reduces unemployment. When output falls, firms lay off workers, raising unemployment.

Okun's Law

We can be more precise about this relationship. In the 1960s, economist Arthur Okun noted a statistical fact that we now call **Okun's law:**

$$\frac{Y - Y^*}{Y^*} = -2(U - U^*) \qquad \textbf{(12.1)}$$

Okun's law captures the relative sizes of output and unemployment fluctuations over the business cycle. The equation says that the output gap falls by 2 percentage points when unemployment rises 1 point above the natural rate.

Suppose the natural rate, U^*, is 5 percent. If actual unemployment is also 5 percent, then Okun's law says the output gap is zero. With unemployment at the natural rate, output equals potential output.

Now suppose the unemployment rate rises to 7 percent. If the natural rate is still 5 percent, the output gap is

$$\frac{Y - Y^*}{Y^*} = -2(U - U^*)$$
$$= -2(7\% - 5\%)$$
$$= -4\%$$

The negative output gap indicates a recession: output is 4 percent below potential.

If unemployment falls to 3 percent, the output gap becomes

$$\frac{Y - Y^*}{Y^*} = -2(U - U^*)$$
$$= -2(3\% - 5\%)$$
$$= +4\%$$

The positive gap indicates a boom: output is 4 percent above potential.

Figure 12.4 shows the evidence for Okun's law. For each year from 1960 through 2007, it plots estimates of the output gap against the deviation of unemployment from the natural rate. We see the close relationship

FIGURE 12.4 Okun's Law, 1960–2007

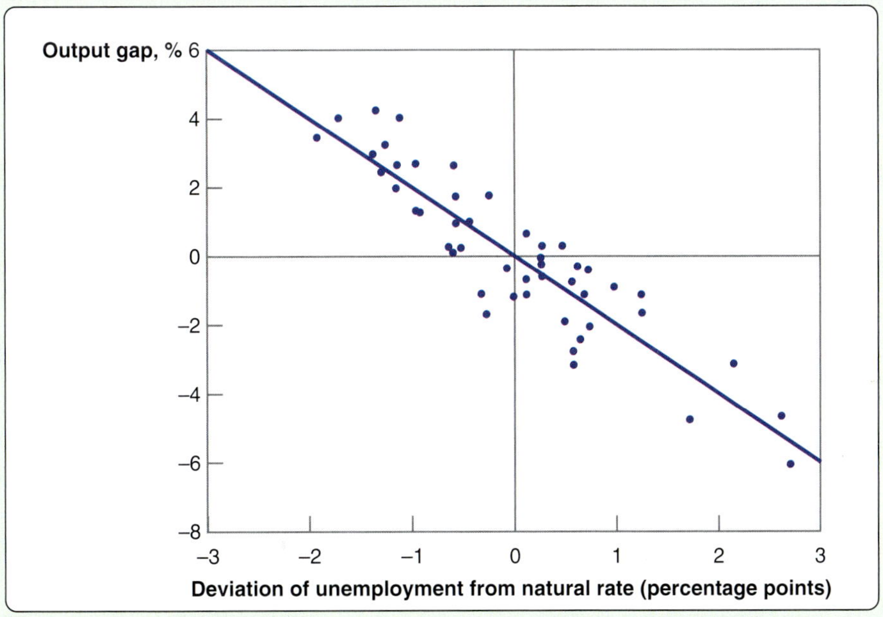

This graph plots the U.S. output gap and the deviation of unemployment from the natural rate. Each dot represents a year. The line through the data has a slope of −2.0, confirming Okun's law: the output gap falls by 2 percentage points when unemployment rises by one point.

Sources: Department of Commerce; Bureau of Labor Statistics; and author's estimates of U^* and Y^*

predicted by Okun's law. The line drawn through the data has a slope of −2.0, confirming that the output gap falls by two percentage points when unemployment rises by 1 point.

We have defined a recession as a period when output is below potential and unemployment is above the natural rate. While common, this definition is not the only one used by economists. You may see the term *recession* used in a somewhat different way, as the next case study explains.

▶The best measure of an economy's output is real GDP. However, this variable is measured only on a quarterly basis, and NBER wants to determine the months in which recessions begin and end. Therefore the committee examines monthly indicators of the economy's strength, such as retail sales and production in the manufacturing sector.

Visit the text Web site for an update on NBER recessions.

CASE STUDY

What Is a Recession?

Suppose you see a headline that says the United States entered a recession in a certain month. This report is probably based on an announcement from the National Bureau of Economic Research (NBER). NBER is a private organization, not a government agency, but its judgments about recessions are widely viewed as "official."

A group of NBER economists, the Business Cycle Dating Committee, decides when recessions begin and end. The committee bases its decisions on the behavior of output. It does *not* seek to determine whether output is above or below potential. Instead, it simply asks whether output is rising or falling—whether the growth rate of output is positive or negative.

For the NBER, a "recession" is a period when output falls by a substantial amount. A period when output rises is an "expansion" (NBER does not use the term *boom*). Since output growth is positive on average, the economy spends more time in expansions than in recessions.

NBER has identified seven recessions between 1960 and 2007, with an average length of 11 months. The last of these recessions occurred from March to November 2001. In early 2008, some economists suggested that another recession was beginning. The Business Cycle Dating Committee was discussing the possibility, but as of mid-2008 it had not decided to announce a recession.

Figure 12.5 illustrates the difference between NBER's

FIGURE 12.5 Two Definitions of Recessions

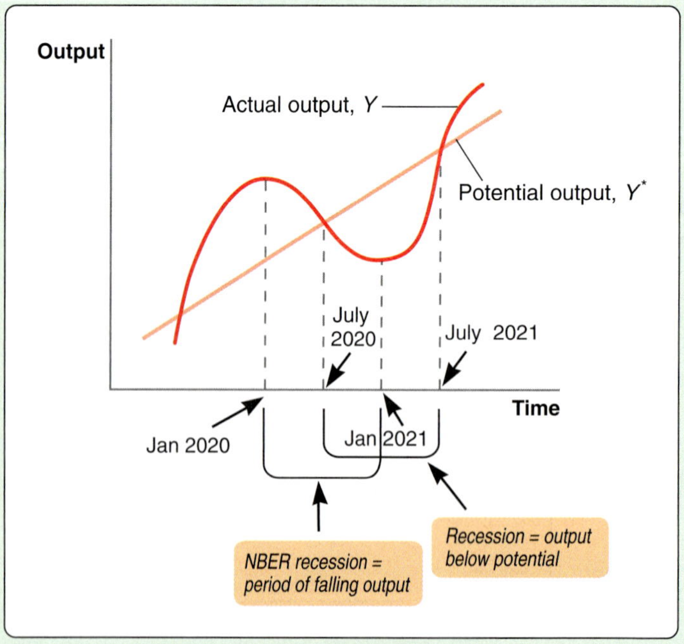

This book defines a recession as a period when output is below potential. In the example shown here, a recession begins in July 2020 and ends in July 2021. The National Bureau of Economic Research defines a recession as a period of falling output. By that definition, a recession begins in January 2020 and ends in January 2021.

definition of a recession and the primary definition in this book. In this example, output starts falling in January 2020. An NBER recession starts then, even though output is still above potential. The recession ends in January 2021, when output starts rising. Using our primary definition, the recession starts later and ends later. It runs from July 2020 to July 2021, the period when output is below potential.

In practice, the difference between the two definitions is not enormous. Historically, whenever output has fallen far below potential, a period of negative output growth occurs around the same time. Thus the dates of NBER recessions give a good idea of when deep recessions have occurred by our definition.

Aggregate Expenditure

What causes booms and recessions? Why do firms sometimes reduce their output and lay off workers? Why do they sometimes hire extra workers and produce more than usual?

The short answer is that these fluctuations are caused by changes in **aggregate expenditure (AE).** This variable is total spending on an economy's goods and services by people, firms, and governments. Total spending varies over time, causing the business cycle.

Aggregate expenditure (AE) Total spending on an economy's goods and services by people, firms, and governments

Figure 12.6 outlines the effects of aggregate expenditure. A rise in spending means higher sales for the firms that produce goods and services. When firms sell more, they respond by increasing their production. So higher expenditure leads to higher output. As we've discussed, higher output means firms need more workers, so unemployment falls. A decrease in aggregate expenditure has the opposite effects. It reduces firms' sales, leading to lower output and higher unemployment.

These ideas were developed by the British economist John Maynard Keynes in his 1936 book *The General Theory of Employment, Interest, and Money*. Before Keynes, economists who studied output movements focused on the economy's productive capacity. In our terminology, they assumed that actual output always equals potential output. They attributed the business cycle to shifts in resources and technologies that change potential output.

Keynes wrote during the Great Depression, when output fell by more than 30 percent in both the United States and Britain. It was obvious to Keynes that potential output had *not* fallen sharply. Workers and factories hadn't disappeared, and firms hadn't forgotten their production methods. Instead,

FIGURE 12.6 Effects of Aggregate Expenditure

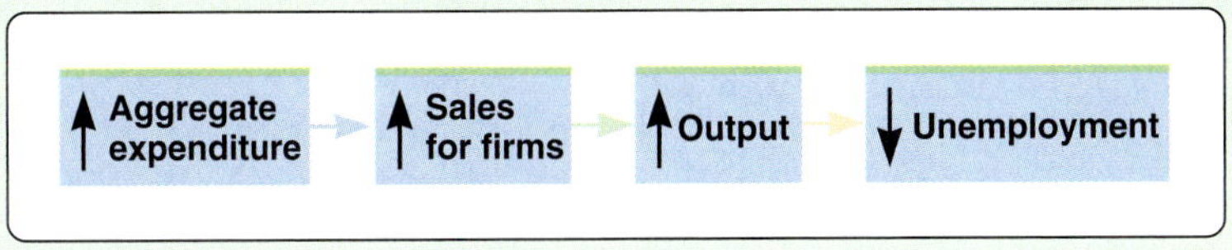

something had pushed actual output below potential. Keynes argued that this factor was a fall in aggregate expenditure, and today most economists agree.

12.2 WHAT DETERMINES AGGREGATE EXPENDITURE?

If the business cycle is caused by shifts in aggregate expenditure, then the next question is what causes expenditure to shift. We now turn to this question.

The Components of Expenditure

To understand aggregate expenditure, the first step is to review the different types of spending in an economy. Aggregate expenditure can be broken into four components, which you probably recall from your principles of economics course:

- *Consumption (C)* covers purchases of goods and services by individuals—everything from loaves of bread to cars to haircuts.
- *Investment (I)* means purchases of physical capital, such as new factories, machines, and houses.
- *Government purchases (G)* includes roads, military jets, and the salaries of government workers (which economists interpret as purchases of the workers' services).
- *Net exports (NX)* is exports minus imports. It measures net purchases of a country's goods and services by foreigners.

▶Section 1.2 discusses the concept of investment, and Section 6.4 discusses net exports.

These four components sum to aggregate expenditure. We assume that output, Y, equals AE:

$$Y = AE = C + I + G + NX \qquad \textbf{(12.2)}$$

Anything that affects one of the spending components affects aggregate expenditure, and therefore affects output.

The Role of the Interest Rate

Many factors affect aggregate expenditure, but one is central: the interest rate. More precisely, what matters is the ex ante real interest rate, $r^{\text{ex ante}}$. Throughout this chapter, we'll denote this variable simply as r. The ex ante real interest rate is the nominal interest rate minus expected inflation: $r = i - \pi^e$ (review Equation 3.8).

Changes in the interest rate have complex effects, but they can be summarized simply: *a rise in the real interest rate reduces aggregate expenditure.* Conversely, a fall in the interest rate raises AE. Let's discuss why.

Effects on Spending The real interest rate affects three of the four components of spending, all but government purchases. We've seen these effects in earlier chapters:

- *Consumption* A higher real interest rate encourages people to save (see Section 4.1). Higher saving means lower spending on consumption.

Spending on durable goods, such as cars and appliances, is especially sensitive to the interest rate. Many consumers borrow to buy these goods, so higher rates make the goods more expensive.

- *Investment* A higher real interest rate makes it more expensive for firms to finance investment projects. Thus investment spending falls (again, see Section 4.1).
- *Net exports* An increase in the real interest rate reduces a country's net capital outflows, which in turn raises the real exchange rate. The higher exchange rate makes the country's goods more expensive relative to foreign goods, reducing net exports (see Section 6.5).

The Consumption Multiplier The effects of a higher interest rate on aggregate expenditure are magnified by the **consumption multiplier.** A fall in spending reduces people's incomes, which in turn reduces their consumption. If firms reduce investment in new factories, for example, construction companies do less business. Construction workers are laid off, losing their pay, and company owners lose profits. With less income, people reduce their spending on goods and services.

Consumption multiplier Effect of income on consumption that magnifies changes in aggregate expenditure

This decrease in consumption affects firms that might not have been affected directly by the rise in interest rates. Sales fall, for example, at the stores where construction workers shop. This fall in spending reduces incomes for store owners and employees, which causes another decrease in consumption. In the end, lower spending spreads through the economy.

Aggregate expenditure (AE) curve The negative short-run relationship between the real interest rate and output

These effects, while complex, are really only the beginning of the story. Higher interest rates also reduce spending for reasons involving the stock market, the banking system, and other parts of the economy. We discuss these other channels in Chapter Thirteen.

▶ Many textbooks in macroeconomics present the AE curve under another name, the *IS curve*. (IS stands for investment and saving, which both influence aggregate expenditure.)

The Aggregate Expenditure Curve

Figure 12.7 summarizes our discussion with a graph of the **aggregate expenditure (AE) curve.** The AE curve shows how the real interest rate affects aggregate expenditure, and hence output. The AE curve slopes down, capturing the negative effects we've discussed. Output can be either higher or lower than potential output (Y^*), depending on the interest rate.

FIGURE 12.7 The Aggregate Expenditure Curve

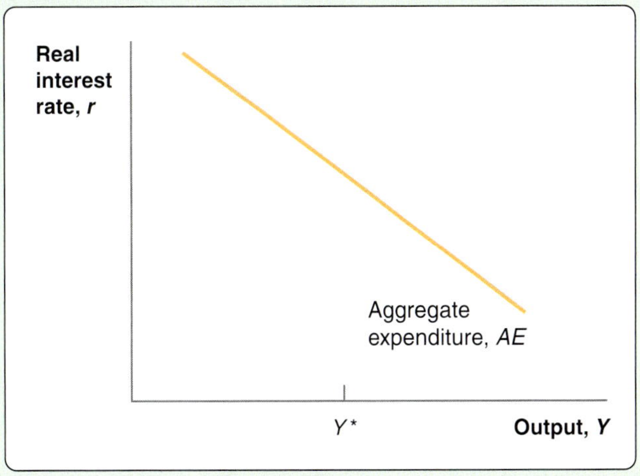

The AE curve captures the negative effect of the real interest rate on aggregate expenditure, which determines output in the short run.

Monetary Policy and Equilibrium Output

If the real interest rate determines aggregate expenditure, what determines the real interest rate? In the short run, the answer is the central bank—in the United States, the Federal Reserve.

Monetary Policy and the Real Rate Chapter Eleven discusses how the central bank controls the interest rate. The central bank chooses an interest-rate target, then adjusts the money supply so that money supply and money demand intersect at the target (review Figure 11.4).

The central bank sets a target for the *nominal* interest rate, i. However, *in the short run, the central bank's control of the nominal interest rate allows it to control the real rate as well.* Again, the real rate is the nominal rate minus expected inflation: $r = i - \pi^e$. Economists disagree about what determines expected inflation, but most believe this variable does *not* shift abruptly when the central bank changes its interest-rate target. Therefore, we'll assume the central bank can take expected inflation as given when it chooses the target.

For a given level of expected inflation, the central bank can set a nominal interest rate that produces the real rate it desires. Say it wants a real rate of 3 percent. If expected inflation is 2 percent, policymakers set a nominal interest rate of 5 percent. The real rate is $5\% - 2\% = 3\%$.

Suppose expected inflation rises at some point to 4 percent. If the central bank wants to maintain a real interest rate of 3 percent, it can do so by raising the nominal rate. A nominal rate of 7 percent produces a real rate of $7\% - 4\% = 3\%$.

Equilibrium Output We can now see how the equilibrium level of output is determined in the short run. As shown in **Figure 12.8,** output depends on the AE curve and the central bank's choice of the real interest rate. In effect, the central bank picks a point on the AE curve.

The figure shows an example in which equilibrium output is below potential output. Output could be at or above potential if the central bank chose a lower interest rate.

Shifts in Monetary Policy At this point, we can understand one reason that output fluctuates over the business cycle: shifts in monetary policy. Output rises or falls when the central bank changes the real interest rate.

Figure 12.9 gives an example. Initially the central bank chooses a real interest rate of r_1, which implies that output equals potential output. Then the central bank raises the interest rate to r_2, and output falls below potential. The central bank has caused a recession.

You may wonder why a central bank would ever behave this way. If output is at potential, why reduce it? The short answer is that a recession may be necessary to control inflation. We'll discuss this point later in the chapter.

Expenditure Shocks

The AE curve captures the effects of the real interest rate on expenditure. Now we turn to other factors. Any event that changes aggregate expenditure for a given interest rate is called an **expenditure shock.** An expenditure shock causes the AE curve to shift.

Expenditure shock Event that changes aggregate expenditure for a given interest rate, shifting the AE curve

An Example One kind of expenditure shock is a change in government spending. For example, the government might increase military spending

FIGURE 12.8 Equilibrium Output

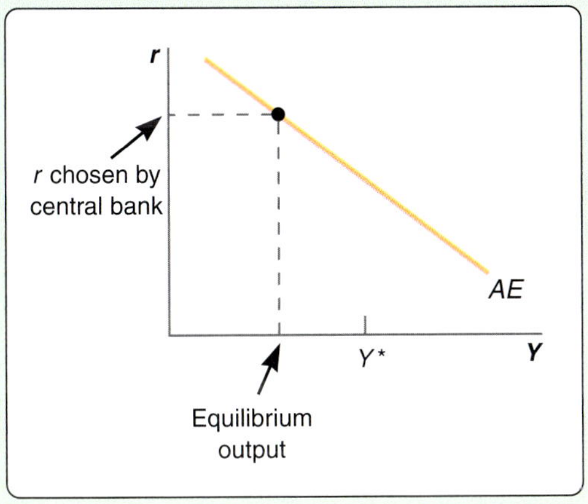

In the short run, equilibrium output is determined by the AE curve and the real interest rate chosen by the central bank. In this example, output is below potential output.

FIGURE 12.9 A Shift in Monetary Policy

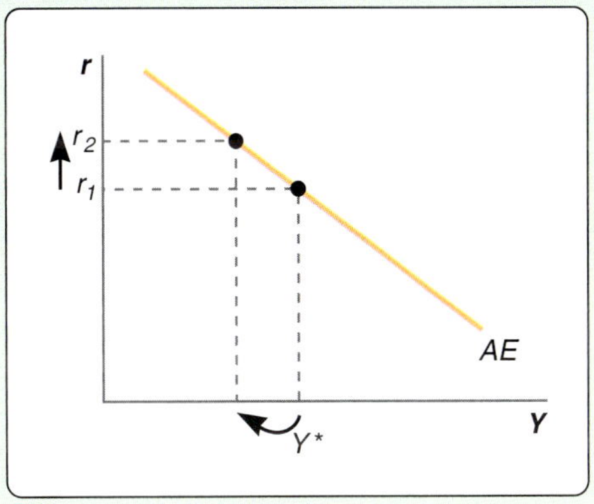

In this example, the central bank initially chooses a real interest rate of r_1, which makes output equal potential output. Then the central bank raises the interest rate to r_2, pushing output below potential.

during a war. This action raises the government purchases component (G) of aggregate expenditure.

Figure 12.10 shows the effects of this shock. For any given interest rate, higher government purchases mean that aggregate expenditure is higher. Therefore, the AE curve shifts to the right, from AE_1 to AE_2.

Assume for now that the central bank keeps the real interest rate constant. In this case, the shift in the AE curve raises equilibrium output. In our example, output rises from below potential to above potential: the expenditure shock moves the economy from a recession to a boom.

FIGURE 12.10 An Expenditure Shock

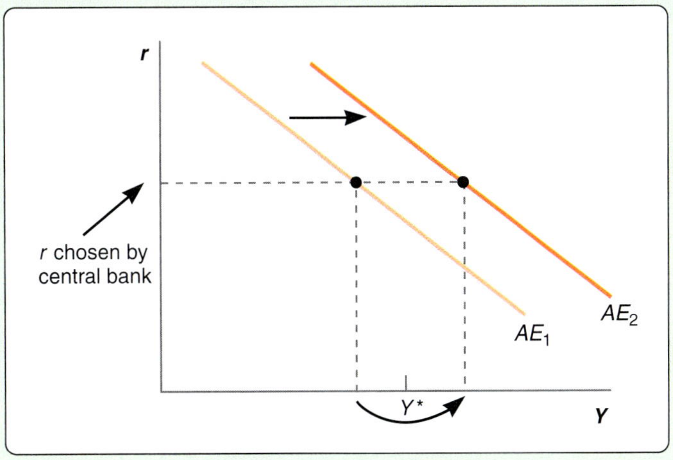

A positive expenditure shock, such as a rise in military spending, shifts the AE curve to the right. If the central bank holds the real interest rate constant, equilibrium output rises. In this example, output rises from a level below potential to a level above potential.

Types of Expenditure Shocks

Each of the four components of spending can shift for various reasons, so there are many kinds of expenditure shocks. Shocks can raise spending, shifting the AE curve to the right, or reduce spending, shifting it to the left. In each case, output changes if the central bank keeps the interest rate constant, as in Figure 12.10.

Let's examine some types of shocks that have occurred in the United States and elsewhere.

- *Government spending* We already mentioned the effect of higher military spending. In U.S. history, an important example is the Vietnam War. In the late 1960s, rising spending on the war shifted the AE curve to the right, contributing to an economic boom. (As a percentage of GDP, spending on the Iraq War has been lower than spending on Vietnam, so the impact on AE has been smaller.)
- *Taxes* A tax increase means consumers have less income left to spend. Consumption falls, shifting the AE curve to the left. The reverse happens if taxes are reduced. In 2008, fears of a recession led to the Economic Stimulus Act, which mandated rebates for most taxpayers. A middle-income family of four received $1800. The goal of this policy was to shift AE to the right and raise output.
- *Consumer confidence* Consumption depends partly on public confidence in the economy. If consumers fear trouble, they save more for a rainy day when their incomes might fall. An unusually large drop in confidence occurred in August 1990, when Iraqi forces under Saddam Hussein invaded Kuwait. Oil supplies were interrupted, and people feared the onset of a major oil crisis like those of the 1970s. Consumption fell sharply, shifting the AE curve to the left. This shock helped cause a recession in 1990–91.
- *New technologies* Investment spending depends partly on whether firms see good investment opportunities. In the late 1990s, many firms believed that computers and related technologies would boost productivity. Investment in computers soared, shifting the AE curve to the right and raising output. The euphoria about new technologies died down around 2000, and firms reduced investment. This shock helped cause a recession in 2001–2002.

▶The changes in investor sentiment that shifted aggregate expenditure also caused stock prices to rise in the late 1990s and fall in the early 2000s, events detailed in the case study on the Millennium Boom in Section 3.4.

- *Changes in bank lending* Many firms depend on banks to finance investment. Sometimes banks reduce their lending sharply, an event called a **credit crunch,** and firms are forced to cut investment. This happened in the aftermath of the Savings & Loan crisis of the 1980s. Defaults during the crisis made banks wary of all but the safest borrowers, and regulators started reviewing loans more critically. Investment fell, shifting the AE curve to the left and contributing to the 1990–91 recession. Another credit crunch followed the subprime mortgage crisis of 2007.

Credit crunch A sharp reduction in bank lending

▶Chapters Thirteen and Eighteen discuss the credit crunch that began in 2007 in detail.

- *Foreign business cycles* Booms and recessions are contagious: a change in one country's output affects other countries' output. This effect is important for a country such as Canada, which sells a large fraction of its GDP to the United States. A U.S. recession reduces spending by U.S. consumers, including their spending on Canadian goods. For Canada, net exports fall, shifting that country's AE curve to the left and reducing output.

Countercyclical Monetary Policy

In analyzing expenditure shocks, we've assumed the central bank holds the real interest rate constant. In this case, a shock causes output to change. In reality, the central bank may want to keep output constant. If so, it adjusts the interest rate to offset the effect of the expenditure shock. This behavior is called **countercyclical monetary policy.**

Countercyclical monetary policy Adjustments of the real interest rate by the central bank to offset expenditure shocks and thereby stabilize output

Figure 12.11 gives an example. Initially the real interest rate is r_1 and output is at potential. Then there is an expenditure shock—let's say a change in consumer confidence.

In Figure 12.11A, we assume confidence falls, so the AE curve shifts to the left. Output would fall if the interest rate stayed at r_1. But the central bank reduces the interest rate to r_2, keeping output at potential. The lower interest rate raises expenditure, offsetting the effect of lower confidence. In Figure 12.11B, confidence rises and the AE curve shifts to the right. Here the central bank keeps output constant by *raising* the interest rate to r_2.

The Federal Reserve has often engaged in countercyclical policy. In 2007–2008, for example, the Fed believed that a credit crunch was shifting the AE curve to the left, threatening a recession. In response, the Federal Open Market Committee cut its target for the federal funds rate 7 times, moving the target from 5.25 percent in August 2007 to 2.0 percent in April 2008 (see Figure 11.8).

As of mid-2008, it was not clear whether the Fed's actions would prevent a major fall in output. This reflects the fact that reality is more complicated than the graphs in Figure 12.11. In reality, the effects of interest-rate cuts occur with a time lag and vary in size, making monetary policy an imperfect

FIGURE 12.11 Countercyclical Monetary Policy

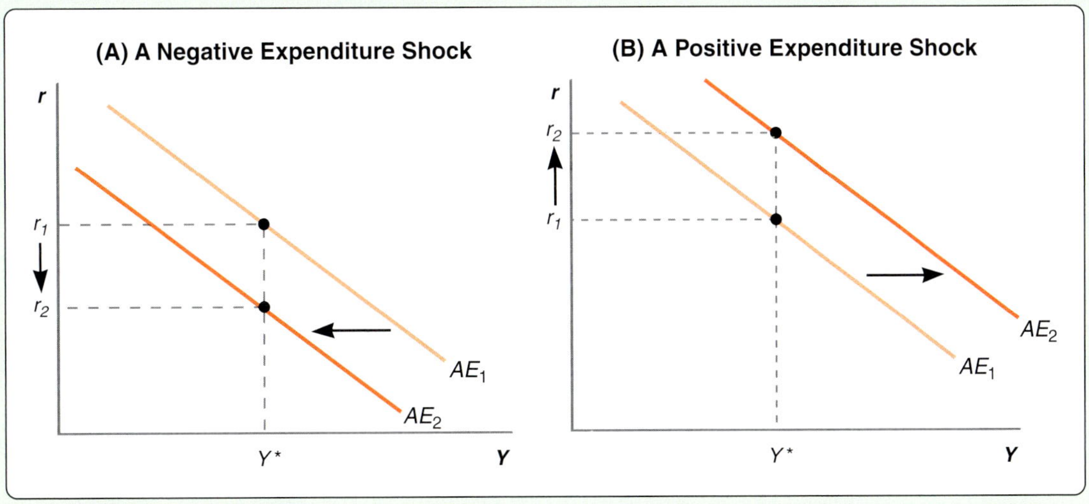

In these examples, output starts at potential and an expenditure shock occurs. The AE curve shifts, but the central bank adjusts the real interest rate to keep output constant. It lowers the real interest rate to offset a negative expenditure shock (A), and it raises the interest rate to offset a positive shock (B).

tool for stabilizing output. We return to countercyclical policy and its limits in Chapters Thirteen and Fifteen.

12.3 FLUCTUATIONS IN THE INFLATION RATE

We now turn to the short-run behavior of the inflation rate. This variable is the average percentage change in the prices of goods and services. For example, the inflation rate for the year 2020 is an average of price changes from 2019 to 2020. These price changes are made by the firms that sell goods and services. Therefore, to understand inflation movements, we must discuss the factors behind firms' pricing decisions.

Suppose you are the manager of a firm. It is the end of 2019, and you are choosing prices for your products in 2020. How much will you raise prices over those of the previous year? We'll discuss three major factors in this decision: expected inflation, output, and supply shocks.

Expected Inflation

When you choose a product price for 2020, one consideration is what other firms will do. Say you expect other firms to raise prices by an average of 5 percent. In other words, you expect a 5 percent inflation rate. As part of this inflation, the costs of your inputs are likely to rise 5 percent. Your workers will want 5 percent raises to keep up with inflation.

Everything else equal, you want to keep your price in line with other prices. If you expect your costs and your competitors' prices to rise by 5 percent, you will raise your price by the same amount. In economic language, you raise your *nominal* price (your price in dollars) to maintain the same *relative* price (your price compared to other prices).

Now suppose that every firm is in the situation we've described: everyone expects 5 percent inflation in 2020. Every firm raises its prices 5 percent to keep up. These price increases mean that inflation turns out to be 5 percent.

This reasoning applies for any level of expected inflation. The inflation rate that firms expect becomes the rate that actually occurs. In symbols,

$$\pi = \pi^e$$

where π is actual inflation and π^e is expected inflation.

What Determines Expected Inflation?

If expected inflation affects actual inflation, then what determines expectations? In 2019, what determines the inflation rate that firm managers expect in 2020?

Earlier chapters of this book introduced two theories about expectations, rational expectations and adaptive expectations. Economists disagree about which theory is better for understanding inflation behavior. Let's review the two theories and then discuss the debate.

Rational Expectations The classical theory of asset prices assumes rational expectations about firms' earnings. This means that expectations are the best possible forecasts based on all public information (review Section 3.2). Many economists also assume rational expectations about inflation.

Under this assumption, any news about inflation affects expectations. For example, since monetary policy affects inflation, expectations depend on the actions and statements of the central bank. If the Fed chair announces a plan to fight inflation, and people believe he will carry it out, then expected inflation falls.

Adaptive Expectations This theory is also known as *backward-looking expectations*. It says that expectations are *not* based on all public information. Instead, expected inflation is determined by just one thing: past inflation. People expect inflation to continue at the rate they've seen recently (review Section 4.3).

We'll focus here on a specific version of adaptive expectations: expected inflation equals inflation over the previous year:

$$\pi^e = \pi(-1) \tag{12.3}$$

where (−1) indicates the previous year. Under this assumption, expected inflation for 2020 is actual inflation over 2019. Problem 12.9 examines adaptive expectations based on inflation over longer time periods.

Is adaptive expectations a reasonable assumption? Supporters make two points:

1. For the firm managers who set prices, adaptive expectations is a convenient way to forecast inflation. Rational expectations means that price setters study all information relevant to inflation, such as the statements of central bank officials. Busy firm managers may not have time for this analysis. Forecasting that inflation will equal past inflation is an easy shortcut.

2. Firms don't lose much from relying on this shortcut. Although adaptive expectations are not the best possible forecasts, they are fairly good ones. In recent U.S. history, inflation has moved slowly from year to year. The change in inflation has been less than 2 percentage points in every year since 1984. So adaptive forecasts of inflation have not been far off.

Choosing an Assumption To analyze the economy, we must choose an assumption about expectations. For most of this chapter, we assume adaptive expectations as in Equation (12.3). This assumption helps keep our analysis simple. In addition, it appears fairly realistic. Research that measures expectations with surveys suggests that inflation expectations in the United States are similar to adaptive expectations.

One such survey is run by the Federal Reserve Bank of Philadelphia. Every 6 months, the bank asks U.S. business economists what inflation rate they expect over the next year. **Figure 12.12** presents data from surveys over the period 1960 to 2007. For each survey, the figure plots the average inflation expectation against inflation over the previous year. We see a strong positive relationship, as predicted by adaptive expectations. This assumption does not fit the data perfectly, but it is a reasonable approximation.

FIGURE 12.12 Inflation Expectations, 1960–2007

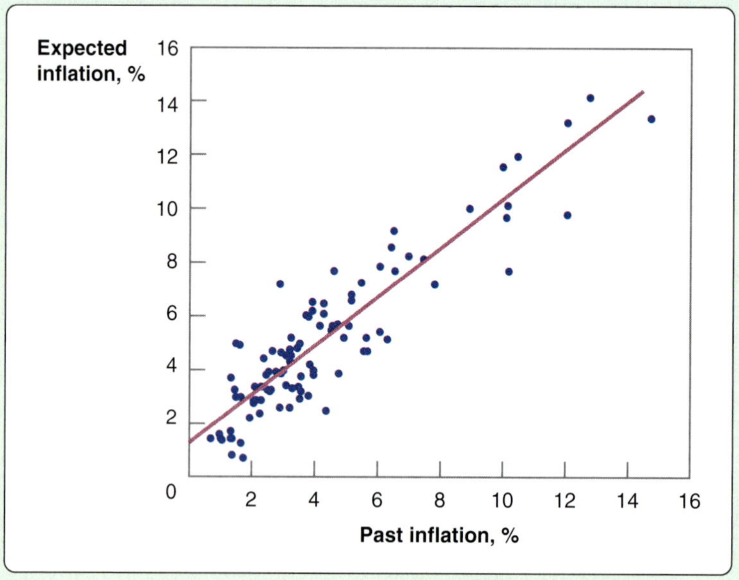

Each point on this graph represents the results of a survey of business economists performed every 6 months. The vertical axis is the average of the inflation rates that survey respondents expect over the next year. The horizontal axis is the actual inflation rate over the previous year. The strong relationship between expected inflation and past inflation suggests that adaptive expectations is a reasonable assumption.

Source: Federal Reserve Bank of Philadelphia

Nonetheless, not all economists accept the assumption of adaptive expectations. Therefore, while we make this assumption for now, we return to the debate over expectations in Chapter Sixteen.

The Effect of Output

Whatever determines expected inflation, it is one variable that affects actual inflation rates. We now turn to another factor, the level of output.

Why Output Matters To understand the role of output, suppose an economy enters a boom. In this situation, a typical firm produces more than usual. High production increases the firm's *marginal cost*—the cost of producing an extra unit of output. Marginal cost rises because firms are straining their productive capacity. In addition, unemployment falls in a boom, making workers more aggressive in pushing for wage increases. Large wage increases further raise marginal costs.

A basic economic principle is that firms adjust prices in line with marginal costs. Therefore, when a boom raises marginal costs, firms raise prices faster than usual.

The reverse happens in a recession. Firms reduce production, so they have unused capacity. Facing high unemployment, workers are less aggressive in pushing for raises. These factors reduce marginal costs, so firms raise prices by less than usual.

The Phillips Curve Remember our earlier assumption that inflation equals expected inflation. We now modify this assumption to account for the effect of output. We assume that inflation equals expected inflation *when output is at potential*. With normal levels of production, firms raise prices at the expected inflation rate to keep relative prices stable.

Movements in output change inflation relative to this baseline. When output exceeds potential, the rise in marginal costs gives firms extra incentives to raise prices. As a result, inflation rises above expected inflation. When output is below potential, lower marginal costs push inflation below expected inflation.

Figure 12.13A captures these ideas in a graph called the **Phillips curve (PC).** This curve shows the short-run relationship between output and inflation. It captures our assumptions that inflation equals expected inflation when output is at potential, and that higher output raises inflation.

Phillips curve The positive short-run relationship between output and inflation; also, the negative short-run relationship between unemployment and inflation

The Phillips curve can also be presented in another way, shown in **Figure 12.13B.** This version of the curve involves unemployment rather than output, and it is a negative relationship. Inflation equals expected inflation if unemployment equals its natural rate, U^*. Inflation rises if unemployment falls below the natural rate, and it falls if unemployment rises.

Why can we draw the Phillips curve in two different ways? The answer is Okun's law (Equation (12.1)), which tells us that output and unemployment move in opposite directions over the business cycle. Low unemployment accompanies high output in an economic boom; a recession means low output and high unemployment. The key idea behind the Phillips curve is that *an*

FIGURE 12.13 The Phillips Curve

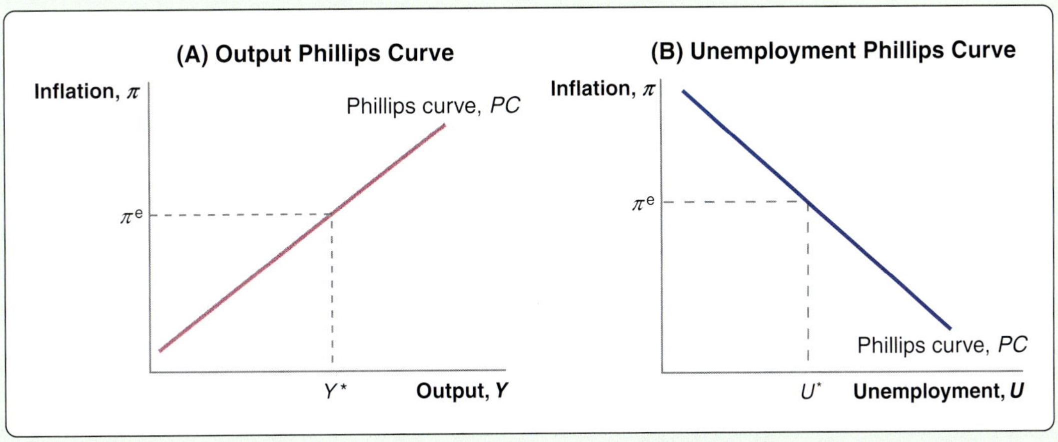

One version of the Phillips curve captures the short-run relationship between inflation and output: inflation equals expected inflation if output is at potential, and higher output raises inflation (A). The Phillips curve can also be expressed as a relationship between inflation and unemployment: inflation equals expected inflation if unemployment is at the natural rate, and higher unemployment reduces inflation (B).

economic boom raises inflation and a recession reduces it. Figure 12.13A captures this idea with a positive effect of output on inflation, and Figure 12.13B captures it with a negative effect of unemployment.

▶ The Phillips curve is named after A.W. ("Bill") Phillips, an economist from New Zealand. In a famous 1958 paper, Phillips noted a negative relationship between unemployment and inflation (as in Figure 12.13B) in British data.

In analyzing the economy, it is sometimes convenient to use the output version of the Phillips curve (Figure 12.13A) and sometimes the unemployment version (Figure 12.13B). Always remember that the two curves express the same basic idea.

Equations for the Phillips Curve We can also express the Phillips curve mathematically. Just as there are two versions of the Phillips curve graph, there are two equations for the Phillips curve. The first relates inflation to output:

OUTPUT PHILLIPS CURVE

$$\pi = \pi^e + \alpha \frac{(Y - Y^*)}{Y^*} \qquad (\alpha > 0) \qquad \textbf{(12.4)}$$

Recall that the term $(Y - Y^*)/Y^*$ is the output gap—the percentage deviation of output from potential. Like Figure 12.13A, Equation (12.4) says that inflation equals expected inflation if output is at potential. When output deviates from potential, inflation moves in the same direction.

The coefficient α is a positive constant that measures how strongly output affects inflation. If $\alpha = 0.5$, for example, then an output gap of 1 percent (meaning output is 1 percent above potential) raises the inflation rate by half a percentage point.

We derive the second Phillips curve equation by combining Equation (12.4) with Equation (12.1), which expresses Okun's law. Equation (12.1) is $(Y - Y^*)/Y^* = -2(U - U^*)$: the output gap equals -2 times the deviation of unemployment from the natural rate. In Equation (12.4), substituting $-2(U - U^*)$ for $(Y - Y^*)/Y^*$ gives us

UNEMPLOYMENT PHILLIPS CURVE

$$\pi = \pi^e + \alpha[-2(U - U^*)]$$

$$\pi = \pi^e - 2\alpha(U - U^*) \qquad \textbf{(12.5)}$$

Like Figure 12.13B, Equation (12.5) says that inflation equals expected inflation if unemployment is at the natural rate and that movements in unemployment push inflation in the opposite direction.

Notice that the coefficient on unemployment in Equation (12.5) is -2 times the output coefficient in Equation (12.4). If $\alpha = 0.5$, for example, the coefficient on unemployment is -1.0. A 1 percentage point rise in the unemployment rate reduces the inflation rate by 1 percentage point.

The Phillips Curve with Adaptive Expectations Remember our assumption of adaptive expectations: $\pi^e = \pi(-1)$. With this assumption, we can write the Phillips curve in a different way. In the output Phillips curve, Equation (12.4), substituting $\pi(-1)$ for π^e gives us

$$\pi = \pi(-1) + \alpha \frac{(Y - Y^*)}{Y^*}$$

Moving $\pi(-1)$ to the left side yields

OUTPUT PHILLIPS CURVE WITH ADAPTIVE EXPECTATIONS

$$\pi - \pi(-1) = \alpha \frac{(Y - Y^*)}{Y^*} \quad (12.6)$$

In this equation, the left side is current inflation minus last year's inflation—in other words, the *change* in inflation. So the output gap determines the change in inflation. When output exceeds potential, the change in inflation is positive: inflation rises. When output is below potential, inflation falls.

Once again, Okun's law lets us replace the output gap with $-2(U - U^*)$. Making this substitution in Equation (12.6) gives us

UNEMPLOYMENT PHILLIPS CURVE WITH ADAPTIVE EXPECTATIONS

$$\pi - \pi(-1) = -2\alpha(U - U^*) \quad (12.7)$$

When unemployment equals the natural rate, the change in inflation is zero: the inflation rate is constant. For this reason, the natural rate is sometimes called the *nonaccelerating inflation rate of unemployment*, or **NAIRU.** Inflation falls when unemployment exceeds the natural rate, and it rises when unemployment is below the natural rate.

NAIRU Acronym for *nonaccelerating inflation rate of unemployment*, the unemployment rate that produces a constant inflation rate; another name for the *natural rate of unemployment*, U^*.

Some Data Does the Phillips curve describe reality? Let's examine the version that relates the change in inflation to unemployment, Equation (12.7). **Figure 12.14** plots the change in U.S. inflation against $U - U^*$, the deviation of unemployment from the natural rate, for each year from 1960 through 2007. $U - U^*$ is calculated using the estimates of U^* in Figure 12.2 (p. 346).

Figure 12.14 shows a negative relation between unemployment and the change in inflation, as predicted by the Phillips curve. The line that best fits this relation has a slope of approximately -1.0. This means the inflation rate falls by 1 percentage point when unemployment is 1 point above the natural rate.

▶If you have taken statistics: We obtain a coefficient of -0.97 when we run a regression of the change in inflation on $U - U^*$, without a constant term. The line in Figure 12.14 is the regression line.

The Phillips curve relation is far from perfect, however. In Figure 12.14, inflation sometimes moves in ways our theory does not predict. In 1974, for example, inflation rose almost 5 points even though unemployment was near the natural rate. In 1980, inflation rose 2 points when unemployment was *above* the natural rate. To understand such episodes, we turn to the final factor that affects inflation.

Supply Shocks

So far we've seen that inflation depends on expected inflation and on output or unemployment. The final factor is supply shocks.

What Are They? A **supply shock, ν** (the Greek letter nu) is an event that causes a major change in firms' production costs. An *adverse supply shock* raises costs, and a *beneficial supply shock* reduces costs. In the short run, these shocks cause changes in the inflation rate.

Supply shock, ν Event that causes a major change in firms' production costs, which in turn causes a short-run change in the inflation rate

FIGURE 12.14 **Evidence for the Phillips Curve, 1960–2007**

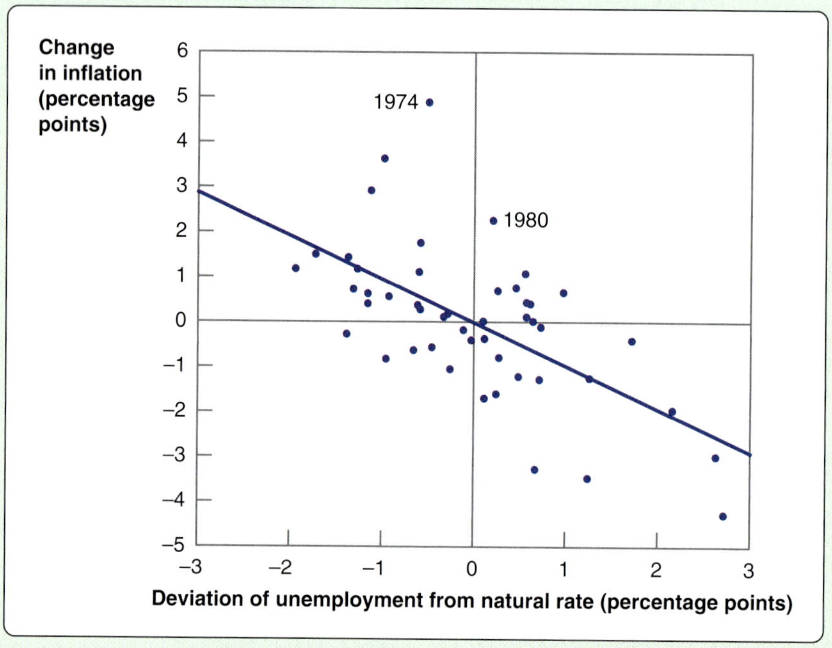

In this graph, the vertical axis is the change in the U.S. inflation rate from the previous year, $\pi - \pi(-1)$. The horizontal axis is the difference between unemployment and the natural rate, $U - U^*$. Each dot represents a year. On average, a one percentage point rise in unemployment reduces the inflation rate by about one point. This negative relationship is predicted by the Phillips curve with adaptive expectations.

Sources: Bureau of Labor Statistics and author's calculations

One kind of supply shock is a change in oil prices. Many firms use oil in their production processes. If oil prices rise, then costs rise for oil users, leading them to increase the prices of their goods by more than usual. The inflation rate rises. A fall in oil prices has the opposite effect, reducing firms' costs and pushing inflation down.

There are many kinds of supply shocks. A shock can stem from a change in the prices of raw materials, such as oil. It can be a jump in wages when firms negotiate new labor contracts. It can be a change in the exchange rate, which affects the costs of importers.

Supply Shocks and the Phillips Curve We can capture the effects of supply shocks in our graph of the Phillips curve. An adverse supply shock raises inflation for any given levels of expected inflation and output. As shown in **Figure 12.15,** the Phillips curve shifts up, from PC_1 to PC_2. A beneficial supply shock has the opposite effect, shifting the Phillips curve down.

In the equation for the Phillips curve, we add the term ν, which captures supply shocks:

FIGURE 12.15 An Adverse Supply Shock

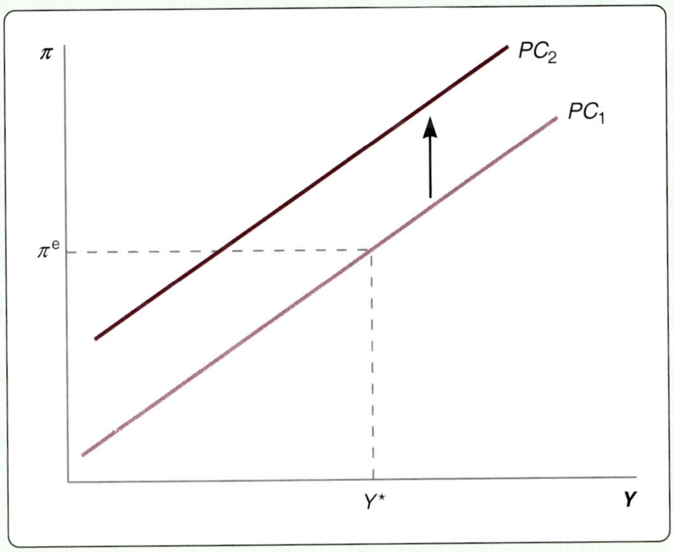

An adverse supply shock, such as a rise in oil prices, causes the Phillips curve to shift up.

THE PHILLIPS CURVE WITH SUPPLY SHOCKS

$$\pi = \pi^e + \alpha \frac{(Y - Y^*)}{Y^*} + \nu \qquad (12.8)$$

If no supply shock occurs, then $\nu = 0$. A positive ν is an adverse shock and a negative ν is a beneficial shock. For example, $\nu = 2\%$ means a shock that raises inflation by 2 percent.

Let's again rewrite the Phillips curve using adaptive expectations, $\pi^e = \pi(-1)$. This assumption leads to

THE PHILLIPS CURVE WITH ADAPTIVE EXPECTATIONS AND SUPPLY SHOCKS

$$\pi - \pi(-1) = \alpha \frac{(Y - Y^*)}{Y^*} + \nu \qquad (12.9)$$

Once again, $\pi - \pi(-1)$ is the change in inflation from the previous year.

Equation (12.9) gives a compact summary of inflation behavior. If output is at potential ($Y = Y^*$) and no supply shock occurs ($\nu = 0$), then the change in inflation is zero. In other words, inflation stays at its previous level. Inflation can rise above its previous level for two reasons: a positive output gap ($Y > Y^*$) or an adverse supply shock ($\nu > 0$). Similarly, inflation can fall because of a negative output gap or a beneficial supply shock.

Many kinds of supply shocks occur, but the most important example is the one we started with: changes in oil prices. Oil prices explain many movements in inflation rates, as the next case discusses.

CASE STUDY

Oil Prices and Inflation

Look at Figure 12.1 (p. 344), which shows U.S. inflation rates since 1960. You can see that inflation rose rapidly at two points during the 1970s, peaking at 11 percent in 1974 and 14 percent in 1980. In each case, a major factor behind the inflation run-up was an increase in world oil prices.

The oil price increases reflected political and military events in the Middle East. The first increase followed the Yom Kippur War of October 1973, in which Egypt and Syria attacked Israel. The United States and Western European countries supported Israel in the war, angering Arab oil producers. OPEC (the Organization of Petroleum Exporting Countries) decided to reduce oil production, and it temporarily banned exports to Israel's supporters. The supply of oil fell sharply, pushing up the price. The price more than doubled in December 1973, from about \$4 per barrel to \$10, spurring inflation throughout the world.

In early 1979, oil prices were stable at about \$15 per barrel. Then a revolution broke out in Iran, a major oil producer. Ultimately Iran's monarch, the Shah, was overthrown and replaced by a fundamentalist Islamic government. In the meantime, the revolution disrupted Iran's oil production, reducing world supply. The price of oil climbed to \$40 per barrel in 1980, and inflation rose again.

Oil prices also explain some of the smaller inflation movements in Figure 12.1. Dissension within OPEC caused a fall in oil prices in 1986, which in turn caused a dip in U.S. inflation. Oil prices rose in 1990, when Iraq invaded Kuwait, and U.S. inflation rose.

More recently, oil prices have been less important for U.S. inflation. The reason is *not* that oil prices have been stable. To the contrary, prices have risen dramatically in recent years, from \$20 per barrel in 2002 to over \$100 in early 2008. This trend reflects falling oil production in parts of the world, such as the North Sea, and fears that output will fall elsewhere. It also reflects rising demand for oil from rapidly growing economies, especially China and India.

Rising oil prices have meant higher gasoline prices for U.S. consumers, but the effects on overall inflation have been modest. The inflation rate edged up from 2 percent in 2002 to around 4 percent in early 2008, hardly a return to 1970s' levels. Evidently oil prices don't affect inflation the way they used to.

What explains this change? One factor is that oil has become less important to the U.S. economy. The manufacturing sector has shrunk and the service sector, which uses less energy, has grown. Since the 1970s, the amount of oil used per unit of aggregate output has fallen by almost half.

Economists speculate about other factors. One theory involves a change in the behavior of inflation expectations. In the 1970s, people expected oil price hikes to raise inflation, and these expectations were self-fulfilling. To match expected inflation, firms throughout the economy raised their prices when they saw oil prices rise, and workers demanded larger wage increases. This behavior magnified the direct effects of oil prices on inflation.

According to this theory, expectations behave differently now: rising oil prices no longer produce self-fulfilling expectations of a large inflation increase. The ultimate reason for this change is the behavior of the Federal Reserve. The Fed has shown a commitment to low inflation, so firms and workers believe that any inflationary blip caused by oil prices will soon be reversed. We return to this idea when we discuss monetary policy in Chapters Fifteen and Sixteen.

12.4 THE COMPLETE ECONOMY

We have used the aggregate expenditure curve to explain output movements and the Phillips curve to explain inflation movements. We now put the two curves together to get a complete view of short-run economic fluctuations.

Combining the Two Curves

Figure 12.16 shows how both output and the inflation rate are determined. The central bank chooses the real interest rate. In Figure 12.16A, the real interest rate and the AE curve determine equilibrium output. Then output and the Phillips curve determine inflation in Figure 12.16B. The figure shows a case in which output is below potential and inflation is less than expected inflation.

We can use the AE and Phillips curves to see how various events affect the economy. Let's consider three examples. In each one, we assume that initially output is at potential and inflation equals expected inflation. Then something happens, and we trace out the effects.

A Rise in the Real Interest Rate In **Figure 12.17A,** the central bank raises the real interest rate from r_1 to r_2. This action moves the economy along the AE curve, pushing output below potential. In **Figure 12.17B,** lower output moves the economy along the Phillips curve, reducing inflation below expected inflation.

This example illustrates a basic tradeoff facing central banks. *Policymakers can reduce inflation by raising the real interest rate, but at the cost of reducing output in the short run.*

FIGURE 12.16 The Complete Economy

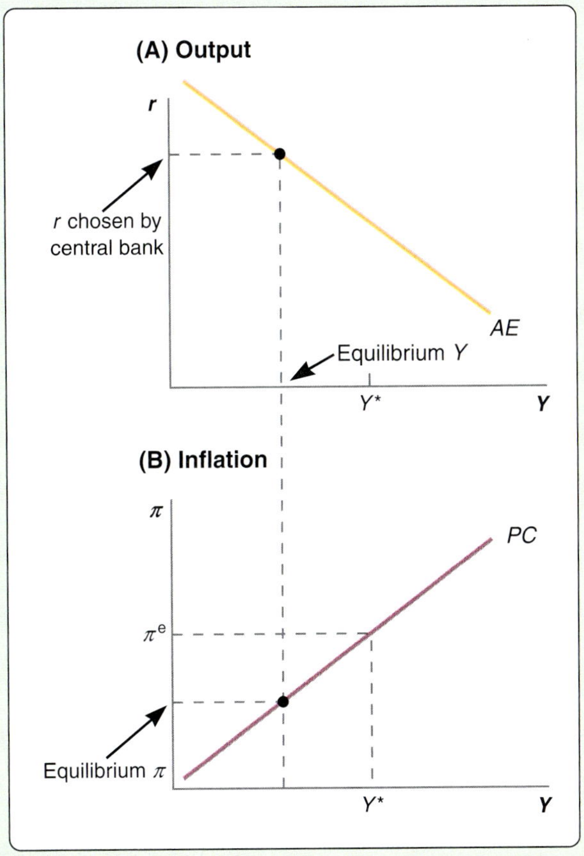

In the short run, the central bank chooses the real interest rate. The real interest rate and the AE curve determine output (A). Output and the Phillips curve determine inflation (B). In this example, output is below potential and inflation is below expected inflation.

FIGURE 12.17 A Rise in the Real Interest Rate

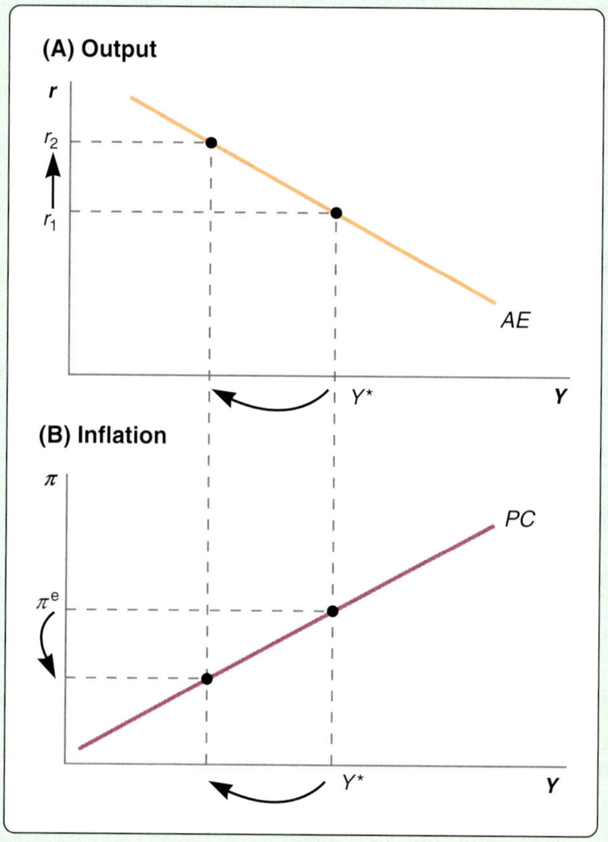

In this example, the real interest rate is initially r_1 and output is at potential. Then the central bank raises the interest rate to r_2, which pushes output below potential (A). The fall in output pushes inflation below expected inflation (B).

An Expenditure Shock **Figure 12.18** shows the effects of a shock that raises aggregate expenditure, such as a tax cut or a rise in consumer confidence. The shock shifts the AE curve to the right in Figure 12.18A. Assuming the central bank keeps the real interest rate constant, output rises above potential. Higher output moves the economy along the Phillips curve to higher inflation in Figure 12.18B.

A Supply Shock Finally, we examine the effects of an adverse supply shock, such as a rise in oil prices. For this shock, we show two possible outcomes based on different reactions by the central bank.

In **Figure 12.19,** the central bank keeps the real interest rate constant. Since the shock does not affect the AE curve, output stays at potential. The adverse supply shock causes the Phillips curve to shift up, leading to higher inflation.

Accommodative monetary policy Decision by the central bank to keep the real interest rate constant when a supply shock occurs, allowing inflation to change

The central bank's behavior in this case is called **accommodative monetary policy.** The central bank responds passively to (accommodates) the supply shock, letting inflation go where the shock pushes it.

FIGURE 12.18 An Expenditure Shock

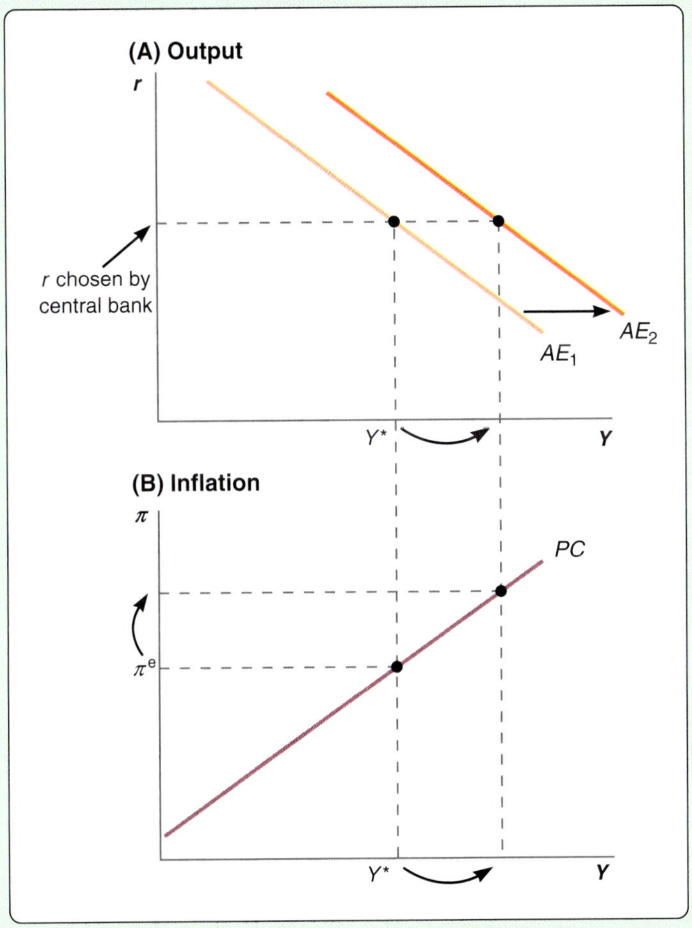

In this example, output is initially at potential. An expenditure shock shifts the AE curve to the right and the central bank holds the real interest rate constant, so output rises above potential (A). The rise in output pushes inflation above expected inflation (B).

In **Figure 12.20,** the central bank chooses **nonacommodative monetary policy.** It acts to keep inflation constant. It raises the real interest rate, which reduces output. The Phillips curve shifts up, but the effect of this shift on inflation is offset by the effect of lower output. Inflation stays at π^e.

Nonaccommodative monetary policy Decision by the central bank to adjust the interest rate to offset a supply shock and keep inflation constant

This example shows that *an adverse supply shock creates a dilemma for the central bank*. Nonaccommodative policy prevents the shock from raising inflation, but at the cost of lower output. Sometimes central banks are unwilling to accept this cost to the economy, so they accommodate the shock and allow inflation to rise.

The Economy Over Time

We've seen how various events affect the economy at a point in time. This is not the end of the story, because these events also affect the future. Here we examine how the economy evolves over time.

FIGURE 12.19 An Adverse Supply Shock with Accommodative Policy

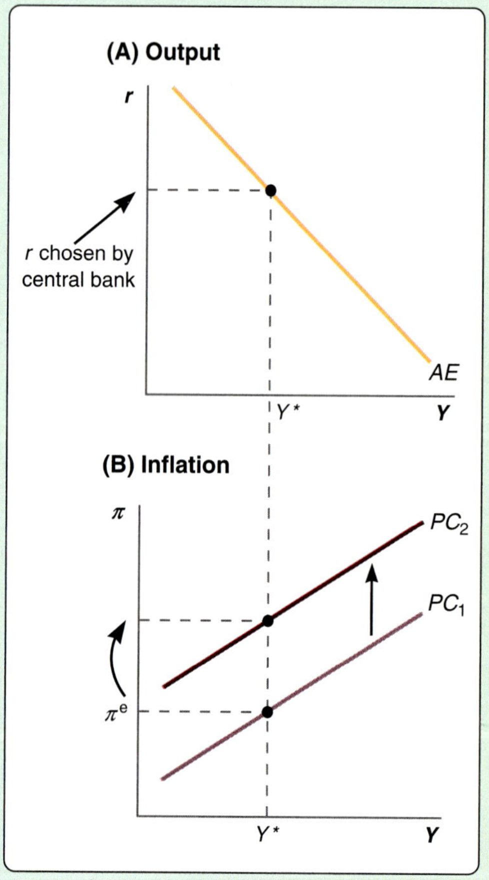

An adverse supply shock causes the Phillips curve to shift up. Here, the central bank does not change the real interest rate, so output remains constant (A). With constant output, the Phillips curve shift raises inflation above expected inflation (B).

FIGURE 12.20 An Adverse Supply Shock with Nonaccommodative Policy

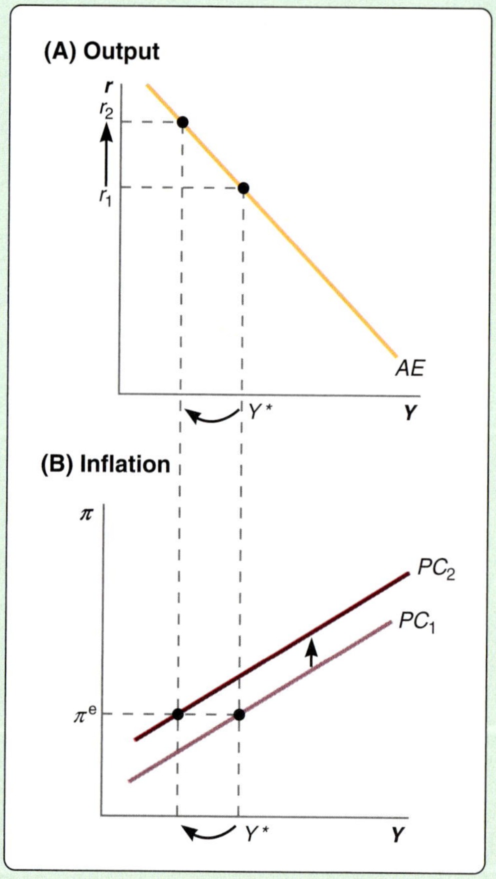

Here, the central bank responds to an adverse supply shock by raising the real interest rate. This action reduces output (A). Lower output offsets the shift in the Phillips curve, keeping inflation at its expected level (B).

The link from the present to the future occurs through the Phillips curve. With our assumption of adaptive expectations, the Phillips curve says that current inflation depends on last year's inflation. So anything that affected inflation last year also affects inflation this year. Similarly, anything that affects inflation this year will affect inflation next year. Let's consider two examples of how the economy might behave over time.

A Rise in the Real Interest Rate Assume the economy starts with output at potential and no supply shocks. In this situation, the Phillips curve implies that inflation is constant over time. Then the central bank raises the real interest rate. Specifically, assume the central bank raises the interest rate in 2020. It keeps the interest rate high in 2021, and then returns it to the initial level in 2022. **Figure 12.21A** shows the movements in the interest rate.

Figure 12.21B shows the behavior of output. As we've seen before, a higher interest rate moves the economy along the AE curve, reducing output. In 2020 and 2021, when the interest rate is high, output is below potential. When the interest rate returns to its initial level in 2022, output returns to potential.

Figure 12.21C shows the behavior of inflation. With adaptive expectations, the Phillips curve says that output affects the *change* in inflation (see Equation (12.6)). With output below potential, the change in inflation is negative in 2020 and 2021, which means the *level* of inflation falls. When output returns to potential in 2022, the change in inflation becomes zero. This means inflation stays constant at the level it reached in 2021.

This scenario exemplifies the monetary policy of **disinflation,** a temporary rise in the real interest rate that reduces inflation. A central bank adopts such a policy if it thinks the inflation rate is too high. The cost of disinflation is lower output. The good news is that *a temporary fall in output reduces inflation permanently.* Once inflation reaches an acceptable level, the central bank can reverse its interest-rate increase. At that point, output returns to potential and inflation stays low.

FIGURE 12.21 A Disinflation

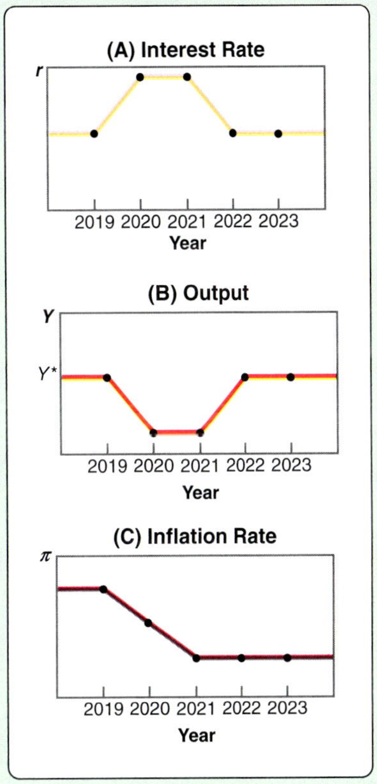

In this example, the economy starts with output at potential and stable inflation. In 2020, the central bank raises the real interest rate temporarily (A), which pushes output below potential (B). The inflation rate falls while output is below potential and then levels off (C).

Disinflation Monetary policy of reducing inflation by temporarily raising the real interest rate

An Adverse Supply Shock Assume again that the economy starts with output at potential and steady inflation. In 2020, a supply shock occurs: oil prices jump up. If we denote supply shocks with ν, then $\nu > 0$ in 2020 and $\nu = 0$ in all other years.

As we've seen before, the effects of supply shocks depend on the response of the central bank. **Figure 12.22** shows an accommodative policy. The central bank keeps the interest rate constant despite the shock, so output stays constant. Inflation jumps up in 2020 because the Phillips curve shifts, as in Figure 12.19 on p. 370.

Notice that inflation stays high after 2020. With output at potential and no further shocks, the change in inflation is zero. Inflation stays where it was pushed by the shock in 2020. *An accommodative monetary policy allows a supply shock to raise inflation permanently.*

Figure 12.23 shows nonaccommodative policy. The central bank raises the real interest rate in 2020 and output falls. Inflation stays constant in 2020, as the effect of lower output offsets the Phillips curve shift, as in Figure 12.20

FIGURE 12.22 A Supply Shock with Accommodative Policy: Effects over Time

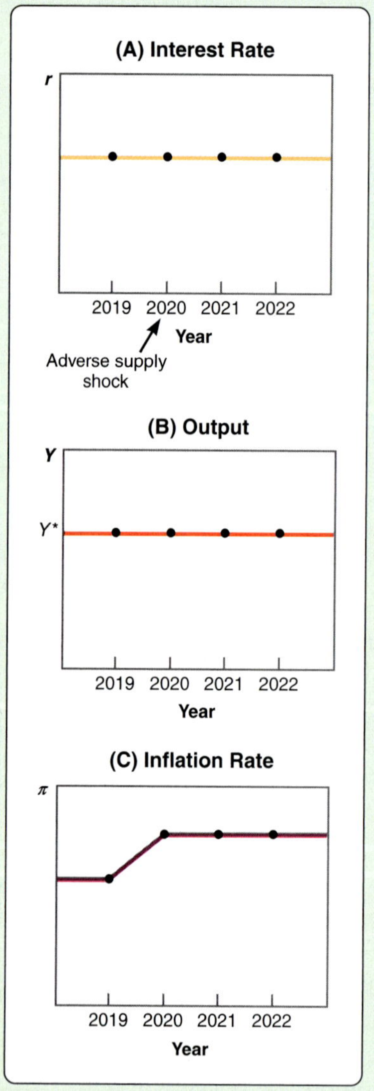

With accommodative policy, an adverse supply shock raises inflation permanently.

FIGURE 12.23 A Supply Shock with Nonaccommodative Policy: Effects over Time

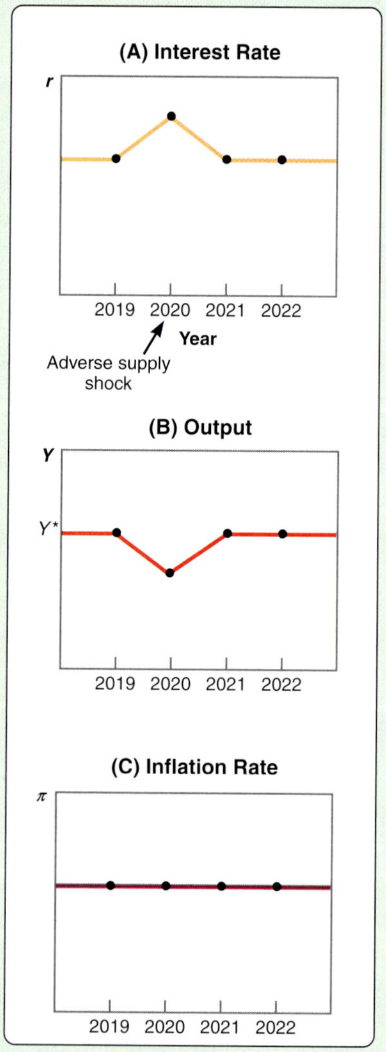

Nonaccommodative policy prevents an adverse supply shock from raising inflation, but it reduces output temporarily.

on p. 370. In 2021, the central bank reduces the interest rate and output returns to potential. As with accommodative policy, inflation stays constant after 2020—but here, it is constant at its original level. Nonaccommodative policy prevents inflation from ratcheting up.

We've worked hard to develop a theory of economic fluctuations, one based on the AE and Phillips curves. The payoff is that the theory helps explain fluctuations in real economies, as the next case study shows.

JUMBO CASE STUDY

The U.S. Economy, 1960–2007

We began this chapter with figure 12.1 (page 344), which shows fluctuations in U.S. unemployment and inflation since 1960. We've touched on parts of this history over the course of the chapter. Here we pull everything together and tell the story of the economy over the past half-century—a story of expenditure shocks, supply shocks, and shifts in monetary policy.

The 1960s This decade began with a mild recession, which you can see in Figure 12.1. Unemployment peaked at 7.1 percent in May 1961. The Fed reduced the real interest rate and the economy recovered.

In the mid-1960s, two shocks shifted the AE curve outward. One was the "Kennedy tax cuts" of 1964. The tax cuts were proposed during the early 1960s recession but took effect after the economy had recovered. The second shock was an increase in government spending. The Johnson administration spent heavily on both its "Great Society" domestic programs and the Vietnam War.

Initially, the Fed did not act to offset the AE shift, so output rose above potential (as in Figure 12.10). As predicted by Okun's law, unemployment fell below the natural rate, reaching 3.4 percent in September 1968. As predicted by the Phillips curve, the economic boom raised inflation from 1.3 percent in 1964 to 5.7 percent in 1970. The Fed finally responded with a sharp interest-rate hike in 1969.

The 1970s This was a dark period in U.S. economic history. It started with a mild recession caused by the 1969 interest-rate increase. Inflation fell slowly, but the Nixon administration became impatient and adopted a radical policy: price controls. In August 1971, prices were frozen for 90 days; after that, large firms needed permission from a government agency to raise prices.

At the same time, the Fed lowered interest rates, creating an economic boom. (Some historians think that Arthur Burns, the Fed chairman, was trying to help President Nixon get reelected.) Normally, the boom would have pushed inflation up, but the price controls held it down artificially.

▶Chapter Sixteen discusses the relationship between President Nixon and Fed Chairman Burns.

In 1973, things started to fall apart. The price controls were relaxed, allowing inflation to pick up. An oil price shock occurred around the same time. So did another adverse supply shock: a sharp increase in food prices caused by bad weather.

Initially, the Fed accommodated these shocks, not wanting to raise unemployment. Inflation rose to 11 percent in 1974. At that point the Fed became alarmed and raised interest rates sharply. This action produced a disinflation like the one in Figure 12.21. High interest rates caused a recession: output fell and the unemployment rate rose to 9.0 percent in mid-1975. The recession pushed inflation down to 5.8 percent in 1976.

With unemployment rising, the Fed switched gears again and lowered interest rates. Arthur Okun described the Fed's behavior as "stop–go monetary policy." In retrospect, it appears the Fed reduced rates too much. Low rates pushed output above potential, raising inflation over 1977–78. Then in 1979, disaster struck again: the second oil shock of the decade. Inflation was 11.4 percent in 1979 and 13.5 percent in 1980.

▶ See the case study in Section 11.5 for more on Paul Volcker's tactics for fighting inflation.

Many historians criticize the Fed for allowing inflation to get out of control in the 1970s. They deride the passivity of William Miller, who was Fed chairman in 1978–79. In August 1979, however, Miller was replaced by Paul Volcker, a man determined to beat inflation. This appointment led to dramatic events in the early 1980s.

The 1980s Volcker's Fed raised interest rates sharply in late 1979 and early 1980. Around the same time, the Carter administration temporarily imposed "credit controls"—regulations that discouraged the use of credit cards and other consumer borrowing. This action decreased consumption spending, shifting the AE curve to the left; along with higher interest rates, it pushed output down and unemployment up.

The Fed briefly reduced rates in mid-1980, but then, determined to beat inflation, raised them to very high levels. In mid-1981, the nominal federal funds rate exceeded 17 percent and the real rate was almost 8 percent.

The spike in interest rates caused the deepest recession since the Great Depression: unemployment reached 10.8 percent in late 1982. With unemployment high, inflation fell quickly, leveling off around 4 percent in 1983–84. At that point the Fed lowered interest rates and unemployment headed back toward 6 percent. This episode is a classic example of a disinflation: a temporary rise in interest rates reduced inflation permanently, at the cost of a recession.

The rest of the 1980s were fairly tranquil. Inflation stayed around 4 percent and unemployment drifted down. The only significant supply shock was a beneficial one—an oil price decrease in 1986. At the end of the decade, strong spending on consumption and investment shifted the AE curve out, pushing output a bit above potential and reducing unemployment to 5.0 percent. Inflation crept above 5 percent and the Fed responded by raising interest rates in 1989.

The 1990s A recession started in 1990, caused partly by the 1989 interest-rate increase. Two other factors were negative expenditure shocks that we've mentioned before: the fall in consumer confidence when Iraq invaded Kuwait, and the credit crunch that followed the S&L crisis.

The recession was fairly mild, with unemployment peaking at 7.8 percent in June 1992. Inflation fell below 3 percent. In 1992–93, the Fed reduced the nominal federal funds rate to 3 percent and the real rate to around zero. The economy recovered and seemed headed toward a stable regime of low inflation and unemployment around 6 percent.

Starting in the mid-1990s, the economy exceeded expectations. Unemployment fell below 6 percent in 1994 and kept falling. It reached 3.8 percent in April 2000. Economists believed that a boom was occurring, with unemployment below the natural rate. They warned that inflation would rise—but instead, inflation fell slightly.

In retrospect, it appears that the natural rate of unemployment fell because of high productivity growth (see the case study in Section 12.1). A lower natural rate allowed actual unemployment to fall without spurring inflation. Productivity improvements also produced fast growth in output and wages. Many observers raved about the "New Economy" and the "Roaring 90s."

The 2000s The economy slowed in the early 2000s, dampening the euphoria about the New Economy. A recession started in 2001. One cause was a fall in investment when companies scaled back their computer spending. Consumption also fell because the stock market fell, reducing people's wealth. Unemployment peaked at 6.4 percent in June 2003. This rate was low compared to previous recessions, but it was significantly above the natural rate.

Inflation was low entering the 2000s, and the recession pushed it lower. Inflation was about 1 percent in 2003. Economists started fretting about the possibility of zero or negative inflation—*deflation*. We discuss the dangers of deflation in Chapter Fourteen.

Responding to the recession, the Fed reduced interest rates steadily. The federal funds rate fell from 6.5 percent in 2000 to 1.0 percent in late 2003. Low interest rates stimulated spending; car sales, for example, were boosted by "zero-percent financing." Tax cuts proposed by the new Bush administration, which were enacted in 2001 and 2002, also stimulated spending.

By the end of 2003, unemployment was falling. As the economy recovered, fears of deflation waned and the Fed raised interest rates. In 2005–2006, the economy seemed to settle into an equilibrium, with unemployment around 5 percent and inflation around 2 percent. The federal funds rate reached 5.25 percent in June 2006 and stayed there until August 2007.

Then the subprime mortgage crisis hit the economy, causing a credit crunch and shaking consumer confidence. Fearing a recession, the Fed responded aggressively: between August 2007 and April 2008, it reduced the federal funds rate from 5.25 percent to 2.0 percent. Congress and the president also sought to stimulate the economy with the tax rebates of 2008.

Online Case Study:
An Update on the U.S. Economy

Conclusion: What Causes the Business Cycle?

At the start of this chapter, we saw that voters judge presidents based on inflation and unemployment. Our historical review shows, however, that presidential policies are secondary factors in economic fluctuations. Two other factors are the most important.

One is luck. The 1970s were grim, for example, because productivity slowed down and wars disrupted oil supplies. These events were outside the control of economic policymakers. Similarly, the strong economy of the 1990s resulted largely from fortuitous advances in computer technologies.

The other key factor is monetary policy. Economist Rudi Dornbusch wrote in 1997 that "no recovery [since 1945] has died in bed of old age—the Federal Reserve has murdered every one of them." He meant that the Fed has intentionally caused recessions to reduce inflation. The most clear-cut example is the Volcker disinflation of the early 1980s. The Fed has also *ended* recessions by cutting interest rates. This impact on the business cycle is one reason this book devotes a lot of ink to the Fed.

12.5 LONG-RUN MONETARY NEUTRALITY

We have seen that monetary policy has powerful effects on the economy. By changing the nominal interest rate, the Fed can change the real interest rate, which in turn affects output, unemployment, and inflation. However, there is an important qualification: most of these effects are temporary. They occur in the short run but not in the long run. Practically speaking, most effects of monetary policy disappear within a few years.

Specifically, in the long run monetary policy does not affect *real variables*. These are variables adjusted for inflation, such as real GDP and real interest rates. In the long run, policy affects only variables that are *not* adjusted for inflation, such as nominal GDP, nominal interest rates, and inflation itself. This idea is the principle of **long-run monetary neutrality.**

Long-run monetary neutrality Principle that monetary policy cannot permanently affect real variables (variables adjusted for inflation)

The analysis in Section 12.4 illustrates long-run neutrality. For example, recall what happens during a disinflation (see Figure 12.21). The central bank raises the real interest rate and output falls, but these effects are temporary. Only inflation changes in the long run. Here, we go beyond examples to discuss the basic forces behind long-run neutrality.

Long-Run Output and Unemployment

Let's first consider the behavior of output. Look again at Figure 12.3A on p. 348, which shows how output changes over time. The long run path of output, Y, is determined by potential output, Y^*. Output deviates from potential during booms and recessions, but it returns to potential in the long run.

Potential output is the normal level of output the economy produces and depends on such factors as the labor force, the capital stock, and technology. Potential output is *not* influenced by monetary policy. When the central bank changes the interest rate, it affects aggregate expenditure but not the economy's productive capacity. Therefore, the central bank's action affects Y but not Y^*. Since Y^* determines output in the long run, monetary policy does not affect output in the long run.

The unemployment rate is also independent of monetary policy in the long run. Okun's law (Equation (12.1)) implies that if output is at potential, then unemployment is at its natural rate. Since output equals potential output in the long run, unemployment equals the natural rate in the long run. And the natural rate depends on features of the labor market that monetary policy does not influence.

A Permanent Boom?

We can also explain long-run neutrality in a different way. Suppose a central bank ignores this concept and tries to change output permanently. Let's say it lowers the real interest rate, pushing output above potential. It keeps the real rate low indefinitely, so output stays high indefinitely. What happens to the economy?

The answer comes from the Phillips curve. When output exceeds potential, the inflation rate rises above its previous level. As long as output stays high, inflation continues to rise. The inflation rate reaches higher and higher levels and eventually becomes astronomical.

A central bank is not likely to let this happen. At some point, inflation will rise high enough that policymakers won't tolerate further increases. They will do what's necessary to stabilize inflation: raise the real interest rate and return output to potential. Accelerating inflation forces the central bank to abandon the goal of raising output permanently.

▶ This reasoning does not hold absolutely all the time. Occasionally, inflation reaches astronomical levels, yet the central bank doesn't act to stabilize it. A recent example is Zimbabwe, where the annual inflation rate was over 100,000% in 2007. In such a situation, the normal workings of the economy break down; the central bank certainly doesn't succeed in keeping output high. We return to this topic in Chapter Fourteen.

The Neutral Real Interest Rate

Like output and unemployment, the real interest rate is independent of monetary policy in the long run. **Figure 12.24** shows why. Given the AE curve, a unique real interest rate makes output equal potential output, Y^*. This interest rate is called the **neutral real interest rate (r^n),** since it implies neither a boom nor a recession.

Neutral real interest rate (r^n) The real interest rate that makes output equal potential output, given the aggregate expenditure curve

In the long run, the central bank must move output to potential; to do so, it must move the real interest rate to the neutral rate. As shown in the figure, the neutral rate is determined by potential output and the position of the AE curve, factors that the central bank doesn't control.

Chapter Four also discusses real interest rates. In that chapter, we explain the long-run behavior of the real rate with the *loanable funds theory*. Here, we say that the long-run real rate equals the neutral rate. It may seem we have two different theories of long-run interest rates, but that's not really true. The factors that raise or lower the interest rate in the loanable funds theory have the same effects on the neutral rate in the AE/PC model. The appendix to this chapter develops this point.

FIGURE 12.24 The Neutral Real Interest Rate

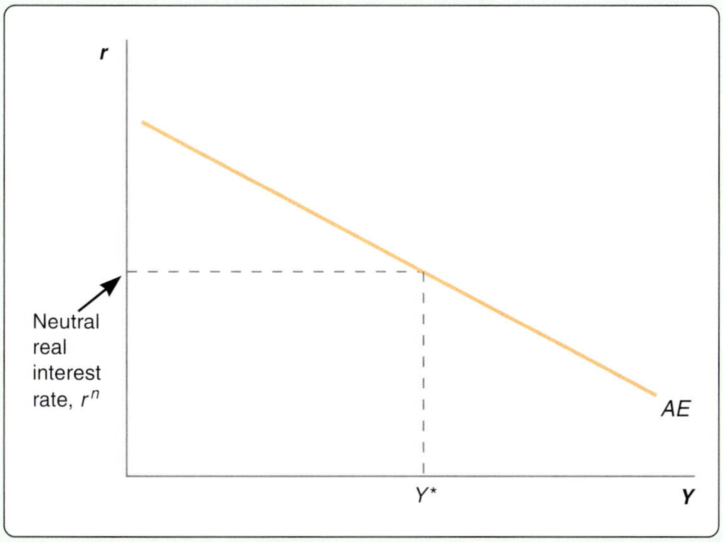

The neutral real interest rate is the rate that makes output equal potential output.

Summary

- This chapter analyzes short-run economic fluctuations using the aggregate expenditure/Phillips curve model.

12.1 The Business Cycle

- The long-run level of output is potential output, which is determined by the economy's resources and technology. The long-run unemployment rate is the natural rate, which is determined by problems in the labor market.
- In the short run, output fluctuates around potential output and unemployment fluctuates around the natural rate. Over this business cycle, output and unemployment move in opposite directions (Okun's law). In an economic boom, output exceeds potential and unemployment is below the natural rate; the opposite occurs in a recession.
- The business cycle is caused by fluctuations in aggregate expenditure—total spending on the economy's goods and services. When aggregate expenditure rises, firms sell more, leading them to increase their output. To produce more they hire more workers, reducing unemployment. The opposite effects occur when aggregate expenditure falls.

12.2 What Determines Aggregate Expenditure?

- Aggregate expenditure is the sum of consumption, investment, government purchases, and net exports. A rise in the real interest rate reduces three of these components (*C, I,* and *NX*) and therefore reduces aggregate expenditure and output. The AE curve summarizes the negative relationship between the interest rate and output.
- In the short run, the central bank's control of the nominal interest rate allows it to control the real interest rate as well. Equilibrium output is determined by the AE curve and the real interest rate chosen by the central bank.
- An expenditure shock is an event that changes aggregate expenditure for a given real interest rate. Expenditure shocks include changes in government spending or taxes, shifts in consumer confidence, new technologies that spur investment, changes in bank lending, and foreign booms and recessions. An expenditure shock shifts the AE curve, and output changes if the central bank holds the real interest rate constant.
- Countercyclical monetary policy can offset expenditure shocks, keeping output stable. Policymakers offset negative shocks by reducing the real interest rate and positive shocks by raising the interest rate.

12.3 Fluctuations in the Inflation Rate

- Firms increase their prices to keep up with the inflation rate they expect in the future, so expected inflation is one determinant of actual inflation.
- Economists debate whether expectations of inflation are rational or adaptive. Adaptive expectations are roughly consistent with evidence from surveys.
- An economic boom raises inflation above expected inflation, and a recession reduces inflation below expected inflation. This relationship is summarized by the Phillips curve, which can be expressed *either* as a positive relationship between output and inflation *or* as a negative relationship between unemployment and inflation.
- If inflation expectations are adaptive, the Phillips curve implies a positive relationship between output and the *change* in inflation, and a negative relationship between unemployment and the change in inflation.
- A supply shock is an event that causes a major change in firms' production costs. It causes the Phillips curve to shift, changing the level of inflation for given levels of output and expected inflation.
- Historically, the most important type of supply shock is a change in oil prices. Increases in oil prices caused jumps in U.S. inflation in the 1970s. However, the effects of oil prices on inflation have diminished over time.

12.4 The Complete Economy

- In the AE/PC model, the central bank chooses the real interest rate; the interest rate and the AE curve determine output; and output and the Phillips curve determine inflation. Economic fluctuations arise from expenditure shocks, supply shocks, and shifts in monetary policy.
- In a disinflation, the central bank raises the real interest rate temporarily. This action causes a temporary fall in output and a permanent fall in inflation.
- When an adverse supply shock occurs, accommodative monetary policy allows inflation to rise

permanently. Nonaccommodative policy prevents inflation from rising but reduces output temporarily.

- The AE/PC model captures U.S. economic fluctuations since the 1960s. The main factors behind these fluctuations are shifts in monetary policy and lucky or unlucky events outside the control of policymakers.

12.5 Long-Run Monetary Neutrality

- Although monetary policy influences the business cycle, it does not affect output or unemployment in the long run.
- The long-run real interest rate is the neutral rate, the rate that makes output equal potential output. Monetary policy does not affect the neutral interest rate.

Key Terms

accommodative monetary policy, p. 368

aggregate expenditure (AE), p. 351

aggregate expenditure (AE) curve, p. 353

aggregate expenditure/Phillips curve (AE/PC) model, p. 344

business cycle, p. 344

consumption multiplier, p. 353

countercyclical monetary policy, p. 357

credit crunch, p. 356

disinflation, p. 371

economic boom, p. 348

expenditure shock, p. 354

long-run monetary neutrality, p. 376

NAIRU, p. 363

natural rate of unemployment, U^*, p. 345

neutral real interest rate, r^n, p. 377

nonaccommodative monetary policy, p. 369

Okun's law, p. 348

output gap, p. 348

Phillips curve, PC, p. 361

potential output, Y^*, p. 345

recession, p. 348

supply shock, v, p. 363

unemployment rate, U, p. 345

Questions and Problems

1. Suppose potential output grows 2 percent per year and the natural rate of unemployment is constant at 6 percent. In 2020, the unemployment rate is 7 percent.
   a. Assuming Okun's law, what is the output gap in 2020?
   b. If output grows 5 percent from 2020 to 2021, what is unemployment in 2021?
2. Suppose the growth rate of potential output rises. The behavior of the output gap (the fluctuations of output around potential) does not change. Do NBER recessions become more or less common? Explain.
3. Suppose a country bans trade with other countries, so net exports are always zero. How would this affect the slope of the AE curve? Explain.
4. Suppose the Fed raises the real interest rate and consumer confidence falls around the same time (as occurred in 1990). Show with a graph what happens to the AE curve and to output.
5. Suppose the economy starts with output at potential. Then a supply shock occurs: oil prices rise sharply. The Fed is *partly* accommodative: it raises the real interest rate, but not by enough to keep inflation from rising. Show with graphs what happens to the AE and Phillips curves, and to output and inflation.
6. Suppose oil prices jump up and the Fed is completely accommodative: it keeps the real interest rate constant. How must the Fed adjust the nominal interest rate? How must it adjust the money supply? Explain.

7. Suppose again that oil prices increase. This has two effects: (a) firms' costs jump up and (b) since more of consumers' income goes to pay for oil imports, there is less to spend on U.S. goods. (We emphasized (a) but ignored (b) in the chapter.) Assume the Fed holds the real interest rate constant. Show what happens to the AE and Phillips curves, and to output and inflation.

8. Suppose the economy starts with output at potential and constant inflation. In 2020, oil prices jump up. Initially, the Fed is accommodative. In 2023, a new Fed chair is appointed and resolves to return inflation to the level before 2020. Show with graphs what happens over time to the real interest rate, output, and inflation.

9. Suppose that expected inflation is the average of inflation over the two previous years:

$$\pi^e = \left(\frac{1}{2}\right)[\pi(-1) + \pi(-2)].$$

   a. Write the equation for the Phillips curve in this case.

   b. Redo the disinflation example in Figure 12.21. Assume the path of the real interest rate is the same as before. Is the path of output different with the new Phillips curve? The path of inflation? Explain.

10. The United States was on a gold standard from 1879 to 1914. During that period, the average inflation rate was about zero. Inflation was sometimes positive and sometimes negative, and there was no relation between inflation in one year and the next. Each year inflation was equally likely to be positive or negative, regardless of past inflation.

   a. For the gold-standard era, is the assumption of adaptive expectations a good one? If not, what assumption about inflation expectations would be more reasonable?

   b. Write the Phillips curve for the alternative assumption about expectations.

   c. Suppose the real interest rate rises temporarily, as in Figure 12.21. Compare the effects on inflation under adaptive expectations and under the alternative assumption in parts (a) and (b).

11. The data in Figure 12.14 suggest an unemployment coefficient of approximately −1.0 in the Phillips curve. That is, the Phillips curve is

$$\pi - \pi(-1) = -(1.0)(U - U^*)$$

Assume the natural rate, U^*, is 5 percent. Actual unemployment is 5 percent in 2020, 7 percent in 2021, 6 percent in 2022, and 5 percent in 2023. Inflation is 5 percent in 2020. What is inflation in 2023? (Assume there are no supply shocks.)

Online and Data Questions

www.worthpublishers.com/ball

12. From the text Web site, get data for the period 1960–2007 on the output gap in Japan and the deviation of unemployment from Japan's natural rate.

   a. Plot these data. Does Okun's law hold in Japan? How does this relation differ in Japan and in the United States?

   b. Japan has a tradition of "lifetime employment." Firms are reluctant to lay off workers, even in recessions. Can this behavior explain your findings in part (a)?

13. From the text Web site, link to the site of the Federal Reserve Bank of St. Louis; also, see the "Guide to St. Louis Fed Data." Get annual data on the inflation rate, the interest rate on 3-month Treasury bills, and the unemployment rate.

   a. According to the AE curve and Okun's law, what is the relationship between the real interest rate and unemployment?

   b. Using data from 1960 to the present, plot the unemployment rate against the real interest rate, defined as the nominal T-bill rate minus inflation. That is, make a graph with the unemployment rate on one axis, the real interest rate on the other, and a point for each year. What relationship, if any, do you see?

c. Are the relationships in parts (a) and (b) similar or different? If they are different, try to explain why. Do the results in (b) show that our theory about the AE curve is wrong?

A Small Research Project

14. Interview a few people who are not economists but are old enough to remember the 1970s. Ask them what caused the high inflation of the 1970s and the deep recession of the early 1980s. Also ask about the 1990s—why there was a recession at the start of the decade and a roaring economy at the end. Do their answers agree with this chapter? If not, whom do you believe?

APPENDIX: THE LOANABLE FUNDS THEORY AND THE NEUTRAL INTEREST RATE

Chapter 4 explains the long-run behavior of the real interest rate with the loanable funds theory. In the AE/PC model, the long-run real interest rate equals the neutral interest rate. Here we compare these two theories of long-run interest rates. They prove to be similar: factors that affect the interest rate in the loanable funds theory also affect the neutral rate in the AE/PC model.

In the loanable funds theory, the real interest rate is determined by the supply and demand for loans, which in turn depend on three factors: investment, saving, and net capital inflows (NCI). As detailed in Section 4.2, higher investment at a given interest rate raises the equilibrium interest rate. Higher saving or net capital inflows at a given interest rate reduce the equilibrium rate. To summarize, the loanable funds theory says

$$\begin{aligned} &\uparrow \text{investment} \rightarrow \uparrow r \\ &\uparrow \text{saving} \quad\;\; \rightarrow \downarrow r \\ &\uparrow \text{NCI} \quad\;\;\;\; \rightarrow \downarrow r \end{aligned}$$

Figure 12A.1 examines how investment, saving, and net capital inflows affect the neutral real interest rate, as determined by the AE curve and potential output. **Figure 12A.1A** shows the effect of investment. As discussed in Section 12.2, a rise in investment for a given interest rate shifts the AE curve to the right. This AE shift raises the neutral real interest rate.

Figure 12A.1B shows the effects of saving and net capital inflows. Consider saving first. Saving rises for a given interest rate if consumers reduce their spending, or if the government reduces its spending or raises taxes. Any of these events shifts the AE curve to the left, reducing the neutral interest rate.

To see the effect of net capital inflows, we must remember a point from Chapter 6: a rise in net capital inflows (or equivalently, a fall in net capital outflows) raises the real exchange rate. The relevance here is that a higher real exchange rate reduces net exports, one of the components of aggregate

FIGURE 12A.1 Determinants of the Neutral Real Interest Rate

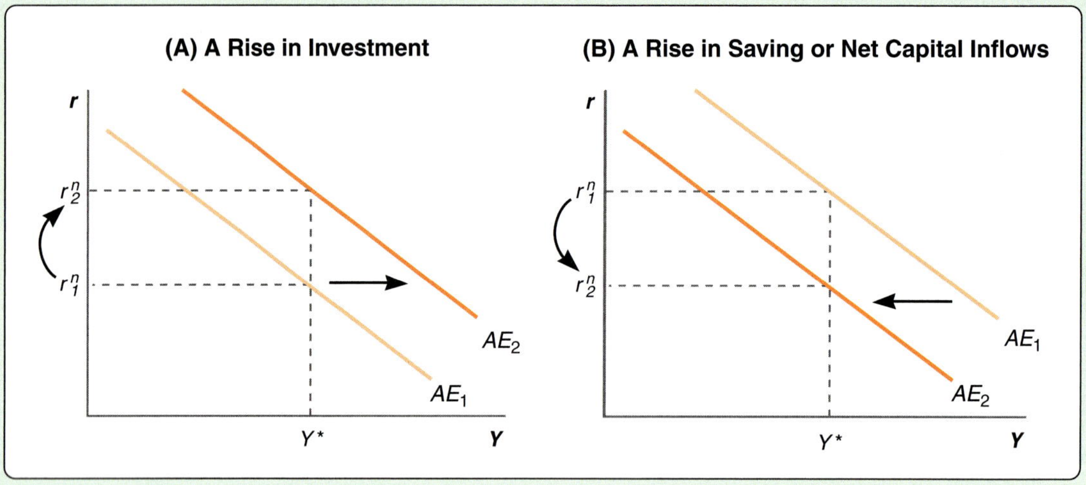

A rise in investment shifts the AE curve to the right, raising the neutral real interest rate (A). A rise in saving or in net capital inflows shifts the AE curve to the left, reducing the neutral rate (B). The effects of investment, saving, and capital flows match their effects on the real interest rate in the loanable funds theory.

expenditure. Lower net exports shift the AE curve to the left, reducing the neutral interest rate.

The general lesson from Figure 12A.1 is that investment, saving, and net capital inflows affect the neutral real interest rate in the same ways they affect the interest rate in the loanable funds theory.

chapter thirteen

13

Economic Fluctuations, Monetary Policy, and the Financial System

- **13.1** MONETARY POLICY AND THE TERM STRUCTURE
- **13.2** THE FINANCIAL SYSTEM AND AGGREGATE EXPENDITURE
- **13.3** THE MONETARY TRANSMISSION MECHANISM
- **13.4** TIME LAGS
- **13.5** TIME LAGS AND THE EFFECTS OF POLICY

The U.S. economy entered a recession in 2001. The causes included a fall in investment, especially spending on computers, and a stock market slump that reduced consumption. Shocks like these cause aggregate expenditure to fall.

Chapter 12 discussed how the Fed can offset expenditure shocks. The story there is simple. If an adverse shock occurs, shifting the AE curve to the left, the Fed reduces the real interest rate. With the appropriate rate cut, aggregate output remains constant. According to this theory, expenditure shocks need not cause recessions.

Bill Pugliano/Getty Images

Changes in asset prices, including house prices, help to cause economic booms and recessions.

Reality is more complicated. In 2001, the Fed quickly recognized the adverse expenditure shocks. It started cutting the federal funds rate in January and kept cutting it: over the year, the funds rate fell from 6.5 percent to 1.75 percent. Nonetheless, the economy slumped. An NBER recession occurred from March to November. The unemployment rate rose from 3.9 percent in December 2000 to 5.7 percent a year later.

In time, the Fed's actions did produce an economic recovery. In 2002, low interest rates spurred rapid growth in auto sales and housing construction. Other components of spending followed, and real GDP grew 3.7 percent over 2003. Unemployment peaked at 6.3 percent in June 2003 and then drifted down, falling below 5 percent in 2005.

The AE curve says simply that a higher interest rate reduces aggregate output. This chapter delves more deeply into the actual process through which monetary policy affects output—what economists call the **monetary transmission mechanism.** The process involves both major parts of the financial system: financial markets and banks.

Monetary transmission mechanism Process through which monetary policy affects output

The steps in the monetary transmission mechanism take time to unfold. As a result, significant lags occur between central banks' policy actions and the actions' ultimate effects on output and inflation. These time lags make it harder for central banks to stabilize the economy.

In this chapter, we also look closely at some of the expenditure shocks that buffet economies. Specifically, we examine shocks that arise within the financial system, such as asset-price crashes and bank failures. Previous chapters have discussed the causes of these events and the costs to savers and government insurance funds. This chapter emphasizes the effects on aggregate expenditure. We'll see that problems in the financial system are a leading cause of recessions.

13.1 MONETARY POLICY AND THE TERM STRUCTURE

We first examine the effects of monetary policy on interest rates. The model presented in Chapter 12 assumes just one interest rate. The Fed influences aggregate expenditure by adjusting this rate. In reality, there are lots of interest rates, and they can move in different directions.

The rates that affect aggregate expenditure are mainly intermediate and long-term rates. For example, most cars are bought with 5-year loans, so the rate on these loans affects car sales. Ten-year rates affect firms' investment, which is often financed with 10-year corporate bonds. In contrast, the Fed controls a very short-term interest rate: the federal funds rate. This rate applies to 1-day loans. It does not directly affect firms and consumers, because they do not finance their spending with 1-day loans.

Does this mean the Fed is irrelevant to the economy? No, because changes in the federal funds rate affect longer-term rates. Since longer rates affect spending, the Fed affects spending indirectly. Let's see how this works.

The Term Structure Again

Section 4.4 discusses the relationships among short-term and long-term interest rates, known as the *term structure*. We analyzed the term structure with the expectations theory. This theory will help us understand how the Fed affects interest rates.

The expectations theory is summarized by Equation (4.4), which gives the interest rate on an n-period bond in period t, denoted $i_n(t)$:

$$i_n(t) = \frac{1}{n}[i_1(t) + Ei_1(t+1) + \cdots + Ei_1(t+n-1)] + \tau_n$$

where $i_1(t)$ is the current one-period rate, $Ei_1(t+1)$ is the one-period rate expected at $t+1$, and so on. The variable τ_n is a term premium, which compensates for the risk from long-term bonds. The equation says the n-period rate equals the average of one-period rates expected over the next n periods, plus the term premium.

As a specific case, let's examine the relation between the 1-year interest rate and the federal funds rate. Since the federal funds rate is a 1-day rate, let's say a "period" is a day. Then $i_1(t)$ is the current federal funds rate. The 1-year rate is a 365-period rate. Applying Equation (4.4), the 1-year rate is

$$i_{365}(t) = \frac{1}{365}\left[i_1(t) + Ei_1(t+1) + \cdots + Ei_1(t+364)\right] + \tau_{365}$$

The 1-year rate is the average of expected federal funds rates over the next year, plus the term premium for 1-year bonds.

A Policy Surprise

To see how the Fed affects interest rates, let's consider an example. Suppose the federal funds rate is initially 3 percent. Bond traders expect the rate to stay at 3 percent for the next year. However, at a meeting on April 1, the Federal Open Market Committee surprises everyone: it raises the federal funds rate by half a percentage point, to 3.5 percent. What happens to longer-term rates?

The One-Year Rate Let's start with the 1-year rate. The 1-year rate on April 1 is the average of that day's federal funds rate and expected rates from April 2 through March 31 of the next year, plus the term premium. The funds rate on April 1 has a weight of only 1/365 in the average. When the Fed raises this rate by 0.5 percent, the *direct* effect on the 1-year rate is small: it rises by only (1/365)(0.5%), or 0.001%.

But the 1-year rate is likely to rise much more than this. The reason is that the current federal funds rate affects expected future rates. Remember that the funds rate usually stays constant between FOMC meetings, which occur every 42 days (six weeks). If the funds rate rises to 3.5 percent on April 1, it is likely to stay there until the next FOMC meeting, on May 13. Before the Fed's surprise, expected funds rates from April 2 to May 13 were 3 percent, but afterward they are 3.5 percent. Thus the Fed's action raises the first 42 terms in the formula for the 1-year rate.

In addition, when the FOMC meets on May 13, it is unlikely to change the funds rate back to 3.0 percent. The Fed rarely reverses course quickly after an interest-rate change. Indeed, an increase in the funds rate is often followed by further increases as the Fed slowly tightens policy.

▶Figure 11.8 on p. 337 shows changes over time in the FOMC's target for the federal funds rate.

Therefore, when the Fed raises the funds rate on April 1, its action is likely to raise the expected rate over the entire next year. The action increases all 365 terms in the formula for the 1-year interest rate, not just the first term or the first 42 terms. With all the terms rising, the 1-year rate jumps up substantially.

Figure 13.1 gives an example of how the 1-year rate might react when the FOMC raises the federal funds rate. Figure 13.1A shows the expected path of the funds rate before and after the Fed's action. Before the action,

FIGURE 13.1 The Federal Funds Rate and the 1-Year Rate: An Example

(A) Expected Path of Federal Funds Rate as of April 1

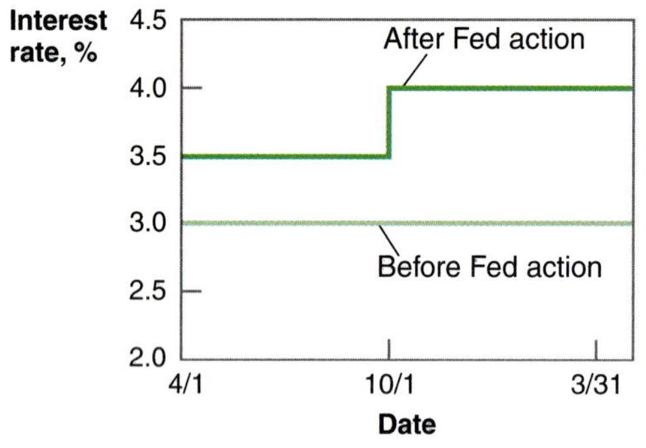

(B) One-year Rate on April 1, %

	Average of expected federal funds rate		Term premium		1-year rate
Before Fed action	3.0	+	1.0	=	4.0
After Fed action	3.75	+	1.0	=	4.75

On April 1, the Fed unexpectedly raises the federal funds rate from 3.0 percent to 3.5 percent. This action raises bond traders' expectations of the funds rate over the next year, causing the 1-year interest rate to rise.

bond traders expect the funds rate to be 3.0 percent over the next year. But when they see the rate rise to 3.5 percent on April 1, they decide that the Fed is tightening policy. Now they expect the funds rate to stay at 3.5 percent for six months, until October 1, and then rise to 4.0 percent for the following six months.

Figure 13.1B calculates the 1-year interest rate. For this example, we assume that the term premium τ is 1.0 percent. Before the Fed acts, the average expected funds rate over the next year is 3.0 percent; adding the term premium, the 1-year rate is $3.0\% + 1.0\% = 4.0\%$. After the Fed acts, the average expected funds rate is $(1/2)(3.5\% + 4.0\%) = 3.75\%$; with the term premium, the 1-year rate is 4.75%. In this example, the 0.5 percentage-point rise in the federal funds rate has caused the 1-year rate to rise by 0.75 percentage points.

Longer-Term Rates A surprise change in the federal funds rate also affects rates at maturities beyond a year. It may be several years before the policy change is reversed. The Fed's action can strongly affect the 5-year interest rate, for example, because it changes the expected funds rate over much or all of the next 5 years.

Fed actions have less effect on very long-term interest rates. The 30-year rate, for example, depends on expected funds rates over the next 30 years. Any policy the Fed is pursuing today is likely to end much sooner than 30 years from now. Thus current actions have little effect on most of the expected rates that determine the 30-year rate.

A Historical Example An episode that illustrates these ideas occurred in January 2008. At that time, the Fed was cutting interest rates in an effort to head off a recession (review Section 12.5). The FOMC had reduced its target for the federal funds rate from 5.25 percent in August 2007 to 4.25 percent in December.

However, policymakers started worrying that interest rates were not falling quickly enough to stimulate spending. The next FOMC meeting was not scheduled until January 29, but on January 21 Chairman Bernanke convened a videoconference. The FOMC decided to reduce the fed funds rate immediately by 0.75 percentage points, to 3.5 percent.

Figure 13.2 shows what happened to interest rates on Treasury securities of various maturities, that is, to the yield curve. On January 22, bond traders realized that the funds rate was falling faster than they had expected. They lowered their expectations of future rates, causing short and intermediate rates to fall. The 3-month rate fell by 0.51 percentage points and the 2-year rate fell by 0.28 points. However, as our analysis predicts, there was little effect on 20- and 30-year interest rates.

Expected Policy Changes

We have seen that a change in the federal funds rate can trigger changes in rates for longer maturities. This does not always happen, however. For other rates to jump when the funds rate changes, the change must be a surprise. If everyone expects in March that the FOMC will raise the funds rate on April 1, then bond traders learn nothing new when the increase occurs. They have no reason to change their expectations about the future, which determine longer-term rates.

Why might people expect a change in the federal funds rate? Fed officials never announce precisely what future rates will be, but they offer hints. When the FOMC sets the current federal funds target, it issues a

FIGURE 13.2 Effect of a Cut in the Federal Funds Rate on the Yield Curve

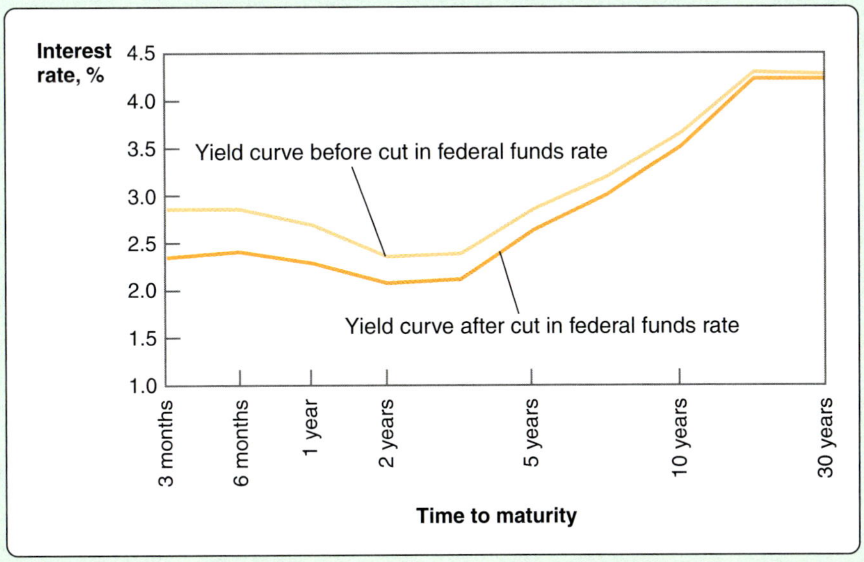

On January 22, 2008, the FOMC unexpectedly reduced its target for the federal funds rate from 4.25 percent to 3.5 percent. This action reduced short-term interest rates significantly but had little effect on very long-term rates.

Source: U.S. Treasury Department

statement discussing its action and what it might do in the future. FOMC members also make speeches that provide clues about their plans.

In addition, bond traders can sometimes infer what the Fed will do from the state of the economy. If a recession is beginning, for example, it is likely that the Fed will respond by reducing the funds rate. If bond traders correctly predict the Fed's actions, then longer-term rates do not jump when the funds rate changes.

The Effects of Changing Expectations This does *not* mean that expected changes in the funds rate are irrelevant to longer-term rates. The Fed's actions still matter if they are expected, but their effects occur *before* the actions themselves.

To see this point, suppose it is March 15. The funds rate is 3 percent, and everyone expects it to stay at 3 percent. Then the Fed Chair makes a speech suggesting that policy needs to tighten. Based on this speech, bond traders think the FOMC is likely to raise the funds rate to 3.5 percent at its meeting on April 1. As usual, they expect the rate to stay at this level for a substantial period of time, or even rise further. How does this affect the 1-year interest rate on March 15?

The 1-year rate on March 15 depends on expected funds rates from then until March 14 of the next year. The Fed Chair's speech does not affect expected rates for the first 17 days, before the FOMC meeting. However, it raises expected rates from April 1 to next March 14.

Thus the March 15 speech raises 348 of the 365 expected 1-day interest rates that determine the current 1-year rate. The 1-year rate jumps up substantially on March 15. If the Fed raises the funds rate as expected on April 1, the 1-year rate does *not* jump on that day—it has responded in advance.

A Historical Example The 1-year interest rate moved before Fed actions in 2004. **Figure 13.3** shows the federal funds target and the 1-year rate for the first nine months of 2004. At the start of the year, the funds target was 1 percent. It had reached this level as the Fed eased policy in response to slow growth over 2001–2003, described in the introduction to this chapter. The 1-year rate was about 1.25 percent.

For three months, the 1-year rate stayed near 1.25 percent. Then good economic news started arriving. In April, May, and June, the government released statistics showing that employment was growing more quickly than before. Bond traders began to expect that signs of recovery would lead the Fed to tighten policy.

The FOMC encouraged this view. In a May 4 statement, it noted the news of stronger growth and stated that "at this juncture, policy accommodation [i.e., low rates] can be removed at a pace that is likely to be measured." Expectations of future funds rates rose, pushing the 1-year rate above 2 percent in June.

In July, the FOMC started raising the funds rate as expected. By the end of September, the funds rate had climbed to 1.75 percent in three steps. Over this period, the 1-year rate was fairly stable. It did not jump on days when the funds rate rose, because the FOMC's actions were not surprises.

FIGURE 13.3 Interest Rates in 2004

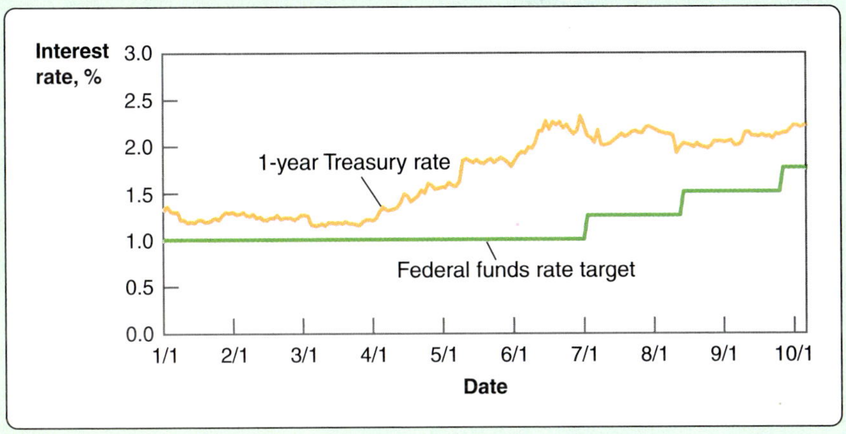

In the middle of 2004, bond traders began to expect that the Fed would raise its target for the federal funds rate. This expectation caused the 1-year interest rate to rise before the Fed acted.

Sources: Federal Reserve Board; U.S. Treasury Department

So far, we have used historical examples to illustrate the effects of Fed actions on interest rates. A number of economists have conducted broader statistical studies on this topic. They examine whether interest rates respond to the federal funds rate in the ways predicted by the expectations theory of the term structure. The next case study describes some of this research.

CASE STUDY

Measuring the Effects of Monetary Policy on the Term Structure

Kenneth Kuttner of Oberlin College studied the effects of FOMC actions in a paper published in 2001.* Kuttner examined all changes in the federal funds target that occurred between 1989 and 2000—a total of 42 changes. He measured the average responses of the yield curve on days when the target changed.

▶We met Kenneth Kuttner in Section 3.3, which discusses his research with Ben Bernanke on the effects of FOMC actions on stock prices.

Only *unexpected* changes in the funds rate should affect longer-term rates. So a key part of Kuttner's study was determining the rates that bond traders expected. Kuttner measured expected rates with data from the federal funds futures market. The interest rate in a futures contract is a good measure of the rate expected on the day the contract will be executed.

▶See section 5.6 for a review of futures contracts.

For each day the funds rate changed, Kuttner subtracted the change predicted by a futures rate from the actual change. The difference is the unexpected change in the funds rate. If the Fed raises the funds rate by 0.5 percentage points when the expected change is 0.25 points, the unexpected change is $0.50 - 0.25 = 0.25$ percentage points.

Kuttner then used the statistical technique of linear regression to measure the average effects of unexpected funds-rate changes on longer-term rates. He found, for example, that the 1-year rate rises by 0.72 times the unexpected

FIGURE 13.4 Typical Effects on the Yield Curve of an Unexpected Rise in the Federal Funds Rate

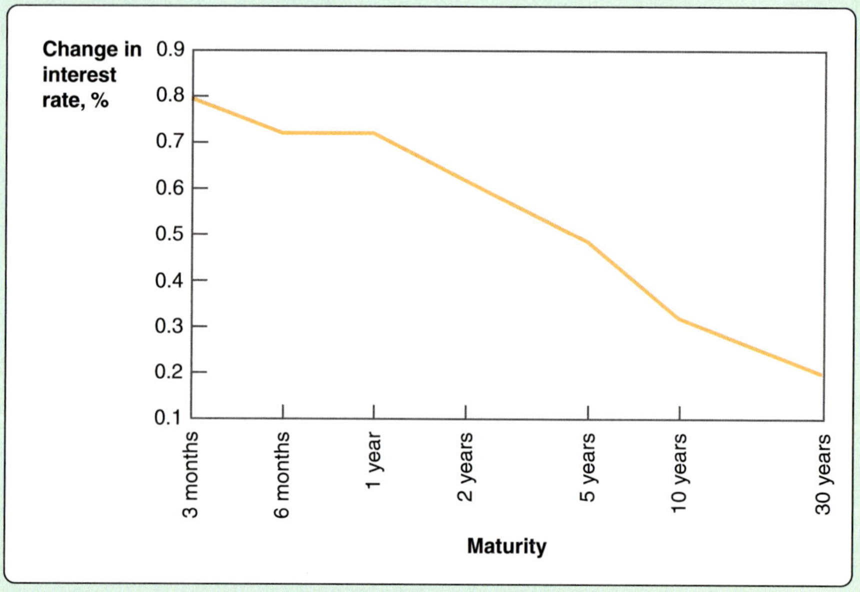

This graph shows the effects of a 1 percentage point unexpected increase in the funds rate. As predicted by the expectations theory of the term structure, interest rates rise substantially at short and intermediate maturities, but the effects die out at long maturities.

Source: Adapted from Kenneth Kuttner, "Monetary Policy Surprises and Interest Rates: Evidence from the Fed Funds Futures Market," *Journal of Monetary Economics*, June 2001

change in the funds rate. If the funds rate unexpectedly rises by 0.25 percentage points, the 1-year rate rises by $(0.72) \times (0.25) = 0.18$ percentage points.

Figure 13.4 summarizes Kuttner's results. It shows the effects of a surprise change in the funds rate on interest rates of various maturities. As predicted by the expectations theory of the term structure, changes in the funds rate cause substantial changes in short and intermediate rates.

As the theory also predicts, the effects die out for long maturities. The change in the 3-month rate is 0.79 times as large as the change in the funds rate, but the change in the 30-year rate is only 0.19 times as large. Research such as Kuttner's has increased economists' confidence in the expectations theory of the term structure.

* See Kenneth Kuttner, "Monetary Policy Surprises and Interest Rates: Evidence from the Fed Funds Futures Market," *Journal of Monetary Economics*, June 2001.

13.2 THE FINANCIAL SYSTEM AND AGGREGATE EXPENDITURE

Chapter 1 discussed the role of the financial system in long-run economic growth. Financial factors are also important in short-run fluctuations. The reason is that financial markets and the banking system influence aggregate expenditure. These influences are important for two reasons.

1. Events in the financial system are one of the initial causes of output fluctuations. We'll see that asset-price crashes and banking crises have caused recessions in the United States and elsewhere.
2. The financial system is part of the monetary transmission mechanism. Actions by the central bank affect not only interest rates but also asset prices and bank lending. These effects magnify the response of output to policy actions.

Changes in Asset Prices

The prices of many assets change greatly over time. For example, stock prices fluctuate due to changes in companies' expected earnings and to the growth and collapse of bubbles (review Sections 3.3–3.5). House prices also experience steep rises and falls.

Generally, an increase in asset prices raises aggregate expenditure. In graphic terms, the AE curve shifts to the right: output is higher for any given real interest rate. Asset prices affect expenditure in several ways involving the behavior of consumption and investment.

An increase in asset prices shifts the AE curve to the right.

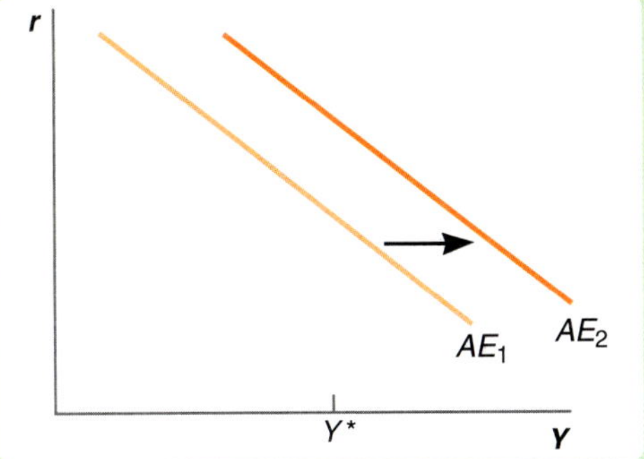

Wealth and Consumption Changes in asset prices affect people's wealth. If stock prices rise 20 percent, for example, the values of people's stock holdings rise 20 percent. Greater wealth leads people to spend more on goods and services. Thus a rise in asset prices raises consumption, one of the four components of aggregate spending.

Economists have studied data on consumption to measure this effect. According to current estimates, a \$1.00 rise in wealth raises consumption by about \$0.04 (four cents). Given the large swings in asset prices, this effect can be important.

For example, the value of U.S. stocks held by individuals and mutual funds was 58 percent of a year's GDP in 1994. This value was 131 percent of GDP in 1999, so it rose by 73 percent of GDP. Multiplying this increase by 0.04 yields 2.9 percent of GDP, which for 1999 is \$270 billion. This gives us an idea of how much rising stock prices raised consumption in the late 1990s. The rise in consumption explains much of the economic boom during this period.

In the early 2000s, stock prices fell. However, house prices rose rapidly in much of the United States, increasing the wealth of homeowners. The housing boom helped to sustain consumption, dampening the recession of 2001.

House prices peaked in June 2006 and then starting falling. In June 2008, the average U.S. house price was 18% below its peak value.[1] The effect of

[1] This figure is based on house-price data constructed by Karl Case of Wellesley College and Robert Shiller of Yale University, available at www2.standardandpoors.com.

Online Case Study: An Update on Asset Prices and Consumption

house prices on consumption was one reason that some economists were predicting a recession in 2008.

Stock Prices and Investment Changes in asset prices also affect the investment component of aggregate expenditure. One reason is that firms can finance investment by issuing new stock. If a firm's stock price rises, it receives more for each share that it sells. It can raise a given amount of money from fewer shares, so the current owners give up a smaller fraction of their stakes in the firm. In effect, raising funds through stock becomes cheaper. With cheaper financing, firms are more likely to undertake new investment projects.

Effects on Net Worth and Collateral Changes in asset prices also affect spending by changing the availability of bank loans. Recall from Section 7.7 that banks require borrowers to post collateral or maintain certain levels of net worth. These requirements help overcome the problems of adverse selection and moral hazard: borrowers are less likely to undertake risky projects if their assets are at stake. In addition, banks reduce their losses from defaults by seizing borrowers' assets.

A rise in asset prices raises collateral and net worth. A firm's net worth is the total value of its stock, so it rises when stock prices rise. Likewise, higher real estate prices raise the value of buildings that firms use as collateral. As a result, banks become more willing to lend: fewer firms are credit-rationed, and interest rates are lower. Greater lending leads to higher investment. Conversely, a fall in asset prices reduces collateral and net worth, so lending and investment fall.

Higher real estate prices also increase lending to individuals. If a person's house rises in value, she can obtain a *home equity loan*, which uses the house as collateral. People use home equity loans for spending such as vacations and home improvements, further increasing aggregate expenditure. When house prices fall, people lose access to home equity loans, dampening expenditure.

Changes in Bank Lending Policies

Bank lending shifts when asset prices change. Lending also shifts as a result of events within the banking system. Banks may become more willing to lend, increasing investment, or less willing, reducing investment. A sharp fall in lending—a credit crunch—can significantly reduce aggregate expenditure.

Why might banks change their lending policies? There are three main reasons:

1. *Risk Perceptions* Banks refuse to lend to borrowers who appear too risky. Sometimes events cause banks to change their assessment of risk. This happens, for example, when they experience a large number of defaults. If many real estate loans go bad, banks may decide that these loans are riskier than they thought and reduce lending to home buyers and real estate developers.

2. *Regulation* Bank regulators usually discourage lending with too much risk. However, regulations change over time, becoming more or less stringent. When regulators become more tolerant of risky loans, lending is likely to rise.

3. *Capital* Capital requirements set a minimum for a bank's equity ratio, the ratio of capital to assets (review Section 10.5). Capital falls if banks suffer losses for any reason, such as a rise in defaults. When this happens, banks must reduce their assets, including loans, to maintain the required equity ratio. A fall in capital that forces banks to reduce lending is called a **capital crunch.** A capital crunch is one possible cause of a credit crunch.

Capital crunch A fall in capital that forces banks to reduce lending

As mentioned in Section 12.2, a credit crunch hit the United States after the Savings and Loan crisis, contributing to the recession of 1990–1991. In that episode, bank lending fell for all three reasons we have discussed. Having been burned by defaults, banks started perceiving borrowers as more risky. Regulators embarrassed by the S&L crisis pushed banks to be conservative. And banks' losses from defaults created a capital crunch.

Another credit crunch arose from the subprime mortgage crisis of 2007–2008. Once again, both risk perceptions and regulation played a role. Banks and finance companies became more conservative in approving mortgages, and the Federal Reserve mandated an end to "no documentation" loans.

In this episode, banks also cut non-real-estate lending that they saw as especially risky. For example, they reduced the number of large loans to private equity firms seeking to take over companies. As of mid-2008, however, it was not clear whether the credit crunch would substantially reduce other kinds of lending, such as consumer and business loans.

▶Another aspect of the 2007–2008 episode was a reluctance of banks to lend to other financial institutions, including other banks, because of worries about the institutions' solvency. Chapter 18 details this part of the credit crunch.

The next case study discusses a topic we have mentioned before: Japan's "Great Recession" of the 1990s and 2000s (see Sections 4.5 and 10.7). The Japanese experience illustrates the effects of both asset prices and banking problems on aggregate expenditure.

CASE STUDY

Asset Prices, Banking, and the Japanese Slump

Figure 13.5A shows the growth rate of output in Japan from 1981 through 2007. From 1981 through 1991, output growth averaged 4.0 percent per year. Then the economy stagnated, with average growth of 0.9 percent from 1992 through 2002. Slow growth produced rising unemployment, political discontent, and a higher suicide rate, among other problems. The economy recovered somewhat over 2003–2007, with growth averaging 2.1 percent.

What caused the Japanese slump? The story starts in the 1980s, when the economy was booming but banks encountered problems. As in other countries, deregulation and competition from securities markets cut into traditional sources of bank profits. For example, loans to large firms fell when Japan's commercial-paper market was created in 1988.

Government regulations prevented Japanese banks from moving into new lines of business, such as derivatives and investment banking, which banks in other countries used to boost profits. Low profits during the 1980s prevented Japan's banks from building up capital. In addition, banks replaced the lending business they lost by increasing real estate loans. This set the stage for problems during the 1990s.

Optimism about the Japanese economy in the 1980s fueled rapid growth in asset prices. In retrospect, the asset-price boom appears to have been an irrational bubble, and it eventually burst. The Japanese stock index, the Nikkei, crashed in 1990, and stock prices continued to fall through 2003. The Nikkei index fell by a total of 72 percent (**Figure 13.5B**). Japanese land prices peaked in 1991 and then fell by 52 percent through 2007. These price collapses are larger than anything the U.S. has experienced.

The collapse in Japan's asset prices had severe effects on the country's banks. Capital levels, which were already low at the end of the 1980s, were reduced further by defaults on real estate loans. Borrowers' collateral and net worth fell sharply, leading to greater credit rationing. After growing rapidly in the 1980s, bank lending stagnated after 1990 (**Figure 13.5C**).

FIGURE 13.5 Japan's Financial Crisis and Economic Stagnation

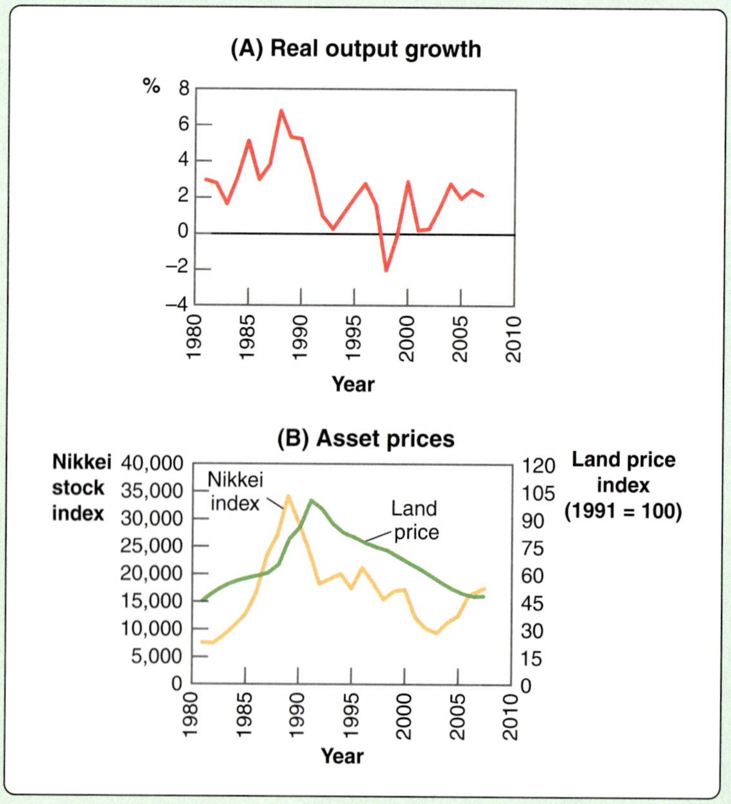

FIGURE 13.5 Continued

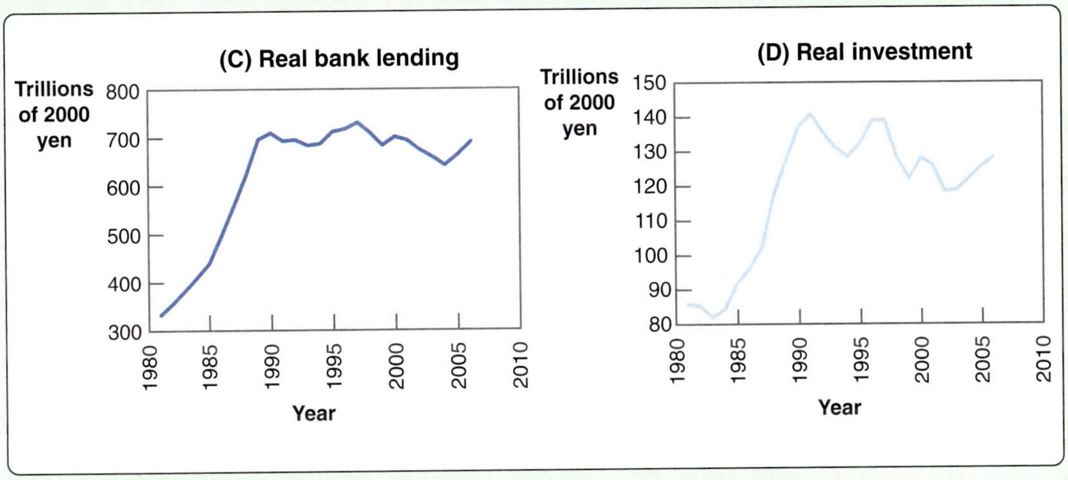

Japanese output grew rapidly in the 1980s and then stagnated from 1992 through 2002 (A). The output slump reflected a collapse in asset prices (B) and stagnation in bank lending (C), which curtailed investment (D).

Sources: International Monetary Fund; Bank of Japan; OECD

Japanese firms rely mainly on banks rather than securities markets to raise funds for investment. Thus the stagnation in lending produced stagnation in investment (**Figure 13.5D**). Investment and consumption were also reduced directly by the crash in asset prices, and Japan entered its long slump.

Once the slump began, the Japanese economy fell into a vicious cycle. Banking problems weakened it. At the same time, the weak economy reduced firms' earnings, leading to more defaults on bank loans. These defaults further weakened the banks.

In the late 1990s, Japanese savers started to fear that banks were becoming insolvent and moved their money to cash and government savings accounts. Foreign banks started charging default premiums on loans to Japanese banks. Finding it harder to raise funds, Japanese banks cut back further on loans, and investment fell again.

As we discussed in Section 10.7, Japanese regulators treated banks leniently. They allowed banks to keep bad loans on their balance sheets to maintain the appearance of solvency. Many economists think this practice exacerbated Japan's problems. Unprofitable firms continued to receive funds from banks, meaning less was available for firms with good investment projects. In particular, too much lending was directed to construction firms, while the manufacturing industry was starved for loans. This misallocation of lending reduced the productivity of the Japanese economy.

Eventually, regulators became stricter, forcing banks to write off bad loans. The total level of bad loans fell over 2003–2007, contributing to the modest economic recovery of that period. The recovery was also spurred by a rise in Japanese exports, the result of a weak yen and high demand from trading partners such as China.*

* For more on Japan's experience, see Kenneth Kuttner and Adam Posen, "The Great Recession: Lessons for Macroeconomic Policy from Japan," *Brookings Papers on Economic Activity*, 2001:2; and Takeo Hoshi and Anil Kashyap, "Japan's Financial Crisis and Economic Stagnation," *Journal of Economic Perspectives*, Winter 2004.

The Investment Multiplier

We have seen that events in the financial system cause shifts in aggregate spending. The financial system is also important for economic fluctuations in another way. It creates a multiplier that magnifies the effects of expenditure shocks, even when the shocks themselves are unrelated to the financial system.

This multiplier involves the behavior of investment. In general, a firm can finance investment either with profits it has earned or by borrowing. We have seen, however, that asymmetric information makes borrowing difficult. Some firms are credit-rationed because lenders think they are too risky. Even if a firm can borrow, it pays an interest rate that includes a premium to compensate for default risk.

These problems disappear if the firm has sufficiently high earnings. It can use these earnings to pay for investment projects. Since the firm does not need an outside lender, there is no risk of credit rationing, and no need to pay the interest-rate premium arising from asymmetric information. In sum, high earnings make it easier and cheaper to finance investment.

Investment multiplier Effect of firms' earnings on investment, which magnifies fluctuations in aggregate expenditure

We can now understand the **investment multiplier** and its role in economic fluctuations, illustrated in **Figure 13.6.** Suppose aggregate expenditure rises for any reason—say, an increase in government spending or consumer confidence. This event causes an economic boom. In a boom, firms sell more and their earnings rise.

With higher earnings, firms can finance investment more cheaply. As a result, they increase investment spending, magnifying the economic boom. Firms' earnings rise even more, they undertake even more investment, and so on.

FIGURE 13.6 The Investment Multiplier

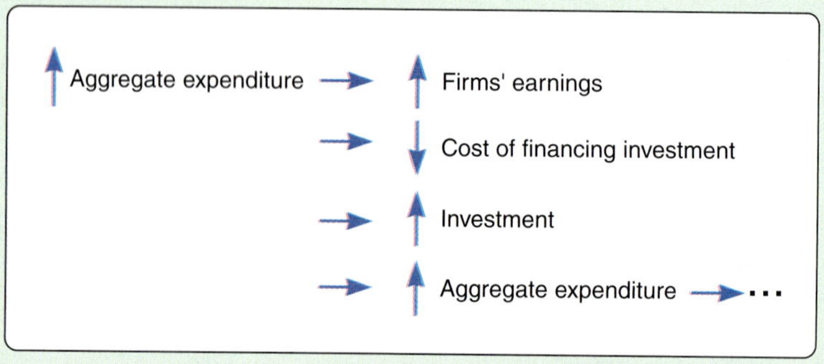

The investment multiplier magnifies fluctuations in aggregate expenditure.

The investment multiplier also works in reverse. If aggregate expenditure falls for any reason, firms' earnings fall, reducing investment. Thus the feedback between earnings and investment magnifies both booms and recessions.

13.3 THE MONETARY TRANSMISSION MECHANISM

We now have the background to understand the monetary transmission mechanism, the process through which monetary policy affects output. This process includes the effects of asset prices and bank lending on expenditure that we've just described.

Figure 13.7 summarizes the monetary transmission mechanism. It shows how the Fed affects the economy when it changes its target for the federal funds rate. We have already discussed most of the individual steps in this process; the figure shows how they all fit together.

Figure 13.7 shows what happens when monetary policy tightens, meaning the Fed raises its federal funds rate target, as shown at the left. This action triggers a series of events that lead to lower output, shown at the right in the figure. Bear in mind that everything works in reverse if the Fed lowers its federal funds rate target, leading to higher output.

FIGURE 13.7 The Monetary Transmission Mechanism

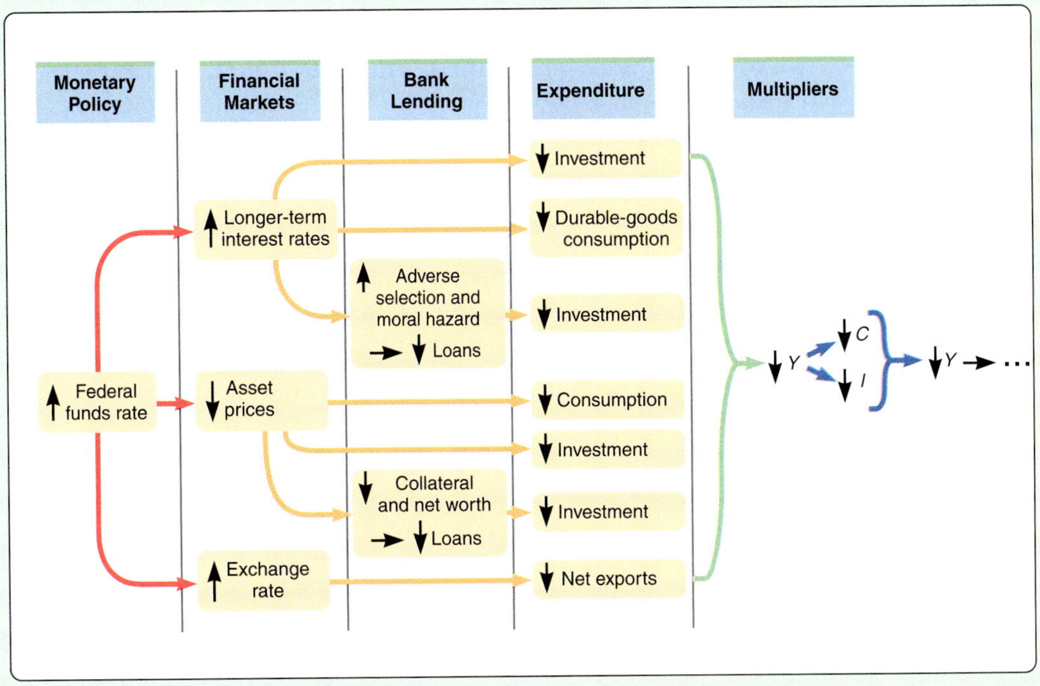

An increase in the federal funds rate reduces output through many channels. A decrease in the federal funds rate has the opposite effects.

Effects in Financial Markets

When the federal funds rate rises, several effects occur in financial markets, as summarized in Figure 13.7:

- The rise in the funds rate causes longer-term interest rates to increase. As we discussed in Section 13.1, this occurs either at the time of the Fed's action or earlier, depending on whether the action is expected.
- As we discussed in Chapter 3, increases in interest rates reduce the present value of future earnings from assets. Thus they reduce asset prices, such as stock prices.
- As we discussed in Chapter 6, higher interest rates attract capital inflows from abroad and reduce capital outflows. As a result, the exchange rate appreciates.

Effects on Bank Lending

When the Fed tightens, the effects in financial markets have further effects, summarized in the column headed "Bank lending" in Figure 13.7:

- As we discussed in Chapter 7, a rise in interest rates worsens the problems of adverse selection and moral hazard in loan markets. With higher rates, a larger proportion of loan applicants become risky. Banks respond by reducing their lending.
- The fall in asset prices also reduces lending, because it reduces borrowers' collateral and net worth.

Effects on Expenditure

The effects of policy on financial markets and banks influence aggregate expenditure in many ways:

- Higher interest rates discourage firms and consumers from borrowing, so they spend less on investment (including housing) and on durable goods.
- Lower asset prices reduce consumption by reducing consumers' wealth.
- Lower asset prices reduce investment by making it more expensive for firms to raise funds by issuing new stock.
- The decrease in bank lending reduces investment.
- The appreciation of the exchange rate reduces net exports.

Multiplier Effects

Finally, the decrease in aggregate spending is magnified by two multipliers:

- The consumption multiplier: As discussed in Section 12.2, lower spending means lower income for consumers. Lower income produces a further fall in consumption.
- The investment multiplier: As discussed in Section 13.2, lower spending means lower earnings for firms. With lower earnings, firms reduce investment.

Some Lessons

Examining the monetary transmission mechanism yields two broad lessons. First, monetary policy affects aggregate spending through many channels. This fact helps explain why policy has large effects on the economy. Second, policy has especially strong effects on certain sectors of the economy. In these sectors, spending is sensitive to the financial variables that policy influences, such as interest rates and bank loans. For example, policy has strong effects on investment because it affects investment through many channels.

The next case study discusses another way in which monetary policy affects some parts of the economy more than others.

CASE STUDY

Monetary Policy, Inventories, and Small Firms

A tightening of monetary policy reduces aggregate spending partly by reducing bank loans. Lending falls because higher interest rates and lower asset prices exacerbate the problem of asymmetric information between borrowers and lenders. Mark Gertler of New York University and Simon Gilchrist of Boston University helped convince economists of this effect in a well-known 1994 paper.*

Gertler and Gilchrist started with a point that we discussed in Section 7.5: asymmetric information is a bigger problem for small firms than for large firms. General Electric is sufficiently well known that it can always issue bonds or borrow from banks; Joe's Hardware Store can't issue bonds, and banks are wary because they don't know Joe. Joe's Store may get a loan in normal times. But if monetary policy tightens, worsening moral hazard and adverse selection, Joe may be denied credit. Monetary policy thus has bigger effects on lending and investment for smaller firms.

Gertler and Gilchrist tested this idea by examining a particular kind of investment: inventories. To operate, many firms must accumulate inventories of materials or of the goods they sell. Joe's Hardware, for example, must buy hammers and nails to stock its shelves. Like other investment, inventories are often financed by borrowing. Large firms usually issue commercial paper, and small firms get short-term bank loans.

Gertler and Gilchrist measured the response of this borrowing and of inventories to monetary tightenings. Specifically, they examined seven dates from the 1940s through the 1980s when the Fed raised interest rates to fight inflation. They compared the effects on small and large firms, as defined by their levels of assets (above or below $200 million in 1986). For each group of firms, Gertler and Gilchrist traced the average paths of short-term borrowing and inventories in the three years after a tightening.

Figure 13.8 shows the results. A monetary tightening has little effect on inventory investment by large firms. Borrowing by these firms *rises* temporarily (Figure 13.8A). Borrowing rises because the Fed's tightening slows the economy. Firms' revenues fall, leading them to borrow more to cover inventories and other costs. Large firms can increase their borrowing because they are well known to lenders.

FIGURE 13.8 Effects of a Monetary Tightening on Large and Small Firms

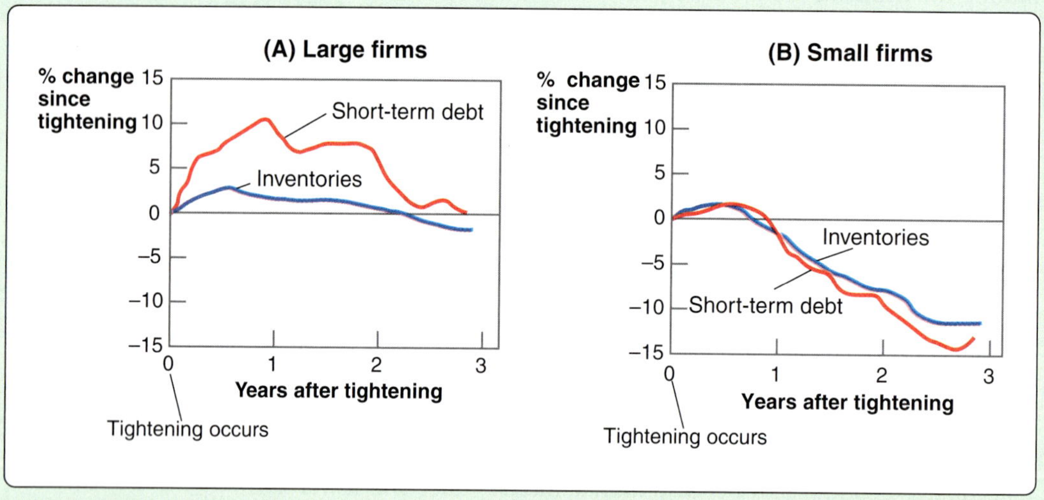

A tightening of monetary policy slows the economy, reducing firms' revenue. Large firms compensate with greater short-term borrowing and their inventory investment does not change significantly (A). By contrast, small firms face increased credit rationing. Their borrowing falls and they are forced to cut inventories (B).

Source: Adapted from Mark Gertler and Simon Gilchrist, "Monetary Policy, Business Cycles, and the Behavior of Small Manufacturing Firms," *Quarterly Journal of Economics*, May 1994

A monetary tightening has very different effects on small firms (Figure 13.8B). They may want to borrow more, but they can't: their borrowing falls as lenders ration credit. Inventories fall because small firms are unable to finance them. Gertler and Gilchrist also show that lower inventories lead to lower sales.

This research demonstrates the importance of asymmetric information in loan markets. If this problem didn't exist, small firms would be more like large firms. Monetary policy would have little effect on their short-term borrowing or inventories. Policy would probably have less effect on other investment as well.

* See Mark Gertler and Simon Gilchrist, "Monetary Policy, Business Cycles, and the Behavior of Small Manufacturing Firms," *Quarterly Journal of Economics*, May 1994.

13.4 TIME LAGS

We now turn to another aspect of monetary policy: the timing of its effects. If the Fed tightens or loosens policy, how long does it take for the economy to respond?

In the AE/PC model developed in Chapter 12, we assume that an increase in the interest rate moves the economy along the AE curve. Output falls immediately. And when output falls, the Phillips curve says that inflation falls immediately. Thus, in the model, the Fed controls the current levels of output and inflation.

In reality, monetary policy affects the economy through processes that take time. It takes time for the interest rate to affect output, and for output to affect inflation. These time lags reduce the Fed's ability to control the economy.

In the basic AE/PC model, an increase in the real interest rate reduces output and inflation immediately.

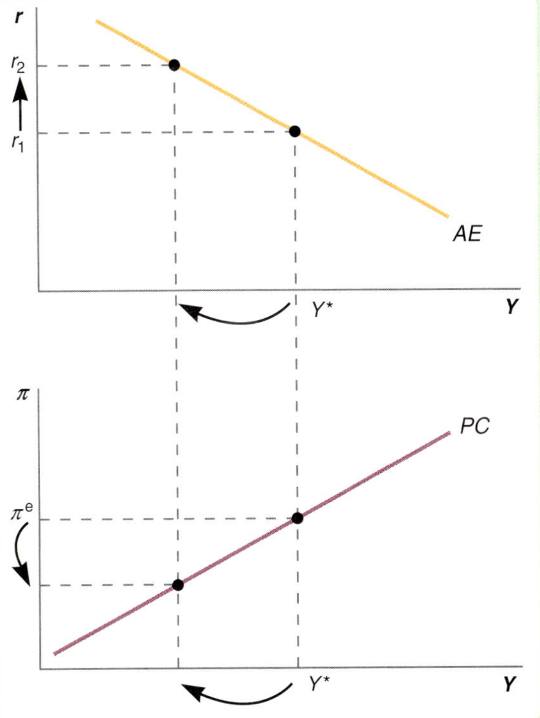

Lags in the AE Curve

Figure 13.7 on page 397 shows the process behind the AE curve. A change in the federal funds rate affects financial variables, such as interest rates, stock prices, and exchange rates. Then these variables affect spending through various channels.

The first parts of this process—the effects in financial markets—are quick. Interest rates and asset prices react on the day of a Fed action, or even earlier if the action is expected. However, the rest of the process is slower, so it takes time for the Fed's action to affect spending.

To understand this slow adjustment, recall that many effects of monetary policy involve investment. Investment projects take time to plan and implement. If the Fed reduces interest rates, firms do not start building new factories and houses on the same day. Instead, low rates affect planning about what projects to undertake in the coming months and years. Similarly, it takes time to adjust investment plans when stock prices rise or banks increase their lending.

Other types of spending also take time to adjust to financial variables. For example, if a firm imports materials from abroad, a depreciation of the currency makes the materials more expensive. The firm might switch to a domestic supplier, reducing the economy's imports and raising net exports. But it takes time for the firm to find the new supplier; it does not stop importing the day the exchange rate changes.

The multiplier effects in Figure 13.7 also take time to unfold. For example, when people see their incomes rise, it takes time for them to adjust their consumption patterns. Because of all these lags, it can be a year or more before a change in monetary policy has its main effects on output.

Lags in the Phillips Curve

The Phillips curve shows that the level of output affects the inflation rate. High output causes firms to raise prices more quickly, and low output does the reverse. However, this process also takes time. As a result, monetary policy affects inflation with a long lag. It can take a year for policy to affect output and then another year for output to affect inflation.

This additional lag arises because firms' price setting adjusts slowly. Many firms review their price decisions only once or twice a year. If output changes, it takes time for firms to recognize the situation and start raising prices more quickly or slowly.

In addition, changes in inflation are slowed by the interactions among different firms. If the economy is booming, for example, firms would like to raise prices quickly. However, each firm fears it will lose sales if its price rises too far above its competitors' prices. No firm wants to go first in making a big adjustment. Inflation edges up slowly as some firms make small adjustments and others copy them.

Evidence

Economic history reveals the time lags in the effects of monetary policy. For example, as discussed at the start of this chapter, the Fed's easing during the 2001 recession affected spending mainly in 2002 and 2003. Another example is the tightening that Fed Chairman Paul Volcker used to end the inflation of the 1970s (see Section 12.4). Volcker started raising interest rates late in 1979. The biggest effects on output occurred in the recession of 1981–1982. Inflation fell mainly in 1982–1983.

Economists also use statistical techniques to measure the lags in policy effects. This research includes a 2004 paper by Christina Romer and David Romer of the University of California, Berkeley.[2] Romer and Romer examine changes in the FOMC's federal-funds target from 1969 through 1996. They first isolate changes in the target that were policy surprises given the state of the economy. Then they trace the paths of output and inflation after each target change and average them to find the typical effects of policy.

Figure 13.9 shows Romer and Romer's results. They find that a monetary tightening causes output to fall gradually. The maximum impact is felt

FIGURE 13.9 Effects of a Monetary Tightening

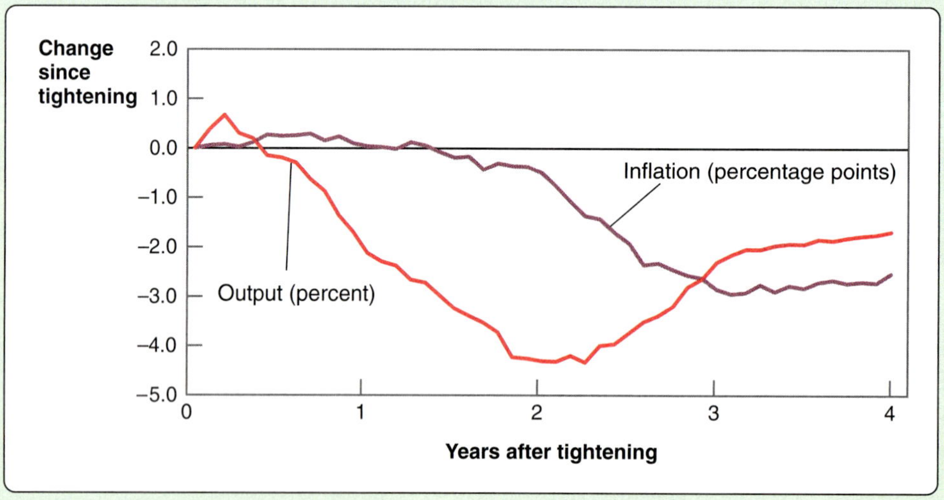

This graph shows the effects of a 1 percentage point increase in the FOMC's target for the federal funds rate. Such an action affects output with a substantial time lag, and it affects inflation with an even longer lag.

Source: Adapted from Christina Romer and David Romer, "A New Measure of Monetary Shocks: Derivation and Implications," *American Economic Review*, September 2004

[2] See Christina Romer and David Romer, "A New Measure of Monetary Shocks: Derivation and Implications," *American Economic Review*, September 2004.

between 22 and 27 months after the Fed's action, and then output starts recovering slowly. As we should expect, it takes longer for the tightening to affect inflation. There is almost no impact for the first 18 months; then inflation falls slowly and levels off after 36 months.

13.5 TIME LAGS AND THE EFFECTS OF POLICY

The time lags we've discussed make it harder for central banks to stabilize the economy. To see how, let's add time lags to the AE and Phillips curves from Chapter 12 and see how they change the effects of monetary policy.

In the AE curve (**Figure 13.10A**), output is still determined by the real interest rate—but here it is the rate a year ago rather than the current rate. The real rate one year ago is denoted $r(-1)$. This change means that it takes monetary policy a year to affect output, roughly capturing the lag we see in reality.

Similarly, in the Phillips curve (**Figure 13.10B**), inflation depends on output in the previous year, $Y(-1)$, rather than current output. As before, inflation also depends on expected inflation. We assume throughout this discussion that expected inflation equals the previous year's inflation rate, $\pi(-1)$.

With these modifications, we will analyze two policies we've discussed before: a disinflation and a countercyclical response to an expenditure shock.

A Disinflation

Figure 12.21 examined a disinflation, a temporary rise in the real interest rate that reduces inflation. Here we investigate how time lags in the AE and Phillips curves change the disinflation process. A rise in the interest rate still reduces inflation, but not as quickly as before.

FIGURE 13.10 The AE/PC Model with Time Lags

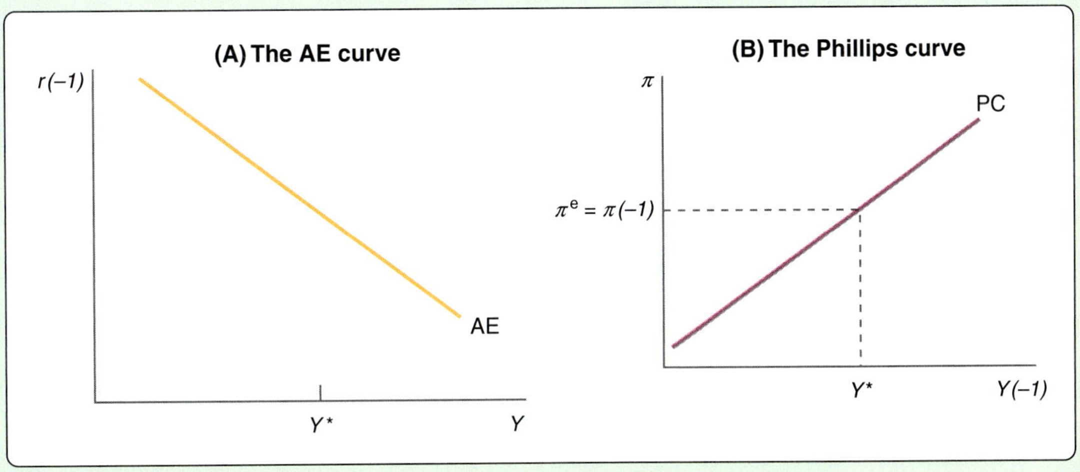

It is realistic to add time lags to the AE/PC model. Output depends on the real interest rate in the previous year (A), and inflation depends on output in the previous year (B).

We assume the economy starts with output at potential and constant inflation. As shown in **Figure 13.11A,** the central bank raises the real interest rate in 2020, keeps it high in 2021, and returns it to the initial level in 2022. This interest-rate path is the same as in Figure 12.21A.

Figure 13.11B shows the behavior of output under our assumption of time lags. For comparison, the figure also shows the output path when the AE and Phillips curves *don't* have lags. The difference between the two cases is clear.

With no time lags, output is low in the years when the interest rate is high, 2020 and 2021. But when the AE curve has a lag, output depends on the previous year's interest rate, not the current rate. Therefore, the high rate in 2020 reduces output in 2021, and the high rate in 2021 reduces output in 2022. Output returns to potential in 2023, the year after the interest rate returns to its initial level.

Figure 13.11C shows the behavior of inflation. With no time lags, inflation falls in the years when output is below potential. But when the Phillips curve has a lag, low output reduces inflation a year later. Since output is low in 2021 and 2022, inflation falls in 2022 and 2023.

Together, the lags in the AE and Phillips curves slow disinflation by two years. Without lags, inflation reaches its final level in 2021; with lags, this occurs in 2023.

FIGURE 13.11 A Disinflation with Time Lags

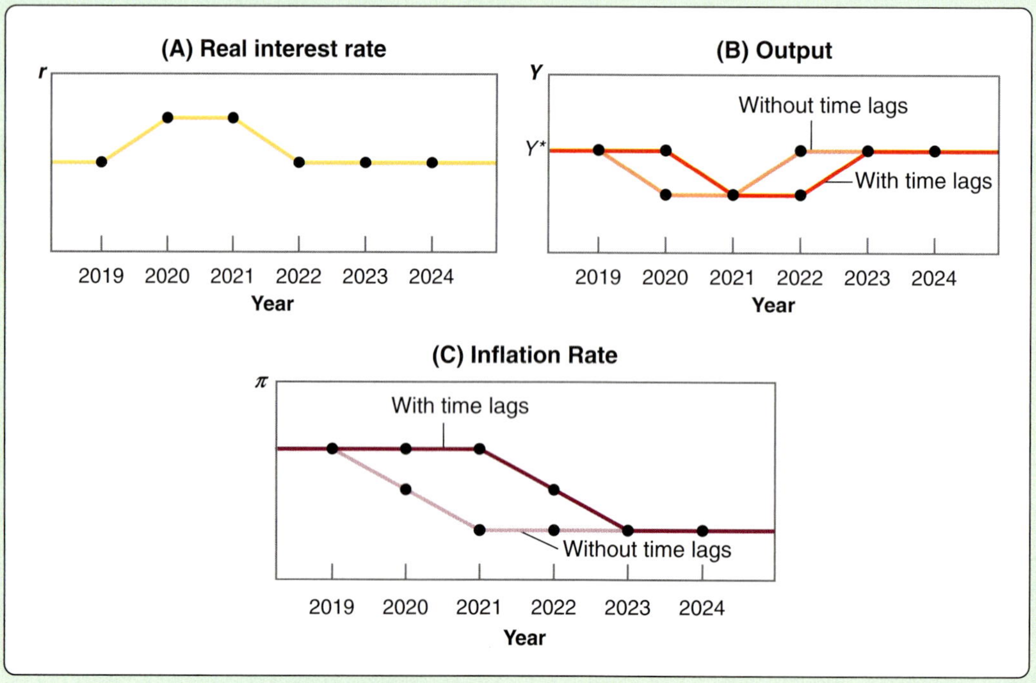

Time lags in the AE and Phillips curves slow down the process of disinflation.

Countercyclical Policy

An expenditure shock, such as a change in consumer confidence or in government spending, affects output and inflation if the central bank does not react. However, in the AE/PC model with no time lags, policymakers can eliminate these effects completely. If an expansionary shock occurs, for example, a sufficient rise in the real interest rate keeps output constant (see Figure 12.11B). With no movement in output, inflation is constant as well.

With time lags, countercyclical policy is a messier process. An expenditure shock causes fluctuations in output and inflation, even if the central bank responds immediately.

Suppose again that the economy starts with output at potential and constant inflation. In 2020, an expenditure shock shifts the AE curve to the right (for example, government spending rises to finance a war). This shock is temporary: in 2021, the AE curve shifts back to its initial position. Policymakers know in 2020 that the shock is temporary.

Assume the central bank follows the countercyclical policy shown in **Figure 13.12A.** In 2020, when the expenditure shock occurs, the central bank raises the real interest rate. In 2021, when the shock disappears, policymakers return the interest rate to its initial level. Let's examine the effects of these actions, once again comparing the model with and without time lags.

Figure 13.12B shows the behavior of output. In the no-lag case, we assume the interest-rate increase in 2020 is the right size to offset the AE shift. As a result, output stays at potential. Output also remains constant in 2021, when the shock disappears and the AE curve returns to its initial position.

To understand the behavior of output with time lags, it's helpful to examine the AE curve. In 2020, the curve shifts out, as shown in **Figure 13.13A.** The high interest rate in 2020 doesn't

FIGURE 13.12 Countercyclical Policy with Time Lags

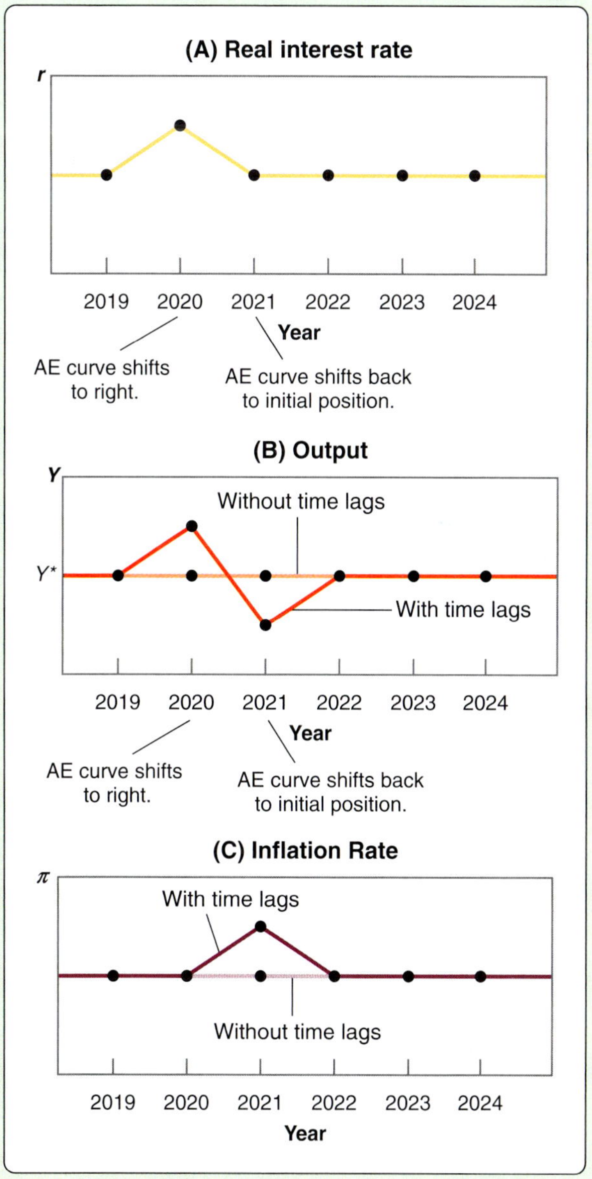

Time lags in the AE and Phillips curves make it more difficult for the central bank to stabilize the economy. Despite countercyclical policy, an expenditure shock causes short-run movements in output and inflation.

FIGURE 13.13 Determining the Output Path in Figure 13.12B

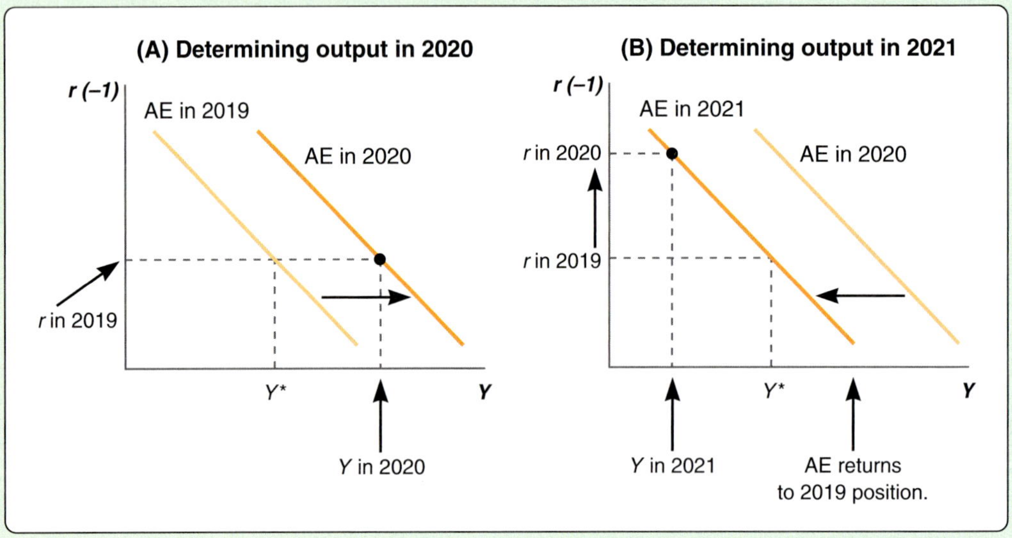

affect spending in that year: what matters is $r(-1)$, the interest rate in 2019. For that interest rate, the AE shift raises output above potential.

In 2021, the AE curve shifts back in (**Figure 13.13B**). For that year, $r(-1)$ is the interest rate in 2020, which was high. The combination of a high $r(-1)$ and the inward AE shift push output *below* potential.

So the economic boom in 2020 is followed by a recession in 2021. Output returns to potential in 2022, the year after the interest rate returns to its initial level. Figure 13.12B shows this output path.

Figure 13.12C shows the behavior of inflation. In the no-lag case, the inflation rate never changes, because output stays at potential. With time lags, the movements in output affect inflation a year later. The boom in 2020 causes inflation to rise in 2021; the recession in 2021 pushes inflation back down in 2022. The expenditure shock has no long-run effect on inflation, but it causes short-run volatility.

In the time-lag case, one might ask why the central bank raises the interest rate in 2020. This action doesn't affect the economy in that year, and it causes a recession in 2021. If policymakers can't offset the expenditure shock when it occurs, why not keep the interest rate constant? The answer is that passive policy would allow a permanent rise in inflation, which the central bank might find unacceptable. Problem 13.6 explores this point.

CASE STUDY

Fiscal versus Monetary Policy

Policymakers have two tools for stabilizing the economy. You probably learned about them in an introductory economics course. One tool is monetary policy, which is controlled by the Federal Reserve. The other is **fiscal policy,** the choice of taxes and government spending. Fiscal policy is controlled by Congress and the president.

Fiscal policy The government's choice of taxes and spending

If we ignore time lags, either monetary or fiscal policy can offset an expenditure shock. **Figure 13.14** shows a negative shock to spending, which shifts the AE curve to the left, from AE_1 to AE_2. In response to this shock, the Fed can reduce the real interest rate (Figure 13.14A). Alternatively, the Fed can do nothing while the president and Congress adjust fiscal policy. An expansionary policy—either a tax cut or a rise in government spending—shifts the AE curve back to the right (Figure 13.14B). Either type of policy keeps output constant.

In practice, monetary policy is used more often than fiscal policy to stabilize the economy. When an expenditure shock occurs, it's likely that the Fed responds, not the president and Congress. The reasons involve time lags. We've seen that lags reduce the effectiveness of monetary policy as a stabilization tool. Most economists believe, however, that the problem is worse for fiscal policy.

To discuss this issue, we must first distinguish between two kinds of time lags. The **inside lag** is the time it takes policymakers to recognize a shock and respond to it. The **outside lag** is the time it takes the policy response to affect the economy. When a shock occurs, the inside lag comes first and the outside lag second, as shown in **Figure 13.15**.

Inside lag Time between a shock and the policy response

Outside lag Time between the policy response and its effects on the economy

This chapter has emphasized the outside lag in monetary policy: the lag between a Fed action (a change in the federal funds rate) and the effects on

FIGURE 13.14 Two Types of Countercyclical Policy

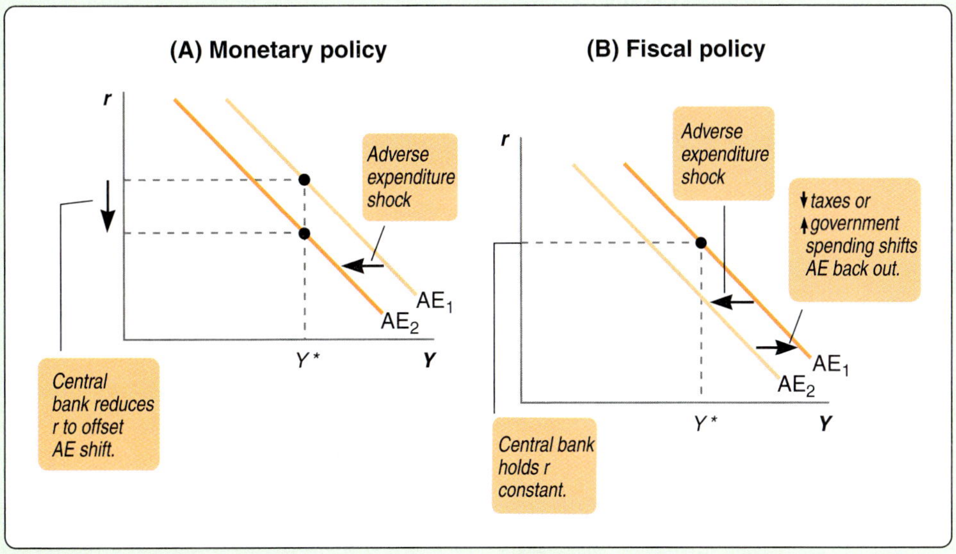

The Federal Reserve can offset an adverse expenditure shock by reducing the real interest rate (A). Alternatively, Congress and the president can offset the shock by raising government spending or cutting taxes (B).

FIGURE 13.15 Inside and Outside Time Lags

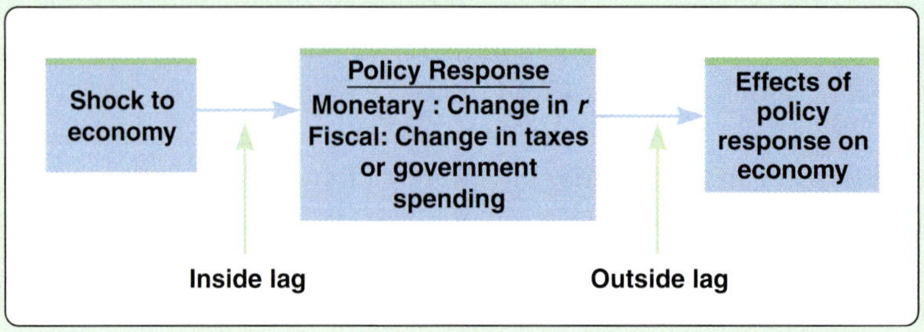

Two kinds of time lags reduce policymakers' ability to stabilize the economy.

output and inflation. This lag can be substantial, partly because it takes time for firms to adjust investment plans when interest rates change. The outside lag is generally *shorter* for fiscal policy. A rise in government spending directly raises aggregate expenditure. A tax cut raises people's after-tax incomes, leading fairly quickly to higher consumption.

The story about inside lags is very different. For monetary policy, this lag is short. As discussed in Section 13.1, the FOMC meets every six weeks to adjust policy. Fed economists monitor the economy constantly, so FOMC decisions reflect the most recent developments.

In contrast, fiscal policy moves slowly. Changes in government spending or taxes must be introduced in Congress, debated, passed, and signed by the president. Major changes are usually controversial, and it can take years to build political support. Consequently, fiscal policy is not used commonly to offset expenditure shocks.

As mentioned in Section 12.2, fiscal policy *was* used as a stabilization tool in 2008. Amid fears of a recession, President Bush and Congress agreed on a package of tax cuts, which took the form of rebates mailed to citizens or deposited in their bank accounts. A family of four received up to $1800; total rebates were $152 billion, or a bit more than 1 percent of GDP.

This episode illustrates the inside lag in fiscal policy. People started worrying about the economy in Summer 2007, when the subprime mortgage crisis became apparent. Politicians proposed tax cuts, but it took until February 2008 to enact the rebate plan. Then it took time for the Treasury to implement the plan: rebates reached consumers between May and July.

In contrast, the Fed responded quickly to the subprime crisis. It started cutting interest rates in August 2007, nine months before the Treasury issued the first rebates. The Fed's action illustrates the short inside lag that makes monetary policy the primary stabilization tool.

Summary

- The monetary transmission mechanism is the process through which monetary policy affects output. It involves both major parts of the financial system, financial markets and banks.

13.1 Monetary Policy and the Term Structure

- The Federal Reserve controls a 1-day interest rate—the federal funds rate. The rates that influence spending are longer-term rates. However, the Fed does affect spending indirectly, because the federal funds rate affects longer-term rates.
- According to the expectations theory, longer-term rates depend on the current federal funds rate and on expectations of future rates. The direct effect of the current rate is small. But a change in the current funds rate can change longer-term rates substantially by changing expectations of future rates. This occurs because the Fed does not reverse changes in the funds rate quickly.
- A change in the funds rate must be unexpected to cause longer-term rates to change substantially at the same time. An expected change causes longer-term rates to move before the change occurs. Financial markets can often predict changes in the funds rate based on the state of the economy and statements by Fed officials.
- Kenneth Kuttner has estimated that a surprise increase in the funds rate of 1 percentage point raises longer-term rates by amounts ranging from 0.79 percentage points for the 3-month rate to 0.19 points for the 30-year rate.

13.2 The Financial System and Aggregate Expenditure

- Events in the financial system are a leading cause of short-run economic fluctuations.
- A rise in asset prices raises aggregate expenditure because higher wealth stimulates consumption, higher stock prices encourage investment, and higher net worth and collateral produce greater lending by banks.
- Events in the banking industry cause shifts in bank lending that influence aggregate spending. These events include changes in risk perceptions, in regulation, and in bank capital.
- Japan experienced a deep economic slump during the 1990s and early 2000s. The causes of the slump included banking problems and crashes in asset prices.
- Economic fluctuations are magnified by the investment multiplier: a rise in aggregate spending raises firms' earnings, which provides them with cheap funds for investment, which raises investment, which further increases aggregate spending.

13.3 The Monetary Transmission Mechanism

- Monetary policy affects aggregate spending through a complex process. A change in the federal funds rate affects longer-term interest rates, asset prices, and exchange rates. These financial variables affect various components of spending, both directly and through effects on bank lending. Changes in spending are magnified by the consumption multiplier and the investment multiplier.
- Gertler and Gilchrist find that monetary policy has larger effects on small firms than on large firms. This finding confirms the importance of bank lending in the monetary transmission mechanism.

13.4 Time Lags

- It takes around a year for a shift in monetary policy to exert its main effects on output. It also takes around a year for a change in output to exert its main effects on inflation.

13.5 Time Lags and the Effects of Policy

- Time lags make monetary policy less effective in stabilizing the economy. They slow down the process of disinflation, and they make it harder to offset the effects of expenditure shocks.
- In theory, either fiscal or monetary policy can be used to stabilize the economy. In practice, the job usually falls to monetary policy, because the political process makes it hard to adjust fiscal policy quickly.

Key Terms

capital crunch, p. 393

fiscal policy, p. 407

inside lag, p. 407

investment multiplier, p. 396

monetary transmission mechanism, p. 384

outside lag, p. 407

Questions and Problems

1. Suppose the federal funds rate is 3 percent. Bond traders expect it to remain at that level for three months and then rise to 3.5 percent for nine months. However, the FOMC raises the rate to 3.5 percent immediately. After this action, traders expect the funds rate to stay at 3.5 percent for a year. How does the FOMC's action affect the 3-month interest rate, the 6-month rate, and the 1-year rate?

2. Suppose that bond traders expect an increase in the federal funds rate, but the FOMC surprises them by keeping it constant. What happens to longer-term rates? Explain.

3. Describe all the ways that a rise in stock prices affects aggregate expenditure. Do the same for a rise in housing prices. Do stock prices have some effects that housing prices don't, or vice versa?

4. The riskiness of banks' assets fluctuates over time. For example, default risk on loans rises and falls.
   a. How are banks likely to adjust their equity ratios (their ratios of capital to assets) when the riskiness of assets changes? Explain. (*Hint*: See Section 9.6)
   b. How do the adjustments in Part (a) affect the sizes of booms and recessions? Explain.

5. Economists have found that recent earnings have larger effects on investment for small firms than for large firms. What might explain this fact?

6. Figure 13.12 shows what happens if the AE curve shifts out temporarily and the central bank raises the real interest rate. Now suppose the same shock occurs but the central bank keeps the interest rate constant. Assuming lags in the AE and Phillips curves, show what happens over time to output and inflation. Discuss the pros and cons of raising the interest rate in response to the shock.

7. Consider the expenditure shock in Figure 13.12: the AE curve shifts to the right in 2020 and returns to its initial position in 2021. Suppose the central bank anticipates the shock: in 2019, it knows what will happen in the following two years. Assuming lags in the AE and Phillips curves, can the central bank keep output and inflation constant? If it can, explain how; if it can't, explain why not.

8. Consider the AE/PC model with time lags. Suppose the economy starts with output at potential and constant inflation. In 2020, an adverse supply shock occurs, shifting the Phillips curve up.
   a. Show the paths of output and inflation over time if the central bank keeps the real interest rate constant.
   b. Can the central bank prevent inflation from rising temporarily as a result of the supply shock? Can it prevent inflation from rising permanently? Explain.
   c. Suppose policymakers want to return inflation to its 2019 level as quickly as possible, and then keep inflation constant. What path should policymakers choose for the real interest rate? What are the resulting paths of output and inflation?

Online and Data Questions

www.worthpublishers.com/ball

9. From the text Web site, get Bernanke and Kuttner's data on expected and unexpected changes in the federal funds rate by the FOMC. (You may recall these data from Problem 3.12.) Choose one day when the expected change in the funds rate was large and the unexpected change was small, and one day when the opposite was true. Then link to the site of the Federal Reserve Bank of St. Louis, which has daily data on the interest rate on 1-year Treasury bonds. For each of the days you selected from the Bernanke-Kuttner data, compute the change in the 1-year interest rate from the day *before* the FOMC's action to the day *after* the action. Can you explain why the change in the 1-year rate was larger in one case than in the other?

10. Link from the text Web site to the online Economic Report of the President and get annual data on real GDP and real investment. Calculate the growth rates of the two variables for each year since 1960. (A variable's growth rate in a given year is the percentage change from the previous year.) Which is more volatile, GDP or investment? What might explain the difference in volatility?

chapter fourteen 14

Inflation and Deflation

- 14.1 MONEY AND INFLATION IN THE LONG RUN
- 14.2 WHAT DETERMINES MONEY GROWTH?
- 14.3 THE COSTS OF INFLATION
- 14.4 DEFLATION AND THE LIQUIDITY TRAP

Three Lions/Getty Images

Germany, 1923: Hyperinflation provided children with new toys.

U.S. inflation caused great concern when it rose above 10 percent in the 1970s. In 1974, President Gerald Ford called inflation "Public Enemy Number One." Voters' unhappiness with inflation contributed to Ford's loss to Jimmy Carter in the 1976 presidential election, and then to Carter's loss to Ronald Reagan in 1980.

By worldwide standards, however, U.S. inflation in the 1970s was hardly extreme. **Table 14.1** on p. 414 illustrates the spectacular variation in inflation rates across countries and time periods. Inflation can be negative, as it was in Japan from 1999 through 2005. A sustained period of negative inflation is called **deflation.** When inflation is positive, it can average less than 3 percent per year (as in the United States in the 2000s), more than 500 percent (as in Argentina in the late 1980s), or any level in between.

For briefer periods, economies can experience **hyperinflation.** This is defined as inflation above 50 percent per *month,* which means about 13,000 percent per year.[1] In the famous German hyperinflation, annual inflation reached 855 million percent in 1923. In Serbia in 1993, in the midst of the Bosnian war, inflation was 116 *trillion* percent (that's 116,000,000,000,000%).

Deflation Sustained period of negative inflation

Hyperinflation Inflation of more than 50 percent per month (or roughly 13,000 percent per year)

[1] This definition of hyperinflation was proposed by Phillip Cagan of Columbia University in "The Monetary Dynamics of Hyperinflation," in Friedman (ed.), *Studies in the Quantity Theory of Money,* University of Chicago Press, 1956.

TABLE 14.1 Some Inflation Rates

Country	Period	Average Annual Inflation Rate
U.S.	1870s	−1.8%
Japan	1999–2005	−0.5
U.S.	2000–2007	2.7
U.S.	1970s	7.8
Italy	1970s	13.9
Turkey	1990s	76.1
Russia	1992–2000	121.3
Argentina	1985–1990	559.1
Germany	1923	855 million
Serbia	1993	116 trillion

Sources: International Monetary Fund; Milton Friedman and Anna Schwartz, *Monetary Trends in the United States and the United Kingdom: Their Relation to Income, Prices, and Interest Rates 1867–1975*, University of Chicago Press, 1982; Thomas J. Sargent, "The Ends of Four Big Inflations," in Hall (ed.), *Inflation*, University of Chicago Press, 1983; Pavle Petrović et al., "The Yugoslav Hyperinflation of 1992–1994: Causes, Dynamics, and Money Supply Process," *Journal of Comparative Economics*, June 1999

These astronomical inflation rates make money virtually worthless—at least for purchasing goods and services. In hyperinflations, people find other uses for money. In the German episode, children used blocks of currency as toys, and families saved on firewood by burning money in their stoves.

What determines the level of inflation? Why is it sometimes low or even negative and sometimes ridiculously high? This chapter addresses these issues. We start with one basic principle: *in the long run, inflation is determined by the growth rate of the money supply.* If a country experiences high inflation for a sustained period, its central bank is expanding the money supply rapidly.

▶Mathematical note: If the monthly inflation rate in decimal form is π^{month}, the annual rate is $(1 + \pi^{month})^{12} - 1$. A monthly rate of 50 percent means $\pi^{month} = 0.5$. This implies an annual rate of $(1 + 0.5)^{12} - 1 = 128.75$ in decimal form, or 12,875 percent.

This idea leads to further questions. What determines the growth rate of the money supply? Why do some central banks increase the money supply quickly if that produces high inflation? How does deflation occur?

Finally, this chapter asks how inflation affects the economy. Was the U.S. harmed a generation ago when inflation rose to 10 percent? What happens to economies with hyperinflation?

14.1 MONEY AND INFLATION IN THE LONG RUN

Monetary policy affects both real variables, such as output, and nominal variables, such as inflation. The effects on real variables, however, are transitory. Monetary policy influences output in the short run, but it is neutral in the long run (see Section 12.5).

In contrast, monetary policy has its strongest effects on inflation in the long run. Various expenditure and supply shocks cause year-to-year movements in the inflation rate. But *average* inflation over a decade or more is tied closely to the growth of the money supply. Let's see why.

Velocity and the Quantity Equation

Remember the basic purpose of money: it is a medium of exchange. People spend money to acquire goods and services. The reason that the money supply affects inflation is that it affects the level of spending in the economy.

Velocity of money Ratio of nominal GDP to the money supply ($V = PY/M$); shows how quickly money moves through the economy

To see this point, we need to introduce a new concept: the **velocity of money.** This variable is the ratio of total spending in the economy to the money supply:

$$V = \frac{\text{total spending}}{M}$$

If spending is \$500 and the money supply is \$100, then velocity is 500/100 = 5.

An economy's total spending is measured by nominal GDP. This variable equals the price level (P) times real output (Y). Therefore, velocity is

▶See the Chapter 1 appendix to review nominal GDP.

$$V = \frac{PY}{M}$$

Velocity measures how quickly money circulates through the economy. Specifically, velocity is the number of times a typical dollar is spent over a year. If $V = 5$, then a dollar is spent five times. Someone spends the dollar in a store, the store owner spends it somewhere else, and it changes hands three times after that.

Economists often rearrange the definition of velocity, bringing M to the left side:

QUANTITY EQUATION OF MONEY

$$MV = PY \qquad (14.1)$$

This is the **quantity equation of money.** The quantity equation says that total spending in the economy (PY) equals the money supply (M) times the number of times each dollar is spent (V). If M is \$100 and V is 5, total spending is \$500.

Quantity equation of money Relationship among the money supply, velocity, and nominal GDP: $MV = PY$

The concept of velocity is closely related to the concept of money demand—the amount of money that individuals and firms choose to hold (see Section 4.3). When the market for money is in equilibrium, the money supply, M, equals money demand, M^d. We can rewrite the definition of velocity as

$$V = \frac{PY}{M^d}$$

This equation says that, for a given level of nominal GDP, there is an inverse relationship between velocity and money demand. Factors that raise money demand also reduce velocity.

For example, suppose ATMs become more common. People start carrying less cash because they can get it easily when needed. This change reduces money demand for a given level of nominal GDP, so velocity rises. Say money holdings fall from \$100 to \$80. If GDP is still \$500, velocity rises from 5 to 6.25, because 500/80 = 6.25.

Deriving the Inflation Rate

The inflation rate is defined as the growth rate of the price level, which means the percentage change from one year to the next. With a little algebra, we can derive an equation for inflation from Equation (14.1), the quantity equation of money.

Since the quantity equation always holds, the percentage change in the left side, MV, must equal the percentage change in the right side, PY:

$$\%\text{ change in } (MV) = \%\text{ change in } (PY)$$

Mathematically, the percentage change in MV is the sum of the percentage changes in M and V; the percentage change in PY can be decomposed in the same way. Therefore,

▶Mathematical note: Formally, Equation (14.2) is a first-order Taylor approximation. It is accurate if the various percentage changes are not too large.

$$(\%\text{change in } M)+(\%\text{change in } V)=(\%\text{change in } P)+(\%\text{change in } Y) \quad \textbf{(14.2)}$$

In Equation (14.2), notice that the first term on the right, % change in P, is the inflation rate. As usual, we denote inflation by π. Rearranging terms yields a formula for π:

$$\pi = (\%\text{change in } M) + (\%\text{change in } V) - (\%\text{change in } Y) \quad \textbf{(14.3)}$$

Equation (14.3) says that inflation is determined by the percentage changes, or growth rates, of three variables: the money supply, velocity, and real output.

In the long run, two of the growth rates in Equation (14.3) are outside the control of the central bank:

- Output growth depends on factors that affect the economy's productivity, such as new technologies. Long-run neutrality means that monetary policy is irrelevant.

▶For the calculation of velocity growth, the money supply is defined as M1 adjusted for sweep accounts (see Section 2.4).

- Long-run changes in velocity are driven primarily by changes in transaction technologies—the methods people use to acquire and spend money. As discussed earlier, velocity moves in the opposite direction from money demand. In the United States, innovations such as ATMs have slowly reduced money demand, so velocity has risen. The growth rate of velocity averaged 2.1% from 1960 through 2007. This long-run growth rate, like long-run output growth, is independent of monetary policy.

In contrast, the central bank chooses the growth rate of the money supply. For given levels of output growth and velocity growth, there is a one-for-one effect of money growth on inflation. In the long run, the central bank can raise or lower inflation by changing money growth.

The Data

We've seen that central banks influence inflation through their choices of money growth. These choices vary widely across countries and time periods. Money growth rates are sometimes negative, sometimes close to zero, and sometimes hundreds or thousands of percent. This variation causes big differences in inflation.

This point is obvious when we examine some data. **Figure 14.1** presents data for 52 countries during the period 1980–1990. For each country, the figure shows the average growth rate of the money supply (the M1 measure) and average inflation. We see a close relation: the countries with high inflation rates are those with high money growth.

The relationship in Figure 14.1 is not perfect: the data points do not fall exactly on a straight line. The reason is that inflation is influenced by the

FIGURE 14.1 Inflation and Money Growth Across Countries

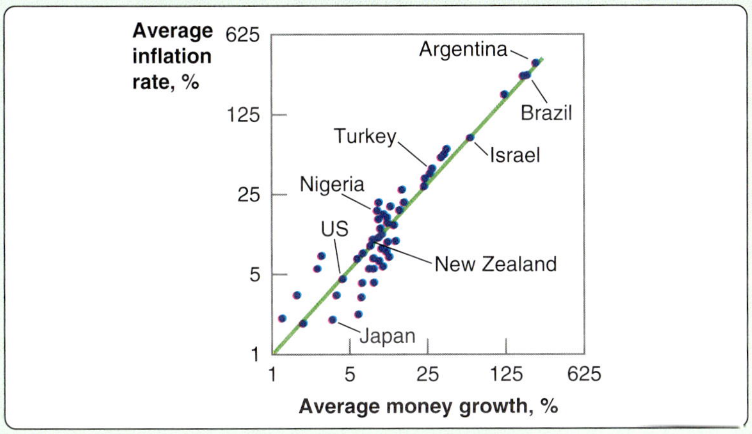

For the period 1980–1990, this graph plots the average growth rate of the money supply (as measured by M1) and the average inflation rate in 52 countries. Differences in money growth explain most cross-country differences in inflation.

Source: International Monetary Fund

growth rates of output and velocity (see Equation (14.3)). However, these growth rates vary much less across countries than does money growth. As a result, money growth explains most differences in inflation.

Figure 14.2 illustrates our point another way. It shows money growth and inflation in one country, the United States, in different decades. We again see a strong relation between the two variables. Decades of high money growth, such as the 1910s and 1970s, are decades of high inflation. Low money growth in the 1930s produced deflation.

As we have discussed, the relation between money growth and inflation holds *in the long run*—practically speaking, over periods of a decade or more. It may not hold for shorter periods. To illustrate this point, **Figure 14.3** presents data for individual years rather than decades. Specifically, it shows inflation and money growth for each year between 1990 and 2007. There is little relation between year-to-year fluctuations in the two variables. This reflects the short-run influence of expenditure and supply shocks on inflation.

The great economist Milton Friedman said that "inflation is always and everywhere a monetary phenomenon." The data show that Friedman is right—as long as we add "in the long run" to the end of his statement.

The Phillips Curve Again

Section 12.4 explains the behavior of inflation with a Phillips curve: inflation depends on past inflation, output, and supply shocks. Here, we say that average inflation is determined by money growth. Superficially, these two theories sound different, and people sometimes interpret them as contradictory. In fact, they fit together nicely.

FIGURE 14.2 U.S. Inflation and Money Growth Across Decades

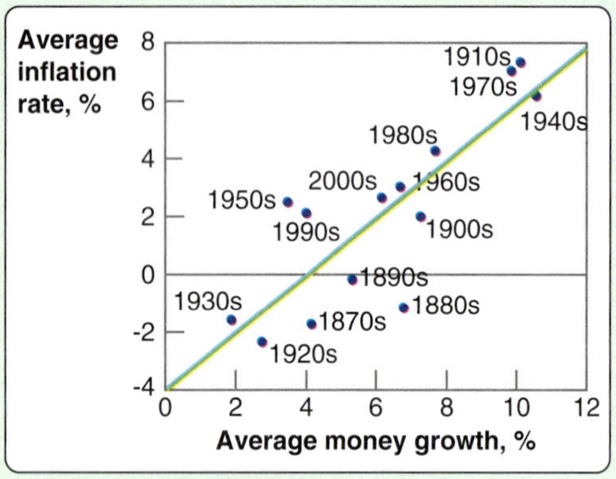

This graph plots the average growth rate of the money supply and the average inflation rate for each decade from the 1870s to the 2000s. The money supply is measured by M2 because M1 data are not available so far back in time. Differences in money growth explain most differences in inflation across decades.

Sources: Milton Friedman and Anna Schwartz, *Monetary Trends in the United States and the United Kingdom: Their Relation to Income, Prices, and Interest Rates 1867–1975*, University of Chicago Press, 1982; and Federal Reserve Board. The data point for the 2000s covers 2000–2007

FIGURE 14.3 U.S. Inflation and Money Growth Across Individual Years

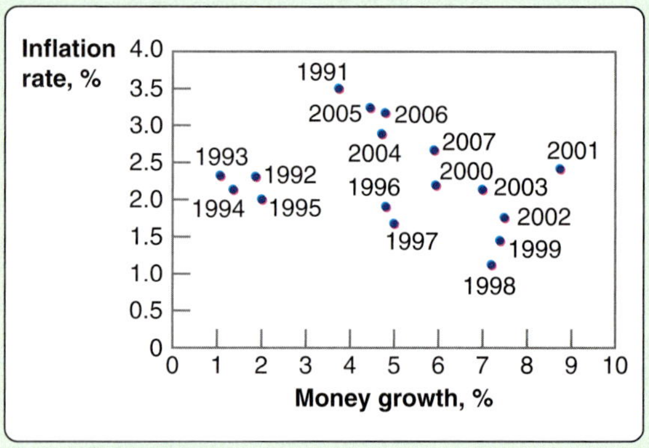

This graph plots the growth rate of M2 and the inflation rate in each year from 1991 through 2007. Differences in money growth do *not* explain differences in inflation across individual years.

Source: Federal Reserve Board

Specifically, the Phillips curve is part of the mechanism by which money growth produces inflation. Using the quantity equation of money, $MV = PY$, we've shown algebraically that these two variables are linked. In economic terms, however, the link is not direct. If the central bank increases the rate of money growth, it is *not* the case that firms observe this action and respond directly by raising prices faster. Instead, higher money growth sets off a chain of events that involves the Phillips curve.

Figure 14.4 outlines these events, which should be familiar from Chapters 11 and 12. In the money market, higher money growth pushes down the nominal interest rate, which reduces the real rate for a given level of expected inflation. The lower real rate moves the economy along the aggregate expenditure curve, raising output. Finally, higher output moves the economy along

FIGURE 14.4 From Money Growth to Inflation

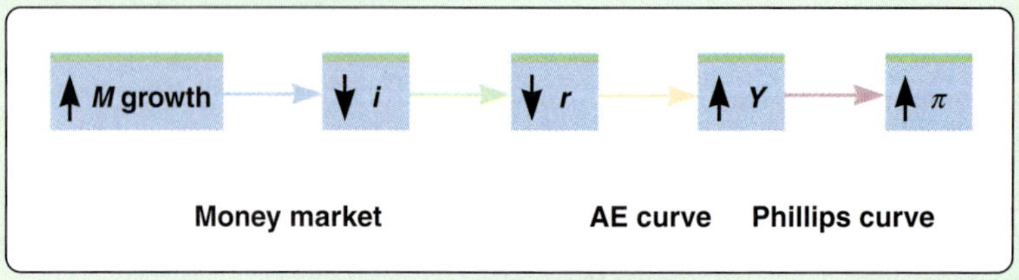

A rise in money growth sets off a series of effects that raise inflation. A fall in money growth has the opposite effects, reducing inflation.

the Phillips curve, raising the inflation rate. In the end, we confirm this chapter's central idea: higher money growth leads to higher inflation.

Chapter 12 discusses some of the steps in Figure 14.4: the links from interest rates to output to inflation. That discussion leaves out the first step, from money growth to interest rates, because we assume a policy of interest-rate targeting. Under this policy, however, money growth is always adjusting in the background. A long-run rise in inflation requires an increase in money growth.

For details on the behavior of money growth under interest-rate targeting, see the Chapter 14 appendix at the text Web site.

14.2 WHAT DETERMINES MONEY GROWTH?

At one level, the question "What determines inflation in the long run?" has a simple answer: the growth rate of the money supply. However, this answer raises another question: what determines money growth? Why is it sometimes slow and sometimes fast, producing the different inflation rates that we see?

The answer to this question is more complex. Different factors determine money growth in different circumstances. **Table 14.2** summarizes the main cases that we will discuss. As shown in the table, one key issue is whether an economy uses commodity money or fiat money.

▶Section 2.2 compares commodity money and fiat money and discusses the uses of each over U. S. history.

Commodity Money

Commodity money, such as gold coins or paper money exchangeable for gold, has intrinsic value. With commodity money, the money supply is determined by how much of the commodity is produced.

One example of a commodity money system is the classical gold standard, which existed in the United States from 1879 to 1913. During that period, money was mainly gold certificates. If you turned in gold to the government, you received gold certificates at a rate of $20.67 per ounce. If you held gold certificates, you could trade them back to the government for gold.

Under this system, the government did not try to control the money supply. Instead, money growth was determined by how much gold people exchanged for gold certificates. This was the amount of gold produced minus the amount people kept for "nonmonetary" uses, such as making jewelry.

Ultimately, the main factor determining money growth was developments in the mining industry. In the first half of the gold-standard period,

TABLE 14.2 Determinants of Money Growth and Inflation

Commodity Money	Fiat Money
Production of the commodity (e.g., U.S. gold standard, 1879–1913)	Choice of the central bank • Often central banks keep inflation low (e.g., U.S., 2000s) • Desire for high output → high inflation (e.g., U.S., 1970s) • Government budget deficits → very high inflation (e.g., Zimbabwe, 2000s)

mines produced new gold at a slow rate. As a result, money growth was low for most of the period from 1879 to 1897.

At the end of the nineteenth century, gold was discovered in Colorado, Alaska, and South Africa. In addition, new mining techniques made it easier to extract gold from ore. Gold production boomed, causing rapid money growth from 1897 to 1913.

The slow money growth of the early gold-standard period led to deflation: the inflation rate averaged −1 percent from 1879 to 1897. From 1897 to 1913, higher money growth produced average inflation of +2 percent.

These inflation developments had important effects on the economy, which in turn produced political conflict. The next case study discusses politics in the 1890s.

CASE STUDY

The Free Silver Movement

Issues in money and banking have sparked political controversy throughout U.S. history. Supporters of large banks, centered traditionally in Eastern cities, have battled antibank populists in farming regions. Chapter 10 discusses some of the episodes in this saga, such as the fight over the Second Bank of the United States in the 1830s and the fight over bank branching in the early 1900s.

One of the biggest battles occurred during the gold-standard era. The underlying cause was the deflation from 1879 to 1896. This deflation was unforeseen: people did not expect inflation to be negative. In other words, actual inflation over the period (π) was lower than expected inflation (π^e).

This divergence meant that the ex post real interest rate, $i - \pi$, was higher than the ex ante real rate, $i - \pi^e$ (review Section 3.6). In real terms, debtors paid more on their loans than they expected when the loans were made.

Farmers in the western United States had large debts to banks. The 1880s and 1890s were tough times for this group because of poor agricultural conditions, including drought and infestations by insects. Rising debt burdens caused by deflation pushed many farmers into bankruptcy.

Farmers and their political allies wanted to raise the inflation rate, which would reduce real interest rates. They understood that inflation required faster money growth and that the gold standard was keeping money growth low.

Bimetallism Monetary system in which money is backed by both gold and silver

Consequently, supporters of higher inflation pushed for a monetary system called **bimetallism** (literally, two metals). In this system, the government would issue money backed by silver as well as by gold. Specifically, a dollar could be issued for *either* 0.0484 ounces of gold or 0.774 ounces of silver (making silver worth 1/16 as much as gold). Silver mining was booming during this period, so bimetallism would have caused a large increase in the money supply.

The debate over bimetallism came to a head in the presidential campaign of 1896. The Republicans nominated William McKinley, who supported the gold standard. The Democrats nominated William Jennings Bryan, known as "the Great Commoner" for his populist views. Bryan's primary campaign issue was "Free Silver," meaning bimetallism.

At the Democratic convention in Chicago, Bryan made one of the most famous speeches in American political history, expressing his views on monetary policy with a dramatic Biblical metaphor. Referring to his opponents, the Eastern bankers, Bryan said, "We will answer their demand for a gold standard by saying to them: You shall not press down upon the brow of labor this crown of thorns, you shall not crucify mankind upon a cross of gold."

In the 1896 election, Bryan carried the South and West and lost badly in the East. The election turned on Midwestern states such as Ohio and Michigan, whose economies were shifting from agriculture to industry. McKinley carried these states, giving him the presidency. The gold standard was secure.

Ironically, Bryan's supporters ultimately got what they wanted: inflation. Deflation ended because of the happenstance that gold production rose after 1896. With this development, the fervor for bimetallism waned (although Bryan was twice more the Democratic presidential candidate, in 1900 and 1908).

Fiat Money and Inflation

Today, economies use fiat money—pieces of paper that are not exchangeable for any commodity. The supply of fiat money is controlled by an economy's central bank, not its mining industry. As we discuss in Section 11.5, the central bank has the tools to increase the money supply at whatever rate it chooses.

As noted in Table 14.2, central banks often choose low levels of money growth. The reason is obvious: to keep inflation low. For example, the Federal Reserve has kept money growth low in recent years, producing average inflation rates below 3 percent in the 1990s and 2000s.

In other cases, central banks choose higher money growth. We've seen that the Fed allowed money to grow rapidly in the 1970s, producing average inflation of 8 percent. Central banks in some countries have produced hyperinflation.

Such experiences may appear puzzling. Central bank officials dislike high inflation. Most understand the link between inflation and money growth. So why don't they always choose low money growth and low inflation? One answer is that rapid money growth can raise output temporarily.

The Output–Inflation Trade-off

One step on the path from money growth to inflation is a rise in output, which raises inflation through the Phillips curve (see Figure 14.4). This output boom increases people's incomes and reduces unemployment. This prospect tempts central banks to follow inflationary policies.

Section 12.4 uses the Phillips curve to show how accommodative policy leads to higher inflation. The Chapter 14 appendix at the text Web site shows how money growth rises during this process.

▶A Disinflation: $\downarrow M$ growth $\rightarrow \uparrow i \rightarrow \uparrow r \rightarrow \downarrow Y \rightarrow \downarrow \pi$

A central bank also allows inflation to rise if it accommodates an adverse supply shock, such as a rise in oil prices. Here the aim of policymakers is not to raise output, but merely to keep it from falling below potential. With an adverse supply shock, however, stable output requires an increase in money growth and inflation.

Finally, once money growth and inflation are high, central banks may keep them high. We've seen that a policy of reducing inflation—a disinflation—causes a temporary output loss. In a disinflation, the process in Figure 14.4 works in reverse: along the path from lower money growth to lower inflation, interest rates rise and output falls. If policymakers are unwilling to pay this cost, they keep money growth high and live with inflation.

The factors we've outlined help explain U.S. inflation in the 1970s. Large supply shocks occurred in 1973 and 1979—the two OPEC oil-price increases. The Fed accommodated these shocks, allowing money growth and inflation to rise. Then, under Chairmen Burns and Miller, the Fed was unwilling to reduce output to disinflate. Inflation fell only after Paul Volcker was appointed chairman in 1979; Volcker decided enough was enough, reduced money growth, and accepted a deep recession (review Section 12.4).

The output–inflation trade-off helps explain many episodes of inflation. However, it is *not* the main reason for very high inflation. Policymakers may allow 10 percent inflation to keep output high, but this motive doesn't explain 500 percent inflation in Argentina or hyperinflation in Serbia. Something else is going on in these cases.

Seigniorage and Very High Inflation

What explains inflation in the hundreds or thousands of percent? The short answer is government budget deficits. Governments frequently spend more than they raise in taxes, creating deficits. Most often, governments cover deficits by issuing bonds—in other words, by borrowing. This borrowing pushes up interest rates, which reduces investment and hurts economic growth (review Section 4.2). However, deficits financed by bonds do *not* necessarily cause inflation. For example, the U.S. government has run large deficits in the 2000s, but inflation has stayed low.

Sometimes, however, governments with deficits have trouble selling bonds. This occurs when savers fear the government will default on its debt. This fear arises when debt reaches a high level, especially if the government or those of similar countries have defaulted in the past.

When private savers refuse to buy government bonds, the government turns to another buyer: the central bank. Some central banks are legally required to buy the bonds; others do so voluntarily to keep the government functioning. Purchases of bonds by the central bank cause an increase in the monetary base (review Section 11.2). The increase in the base raises the money supply. When the government runs large deficits, the money supply rises rapidly, fueling inflation.

Formally, the government is borrowing money when it sells bonds to the central bank. However, the central bank is set up by the government, and it gives back the interest it earns from government bonds. So when the government sells bonds to the central bank, it does not really create a debt to an outside entity. In effect, the central bank just creates money and gives it to the government. Financing deficits this way is known as **printing money.** The money that the government receives is called **seigniorage revenue** (after the *seigneurs,* or feudal lords, who created money in the Middle Ages).

Printing money Financing government budget deficits by selling bonds to the central bank

Seigniorage revenue Revenue the government receives from printing money

Budget deficits have caused high inflation in much of the world. Some examples:

- In the 1980s, populist governments in Latin America spent large amounts on programs for the poor, yet raised little revenue because of tax evasion. At first they financed budget deficits by borrowing; they had trouble selling bonds, but they received loans from U.S. banks. These loans were cut off after Mexico defaulted on its debt in 1982. At that point, countries such as Argentina and Brazil turned to seigniorage revenue, producing inflation rates of hundreds and thousands of percent per year.

- In the 1990s, three- and four digit inflation occurred in Russia and other countries that had recently abandoned Communism. Budget deficits were caused partly by subsidies to unprofitable firms left over from the old regime. Savers were wary of lending to countries with uncertain futures, so seigniorage revenue was needed. In 1993, the inflation rate was 256 percent in Romania, 875 percent in Russia, and 4735 percent in Ukraine.

Beyond inflation of "only" a few thousand percent lies hyperinflation. Most hyperinflations have occurred during or after wars, especially World Wars I and II. Wars destroy economies and create political turmoil, leading to huge budget deficits. Money growth explodes, producing inflation rates that sound like science fiction.

Two hyperinflations have occurred since 1990:

- In the early 1990s, Serbia set the all-time record for hyperinflation. In this episode, the war in Bosnia fueled high government spending. At the same time, output fell sharply because trade was interrupted by the breakup of Yugoslavia and by embargoes imposed as punishment for the war. Falling output reduced tax revenue, and the deficit rose to a staggering one-third of GDP. Serbia's government financed its deficit by printing money, producing an inflation rate in the hundreds of trillions in 1993.

- In 2008, Zimbabwe was in the midst of hyperinflation. Output had collapsed since 2000 as a result of the disastrous policies of President Robert Mugabe,

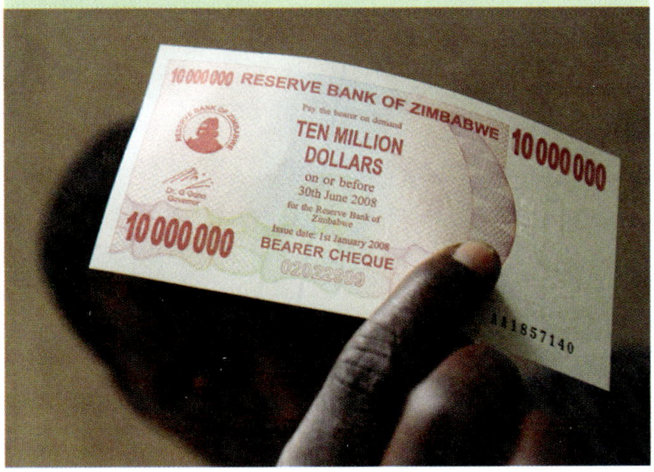

A 10-million-dollar note issued by the Reserve Bank of Zimbabwe. When it was printed in January 2008, it could buy six loaves of bread; a few months later, it was nearly worthless.

AP PHOTO/Tsvangirayi Mukwazhi

including a chaotic land redistribution, protectionist trade policies, controls on exchange rates, and political repression that destabilized the country. Tax revenue plummeted and, as in Serbia, the government budget deficit reached a third of GDP. The inflation rate was around 100 percent in 2001, climbed to 1000 percent in 2006, and then exploded. Inflation exceeded 100,000 percent in 2007 and it was still rising in 2008.

The next case study examines history's most famous hyperinflation.

CASE STUDY

The German Hyperinflation

After World War I, the German government spent heavily to rebuild its country. Under the Treaty of Versailles, it also paid large reparations—about 6 percent of its GDP—to the victors in the war. All this spending produced large budget deficits, which were financed by printing money. The result was inflation of 167 percent in 1921 and 4130 percent in 1922.

Berlin, Germany, 1923: A woman lights her stove with millions of deutsche marks, the German currency.

In 1923, things fell apart. Germany fell behind on its reparations payments, leading France to occupy the industrial Ruhr Valley. German output fell sharply, reducing tax revenue. Workers in the Ruhr went on strike to protest the occupation, and the German government paid their wages.

Tax receipts covered only 11 percent of government spending, so huge levels of seigniorage were needed. Money growth and inflation exploded. Monthly inflation was about 100 percent in January 1923 and rose to 30,000 percent in October. This inflation rate meant that prices doubled every four days. For all of 1923, inflation was 855 million percent.

This period produced amazing stories. Bar patrons ordered two beers at a time, because the price of the second was likely to rise before they finished the first. Cash lost so much of its value that people used it to make toys, as shown at the beginning of this chapter, or to heat their homes, as shown in the accompanying photo.

Huge amounts of money were needed to buy goods. One man went to buy a loaf of bread, pushing his cash in a wheelbarrow. He carelessly left it outside when he entered the store. When he came out, he found that someone had dumped out the cash and stolen the wheelbarrow.

Just as budget deficits caused the hyperinflation, it ended when deficits were eliminated. At the end of 1923, the German government fired a third of its workers and raised taxes. Around the same time, the Allies agreed to reduce reparations and leave the Ruhr. In 1924, the German government ran a budget surplus. Inflation in 1924 was 4 percent.

History is full of dramatic episodes of high inflation. However, as the next case discusses, such episodes are becoming more rare.

CASE STUDY

The Worldwide Decline in Inflation

Figure 14.5 shows the behavior of inflation in several groups of countries in recent decades. Each group's inflation rate is an average of inflation in individual countries, weighted by the country's real GDP. The figure shows that inflation has fallen throughout the world.

In the most advanced economies, (Figure 14.5A), average inflation was 9 percent in the early 1980s. It fell to 2 percent in the late 1990s and has remained near 2 percent in the 2000s. In developing economies (Figure 14.5B), inflation was high in the 1990s but has fallen since then. For example, inflation in Latin America and the Caribbean averaged 254 percent over 1990–1994 and 6 percent in 2005–2007.

Why have inflation rates fallen? Recall that different factors explain different levels of inflation. The stories behind the inflation decreases in advanced economies and in countries with higher initial inflation differ.

▶ As we've noted, Zimbabwe is an exception to the trend toward low inflation. Another exception, though less extreme, is Venezuela. In 1999, Venezuela elected a populist president, Hugo Chavez, and he raised government spending. Venezuela's inflation rate was about 25 percent in 2008.

In advanced economies such as the United States, inflation has fallen largely because policymakers have changed their views about the economy. There have been two related developments.

First, policymakers have become convinced of the long-run neutrality of monetary policy. In the 1960s, many believed that expansionary policy would raise both inflation and output permanently. Policymakers were willing to accept some inflation to keep output high.

In a famous 1968 address, Milton Friedman argued that the effects on output are transitory—the idea of long-run neutrality that we discussed in Section 12.5. It took awhile for Friedman to persuade policymakers, but most were convinced by the early 1980s. Long-run neutrality makes disinflation more attractive: it requires only a temporary sacrifice of output, not a permanent one. A growing belief in this idea prompted central banks in the U.S. and Europe to disinflate in the 1980s.

The second development is that experience with inflation has made policymakers dislike it more. Policymakers of the 1960s and 1970s had lived through the Great Depression of the 1930s. Because of this experience,

FIGURE 14.5 The Worldwide Fall in Inflation

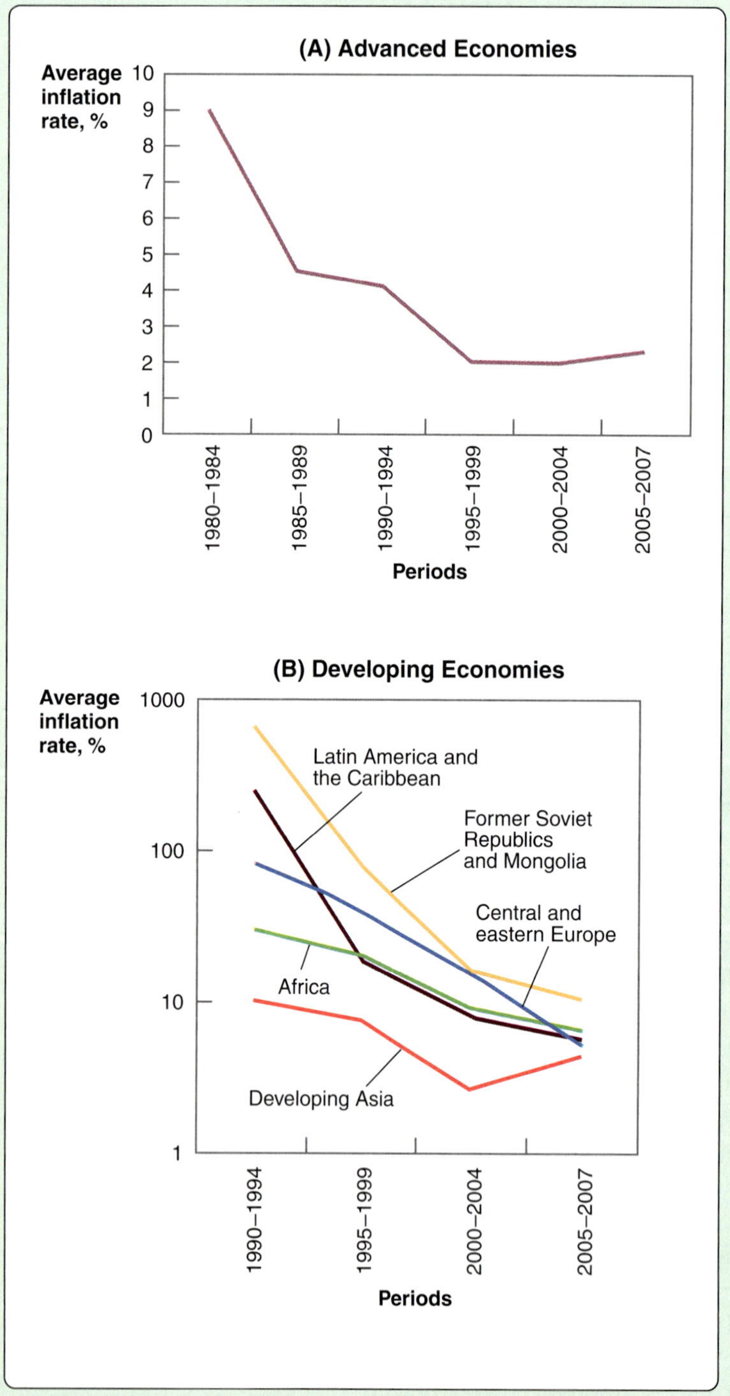

Around the world, inflation has fallen in recent decades. It started falling in advanced economies in the 1980s (A) and in developing economies in the 1990s (B). Both graphs chart average inflation rates in groups of countries over five-year periods and over the three-year period from 2005 through 2007.
Source: International Monetary Fund

they put a priority on keeping unemployment low. When adverse supply shocks occurred in the 1970s—the OPEC oil-price hikes—central banks accommodated them. This policy avoided recessions but allowed inflation to rise.

Eventually, high inflation created a backlash against overly expansionary policy. Today, the inflationary 1970s have replaced the Depression as the "bad old days" that policymakers are determined not to repeat. Since the 1970s, central banks in developed countries have been willing to endure recessions to reduce inflation and keep it low.

In developing countries as well, experience with inflation—often very high inflation—has made policymakers determined to reduce it. Remember, though, that the underlying cause of very high inflation is budget deficits. To reduce inflation, governments have had to reduce deficits.

In many countries, populist governments have been replaced by more conservative ones that reduced spending. In Latin America, for example, average deficits fell from 4.6 percent of GDP over 1970–1989 to 2.7 percent over 1990–2002. In addition, economic reforms have convinced foreigners to lend more to developing countries, reducing the need for seigniorage to finance the deficits that remain.

Peru is one country that reduced inflation dramatically. A left-wing president, Alan Garcia, was elected in 1985. He raised food subsidies and wages for government workers, and the budget deficit reached 9 percent of GDP. Inflation rose to 40 percent per month—almost hyperinflation.

In 1990, a new president, Alberto Fujimori, shifted course. He eliminated subsidies and fired government workers. He cracked down on tax evasion, raising tax revenues from less than 5 percent of GDP in 1990 to 12.5 percent in 1999. Additional revenues came from sales of state-owned firms. These policies produced a budget surplus, and inflation fell to 2 percent per year in 2000. Inflation remained low under Fujimori's successor as president, Alejandro Toledo.

In 2006, Alan Garcia was again elected president. Many people feared that Garcia would produce high inflation, as he had two decades before. But Garcia had learned his lesson. "Do you think," he asked, "I want my tombstone to read 'He was so stupid that he made the same mistakes twice?' " The second Garcia administration has limited government spending and kept the inflation rate close to 2 percent.

Online Case Study:
An Update on Worldwide Inflation

14.3 THE COSTS OF INFLATION

So far we have discussed the causes of inflation. We now turn to its effects. Does inflation harm the economy, and if so how? What levels of inflation are acceptable and what levels are dangerous?

Central bankers believe that inflation is very harmful. Jean-Claude Trichet, the president of the European Central Bank, has called inflation "a betrayal of the people." However, policymakers are often vague in describing *why* inflation is so bad. This reflects the fact that no one fully understands its effects.

Nobody knows, for example, whether annual inflation rates of 5 or 10 percent are truly harmful. Economists have researched this issue, but we have not made much progress. As economist Paul Krugman has put it, "one of the dirty little secrets of economic analysis is that even though inflation is universally regarded as a terrible scourge, efforts to measure its costs come up with embarrassingly small numbers."[2]

The Inflation Fallacy

You may find the last paragraph puzzling. Many people consider it obvious why inflation is harmful. Inflation means that prices of goods and services rise—things become more expensive. People cannot afford to buy as much as before, so their standard of living suffers. In a 1996 survey, 77 percent of the U.S. public agreed with the statement that inflation "hurts my real buying power, making me poorer."

Economists have a different view. When surveyors presented the same statement to economics professors, only 12 percent agreed. Harvard's Gregory Mankiw has called the statement "the inflation fallacy." Economists don't see a necessary connection between inflation and changes in living standards.[3]

[2] See Paul Krugman, *The Age of Diminished Expectations,* MIT Press, 1997.

[3] The survey on attitudes toward inflation is presented in Robert J. Shiller, "Why Do People Dislike Inflation?," in Romer and Romer (eds.), *Reducing Inflation: Motivation and Strategy,* University of Chicago Press, 1997.

The reason is that inflation increases *all* the economy's prices—including wages and salaries. Workers demand wage increases to compensate for inflation, and firms can afford to raise wages because prices are higher. If inflation rises by 1 percent, wage growth normally rises by 1 percent as well. Wages keep pace with inflation, so people can afford the same things as before.

To put it differently, a worker's standard of living depends on her *real* wage—the ratio of her wage to the aggregate price level. Inflation raises the numerator and denominator of this ratio by the same amount, so the real wage is unchanged. The real wage is determined by other factors, such as the worker's productivity.

History supports this reasoning. When U.S. inflation fell from 10 percent to 4 percent in the early 1980s, wage growth slowed as well. Both before and after disinflation, real wages grew about 1 percent per year, reflecting growth in productivity. Lower inflation had no obvious benefit for living standards.

Very High Inflation

This does *not* mean that economists consider inflation harmless. While inflation does not directly reduce living standards, it can hurt the economy in subtler ways. We'll discuss some of the adverse effects of inflation that economists have identified.

As you might expect, inflation costs are easiest to identify when inflation is very high—in the hundreds of percent or more. Effects of high inflation include "shoe leather costs," distracted firms, relative-price variability, and income inequality.

Shoe Leather Costs With high inflation, money loses its value quickly. Anyone who holds a significant amount of money sees his wealth eroded. As a consequence, people try to minimize their money holdings. Lower money holdings mean that transactions become harder, making life less convenient (see Section 4.3).

This effect is important at high inflation rates. To avoid holding cash, people visit their banks frequently, causing long lines. If people lack bank accounts, as is common in developing countries, they rush to buy goods as soon as they receive their pay. They buy things they don't really want just to get rid of cash. These effects of inflation are called **shoe leather costs**—a metaphor referring to the shoe leather worn out on trips to the bank.

Shoe leather costs Inconveniences that result from holding less money when inflation is high

Distracted Firms High inflation causes headaches for the managers of firms. They must push their customers to pay bills promptly, before inflation erodes the value of payments. At the same time, they can reduce costs by delaying payments to other firms. Like people, firms try to minimize money holdings; they constantly move cash into bank accounts with interest that compensates for inflation.

These activities consume managers' time and attention. Coping with inflation leaves less time for normal business activities, such as developing new products or improving productivity. It is difficult to quantity this effect, but some economists think it hurts economic growth.

Relative-Price Variability When inflation is high, all firms raise their prices by large amounts. But they do so at different times. At any moment, some prices are abnormally high compared to others, just because they have adjusted more recently. In other words, inflation causes dispersion in relative prices.

Research has confirmed this effect. For example, an Argentine study found that high inflation increases the variation in prices across different grocery stores. Price differences distort consumers' purchases and firms' sales, harming economic efficiency. And consumers must spend more time comparing prices to get a good deal.[4]

Income Inequality High inflation hurts the overall economy, but the biggest problem may be the unevenness of its effects. Studies from Latin America show that inflation increases the inequality between rich and poor.

One reason is that the poor have relatively large money holdings. They receive their wages in cash and have no bank accounts, so inflation is costly. By contrast, the rich have access to bank accounts with high nominal interest rates that compensate for inflation.

There are also differences in wage adjustment. The salaries of professional workers are often indexed to inflation, meaning they change automatically to preserve their real value. The wages of unskilled workers are slower to adjust when inflation accelerates.

CASE STUDY

Life in Inflationary Brazil

In the 1960s and 1970s, annual inflation in Brazil fluctuated between 28 percent and 77 percent. In the 1980s, it rose steadily, reaching 273 percent in 1985 and 3467 percent in 1990. During the 1980s, Brazil experienced many of the effects of high inflation that we have discussed.

Much effort was directed toward minimizing money holdings. Middle-class Brazilians had "overnight" bank accounts with interest rates adjusted daily to keep up with inflation. However, they could not write checks on these accounts. A typical person visited her bank twice a week and waited in long lines to shift funds to her checking account. People tried to carry the minimum amount of cash to finance daily spending—but frequent price changes made it hard to know how much was needed. Bus fares, for example, often rose from one day to the next.

Many people were paid at the beginning of the month. They rushed to grocery stores to buy a month's food before prices rose. Early in the month, the wait in the grocery checkout line was an hour. People bought extra refrigerators to store their food purchases.

Relative prices varied erratically. Brazilian economist Eliana Cardoso has given some colorful examples: "In the last week of December, 1989, a Chevette cost the same as 42 standard-size brassieres, and a refrigerator the same as a

[4] See Mariano Tommasi, "Inflation and Relative Prices: Evidence from Argentina," in Sheshinski and Weiss (eds.), *Optimal Pricing, Inflation, and Costs of Price Adjustment,* MIT Press, 1993.

FIGURE 14.6 The Real Minimum Wage in Brazil, 1977–1990

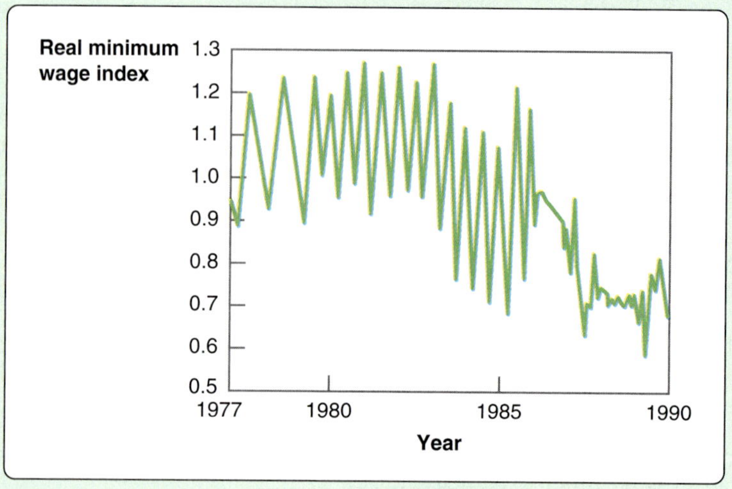

This graph shows an index of Brazil's real minimum wage, with the level in January 1978 defined as 1.0. In the early 1980s, the real wage fluctuated as inflation pushed it down and increases in the nominal wage pushed it back up. In the late 1980s, inflation accelerated and nominal wage adjustments did not keep pace, so the real wage fell.

Source: Adapted from Rudiger Dornbusch et al., "Extreme Inflation: Dynamics and Stabilization," *Brookings Papers on Economic Activity* 1990: 2

linen shirt. The same bottle of wine cost 50 cruzados in one supermarket and 15 cruzados in another." On the bright side, confusion about prices benefited producers of electronic calculators, whose sales doubled from 1988 to 1989.*

As we have discussed, the costs of high inflation are greatest for the poor. In Brazil, the salaries of professional workers were adjusted every month to keep up with inflation. The poor were not protected as well.

Figure 14.6 shows the real minimum wage in Brazil over the 1980s. This wage was reduced by inflation and periodically increased through an increase in the nominal wage. In the early 1980s, the nominal wage was increased twice a year. Workers lost purchasing power between wage adjustments, but it was eventually restored. In the late 1980s, however, inflation accelerated and wage adjustments did not keep pace. By 1989, the real minimum wage fell to around 60 percent of its 1980 level.

* The anecdotes in this case study come from Eliana Cardoso, "Brazil: From Inertia to Megainflation," in Bruno and Fischer (eds.), *Lessons of Economic Stabilization and Its Aftermath*, MIT Press, 1991; and from personal communication with Cristina Terra, another Brazilian economist.

Moderate Inflation

Inflation causes concern even when it is far below the levels Brazilians experienced. We saw that President Ford declared U.S. inflation "Public Enemy Number 1" when it reached 11 percent in 1974. Polls from the 1970s show that the public also viewed inflation as the country's worst problem.

However, most costs we have discussed so far do not appear important for moderate inflation rates—say 10 percent or below. For example, cash loses its value only slowly, so people do not go to much trouble to hold less of it. And U.S. studies find that moderate rises in inflation do *not* raise income inequality.

Some economists conclude that 10 percent inflation is not much of a problem. In this view, public distaste for inflation simply reflects the inflation fallacy. Other economists disagree, suggesting ways that even moderate inflation is harmful. Two costs stand out as possibly most important: increased uncertainty, and distortions of the tax system.

Inflation Uncertainty One view is that 10 percent inflation would *not* be a problem if it were steady—if prices rose exactly 10 percent year after year. In practice, however, the inflation rate bounces around. And studies have found that the variability of inflation is higher when its average level is high. In other words, as inflation rises, it becomes less stable. It is harder to predict future inflation.

Uncertainty about inflation creates risk in loan markets. When inflation changes unpredictably, the ex post real interest rate differs from the ex ante rate (recall the discussion of the late nineteenth century on p. 420). Wealth is redistributed between borrowers and lenders.

This redistribution can harm the economy. An example is the Savings and Loan crisis of the 1980s described in Section 9.6. One cause of the crisis was the unexpected rise in inflation in the 1970s, which reduced ex post real interest rates. Banks' losses in this episode drove many into insolvency, requiring a costly government bailout.

In addition, uncertainty about inflation discourages both borrowers and lenders from entering the loan market. Each group is deterred by the risk of redistributions. The financial system becomes less effective at channeling funds to investors, hurting economic growth.

Inflation and Taxes The final inflation cost we'll discuss involves taxation. When inflation rises, people pay higher taxes on the income they earn from savings.

For example, consider the interest you earn on a bank account. Suppose inflation rises and the nominal interest rate rises by the same amount. Before taxes, the real interest rate is the same as before. (This is the Fisher effect from Section 4.2.) In most countries, however, you pay taxes based on your nominal interest income. This income has risen, so you pay higher taxes on the same real income.

As another example, suppose you purchase a share of stock and sell it for a higher price five years later. You pay a capital gains tax on your profit—the difference between the prices when you buy and sell. When inflation occurs, it causes the price of the stock to increase over time, raising the capital gain in nominal terms. Once again, taxes are based on nominal quantities, so you pay more.

Some economists think that taxes on interest and capital gains discourage saving. When inflation raises these taxes, saving falls. The result is lower investment and lower economic growth.

CASE STUDY

The After-Tax Real Interest Rate

After-tax real interest rate ($\hat{r}$) The interest rate adjusted for both taxes and inflation: $\hat{r} = (1 - \tau)r - \tau\pi$

Previously, we've measured the return on saving with the real interest rate, defined as the nominal rate minus inflation. This concept ignores taxes. When interest income is taxed, the return on saving is the **after-tax real interest rate, $\hat{r}$.** This variable adjusts for the losses from both inflation and taxes. Examining it will help us understand the costs of inflation.

As usual, let i be the nominal interest rate and π be inflation. The real interest rate ignoring taxes is $r = i - \pi$. Finally, let τ (the Greek letter tau) be the tax rate. Savers pay a fraction τ of their nominal interest income in taxes.

After taxes, savers receive a nominal interest rate of $(1 - \tau)i$. For example, if the pretax nominal rate is 10 percent and τ is 0.3, the after-tax nominal rate is $(0.7)(10\%) = 7\%$. Someone with \$100 in the bank receives nominal interest of \$10, pays \$3 in taxes, and is left with \$7.

To get the after-tax real interest rate, we subtract inflation from the after-tax nominal rate:

$$\hat{r} = (1 - \tau)i - \pi$$

Since $i = r + \pi$, we can rewrite the equation for $\hat{r}$ as

$$\hat{r} = (1 - \tau)(r + \pi) - \pi$$

Then a little algebra gives us

$$\begin{aligned}\hat{r} &= (1 - \tau)r + (1 - \tau)\pi - \pi \\ &= (1 - \tau)r - \tau\pi \qquad \textbf{(14.4)}\end{aligned}$$

Equation (14.4) shows how inflation affects the return on savings. Assume that the Fisher effect holds, so inflation has no effect on r, the pretax real interest rate. With this assumption, a 1-point rise in π reduces the after-tax real rate by τ.

This effect can be large. Suppose that r is 4 percent and τ is 0.3. If inflation is zero, then equation (14.4) implies

$$\begin{aligned}\hat{r} &= (1 - 0.3)(4\%) - (0.3)(0) \\ &= 2.8\%\end{aligned}$$

For the same r and τ, if inflation is 10 percent, then

$$\begin{aligned}\hat{r} &= (1 - 0.3)(4\%) - (0.3)(10\%) \\ &= -0.2\%\end{aligned}$$

In this example, inflation wipes out the real return on savings: the negative $\hat{r}$ means that savers lose slightly more from taxes and inflation than they receive in interest. Inflation substantially reduces the incentive to save.

14.4 DEFLATION AND THE LIQUIDITY TRAP

In the 2000s, inflation has been low in most of the world (see Figure 14.5). In some places, inflation has been so low that economists worry about the opposite problem: deflation.

Japan experienced deflation from 1999 to 2005. In the United States, inflation fell to about 1 percent in 2003. It crept back up during the economic recovery of 2004–2005, but deflation was only narrowly averted.

Why do economists worry about deflation? Why might it occur, and what problems might it cause? Once again, in answering these questions we must distinguish among different times and places.

Money Growth Again

The central point of this chapter is that money growth determines inflation. Historically, this principle has explained negative as well as positive inflation. Deflation arises when money growth is low.

In the United States, low money growth caused deflation from 1879 to 1897, during the gold standard period (see Section 14.2). Deflation also occurred from 1930 to 1933, when the money supply fell sharply and inflation averaged −7 percent. The money supply fell because bank panics reduced the money multiplier (review Section 11.4).

Notice that these examples are not recent. Today, there is little risk of deflation caused by low money growth. Central banks know how to control the money supply, and they don't want deflation. If faced with this prospect, they are likely to increase money growth.

The Liquidity Trap

Yet there is still a scenario that can produce deflation. Deflation can occur if the economy falls into a **liquidity trap,** a situation in which the central bank loses its usual ability to control inflation. Let's discuss how this might happen.

Liquidity trap Situation in which output is below potential at a nominal interest rate of zero (a real interest rate of $-\pi$), eliminating the central bank's usual ability to raise output and inflation

Lower Bounds on Interest Rates Recall how the central bank influences short-run economic fluctuations. It sets a target for the nominal interest rate, which helps determine the real interest rate. The real rate affects output through the AE curve, and output affects inflation through the Phillips curve (review Figure 12.16).

In discussing this mechanism, we have assumed that the central bank can set interest rates at whatever levels it chooses. In fact, there is a limit on the central bank's options: it must set a nominal rate of zero or higher. A negative nominal interest rate is impossible.

It is easy to see why. A negative nominal rate means someone pays \$100 for a bond that pays back *less* than \$100 in the future. A saver would never buy such a bond, because she can do better holding cash. If she puts a \$100 bill in a safe deposit box, it is still worth \$100 in the future.

The bound on the nominal interest rate implies a bound on the real rate as well, one that depends on inflation. The real interest rate r is $i - \pi$. Since i cannot go below zero, the real rate cannot go below $-\pi$. For example, if π is 2 percent, the real rate can't be less than -2 percent. If π is 3 percent, the real rate can't be less than -3 percent.

This constraint doesn't matter if the central bank wants an interest rate above the bound. This is usually the case. But a problem can arise if an adverse expenditure shock occurs, causing a recession. To end the recession the central bank must reduce the real interest rate, and the lower bound may get in the way.

Figure 14.7 illustrates this point. The economy starts with output at potential, but then a shock pushes the AE curve to the left. To keep output from falling, the central bank would have to reduce the real interest rate to the level labeled $r^{\#}$. But $r^{\#}$ is less than $-\pi$, the lower bound on the real interest rate. The best that policymakers can do is to reduce the real rate to $-\pi$. With that interest rate, output falls to the level labeled Y', which is below potential.

This situation is a liquidity trap. The term was coined by John Maynard Keynes, who first warned of the problem. Keynes argued that the risk of a

FIGURE 14.7 A Liquidity Trap

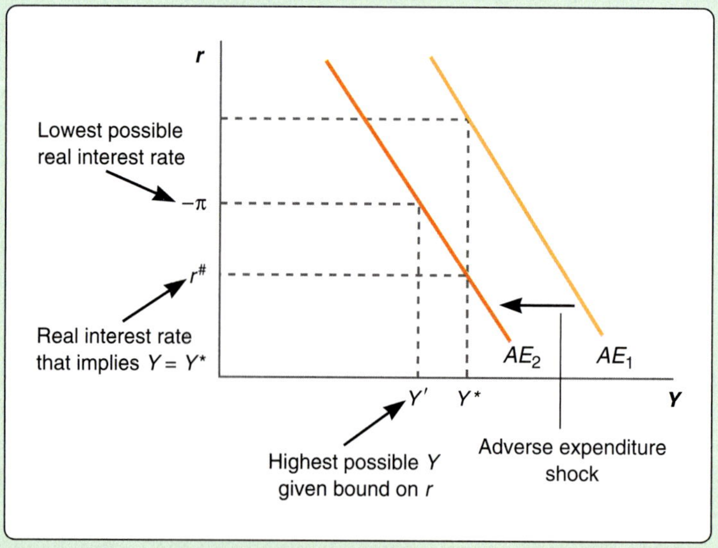

In this example, output starts at potential (Y^*), but then a shock pushes the AE curve to the left. To keep output constant, the central bank would have to reduce the real interest rate to $r^{\#}$, but this is impossible. The real interest rate cannot fall below $-\pi$, which exceeds $r^{\#}$ in this example. With $r = -\pi$, output is Y', which is below Y^*.

liquidity trap makes monetary policy an unreliable tool for combating recessions.

The Role of Deflation We can now see the danger of deflation. The lower bound on the real interest rate is $-\pi$. This bound is negative if $\pi > 0$, but it is positive under deflation. If inflation is -2 percent, for example, the lower bound on the real interest rate is $+2$ percent. A positive bound makes it more likely that the central bank won't be able to end a recession.

U.S. history helps us appreciate this point. In recent decades, the Fed has consistently ended recessions by cutting interest rates (see Section 12.4). Often, the real rate has fallen to about zero. In 2003, for example, the Fed reduced the nominal interest rate to 1.0 percent when inflation was also about 1 percent. By contrast, if deflation occurred, the real interest rate would have to be positive. The Fed couldn't reduce the real rate as much as it has in past recessions.

Danger also exists if the inflation rate is positive but low. Say inflation is 1 or 2 percent, and an adverse expenditure shock occurs. Time lags mean the central bank can't offset this shock immediately (review Section 13.4). Output is likely to fall for some time, reducing inflation. Since inflation started at a low level, it may fall below zero. Deflation has begun, with the risk of a liquidity trap.

If an economy enters a liquidity trap, it is hard to get out. A vicious cycle can arise, with deflation and the liquidity trap reinforcing one another. **Figure 14.8** outlines this scenario. Deflation raises the bound on the real interest rate, which means the central bank can't raise output. Low output causes further deflation through the Phillips curve. Further deflation keeps

FIGURE 14.8 A Vicious Cycle

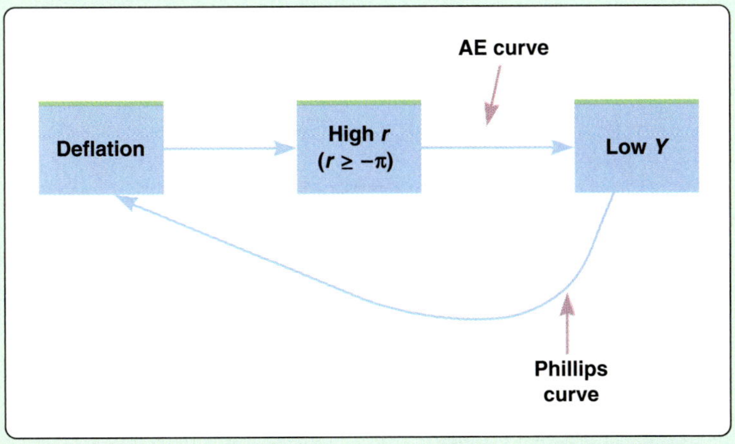

A liquidity trap with deflation and low output can perpetuate itself. Deflation raises the lower bound on the real interest rate, $-\pi$; a high real interest rate keeps output low; and low output causes further deflation.

the real interest rate high, which keeps output low, and so on. The economy can be stuck in this cycle indefinitely.

The Irrelevance of Money Growth We've seen how an economy can get stuck in deflation. However, this idea may seem inconsistent with the first part of this chapter, where we stressed the long-run link between inflation and money growth. If inflation is negative, why can't the central bank push it above zero by raising money growth?

The answer is that the normal money growth–inflation relation breaks down in a liquidity trap. Remember Figure 14.4, which shows how money growth affects the economy. Higher money growth pushes down interest rates, which raises output, which raises inflation. A liquidity trap breaks the first link in this chain: higher money growth does *not* reduce interest rates, because they are already at their lower bounds. Since interest rates do not fall, output does not rise and neither does inflation.

Figure 14.9 shows what happens in the money market. The money demand curve usually slopes down, but it becomes flat at a zero nominal interest rate. The horizontal demand curve means that people are willing to hold any amount of money. The usual reason for holding other assets—to earn interest—disappears if the interest rate is zero.

On the flat part of the money demand curve, the money supply has no effect on the nominal interest rate. If the central bank raises the money

FIGURE 14.9 The Market for Money in a Liquidity Trap

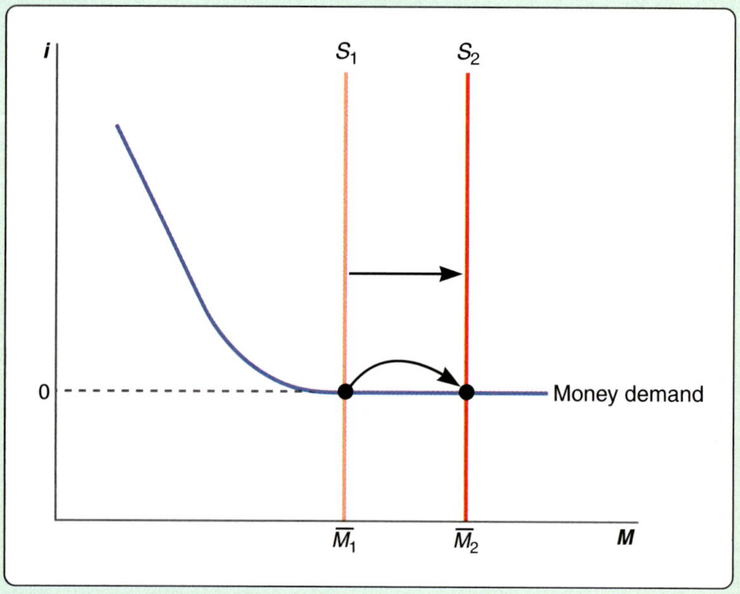

The money demand curve becomes horizontal at a nominal interest rate of zero. In a liquidity trap, money-market equilibrium occurs on the horizontal part of money demand, and an increase in the money supply does not change the interest rate.

supply from $\overline{M}_1$ to $\overline{M}_2$, the equilibrium interest rate remains at zero. We see again that the usual effects of monetary policy disappear.

Is there any way to escape a liquidity trap? Keynes, who pointed out the problem, also suggested a solution: expansionary fiscal policy. An increase in government spending or a tax cut shifts out the AE curve, raising output at the current real interest rate (see Figure 13.14). A high enough output level raises inflation through the Phillips curve; deflation ends and the bound on the real interest rate falls below zero.

Sometimes, however, governments are unwilling to cut taxes or raise spending. In this case, deflation can persist for a long time. This brings us to the case of Japan.

CASE STUDY

Japan's Liquidity Trap

Section 13.2 discussed Japan's deep recession of the 1990s and early 2000s. **Figure 14.10A** captures this slump by comparing Japan's output to estimates of its potential output. The estimates are based on the assumptions that actual and potential output were equal in 1990 and that potential has grown 2 percent per year since then.* The difference between the two variables—Japan's output gap—reached 14 percent in 2003.

The initial causes of Japan's recession were banking problems and a collapse in asset prices. Over the 1990s, the slump was exacerbated by other expenditure shocks, including a fall in consumer confidence, reduced exports during the East Asian financial crisis, and a tax increase in 1997.

A predicted by the Phillips curve, Japan's recession reduced inflation. As

FIGURE 14.10 Japan's Liquidity Trap

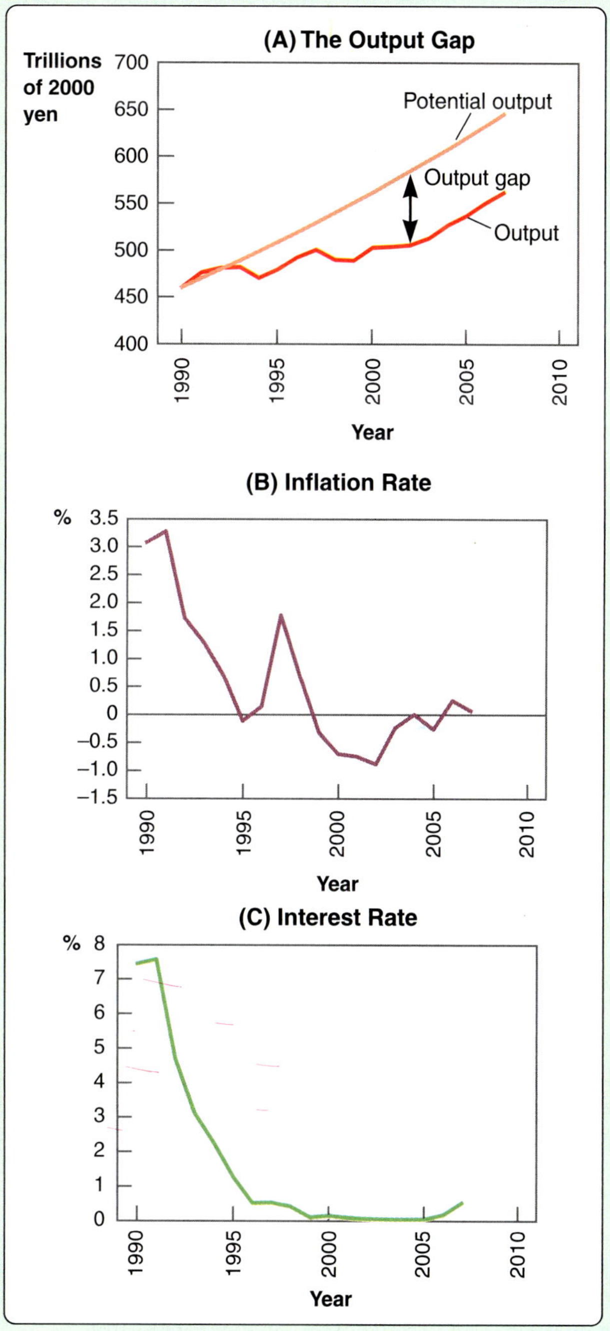

Japan's output gap became negative in the 1990s and reached −14 percent in 2003 (A). The negative output gap reduced inflation, which fell below zero in 1999 (B). The Bank of Japan sought to raise output by lowering the interest rate it targets, the call money rate, but this rate reached zero in 1999 (C). The economy entered a liquidity trap that lasted until 2006, when signs of recovery led the BOJ to raise the interest rate slightly.

Source: International Monetary Fund

shown in **Figure 14.10B**, the inflation rate fell below zero in 1999 and remained negative through 2005. Japan experienced deflation.

The Bank of Japan tried to raise output through countercyclical policy. As shown in Figure **14.10C**, the BOJ started reducing the interest rate that it targets, the call-money rate, in 1992. However, lower rates did not stimulate spending enough to offset the adverse shocks to the economy. In 1999, the nominal interest rate fell below 1/10 of a percent: for practical purposes, it was zero. At that point, Japan was stuck in a liquidity trap. Output was below potential, but further interest-rate cuts were impossible.

With the interest rate at zero, the Bank of Japan performed large, expansionary open-market operations. As a result, M1 in Japan grew by 14 percent in 2001 and by 24 percent in 2002. However, as predicted by our analysis of liquidity traps, rapid money growth did not raise output or inflation.

As the recession dragged on, some economists advocated Keynes's solution, a fiscal expansion. However, Japan's government debt was so high that its bond rating was falling (review Section 4.5). The government rejected a fiscal expansion that would raise debt further; indeed, it sought to reduce debt through a fiscal *contraction,* the tax increase of 1997.

Japan's economy has improved somewhat since 2003: output is still below potential, but the gap is narrowing. As discussed in Section 13.2, growth has been spurred by rising exports and banking reforms. Believing the worst is over, the Bank of Japan raised its interest rate target from 0 to 1/4 of a percent in 2006, and to half a percent in 2007. Some economists have criticized these actions, however. They think it is premature to raise interest rates because Japan's recovery is fragile.

* A number of economists have argued that these assumptions are reasonable. See, for example, Takeo Hoshi and Anil Kashyap, "Japan's Financial Crisis and Economic Stagnation," *Journal of Economic Perspectives,* Winter 2004.

Summary

- Inflation varies tremendously across countries and time periods. It ranges from negative levels (deflation) to hyperinflation (monthly inflation above 50 percent).

14.1 MONEY AND INFLATION IN THE LONG RUN

- The velocity of money is the ratio of nominal GDP to the money supply. It measures how quickly money circulates through the economy. Factors that raise money demand also reduce velocity.
- The quantity equation of money is $MV = PY$: the money supply times velocity equals nominal GDP.
- Long-run inflation is determined by the growth rates of the money supply, velocity, and real output. The central bank can raise or lower inflation by changing money growth.
- Empirically, there is a close relation between money growth and inflation across countries and across decades within a country. However, this relation does not explain short-run, year-to-year inflation movements.
- Money growth influences inflation through a chain of effects: higher money growth reduces interest rates, which raises output, which raises inflation.

14.2 WHAT DETERMINES MONEY GROWTH?

- When money is backed by a commodity, money growth and inflation are determined by how much of the commodity is produced.

- Under the gold standard in the United States, low gold production led to deflation in the late nineteenth century. The adverse effects on debtors spurred a campaign for bimetallism, a system in which money is backed by gold and silver. Bimetallism was not adopted, but increased gold production eventually ended deflation.
- With fiat money, central banks choose the growth rate of the money supply. Often they choose low money growth to keep inflation low.
- Sometimes central banks allow money growth and inflation to rise to avoid a fall in output. For example, U.S. inflation rose in the 1970s because the Fed accommodated adverse supply shocks, and it stayed high because the Fed was unwilling to pay the costs of disinflation.
- The underlying cause of very high inflation is government budget deficits. If governments cannot borrow, they finance deficits with seigniorage revenue—by printing money. The money supply rises rapidly, fueling inflation. One famous example is the German hyperinflation of 1923.
- Today, inflation is low in most of the world. It fell in developed countries in the 1980s as policymakers decided to pay the output costs of disinflation. It fell in developing countries in the 1990s as conservative governments cut budget deficits.

14.3 THE COSTS OF INFLATION

- Many people believe that inflation erodes living standards, but this view is fallacious. A rise in inflation causes a parallel rise in nominal wage growth, so real wages are not affected.
- Very high inflation causes inconvenience as people hold less money (shoe leather costs), distracts firms from their business, causes variability in relative prices, and worsens income inequality.
- The costs of moderate inflation are unclear. Possible costs include effects of inflation uncertainty and distortions of the tax system. Inflation reduces the after-tax real interest rate, which may discourage saving.

14.4 DEFLATION AND THE LIQUIDITY TRAP

- In the past, deflations have been caused by low money growth, as in the U.S. in the 1890s and 1930s.
- A liquidity trap means that output is below potential when the nominal interest rate is zero. The central bank loses its usual ability to end a recession, because a rise in money growth doesn't affect interest rates.
- Deflation increases the risk of a liquidity trap. An economy can fall into a vicious cycle of recession, deflation, and high real interest rates.
- Japan experienced a liquidity trap in the early 2000s. The nominal interest rate was zero from 1999 to 2006.

Key Terms

after-tax real interest rate, p. 432
bimetallism, p. 420
deflation, p. 413
hyperinflation, p. 413
liquidity trap, p. 433
printing money, p. 423
quantity equation of money, p. 415
seigniorage revenue, p. 423
shoe leather costs, p. 428
velocity of money, p. 414

Questions and Problems

1. Suppose that country A and country B have the same rate of money growth and velocity is constant in both. Output growth is higher in country A. Which country has higher inflation? Explain.
2. In Figure 14.1, the relation between money growth and inflation is less perfect among countries with inflation below ten percent than it is among countries with higher inflation. What might explain this difference?

3. Should the United States return to the gold standard? What might be the advantages and disadvantages?

4. [Advanced] Assume that a central bank's nominal seigniorage revenue equals the change in the money supply, denoted ΔM. Real seigniorage revenue is $\Delta M/P$. Assume the inflation rate equals the growth rate of the money supply, which is $\Delta M/M$.
   a. What is the rationale for these assumptions? Are they realistic?
   b. Write real seigniorage revenue in terms of the inflation rate and the real money supply, M/P.
   c. When inflation rises, what happens to the real money supply and to seigniorage revenue? (*Hint:* In equilibrium, money supply must equal money demand.)
   d. Sometimes a small increase in the government budget deficit produces a large increase in inflation. Explain this fact using the answer to part (c).

5. Suppose all firms in an economy adjust prices once per year. Half the firms adjust prices in January, and half adjust in July. Suppose inflation rises from zero to 10 percent per year. What is the likely effect on the variability of relative prices? Explain.

6. Consider the market for loanable funds, which determines the real interest rate in the long run (see Section 4.1).
   a. As usual, draw the supply and demand for loans as functions of the *pretax* real interest rate, r.
   b. Suppose savers are taxed on their nominal interest income. If inflation rises, what happens to the supply and demand curves in part (a)?
   c. What happens to the equilibrium levels of the pretax real interest rate, loans, and investment?

7. Suppose the pretax real interest rate (r) is 2 percent, the tax rate (τ) is 0.4, and the inflation rate (π) is 8 percent. Calculate the after-tax real interest rate ($\hat{r}$).

8. What inflation rate would make the after-tax real interest rate equal the pretax real rate (that is, what inflation rate implies $\hat{r} = r$)? Explain.

9. Explain the difference between deflation and disinflation.

10. "Inflation is always and everywhere a monetary phenomenon, but deflation is not." Comment.

11. How does each of the following events affect the risk of a liquidity trap?
    a. The central bank decides to push long-run inflation to zero.
    b. The neutral real interest rate rises (see Section 12.5 for a review of the neutral rate).
    c. The government introduces a tax on people's holdings of currency. Other assets are not taxed.

Online and Data Questions

www.worthpublishers.com/ball

12. Link from the text Web site to the St. Louis Fed site for data on (1) nominal GDP and (2) interest rates on 3-month Treasury bills. Link to sweepmeasures.com for data on M1 adjusted for sweep accounts (use the series labeled M1RS).
    a. Using these data, compute the velocity of money for each year from 1980 to the present. Make a graph showing velocity and the T-bill rate over time.
    b. Does velocity fluctuate from year to year? What might explain these movements?
    c. What is the long-run trend in velocity? What might explain this trend?

13. Link from the text Web site to the site of the International Labour Organization, whose LABORSTA database reports consumer price indices for most of the world's countries. For a recent year, identify the country with the highest inflation rate (that is, the largest percentage change in its price index). Do some research and explain why inflation is high in that country.

14. [Advanced] From the St. Louis Fed Web site, get annual data on U.S. inflation from 1960 to the present.
    a. For each decade from the 1960s to the 2000s, calculate the mean and variance of inflation over the decade. For example, calculate the mean and variance for the 10 years from 1960 through 1969.
    b. Make a graph that plots the mean of inflation against the variance, with a point for each decade. What is the relation between the two variables?
    c. What might explain the relation found in part (b)?

chapter fifteen 15

Policies for Economic Stability

- 15.1 CHOOSING THE LONG-RUN INFLATION RATE
- 15.2 INFLATION AND OUTPUT STABILITY
- 15.3 THE TAYLOR RULE
- 15.4 THE TAYLOR RULE IN THE AE/PC MODEL
- 15.5 UNCERTAINTY AND POLICY MISTAKES
- 15.6 MAKING INTEREST-RATE POLICY
- 15.7 MONETARY POLICY AND FINANCIAL EVENTS

Martin Sundberg/Getty Images

These sailors are leaning against the wind. We'll see the relevance to monetary policy in section 15.3.

Suppose you do very well in your money and banking course. You embark on a brilliant career as an economist or banker. Eventually, you are appointed chair of the Board of Governors of the Federal Reserve System. In this job, you run the monetary policy of the United States. What should you do?

The U.S. Congress has provided some guidance. Congress created the Federal Reserve in 1913. It prescribed goals for the Fed in the Employment Act of 1946 and the Humphrey-Hawkins Act of 1978. On its Web site, the Fed summarizes these goals as "maximum sustainable output growth," "maximum employment," "stable prices," and "moderate long-term interest rates."[1]

Unfortunately, these goals are a bit vague. As the new Fed chair, you may have some questions. What exactly do the goals mean—for example, what is the "maximum" level of employment? Can the Fed really achieve all the goals? How? What if one goal conflicts with another?

Part V of this book—the last four chapters—surveys current thinking about monetary policy. We discuss the goals of the Fed and other central banks, their strategies for pursuing these goals, and the challenges they face.

[1] See *The Federal Reserve System: Purposes and Functions,* Chapter 2, www.federalreserve.gov.

This chapter discusses two basic tasks of a central bank. The first is to choose the long-run level of inflation. As we saw in Section 14.1, the central bank controls this variable because it controls the money supply. We'll discuss the question of what long-run inflation rate is best.

The central bank's second task is to stabilize the economy. As we discuss in Chapter 12, expenditure and supply shocks cause output and inflation to fluctuate around their long-run levels. Central banks can dampen these movements with the right policies—or exacerbate them with policy mistakes. We'll discuss the pros and cons of alternative stabilization policies.

We've seen that most central banks target a short-term interest rate. In this regime, stabilization policy takes the form of interest-rate adjustments. We'll discuss theories of how central banks should move their targets in response to economic developments. We'll also discuss practical aspects of U.S. policy—how people at the Fed analyze the economy and choose targets for the federal funds rate.

15.1 CHOOSING THE LONG-RUN INFLATION RATE

Economic shocks cause short-run movements in the inflation rate, which central banks cannot eliminate. But central banks control long-run inflation—the average level around which inflation fluctuates. What long-run inflation rate should policymakers choose?

Congress has told the Federal Reserve to seek "stable prices." In response, the Fed has kept inflation low in recent decades. Central banks in most other countries have also produced low inflation (see the case study in Section 14.2).

The Fed's mandate also includes "moderate long-term interest rates"—which means nominal rates that are not too high. However, this is not really a separate goal. The Fisher equation, Equation (4.1), says that the nominal interest rate is the real rate plus expected inflation: $i = r + \pi^e$. The Fed doesn't influence the real rate in the long run, but it does influence expected inflation. If it consistently keeps actual inflation low, then expected inflation will also be low, holding down the nominal interest rate. If the Fed produces "stable prices," it produces moderate interest rates as well.

The precise meaning of "stable prices" is debatable. Some economists define this term as the complete absence of inflation. They argue that the long-run inflation rate should be zero. Others believe that a low but positive rate—say 1 percent or 2 percent—also constitutes price stability, and that a little inflation is good for the economy. Let's discuss these two points of view.

The Case for Zero Inflation

The case for zero inflation is simple. Inflation has harmful effects on the economy. For example, it causes variability in relative prices, and its interaction with the tax system discourages saving (see Section 14.3). The lower the inflation rate, the smaller these distortions. They are minimized if inflation is pushed all the way to zero.

Unfortunately, your work is far from done. The economy will not stay tranquilly in long-run equilibrium. It will be buffeted by expenditure and supply shocks—changes in fiscal policy, consumer confidence, oil prices, and so on—causing short-run fluctuations in output and inflation. As Fed chair, you can't eliminate these fluctuations completely. But part of your job is to dampen them as much as possible, keeping output and inflation close to their long-run levels.

The rest of this chapter discusses central banks' methods for stabilizing output and inflation. Let's first look more closely at why stability is desirable.

Inflation Stability

Inflation has a number of different costs. Some depend on the long-run level of inflation, but others depend on inflation variability. If the long-run inflation rate is 2 percent, for example, the resulting distortions are minimized if inflation stays close to that level. The economy suffers more if inflation bounces much above and below 2 percent from year to year.

▶ We can express these ideas with terms you may know from statistics. The long-run level of inflation is the *mean* of the inflation rate. Fluctuations around the long-run level determine the *variance* of the inflation rate. Some costs of inflation depend on the mean and some on the variance.

Why is unstable inflation costly? One reason, discussed in Section 14.3, is the effect on loan markets. Variability in inflation causes variability in ex post real interest rates, which increases risk for both borrowers and lenders. Greater risk reduces the level of lending, hurting investment and economic growth.

Unstable inflation also exacerbates the problem of relative price variability. If inflation is steady, firms adjust prices periodically to keep up with it, and different prices tend to stay in line with one another. If inflation is unpredictable, by contrast, firms are likely to make different guesses about appropriate price adjustments. Some firms raise prices more quickly than others, causing inefficient movements in relative prices.

Output Stability

Congress tells the Fed to seek "maximum sustainable output growth" and "maximum employment." However, the Fed's ability to influence output and employment is limited: monetary policy does not affect these variables in the long run. This is the principle of long-run neutrality discussed in Section 12.5.

Monetary policy *does* affect short-run movements in output and employment. Central banks try to minimize the year-to-year fluctuations of these variables around their long-run levels. In other words, central banks try to dampen the business cycle.

Figure 15.1 illustrates this idea. It shows the path of an economy's output when the central bank succeeds in stabilizing output, and when it doesn't. Note that potential output, which determines output in the long run, follows the same path in the two cases. Potential output is not affected by monetary policy. The difference between the two scenarios is that successful policy keeps output closer to potential.

Central banks want to stabilize unemployment as well as output. But recall Okun's law (Equation (12.1)): output and unemployment move together closely over the business cycle. Reducing fluctuations in output

FIGURE 15.1 Reducing the Business Cycle

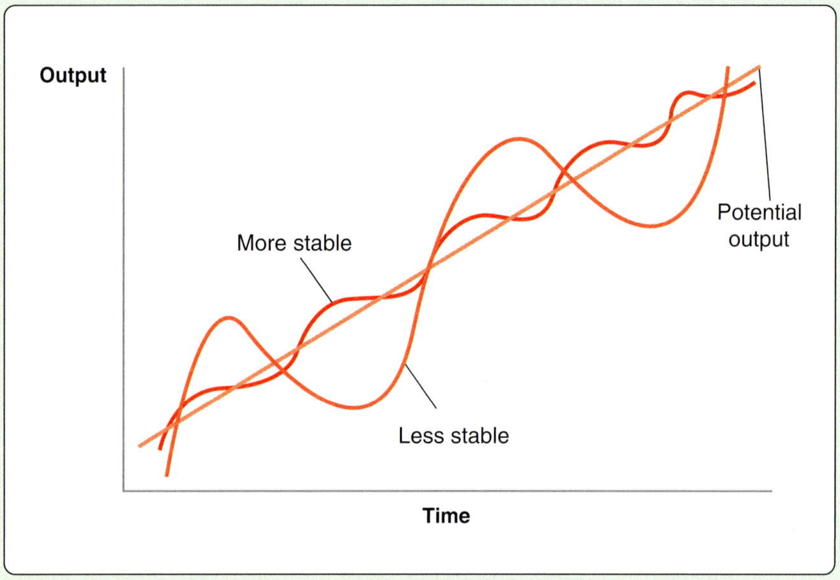

One goal of monetary policy is to dampen fluctuations in aggregate output, keeping it close to potential output.

automatically reduces fluctuations in unemployment. So the two goals are really the same, just as the goals of price stability and moderate interest rates are the same.

Balancing the Goals

Central banks want to stabilize both output and inflation. Sometimes the right policies can achieve both goals, but sometimes the goals conflict. As we'll see, a policy that stabilizes output can destabilize inflation, and vice versa. In such situations, the central bank must decide which type of stability is more important.

This is another unresolved question. As we discuss in section 14.3, economists don't understand the effects of inflation very well. Thus we don't know how important it is to stabilize inflation. The benefits of output stability are also unclear, as the next case study relates.

CASE STUDY

How Costly Is the Business Cycle?

Stabilizing output means reducing the size of the business cycle. Is this desirable? At first glance, the answer might seem obvious. The business cycle includes recessions when output falls and unemployment rises. Recessions create hardship for people who find themselves with lower income or even without a job. Clearly it is desirable to reduce the size of recessions.

However, the business cycle includes economic booms as well as recessions. Both are dampened if the business cycle is reduced. This is shown in Figure 15.1: with greater stability, output falls less in recessions and rises less in booms. By Okun's law, unemployment rises less in recessions and falls less in booms. It is not clear that there are large overall benefits.

Consider an example. Suppose the natural rate of unemployment is 5 percent. Initially, there is a sizable business cycle. Half the time the economy is in recession, with 7 percent unemployment, and half the time it experiences a boom, with 3 percent unemployment. On average, unemployment equals the natural rate of 5 percent.

Now suppose the central bank manages to eliminate the business cycle, so unemployment is 5 percent at all times. Obviously, this stabilization does not reduce average unemployment. It just smooths unemployment over time, moving some of it from recession years to boom years. Some economists argue that this doesn't benefit society very much.

Others disagree, arguing that stabilization is highly beneficial. In their view, we can't determine the value of stabilization simply by examining average unemployment, because unemployment has different costs in different circumstances. In particular, it's worse for a worker to be unemployed during a recession, when many other workers are also unemployed, than during a period when unemployment is at or below its natural rate.

To see this point, think about a worker who becomes unemployed, losing his normal source of income. This person can support himself temporarily with savings and unemployment insurance, but these are exhausted at some point. A spell of unemployment can produce severe hardship if it drags on for a long time. And this is most likely to happen during a recession, when many people are looking for work and jobs are scarce. If a worker loses his job when the economy is healthy, he has a better chance of finding a new job quickly.

If this argument is correct, then dampening the business cycle benefits society even if it doesn't reduce the average unemployment rate. It is desirable to move unemployment from recessions to booms because unemployment is less painful in booms. This reasoning is speculative, however, and the costs of business cycles remain controversial. In the end, these costs are much like the costs of inflation: many economists think they are large, but nobody has identified them precisely.*

* For an in-depth discussion of the costs of business cycles, see Chapter 10 of David Romer, *Advanced Macroeconomics* (3rd ed.), McGraw Hill, 2006.

15.3 THE TAYLOR RULE

Now that we've discussed the goals of output and inflation stability, let's see how central banks try to achieve these goals. Most central banks use a short-term interest rate as their policy instrument. As a result, stabilization policy takes the form of interest-rate adjustments. Central banks must decide when to raise or lower interest rates, and by how much.

Martin's Metaphor

When shocks push output and inflation away from their long-run levels, the central bank adjusts the real interest rate to push them back. In a recession, for example, the central bank cuts the interest rate to return output to potential. If inflation rises, the central bank raises the interest rate to slow the economy and push inflation down.

This is an old idea. In the 1950s, Federal Reserve Chair William McChesney Martin expressed it with a metaphor based on sailing. He said the Fed's job is to "lean against the wind"—where "wind" means movements in inflation and output.

Martin's metaphor captures the basic idea of stabilization policy, but it does not yield very precise instructions for central banks. When exactly should they lean against the wind, and how hard should they lean? In other words, what interest rate should they set in various circumstances? Economists have long debated these questions.

Taylor's Formula

A breakthrough in analyzing stabilization policy came in 1993, in a paper by John Taylor of Stanford University. Much of current thinking about stabilization is based on the **Taylor rule** proposed in that paper. Taylor's insight was to express the idea of leaning against the wind in a simple equation. The equation gives a precise rule, or formula, for setting the interest rate:[3]

Taylor rule Formula for adjusting the interest rate to stabilize the economy: $r = r^n + a_y\tilde{Y} + a_\pi(\pi - \pi^T)$

THE TAYLOR RULE

$$r = r^n + a_y\tilde{Y} + a_\pi(\pi - \pi^T) \qquad \textbf{(15.1)}$$

In this equation, r is the ex ante real interest rate, $i - \pi^e$. In the short run, the central bank's control of the nominal interest rate allows it to control this real rate as well (review Section 12.3). Under the Taylor rule, the central bank sets r based on several factors:

▶ We can also define the Taylor rule with a formula for the nominal interest rate. Substituting the definition of r, $i - \pi^e$, into (15.1) leads to $i = \pi^e + r^n + a_y\tilde{Y} + a_\pi(\pi - \pi^T)$. This equation and (15.1) are two ways of expressing the same policy.

- The neutral real interest rate, r^n. This term is the interest rate that makes output (Y) equal potential output (Y^*).
- The output gap, $\tilde{Y}$. This variable is the percentage deviation of output from potential: $\tilde{Y} = (Y - Y^*)/Y^*$.
- The *inflation gap*, $\pi - \pi^T$. The term π^T is the central bank's long-run inflation target—either explicit or implicit. The inflation gap is the current deviation of inflation from the target.
- The coefficients a_y and a_π. These terms are positive constants that measure how strongly the interest rate responds to the output and inflation gaps. If $a_y = 0.5$, for example, then a one percentage point rise in the output gap raises the interest rate by half a percentage point.

[3] See John Taylor, "Policy Rules in Practice," *Carnegie-Rochester Conference Series on Public Policy,* December 1993.

To understand the Taylor rule, suppose first that the economy is in long-run equilibrium. The output gap is zero and inflation is at its target: $\pi = \pi^T$. In this situation, the last two terms in the rule are zero, so the rule says $r = r^n$. The central bank sets the interest rate to the neutral level to maintain the status quo.

Now suppose that output changes. If the output gap rises above zero—there is an economic boom—the Taylor rule says to raise the interest rate above r^n. If the output gap is negative, the rule says to reduce the interest rate. In each case, the central bank leans against the wind.

The Taylor rule also prescribes interest-rate adjustments when the inflation rate departs from its long-run level. Once again the central bank leans against the wind, raising the real interest rate when inflation rises and reducing it when inflation falls.

Applying the Rule

To use the Taylor rule, we must assign numbers to some of its terms. Let's assume the central bank's inflation target, π^T, is 2 percent. The neutral real interest rate is 1.8 percent. These numbers are reasonable estimates for the United States in recent years.

For the coefficients in the Taylor rule, assume $a_y = 1.0$ and $a_\pi = 0.5$. We will see that these numbers fit the behavior of the Fed. With our assumptions, the Taylor rule (Equation (15.1)) becomes

$$r = 1.8 + 1.0\tilde{Y} + 0.5(\pi - 2.0) \tag{15.2}$$

Equation (15.2) prescribes a real interest rate for any state of the economy. For example, suppose the output gap is 1 percent and the inflation rate is 3 percent. Then the equation says

$$\begin{aligned} r &= 1.8 + 1.0(1.0) + 0.5(3.0 - 2.0) \\ &= 3.3 \end{aligned}$$

In this example, output is above potential and inflation is above its target. To slow the economy, the central bank chooses a real interest rate of 3.3 percent, which is higher than the neutral rate.

The Rule in Action

The Taylor rule is not just a theoretical idea about monetary policy. It has become famous because it appears to capture the actual behavior of the Federal Reserve. Over the last two decades, the interest rates chosen by the Fed have usually been close to the rates prescribed by the Taylor rule.

Figure 15.2 demonstrates this point. For the period from 1987 through 2007, the figure shows the real interest rates implied by the Taylor rule. The calculations assume the specific version of the rule in Equation (15.2), with coefficients of $a_y = 1.0$ and $a_\pi = 0.5$. The figure also shows the actual path of the real federal funds rate chosen by the Federal Open Market Committee. The two series move together fairly closely, suggesting that the Taylor rule is a good summary of Fed policy.

FIGURE 15.2 The Fed and the Taylor Rule

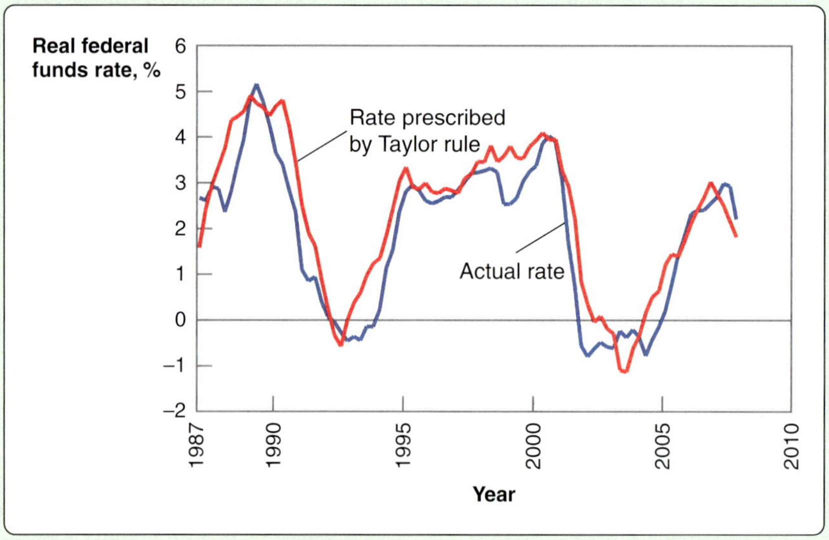

This graph compares the real federal funds rate over 1987–2007 to the rate implied by the Taylor rule in Equation (15.2). The Taylor rule is a fairly good approximation to how the Fed sets interest rates. Visit the text Web site for details on the measurement of the real interest rate, inflation, and the output gap.

Sources: Federal Reserve Bank of St. Louis and author's calculations

To be clear, the FOMC does not consciously follow the Taylor rule. It does not use any simple formula to choose interest rates. Instead, as we discuss in Section 15.6, policymaking is a complicated process in which Fed economists analyze hundreds of variables. Nonetheless, this process usually produces interest rates that are close to those implied by the Taylor rule. The rule seems to capture the most important factors behind policy choices.

Since Taylor's article, economists have applied his idea to many countries. It appears that some version of the Taylor rule fits the behavior of many central banks. However, the coefficients in the rule, a_y and a_π, are not always the same.

15.4 THE TAYLOR RULE IN THE AE/PC MODEL

We've seen that the Taylor rule captures much of the behavior of monetary policy in the United States and elsewhere. We've also discussed the basic rationale for the rule: by leaning against the wind, monetary policy stabilizes output and inflation. We can explore the Taylor rule in more depth using the AE/PC model of economic fluctuations. The model shows how the Taylor rule stabilizes the economy when expenditure and supply shocks occur. It also shows how the choices of a_y and a_π, the coefficients in the rule, affect the economy.

An online appendix to this chapter analyzes the Taylor rule in the AE/PC model. This analysis uses a version of the model with time lags, which capture the fact that central banks can't shift output or inflation immediately. Here we summarize some of the results of the analysis. Consult the appendix if you are interested in the precise assumptions and math behind the results.

An Example

TABLE 15.2 Two Possible Taylor Rules

TR-I (more aggressive)
$r = 2.5 + 1.0\tilde{Y} + 1.0(\pi - 2.0)$
TR-II (less aggressive)
$r = 2.5 + 0.5\tilde{Y} + 0.5(\pi - 2.0)$

Initially we examine one specific version of the Taylor rule, labeled TR-I in **Table 15.2**. We assume the neutral real interest rate is 2.5 percent and the inflation target is 2.0 percent. The coefficients on output and inflation, a_y and a_π, are both 1.0.

To see the implications of this rule, suppose that in 2019 the economy is in long-run equilibrium: the output gap is zero (Figure 15.3A) and the inflation rate equals the target of 2 percent (Figure 15.3B). In 2020, an adverse supply shock occurs. This shock causes inflation to jump from 2 percent to 4 percent.

Figure 15.3 shows how monetary policy and the economy respond to the shock. Because the inflation rate rises in 2020, the Taylor rule prescribes an increase in the real interest rate. Specifically, since the coefficient a_π is 1.0, the 2-point rise in inflation implies an interest rate increase of 2 points. The central bank raises the interest rate from 2.5 percent, the neutral level, to 4.5 percent (Figure 15.3C).

Because of time lags, the interest rate increase in 2020 does not affect output or inflation in that year. However, through the AE curve, the high interest rate in 2020 reduces output in 2021. Through the Phillips curve, low output reduces inflation in 2022. At that point, inflation is back to the 2 percent target and the output gap is zero. This example illustrates a general point: *when a shock pushes the economy away from long-run equilibrium, the Taylor rule guides it back.*

In this example, the interest rate increase lasts for only one year: r rises in 2020 but returns to r^n in 2021. To understand why, notice that output is below potential in 2021, which reduces r in the Taylor rule. But inflation is still above target in 2021, which increases r. The two effects cancel, implying $r = r^n$. In 2022, r stays at r^n because the economy is back in long-run equilibrium.

Choosing the Coefficients

The effects of the Taylor rule depend on the coefficients a_y and a_π—on how strongly policy leans against the wind. Economists debate which coefficients are best. To see some of the issues involved, let's compare the two Taylor rules

FIGURE 15.3 The Taylor Rule and a Supply Shock

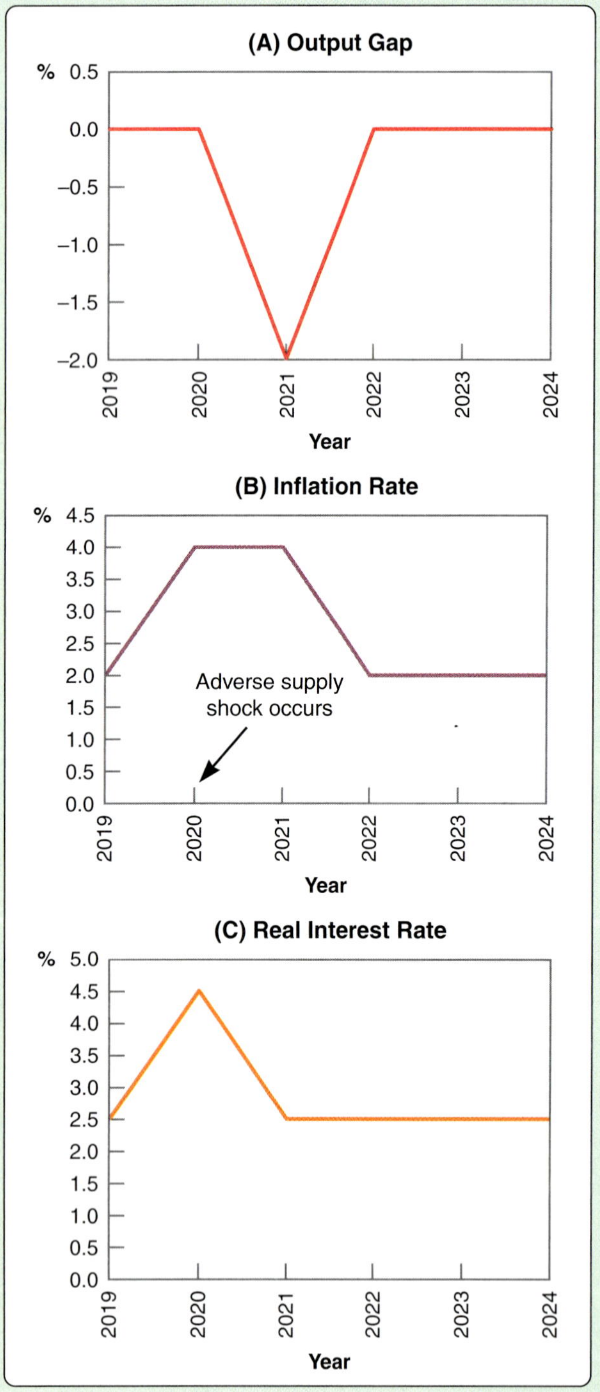

In this example, a supply shock raises inflation by 2 percentage points in 2020. The central bank follows the Taylor rule TR-I in Table 15.2, which guides the economy back to long-run equilibrium.

in Table 15.2. We assumed TR-I in our previous example. The other rule, TR-II, has smaller coefficients: both a_y and a_π are 0.5 rather than 1.0. Smaller coefficients mean that *r* changes by less for given movements in output and inflation. The central bank responds less aggressively to economic fluctuations with TR-II than with TR-I.

In comparing the two rules, we examine the same shock as before: in 2020, an adverse supply shock raises inflation from 2 percent to 4 percent. **Figure 15.4** shows the economy's path with TR-II and compares it to the path with TR-I, which we saw previously in Figure 15.3.

Like TR-I, TR-II returns the economy to long-run equilibrium. However, this process is more gradual. When inflation rises in 2020, the smaller a_π in TR-II implies a smaller rise in *r*. Output doesn't fall as sharply, and in 2022 inflation is still above target. Since inflation falls more slowly with TR-II, *r* must stay above r^n longer.

Which version of the Taylor rule is better? The answer is ambiguous. The more aggressive rule, TR-I, does a better job of stabilizing inflation. When a supply shock pushes inflation above the 2 percent target, the rule pushes it back quickly. With TR-II, inflation stays above target longer.

On the other hand, the more aggressive TR-I is worse for stabilizing output. Policy tightens sharply when the supply shock occurs, causing a deep recession in 2021. Output follows a smoother path with the less aggressive TR-II.

This example illustrates a general principle: *central banks face a trade-off between output stability and inflation stability*. The Taylor rule that is best for achieving one of these goals is not best for achieving the other. As we've discussed, economists are unsure about the relative importance of the two goals, so it's hard to know which rule is best overall.

15.5 UNCERTAINTY AND POLICY MISTAKES

The AE/PC model captures some of the trade-offs that central banks face in trying to stabilize the economy. Yet the model is a simplification of reality. Running monetary policy in a real economy is much harder than analyzing policy with the model.

A major reason is uncertainty about the economy's behavior. When we examine policy options, we usually assume that we know the precise AE and Phillips curves that determine output and inflation. In reality, policymakers do not have textbooks in which they can look up these curves. Central bank economists try to estimate the behavior of the economy, but their estimates may be wrong.

These misestimates can lead to policy mistakes. Actions that stabilize the economy under certain assumptions may destabilize it if the assumptions are incorrect. Thus well-intentioned policies can backfire. Let's discuss some examples of this problem. In these examples, we assume that the AE/PC model is an accurate description of the economy, and that policymakers know this. However, they are mistaken about important details of the model.

A Mistake About the AE Curve

One type of mistake involves the slopes of the AE and PC curves—how flat or steep they are. The slope of the AE curve shows how much a rise in the real interest rate reduces output, and the slope of the Phillips curve shows how much a rise in output raises inflation. These slopes determine how strongly the economy responds to policy actions.

Let's focus on the AE curve. Economists try to measure its slope by observing how much output changes when interest rates change. This is tricky, however, because output is also influenced by expenditure shocks, such as shifts in fiscal policy or consumer confidence. When output changes, it is difficult to disentangle the effects of interest rates from other factors.

FIGURE 15.4 Choosing the Taylor Rule Coefficients

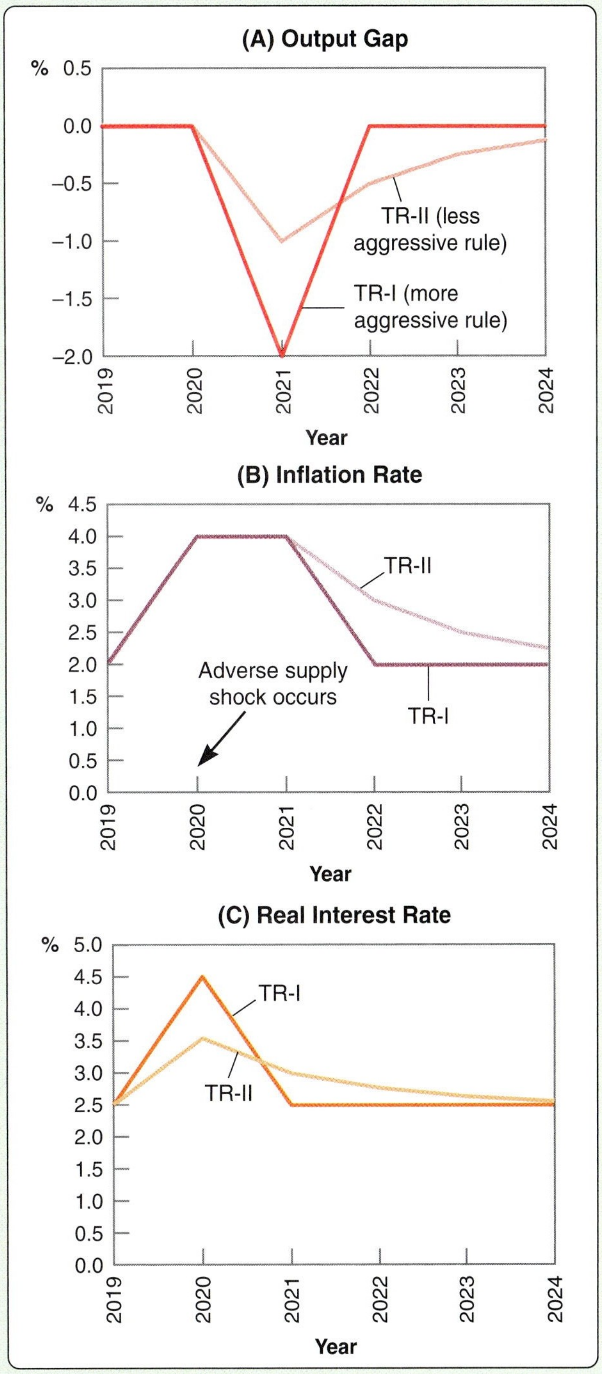

This figure compares the effects of an adverse supply shock under two Taylor rules, TR-I and TR-II. TR-I is more aggressive: it prescribes larger interest-rate adjustments for given movements in output and inflation. This rule is better for stabilizing inflation, but the less aggressive rule is better for stabilizing output.

In addition, the AE coefficient may change over time. Interest rates affect expenditure through complex channels, which may change as the financial system evolves (see Figure 13.7). Estimates of interest-rate effects based on past experience may not be reliable.

An Example of a Mistake **Figure 15.5** illustrates this problem. For simplicity, we examine an AE curve without a time lag: expenditure depends on the current real interest rate. The figure shows two versions of the curve. One is the *true* AE curve that describes how the economy works (AE^{TRUE}). The other is an AE curve *estimated* by central bank economists (AE^{EST}), which unfortunately differs from the true curve.

In this example, the estimated curve is steeper than the true curve. This means that the central bank underestimates the effect of the real interest rate on output. For example, suppose the interest rate rises from the neutral level, r^n, to a higher level, r'. The central bank, believing in its estimated AE curve, thinks the higher interest rate will reduce output from potential, Y^*, to Y'. The true AE curve shows that output actually falls by more, to Y''.

The Response to a Shock Suppose the economy starts with r at r^n, and output at potential. Then a positive expenditure shock occurs, say an increase in government spending. The shock raises output by an amount Δ (Greek letter delta) for any given interest rate. Assume the central bank measures this shock correctly.

FIGURE 15.5 A Mistake About the AE Curve

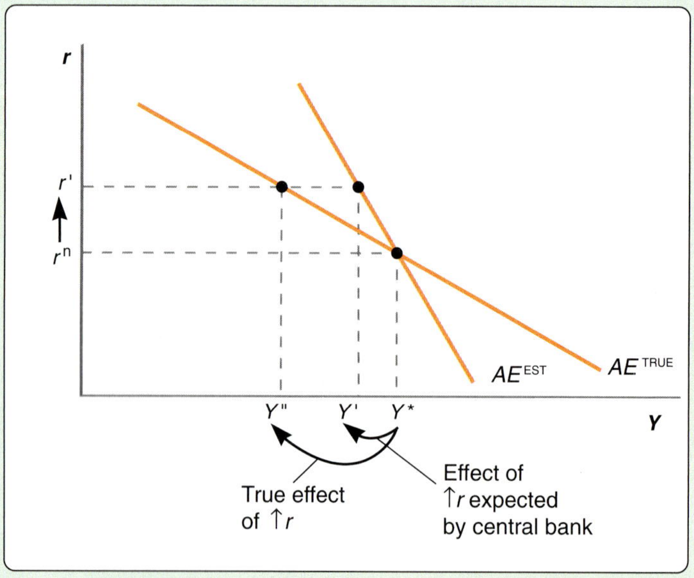

In this example, the AE curve estimated by the central bank is steeper than the true AE curve. This means the central bank underestimates the effect of changing the interest rate. It thinks an increase in r from r^n to r' will reduce output to Y'; in fact, output falls to Y''.

FIGURE 15.6 Effects of a Mistake

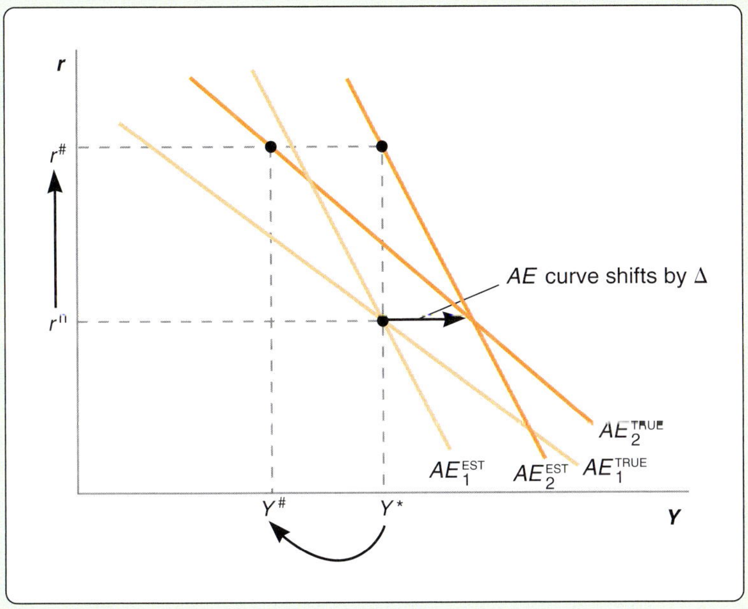

Here, a shock shifts the AE curve to the right by Δ, and the central bank raises the interest rate from r^n to $r^{\#}$. Based on their estimated AE curve, policymakers think their action will keep output at potential. The true effect is to reduce output to $Y^{\#}$.

The central bank doesn't want output to rise, because that would lead to higher inflation through the Phillips curve. So policymakers decide to offset the expenditure shock by raising the real interest rate. Unfortunately, their mistake about the slope of the AE curve leads them astray.

Figure 15.6 shows what happens. The central bank knows a shock has raised spending by Δ, meaning the AE curve has shifted right by that amount. It *thinks* the curve that has shifted is the steep one, AE^{EST}. Given that belief, an interest rate of $r^{\#}$ will keep output at potential. So the central bank raises r to $r^{\#}$.

What's really happened is that the flat curve, AE^{TRUE}, has shifted by Δ. When the interest rate rises to $r^{\#}$, output does *not* stay at potential. Instead, it falls below potential, to $Y^{\#}$. The central bank's reaction to the expenditure shock has caused a recession. The lesson: *When the central bank makes a mistake, an effort to stabilize the economy can actually destabilize it.*

Mismeasurement of the Output Gap

Another kind of mistake is mismeasurement of the output gap, $\tilde{Y}$. We've assumed that policy responds to this variable, which is the percentage difference between actual and potential output. In reality, central banks don't know the output gap because they don't observe potential output. They try to estimate the gap, but once again their estimates may be wrong.

A common way to estimate the output gap is to use Okun's law, Equation (12.1):

$$\tilde{Y} = -2(U - U^*)$$

where U is unemployment and U^* is the natural rate. With this approach, estimates of the output gap depend on estimates of U^*. Economists are often unsure of the current natural rate, leading to mismeasurement of the gap.

An Example of a Mistake Suppose the central bank uses Okun's law to estimate the output gap. It thinks the natural rate is 5 percent, so it plugs this number into Okun's law. It gets an estimate of the gap that we'll denote with the symbol $\hat{\tilde{Y}}$:

$$\hat{\tilde{Y}} = -2(U - 5.0)$$

Unfortunately, the central bank is wrong about the natural rate. The true natural rate is 6 percent, so the true output gap is

$$\tilde{Y} = -2(U - 6.0)$$

To understand this mistake, combine the expressions for $\hat{\tilde{Y}}$ and $\tilde{Y}$:

$$\hat{\tilde{Y}} - \tilde{Y} = [-2(U - 5.0)] - [-2(U - 6.0)]$$

This equation reduces to

$$\hat{\tilde{Y}} - \tilde{Y} = -2.0$$

or

$$\hat{\tilde{Y}} = \tilde{Y} - 2.0 \qquad \textbf{(15.3)}$$

The central bank's estimate of the output gap is always 2 percentage points below the true gap.

For example, suppose in some year the unemployment rate U is 6 percent. This is the true natural rate, so $U - U^*$ is zero and the true output gap is zero. In this situation, the central bank thinks the gap is -2 percent, which means a recession. It believes output is below potential because unemployment exceeds 5 percent, its estimate of the natural rate.

The Effect on Policy To see the effects of this mistake, assume the central bank follows a Taylor rule, specifically TR-II in Table 15.2. However, in applying the rule, policymakers use their estimates of the output gap, $\hat{\tilde{Y}}$. They can't respond to the true gap, $\tilde{Y}$, because they don't observe this variable. With this change, TR-II becomes

$$r = 2.5 + (0.5)\hat{\tilde{Y}} + (0.5)(\pi - 2.0) \qquad \textbf{(15.4)}$$

Recall that $\hat{\tilde{Y}}$ is always 2 percentage points less than the true output gap, $\tilde{Y}$. Because the coefficient on the output gap is 0.5, underestimating it by 2 points reduces the real interest rate by 1 point. Mismeasurement makes monetary policy more expansionary.

Effects on the Economy Suppose in 2020 the economy is in long-run equilibrium. Output is at potential—the true output gap is zero—and inflation is at the target of 2 percent. In this example, no expenditure or supply shocks hit the economy. If the central bank measured the output gap correctly, it would set the interest rate at the neutral level, keeping output and inflation constant.

Mismeasurement of the output gap produces a different outcome, which is shown in **Figure 15.7**. The figure shows the paths of the interest rate, inflation, and two versions of the output gap—the true gap, $\tilde{Y}$, and the central bank's estimate, $\hat{\tilde{Y}}$. The figure is derived using equations for the AE and Phillips curves in the online appendix to this chapter.

In 2020, the true output gap is zero but the central bank perceives a gap of −2 percent. Following its Taylor rule, equation (15.4), the central bank sets a real interest rate of 1.5%, 1 point below the neutral rate. Policymakers think they are setting a low interest rate to end a recession.

Through the AE curve, the low interest rate pushes the true output gap above zero. The positive output gap raises inflation through the Phillips curve. This situation persists for a number of years. Even as the economy experiences an inflationary boom, the central bank *thinks* a recession is occurring: after 2020, $\tilde{Y}$ is positive but $\hat{\tilde{Y}}$ is negative. The central bank keeps r below r^n and the boom continues.

This process finally ends when inflation rises to 4 percent. At that point, the central bank *still* thinks the output gap is negative, which reduces the interest rate in the Taylor rule. But inflation exceeds the 2 percent target,

FIGURE 15.7 Mismeasurement of the Output Gap

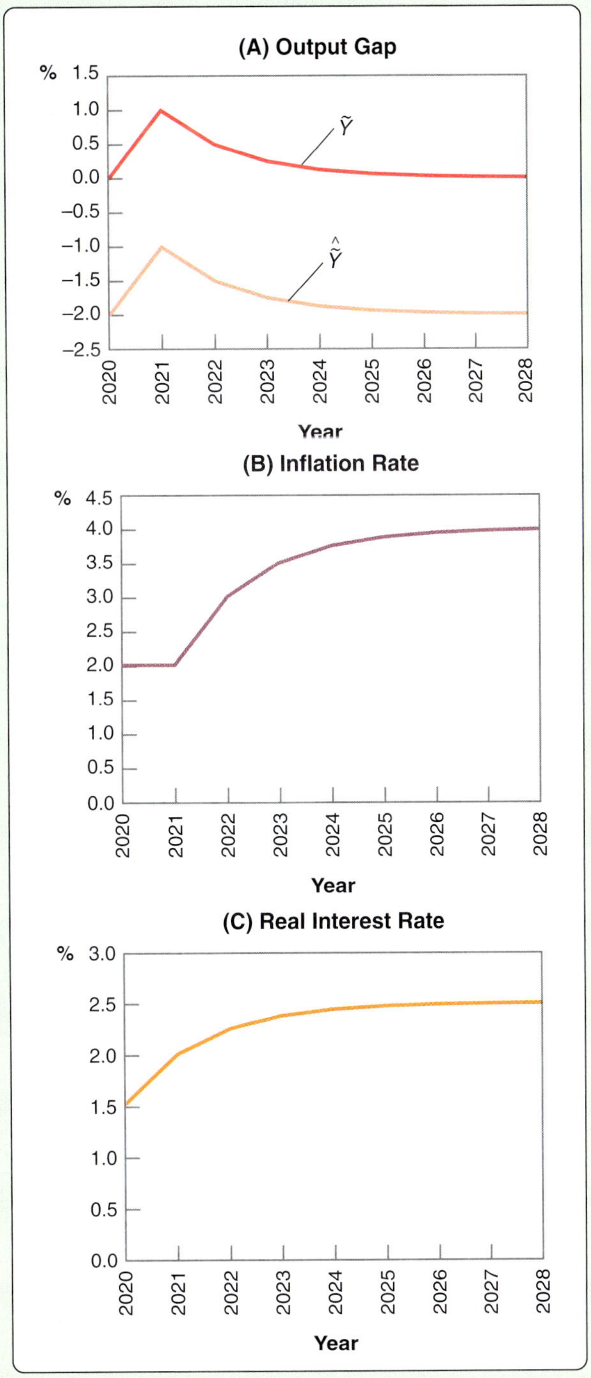

Here the central bank underestimates the natural rate of unemployment. As a result, its estimates of the output gap ($\hat{\tilde{Y}}$) are less than the true gap ($\tilde{Y}$). Policymakers perceive a negative output gap when the true gap is zero or positive, leading to overexpansionary policy. The central bank's inflation target is 2 percent, but its mistake pushes inflation to 4 percent.

which raises the interest rate. Specifically, $\hat{\tilde{Y}} = -2.0\%$ and $\pi = 4.0\%$, so Equation (15.4) implies

$$\begin{aligned} r &= 2.5 + (0.5)(-2.0) + (0.5)(4.0 - 2.0) \\ &= 2.5 \end{aligned}$$

The negative $\hat{\tilde{Y}}$ and the high inflation rate offset one another, implying an interest rate of 2.5 percent, the neutral rate. With $r = 2.5\%$, the true output gap is zero and inflation stabilizes—but at 4 percent, not the central bank's 2 percent target.

Summary In this example, the central bank's basic mistake is that it thinks the natural rate of unemployment is lower than it really is. By Okun's law, this mistake produces underestimates of the output gap, which lead to overly expansionary monetary policy. The ultimate effect is to push inflation above the central bank's target.

Mismeasurement of the output gap is not just a theoretical idea. It helps explain important episodes in economic history, as we discuss in the next two case studies. The first is from the 1970s, the second from the 1990s.

CASE STUDY

The Fed and the Great Inflation

Since World War II, the U.S. inflation rate has usually been low. The big exception is the 1970s. In the "Great Inflation" of 1973–1980, inflation averaged 9 percent per year. The memory of this episode is still fresh for Fed officials. One reason for the Fed's current commitment to low inflation is a desire not to repeat the 1970s.

What caused the Great Inflation? Section 12.3 discusses one factor: supply shocks. Jumps in food and energy prices caused inflation to spike up in 1973–1974 and in 1979. However, most economists don't think these shocks are the whole story. They also blame the Fed for overly expansionary monetary policy.

We can see why by examining history. Inflation started its rise in the late 1960s, well before the oil and food shocks. In addition, inflation accelerated from 1976 through 1978, when there were no shocks. In both these periods, inflation was pushed up by output booms, which in turn were fueled by low real interest rates. The real federal funds rate was negative during much of the 1970s.

Why was policy so expansionary? Economic historians agree that the Fed did not raise inflation on purpose. It tried to keep inflation low, but it made mistakes. In particular, its behavior can be captured by a version of the Taylor rule, but one with an inflationary flaw.

While there is consensus that the Fed erred in the 1970s, there is disagreement about the nature of its mistakes. Economists have proposed two different stories about what went wrong.

Perverse Inflation Responses? John Taylor has proposed one of the stories. He suggests that the Fed followed his rule in the 1970s, but with inappropriate coefficients. In particular, a_π, the response to inflation, was negative. This meant that a rise in inflation caused the Fed to *reduce* the real interest rate. The Fed was leaning with the wind rather than against it.

Why would the Fed behave this way? Because it was confused about nominal and real interest rates. The rate set directly by the Fed is a nominal rate. When inflation rose, the Fed increased this rate. Specifically, Taylor finds that each 1-point rise in inflation caused the nominal federal funds rate to rise by 0.8 points. The Fed thought it was tightening policy.

But what really matters is the real interest rate, the nominal rate minus expected inflation: $r = i - \pi^e$. During the 1970s, the rise in actual inflation caused a parallel rise in expected inflation, as suggested by the assumption of adaptive expectations. When π rose 1 point, π^e rose roughly 1 point as well. With i rising 0.8 points in response, r *fell* by 0.2 points. So a_π, the effect of inflation on the real interest rate, was -0.2.

In Taylor's story, the negative a_π created an inflationary spiral. Initially, economic shocks raised inflation a little bit. With $a_\pi < 0$, higher inflation caused the Fed to lower the real interest rate. The lower real rate caused an output boom, raising inflation further. The more inflation rose, the more the real rate fell, and vice-versa. This process continued until Paul Volcker was appointed Fed chair in 1979. Volcker responded aggressively to inflation—he raised a_π above zero—and this brought inflation under control.

Mismeasurement of the Output Gap? Another explanation for the Great Inflation was proposed by Athanasios Orphanides, a former Fed economist (now governor of the Central Bank of Cyprus). In this story, the Fed made a mistake that we have recently discussed: it mismeasured the output gap. As in our theoretical example, this occurred because the Fed's estimate of the natural rate of unemployment was too low. This mistake led to overexpansionary policy, which pushed inflation above the Fed's target, as in Figure 15.7.

To understand the mistake, recall the history of the natural rate (see Figure 12.2 on p. 346). The natural rate was 5 percent or less in the 1960s, but rose to about 6 percent in the 1970s. In Orphanides's story, the Fed didn't recognize this change. This is not surprising, as economists had not yet developed methods for estimating the natural rate. Orphanides points to statements by Fed officials suggesting that they still believed in a 5 percent natural rate in the 1970s.

Orphanides has reexamined John Taylor's work on the Taylor rule for the 1970s. When Taylor determined which rule fits the Fed's behavior, he used the most recent estimates of output gaps in the 1970s, which were probably close to the true gaps. Orphanides, by contrast, uses "real-time" output gaps—the flawed estimates that the Fed used when it made its decisions. These estimates come from internal Fed documents from the 1970s. In our notation, Orphanides examines the Fed's reaction to $\hat{\tilde{Y}}$, not $\tilde{Y}$.

With this approach, Orphanides finds that the a_π coefficient in the Taylor rule was positive in the 1970s. Thus, he argues, the Fed did *not* make the mistake of reducing the real interest rate when inflation rose. Its mistake was in how it measured economic conditions, not in how it responded to the conditions that it perceived.*

* See John Taylor, "An Historical Analysis of Monetary Policy Rules," in Taylor (ed.), *Monetary Policy Rules,* University of Chicago Press, 1999; and Athanasios Orphanides, "Historical Monetary Policy Analysis and the Taylor Rule," *Journal of Monetary Economics,* July 2003.

CASE STUDY

The Fed and the Roaring 90s

Let's turn from the 1970s to a happier time: the late 1990s. This was another period when the natural rate of unemployment changed, making it tricky to measure the output gap. But this time, the natural rate fell rather than rose. And this time, the Fed caught on quickly to the change.

The natural rate was around 6 percent from the 1970s through the early 1990s. Then it started falling, and it was under 5 percent at the end of the decade. A likely cause was the productivity acceleration of the late 1990s.

Actual unemployment rose to 8 percent in the recession of 1990–91, then fell as the economy recovered. In 1994, unemployment was 6 percent, close to the apparent natural rate. At the same time, inflation was close to the Fed's implicit target of about 2 percent, and the real interest rate was close to the neutral level. The economy seemed to be in long-run equilibrium, and economists predicted that unemployment would stay near 6 percent.

But unemployment kept falling. It reached 5 percent in 1997 and 4 percent at the end of 1999. Many economists assumed that the natural rate was still 6 percent, so 4 percent unemployment meant a major output boom. They expected the Fed to tighten policy in accordance with the Taylor rule.

Yet the Fed didn't tighten. Instead, it kept the real interest rate steady through the late 1990s (see Figure 15.2). At the time, many economists and journalists suggested that the Fed was making a mistake. It was allowing the boom to continue, which would lead eventually to higher inflation.

In retrospect, these worries appear largely unfounded. The natural rate was falling, so actual unemployment could fall without creating a large gap between the two. In other words, with U and U^* both falling, $U - U^*$ stayed close to zero. There was only a mild output boom, so inflation rose only a little.

Today, many economists praise the Fed's policy in the late 1990s. If the Fed had tightened, as many suggested, it would have kept unemployment higher than necessary. And it might have pushed inflation down too far, worsening the risk of deflation in the early 2000s.

How did the Fed know the natural rate was falling? It appears that Fed officials recognized the rise in productivity growth and guessed correctly that this might affect the natural rate. In addition, Fed economists used sophisticated statistical techniques to estimate the natural rate. This work was part of the Fed's ongoing efforts to learn about the economy, which we discuss next.

Coping with Uncertainty

We've seen that uncertainty about the economy can lead central banks into costly mistakes. What can be done about this problem? Let's discuss some possible answers.

Learning About the Economy The best way to deal with uncertainty is to reduce it. Central banks are less likely to make mistakes if they gain a better understanding of the economy. To this end, economists at central banks do extensive research. The Federal Reserve System employs about 500 economists, half at the Board of Governors and half at the 12 Fed Banks. The Fed also hires university professors as part-time consultants.

As part of this work, economists at the Board of Governors have developed a model of the U.S. economy. This model is a system of equations that describe the determinants of output, inflation, and other aggregate variables. It is called the FRB/US model, where FRB stands for Federal Reserve Board. It is commonly pronounced "Furbus."

The FRB/US model is similar in spirit to this book's AE/PC model, but much more complicated. There are hundreds of equations rather than two. For example, rather than one equation for aggregate expenditure, there are separate equations for different kinds of consumption, such as durables and nondurables; different kinds of investment, such as housing and inventories; and so on. All these equations must be combined to determine total spending.

Fed economists constantly refine the FRB/US model based on economic theory and new data. They use statistics to get the best possible estimates of the model's coefficients, such as coefficients capturing the effects of interest rates on spending.

Cautious Interest-Rate Movements Research reduces uncertainty but cannot eliminate it. Central bankers will never know the exact equations describing their economies. How should this fact influence policy?

A common answer is that central banks should move interest rates cautiously. When doubtful about the right response to a shock, they should choose a small adjustment. Alan Blinder, a former vice chair of the Fed, summarized this idea by saying, "the Fed should decide what policy is best and then do less."

The reason for caution is to avoid changing interest rates too much. We saw the danger of overadjustment in one of our examples of policy mistakes, the one in which the central bank misestimates the slope of the AE curve. This mistake led policymakers to raise the interest rate too much in response to an expenditure shock, causing a recession (Figure 15.6). Such an outcome is less likely if the central bank "does less."

Caution means a central bank may not offset a shock fully when it occurs. However, policymakers can make another adjustment later if more action is needed. The delay slows the economy's return to long-run equilibrium, but many economists think it's worth paying this price to guard against overadjustment.

Policymakers seem to take these ideas to heart. When shocks occur, central banks rarely respond with large, immediate changes in interest rates. Instead, they practice **interest-rate smoothing.** They change rates by a small amount at a time, making a series of adjustments if they eventually want a large change.

Interest-rate smoothing Central banks' practice of moving interest rates through a series of small changes

When the Fed shifts policy, it usually changes its target for the federal funds rate by 1/4 of a percentage point at a time. For example, as the economy recovered from the recession of the early 2000s, the Fed raised its target by 1/4 point on 17 occasions. Overall, the target rose from 1.0 percent in 2004 to 5.25 percent in 2006 (see Figure 11.8).

▶ The Fed departed somewhat from interest-rate smoothing in early 2008, when it reduced the federal funds rate by 3/4 of a point on two occasions. We discuss this episode in Section 15.7 and Chapter 18.

Smaller Responses to Output Gaps? We've seen that mismeasurement of the output gap can lead to costly mistakes in policy. It is difficult to measure the gap because central banks don't observe potential output or the natural rate of unemployment. The inflation rate is measured much more accurately.

Some economists conclude that policy should not respond much to output gaps. In the Taylor rule, the inflation coefficient a_π should be large, but the output coefficient a_y should be small. Athanasios Orphanides argues that a small a_y would prevent the kind of mistake the Fed made in the 1970s. At the same time, a large a_π would keep the economy reasonably stable.

Other economists disagree. They think that a low coefficient on the output gap would allow recessions to drag on for a long time. It is better to measure the gap imperfectly than to ignore the gap. Policymakers should be cautious in the sense of smoothing interest rates, but eventually they should respond strongly to estimated output gaps.

Most central banks have *not* been convinced to deemphasize output gaps. The Fed, for example, reduced interest rates significantly in response to the negative gaps of the early 2000s (see Figure 15.2). The Taylor rule that fits the Fed's behavior has a sizable coefficient on the gap.

15.6 MAKING INTEREST-RATE POLICY

Much of this chapter has focused on the Taylor rule, but this rule is only an approximation of how central banks behave. Policymakers choose interest rates through a process that is far more complex than applying a formula. Sometimes this process produces significant deviations from the Taylor rule. We now discuss some details of the policy process.

The broad approach is similar at many central banks. A committee of top officials meets periodically to set policy. In the United States, the Federal Open Market Committee meets every 6 weeks. At the European Central Bank, the Governing Council meets once a month. At these meetings, policymakers discuss the state of the economy and then choose an interest-rate target. The policy committee is supported by a staff of economists that continuously monitors the economy, makes forecasts, and analyzes policy options. It reports on this work to policymakers before each of their meetings.

At the Federal Reserve, much of the staff's analysis is summarized in three books that it presents to the FOMC. These books have bureaucratic-sounding names, such as "Summary of Commentary on Current Economic Conditions by Federal Reserve District." But they are better known by the colors of their covers: they are the Green Book, the Blue Book, and the Beige Book. We will discuss what's in these books and how they are produced.

Monitoring the Economy

The first job of Fed economists is to monitor the state of the economy. Much of this task consists of estimating the current level of output. We've already discussed the fact that the Fed doesn't observe potential output, Y^*. At any point in time, it also doesn't know actual output, Y. The reason is that data on the main measure of output, real GDP, are produced with a substantial time lag.

Specifically, GDP is calculated quarterly, but the final number for a quarter is not published until the end of the following quarter. For example, GDP for the first quarter of the year, January through March, is not reported until the end of June. So economists never know the current level of GDP.

Outside the Fed, economists wait for complete data before analyzing events. For example, the NBER announces the starts and ends of recessions many months after they occur (see Section 12.1). But the Fed can't wait. Its policies offset the effects of shocks with a lag, and the lag is worsened if actions are delayed.

So Fed economists try their best to estimate current output. To do so, they examine data series that are calculated monthly, and with relatively short lags. These series include retail sales, employment, and industrial production. These variables tend to move in the same direction as GDP, so they provide hints about GDP before that variable is calculated.

Every Monday, economists on the staff of the Fed Board in Washington brief the governors about data released during the previous week. They also interpret the data. For example, if retail sales have fallen, they discuss what that means. Does it suggest the economy is slowing? Or does it just reflect the big snowstorm that curtailed shopping last month?

The analysis of the board's economists is summarized every 6 weeks in the Green Book. This document includes estimates of the current level of GDP based on all available data. The Green Book is distributed to the FOMC 5 days before its meetings.

While economists at the board are preparing the Green Book, economists at the Fed Banks are briefing their presidents. At each bank, the staff studies the economy of its Federal Reserve District as well as the national economy. At the FOMC meeting, the bank president may report on his or her district.

Each Federal Reserve Bank also contributes to the Beige Book. This document is a collection of anecdotes about various industries that are doing well or badly in different parts of the country. Sometimes changes in the economy show up in these stories before they are reflected in national data.

Forecasts

In addition to analyzing the current economy, the Fed staff forecasts its future. Each Green Book presents forecasts of output and inflation over the next 2 years.

Forecasts are important because policymakers would like to respond preemptively to shifts in the economy. If they can predict movements in output and inflation, they can adjust interest rates in advance. This reduces the problems caused by lags in the effects of policy, allowing the Fed to stabilize the economy more effectively.

One tool for forecasting is the FRB/US model of the economy. In this model, most variables depend on past values of other variables—as in the AE/PC model with time lags. For example, current investment depends on past investment, GDP, and interest rates. Because of these linkages, an analyst can plug current data into the equations to get forecasts.

Forecasts from the FRB/US model do not go directly into the Green Book. The Green Book forecasts are "judgmental": they are chosen by people rather than by equations in a computer. Within the Fed staff, different economists forecast different variables, such as consumption and investment. These people take account of the forecasts from FRB/US, but they also examine other information that they think is relevant.

This information can include many factors. For example, the consumption forecaster may examine surveys of consumer confidence, which some economists think are good predictors of consumption. The forecaster may use various statistical techniques to forecast consumption, supplementing the forecasts from the FRB/US model. She may consider anecdotal evidence, such as retailers' predictions about holiday sales.

The preceding paragraph is somewhat speculative. The Fed publishes the equations of the FRB/US model, but it doesn't say how judgmental forecasts are made. Fed economists are not allowed to reveal this information. Outsiders must rely on bits of gossip to get a rough picture of the forecasting process. This reflects the imperfect transparency of Fed policymaking, which we discuss in Chapter 16.

A "forecast coordinator" oversees the many economists working on forecasts, with the goal of ensuring that different forecasts fit together. There can be conflicts: one economist might forecast that net exports will fall because of rising imports of consumer goods, while another forecasts a big fall in consumption, for example. The various forecasters hold meetings to work out these differences. When the coordinator is satisfied with the forecasts, they go into the Green Book.

Policy Options

The day after FOMC members receive the Green Book, they receive the Blue Book. This document is prepared by the Division of Monetary Affairs at the Board of Governors. It helps prepare the FOMC to choose a target for the federal funds rate.

The first part of the Blue Book reviews events in financial markets since the last FOMC meeting. What has happened to asset prices and long-term interest rates? How did long-term rates react to the committee's last decision? Based on federal funds futures, what do markets expect the committee to do next? This information helps policymakers gauge the likely effects of their next decision.

Then the Blue Book discusses policy options. It outlines three possible interest-rate decisions that appear reasonable in current circumstances. These options might be a 1/4 percent cut in the federal funds rate, no change, and a 1/4 percent increase. If it seems clear the FOMC is leaning toward tightening, the options might be no change or a 1/4 or 1/2 percent increase.

The Blue Book discusses the pros and cons of each choice. In analyzing a rate increase, for example, it might discuss evidence that the economy is growing too quickly and contrast that with evidence that growth is slowing. The Blue Book also proposes language for the FOMC statement that will accompany the interest-rate announcement.

The FOMC Meeting

The policy process culminates every 6 weeks with a meeting of the Federal Open Market Committee. The committee gathers at board headquarters in Washington, typically on a Tuesday from 9:00 AM to 2:15 PM. The committee consists of the seven Fed governors and five of the twelve Fed bank presidents. The other presidents attend the meeting and participate in the discussion, but they can't vote on the interest-rate decision. Top members of the Fed staff are also present.

▶ An FOMC meeting is pictured on p. 313.

The meetings have a formal structure that determines who speaks when. In the first part of the meeting, participants review the state of the economy without explicitly discussing policy options. The director of the board's Division of Research and Statistics summarizes the material in the Green Book and takes questions. Then the bank presidents take turns giving their views on the economy, both nationally and in their regions. Finally, there are remarks by each of the governors, with the chair speaking last.

Then the meeting turns to policy. The director of the Division of Monetary Affairs summarizes the three proposals in the Blue Book and their rationales. Once again, each president and governor takes a turn making comments. The chair summarizes the discussion and makes a final proposal for an interest-rate target. He also proposes language for a brief statement in which the committee will explain its decision. The statement might say, for example, that the Fed is raising interest rates because it sees a risk of higher inflation.

After hearing the chair's proposal, the 12 FOMC members vote to accept or reject it. For practical purposes, however, the outcome is decided before the vote. A chair's proposal has never been defeated, and it is rare to have more than one or two dissents. Committee members usually defer to the chair unless they have strong objections. Also, the chair gauges the opinions of others during the discussion and makes a proposal that he knows will pass.

After the interest-rate vote, the committee sometimes discusses longer-term issues. For example, at several meetings in recent years, the committee has discussed the pros and cons of adopting an explicit inflation target. At 2:15, the meeting ends and the board's press office announces the new interest-rate target. The news flashes across computer screens around the world, often causing immediate changes in asset prices and interest rates.

Online Case Study: An FOMC Meeting

15.7 MONETARY POLICY AND FINANCIAL EVENTS

This chapter has reviewed central banks' efforts to stabilize output and inflation. We've seen that policymakers adjust interest rates based on current estimates of these variables and forecasts of their future paths. Often, policy actions are close to those prescribed by the Taylor Rule.

However, output and inflation are not the only variables that influence monetary policy. In some time periods, an important factor is developments in the financial system. Adverse events, such as asset-price crashes or failures of financial institutions, lead central banks to reduce interest rates. Some economists think policymakers should also *raise* interest rates when asset-price bubbles occur, but this idea is controversial.

Responses to Financial Crises

Financial crisis Major disruption of the financial system, typically involving crashes in asset prices and failures of financial institutions

Sometimes the economy is threatened by a **financial crisis**, a major disruption of the financial system that typically involves crashes in asset prices and failures of financial institutions. If a crisis occurs or policymakers fear that one is on the way, the central bank is likely to lower interest rates. In the United States, such an episode occurred in the summer of 1998, when Russia defaulted on its sovereign debt and a huge hedge fund, Long Term Capital Management, nearly failed. The Fed responded by cutting the federal funds rate by 3/4 of a point. In Figure 15.2 on p. 452, you can see a temporary decrease in the real funds rate in 1998–1999. You can also see that this decrease was a deviation from the Taylor rule.

A major financial crisis threatened the U.S. economy in 2007–2008. The subprime mortgage crisis triggered a decrease in asset prices and weakened financial institutions, endangering their solvency. We discuss this episode in detail in Chapter 18.

Here we focus on the Fed's interest-rate adjustments. **Figure 15.8** compares the real federal funds rate over 2007 and the first half of 2008 to the

FIGURE 15.8 Deviating from the Taylor Rule, 2007–2008

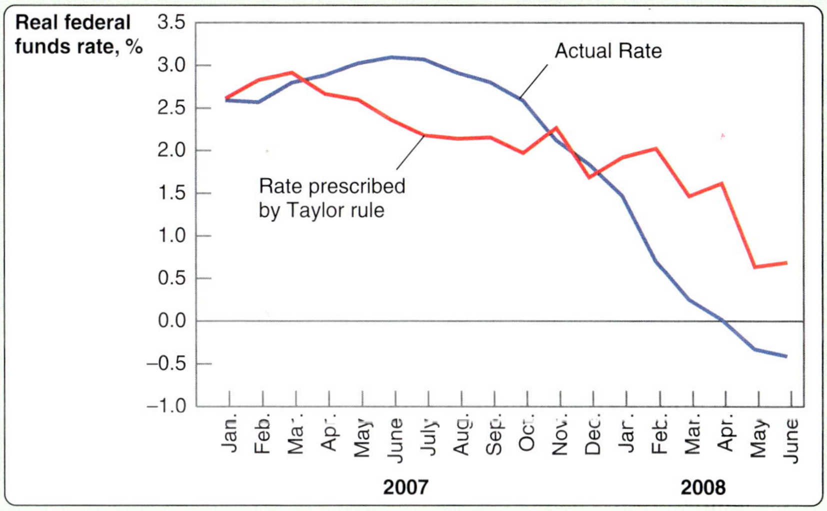

The Fed reduced interest rates sharply in response to the financial crisis of 2007–2008.

rate prescribed by the Taylor rule (Equation (15.2)). From July 2007 to June 2008, the Taylor rule implies an interest rate cut of 1.5 percent (from 2.2 percent to 0.7 percent), reflecting a modest slowdown in the economy. The actual response of the Fed was more aggressive: it cut the real interest rate by 3.5 percent.

Why do central banks respond aggressively to financial crises? There are two related reasons:

1. A financial crisis is likely to reduce output in the near future. Among other reasons, a crisis shakes consumer confidence, leading to lower consumption, and it reduces bank lending, leading to lower investment. This process takes time to unfold. Given the lags in policy effects, the central bank wants to act preemptively. It lowers rates when it sees a financial crisis developing rather than waiting for output to fall.

2. During a financial crisis, there is a risk that the crisis will suddenly worsen. In 1998, the Fed feared that problems at Long Term Capital Management could spread to other financial institutions. Similarly, the Fed feared widespread failures of financial institutions in 2007–2008. Because of such risk, a central bank is likely to respond more strongly to a financial crisis than is justified by the current situation. Policymakers provide extra stimulus to the economy as insurance against worst-case scenarios.

Responses to Bubbles

Clearly, central banks respond to problems in financial markets, including large falls in asset prices. Some economists argue that this policy should have a complement: the central bank should react to unusually large *increases* in asset prices. In particular, it should raise interest rates if a bubble pushes asset prices above the assets' true values.

To understand this issue, we must make a distinction. Asset prices affect output through various channels, including the effect of wealth on consumption and the effect of stock prices on investment. Because central banks respond to output movements, they respond indirectly to asset prices. The controversial question is whether they should also respond *directly*. For a given level of output, should a central bank raise interest rates by more than normal if it perceives an asset-price bubble? Let's examine both sides of this issue.

Why Respond to Asset Prices? The affirmative argument is based on the link between asset-price bubbles and subsequent crashes. A bubble is driven by self-fulfilling expectations of rising prices. At some point, expectations shift and prices fall, sometimes rapidly. Just as high asset prices raise output, falling prices can cause a recession. Falling stock prices contributed to the U.S. recession of the early 2000s, and falling house prices threatened the economy in 2007–2008. Japan's stagnation in the 1990s began with crashes in both stock and real estate prices.

When a crash occurs, the central bank lowers interest rates. But this response may be too late to prevent a recession, because of the lags in policy effects. Rather than react to crashes, central banks would do better to prevent them from occurring. They can do this by dampening the bubbles that precede crashes. If asset prices don't rise to irrationally high levels, they won't plummet when markets come to their senses.

And central banks have a tool for dampening bubbles: interest-rate increases. Higher rates reduce asset prices by reducing the present value of future asset income (see Section 3.3). So when central banks see a bubble developing, this argument goes, they should lean against it with tighter policy.

Why Not Respond to Asset Prices? Many economists are skeptical that monetary policy should respond to asset prices. They point out several problems with this idea.

- To respond to bubbles, central banks must identify them. This is hard. Rapid increases in asset prices might reflect bubbles, or they might reflect increases in expected earnings. In the late 1990s, some economists argued that stock prices were rising because the productivity acceleration raised firms' expected profits. Economists can be sure of a bubble only when they see it end—and then it's too late to prevent the bubble.
- The effects of interest rates on bubbles are unpredictable. Depending on market sentiment, an increase in rates might have little effect on

asset prices. Or it might shake confidence and cause a big decline. In the worst case, an attempt to contain a bubble might cause the kind of crash that the central bank wants to prevent.

- A policy tightening aimed at asset prices has adverse side effects. It reduces aggregate expenditure and raises unemployment. It is unwise to accept this cost when the benefits of the policy are uncertain.

Fed Policy Fed officials have weighed the arguments about responding to bubbles and found the negative case more persuasive. Under Chairman Alan Greenspan, the Fed ignored advice to lean against the stock market boom of the 1990s. In the 2000s, Greenspan and then Ben Bernanke kept interest rates low as house prices rose rapidly.

Bernanke's behavior is not surprising, because he has long argued that monetary policy should not respond to bubbles. In 2001, when Bernanke was still a professor, he and Mark Gertler wrote that responding to bubbles would have "dangerously unpredictable effects" and "no significant benefits."[4]

Many observers criticize the Fed on this issue. They note the problems caused by decreases in stock and house prices and blame them on the Fed's inaction during bubbles. In 2007, *The Economist* magazine criticized the Fed for low interest rates during the housing bubble, alleging, "loose monetary policy is partly responsible for the mess the central bankers are now trying to clear up." Stephen Roach of Morgan Stanley, the investment bank, also criticized the Fed along with other central banks: "For the second time in seven years, the bursting of a major asset bubble has inflicted great damage on world financial markets. In both cases—the equity bubble of 2000 and the credit bubble of 2007—central banks were asleep at the switch."[5] It remains to be seen whether such criticism will influence Fed policy during future bubbles.

[4] Ben Bernanke and Mark Gertler, "Monetary Policy and Asset Price Volatility," in *New Challenges for Monetary Policy*, Federal Reserve Bank of Kansas City, 1999.

[5] Stephen Roach, "The Failure of Central Banking," CNN Money Crisis Counsel, August 2007, money.cnn.com.

Summary

- A central bank's tasks include choosing a long-run level for the inflation rate and dampening fluctuations in inflation and output.

15.1 Choosing the Long-Run Inflation Rate

- Some economists believe that zero is the ideal level for long-run inflation. Others advocate a low but positive inflation rate to avoid the costs of disinflation and reduce the risk of a liquidity trap.
- In practice, many central banks target inflation rates around 2 percent, either explicitly or implicitly. Fed Chairman Ben Bernanke's "comfort zone" for inflation is 1–2 percent.

15.2 Inflation and Output Stability

- Central banks seek to stabilize the inflation rate at its long-run level. They also seek to stabilize output—to dampen the business cycle. However, these goals sometimes conflict, and economists are unsure of their relative importance.

15.3 The Taylor Rule

- Central banks have long followed the principle of "leaning against the wind": they adjust interest rates to offset movements in output and inflation.
- The Taylor rule, invented in 1993, captures the idea of leaning against the wind in a formula. The rule prescribes a real interest rate based on the neutral real rate, the output gap, and the deviation of inflation from target.
- Over the last two decades, the interest rates set by the Fed have usually been close to those prescribed by the Taylor rule.

15.4 The Taylor Rule in the AE/PC Model

- In the AE/PC model, the Taylor rule guides the economy back to long-run equilibrium after a shock occurs.
- The behavior of the economy depends on a_y and a_π, the Taylor rule's coefficients on output and inflation. Different coefficients are best for stabilizing output and for stabilizing inflation, so it's not clear which coefficients are best overall.

15.5 Uncertainty and Policy Mistakes

- Central banks' uncertainty about the economy can lead to policy mistakes. Policymakers may adjust the interest rate too much in response to a shock, destabilizing the economy.
- If the central bank underestimates the output gap, its policy is overly expansionary, and inflation rises above target. Such a mistake may help to explain the high inflation of the 1970s.
- Central banks try to reduce their mistakes through research on the economy. They also practice interest-rate smoothing to avoid overreacting to shocks.

15.6 Making Interest-Rate Policy

- The Federal Reserve employs hundreds of economists who monitor the economy and forecast its future. This analysis is summarized in the Green Book prepared for the Federal Open Market Committee. Fed economists also prepare the Blue Book, which analyzes policy options for the FOMC, and the Beige Book, which discusses conditions in various industries around the country. The FOMC meets every 6 weeks to review the state of the economy and choose a target for the federal funds rate.

15.7 Monetary Policy and Financial Events

- Financial crises lead the Fed to reduce interest rates. Rates typically fall by more than the Taylor rule prescribes.
- Some economists argue that central banks should raise interest rates to dampen asset-price bubbles. This idea is controversial, however, and the Fed has not adopted it.

Key Terms

Explicit inflation target, p. 446

Financial crisis, p. 468

Implicit inflation target, p. 446

Interest-rate smoothing, p. 464

Taylor rule, p. 450

Questions and Problems

1. Suppose the neutral real interest rate is 3 percent in Country A and 1 percent in Country B.
   a. What might explain this difference? (*Hint:* See Chapter 12 Appendix.)
   b. If the central banks of the two countries choose the same inflation target, which country is at greater risk of a liquidity trap? Explain.

c. Should the two countries choose the same inflation target? Explain.

2. Suppose an economist has a bright idea: a central bank should lean against the wind when output falls, but *not* when it rises. That is, policymakers should lower the interest rate below the neutral level when a recession occurs, but not raise it in a boom.
   a. Why might this plan appear attractive?
   b. Would it be wise for a central bank to adopt the plan? (*Hint:* Think about the Phillips curve.)

3. We have assumed that the coefficients in the Taylor rule, a_y and a_π, are both positive. Under this assumption, the rule guides the economy back to long-run equilibrium after a shock. The output gap $\tilde{Y}$ eventually returns to zero and inflation returns to its long-run level π^T.
   a. Suppose the inflation coefficient a_π is positive but the output coefficient a_y is zero. Does the economy still return to equilibrium with $\tilde{Y} = 0$ and $\pi = \pi^T$ after a shock? Explain.
   b. How is the answer to the previous question different if a_y is positive and a_π is zero? Explain.

4. Suppose the central bank measures the output gap accurately, but mismeasures the neutral real interest rate. It believes the neutral rate is 1 percent, but the true neutral rate is 3 percent. If the central bank follows the Taylor rule, how does its mistake affect the interest rates it sets and the behavior of output and inflation? Explain.

5. Recall the example in Figure 15.6, in which the central bank responds to an expenditure shock. Suppose policymakers know the true slope of the AE curve but mismeasure the shock: they think the curve shifts to the right by 2Δ, twice the actual shift. How will the central bank adjust the interest rate if it wants to keep output at potential? What will really happen to output? Explain.

6. Consider a variation on the Taylor rule:

$$r = (0.25)r^{\text{TAYLOR}} + (0.75)r(-1)$$

where r is the real interest rate in a quarter, r^{TAYLOR} is the interest rate implied by the Taylor rule, and $r(-1)$ is the interest rate in the previous quarter. Call this rule TR-S.
   a. Compare the behavior of the interest rate under TR-S to its behavior under the basic Taylor rule. (*Hint:* What might "S" stand for?)
   b. Is TR-S a realistic description of central banks' behavior? Why might they follow such a rule rather than the basic Taylor rule?

7. Suppose the Fed had a policy of responding to asset-price bubbles. Under this policy, it would have set higher interest rates than it actually did during the stock market boom of the late 1990s and the housing bubble of the 2000s.
   a. For the period 1990–2007, draw a graph showing roughly what interest rates the Fed would have chosen under the antibubble policy. Compare this hypothetical interest-rate path to the actual path of rates (see Figure 15.2).
   b. How would the antibubble policy have changed the behavior of output and inflation? Draw rough graphs comparing the likely paths of these variables to the paths they actually followed. (See pp. 374–375 for a summary of the actual paths.) In this part of the question, assume the antibubble policy was unsuccessful: stock and house prices rose rapidly despite higher interest rates.
   c. Now suppose the hypothetical policy succeeded: it dampened the stock market and housing bubbles. How does this change the answer to part (b)?

Online and Data Questions

www.worthpublishers.com/ball

8. [Advanced] Suppose the economy is in long-run equilibrium in 2019. In 2020, an adverse expenditure shock reduces output by 2 percent.

a. Assume the central bank uses TR-I in Table 15.2. Using the equations for the AE and Phillips curves in the online appendix, derive the paths of output, inflation, and the interest rate from 2020 until the economy is back in long-run equilibrium.

b. Redo the calculations in part (a) assuming TR-II. Which of the two rules is better for stabilizing output? For stabilizing inflation? Explain.

9. Link from the text Web site to the site of the Federal Reserve Board, which includes minutes from FOMC meetings. Pick a recent meeting at which the committee changed its federal funds rate target.

a. Based on the minutes, briefly summarize the rationale for the target change.

b. Does the FOMC's action appear consistent with the Taylor rule? Explain.

c. Did any members dissent from the committee's decision? If so, why did they dissent?

chapter sixteen 16

Monetary Institutions and Strategies

- 16.1 TIME CONSISTENCY AND INFLATION
- 16.2 CENTRAL BANK INDEPENDENCE
- 16.3 MONETARY POLICY RULES
- 16.4 INFLATION TARGETS
- 16.5 COMMUNICATION BY CENTRAL BANKS

When the Federal Open Market Committee meets, most of the meeting focuses on an immediate policy decision: the choice of a target for the federal funds rate. However, after this decision is made, the committee sometimes discusses longer-term issues about monetary policy. For example, since Ben Bernanke became Fed chair, several meetings have discussed whether the Fed should adopt an explicit inflation target.

DENNIS BRACK/Bloomberg News/Landov

Congressman Barney Frank (D-MA), chair of the House Committee on Financial Services, addresses Ben Bernanke at a 2007 hearing. Chairman Bernanke and Chairman Frank don't always see eye-to-eye on monetary policy.

This book's discussion of monetary policy is following a similar structure. Like the main part of an FOMC meeting, Chapter 15 focused on setting interest-rate targets. We discussed the process through which these targets are chosen and the factors that lead policymakers to raise or lower them. Like the end of an FOMC meeting, this chapter turns to longer-term policy issues. Some of these concern strategic decisions that the Fed and other central banks must make. Others are issues facing the governments that establish central banks and determine their powers.

One issue is central bank independence. In most of the world, governments have given central banks great freedom to run monetary policy. Elected political leaders have little control over interest-rate adjustments. Some people think this is undemocratic, but most economists support central bank independence. We discuss why.

We also discuss limits on central banks' authority. Independence gives these institutions enormous power over the economy. Some economists think this power should be constrained by a policy rule—a rule that tells the central bank what to do in various circumstances. We survey the debate over what rule, if any, should govern monetary policy. Currently, much of this debate focuses on explicit inflation targeting, a policy adopted by many countries over the last two decades.

A final issue we consider is communication by central banks. Traditionally, central banks have been secretive about their decision making, but recent years have seen a trend toward openness. Today, policymakers provide the public with lots of information about what they are doing and why. We discuss the reasons for this change and debates over what information central banks should release.

To address all these issues, we begin with some economic theory. The behavior of central banks in recent decades has been greatly influenced by theoretical research—specifically, theories of *time-consistency problems* in monetary policy. We discuss these theories, which underlie developments around the world in central bank independence, policy rules, and communication.

16.1 TIME CONSISTENCY AND INFLATION

Economics professors develop abstract theories and publish them in scholarly journals. Sometimes the only people who pay attention are other economics professors. But other times, academic theories are taken to heart by real-world policymakers and actually prompt them to change their behavior. The theory of time-consistency problems in monetary policy is one of the best examples.

This theory follows from a more basic idea, the idea that people have rational expectations about inflation. We introduced that concept in Section 12.3. We need to review rational-expectations theories before defining the time-consistency problem.

Rational Expectations and the Phillips Curve

The behavior of inflation depends on expectations. This idea is captured by the Phillips curve, Equation (12.4):

$$\pi = \pi^e + \alpha\tilde{Y}$$

▶ In mathematical terms, $\tilde{Y} = (Y - Y^*)/Y^*$, where Y is output and Y^* is potential output.

▶ To keep the analysis here as simple as possible, we use a version of the Phillips curve without supply shocks. We also ignore the time lag in the effect of output on inflation (see Section 13.4).

Recall that π is inflation, π^e is expected inflation, $\tilde{Y}$ is the output gap (the percentage deviation of output from potential), and α is a coefficient showing how strongly output affects inflation. Expected inflation enters this equation because firms raise prices to match price increases they expect from other firms.

There are two leading theories of inflation expectations. One is adaptive expectations, which says that expectations are determined by past inflation. Much of this book uses a simple version of this theory in which expected inflation equals inflation over the previous year: $\pi^e = \pi(-1)$ (Equation (12.3)).

The other theory is rational expectations, which says that people make the best possible forecasts of inflation based on all available information. The behavior of the central bank is a key part of this information. If the central bank tightens policy, for example, then expected inflation is likely to fall.

The concept of rational expectations was introduced in a 1961 paper by John Muth of Carnegie-Mellon University. At first the idea had little impact, but that changed in the 1970s, when the "rational-expectations revolution" swept macroeconomics. This movement was led by Robert Lucas of the University of Chicago, who won a Nobel Prize for his work in 1995. (Since Milton Friedman's death in 2007, Lucas is arguably the most influential living macroeconomist.)

In Lucas's view, rational expectations follows from the basic economic principle that firms maximize profits. Remember why expectations matter: firms base price increases on the increases they expect from other firms. If expectations are mistaken, firms set the wrong relative prices, and this reduces profits. So when firms choose prices, they have incentives to forecast inflation as well as possible—to form expectations rationally.

Not all economists accept this argument. Some believe that adaptive expectations is a more realistic assumption than rational expectations. Nonetheless, there is no doubt that rational-expectations theories have been hugely influential, in part by providing foundations for time-consistency theories.

The Time-Consistency Problem

Ultimately we will use time-consistency theories to explain the behavior of inflation. But first, we must step back and discuss the basic concept of a **time-consistency problem**. This problem arises in many contexts. It occurs when someone has incentives to make a promise, but then to renege on the promise later. Other people understand this inconsistency, so they don't believe the promise when it's made.

Time-consistency problem Situation in which someone has incentives to make a promise but later renege on it; because of these incentives, others don't believe the promise

To illustrate this idea, let's put aside the topic of monetary policy and consider family life. Suppose a family is preparing for a holiday visit to Grandpa and Grandma's house, where the kids will receive lavish presents. Dad wants the kids to clean their rooms before the trip. To get them to comply, he makes a threat: if the rooms aren't cleaned, the family will stay home. If the kids believe the threat, they will promptly clean up. They don't like cleaning, but they won't do anything to jeopardize their presents.

Unfortunately for Dad, his threat is not time-consistent. If the kids refuse to clean their rooms, he will relent and take them to their grandparents anyway. Otherwise, Grandpa and Grandma will be left with dinner on the table and get angry at Dad, which he can't stand. The kids, of course, are smart enough to understand this. They realize that Dad is bluffing, so they ignore him and play video games until it's time to leave. Their rooms stay messy.

Time-consistency problems arise in economic policy as well as in families. Suppose a government wants firms to build factories, making the economy more productive. The government might encourage this investment by promising not to tax firms' profits from the factories. But this promise is not time-consistent. Once the factories are built, the government will be tempted to enact taxes to raise revenue. Knowing this, firms may not build the factories.

How the Time-Consistency Problem Increases Inflation

How is time consistency relevant to monetary policy? This question was answered in a 1977 paper by Finn Kydland of Carnegie-Mellon University and Edward Prescott, then of the University of Minnesota (now at Arizona State University). According to Kydland and Prescott, the time-consistency problem explains why central banks sometimes produce high inflation, and solving the problem is the key to controlling inflation. Kydland and Prescott won the Nobel Prize in 2004.

The Puzzle of High Inflation To understand the Kydland-Prescott argument, recall our discussion in Chapter 14 of why central banks create inflation. A traditional explanation is that disinflation is costly. If inflation is high, the central bank can reduce it by tightening policy, but this action reduces output in the short run. Sometimes policymakers are unwilling to pay this price.

This reasoning rests on the assumption of adaptive expectations. With that assumption, we can write the Phillips curve as $\pi = \pi(-1) + \alpha\tilde{Y}$ (Equation (12.6)). Inflation equals past inflation if the output gap is zero; to reduce inflation, the central bank must push output below potential.

The assumption of rational expectations undermines the traditional explanation for inflation, because it implies that disinflation can be costless. If the central bank plans to reduce inflation, it can first announce its intention to the public. If people believe the announcement, then expected inflation falls. From the Phillips curve, a fall in expected inflation reduces actual inflation, even if the output gap is zero. Since disinflation doesn't require an output loss, the central bank has no reason to produce high inflation.

Figure 16.1 illustrates this point. We assume that expected inflation starts at a high level, implying an initial Phillips curve of PC_1. The central bank wants to reduce inflation to the level it considers best, π^{ideal}. You might think of π^{ideal} as 2 percent, the inflation rate that many central banks target. Policymakers announce that inflation will fall to π^{ideal}, causing expected inflation to fall and shifting the Phillips curve down to PC_2. With this Phillips curve, the central bank can produce inflation of π^{ideal} while keeping output at potential.

The late 1970s, when Kydland and Prescott published their article, was the height of the rational-expectations revolution. Ironically, it was also a period when the U.S. inflation rate reached double digits and policymakers seemed unable to reduce it. Economic theory was saying that inflation

FIGURE 16.1 Rational Expectations and Costless Disinflation

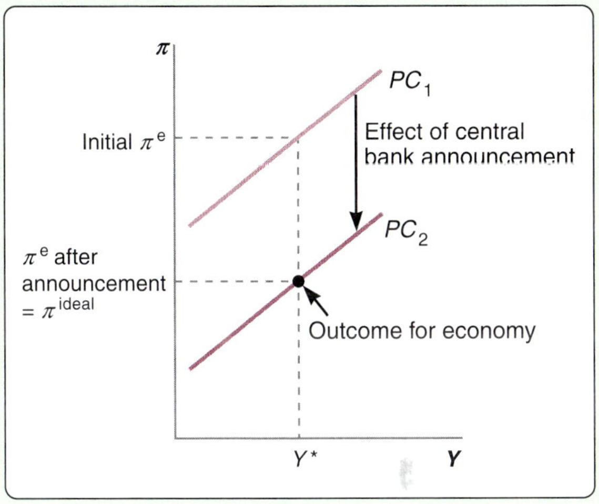

Expected inflation is initially high, but the central bank announces it will reduce inflation to π^{ideal}. Expectations are rational and the public believes the announcement, so expected inflation falls. The Phillips curve shifts down, allowing the central bank to reduce inflation without reducing output.

FIGURE 16.2 The Inflation-Surprise Decision

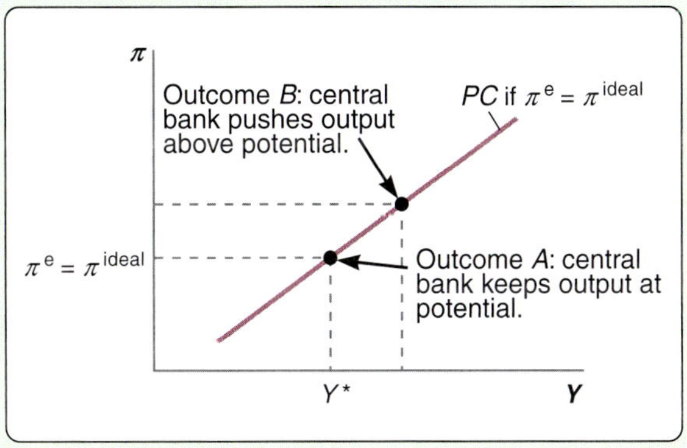

If expected inflation equals π^{ideal}, the central bank chooses between two outcomes for the economy, shown here by the points labeled *A* and *B* on the Phillips curve. In the Kydland-Prescott theory, policymakers are likely to choose outcome *B*, which implies that a promise of $\pi = \pi^{ideal}$ is not time-consistent.

is easy to eliminate, but real-world inflation was stubbornly high. Kydland and Prescott sought to resolve this paradox—to explain how high inflation can occur despite rational expectations.

Answering the Puzzle In the Kydland-Prescott theory, the central bank would like to follow the anti-inflation policy shown in Figure 16.1. It would like to promise low inflation, so that expected inflation falls. Unfortunately, this policy is not time-consistent. The central bank has an incentive to renege on its promise, just like a Dad issuing threats to his kids.

This incentive arises from the Phillips curve. Once expected inflation is set, there is a trade-off between output and inflation. If expected inflation is low, the central bank has an incentive for expansionary policy—a decrease in interest rates. This policy causes an output boom but also raises inflation above the expected level.

Figure 16.2 illustrates this point. We assume for the moment that the central bank has promised an inflation rate of π^{ideal} and the public believes this promise. So π^e in the Phillips curve is π^{ideal}. In this situation, the central bank has two options. One is to keep output at potential, producing the inflation rate that's expected. In this

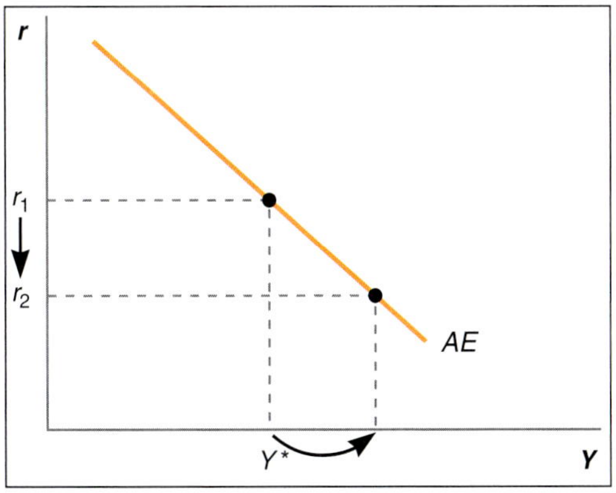

In the short run, the central bank can raise output above potential by reducing the real interest rate.

case, the economy ends up at outcome *A* in Figure 16.2. The other option is to raise output above potential, which the central bank can do by lowering interest rates. Raising output moves the economy along the Phillips curve to outcome *B*, with an inflation rate somewhat above π^{ideal}. In this case, the public's inflation expectations turn out to be wrong.

Will the central bank choose point *A* on the Phillips curve or point *B*? We will call this choice the *inflation-surprise decision*. According to Kydland and Prescott, policymakers are likely to choose point *B*, where output exceeds potential and inflation is higher than the public expects. An increase in output has large benefits: people's incomes rise and unemployment falls. Policymakers don't like the higher inflation, but they may decide this is an acceptable cost of producing an economic boom.

You may see what's coming. The public understands the central bank's incentives. If policymakers promise inflation of π^{ideal}, people realize the policymakers are likely to renege, so everyone ignores the promise. The situation in Figure 16.2, with $\pi^e = \pi^{\text{ideal}}$, never arises. Instead, as shown in **Figure 16.3**, expected inflation is high. Through the Phillips curve, high expected inflation produces high actual inflation. We call this outcome the *high-inflation trap*.

In Figure 16.3, we assume the central bank keeps output at potential. Notice that policymakers still have the option of raising output and moving along the Phillips curve. But this option is less appealing than it was in Figure 16.2. In the high-inflation trap, expected inflation is high. This means inflation is a serious problem even if policymakers keep it at the expected level. Pushing inflation even higher would have large costs, so policymakers don't do it.

Kydland and Prescott's argument is subtle. If you want to explore it further, go to the Chapter 16 Online Appendix at the text Web site.

FIGURE 16.3 The High-Inflation Trap

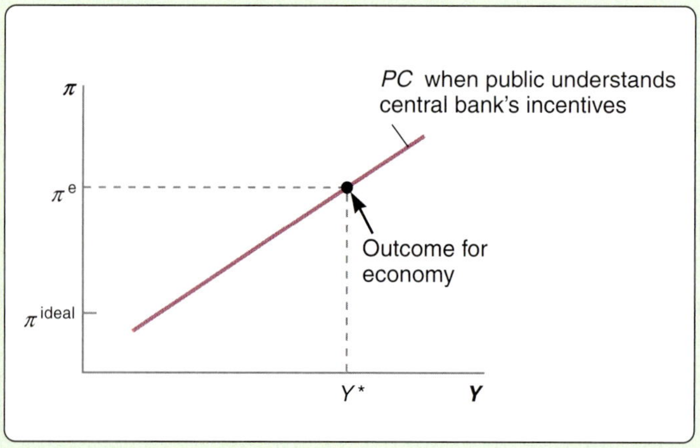

When the public understands the central bank's incentives, both expected and actual inflation are high.

Solving the Time-Consistency Problem

In the Kydland-Prescott theory, the time-consistency problem dooms the economy to high inflation. But is the situation really hopeless? Is there any way for central banks to solve the time-consistency problem? These questions have stimulated much analysis. Economists have suggested several methods for reducing the problem.

Conservative Policymakers One idea was suggested in 1983 by Kenneth Rogoff, a young economist at the Federal Reserve Board (now an older Harvard professor). This idea is based on the fact that governments appoint the policymakers who run central banks. The U.S. president, for example, appoints the chair of the Federal Reserve. Rogoff suggests that governments can solve the time-consistency problem via their choices of policymakers.

The criterion for choosing policymakers is their views about inflation. Economists have not reached a consensus about how inflation affects the economy. Some believe it does severe damage, while others think the costs are modest, as we discussed in Chapter 14. Rogoff uses the term *conservative* for those who strongly dislike inflation. These people think it is more important to keep inflation low than to stimulate output. Rogoff argues that governments should appoint **conservative policymakers** to run central banks.

Conservative policymaker
Central bank official who believes it is more important to keep inflation low than to stimulate output

To see how this strategy solves the time-consistency problem, look again at the surprise-inflation decision in Figure 16.2. In this scenario, the public expects inflation of π^{ideal}. Kydland and Prescott say the central bank will create an output boom that raises inflation above π^{ideal}. But that won't happen if policymakers are conservative. Conservatives won't raise output, because they believe the benefits of doing so are outweighed by the costs of higher inflation. If the public expects inflation of π^{ideal}, that's what they get.

▶ As you know, people use the word *conservative* to describe viewpoints on many issues, from tax policy to Supreme Court decisions. However, Rogoff's definition of the term has caught on in discussions of monetary policy.

Therefore, if policymakers are conservative, the time-consistency problem disappears. The central bank can promise inflation of π^{ideal} and people will believe it. Then policymakers produce the promised inflation rate by keeping output at potential. They achieve the low-inflation outcome in Figure 16.1, which eludes less conservative policymakers.

Remember this in case you become president of the United States. If Rogoff's analysis is correct, then you should choose conservatives to run the Fed. Note that you, the president, should appoint conservatives even if you are *not* conservative yourself. You might care more about output than inflation, but it would be foolish to appoint a Fed chair who shares your concern. Such an appointment would lead to the high-inflation trap in Figure 16.3. A conservative will produce lower inflation without reducing output.

Reputation Conservative policymakers are one hope for escaping high inflation. Another is central bankers' concern for their reputations. Regardless of whether policymakers are conservative in Rogoff's sense of the term, they would like people to *believe* they are conservative. This concern can solve the time-consistency problem.

To see this point, suppose a new Fed chair is appointed. Initially, the public doesn't know this person's views about inflation—policymakers don't wear labels saying whether they're conservative. The public judges the chair based on her performance in office. If the chair produces low inflation, she gains a reputation as a conservative and the public expects low inflation in the future. Conversely, a record of high inflation produces high expected inflation.

High expected inflation is bad for the economy. It shifts the Phillips curve up, raising actual inflation for any given output gap. This shift worsens the trade-off facing policymakers. So any Fed chair would like to gain a conservative reputation that keeps expected inflation low.

This desire influences the surprise-inflation decision in Figure 16.2. As before, expansionary policy has the benefit of raising output and the cost of raising inflation. But now it has an additional cost: it damages the chair's reputation as an inflation fighter, hurting the economy in the future. Even if the Fed chair is *not* conservative, this additional cost may tip her decision away from expansionary policy. Like a true conservative, she keeps inflation at π^{ideal} if that's what the public expects. This eliminates the time-consistency problem, making low inflation feasible.

In this theory, it is desirable for policymakers to care a lot about their reputations. This happens if policymakers have long time horizons—if they put a large weight on how their actions today affect the future. Then the costs of raising expected inflation are a strong deterrent to inflation.

One way to encourage long horizons is to give long terms in office to central bank officials. If policymakers come and go, each may decide to do what's best for the economy while he's in charge—and that leads to the high-inflation trap. If a policymaker will be around for a long time, he cares more about his reputation.

A Policy Rule The last solution to the time-consistency problem is the simplest. The government imposes a rule requiring the central bank to produce low inflation. Kydland and Prescott advocated such a rule in their 1977 article.

Suppose again you are the U.S. president. Don't worry about whom you appoint as Fed chair or the length of the chair's term. Instead, ask Congress to pass a law requiring the Fed to produce an inflation rate of π^{ideal}. The law might say that any Fed chair who produces inflation significantly above π^{ideal} is fired. Or, to be really safe, the punishment could be 20 years in Federal prison.

This law quickly eliminates the time-consistency problem. To avoid punishment, Fed chairs will try hard to keep inflation at π^{ideal}, even if they think higher inflation would benefit the economy. That is, the rule forces policymakers to act conservative even if they are not. Understanding this, the public will expect inflation of π^{ideal}.

16.2 CENTRAL BANK INDEPENDENCE

The United States is a representative democracy. Most decisions about economic policy are made by elected officials. For example, fiscal policy—taxation and government spending—is determined by Congress and the president. If the majority of citizens don't like these leaders' policies, they can vote them out of office.

Monetary policy is a critical part of economic policy, with strong effects on people's jobs and incomes. But unlike taxes and spending, monetary policy is not determined by elected government officials. It is run by the independent Federal Reserve System, most of whose leaders have never won an election.

Politicians and economists have long debated whether central banks should be independent of governments. Today, a consensus holds that independence is good. We will see that this belief reflects the Kydland-Prescott theory of time consistency and inflation.

The Independent Federal Reserve

The U.S. Constitution gives Congress the power to create money. But Congress has delegated this job to the Federal Reserve, which it established in 1913. As we discussed in Section 11.1, the government has little control over Fed officials. Governors of the Fed System are chosen by the U.S. president initially, but they serve 14-year terms and can't be fired. Presidents of Federal Reserve Banks are chosen by the banks' boards of directors, without any input from elected officials.

In addition, the U.S. government has an informal tradition of treating the Fed as independent and nonpolitical. Fed governors are likely to be chosen for technical expertise in monetary policy rather than political connections. Ben Bernanke's appointment as Fed chair is a clear example. Bernanke had served briefly as a Bush administration economist, but he spent most of his career as a professor at Stanford and Princeton universities. He made his name by publishing papers in academic journals, and he was not active in politics.

▶At least, Bernanke was not active in *national* politics. While at Princeton, he was twice elected to the school board of Montgomery Township, NJ.

Another tradition is that Fed chairs serve for a long time. The U.S. president has the right to replace the chair every 4 years, but often forgoes this opportunity—even if the president and the Fed chair belong to different political parties. Alan Greenspan was chair from 1987 to 2006, when he retired at age 79. He was appointed by Republican Ronald Reagan and reappointed by Democrat Bill Clinton, as well as both Republican Bushes. Before that, Paul Volcker was appointed by Democrat Jimmy Carter and reappointed by Reagan.

Recent administrations have helped strengthen the Fed's independence by resisting the temptation to give it advice or criticize its actions publicly. In 1999, President Clinton said, "I've made a real practice of trying not to comment on interest rate changes and trying to let Chairman Greenspan and the Fed do their work and I would do mine." President George W. Bush followed the same policy. Reporters ask administration officials about their views on Fed policy, but generally they don't get an answer.

Another factor behind the Fed's independence is its income. Most government agencies depend on funding from Congress. Members of Congress can use the threat of budget cuts to influence agencies' policies. The Fed, however, does not need congressional appropriations. As we saw in Section 11.2, the Fed creates money and trades it for government bonds, which produces a large flow of interest income (ranging around \$20–\$40 billion in recent years). The Fed uses part of this income to fund its operations, then returns the rest to the U.S. Treasury. Like an independently wealthy person, the Fed is free to do what it chooses without fear that someone will punish it financially.

Congress does monitor what the Fed does. Congressional acts require the Fed chair to testify twice a year before the Senate Banking Committee and the House Committee on Financial Services. The chair is asked to explain the Fed's policies, and committee members sometimes criticize the chair or ask sharp questions. But this is just talk—under current law, Congress can't force the Fed to change its policies.

Independence Around the World

Before the 1990s, most central banks were less independent than the Federal Reserve. The Bank of England was an extreme example, as it had no authority to set interest rates. Rates were chosen instead by a government official, the chancellor of the exchequer (the British equivalent of the U.S. secretary of the treasury). The central bank had only a technical job: it performed open-market operations to produce the interest rates chosen by the chancellor.

Other central banks were more independent than the Bank of England but less independent than the Fed. In Japan, interest rates were chosen by the Policy Board of the Bank of Japan. However, the board was not entirely independent: it included one official from the government's ministry of finance and another from its economic planning agency. In addition, the government had the authority to fire the governor of the bank.

In continental Europe, countries such as Germany and Switzerland had highly independent central banks. But in countries such as France and Italy, governments had the right to veto central-bank decisions.

This landscape has changed drastically in the last two decades. Around the world, governments have enacted legislation to make their central banks more independent. This movement started in New Zealand, where a 1989 law changed the central bank from one of the least independent in the world to one of the most independent. In 1997, the UK shifted interest-rate decisions from the chancellor of the exchequer to the Bank of England. In 1998, Japan eliminated most of the government's influence over the Bank of Japan. Many Latin American countries also granted independence to their central banks during the 1990s. Today, U.S.-style independence is the worldwide norm.

The European Central Bank (ECB) is highly independent. The ECB was established in 1999 by the Maastricht Treaty, an agreement among the 11 countries that first adopted the euro as their currency. The governments of these countries agreed to give up all authority over monetary policy. The ECB's independence has unusually strong foundations because it does not depend on legislation in any one country. The Maastricht Treaty can be changed only by agreement of all the countries that signed it.

Even today, not *all* central banks are independent. For example, the People's Bank of China must receive approval for major decisions from the State Council, part of the Chinese government. Officials at the People's Bank have argued for greater independence, as have outside economists and the International Monetary Fund, but so far the government has not relaxed its control.

What explains the trend toward central bank independence? Why do economists urge China to follow this trend? Policymakers have debated the pros and cons of independence for many years. In the 1990s, many countries decided that the pro-independence side had the stronger arguments. Let's survey both sides of this debate.

Opposition to Independence

Many people have criticized the independence of the Fed. Their central argument is a political one: in a democracy, elected officials should control economic policy. At a minimum, Congress should have greater influence over the Fed.

One person with this view is Congressman Barney Frank, Democrat of Massachusetts, who is pictured on p. 475. In 2007, Frank became chair of the House committee that oversees the Fed. In a 2007 speech, Frank criticized the idea that "the Fed somehow should be above democracy." He asserted a role for Congress in monetary policy, saying sarcastically, "God forbid anybody in elected office should talk about whether or not we need a 25-basis-point increase in interest rates. Somehow that's sacrosanct. No, it isn't. It's public policy."

For many critics of Fed independence, a desire for democracy is mixed with another concern. They fear that the priorities of central banks are those of financial interests, not ordinary citizens. These critics follow in a long tradition of populists, such as Andrew Jackson, who distrust central banks. (Recall the story of Jackson and the Second Bank of the United States in Section 8.2.)

Today's populists argue that the Fed is too concerned with fighting inflation, which Wall Street dislikes. It does not care enough about promoting employment, which is more important for ordinary people. For example, at a 2007 hearing, Barney Frank reminded Ben Bernanke that Congress has set "maximum employment" as one of the Fed's goals. Frank said, "I am concerned there are people at the Fed who don't really accept that."

Periodically, members of Congress propose legislation that would reduce the Fed's independence. In 1991, Lee Hamilton of Indiana proposed that Fed bank presidents be removed from the FOMC, leaving only the Fed governors. In his view, the power of Bank presidents is particularly undemocratic, because they are not appointed by elected officials. Hamilton also proposed that the secretary of the treasury be *added* to the FOMC. In

1996, Senators Dorgan and Reid of North Dakota proposed that Congress assume authority over the Fed's budget.

More recently, Congressman Frank has advocated greater oversight of the Fed, saying his committee will "pay a little more attention" to the Fed's actions. To this end, Frank has expanded the semiannual hearings that review Fed policy. After the Fed chair testifies, the committee hears from people with different viewpoints, such as liberal economists and representatives of labor unions.

Under current law, congressional critics can't force the Fed to change its policies. Proposed legislation to reduce the Fed's independence has not passed, and no new legislation appears imminent. The majority of Congress is satisfied with the status quo.

Nonetheless, the opposition to independence has probably influenced the Fed. It reminds the Fed that its power is derived from legislation that Congress could change. It would be risky for the Fed to pursue policies that too many in Congress oppose. At a minimum, unpopular policies will lead to harsh questions at congressional hearings. At worst, proposals to limit the Fed's independence could gain enough support to pass. We'll see later how fear of political criticism has influenced the Fed's behavior.

The Traditional Case for Independence

What are the arguments for central bank independence? At a philosophical level, supporters argue that Fed independence is not really undemocratic. Congress still has ultimate authority over monetary policy. Congressional acts prescribe the goals of policy, and it was Congress's choice to assign the pursuit of these goals to the Fed.

Most important, proponents of independence believe that it leads to better monetary policy. The arguments about why have evolved over time. A long-standing argument is that independence protects the Fed from political pressures for unwise policies—in particular, policies that produce high inflation.

This argument is clearest if we assume the Phillips curve from Section 13.4: $\pi = \pi(-1) + \alpha\tilde{Y}(-1)$. This version of the Phillips curve is based on the assumption of adaptive expectations, which makes inflation depend on past inflation. The equation also assumes that output affects inflation with a 1-year lag, which will be important here.

Economic events affect politics as well. Presidential elections are influenced heavily by the state of the economy in election years. Suppose you are the U.S. president and you want to be reelected. Suppose also that the Fed is *not* independent: you can tell it what to do. You can help yourself by ordering a monetary expansion, one that causes an economic boom during election year. The boom will cause inflation to rise, but with a lag; if you time it right, inflation will rise *after* the election. On election day voters will see a booming economy and stable inflation and reward you with another term.

Unfortunately, this strategy is bad for the economy in the long run. Inflation rises after the election. And with the Phillips curve we have assumed, the increase in inflation is permanent. Future policymakers must either live with high inflation indefinitely or cause a recession to disinflate. Either way, your reelection has a high cost.

This scenario is less likely if the central bank is independent. Fed policymakers don't have to run for reelection. They are free to concentrate on the long-run health of the economy, not its performance in any particular year. They won't expand policy if the future inflationary costs exceed the short-run benefits.

Independence and Time Consistency

The arguments we have discussed have been around for many decades. In the 1980s and 1990s, supporters of central bank independence added new arguments. These do *not* involve elections; instead, they are based on Kydland and Prescott's time-consistency problem. Economists argue that central bank independence reduces this problem for two reasons.

Conservative Central Bankers Ironically, the first argument is closely related to an argument *against* central bank independence. Populists complain that Fed officials are out of step with the public in caring too much about inflation and not enough about output and employment. In Rogoff's terminology, Fed officials are too conservative. Elected leaders are more likely to share the public's concerns, so they should control monetary policy.

In the Kydland-Prescott theory, however, conservatism is a virtue. It helps central banks to escape the time-consistency problem. Turning monetary policy over to less-conservative politicians would worsen this problem, leading to higher inflation without any gain in output. So everyone, even populist members of Congress, should want conservative central bankers to run policy.

Long Horizons The time-consistency problem can be solved if policymakers establish reputations for hating inflation. As we have discussed, this is more likely to happen if policymakers have long time horizons. Economists argue that central bankers have longer horizons than politicians, giving them a better chance of escaping the time-consistency trap.

Long horizons partly reflect long periods in office. We've seen that Fed governors have 14-year terms and that Alan Greenspan was chair for nearly 19 years. If Fed officials acquire reputations for producing high inflation, they know this will raise inflation expectations for a long time. So policymakers have strong incentives to keep inflation low.

In addition, central banks can acquire reputations that are not tied to individual people. This occurs because policy is made by groups of people whose terms in office overlap. In particular, most economists agree that the Fed has a reputation for low inflation after nearly three decades of producing it. As an institution, a central bank has a very long horizon, because its authority lasts indefinitely. So policymakers care a lot about preserving an anti-inflation reputation.

Evidence on Independence and Inflation

The different arguments for central bank independence have a point in common: they imply that independence reduces inflation. Inflation falls because policymakers don't need to get reelected or because the time-consistency problem is reduced. In the 1980s and 1990s, economic researchers tested these theories by comparing different countries. Most concluded that independence really does reduce inflation.

The first step in this research was to measure the independence of central banks. Economists created numerical ratings of independence based on various factors. For example, a central bank received points if its top policymakers served long terms and could not be fired. It lost points if monetary-policy boards included government officials, or if the government had veto power over central bank decisions.

Once researchers measured central bank independence in various countries, they compared it to inflation. **Figure 16.4** shows one set of results, from a 1993 study by Harvard's Alberto Alesina and Lawrence Summers. The figure plots an index of independence against average inflation for the period 1955–1983, revealing a strong negative relation. For the period before 1983, the countries with the most independent central banks, Germany and Switzerland, had the lowest inflation. The least independent banks, in New Zealand and Spain, produced the highest inflation.

FIGURE 16.4 Central Bank Independence and Inflation, 1955–1988

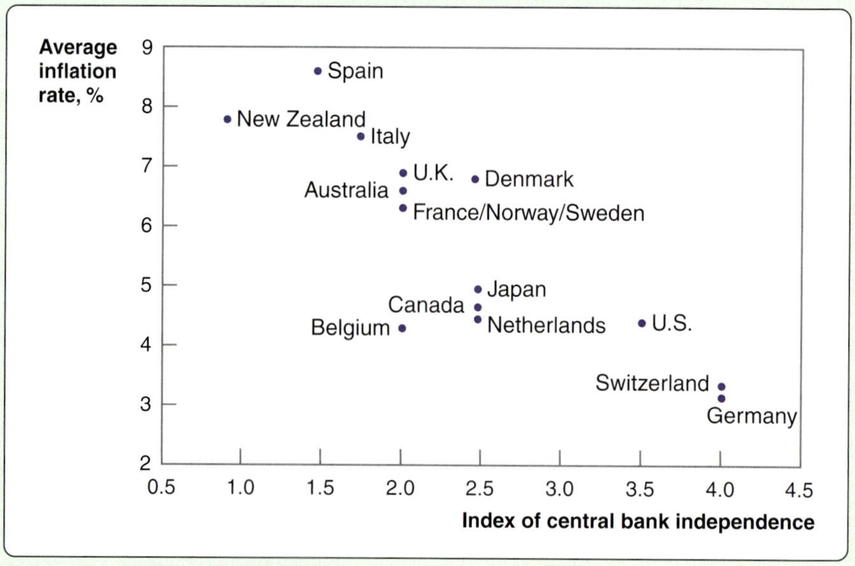

A comparison of central bank independence and average inflation among 16 countries reveals that countries with more independent central banks have lower inflation.

Source: Alberto Alesina and Lawrence H. Summers, "Central Bank Independence and Macroeconomic Performance: Some Comparative Evidence," *Journal of Money, Credit, and Banking*, May 1993

Some economists question these results, pointing out that a correlation between two variables does not prove that one causes the other. It could be that some third factor determines both independence and inflation. In particular, some countries may simply dislike inflation more than others.

One commonly cited example is Germany. Polls in that country find that people consider inflation very harmful, an attitude that may reflect the scarring experience of the 1920s' hyperinflation (see Section 14.2). Because Germans hate inflation, their central bank kept inflation low. The government supported this policy by making the central bank independent, but this was not the underlying cause of low inflation. Granting the same independence to Spain's central bank would not have reduced inflation to German levels, because Spaniards don't hate inflation as much as Germans do.

Despite this argument, governments in most countries have become convinced that central bank independence does reduce inflation. They interpret the relationship in Figure 16.4 as causal. Evidence like this is a major reason for the trend toward independence since 1989.

16.3 MONETARY POLICY RULES

Independent central banks have great power over the economy. How freely should they exercise this power? Should central banks be able to adjust policy in any way they like, or should their actions be constrained? This is a classic controversy in economic policy. In economists' language, the question is whether central banks should use discretionary policy or follow a monetary policy rule.

Two Approaches to Policy

Discretionary policy means the central bank acts at each point in time based on its judgment of what's good for the economy. This is how the Fed currently operates. The FOMC meets every 6 weeks to set the federal funds rate. At each meeting, committee members examine whatever information they think is relevant and decide what interest rate is best in the current situation.

Discretionary policy Monetary policy that is adjusted at each point in time based on the judgment of the central bank

A **monetary policy rule**, by contrast, is a simple rule or formula that tells the central bank what to do. When such a rule is in place, the job of policymakers is to follow the rule, not to use their judgment about what actions are best.

Monetary policy rule A simple rule or formula that tells the central bank how to run policy

One policy rule was proposed by the great economist Milton Friedman. Under this rule, the central bank increases the money supply by a fixed percentage every year. A different rule might dictate that money growth varies over time according to some formula. If the central bank uses an interest rate as its policy instrument, a rule could say how the interest rate is set.

Where does a policy rule come from? It could be imposed on the central bank by legislation or even a constitutional amendment. But a central bank can also adopt a rule on its own. Policymakers can announce the rule and commit themselves to follow it rather than use discretionary policy.

The traditional distinction between rules and discretion has been somewhat muddied by the work of John Taylor. Fed policies since 1987 can be captured approximately by a "Taylor rule" in which the interest rate adjusts to output and inflation. But the Fed has *not* followed a rule in the sense of the rules vs. discretion debate. Policymakers don't consciously use Taylor's formula, and sometimes they deviate from it significantly.

▶To review the Taylor rule, see Chapter 15.

Which is better, a policy rule or discretion? It might seem obvious that discretion is preferable. Under this approach, the central bank always chooses the policy that appears best in current circumstances. A rule may force the central bank *not* to choose the policy that appears best. How can that be a good idea?

Like the case for central bank independence, the case for rules comes in older and newer styles. And once again, the newer arguments are based on Kydland and Prescott's time-consistency problem.

Traditional Arguments for Rules

The classic case for policy rules was developed in the 1960s by Milton Friedman and his followers. These economists are called **monetarists**. Monetarists believe that monetary policy has strong effects on output and inflation. In theory, this means that policy can be an effective tool for stabilizing the economy. But in practice, monetarists believe, central banks misuse this tool. Their discretionary policies do more harm than good, so they should be constrained by rules.

Monetarists School of economists who believe that monetary policy has strong effects on the economy and that policy should be set by a rule

Monetarists point out two problems with discretionary policy, both related to ideas we've discussed before. Policymakers can make well-intentioned mistakes, and they can succumb to political pressure.

Well-Intentioned Mistakes

Central bankers are uncertain about the economy. They may misjudge parameters such as the natural rate of unemployment or the effects of interest rates on spending. Because of these mistakes, efforts to stabilize the economy can backfire and destabilize it. It would be better, monetarists conclude, if a rule prevented the central bank from attempting stabilization.

▶Section 15.5 discusses central bankers' uncertainty about the economy.

Milton Friedman expressed these ideas with a metaphor. In 1960 he wrote:

> *What we need is not a skilled monetary driver of the economic vehicle continuously turning the steering wheel to adjust to the unexpected irregularities of the route, but some means of keeping the monetary passenger who is in the back seat as ballast from occasionally leaning over and giving the steering wheel a jerk that threatens to send the car off the road.*[1]

A monetary rule is a way of keeping the Fed's hands off the steering wheel.

Support for these ideas grew during the 1970s. During that period, the Fed appeared to jerk the steering wheel: it overreacted to movements in output and inflation. It allowed inflation to rise in the early 1970s, perhaps because it underestimated the natural rate of unemployment. It then became alarmed by inflation and tightened sharply, causing a deep recession

[1] Milton Friedman, *A Program for Monetary Stability,* Fordham University Press, 1960.

in 1974–75—at which point it loosened again, causing another rise in inflation. The decade ended with another sharp tightening, the start of the Volcker disinflation. These policy shifts were meant to stabilize the economy, but critics think they did the opposite.

Political Influence The other traditional argument against discretion is that it allows politics to influence monetary policy. As we have discussed, politicians would like monetary expansions before elections, even if these actions hurt the economy in the long run. They may pressure the central bank for overly expansionary policies.

Central bank independence is meant to solve this problem. However, this solution has not always worked. Recent presidents have respected the Fed's independence, but some of their predecessors have not. Some historians argue that presidents have been able to influence the Fed to an unhealthy extent. This could not happen if the Fed's hands were tied by a policy rule. The next case study discusses a famous episode of presidential pressure on the Fed.

CASE STUDY

Nixon and Burns

Richard Nixon understood the effects of monetary policy on elections. In his book *Six Crises*, he complained that a Fed tightening had slowed the economy before the 1960 presidential election. Voters blamed the Eisenhower administration, in which Nixon was vice president. Nixon thought this contributed to his narrow loss to John Kennedy.

Once Nixon became president in 1968, he didn't want monetary policy to interfere with his reelection. William McChesney Martin's term as Fed chair expired in 1970, and Nixon replaced him with Arthur Burns. Burns was a highly respected economist and long-time Nixon advisor. At the time of his Fed appointment, Burns was part of Nixon's White House staff. Some historians suggest that Nixon chose a Fed chair whom he thought would follow his wishes.

AP/Wide World Photos

Richard Nixon (center) consults with his economic advisors during the 1968 presidential campaign. The group includes Arthur Burns (second from right) and Milton Friedman (second from left).

Clearly, Nixon tried to influence Burns's policies. At the ceremony to announce Burns's appointment, Nixon said, half-jokingly, "I respect his independence. However, I hope that independently he will conclude that my views are the ones that should be followed." When his audience applauded, Nixon said, "You see, Dr. Burns, that is a standing vote for lower interest rates and more money."

In private, Nixon gave Burns blunt advice. A biographer of Burns quotes Nixon as telling him, "You see to it: no recession." In a letter to Burns, Nixon acknowledged why this was so important: "I must register with you, as strongly as I can, my concern that what really determines the result of an election is not interest rates, but unemployment statistics around election time." White House aides sometimes called Burns to reiterate the president's desire for expansionary policy.

According to William Safire, a Nixon speechwriter, the administration used the press to pressure Burns. When Burns resisted Nixon's policy suggestions, the White House planted a false and unflattering story that Burns was seeking a pay raise. Administration officials also suggested they were considering legislation to increase the number of Fed governors, which would have diluted Burns's power.

Was this pressure effective? In retrospect, monetary policy was clearly too loose before the 1972 election. The economy grew too rapidly, helping to fuel the high inflation of the mid-1970s. Some historians think the Fed made an honest mistake because it mismeasured the natural rate of unemployment (see section 15.5). But others think Burns was overly eager to help Nixon. They point out that Burns resisted proposals by other Fed governors to tighten policy.*

* For more on this episode, see Burton A. Abrams, "How Richard Nixon Pressured Arthur Burns: Evidence from the Nixon Tapes," *Journal of Economic Perspectives*, Fall 2006.

Time Consistency Again

The case for monetary policy rules was bolstered by Kydland and Prescott's analysis of the time-consistency problem. This problem arises under discretionary policy, which gives the central bank power to loosen policy whenever it wants. As we have discussed, a policy rule is a simple solution to the problem. A rule can force the central bank to produce low inflation. The time-consistency problem disappears.

Notice that this argument is quite different from the traditional arguments for rules. Suppose that central banks pay no attention to politicians. And suppose they don't make mistakes—they understand exactly how their policies affect the economy. The time-consistency problem still causes central banks with discretion to produce too much inflation.

Money Targets

Suppose you are convinced that central banks should follow a policy rule. What rule is best? Thinking on this topic has changed over time. From the 1960s to the 1980s, the leading proposal was Milton Friedman's rule of fixed money growth.

Currently, most central banks use an interest rate as their policy instrument. They set targets for the interest rate and adjust the money supply to hit the targets. Friedman and the monetarists argued that central banks should instead target the money supply and let markets determine interest rates.

▶Section 11.5 discusses interest-rate targeting and the rationale for this policy.

Further, they proposed a simple rule for money targets: the targets should grow over time at a low, constant rate, such as 3 percent per year. Each year, the central bank should raise the money supply 3 percent above its level in the previous year. Money growth determines inflation in the long run, so low money growth would keep average inflation low. In addition, the monetarists argued, the constancy of money growth would promote stability in output and inflation.

Crucially, the monetarist rule implies that central banks do *not* "lean against the wind" of output and inflation movements. In a recession, a central bank with discretion is likely to raise money growth to stimulate aggregate spending; in a boom, it slows money growth. The monetarist rule forbids these variations in money growth, because they are likely to backfire and destabilize the economy.

Today, few economists advocate a fixed growth rate for the money supply—or any policy based on money targets. Most economists believe that money demand is unstable, which implies that money targets destabilize output. In the United States, money targeting was discredited by the experience of 1979–1982, when the Fed tried this policy and output fluctuated sharply.

Most other central banks have also dismissed the idea of money targets. But there is a major exception: the European Central Bank. The ECB announces targets for money growth, although it doesn't try to hit them precisely. We discuss the ECB's approach in an upcoming case study.

16.4 INFLATION TARGETS

During the 1980s, many central bankers were unsure of the best approach to monetary policy. They were convinced of the dangers of discretion. But they didn't like the monetarist rule of fixed money growth, both because of instability in money demand and because they were reluctant to give up entirely on leaning against the wind. So central bankers searched for new policy ideas.

Today, many central bankers think they have found a good way to run policy: explicit inflation targeting. Policymakers announce that they want to keep inflation near a certain level, such as 2 percent, or in a certain range, such as 1–3 percent. They also declare that achieving this goal is the primary focus of policy.

Explicit inflation targets were first introduced by New Zealand in 1989 and Canada in 1990. Since then, inflation targeting has spread around the world, and many economists advocate it for the United States. Let's discuss how inflation targeting works and the arguments for and against this policy.

How Inflation Targeting Works

Inflation targeting is a different type of policy from money or interest-rate targeting. "Targeting" in those cases refers to the choice of a policy instrument, a variable the central bank controls precisely.

An inflation target, by contrast, is a goal for the economy that the central bank can't achieve perfectly. Inflation is influenced by economic shocks, which policy can offset only with a lag. So inflation inevitably fluctuates somewhat around the target. This imprecision is one reason that countries sometimes announce a target range rather than a single number.

A related feature of inflation targeting is that it is forward-looking. The lags in policy effects mean that central banks can't raise or lower current inflation if it is off-target. Instead, they try to push future inflation toward the target.

Adjusting Interest Rates Most central banks use an interest rate as their policy instrument, including most central banks with inflation targets. Thus, in common terminology, many central banks are both interest-rate targeters *and* inflation targeters. They use their interest-rate instrument to pursue their goal for inflation.

Because of time lags, a major part of inflation targeting involves forecasting inflation. Central bank economists forecast inflation using various economic models and statistical methods (see Section 15.6). They try to predict how inflation would respond to different choices of interest rates. Policymakers choose interest rates that imply forecasts of inflation heading toward the target.

Figure 16.5 gives an example of inflation targeting in the Republic of Laurencia. The Central Bank of Laurencia has an inflation target of 2 percent,

FIGURE 16.5 Inflation Targeting in Laurencia, 2020

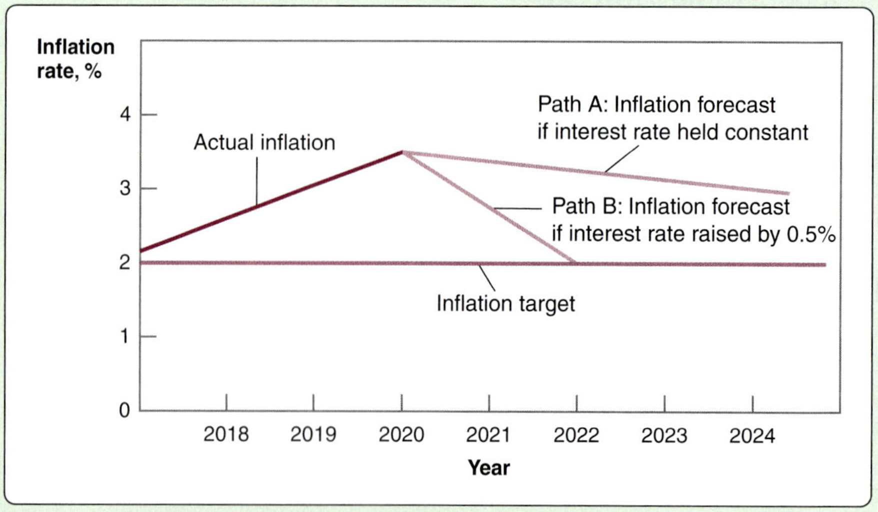

Laurencia has an inflation target of 2%, but in 2020 actual inflation is 3.5%. Central bank economists forecast that inflation will stay high if the interest rate is held constant. Policymakers raise the interest rate, pushing inflation forecasts back to the target.

but in 2020 a rise in world oil prices has pushed inflation to 3.5 percent. If the bank keeps interest rates constant, its economists forecast that inflation will follow Path A, staying well above 2 percent. So the bank needs to raise rates.

The bank's economists estimate that a half-point rise in interest rates will shift inflation to Path B, which leads back to the target in 2022. So the bank raises rates by this amount. Depending on shocks after 2020, inflation in 2022 may end up higher or lower than forecasted, so the bank may continue to miss its target. But it will keep adjusting interest rates to push inflation in the right direction.

Flexible Targets Economists distinguish between two types of inflation targeting. *Strict* targeting means that hitting the inflation target is the central bank's only goal. If shocks push inflation away from the target, policy pushes it back as quickly as possible.

Flexible targeting means the central bank is not concerned *only* with inflation. It also pays attention to the goal of output stability. As a result, it may tolerate some deviations from the inflation target. If inflation is above target, for example, policymakers may reduce it slowly. They don't disinflate quickly, because that would require a sharp increase in interest rates and a sharp fall in output.

In practice, it appears that central banks choose flexible inflation targeting. No central bank ignores output stabilization entirely. The Bank of England has expressed a typically flexible attitude, saying that strict targeting would create "unnecessary uncertainty and volatility." The bank's goal is that "inflation can be brought back to target within a reasonable time period without creating undue instability in the economy."[2]

An open question is just how flexible targeters should be. How long is it acceptable for inflation to vary from the target? How much output volatility is acceptable to control inflation? Central banks have not given clear answers to these questions. The Bank of England, for example, does not define the "reasonable time period" in which inflation should return to target.

Because of this vagueness, inflation targeting is not as rigid as a traditional policy rule, such as money targeting. It allows more leeway for policymakers to use their judgment. Policy under inflation targeting is sometimes called "constrained discretion," meaning it is a compromise between a monetary policy rule and purely discretionary policy.

The Spread of Inflation Targeting

The 1990s were a momentous period for monetary policy. Many central banks became more independent during that decade, as we saw in Section 16.2. At the same time, many countries adopted explicit inflation targeting.

Figure 16.6 presents a time line showing when countries adopted inflation targeting. So far, this has occurred in three waves. Starting with

[2] "Monetary Policy Framework" at www.bankofengland.co.uk

FIGURE 16.6 The Spread of Inflation Targeting

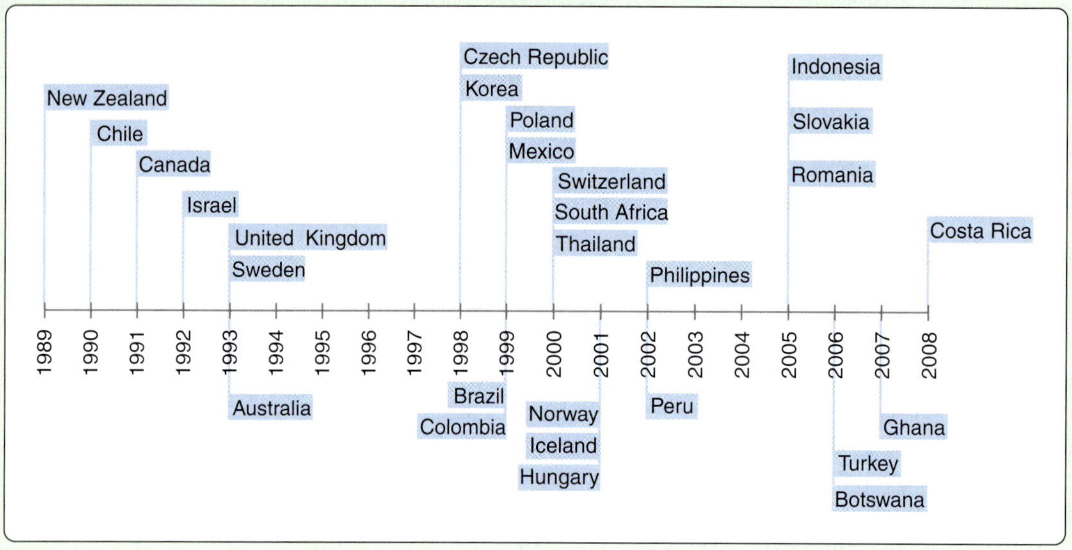

New Zealand, seven countries adopted inflation targeting between 1989 and 1993. Fourteen countries adopted the policy between 1998 and 2002, and seven more joined the club between 2005 and 2008. Adopters range from the U.K. and Canada to countries throughout the developing world.

In some countries, the decision to adopt inflation targets was made by the central bank. At some point, central bank officials simply announced that they would start targeting a certain inflation rate. In other countries, the government has imposed inflation targeting on the central bank. One example is the United Kingdom. The British government has granted independence to the Bank of England in the sense that the bank sets interest rates. But the chancellor of the exchequer still tells the bank what goal to pursue in adjusting rates. Currently, the bank is required to target 2 percent inflation.

Another variation is for inflation targets to be chosen jointly by the government and the central bank. In Canada, for example, the government's finance minister and the central bank governor sign periodic agreements on targets. A 2006 agreement extended the current target range, 1–3 percent, through 2011.

Monitoring the Policy When inflation targeting is established, it is usually accompanied by another change: the central bank starts publishing more information about its policies. One purpose is to assure the government and the public that policymakers are doing their best to achieve the announced targets. Typically, the central bank publishes an "Inflation Report" every 3 months. These reports present forecasts of inflation and discuss what interest rates are needed to push inflation to its target. For example, the Bank of England publishes a detailed report that usually runs about 50 pages in length.

In some countries, the central bank must provide a formal explanation if inflation deviates significantly from target. If the Bank of England misses its 2 percent target by more than 1 percentage point, the governor must write an open letter to the chancellor of the exchequer discussing what happened and how the bank will rectify the situation. This requirement was triggered for the first time in April 2007, when inflation reached 3.1 percent.

The text Web site links to the Bank of England site, where you can find inflation reports and the open letter from the governor to the chancellor.

Inflation Targeting in the United States? The Federal Reserve has not adopted explicit inflation targeting, but many economists think it should. Ben Bernanke's 2005 appointment as Fed chair increased speculation about this possibility, because Bernanke had advocated inflation targeting as an economics professor. Bernanke and Frederic Mishkin of Columbia University coined the term "constrained discretion" in a 1997 paper.[3] After Bernanke took office, he initiated several discussions of inflation targeting at FOMC meetings.

Yet it is not clear whether inflation targeting is in the Fed's future. Some officials oppose the idea, notably Donald Kohn, the Fed's vice chair. Over 2007–2008, the Fed was distracted from the topic by urgent problems arising from the subprime mortgage crisis. It's likely that discussions of inflation targeting will begin again when financial markets are more tranquil.

Why do some people support inflation targeting and others oppose it? Let's turn to the pros and cons of this policy.

The Case for Inflation Targeting

In some ways, inflation targeting is not very different from policy in nontargeting countries, including the United States. The Fed appears to have an *implicit* inflation target of around 1–2 percent. It tightens policy when inflation rises above this level and loosens when inflation falls, just as it would if the target were explicit. Some economists conclude that it doesn't matter whether central banks announce inflation targets. This action has little effect because it doesn't change policymakers' choices of interest rates.

More broadly, some are lukewarm about inflation targets because central banks have done well without them. In particular, since the 1980s the Federal Reserve has produced low and stable inflation, and usually stable output as well. When economists suggest a new approach for the Fed, a common response is "if it ain't broke, don't fix it."

Yet many economists believe that explicit inflation targets have large benefits. Advocates of inflation targeting make two main arguments: targeting reduces the dangers of discretionary policy, and it anchors inflation expectations.

Locking in Good Policy We've seen that inflation targeting is less rigid than a traditional policy rule. Yet the central bank's behavior is

[3] Ben Bernanke and Frederic Mishkin, "Inflation Targeting: A New Framework for Monetary Policy," *Journal of Economic Perspectives*, Spring 1997.

"constrained" by the commitment to targets. Constraints reduce the dangers of discretionary policy.

In particular, explicit targets help to ensure low inflation rates. If inflation were consistently above target, it would be obvious that the central bank was not doing its job. This would prompt criticism and embarrass policymakers. It would probably endanger their reappointments. All this gives policymakers incentives to keep inflation low.

Another constraint is the requirement that policymakers explain their actions in inflation reports. This requirement reduces the risk of erratic policy or political influence. Under inflation targeting, it would have been hard for Arthur Burns to expand policy to help Richard Nixon. Burns would have been hard-pressed to justify his actions on economic grounds.

What about the argument that current policy "ain't broke"? The answer is that things might change. A president might appoint a Fed chair who is soft on inflation, or someone who is close to the president politically. Inflation targeting would help lock in good policy regardless of who runs the Fed. In the words of Bernanke and Mishkin, inflation targeting would "depersonalize" policy, making success "less dependent on the competence or the convictions of a few individuals."

Anchored Expectations Supporters of inflation targeting argue that it changes the behavior of expectations. This change makes it easier for policymakers to stabilize output and inflation.

The argument starts from the premise that in the absence of inflation targeting, expectations are likely to be adaptive. That is, expected inflation equals past inflation. This implies that any rise in inflation, say from an adverse supply shock, raises expected inflation in the future.

▶ For more on the trade-off between output stability and inflation stability, see Sections 12.4 and 15.4.

This fact creates an unpleasant trade-off for the central bank. A rise in expected inflation feeds through into higher actual inflation, unless the central bank tightens policy and reduces output. Policymakers must destabilize output to prevent changes in inflation from becoming permanent.

But now suppose the central bank announces an inflation target. This commitment changes the behavior of expectations. The public understands that any changes in inflation will be temporary, as policymakers will push inflation back to the target. As a result, expectations become "anchored": the public expects inflation to equal the target even if past inflation did not.

Now it's easy to stabilize inflation. If a supply shock pushes it up, expected inflation stays constant at the target. Thus, once the initial shock disappears, inflation goes back to target automatically. The central bank doesn't need to tighten policy and reduce output. By anchoring expectations, inflation targeting improves the trade-off between inflation stability and output stability.

This theory is controversial. Some economists doubt that inflation targeting changes the basic behavior of people's expectations. They suggest that targeting has *not* changed the policy trade-offs in countries that have adopted it. Debate on this issue is continuing as part of the larger debate about inflation expectations.

Opposition to Inflation Targeting

Why not adopt an inflation target? Many critics of this policy make a simple argument. Central banks such as the Fed should seek to stabilize both output and inflation. Under inflation targeting, policy focuses primarily on inflation, so output stability suffers. For example, if the economy enters a recession, the central bank may not act aggressively to raise output.

Supporters of inflation targeting respond with two counterarguments. First, in many circumstances inflation targeting naturally stabilizes output as well as inflation. This fact follows from the Phillips curve. If output rises above potential, this causes inflation to rise above its target. To contain inflation, the central bank must tighten policy and curtail the output boom. Conversely, a recession causes inflation to fall *below* its target, so the central bank will loosen policy to fight a recession.

Second, as we discussed earlier, inflation targeting is a flexible policy. Policymakers allow temporary deviations from the target when necessary to stabilize output. An inflation-targeting central bank can stabilize output just as well as a nontargeting central bank.

But will it? Skeptics argue that, in practice, inflation targeting leads policymakers to deemphasize output stability. Remember that one argument *for* inflation targeting is that the policy is not *too* flexible. It "constrains" central banks, putting pressure on them to achieve targets or at least explain why they don't. Policymakers may be judged as failures if they miss inflation targets too often or by large amounts.

In contrast, central banks do not announce numerical goals for output, and there are no clear criteria for judging the success of output stabilization. Policymakers feel less pressure to stabilize output than to hit inflation targets, and this asymmetry leads them to sacrifice output too readily. If inflation exceeds its target, for example, policymakers may push it down quickly even if this causes a recession.

Donald Kohn, the Fed vice chair, expressed this view in a 2005 essay. He noted that inflation targeting allows for output stabilization in theory, but

> *in practice, the presumption still is that the numerical [inflation] goal will be hit consistently, with the burden of proof on any deviations—and that presumption must be part of the mind-set of the policymaker. In most inflation-targeting countries the periodic reports of the central bank are called inflation reports, not inflation and output variability reports. . . . Inflation targeting is usually accompanied by elements of accountability linked directly to the inflation target—and to that target alone.*[4]

We conclude our discussion of inflation targeting with two case studies. The first discusses evidence on the effects of the policy, and the second discusses a variation on inflation targeting practiced by the European Central Bank.

---

[4] Donald Kohn, comment on Marvin Goodfriend, "Inflation Targeting for the United States?," in Ben Bernanke and Michael Woodford (eds.), *The Inflation Targeting Debate,* University of Chicago Press, 2005.

CASE STUDY

Targeters and Nontargeters

A number of economists have tried to measure the effects of inflation targeting by examining countries that adopted it. One study was published in 2005 by this author and Niamh Sheridan of the International Monetary Fund.* We examined seven countries that adopted inflation targeting in the early 1990s, comparing their economic performance before and after targeting. We also compared these countries to thirteen others that did *not* adopt inflation targets.

Ball and Sheridan found that performance usually improved after a country introduced inflation targeting. Average inflation fell, and both inflation and output became more stable. Inflation expectations, as measured by economists' forecasts of future inflation, also became more stable.

However, countries that *didn't* adopt inflation targets experienced similar improvements in their economies. This result suggests that the improvements were not caused by targeting. Instead, some positive development—perhaps better policy, perhaps fewer adverse shocks—was common to targeters and nontargeters.

Table 16.1 presents some of Ball and Sheridan's results. The table shows inflation rates for the twenty countries in the study. For each country, it

TABLE 16.1 Inflation Targeting and Average Inflation

		Average Inflation over Pretargeting Period, %	Average inflation over Posttargeting Period, %
Targeters	Australia	5.4	2.6
	Canada	4.4	1.6
	Finland	4.1	1.1
	New Zealand	10.2	1.9
	Spain	5.9	2.5
	Sweden	5.4	1.0
	United Kingdom	5.5	2.4
Nontargeters	Austria	2.7	1.8
	Belgium	2.5	1.7
	Denmark	3.2	2.2
	France	3.1	1.4
	Germany	2.2	1.7
	Ireland	3.1	2.1
	Italy	5.7	3.3
	Japan	1.6	0.1
	The Netherlands	1.6	2.2
	Norway	4.9	2.2
	Portugal	10.6	3.5
	Switzerland	3.3	0.8
	United States	3.7	2.5

Source: Laurence Ball and Niamh Sheridan, "Does Inflation Targeting Matter?," in Bernanke and Woodford (eds.), *The Inflation Targeting Debate*, University of Chicago Press, 2005

presents average inflation for two periods: one from 1985 until the early 1990s, when inflation targeting started; and one from the early 1990s to about 2000 (the exact dates vary across countries).

The table shows that average inflation dropped from the first, pretargeting period to the second, posttargeting period in 19 of the 20 countries in the sample. (The Netherlands was the exception.) These decreases were part of the worldwide trend toward lower inflation, discussed in Chapter 14. The key result is that the decreases were similar for targeters and nontargeters. In each group, inflation in most countries fell to between 1 and 3 percent in the posttargeting period.

One interpretation of Ball and Sheridan's results is that explicit inflation targeting doesn't have much effect on the economy. However, it is too early to draw strong conclusions, as targeting has only a two-decade history. Perhaps nontargeting central banks will perform less well in the future because of the dangers of discretionary policy. If so, future data may show clearer benefits of inflation targeting.

* See Laurence Ball and Niamh Sheridan, "Does Inflation Targeting Matter?," in Bernanke and Woodford (eds.), *The Inflation Targeting Debate,* University of Chicago Press, 2005. For a skeptical evaluation of Ball and Sheridan's evidence, see Mark Gertler's Comment in the same volume.

CASE STUDY

The ECB's Two Pillars

Most central banks can be identified clearly as inflation targeters or nontargeters. The European Central Bank, however, is an intermediate case. The ECB has an inflation target, but it's a fuzzy one: the ECB seeks inflation "below but close to 2 percent." Policymakers haven't said exactly what that means.

In addition, the ECB's approach to interest-rate adjustment differs from pure inflation targeting. Inflation targeters set rates based on forecasts of inflation (see Figure 16.5). The ECB bases interest-rate decisions *partly* on inflation forecasts but also on another variable: the growth rate of the money supply. According to the ECB, inflation forecasts and money growth are the "two pillars" of its policy.

Specifically, the ECB has announced a "reference value" of 4.5 percent for annual growth in M3, a broad measure of the money supply. The ECB's M3 aggregate is comparable to the Fed's M2. If the growth of M3 exceeds 4.5 percent, the ECB is more likely than otherwise to tighten policy; if M3 growth is below 4.5 percent, policy is more likely to loosen.

▶Section 2.4 discusses the Fed's M2 aggregate.

Why respond to money growth? In explaining their policy, ECB officials cite the strong long-run relation between money growth and inflation. Rapid money growth is likely to produce high inflation at some point in the future. So it is prudent to tighten policy, even if short-run forecasts of inflation are low.

More generally, two pillars are better than one because of uncertainty about the economy. Flawed assumptions can lead to inaccurate forecasts of inflation, so it is risky to base policy entirely on these forecasts. Examining money growth is a method of "cross-checking" that reduces the risk of policy mistakes.

Outside the ECB, many economists question the two-pillar approach. One reason is instability in money demand, which has dissuaded other central banks from targeting money. Yet the ECB has resisted suggestions to modify its policy.

The text Web site links to the ECB site, which discusses the two-pillar policy.

16.5 COMMUNICATION BY CENTRAL BANKS

Throughout this chapter, we've seen that expectations about monetary policy affect the economy. Policymakers influence expectations not only by their actions but also by what they say. So a big issue for central banks is how best to communicate with the public.

We've already discussed one question about communication: whether central banks should announce explicit inflation targets. Here we address two other issues: how policymakers can establish anti-inflation reputations and how much information they should release about the policy process.

Reputation

In the Kydland-Prescott theory, policymakers should seek reputations as conservatives, people who hate inflation and are determined to keep it low. Such reputations help overcome the time-consistency problem that produces high inflation. Central bankers around the world have taken this idea to heart.

What determines reputations? The largest factor is past performance: a central banker gains a reputation for low inflation by producing low inflation. However, public statements also matter. Policymakers try to say things that enhance their reputations as inflation fighters.

Alan Greenspan had a strong anti-inflation reputation based on both performance and statements. When Ben Bernanke became Fed chair, he hoped to inherit some of that reputation. Partly for that reason, Bernanke promoted the idea that his policies were similar to Greenspan's. In congressional testimony in 2006, Bernanke said, "My intention is to maintain continuity with the practices of the Federal Reserve in the Greenspan era."

Policymakers at the European Central Bank have tried hard to establish conservative reputations. Since the ECB was created only in 1999, it doesn't have a long track record of fighting inflation. Perhaps for this reason, ECB officials go to great lengths to assure the public of their opposition to inflation.

One example is a 2000 speech by Ottmar Issing, then the ECB's chief economist, on the costs of inflation. As we discussed in Chapter 14, research has not clearly established that moderate inflation has large costs. But you wouldn't know that from Issing's speech. He mentions several economic costs, such as relative price variability. He then continues:

> *[T]he case for price stability goes beyond the purely economic sphere. Price stability, the ability to rely on stable money, is the basis for trust in the interaction between economic agents, trust in property rights, trust in society, and trust in the*

future more generally. Trust in stable money is also the basis for a free society, the ability of people to take decisions and plan their future for themselves. . . . There is a saying that "peace is not everything, but without peace everything else comes to nothing." I am tempted to say the same thing for price stability. Inflation—like war, to which it is often closely associated—destroys the fruit of honest labour, it devalues savings and investment, it erodes the social fabric of society, and ultimately, puts the very foundations of democracy and freedom at risk."[5]

Statements like this help convince the public that the ECB will keep inflation low.

To illustrate the importance of anti-inflation reputations, the next case study shows what can happen if a policymaker doesn't have one.

CASE STUDY

Alan Blinder

In 1994, President Clinton appointed Alan Blinder as vice chair of the Fed. Blinder had strong qualifications: he was a long-time professor at Princeton University and an expert on monetary policy. (He had coauthored several papers with a younger Princeton colleague, Ben Bernanke.) When Blinder was appointed, journalists speculated that he might eventually succeed Alan Greenspan as Fed chair.

But some observers were critical of the appointment. They feared that Blinder was not strong enough in his opposition to inflation. In a 1987 book, he had argued that the Fed sometimes overreacted to inflation. Using a medical analogy, he called inflation "a head cold"—annoying, but not a major disease. As a result, he lacked the anti-inflation reputation sought by many central bankers.

When Blinder was appointed, Chairman Greenspan asked David Mullins, the outgoing vice chair, to review Blinder's writings. Mullins was to report on whether Blinder's views were appropriate for a Fed official. Mullins told Greenspan, "It's not perfect." Then he said, "Don't worry, it's not like he's a Communist or anything. It's just in his early publications he's noticeably soft on inflation." Greenspan's response: "I would have preferred he were a Communist."

Once he took office, Blinder was careful not to compare inflation to a head cold. However, he soon ran into trouble at a Fed conference where he was asked to make concluding comments. The topic of the conference was "Reducing Unemployment," so Blinder talked about the effects of monetary policy on unemployment. A Fed publication summarized his remarks as follows:

[Blinder] pointed out monetary policy could affect short-run cyclical fluctuations in unemployment. Moreover, he argued that central banks should attempt to guide the unemployment rate to the natural rate. He thus viewed the legislative mandate

[5] Ottmar Issing, "The Case for Price Stability," St. Edmund's College Millennium Year Lecture, Cambridge University, 2000. Available at www.ecb.int.

*calling upon the Federal Reserve to pursue both maximum employment and stable prices as being an appropriate charge for central banks.**

These ideas are basic economic principles that we have discussed in this book. It is clear that the Fed tries to stabilize unemployment at the natural rate. (By Okun's law, this is equivalent to stabilizing output at potential.) Nonetheless, Blinder's talk differed from many comments by central bankers in stressing unemployment rather than the battle against inflation. As a result, it strengthened impressions that Blinder was not sufficiently conservative in Rogoff's sense, making him a poor choice to run a central bank.

Journalists played up the idea that Blinder had unconventional views. A front-page story in the *New York Times* said Blinder "publicly broke ranks with most of his colleagues today, saying he believed that the nation's central bank should seek to hold down unemployment in setting interest rates." *Newsweek* columnist Robert Samuelson wrote that Blinder's comments showed he lacked "the moral or intellectual qualities needed to lead the Fed."

Chairman Greenspan chose not to comment on the controversy, which many interpreted as lack of support for Blinder. According to journalist Bob Woodward, the result was a "subtle but deadly sting." The controversy probably cost Blinder any chance of promotion to Fed chair. In 1996 he left the Fed for his old job at Princeton.

Blinder thinks he got a raw deal. In writing about his experience, he points out that the views in his speech were conventional, and that Congress has instructed the Fed to seek high employment as well as low inflation. As Blinder puts it ironically, "My endorsement of the Fed's dual mandate meant that the Vice Chairman of the Federal Reserve was publicly endorsing the Federal Reserve Act. Now there's news for you!"

On the other hand, critics suggest that Blinder's remarks were politically naive. They think the Fed's conservative reputation helps keep inflation low, and that policymakers should be careful not to endanger this reputation.†

* Bryon Higgins, "Reducing Unemployment: Current Issues and Policy Options—A Summary of the Bank's 1994 Symposium," Federal Reserve Bank of Kansas City *Economic Review*, Fourth Quarter 1994.

† For more on this episode, see Bob Woodward, *Maestro: Greenspan's Fed and the American Boom*, Simon and Schuster, 2000; and Alan Blinder, "Central Banking in a Democracy," Federal Reserve Bank of Richmond *Review*, 1996. The *New York Times* article is Keith Bradsher, "Fed Official Disapproves of Rate Policy," August 28, 1994. The Samuelson column is "Economic Amnesia: Alan Blinder Forgets the Dangers of Inflation," September 12, 1994.

Transparency

Transparency Provision to the public of clear and detailed information about policy making

So far we have discussed policymakers' statements about their basic goals. Many central banks go beyond these broad statements to discuss the rationales for specific actions. They refer to this provision of information as **transparency.** For example, the Web site of the European Central Bank says, "Transparency means providing the public with all relevant information on the ECB's strategy, assessments, and policy decisions as well as on its procedures in an open, clear and timely manner."

In the last two decades, many central banks have become more transparent. This trend has accompanied the movements toward central bank independence and inflation targeting. Like these other reforms, transparency is motivated partly by academic theories of inflation expectations.

Transparency can take many forms. Different central banks provide different types of information about their policies. However, several approaches have become common:

- Many central banks issue publications that give the rationale for recent decisions. These publications also discuss the likely course of future policy. In countries with inflation targets, this material is usually included in inflation reports. Other central banks have publications that serve the same purpose, such as the ECB's *Monthly Bulletin*.
- Some central banks publish the economic forecasts produced by their staffs. Typically they provide forecasts of inflation and output over the next two or three years.
- Some central banks publish minutes of the meetings at which interest rates are set. The Fed, for example, publishes minutes of FOMC meetings. This gives the public a picture of the debate behind policy decisions.
- At some central banks, officials hold press conferences to explain their actions and take questions. At the ECB, for example, the president and vice president hold a press conference after each announcement of an interest-rate target.

Why Transparency? Central bankers give several reasons for moving toward transparency:

- One reason is political. Many economists support central bank independence but feel uncomfortable with unelected officials making policy in secret. They believe central bankers should be accountable. Policymakers have a duty to explain their actions to the public, from whom their authority ultimately derives.
- Another motive for transparency is its effect on inflation expectations. As we've seen, policymakers want the public to believe that they will keep inflation low. Broad statements about this intention only go so far. The public is more likely to be convinced if policymakers provide details about what they are doing to control inflation.
- Finally, transparency helps policymakers control long-term interest rates. Aggregate expenditure is influenced by these rates, which in turn depend on expectations of the short-term rates set by central banks (see Section 13.1). A transparent central bank can influence long-term rates by guiding expectations of short-term rates. For example, it can raise long rates by telling the public that short rates will rise in the future.

The Fed's Tradition of Secrecy Transparency hasn't always been popular. Before the 1990s, many central banks were nontransparent. Mystery surrounded policymaking in many countries, including the United States. A 1987 bestseller about the Fed was called *Secrets of the Temple*.

Before 1994, the FOMC did not release any information at the end of a meeting—not even its interest-rate target. The committee ordered open-market operations to achieve the target, but outsiders had to figure out what the target was by observing actual interest rates. Only after 6 weeks, following the *next* FOMC meeting, did the committee release any information. At that point it issued a "Policy Record" giving a broad summary of the meeting.

It was difficult to get more information out of the Fed. The chair was required to testify before Congress, but he described policy only in generalities. Alan Greenspan, the chair from 1987 to 2006, was famous for the nontransparency of his statements—and proud of it. He once said, "Since I've become a central banker, I've learned to mumble with great coherence. If I seem unduly clear to you, you must have misunderstood what I said."[6]

Why this attitude? Probably the main reason was fear of political criticism. The Fed did *not* want to be overly accountable for its actions, so it was reluctant to talk about them.

While undemocratic, this attitude is defensible. As we've discussed, the Fed sometimes needs to do unpopular things for the long-run good of the economy. In particular, it sometimes needs to tighten policy and reduce output to control inflation. If it's obvious what the Fed is doing, it will hear criticism from populist politicians and face threats to its independence. Obfuscation may be necessary for the Fed to do the right thing.

Chapter 11 discussed the example of disinflation in the early 1980s. Fed Chair Volcker knew that a severe tightening of policy was needed to reduce inflation and that this action would be unpopular. Therefore, some historians argue, Volcker tried to confuse people about what he was doing. He shifted from interest-rate targeting to money targeting to make it less obvious that the Fed was responsible for high interest rates.

Moving Toward Transparency Despite this history, the Fed has been influenced by the worldwide trend toward transparency. It has become more transparent over time. This change has occurred through a series of small steps, which are shown in **Figure 16.7.** Some of these steps involve the minutes of FOMC meetings. In 1993 the Fed started releasing minutes 6 weeks after each meeting. In 2004, this delay was reduced to 3 weeks.

The Fed has also expanded the information provided immediately after FOMC meetings. The committee started announcing its interest rate targets in 1994. Since then it has added brief statements discussing its decisions and what it might do in the future. It also announces dissents from committee decisions by individual members.

Since 1979, the FOMC has issued semiannual projections of future output, unemployment, and inflation. Initially, this practice was a response to

[6] Alan Greenspan, Testimony to the U. S. Congress, September 1987.

FIGURE 16.7 The Increasing Transparency of the FOMC

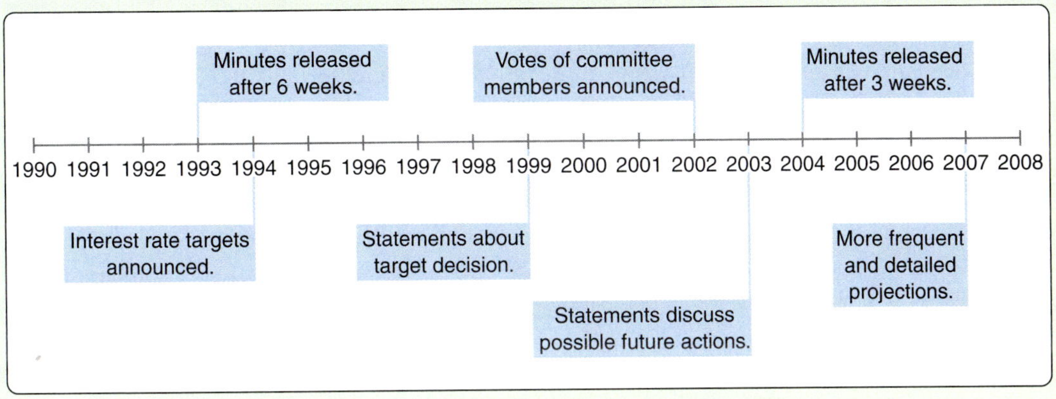

Starting in the 1990s, the FOMC has increased its transparency through a series of small steps.

congressional pressure for greater openness. In 2007, however, the Fed took the initiative to provide more information. It started releasing projections four times a year, increased the number of variables it projects, and extended the horizon for projections from 2 years to 3. It also started publishing explanations for the projections.

Despite these actions, the Fed remains less transparent than many central banks. The Green Book, which includes the detailed economic forecasts of the Fed's staff, is released only after 5 years, for the benefit of historians. Fed officials never hold press conferences. The minutes of policy meetings are less detailed than in some countries, such as the United Kingdom. The Fed still appears somewhat skittish about providing ammunition for its critics.

In announcing the 2007 changes in Fed projections, Chairman Bernanke said, "The communications strategy of the Federal Reserve is a work in progress." It is likely that more items will be added to the time line in Figure 16.7.

Online Case Study: An Update on Fed Transparency

Summary

16.1 Time Consistency and Inflation

- Monetary institutions and strategies have been heavily influenced by Kydland and Prescott's theory of the time-consistency problem facing central banks.
- The problem of time-consistency arises when someone has incentives to make a promise but later renege on it; because of these incentives, others don't believe the promise.
- The time-consistency problem can produce high inflation. If central bankers promise to keep inflation low, they have incentives to renege with expansionary policies that raise inflation. Therefore, the public doesn't believe policymakers' promises, and the economy ends up in a high-inflation trap.
- Possible solutions to the time-consistency problem include the appointment of conservative central bankers, policymakers' concern for their reputations, and rules for monetary policy.

16.2 Central Bank Independence

- The Federal Reserve is independent of the government: elected officials can't control its policies.

Throughout the world, central banks have become more independent over the last two decades.

- Populist politicians argue that central bank independence is undemocratic and that it leads policymakers to overemphasize the problem of inflation relative to unemployment.
- Supporters of independence argue that it protects policymakers from political pressure for unsound policies. It also reduces the time-consistency problem, as central bankers tend to be conservative and to care about their reputations. Research has found that countries with more independent central banks have lower average inflation rates.

16.3 Monetary Policy Rules

- A central bank can either use discretionary policy, adjusting it at each point in time based on policymakers' judgment, or follow a monetary policy rule that tells the bank what to do.
- Milton Friedman and the monetarists argued that policy rules reduce the risks of unstable or politically motivated policies. Modern supporters also argue that rules reduce the time-consistency problem.
- The rule advocated by monetarists was a fixed growth rate for the money supply. Few economists advocate this rule today, largely because of the instability of money demand.

16.4 Inflation Targets

- In the last two decades, about 30 countries have adopted an explicit inflation target. When inflation deviates from the target, the central bank adjusts interest rates to guide it back. Policymakers report regularly to the public on their efforts to control inflation.
- Many economists think the Federal Reserve should adopt an inflation target. Supporters interpret inflation targeting as "constrained discretion," a policy that combines flexibility with the benefits of a monetary rule. Inflation targeting also anchors inflation expectations.
- Other economists oppose inflation targeting, fearing that it causes policymakers to overemphasize inflation stability at the expense of output stability.
- The European Central Bank practices a variation on inflation targeting in which it adjusts policy based on the growth rate of the money supply.

16.5 Communication by Central Banks

- Central bankers try to establish reputations for hating inflation. A policymaker gets in trouble if people perceive him as soft on inflation, as illustrated by the case of Alan Blinder.
- The Fed and other central banks have become more transparent in recent decades. They publish information such as economic forecasts and minutes of policy meetings. Transparency makes central banks accountable to the public, and it improves policymakers' control of inflation expectations and long-term interest rates.

Key Terms

Conservative policymaker, p. 481

Discretionary policy, p. 489

Monetarists, p. 490

Monetary policy rule, p. 489

Time-consistency problem, p. 477

Transparency, p. 504

Questions and Problems

1. Suppose a parent paid your college tuition this year. He or she wants you to get a summer job so you can contribute next year. You would prefer to spend your time with friends at the beach. Your parent says, "There's no way I'll pay for everything next year. If

you don't get a job, you'll have to take a semester off."

Are you likely to take this threat seriously and get a job? Explain why or why not. Answer this question under two different assumptions:

a. You are an only child.

b. You are the oldest of ten children.

2. Suppose the Phillips curve becomes steeper: a given change in output has a larger effect on inflation. How does this affect the time-consistency problem facing the central bank and the likelihood of high inflation? (*Hint:* Think about the inflation-surprise decision in Figure 16.2.)

3. In the Kydland-Prescott theory, it is desirable for central bank officials to hate inflation passionately. Is it also desirable for them to hate unemployment passionately? Explain why or why not.

4. Governors of the Federal Reserve serve overlapping terms in office. When one governor is appointed, the others are at various points in their terms. Suppose a new law mandates that all governors be appointed at the same time for concurrent terms. Would this increase or decrease the risks of discretionary monetary policy? Explain.

5. Consider the relationship between inflation targeting and Taylor rules (Section 15.3).

   a. The adjustment of interest rates under inflation targeting is similar to a Taylor rule. Explain why.

   b. If a central bank shifts from flexible inflation targeting to strict targeting, does the equivalent Taylor rule become more or less aggressive? (A more aggressive rule responds more strongly to movements in output and inflation.)

6. When President Bush announced Ben Bernanke's appointment as Fed chair, the Dow Jones stock index jumped by more than 1 percent in a few minutes.

   a. Why do you think that happened?

   b. If the United States adopted inflation targeting, how might that affect the reaction of the stock market to Fed appointments? Explain.

7. Figures 12.22 and 12.23 on p. 372 show the effects of an adverse supply shock in the AE/PC model. The figure assumes adaptive inflation expectations, $\pi^e = \pi(-1)$, and shows how the economy evolves if the central bank accommodates the supply shock and if it doesn't. Now suppose the central bank adopts an explicit inflation target, π^T. Inflation expectations become anchored at the target: $\pi^e = \pi^T$.

   a. For these expectations, show how the economy responds to a supply shock under an accommodative and a nonaccommodative policy.

   b. Does the anchoring of expectations make it more or less desirable to accommodate the shock? Explain.

8. In 2007, Congressman Barney Frank said the adoption of an explicit inflation target would be a "terrible mistake." Why do you think he believes that?

9. Consider a policy of "output and inflation targeting": the central bank announces numerical targets for both inflation and real GDP. What are the pros and cons of such a policy? No central bank has seriously considered this approach; why not?

10. Suppose the growth rate of Europe's money supply exceeds the ECB's reference value, leading the ECB to raise its interest-rate target. Will this action push money growth toward the reference value? Explain. (*Hint:* Review money and interest-rate targeting in Section 11.6).

11. In 2006, Ben Bernanke said the goals of strong output growth and low inflation "are almost always consistent with each other." Alan Greenspan once called the trade-off between output and inflation "ephemeral."

    a. Are these statements accurate? Explain.

    b. Why do you think the chairmen made these statements?

Online and Data Questions

www.worthpublishers.com/ball

12. The text Web site has data from the Ball-Sheridan study on inflation targeting. One variable is the standard deviation of output growth, which measures the instability of output.
    a. In theory, how might inflation targeting affect output stability? (*Hint:* One could argue for either positive or negative effects.)
    b. What do the Ball-Sheridan data say about this issue? Compare the standard deviation of output growth before and after the early 1990s in countries that adopted inflation targets and countries that didn't.
13. The text Web site links to "Inflation Targeting for the United States?" a 2005 article by economist Marvin Goodfriend, and to a comment on the article by Fed Vice Chair Donald Kohn. Goodfriend supports inflation targeting and Kohn opposes it. Write a brief essay saying which side you agree with and why.

chapter seventeen 17

Monetary Policy and Exchange Rates

- 17.1 EXCHANGE RATES AND STABILIZATION POLICY
- 17.2 COSTS OF EXCHANGE-RATE VOLATILITY
- 17.3 EXCHANGE-RATE POLICIES
- 17.4 FIXED EXCHANGE RATES
- 17.5 CURRENCY UNIONS

AP Photo/Michael Reynolds

July 31, 2007: U.S. Treasury Secretary Henry Paulson and Chinese Vice Premier Wu Yi chat about the dollar–yuan exchange rate.

The Bush Administration's policy was not to criticize the Federal Reserve. But U.S. officials *did* criticize another central bank: The People's Bank of China. They objected to the bank's efforts to hold down the value of China's currency, the yuan.

After meeting with Chinese leaders in 2007, President Bush said, "I emphasized to the delegation that we will be watching very carefully as to whether or not they will appreciate their currency." Treasury Secretary Henry Paulson said bluntly, "the currency needs to appreciate, and it needs to appreciate faster."

Why does China want a weak yuan? How does the People's Bank keep the currency weak? Why do U.S. leaders care? Can they force China to change its policy?

We begin this chapter on exchange-rate policy by discussing why central banks and governments care about exchange rates. Movements in exchange rates create risk for firms engaged in foreign trade and for owners of foreign assets. Exchange-rate fluctuations also interfere with policymakers' efforts to stabilize aggregate output and inflation. Consequently, many central banks try to stabilize exchange rates.

We then discuss *how* central banks influence exchange rates. Their tools include interest-rate changes, foreign-exchange interventions, and controls on capital flows. Sometimes countries cooperate in controlling exchange rates, but sometimes frictions occur, as with China and the United States.

We will see that every exchange-rate policy has pluses and minuses. As a result, exchange-rate policies are controversial around the world. Some central banks tolerate substantial fluctuations in exchange rates, while others try to keep them fixed. An extreme version of fixed rates is a currency union, such as the euro area. Countries in a currency union adopt a common money, making it impossible for exchange rates among the countries to change.

17.1 EXCHANGE RATES AND STABILIZATION POLICY

The relationship between monetary policy and exchange rates is complex. Sometimes changes in policy cause changes in exchange rates. An increase in interest rates by the central bank causes a fall in net capital outflows (capital outflows minus capital inflows). As a result, the currency appreciates. Such exchange-rate movements are part of the transmission mechanism through which monetary policy affects the economy (see Figure 13.7).

On the other hand, many movements in exchange rates are *not* caused by central banks. They can arise, for example, from shifts in the confidence of asset holders or changes in commodity prices. Such events can destabilize the economy, so central banks are likely to react to them. Shifts in monetary policy can be responses to exchange-rate movements as well as causes of these movements.

Exchange Rates and Aggregate Expenditure

▶ The analysis that follows draws on the theory of real exchange-rate fluctuations in Sections 6.4–6.5 and on the theory of aggregate expenditure in Section 12.2.

Let's discuss how a shift in exchange rates might affect an economy and how the central bank might respond. In this example, the underlying shock to the economy is a change in the confidence of asset holders.

Initially, the country of Boversia has a corrupt, inefficient government. But then an election brings better leaders to power. The economic outlook for Boversia improves, making Boversian assets more attractive to savers around the world. Higher confidence reduces Boversia's net capital outflows (NCO).

Figure 17.1A shows the effects of the confidence shift on Boversia's equilibrium real exchange rate (ε) and net exports (*NX*). In this graph, *NX* and *NCO* are measured in units of the local currency, the bover. The fall in net capital outflows means the *NCO* curve shifts to the left. The real exchange rate rises and net exports fall. Net exports fall because a higher real exchange rate makes Boversian goods more expensive relative to foreign goods.

The fall in net exports affects the aggregate expenditure (*AE*) curve, as shown in **Figure 17.1B.** Net exports are one of the four components of spending, along with consumption, investment, and government purchases. So the fall in net exports reduces aggregate expenditure for any given real interest rate (r). The *AE* curve shifts to the left.

FIGURE 17.1 Rising Confidence in Boversia

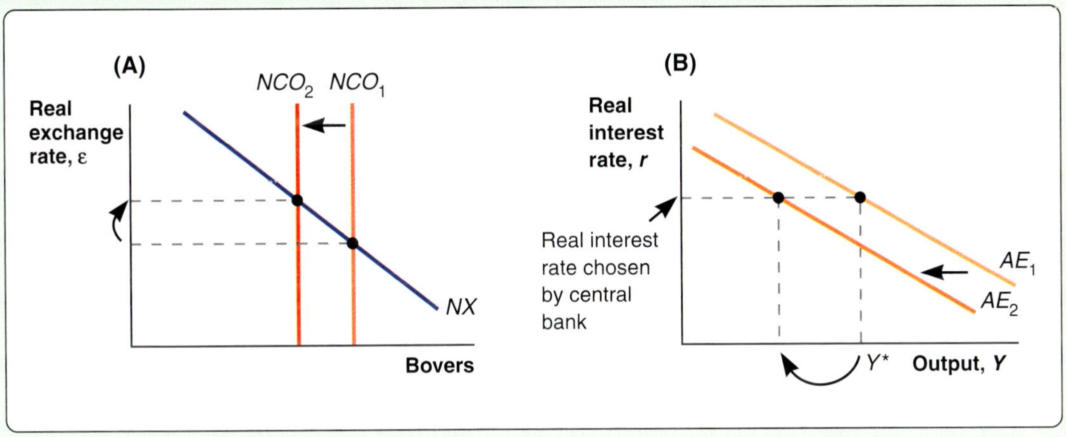

When Boversia's assets become more attractive to foreign savers, its net capital outflows fall and its real exchange rate rises (A). The higher exchange rate reduces net exports, shifting the aggregate expenditure curve to the left. If the central bank holds the real interest rate constant, output falls (B).

Suppose for now that Boversia's central bank holds the real interest rate constant. In this case, the shift in aggregate expenditure reduces output. We assume that output was initially at potential (Y^*), so the *AE* shift pushes it below potential. Notice the irony: when people become more confident in Boversia's future, the short-run effect is a recession.

Confidence in economies can fall as well as rise. A decrease in confidence produces the opposite scenario from Figure 17.1. The *NCO* curve shifts to the right, reducing the real exchange rate, and the *AE* curve shifts to the right, raising output.

As usual, output movements affect inflation through the Phillips curve. When a rise in confidence causes a recession, the inflation rate falls; when lower confidence causes an economic boom, the inflation rate rises. Generally, shifts in confidence and the resulting changes in exchange rates destabilize both output and inflation.

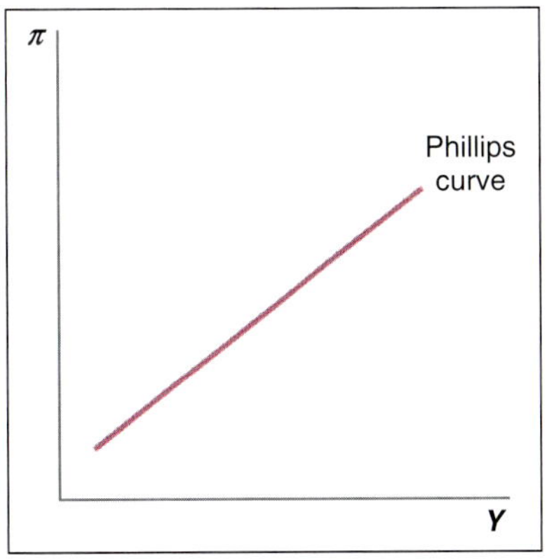

The Phillips curve captures the positive short-run relationship between output and inflation.

Offsetting Exchange-Rate Shocks

Central banks often try to stabilize the economy. When the *AE* curve shifts, policymakers adjust the real interest rate to keep output at potential. Such actions have side effects on exchange rates. **Figure 17.2** examines these effects using our example of increased confidence in Boversia.

The figure is easiest to understand if we start at the right, with Figure 17.2B. Remember that the appreciation of the

FIGURE 17.2 Rising Confidence and Output Stabilization

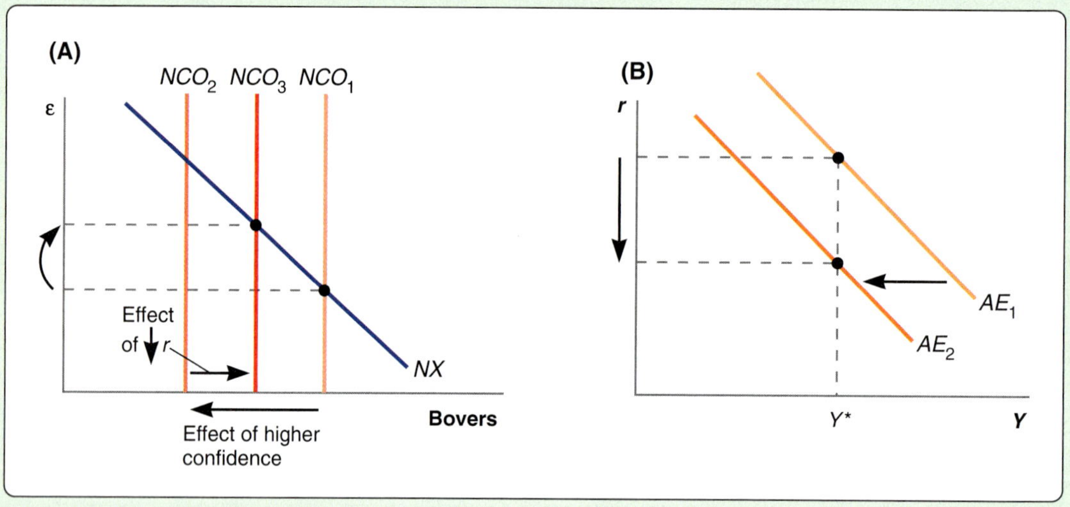

As in Figure 17.1, higher confidence in Boversia shifts both the *NCO* curve and the *AE* curve to the left. But now the central bank reduces the real interest rate to keep output at potential (B). This action shifts the *NCO* curve to the right, but does not fully offset the shift caused by higher confidence. The real exchange rate rises above its initial level (A).

bover has reduced net exports, shifting the *AE* curve to the left. The central bank offsets this shock by reducing the real interest rate, and output remains constant.

The central bank's action also affects the exchange rate, as shown in Figure 17.2A. Higher confidence in Boversia has shifted the *NCO* curve to the left, from NCO_1 to NCO_2. The lower interest rate works in the opposite direction: it makes Boversian assets less attractive, raising net capital outflows. The *NCO* curve shifts to the right, from NCO_2 to NCO_3.

Notice that the rightward shift in the *NCO* curve is smaller than the leftward shift caused by higher confidence in Boversia. Thus the real exchange rate ends up above its initial level. The central bank *could* push the exchange rate down farther by reducing the interest rate more. But this is not necessary to keep output at potential.

To see this point, think about the different components of aggregate spending. The exchange rate ends up higher than its initial level, so net exports are lower. However, the central bank has reduced the interest rate, raising consumption and investment. Higher consumption and investment balance lower net exports, keeping output constant despite the higher exchange rate. **Figure 17.3** summarizes these effects.

As usual, our theoretical analysis only approximates reality. We've ignored problems with stabilization policy such as time lags and uncertainty about policy effects. Because of these problems, real-world central banks can dampen the effects of exchange-rate shifts on output, but not offset them perfectly. Fluctuations in exchange rates inevitably cause some instability in output.

FIGURE 17.3 Effects on Components of Spending

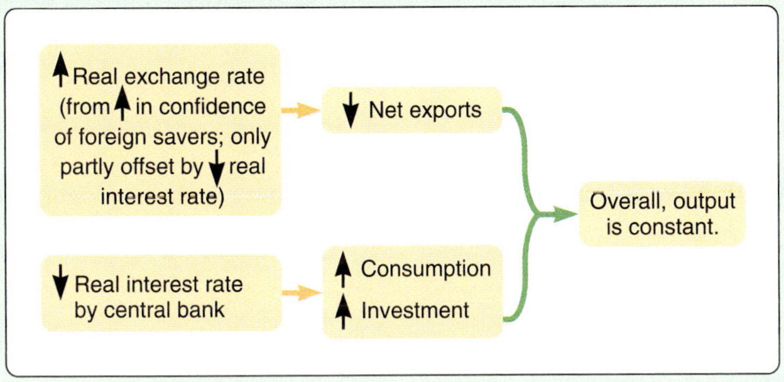

When confidence in Boversia rises and the central bank stabilizes output, the exchange rate rises and the interest rate falls. These changes have offsetting effects on aggregate expenditure.

How important are exchange rates for monetary policy? The answer varies across countries depending on their levels of foreign trade. Trade is especially important for small countries, where exports can be half of GDP or more. This means that changes in exchange rates have big effects on the economy, and central banks react to them strongly.

Trade is less important in the United States, where exports are around 15 percent of GDP. When the Fed chooses interest rates, exchange rates are a secondary factor: it focuses more on developments in the domestic economy. One can often ignore exchange rates in analyzing U.S. policy, while this is impossible for many countries. The next case study discusses a central bank that pays a lot of attention to exchange rates.

CASE STUDY

Canadian Monetary Policy

Canada has a high level of foreign trade: imports and exports are each about 40 percent of GDP. Over 80 percent of Canada's trade is with the United States. So exchange rates are important for Canada's economy, especially the rate between the U.S. and Canadian dollars. The Bank of Canada responds strongly to changes in this rate.

One example comes from the early 2000s. Canada experienced a fall in net capital outflows, the type of event portrayed in Figure 17.1. The underlying cause was declining confidence in the U.S., where the economy was slowing. U.S. assets became less attractive to Canadians, so less capital flowed out of Canada.

As predicted by Figure 17.1, the fall in net capital outflows raised Canada's exchange rate. The Canadian dollar rose from 0.62 U.S. dollars in January 2002 to 0.83 in November 2004. This appreciation reduced Canada's net exports, threatening to cause a recession.

The Bank of Canada responded with low interest rates. Over 2003–2005, the bank kept the nominal rate between 2 and 3 percent; inflation was around the same level, so the real rate was near zero. As in Figure 17.2, low interest rates kept output near potential despite the high exchange rate.

In February 2005, the bank's governor, David Dodge, explained the rationale for low interest rates. They were needed "to provide support for domestic demand [i.e., consumption and investment] to offset the additional drag we expect from net exports." The drag on net exports was the strong currency. Dodge's statement fits perfectly with Figure 17.3, which analyzes the different components of spending.

In other periods, Canada has experienced a *rise* in net capital outflows—the opposite of the shock in Figure 17.1. The exchange rate has fallen and the Bank of Canada has raised interest rates.

An example occurred during the mid-1990s, when Mexico experienced a financial crisis. A large government debt in Mexico produced fears of default, leading to capital flight (a large rise in net capital outflows). This episode made asset holders nervous about Canada, because it also had a large government debt. The Canadian dollar fell from 0.80 U.S. dollars in early 1993 to 0.71 in early 1995.

The fall in the exchange rate threatened to push output above potential, which would raise inflation. The Bank of Canada acted aggressively to prevent this outcome. To slow the economy, it raised its interest-rate target from 5.7 percent in January 1995 to 8.1 percent in February.

These examples illustrate a general policy. Recall that U.S. monetary policy is largely captured by a Taylor rule: the Fed adjusts interest rates based on output and inflation. Researchers find that this rule does not fit Canada. Instead, the Bank of Canada responds to output, inflation, *and* the exchange rate. One study finds that, on average, a 1 percent rise in the Canadian dollar produces an interest-rate cut of 0.2 percentage points.*

* This estimate is from Gergana Danailova-Trainor, *Open Economy Policy Rules*, Johns Hopkins University dissertation, 2004.

17.2 COSTS OF EXCHANGE-RATE VOLATILITY

So far, we have assumed that central banks seek to stabilize aggregate output and inflation. They care about the exchange rate only because this variable affects output and inflation. In reality, central banks also care about exchange rates for other reasons. Fluctuations in exchange rates harm the economy directly, as we discuss now.

Exchange Rates and Risk

▶Table 6.1 on p. 161 summarizes the winners and losers from a currency appreciation.

An appreciation of a country's currency hurts some parts of its economy and helps others. The appreciation benefits individuals and firms that import goods, because imports become less expensive. Exporters are hurt because their products become more expensive for foreigners. Owners of foreign assets are also hurt, because these assets become less valuable in domestic currency.

All the effects of an appreciation work in reverse when a depreciation occurs. In this case, importers lose and exporters and foreign-asset holders gain.

Over time, a country's exchange rate sometimes rises and sometimes falls. So for any firm or asset holder, the effects of exchange-rate changes are sometimes good and sometimes bad. Overall, exchange-rate fluctuations create risk. An exporter can see its profits rise or fall depending on what happens to exchange rates. Similarly, buying foreign assets means gambling on exchange rates. Firms and asset holders dislike this risk.

Firms and asset holders can reduce risk by trading futures contracts for currencies. However, delivery dates in these contracts are seldom more than 6 months in the future. This means it's difficult to hedge against exchange-rate movements that last more than 6 months. For example, if the dollar appreciates over several years, U.S. exporters are inevitably hurt.

Risk and Economic Integration

One way a firm can reduce its exchange-rate risk is to trade less with foreigners. It can seek suppliers in its own country, so its costs don't fluctuate with exchange rates. It can focus on producing for the domestic market rather than expanding its business overseas. The greater the volatility of exchange rates, the greater the incentives to reduce exchange-rate risk. So volatile exchange rates reduce international trade.

Most economists think this effect is very harmful. International trade lets countries specialize in producing goods for which they have a comparative advantage. In addition, imports provide competition for domestic firms, encouraging them to become more efficient. Trade links help new technologies spread around the world. For all these reasons, international trade boosts economic growth. When exchange-rate volatility reduces trade, it hurts growth.

Volatile exchange rates also reduce international capital flows. Savers can avoid exchange-rate risk by purchasing assets in their own country. This incentive to buy domestic assets prevents savings from flowing to the countries where they would be most productive.

For example, suppose a developing country badly needs new factories. American savers can finance this investment by purchasing securities from the country's firms. If the factories are productive, everyone benefits: Americans earn high returns on the securities, the local firms earn profits, and the developing economy grows. But none of this happens if exchange-rate risk deters Americans from buying foreign securities.

17.3 EXCHANGE-RATE POLICIES

We have seen that exchange-rate fluctuations harm economies. As a result, many central banks try to stabilize exchange rates. Some even fix exchange rates at a constant level.

How do central banks control exchange rates? They use several different methods, which are summarized in **Table 17.1.** Choosing among these methods is controversial, as each one has drawbacks.

TABLE 17.1 Exchange Rate Policies and Their Pitfalls

Policy Tool	Drawback
Interest-rate adjustments	May destabilize output
Foreign-exchange interventions	Questionable effectiveness
Capital controls	Impede efficient flow of savings
Policy coordination	Countries unlikely to agree

Interest-Rate Adjustments

We have already seen one tool for controlling exchange rates: interest rates. The central bank can raise the real exchange rate by increasing the real interest rate, or lower the exchange rate by decreasing the interest rate. Therefore, if some event causes the exchange rate to change, the central bank can reverse this movement by adjusting the interest rate.

But there's a catch. The interest-rate adjustments needed to stabilize the exchange rate often differ from those that stabilize output and inflation. As a result, central banks face trade-offs between exchange-rate stability and their other goals.

Recall our example of increased confidence in Boversia. If the central bank doesn't respond, the real exchange rate rises and output falls below potential (see Figure 17.1). Policymakers can stabilize output by reducing the real interest rate. However, this action only *partly* reverses the rise in the exchange rate. The exchange rate remains above its initial level (see Figure 17.2).

Suppose Boversia's central bank wants to prevent *any* change in the exchange rate. Then it must reduce the interest rate by more than it does when stabilizing output. **Figure 17.4** shows this case. The larger interest-rate cut offsets fully the effect of the confidence shift on net capital

FIGURE 17.4 Stabilizing the Exchange Rate

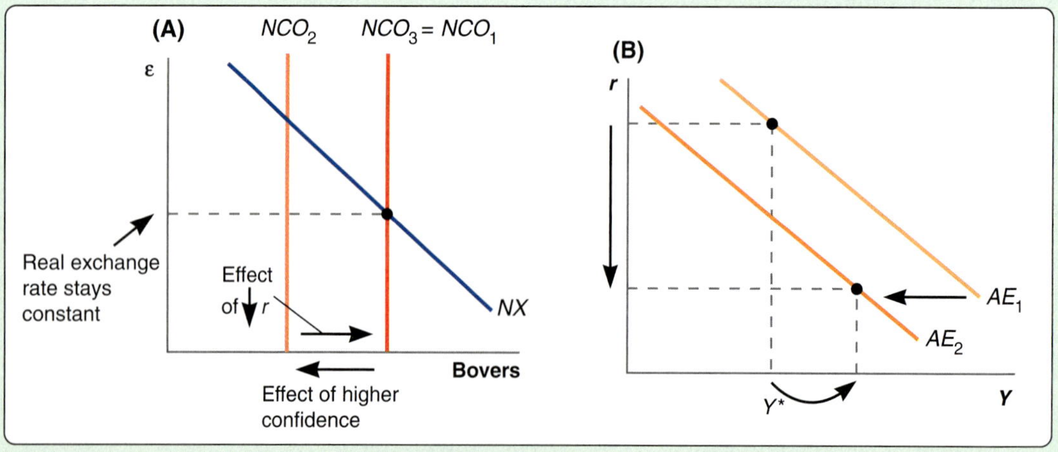

Here, increased confidence shifts the *NCO* curve to the left, but the central bank lowers the interest rate enough to reverse the shift completely. The real exchange rate doesn't change (A). The lower interest rate pushes output above potential despite the inward shift of the *AE* curve (B).

FIGURE 17.5 A Domestic Shock and Output Stabilization

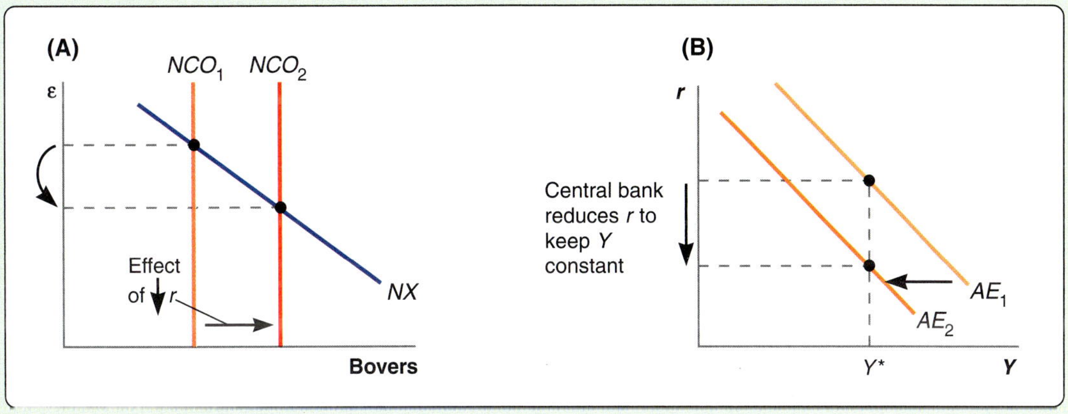

Here, Boversia's *AE* curve shifts in due to a domestic shock. The central bank reduces the real interest rate to keep output constant (B). The lower interest rate shifts the *NCO* curve to the right, reducing the real exchange rate (A).

outflows, stabilizing the exchange rate (Figure 17.4A). The larger interest-rate cut also pushes output *above* potential (Figure 17.4B).

The initial shock in Figure 17.4 is a rise in confidence. If confidence falls, then the process works in reverse. Stabilizing the exchange rate requires a large *increase* in the interest rate, one that pushes output *below* potential. The general lesson is that stabilizing the exchange rate makes output less stable. Output fluctuations also destabilize inflation through the Phillips curve.

Many kinds of economic shocks create trade-offs between exchange-rate stability and output stability. In **Figure 17.5,** we assume that Boversia's *AE* curve shifts in due to some domestic shock—say a tax increase or a fall in consumer spending. This shock has no direct effect on net capital outflows. The central bank can keep output stable by reducing the real interest rate (Figure 17.5B). But this action raises net capital outflows and reduces the exchange rate (Figure 17.5A). If the central bank desires a constant exchange rate, it must keep the interest rate constant and let output fall below potential.

Central banks would like to eat their cake and have it too. They want to stabilize exchange rates without choosing interest rates that destabilize output and inflation. Consequently, policymakers look for alternative ways to influence exchange rates.

Foreign-Exchange Interventions

Central banks sometimes try to influence exchange rates through **foreign-exchange interventions**—purchases or sales of foreign currencies. The central bank trades its own currency for a foreign one, or vice versa.

To make interventions possible, central banks hold **international reserves.** These are stocks of liquid assets denominated in foreign currencies, such as bonds issued by foreign governments. As of 2007, the U.S. Federal Reserve owned about $70 billion of such assets, denominated mainly in euros and yen.

Foreign-exchange interventions Purchases and sales of foreign currencies by central banks

International reserves Liquid assets held by central banks that are denominated in foreign currencies

FIGURE 17.6 Foreign-Exchange Interventions and International Reserves

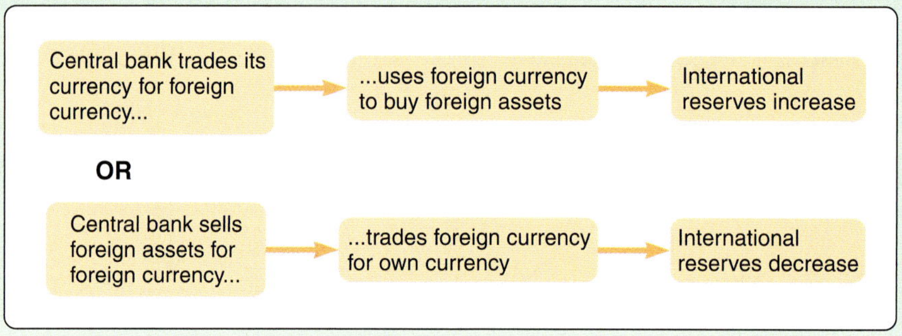

Figure 17.6 shows the relationship between foreign-exchange interventions and international reserves. If a central bank trades its own currency for a foreign one, it uses the proceeds to increase its reserves. For example, the Fed might trade dollars for euros, and use the euros to buy European bonds.

To perform the opposite intervention, a sale of foreign currency, the central bank must first sell some of its foreign assets. The Fed might sell European bonds for euros, then trade the euros for dollars. In this case, the Fed's international reserves fall.

Effects of Interventions Foreign-exchange interventions affect exchange rates because they shift the supply and demand for currencies. If the Fed sells dollars for euros, the supply of dollars increases, reducing the price of the dollar: the dollar depreciates. If the Fed buys dollars, the demand for dollars increases and the dollar appreciates.

We can capture the effects of interventions with our graph of net exports and net capital outflows. **Figure 17.7A** shows what happens if

FIGURE 17.7 Interventions and the Exchange Rate

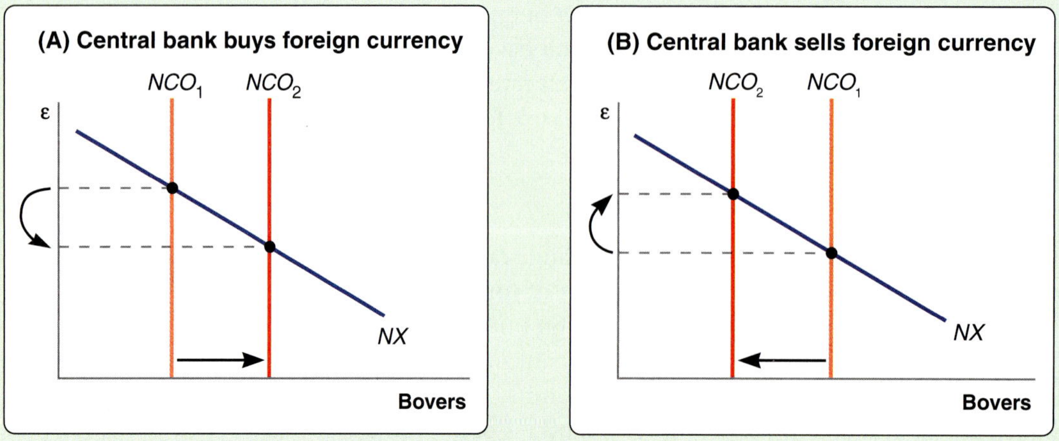

Purchases of foreign currency by the central bank raise net capital outflows and reduce the real exchange rate (A). Sales of foreign currency have the opposite effects (B).

Boversia's central bank buys foreign currency. It uses the foreign currency to purchase foreign assets, which adds to capital outflows. The *NCO* curve shifts to the right, reducing the real exchange rate. Conversely, in **Figure 17.7B,** a sale of foreign currency shifts the *NCO* curve to the left and raises the exchange rate.

Why Interventions? Central banks can control exchange rates by adjusting interest rates, but the side effects on output may be undesirable. The motive for foreign-exchange interventions is to escape this dilemma. Interventions allow policymakers to stabilize output and the exchange rate at the same time.

Suppose once again that a rise in confidence shifts Boversia's *NCO* curve to the left. The central bank can keep the exchange rate constant by reducing the interest rate, but this policy pushes output above potential (see Figure 17.4). The rise in output is unwelcome because, through the Phillips curve, it raises inflation.

The central bank can do better with a foreign-exchange intervention, as shown in **Figure 17.8.** When the *NCO* curve shifts to the left, the central bank buys foreign currency and builds up its international reserves. This action shifts the *NCO* curve back to the right, preventing a change in the exchange rate (Figure 17.8A).

In this example, the *AE* curve doesn't shift (Figure 17.8B). Since the intervention prevents the exchange rate from moving, net exports don't change, and aggregate expenditure is unchanged at a given interest rate. With a fixed *AE* curve, the central bank can keep output constant by holding the real interest rate constant. Its policies stabilize the exchange rate without creating an inflationary boom.

FIGURE 17.8 Interventions and Exchange-Rate Stabilization

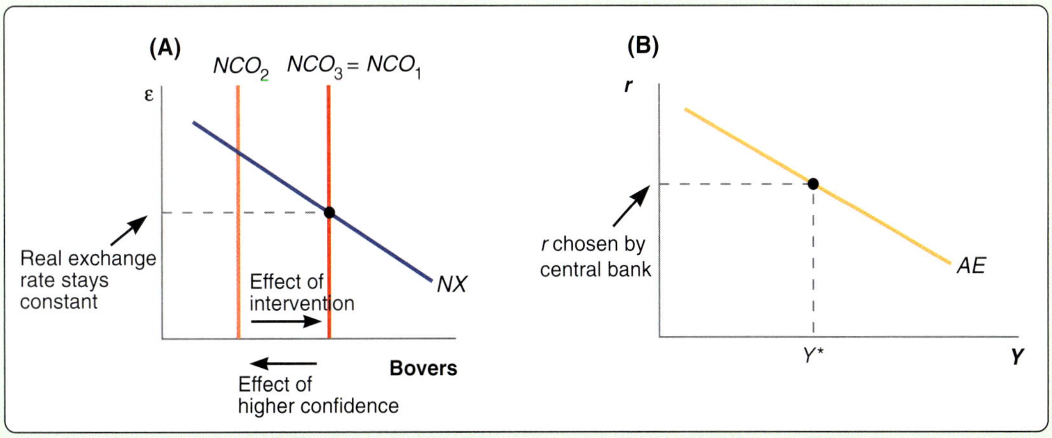

Here, increased confidence shifts the *NCO* curve to the left, but the central bank reverses the shift by purchasing foreign currency. The exchange rate does not change (A). The *AE* curve does not move and the central bank holds the interest rate constant, so output does not change (B).

Who Intervenes? Some countries intervene frequently in currency markets. A leading example over the last decade is Brazil, whose currency is called the real (pronounced ray-al). Over 2000–2002, capital flight reduced the value of the real from 0.55 U.S. dollars to 0.26. Capital flight was caused by fears that a socialist, Luiz Inacio Lula da Silva, would be elected president and adopt policies harmful to economic growth. In 2002, Brazil's central bank purchased $40 billion worth of reals in an effort to stabilize the exchange rate.

Then the situation changed dramatically. Lula *was* elected in 2002, but his policies proved to be moderate. Brazil's economy grew strongly and asset holders gained confidence in the country. Capital flowed in, and the exchange rate rose above 0.4 in 2005. At that point the central bank decided the exchange rate was too high and started selling reals—the opposite of its previous interventions. Over 2005–2007, the central bank's international reserves rose from $54 billion to $180 billion.

East Asian countries have also intervened heavily in foreign-exchange markets. For example, the Bank of Japan sold yen repeatedly during 2003 and 2004 in an effort to hold down the currency's value. The sales totaled $315 billion worth of yen, close to 10 percent of Japan's annual GDP. Policymakers wanted a weaker yen to stimulate net exports and help the economy escape its protracted slump.

▶Sections 13.2 and 14.4 discuss the long Japanese recession of the 1990s and early 2000s.

In contrast to Brazil and Japan, some central banks rarely intervene in currency markets. The Federal Reserve traded currencies frequently in the 1970s and 1980s, but since then it has largely abandoned the practice. As of 2008, the Fed had not intervened since 2000. The same is true of the European Central Bank.

Why don't the Fed and ECB intervene more often? The answer is that they doubt the effectiveness of interventions. We've seen that, in theory, these actions affect exchange rates. Yet many economists argue that the effects are small, so interventions are not useful in practice. The next case study discusses this debate.

CASE STUDY

Do Interventions Work?

Why the skepticism? The answer is that interventions are small relative to the foreign-exchange market. We saw, for example, that Japan traded $315 billion worth of currencies over 2 years. That sounds like a lot of money, but total transactions in currency markets are over $1 trillion per *day*. Interventions are a tiny fraction of these transactions.

Interventions shift the *NCO* curve, as shown in Figure 17.8. However, the size of interventions suggests that the shifts are slight and the effects on exchange rates are small. Interventions can't offset major shocks such as capital flight, as we've assumed up to now.

This reasoning leads many observers to dismiss interventions as useless. For example, in 2007 the Reserve Bank of New Zealand was worried about an appreciation of the New Zealand dollar. In June, reports *The Economist* magazine, the Reserve Bank "decided enough was enough—and let rip with the pea-shooter. It intervened in foreign-exchange markets to weaken the currency." The "pea-shooter" quip reflects the view that interventions don't work. In *The Economist's* opinion, New Zealand needed lower interest rates if it wanted a weaker currency.*

Yet not all economists dismiss interventions. Some suggest that interventions can change exchange rates even if they are small. One theory is that interventions are "signals" of central banks' desire to adjust exchange rates. These signals lead people to expect future actions, such as changes in interest rates, that will affect exchange rates. Expectations of future exchange-rate movements affect current rates.

Others suggest that interventions can trigger self-fulfilling expectations. When people see a central bank buy a currency, they infer that the currency is likely to appreciate. This belief raises demand for the currency, and it does appreciate. This effect can be sizable even if the intervention itself is small.

Motivated by this debate, researchers have tried to measure the effects of foreign-exchange interventions. This work includes a 2006 paper by Rasmus Fatum and Michael Hutchinson of the University of California, Santa Cruz.†
Fatum and Hutchinson studied interventions in the market for yen over the period 1990–2000. They examined 43 episodes during this period when a central bank traded yen for U.S. dollars or dollars for yen. The central bank was usually the Bank of Japan but occasionally the Fed.

For each of the 43 episodes, Fatum and Hutchinson examined the path of the dollar-yen exchange rate in the 5 days after the intervention. They judged the intervention a "success" if the exchange rate moved in the direction intended by the central bank. A sale of yen was a success if the yen depreciated over the next 5 days; a purchase was a success if the yen appreciated.

Fatum and Hutchinson found that 31 of the 43 interventions were successes; only 12 were failures. This rate of success would be unlikely if interventions had no effects. Fatum and Hutchinson concluded that interventions do influence exchange rates.

The debate over interventions continues. One compromise position is that interventions affect exchange rates for periods of a few days, as Fatum and Hutchinson found, but don't influence longer-term movements in rates.

* See *The Economist*, "New Zealand Defends Its Currency," June 14 2007.

† See Rasmus Fatum and Michael Hutchinson, "Effectiveness of Daily Foreign Exchange Market Interventions in Japan," *Journal of International Money and Finance*, May 2006.

Capital Controls

Policymakers also influence exchange rates through **capital controls.** These regulations reduce the flow of savings across countries. Some capital controls restrict capital inflows: they make it harder for foreigners to buy a country's assets. Other controls restrict outflows: they make it harder for a country's residents to buy foreign assets.

Capital controls Regulations that restrict capital inflows or outflows

Both governments and central banks impose capital controls, and the regulations take many forms. Purchases of certain assets may require government approval or be subject to taxes or be forbidden entirely.

The motives for capital controls also vary. Some countries restrict capital outflows to force savers to purchase domestic assets. This provides domestic firms with more funds for investment. Countries sometimes restrict capital inflows for political reasons. They think that foreign ownership of certain assets symbolizes outside domination of their country. For this reason, Mexico's constitution limits foreign ownership of real estate or natural resources.

Effects on Exchange Rates For our purposes, a key function of capital controls is to influence exchange rates. Suppose Boversia imposes new regulations that reduce capital outflows. As shown in **Figure 17.9A,** the *NCO* curve shifts to the left, raising the real exchange rate. In **Figure 17.9B,** restrictions on capital inflows shift the *NCO* curve to the right, reducing the exchange rate.

Countries use capital controls for the same reason that they use foreign exchange interventions: to ease the trade-off between output and exchange-rate stability. If a change in confidence shifts the *NCO* curve, capital controls can shift it back to its initial position. This stabilizes the exchange rate without an interest-rate adjustment that would destabilize output.

An example occurred during the East Asian crisis of 1997–1998 (discussed in Sections 4.2 and 6.4). Asset holders lost confidence in countries such as South Korea, Thailand, and Indonesia. These countries' *NCO* curves shifted to the right, reducing their exchange rates. In most cases, the central bank responded by raising interest rates sharply. These actions dampened the exchange-rate movements but also caused recessions. In Indonesia, for example, the unemployment rate rose to 20 percent.

Malaysia was also hit by capital flight, but it responded differently from its neighbors. In 1998, the government imposed restrictions on capital outflows. Foreigners who owned Malaysian securities were forbidden to sell

FIGURE 17.9 Capital Controls and the Exchange Rate

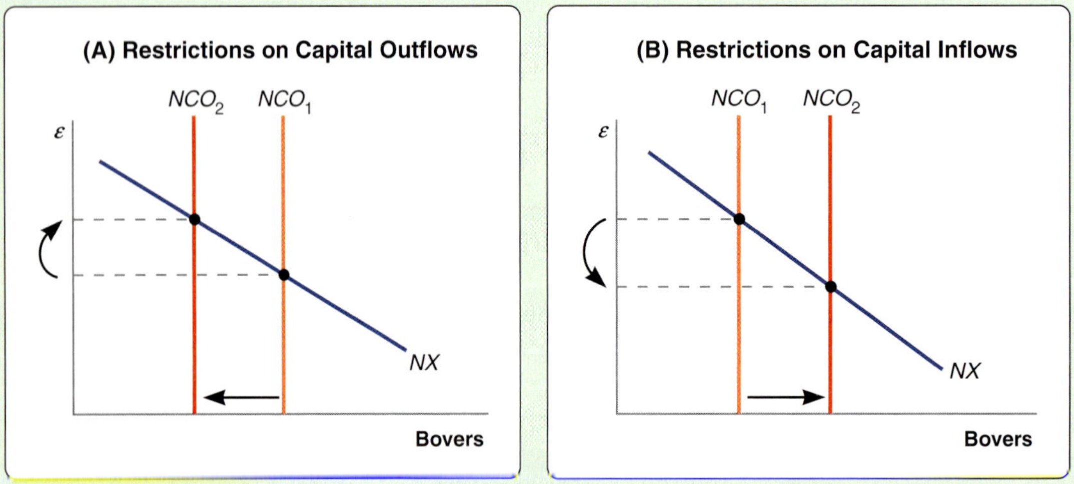

If Boversia's government or central bank imposes restrictions on capital outflows, the *NCO* curve shifts to the left and the exchange rate rises (A). Restrictions on capital inflows have the opposite effects (B).

them for 12 months. Nobody could transfer funds from Malaysian bank accounts to foreign accounts or take significant amounts of cash out of the country.

These rules prevented Malaysia's net capital outflows from rising. Therefore, the exchange rate did not fall, and the central bank did not need to raise interest rates. Indeed, when the government announced the capital controls, it also fixed the exchange rate 10 percent *above* its previous level. At the same time, the central bank reduced its interest-rate target from 9.5 percent to 8 percent to stimulate aggregate spending.

These policies appear to have helped the economy. Malaysia was in a recession in 1998, but it recovered quickly after it began its new policies—unlike the neighboring countries that raised interest rates.

The Critique of Capital Controls Many economists think capital controls are a bad idea. Restrictions on capital inflows make it harder for a country's firms to finance investment. Restrictions on outflows prevent savers from earning high returns on foreign assets. In general, capital controls impede the flow of savings to the countries where savings are most productive.

Economists question capital controls even when they seem to benefit the economy in the short run, as in Malaysia. Critics argue that controls hurt the economy in the long run by reducing foreign investment. Foreigners won't put money in a country if the government might prevent them from taking it back out.

These ideas have persuaded many countries to abolish capital controls. For example, the U.S. government used to tax Americans who bought foreign assets, but this policy ended in 1974.

Many developing countries still have capital controls. India, for example, limits the quantity of foreign assets that a resident can buy in a year. It also limits the interest that foreigners can earn on Indian corporate bonds, discouraging purchases of the bonds. Economists frequently advise India to loosen its capital controls, but it's not clear whether this will happen.

Critics of capital controls gained ammunition from events in Thailand in December 2006. Thailand's central bank was trying to slow an appreciation of its currency, the baht. On December 18, it announced a restriction on capital inflows. Foreign savers who bought Thai assets were required to deposit 30 percent of their funds with the central bank at zero interest.

This action shook confidence in Thai assets. It stopped the rise in the currency, but it also caused a stock market crash: the Thai market fell by 12 percent when the deposit requirement was announced. Fearing further instability, the central bank quickly reversed course. On December 20, it removed the deposit requirement for most foreign savers.

Policy Coordination

Exchange-rate policies inherently involve many countries. If one country acts to strengthen its currency against others, then the other currencies weaken. So countries care about one another's policies. Exchange rates are a perennial topic of discussion among officials of different countries.

In some periods, countries have cooperated in exchange-rate policy. A famous example is the "Plaza Agreement," signed in 1985 at the Plaza Hotel in New York. At the time the dollar was very strong, causing a trade deficit in the United States. This deficit created political pressures for import restrictions, which America's trading partners feared. To reduce the deficit, European countries and Japan agreed to work with the U.S. to weaken the dollar.

Another episode of cooperation occurred in 2000, when the euro was near its all-time low of 0.85 dollars (see Figure 6.8). The European Central Bank, the Fed, and the Bank of Japan tried to boost the euro's value by simultaneously purchasing the currency. However, these actions did not have much effect on exchange rates. The failure of the interventions in 2000 helps explain why the Fed and ECB haven't intervened since then.

In recent years, the United States has not coordinated exchange-rate policies with other countries. Given the questionable effectiveness of interventions, exchange-rate adjustments require changes in interest rates. Most central banks, including the Fed, want complete freedom in setting interest rates. They don't make exchange-rate agreements because such commitments would constrain their choices of interest rates.

Policymakers still discuss exchange rates at international meetings. And they lobby one another in speeches. For example, over 2003–2004, U.S. Treasury Secretary John Snow and Fed Chair Alan Greenspan criticized Japan's exchange-rate policy. Recall that Japan was intervening in currency markets to weaken the yen. The U.S. wanted a stronger yen—and hence a weaker dollar—to stimulate U.S. exports. It is doubtful, however, that outside criticism influenced Japan's policies.

The next case study discusses the country with perhaps the most criticized exchange-rate policy in the world: China.

CASE STUDY

The Yuan

China's economy has grown rapidly since the 1990s, partly as a result of growing exports. To promote exports, Chinese policymakers have worked to hold down the value of their currency, the yuan. A weak yuan makes Chinese goods inexpensive in foreign markets.

China has controlled its exchange rate through two sets of policies. One is restrictions on capital inflows. Before 2002, foreigners were not allowed to buy Chinese securities. The government has loosened this rule, but only slightly: only a handful of foreign financial institutions can buy securities. Foreign banks are not allowed to lend in China.

China's other method for keeping the yuan weak is foreign-exchange interventions. The Bank of China has sold large quantities of yuan and accumulated international reserves. As of 2007, reserves were around \$1.5 trillion and climbing. Sixty percent of the reserves were dollar-denominated assets, such as U.S. Treasury bonds.

These policies have succeeded in keeping the yuan weak. From 1994 to 2005, China's exchange rate was fixed at 0.121 dollars per yuan. Since then the yuan has appreciated, but slowly. In 2007, the exchange rate averaged 0.132, 9 percent above its 2005 level. Economists estimated that this rate would be 30 to 40 percent higher if China didn't restrict capital flows or intervene in currency markets.

As China's economy has grown, the country has become a major trading partner of the United States. A weak yuan means a stronger dollar, which hurts U.S. firms that export or compete with Chinese imports. As a result, many U.S. business leaders and politicians have criticized China's exchange-rate policy.

Steel is one U.S. industry affected by China's policy. For decades the fortunes of this industry have been tied to exchange rates. In recent years the dollar-yuan rate has been crucial, as China has become a major steel producer: it accounted for 36 percent of world output in 2007. Over 2005–2007, the dollar was weak against many currencies but strong against the yuan, raising the price of U.S. steel relative to Chinese steel. The U.S. industry suffered, with steel output falling from 122 million tons in 2004 to 97 million tons in 2007.

Supporters of U.S. steel have complained bitterly about Chinese policy. In 2005, Congressman Pete Visclosky, a Democrat from a steel-producing district in Indiana, said, "Every day China unfairly manipulates its currency, the U.S. steel industry faces a competitive disadvantage." In 2007, the president of the steel industry's lobbying group said that U.S. companies can compete against foreign companies but "we can't compete against other governments."

In 2007, members of Congress proposed several pieces of legislation intended to pressure China to change its policy. Proposed actions included complaints to the World Trade Organization, a ban on purchases of Chinese goods by the U.S. government, and tariffs on all Chinese imports. These proposals were not enacted, however. They were opposed by the Bush administration, which argued that negotiations with China were more likely than punitive legislation to change Chinese policy.

U.S. criticism may have motivated China's 2005 decision to stop fixing its exchange rate at 0.121. This decision was welcomed by many in the United States, who hoped it would lead to a substantial appreciation of the yuan. In hindsight, however, the 2005 action looks more like a public-relations move than a real policy change, as the appreciation that followed was modest.

At times, U.S. criticism has provoked retorts from Chinese officials. In 2004, Li Ruogo, the deputy governor of the People's Bank, remarked, "China's custom is that we never blame others for our own problem. For the past 26 years, we never put pressure or problems on to the world. The U.S. has the reverse attitude, whenever they have a problem they blame others."

Online Case Study:
An Update on Chinese Currency Policy

17.4 FIXED EXCHANGE RATES

We've seen that central banks have several methods for controlling exchange rates, but each has drawbacks (see Table 17.1). Consequently, most central banks allow exchange rates to change over time in response to economic shocks. That is, they choose **floating exchange rates.**

Floating exchange rate Policy that allows the exchange rate to fluctuate in response to economic shocks

Fixed exchange rate Policy that holds the exchange rate at a constant level

However, this policy is not universal. Some central banks choose **fixed exchange rates**: they maintain a constant exchange rate between their currency and another one. Denmark, for example, has a national currency, the krone; it does not use the euro. But Denmark's central bank fixes the value of the krone at about 0.13 euros.

Which is better, fixed exchange rates or flexible rates? This question perennially provokes controversy. One motive for fixed rates is to promote international trade and capital flows. As discussed in Section 17.2, exchange-rate risk deters trade and capital flows; fixed exchange rates eliminate this risk.

This point is just the start of the debate. We will examine several arguments for and against fixing exchange rates, which are summarized in **Table 17.2.** But first, let's discuss the mechanics of *how* a central bank fixes an exchange rate.

TABLE 17.2 A Fixed Exchange Rate: Pros and Cons

Pros	Cons
Promotes trade and capital flows	Loss of independent monetary policy
Controls inflation	Danger of speculative attacks

Mechanics of Fixed Exchange Rates

Suppose the central bank of Boversia decides to fix the value of its currency, the bover. It chooses an exchange rate of 0.5 U.S. dollars per bover (or 2.0 bovers per dollar). How does the central bank maintain this exchange rate?

First, it promises to trade currencies at the chosen rate. If people want to buy bovers, the central bank provides the bovers in return for dollars. It uses the dollars to build up its international reserves. If people want to sell bovers, the central bank uses its reserves to buy them.

The central bank's purchases and sales of bovers are foreign-exchange interventions. Notice, however, that the central bank does not choose the interventions. It acts passively, supplying whatever amounts of currency people want at the fixed exchange rate.

We have seen that foreign-exchange interventions have limited effects on exchange rates. Thus a fixed exchange rate must be backed up by more powerful tools: interest-rate adjustments or capital controls. These policies are the real basis of fixed rates.

To see this, suppose Boversia is hit with capital flight. People sell large quantities of bovers, which normally would push down the exchange rate. At first the central bank can maintain the fixed rate by purchasing bovers with its reserves of dollars. But these reserves are limited and are likely to run out during an episode of capital flight.

When the central bank runs out of reserves, it faces a choice. If it wants to maintain the fixed exchange rate, it must curb capital outflows through higher interest rates or capital controls. If it doesn't adopt these policies, it must let the exchange rate fall.

Devaluation and Revaluation

A fixed exchange rate is a fixed *nominal* rate, such as 0.5 dollars per bover. The exchange rate that matters for the economy is the *real* rate. The relation between the real rate, ε, and the nominal rate, e, is given by Equation 6.1:

$$\varepsilon = \frac{eP}{P^*}$$

where P is the domestic price level and P^* is the foreign price level. In the Boversia example, P is Boversia's price level and P^* is the U.S. price level.

A fixed nominal exchange rate does not imply a fixed real rate. Instead, the behavior of the real rate depends on the price levels P and P^*. Suppose P grows more rapidly over time than P^*; in other words, the domestic inflation rate exceeds the foreign inflation rate. This means the ratio P/P^* rises. With a fixed nominal exchange rate (a fixed e), the rise in P/P^* raises the real rate, ε. Conversely, if P rises more slowly than P^*, the real exchange rate falls.

These changes in real exchange rates can be harmful. A rise in a country's real exchange rate reduces its net exports, which can cause a recession. A fall in the real exchange rate makes imports more expensive, hurting the country's consumers.

To address these problems, countries with fixed exchange rates occasionally change the rates. They adjust nominal rates to offset the effects of inflation on real rates. Suppose again that Boversia fixes its nominal exchange rate against the dollar, and assume its inflation rate exceeds U.S. inflation. P/P^* rises over time, raising the real exchange rate. At some point, Boversia's central bank may cut the nominal exchange rate to push the real rate back down. For example, it might reduce the nominal rate from 0.5 dollars per bover to 0.4.

When a country has a fixed exchange rate, a decrease in this rate is called a **devaluation.** Boversia devalues its currency if it reduces the exchange rate from 0.5 to 0.4. An increase in the exchange rate is a **revaluation.** A devaluation or revaluation is a significant, discrete change. After the change, the exchange rate is fixed at its new level.

Devaluation Resetting of a fixed exchange rate at a lower level

Revaluation Resetting of a fixed exchange rate at a higher level

Loss of Independent Monetary Policy

Let's now return to the pros and cons of fixed exchange rates. We've already discussed one benefit: fixed rates encourage international trade and capital flows (see Table 17.2). The costs arise from the policies needed to control the exchange rate. These policies must include either capital controls or interest-rate adjustments, and each option has costs.

We'll focus on countries without capital controls, those which use interest rates to influence exchange rates. We saw in Section 17.1 that stabilizing exchange rates can conflict with stabilizing output and inflation. A decision to fix the exchange rate means that exchange-rate stability always takes precedence. As a result, the central bank loses its normal ability to stabilize the economy.

Recall the case of an adverse expenditure shock, such as an increase in taxes, that does not directly affect the exchange rate (see Figure 17.5). The central bank could keep output constant by decreasing the interest rate, but this would also decrease the exchange rate. If the central bank is committed to a fixed exchange rate, it must hold the interest rate constant and allow a recession to occur.

Sometimes a fixed exchange rate requires the central bank to change the interest rate. Policymakers must offset shocks that would otherwise cause exchange-rate fluctuations. In particular, they must adjust the interest rate when foreign interest rates change.

Consider again Boversia's fixed exchange rate against the dollar. If the Federal Reserve raises the U.S. interest rate, U.S. assets become more attractive. Normally, higher demand for U.S. assets would raise net capital outflows from Boversia, reducing the exchange rate. To prevent this outcome, Boversia's central bank must raise the domestic interest rate; in effect, it must mimic the Fed's action. This prevents U.S. assets from becoming more attractive compared with Boversian assets, so net capital outflows and the exchange rate don't change.

The upshot is that the Federal Reserve determines interest rates in Boversia as well as in the United States. The Fed sets rates based on U.S. economic conditions, so its policies may be inappropriate for Boversia. Say the U.S. experiences an economic boom at the same time Boversia is in a recession. The Fed is likely to raise interest rates to slow the U.S. economy and prevent inflation from rising. Unfortunately, this action also triggers an interest-rate increase in Boversia, worsening that country's recession.

Controlling Inflation

Many economists cite the loss of independent monetary policy as a disadvantage of fixed exchange rates. However, supporters of fixed rates argue that some countries benefit from the loss of policy independence.

To understand why, recall the argument for monetary rules in Section 16.3. In theory, discretionary monetary policy stabilizes the economy, but in practice it may do more harm than good. A monetary rule prevents incompetent or politically motivated policy.

A fixed exchange rate can be interpreted as one kind of monetary rule. The interest rate must be set to keep the exchange rate constant, so the central bank cannot adjust policy as it chooses. This prevents mischief.

Specifically, fixed exchange rates can prevent high inflation. If Boversia fixes its exchange rate against the dollar, its monetary policy is determined by the Federal Reserve. As a result, its inflation rate will be close to the U.S. inflation rate. As long as the Fed keeps U.S. inflation low, Boversian inflation is also low.

The link between the two countries' inflation rates is complex. U.S. inflation does not directly affect Boversian inflation. Instead, differences in the two inflation rates set off a chain of effects that pushes Boversia's rate toward

FIGURE 17.10 Fixed Exchange Rates and Inflation

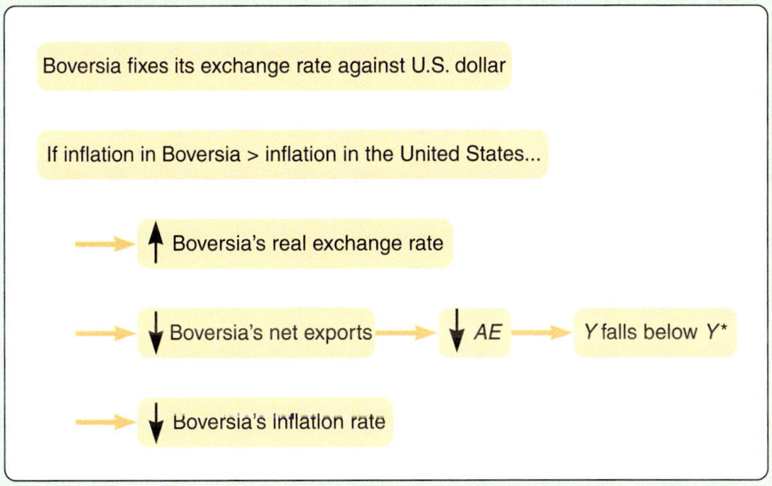

the U.S. rate. **Figure 17.10** outlines this mechanism. We assume that, initially, Boversian inflation exceeds U.S. inflation. With a fixed nominal exchange rate, Boversia's real exchange rate rises. The real appreciation reduces net exports, pushing output below potential. Finally, low output reduces inflation through the Phillips curve. This process continues until Boversia's inflation rate has fallen to the U.S. level, which stabilizes the real exchange rate.

Israel is one country that has used a fixed exchange rate, along with other policies, to reduce inflation. In the early 1980s, Israel financed government budget deficits by printing money, with the predictable result of high inflation (see Section 14.2). The inflation rate peaked at about 500 percent in 1985. At that point, the government cut the deficit. It also fixed the value of its currency, the shekel, against the dollar. Finally, it attacked inflation directly by persuading labor unions to accept smaller wage increases. This combination of policies reduced inflation quickly: Israeli inflation was less than 20 percent in 1986.

Fixed exchange rates are often temporary; countries shift policy once inflation is under control. Israel devalued the shekel in 1987 and again in 1989. Further adjustments followed, and in 2000 Israel let the currency float. It now targets inflation and does not try to control the exchange rate.

The Instability of Fixed Exchange Rates

As we have seen, a fixed exchange rate doesn't last forever. Eventually, policymakers devalue or revalue the currency, or switch to a floating rate. Sometimes these shifts occur suddenly and are not entirely voluntary. They are forced on policymakers by expectations in currency markets.

Suppose again that Boversia fixes its nominal exchange rate against the dollar and that Boversian inflation exceeds U.S. inflation. The real exchange rate rises, producing the chain of effects in Figure 17.10—assuming

FIGURE 17.11 The Instability of Fixed Exchange Rates

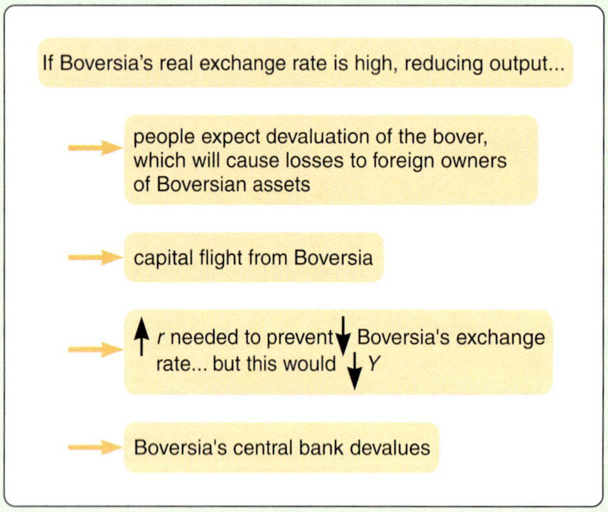

the central bank is committed to the fixed exchange rate.

However, people may doubt this commitment. The process in Figure 17.10 is painful, as it involves a recession. At some point the central bank may decide to stop the process by devaluing the currency. Therefore, as the real exchange rate rises, people start to think that a devaluation is likely.

This expectation triggers a series of effects, which are summarized in **Figure 17.11.** If devaluation does occur, it will hurt foreign owners of Boversian assets, as the assets will be worth less in foreign currencies. To avoid these losses, people start selling the assets. Boversia experiences capital flight.

With capital flight, the central bank quickly loses its international reserves. To maintain the fixed exchange rate, it would have to raise interest rates sharply. But this would reduce aggregate expenditure, magnifying the fall in output caused by the rise in the real exchange rate. To avoid this outcome, the central bank is likely to let the exchange rate fall.

A lesson from Figure 17.11 is that expectations of devaluation can be self-fulfilling. These expectations cause capital flight, which forces devaluation. We've seen before that self-fulfilling expectations are common in the financial system. Expectations of stock market crashes cause crashes, and expectations of bank runs cause runs.

The threat to a fixed exchange rate is increased by currency speculation. Institutions such as hedge funds and investment banks try to predict movements in exchange rates and profit from them (see Section 6.6). If these speculators think Boversia will devalue, they borrow bovers and sell them for other currencies. Then, if devaluation occurs, they can repurchase the bovers for less than they sold them for. The speculators repay their loans and are left with large profits.

Currency speculators don't just predict devaluations, they help cause them. Their sales of bovers increase capital outflows from Boversia, making it more likely the central bank will devalue. The strategy of selling a currency that may be devalued is called a **speculative attack.** The word *attack* captures the idea that speculators try to force a policy change on the central bank.

Speculative attack Strategy of selling a currency with a fixed exchange rate, to force and to profit from a devaluation

The moral of this story is that fixed exchange rates can backfire. The goal is to stabilize exchange rates, but speculative attacks can cause large, sudden changes. Overall, exchange rates may be less volatile if they are allowed to float. The next case study discusses a famous speculative attack.

CASE STUDY

George Soros versus the Pound

For most of their histories, European countries had separate currencies. However, starting in 1979 most of these currencies were tied together by the Exchange Rate Mechanism (ERM). Exchange rates were not absolutely fixed, but almost. Countries agreed on exchange-rate targets and promised not to deviate from the targets by more than a few percent. Policymakers planned eventually to fix rates completely and then adopt a common European currency.

The ERM ran into problems in the early 1990s. The story starts in Europe's largest economy, Germany. East and West Germany were reunified in 1990, and the German government spent heavily to rebuild the East. High government spending caused an economic boom, raising inflation. As we've discussed, Germany's central bank, the Bundesbank, was highly averse to inflation. The Bundesbank raised interest rates to slow the economy and push inflation back down.

The rise in German interest rates threatened to raise the value of Germany's currency, the deutschemark, against other European currencies. Equivalently, it put downward pressure on the other currencies. To prevent depreciation, many countries in the ERM needed to raise their interest rates along with Germany's. But they were reluctant, as their economies weren't booming. The U.K. was especially reluctant: it was in a deep recession, so higher interest rates were the last thing it needed.

This situation produced a crisis. Other countries appealed to Germany to reduce its interest rate so they didn't have to raise theirs, but Germany refused. Speculators began to think that some countries would devalue their currencies or drop out of the ERM entirely. In September 1992, speculators attacked the British pound. A hedge fund run by George Soros borrowed billions of pounds from British banks and used them to purchase deutschemarks.

Initially, the U.K. tried to maintain its exchange rate with higher interest rates. The Bank of England raised its interest-rate target from 10 percent to 12 percent on September 16, and to 15 percent on the 17th. But the attack continued, and policymakers were not willing to raise rates further. They announced that the U.K. was dropping out of the ERM, and let the pound float. The exchange rate fell quickly by 10 percent, and interest rates fell below their pre-attack levels.

The U.K.'s decision benefitted George Soros: his profit from the speculative attack was about 1 billion dollars. (In 1995, the *Wall Street Journal* named Soros one of the eight great investors of the 20th century.) Arguably, the U.K.'s decision also benefitted its own economy. The lower interest rate and exchange rate stimulated aggregate spending, and the U.K. recovered strongly from its recession.

After defeating the pound, speculators attacked several other European currencies. Italy briefly raised its short-term interest rate to 30 percent but then followed the UK out of the ERM. The other ERM countries struggled to maintain the system. In July 1993, they agreed to allow larger fluctuations in exchange rates—rates could deviate from their targets by up to 15 percent. This moved the system closer to fully floating exchange rates.

These events were a setback for plans to unify Europe's currencies. However, the ERM countries eventually narrowed their exchange-rate bands again. They created the euro in 1999. By that time Italy had rejoined the ERM, so it adopted the euro. The U.K. remained outside the system, and it still has its own currency.

A Brief History of Fixed Exchange Rates

Fixed exchange rates used to be the norm, but they are less common today. Let's review some history.

The Gold Standard In the late 19th and early 20th centuries, most major economies were on a gold standard. Each country's currency was worth a certain amount of gold, which implied fixed exchange rates between countries. For example, a U.S. dollar was worth 0.0484 ounces of gold and a British pound was worth 0.2358 ounces. These values implied an exchange rate of $0.0484/0.2358 = 0.2053$ pounds per dollar.

▶ For more on the gold standard, see Sections 2.2 and 14.2.

This system broke down during the Great Depression of the 1930s. During that period, many countries abandoned the gold standard so they could expand the money supply. Without the gold standard, exchange rates fluctuated.

The Bretton Woods System Forty-four countries established a new system of fixed exchange rates in 1944. It was called the *Bretton Woods system* after the New Hampshire resort where the agreement was signed. Under this system, all currencies were fixed against the dollar. Fixed rates were maintained through a combination of interest-rate adjustments, capital controls, and interventions.

At the time, policymakers considered fixed exchange rates essential for international trade. In the 1950s, Milton Friedman started arguing for floating rates. He thought that exchange rates should be determined by free markets, not governments. This view is common today, but most economists dismissed it during the Bretton Woods era.

Under the Bretton Woods system, currencies were sometimes devalued or revalued, and speculative attacks occurred. These events became more frequent in the late 1960s, for two reasons. First, some countries relaxed capital controls, making it harder to control exchange rates. Second, U.S. inflation rose, causing the dollar to appreciate in real terms. People started to think the U.S. would devalue, prompting speculative attacks on the dollar.

In 1971, a speculative attack forced an 8 percent devaluation of the dollar. Another attack produced a 10 percent devaluation in 1973—and then yet another attack began. At that point, the Bretton Woods countries let their currencies float. At the time, floating rates were meant to be temporary, but the fixed-rate system was never reestablished.

Since Bretton Woods Since 1973, the world's advanced economies have generally had floating exchange rates. Policymakers have decided that the benefits of fixed rates are outweighed by the loss of monetary policy and the danger of speculative attacks. Europe's Exchange Rate Mechanism was an exception, but it was a temporary arrangement on the path to monetary union.

From the 1970s through the 1990s, many developing countries fixed their exchange rates against the U.S. dollar. However, speculative attacks forced many of these countries to abandon fixed rates, just as they ended the Bretton Woods system. Fixed rates ended for Mexico in 1994 and for most East Asian countries during the crisis of 1997–1998. Today, most developing countries let their currencies float—although some, such as China, allow only small movements in exchange rates.

Fixed exchange rates are still common among two groups of countries. One is small countries with close links to larger economies. These countries fix exchange rates to increase integration with the larger economy. Small countries on the outskirts of the euro area, such as Denmark and Latvia, fix their exchange rates against the euro. Countries in the Caribbean, such as the Bahamas, fix rates against the U.S. dollar.

The second group is oil exporters, such as Saudi Arabia and Kuwait, which also fix exchange rates against the dollar. The reason is that the price of oil in world markets is set in dollars. If Saudi Arabia's riyal floated against the dollar, changes in the exchange rate would cause changes in oil revenues as measured in riyals. Oil exporters prefer stable revenues.

17.5 CURRENCY UNIONS

A currency union is a group of countries that adopts a single money. The world's largest currency union by far is the euro area. The euro was created by 11 countries in 1999, and 15 countries used the euro in 2008.

We can interpret a currency union as an extreme version of fixed exchange rates. Before the euro, the ERM fixed European rates, but devaluations were possible. The value of France's currency, the franc, might fall relative to Germany's deutschemark, for example. Today, the exchange rate between German and French currency is fixed absolutely at 1.0. Both countries use the euro, and one euro in France is always worth one euro in Germany.

▶Section 2.2 compares a currency union with other extreme forms of fixed exchange rates: dollarization, in which one country unilaterally adopts another's currency, and a currency board, which issues local currency backed by foreign currency.

Why was the euro created? Has it benefitted Europe's economies? Should countries elsewhere create similar currency unions? We conclude this chapter by discussing these questions.

The Euro

Let's start with some background on the creation of the euro, how the euro area is expanding, and how European monetary policy is set.

The Birth of the Euro The process leading to the euro began with a 1991 agreement among the countries in Europe's Exchange Rate Mechanism. The agreement was called the Maastricht Treaty after the Dutch city where it was signed. The ERM countries agreed to reduce fluctuations in exchange rates and eventually fix rates completely. Then they would replace their national moneys with a single currency. The Maastricht Treaty said the new currency should be created by 1999. The speculative attacks of 1992 briefly set back the Maastricht process, but the euro was created on schedule on January 1, 1999.

The Maastricht Treaty determines which countries are eligible to adopt the euro. There are two requirements. First, a country has to be a member of the European Union (EU). The EU is an organization established in 1957 to promote European economic integration. Its members have agreed to remove trade barriers and capital controls, but before 1999, they had separate currencies.

Second, a country adopting the euro has to have good economic policies, as defined by several criteria. For example, the government budget deficit has to be less than 3 percent of GDP, and inflation has to be low. The creators of the euro didn't want to share the currency with unstable economies.

Fifteen countries belonged to the EU in 1999. Two of these, Greece and Sweden, failed to meet the criteria for euro membership. Two others, Denmark and the U.K., met the criteria but chose to retain their national currencies. The remaining 11 countries became the initial members of the euro area. **Figure 17.12** shows these countries, along with countries that adopted the euro later.

The Euro Area Grows In 2001, Greece satisfied the economic criteria in the Maastricht Treaty. It became the 12th country to join the euro area.

Between 2004 and 2007, the European Union admitted 12 new members, mostly countries in Eastern Europe. These countries are eligible to adopt the euro if they meet the economic criteria. As of 2008, three of the new EU countries were using the euro: Slovenia, Cyprus, and Malta.

Many other countries are eager to adopt the euro. As of 2008, some had target dates for adoption, such as 2012 for Bulgaria. Other countries, such as Romania and the Czech Republic, have uncertain prospects because of trouble meeting the Maastricht criteria.

The U.K. and Denmark, which chose not to adopt the euro in 1999, have remained outside the currency union. The U.K. government has talked about adopting the euro some day, but much of the public is opposed. In 2000, Denmark held a referendum on euro membership and 56 percent of the public voted no. Sweden became eligible for the euro in 2003, but here, too, the currency was rejected in a referendum.

European Monetary Policy Monetary policy for the euro area is run by the Eurosystem, the analogue of the Federal Reserve System in the United States. The Eurosystem includes the European Central Bank (ECB) in

FIGURE 17.12 The Euro Area, 2008

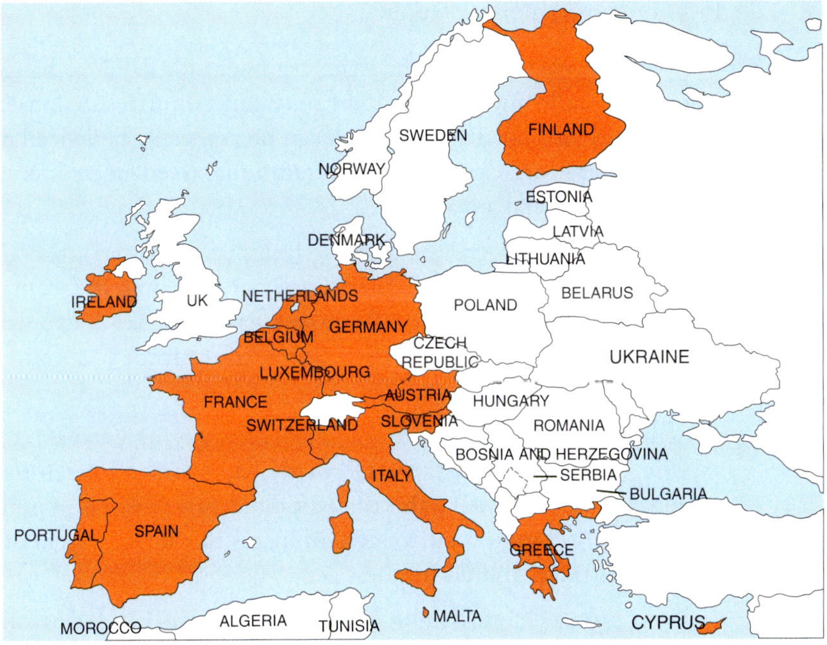

The countries shaded in orange used the euro as their currency in 2008.

Frankfurt and the national central banks (NCBs) of the euro countries. NCBs include Germany's Bundesbank, the Banque de France, and the Banca d'Italia.

Before the euro, the NCBs set monetary policy for their countries. Now their roles are similar to those of Federal Reserve Banks in the United States. NCBs perform central-bank functions such as processing payments and regulating banks (see Table 2.2). They also participate in making monetary policy for the euro area.

The ECB is run by a six-member Executive Board, the equivalent of the Fed's Board of Governors. Members of the board are chosen by agreement of the heads of state of euro countries. The president of the ECB is the chair of the Executive Board. The current president is Jean-Claude Trichet of France, who started an eight-year term in 2003.

Monetary policy is set by the Governing Council of the Eurosystem. Again, there is a close analogy to a U.S. body, the Federal Open Market Committee. The Governing Council has 21 members, the 6 members of the ECB's Executive Board plus the 15 governors of NCBs. The Governing Council meets in Frankfurt once a month. It sets interest-rate targets for the euro area, just as the FOMC sets targets for the United States.

▶ In 2004, the ECB decided that the Governing Council would be limited to 21 members. If more countries adopt the euro, NCB governors will take turns sitting on the council, just as Federal Reserve Bank presidents take turns on the FOMC. Governors from large countries will have more turns than governors from small countries.

The Economics of Currency Unions

Do countries benefit from joining a currency union? Proponents stress that currency unions increase economic integration, while opponents focus on the loss of national monetary policy.

Economic Integration Recall the main argument for fixed exchange rates: they promote trade and capital flows between countries. As an extreme version of fixed rates, a currency union can be especially beneficial for such economic integration. Compared to a traditional fixed-rate system, a currency union has several advantages.

- A currency union creates absolute fixity of exchange rates: 1.0 German euros is always worth 1.0 French euros. People in Germany and France don't have to worry about speculative attacks destabilizing exchange rates. Not even George Soros could force a devaluation of one euro against another.
- A currency union eliminates the costs of changing currencies. Before 1999, French people visiting Germany had to trade French francs for deutschemarks. To make this transaction, they had to stand in line and pay a fee. A common currency eliminates this nuisance, encouraging people to travel and do business across national borders.
- A common currency helps people compare prices across different countries. Consumers can easily tell whether German goods are more or less expensive than French goods because all prices are quoted in euros. This transparency increases competition among firms in different countries, and competition increases economic efficiency.

For all these reasons, the euro's creators hoped it would increase the integration of Europe's economies and speed economic growth. In 2001, French President Jacques Chirac called the euro "the biggest and most significant economic and financial reform in 50 years."

One-Size-Fits-All Policy The main drawback of a currency union is the basic problem with fixed exchange rates: the loss of national monetary policy. If each European country had its own currency and floating exchange rates, its central bank could set interest rates for the country. Instead, the ECB sets a single interest rate for the whole euro area. It can stabilize the area's economies only if the same rate is appropriate for all of them—if "one size fits all."

Critics of the euro argue that different countries need different interest rates. Within the euro area, one country may experience an economic boom at the same time another is in a recession. The first country needs an increase in interest rates to contain inflation, while the second needs lower rates to stimulate spending. The ECB can't pursue both policies at once.

This problem has occurred in practice. For example, during 2003–2004, countries such as Spain and Ireland experienced economic booms and rising inflation. At the same time Germany entered a recession, with unemployment near 10 percent. Over most of this period, the ECB kept interest rates constant—a compromise between the best policies for different countries. As a result, Germany's slump dragged on, and inflation was slow to decline in Spain and Ireland.

The Politics of Currency Unions

We've discussed the economic costs and benefits of currency unions. However, the decision to create the euro was more political than economic. It was part of a broader movement toward European unity.

This movement began after World War II, as European leaders sought to avoid future conflicts. They created institutions to bind countries together, such as the European Union and the North Atlantic Treaty Organization (NATO), the military alliance. A European Parliament meets in Brussels, Belgium; it has little power, but some hope that will change and Europe will move toward full political union.

Supporters of European unity favor any policy that promotes their broad goal. They pushed for the euro as one more step toward unity. When the currency was introduced, Wim Duisenberg, the ECB's first president, described the political importance of the event:

> *The euro is a symbol of stability and unity. Countries from a continent which, throughout the ages, has so often been ravaged by war, have together vowed to uphold the values of freedom, democracy, and human rights. In addition to the economic and political benefits that the euro brings, it will, I believe, help to change the way in which we think about one another as Europeans. . . . The people of Europe have one more fundamentally important thing in common—their money!*[1]

The euro is also a political symbol for Eastern European countries seeking to adopt the currency. These countries are eager to leave behind their Communist histories and tie themselves to Western Europe. When Slovenia adopted the euro in 2007, Prime Minister Janez Jansa said, "The euro isn't important only for our economy, we expect psychological benefits. . . . we are coming closer to the most developed part of the EU and this will give confidence."[2]

Political symbolism helps explain opposition to the euro as well as support. While some politicians dream of a united Europe, others are nationalist. For them, the euro is a threat to countries' identity and strength.

This view is one reason the U.K. opted out of the euro when it was created. Margaret Thatcher, the former prime minister, was a strong critic of the euro. In 1998 she insisted that her Conservative Party "pledge to retain the pound and so maintain control over our destiny as a nation state." In 2001, she said "I would never be prepared to give up our own currency . . . if you have a single currency you give up your independence. You give up your sovereignty. This we must never do."[3]

---

[1] Statement at the unveiling of euro banknotes, European Central Bank, Frankfurt, August 30, 2001.

[2] Interview with Agence France-Presse, December 25, 2006.

[3] Margaret Thatcher, article on BBC.co.uk, September 14, 1998; and speech to Conservative election rally in Plymouth, May 22, 2001.

More Currency Unions?

Several currency unions exist outside Europe. A currency union in West Africa includes eight countries, and one in Central Africa includes six. These groups fix their exchange rates against the euro. The Eastern Caribbean has a currency union of nine small countries.

Economists and politicians have proposed new currency unions in many parts of the world, such as Latin America, East Asia, and all of Africa. Supporters believe the euro has been good for Europe and want the same benefits for their regions. However, there is strong opposition in many places. Much debate about currency unions is likely in the coming years.

The ultimate currency union would be the whole world. If all nations agreed, a world central bank could issue a single world currency. This idea has been advanced by Robert Mundell of Columbia University, the winner of the 1999 Nobel Prize in Economics. Most economists dismiss Mundell's idea, but a world currency could exist someday. If it does, the world will probably have a floating exchange rate against the currencies of any extraterrestial economies we encounter.

Summary

17.1 Exchange Rates and Stabilization Policy

- Economic shocks such as shifts in asset-holders' confidence cause fluctuations in exchange rates. These exchange-rate movements destabilize output and inflation.
- Central banks adjust interest rates to offset the effects of exchange rates on output and inflation. Adjustment to exchange-rate movements is a major part of monetary policy in countries with high levels of foreign trade.

17.2 Costs of Exchange-Rate Volatility

- Fluctuations in exchange rates create risk for importers and exporters of goods and for owners of foreign assets.
- Exchange-rate risk discourages international trade and capital flows, reducing economic efficiency and growth.

17.3 Exchange-Rate Policies

- Central banks have several tools for stabilizing exchange rates, but each has drawbacks.
- A central bank can stabilize exchange rates by adjusting interest rates, but it may destabilize output in the process.
- Some central banks try to influence exchange rates through foreign-exchange interventions (purchases and sales of foreign currency). The effectiveness of interventions is questionable, however.
- Some countries impose capital controls (restrictions on capital inflows or outflows). These regulations help policymakers control exchange rates, but they impede the flow of savings to countries where the savings are most productive.
- Countries sometimes coordinate their exchange-rate policies, but often these policies cause frictions. In the 2000s, the United States has objected to China's policy of keeping its currency weak.

17.4 Fixed Exchange Rates

- A central bank can fix the nominal exchange rate by committing to buy or sell its currency at the fixed rate. It supports this policy with interest-rate adjustments and/or capital controls.
- With a fixed exchange rate, policymakers sometimes devalue or revalue the currency. Often, the reason is to offset drift in the real exchange rate caused by differences between foreign and domestic inflation.

- A country with a fixed exchange rate loses its independent monetary policy. The central bank cannot adjust interest rates to stabilize output.
- A fixed exchange rate can prevent high inflation by tying a country's inflation rate to that of another country.
- Speculative attacks can cause fixed exchange rates to collapse, as in the United Kingdom in 1992.
- From 1944 to 1973, most countries had fixed exchange rates under the Bretton Woods system. Since then, most countries have adopted floating exchange rates.

17.5 Currency Unions

- A currency union is a group of countries that adopts a common money. The euro area is the world's largest currency union.
- The primary advantage of a currency union is greater economic integration. The primary drawback is that the currency union has a single monetary policy, which may not be appropriate for all member countries.
- The impetus for creating the euro was political: a common money symbolizes European unity.

Key Terms

capital controls, p. 523

devaluation p. 529

fixed exchange rate p. 528

floating exchange rate p. 528

foreign-exchange interventions p. 519

international reserves p. 519

revaluation p. 529

speculative attack p. 532

Questions and Problems

1. Suppose that firms in Boversia gain confidence in the economy, so domestic investment rises for any given interest rate. For now, assume that net capital outflows don't change. Using graphs, show what happens to output and the real exchange rate under three assumptions about Boversia's monetary policy:
   a. The central bank holds the real interest rate constant.
   b. The central bank adjusts the real interest rate to keep output constant.
   c. The central bank adjusts the real interest rate to keep the real exchange rate constant.
2. Suppose again that investment rises in Boversia. In this case, assume that higher confidence in the economy also causes a decrease in net capital outflows. Use graphs to answer the following questions:
   a. If the central bank holds the real interest rate constant, what happens to output and the real exchange rate?
   b. If the central bank wants to keep output constant, should it raise or lower the interest rate?
   c. If the central bank wants to keep the exchange rate constant, should it raise or lower the interest rate?
3. Consider the scenario in Figure 17.4: a rise in confidence causes a fall in net capital outflows, and the central bank adjusts the interest rate to keep the exchange rate constant. For this case, explain what happens to each of the components of aggregate spending (consumption, investment, government purchases, and net exports).
4. Suppose government spending rises in Boversia, shifting out the AE curve. The central

bank would like to keep both output and the real exchange rate constant. Using graphs, show how policymakers can accomplish these goals through a combination of an interest-rate adjustment and capital controls.

5. Compare two statements about exchange rates by Treasury Secretary Henry Paulson, both from 2007. (1) "A strong dollar is in our nation's interest." (2) "The currency [China's yuan] needs to appreciate, and it needs to appreciate faster." Are the two statements consistent with one another? Why might the same official make both statements?

6. What is the difference between a depreciation of a currency and a devaluation of a currency? What is the difference between an appreciation and a revaluation?

7. In 2020, Boversia fixes its exchange rate at 0.5 dollars per bover. From 2020 to 2025, Boversia experiences inflation of 5 percent per year, while U.S. inflation is 2 percent per year.
   a. By how much does Boversia's real exchange rate change from 2020 to 2025?
   b. If Boversia wants to return the real exchange rate to its 2020 level, by how much should it devalue or revalue its currency in 2025?

8. Some countries have a "crawling peg" for their nominal exchange rate: they adjust it by a fixed percentage every year. For example, Boversia might reduce its exchange rate against the dollar by 3 percent per year. Why might a country adopt a crawling peg?

9. Boversia has a fixed exchange rate against the dollar. Taxes rise in the United States, reducing U.S. aggregate expenditure. The Federal Reserve adjusts the U.S. interest rate to keep output constant, and Boversia's central bank adjusts its interest rate to keep the exchange rate constant. Using graphs, show what happens to Boversia's output, interest rate, and exchange rate.

10. Under the Maastricht Treaty, a country may adopt the euro only if its government budget deficit is less than 3 percent of GDP. What is the rationale for this requirement? (*Hint:* See Section 14.2.)

11. Suppose the U.S. dollar is abolished. To replace it, each of the 12 Federal Reserve Banks issues a currency for its region. The Boston Fed issues the New England dollar, the Richmond Fed issues the Mid-Atlantic dollar, and so on. What are the costs and benefits of this change?

12. A currency board issues money backed by a foreign currency (review Section 2.2). Like a currency union, a currency board is an extreme version of a fixed exchange rate. Are speculative attacks a danger with a currency board? Explain.

Online and Data Questions

www.worthpublishers.com/ball

13. On the text Web site, examine (i) the behavior of the U.S.-Canada exchange rate over 2005–2007 and (ii) the interest-rate targets chosen by the Bank of Canada over the same period.
    a. Over 2005–2007, did the Bank of Canada respond to movements in the exchange rate in the same way as in earlier periods?
    b. Economists attribute changes in Canada's exchange rate over 2005–2007 to increases in the prices of commodities that Canada exports, including oil and metals. Does this help explain the answer to part (a)? (*Hint:* See the discussion of commodity prices in Section 6.5).

14. Through Internet research, update the information in Figure 17.12. Find out which countries have joined the euro area recently or are likely to join soon. Why are these countries joining while others in the European Union are still left out?

chapter eighteen 18

Financial Crises

- 18.1 THE MECHANICS OF FINANCIAL CRISES
- 18.2 POLICY RESPONSES TO FINANCIAL CRISES
- 18.3 FINANCIAL CRISES IN EMERGING ECONOMIES

During the Great Depression of the 1930s, the U.S. unemployment rate reached 25 percent. Unemployed workers struggled to find sources of income.

Economies are constantly buffeted by shocks to aggregate expenditure and inflation. Central banks usually try to stabilize economies by adjusting short-term interest rates. However, one especially devastating kind of shock requires special responses. This shock is a **financial crisis,** a major disruption of financial markets or the banking system. A financial crisis can cause economic disaster if the central bank doesn't respond effectively.

Financial crises take different forms, but the most common elements are crashes in asset prices and failures of financial institutions. In U.S. history, the worst financial crisis occurred from 1929 to 1933 and included a stock market crash and a series of bank panics. That crisis led to the Great Depression. Much more recently, the subprime mortgage crisis that began in 2007 evolved into a broader financial crisis.

In some periods, including the 1930s, central banks have responded passively to financial crises. At other times, including 2007–2008, central banks have intervened aggressively to contain crises. One way is by serving as lender of last resort: central banks lend to financial institutions that are cut off from other funds, threatening their survival.

Financial crises occur throughout the world. In many countries, key components of crises include capital flight and decreases in exchange rates. Crises of this type have hit emerging economies, such as East Asian countries in the late 1990s and Argentina in the early 2000s. The International Monetary Fund (IMF) typically intervenes in such crises by lending to governments—actions that are highly controversial.

Financial crisis Major disruption of the financial system, typically involving crashes in asset prices and failures of financial institutions

Financial crises are complex events. To understand them, we must understand the workings of financial markets and the banking system, the behavior of the aggregate economy, and the policies of central banks. Previous chapters have discussed these topics separately; here, we pull them together. We'll see that feedbacks among different parts of the financial system and economy are what make financial crises so dangerous.

18.1 THE MECHANICS OF FINANCIAL CRISES

No two financial crises are exactly alike, but most share a few basic features. Let's explore the essential elements of a crisis. We first discuss what happens to the financial system, and then how a crisis affects the rest of the economy.

Events in the Financial System

At the center of most crises are crashes in asset prices, failures of financial institutions, or both.

▶ This discussion draws on earlier coverage of asset-price crashes (Section 3.5), bank insolvencies (Section 9.6), and bank runs (Section 10.1).

Asset-Price Crashes A crash is a sudden, large drop in the prices of assets, such as stocks or real estate. Although nobody is sure what causes crashes, many economists interpret them as the ends of asset-price bubbles. During a bubble, people expect asset prices to rise, which causes high demand for the assets, which makes the expectations of higher prices self-fulfilling. Asset prices rise far above the present value of expected income from the assets.

Then, at some point, sentiment shifts: people start worrying that asset prices are too high. They start selling the assets, pushing prices down. Falling prices shake confidence further, starting a vicious cycle of selling and panic—the crash.

Insolvency A financial institution becomes insolvent if its assets fall below its liabilities. Its net worth, or capital, becomes negative. A commercial bank can become insolvent for reasons including loan defaults and increases in interest rates. When a bank becomes insolvent, regulators are likely to force its closure.

Other kinds of financial institutions can also become insolvent. Hedge funds, for example, borrow money from banks to purchase risky assets. If the prices of these assets decline, a fund's net worth can become negative. The fund is likely to default on its debts and go out of business.

Insolvencies are dangerous because they can spread from one institution to others. This happens because financial institutions have debts to one another. Banks have deposits at other banks, which often exceed the limit on deposit insurance. Banks also lend to one another in the federal funds market, and they lend to hedge funds and investment banks. If one institution fails, its depositors and lenders suffer losses. Net worth drops for these institutions, creating a risk that they, too, will become insolvent.

Liquidity Crises Financial institutions can also fail because they lack liquidity. They are initially solvent, but most of their assets are illiquid: the assets can't be sold quickly for what they're worth. An institution gets in trouble if it doesn't have enough liquid assets to make payments it has promised.

The classic example is a bank run. Depositors lose confidence in a bank and try to withdraw large amounts, exhausting the bank's reserves and liquid securities. The bank must sell illiquid assets at fire-sale prices, and losses on these transactions can push it into insolvency.

Liquidity crises can also occur at nondepository institutions, such as hedge funds and investment banks. These institutions often raise funds through short-term loans and by issuing short-term bonds (commercial paper). To stay in business, they must raise new funds continuously to pay off maturing debts. But creditors can lose confidence and cut off funding. As in a bank run, an institution can be forced into a fire-sale of illiquid assets, leading to insolvency. We return to this point in Section 18.2, where we discuss the 2008 crisis at the investment bank Bear Stearns.

Like insolvencies in general, liquidity crises can spread from one financial institution to another. In this case, the spillovers are largely psychological. If a bank experiences a run, for example, depositors at other banks start worrying about the safety of their funds. They may start making withdrawals, triggering an economy-wide bank panic and widespread failures.

Financial Crises and the Economy

Financial crises have both direct and indirect costs. The direct costs include losses to asset holders when asset prices fall. They also include losses from financial-institution failures. Owners of a failed institution lose their equity, and the institution's creditors lose funds they have lent. When a failed institution is a bank, losses also fall on uninsured depositors and the Federal Deposit Insurance Corporation (FDIC).

While these costs can be large, the greatest dangers from financial crises are their indirect effects. A crisis can set off a chain of events that plunges the whole economy into a recession. **Figure 18.1** summarizes the key parts of this process.

Lending and Spending

A crash in asset prices can cause a sharp fall in aggregate expenditure—channel A in Figure 18.1. One reason is that asset holders suffer a loss of wealth, which leads them to reduce their consumption. A crash also shakes the confidence of firms and consumers, who may interpret it as a sign that the overall economy is in trouble. Uncertain of the future, they put off major decisions about spending until things settle down. In the meantime, consumption and investment fall.

▶ Some of the effects in Figure 18.1 are introduced in Section 13.2, which discusses how events in the financial system affect aggregate expenditure. That discussion illustrates the effects by examining Japan's experience in the 1990s and early 2000s.

Asset-price crashes also reduce bank lending, channel B in Figure 18.1. Lower asset prices mean a fall in borrowers' net worth and collateral, which worsens adverse selection and moral hazard in loan markets. The result is a credit crunch: some borrowers are cut off from loans.

Bank failures also reduce lending, channel C in Figure 18.1. Obviously, banks that fail stop lending. Surviving banks may fear failure and become more conservative in approving loans. They may also increase their liquid assets to guard against runs, leaving fewer funds to lend.

FIGURE 18.1 A Financial Crisis

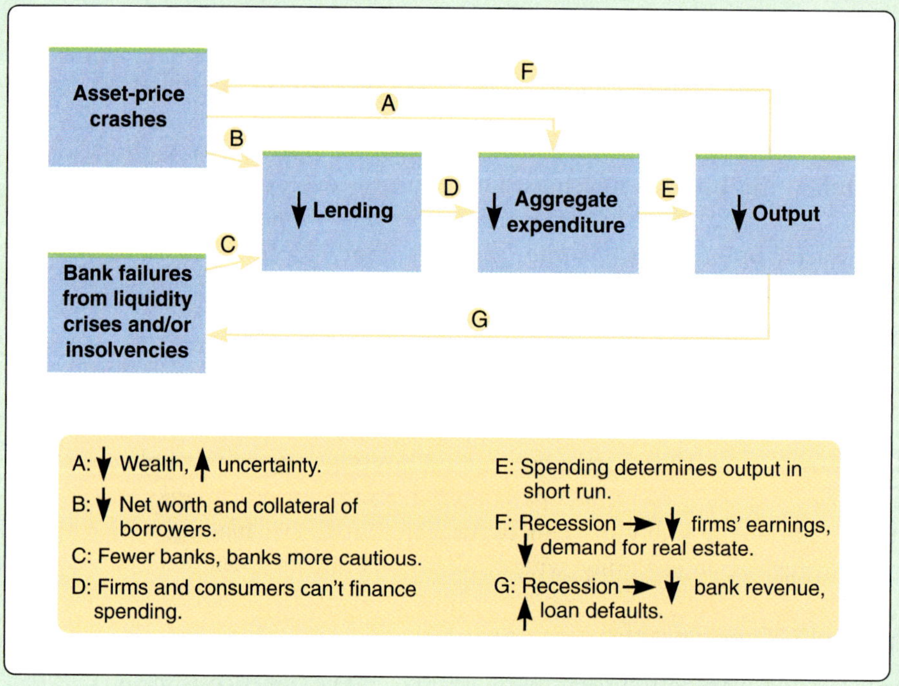

A typical financial crisis is triggered by asset-price crashes or failures of financial institutions. A series of effects leads to a fall in output, which reinforces the causes of the crisis.

Lower bank lending means less spending by firms and individuals who rely on banks for funds, channel D. This effect reduces aggregate expenditure, adding to the direct effect of asset-price crashes. In the short run, expenditure determines output, channel E, so output falls. A crisis can cause a deep recession.

A Vicious Cycle Unfortunately, that's not the end of the story. If a financial crisis causes a recession, the recession can then exacerbate the crisis. Asset prices are likely to fall further, channel F in Figure 18.1. Stock prices fall because the recession reduces firms' expected profits. Lower demand for real estate pushes down real estate prices.

A recession also worsens banking problems, channel G. Banks lose revenue because a recession reduces the demand for loans. Firms go bankrupt, increasing loan defaults. Worries about these problems make bank panics more likely. For all these reasons, bank failures rise.

Because of these feedbacks, a financial crisis can trigger a vicious cycle of falling output and worsening financial problems. Once a crisis starts, it can sustain itself for a long time.

So far we've discussed the most common elements of crises. There are many possible wrinkles—other ways that a crisis can hurt the economy and build on itself. The details vary across different episodes. To illustrate how much can go wrong, let's analyze the worst U.S. financial crisis.

CASE STUDY

Disaster in the 1930s

In U.S. economic history, the Great Depression stands out as a unique disaster. The unemployment rate rose from 3 percent in 1929 to 25 percent in 1933, and it was still 15 percent in 1940. By comparison, the highest unemployment rate since the depression was 10 percent in 1982–1983, during the Volcker disinflation. The depression pushed millions of middle-class families into poverty.

The depression was caused by a series of events starting in 1929, which are summarized in **Figure 18.2.** The episode included all the typical parts of a financial crisis—the events and effects shown in Figure 18.1—plus some less common problems. Channels involving these problems are numbered in Figure 18.2.

Two shocks triggered the crisis. One was the stock market crash of 1929. The Dow Jones index of stock prices fell 13 percent on October 28, 1929, and then kept falling. Overall, the Dow index fell from 365 before the crash to 41 in 1932, a decrease of 89 percent.

The other shock was a series of bank panics from 1930 to 1933. Depositors lost confidence in banks and, with no deposit insurance to protect them, rushed to withdraw funds. President Franklin Roosevelt eventually ended the panics with the bank holiday of March 1933, but more than a third of all U.S. banks failed.

These events reduced bank lending dramatically (channels B and C in Figure 18.2). The stock market crash also created great uncertainty about the economy, as it was an unprecedented event. Uncertainty led firms and consumers to postpone major purchases (channel A). Automobile sales fell sharply, for example.

A special twist in this crisis was a fall in the money supply. Because of the bank panics, people started holding more currency and banks increased their reserves to guard against runs. The currency-deposit and reserve-deposit ratios rose, reducing the money multiplier (Equation (11.2)). The fall in the multiplier reduced the money supply by 33 percent between 1929 and 1933 (channel 1). The fall in the money supply reduced aggregate expenditure (channel 2), reinforcing the effects of the stock market crash and lower bank lending.

As usual in crises, falling output magnified the problems of the financial system, especially the stock market. With the economy depressed, firms' prospects for earnings were bleak. Stock prices stayed low: it took until 1954 for the Dow index to climb back to its 1929 level.

One more series of effects worsened the depression. The fall in the money supply and the output slump caused a sharp deflation (channel 3). From 1929 through 1933, the aggregate price level fell by 22 percent. Deflation increased the real value of debts that were set in nominal terms (channel 4).

FIGURE 18.2 The United States, 1929–1933

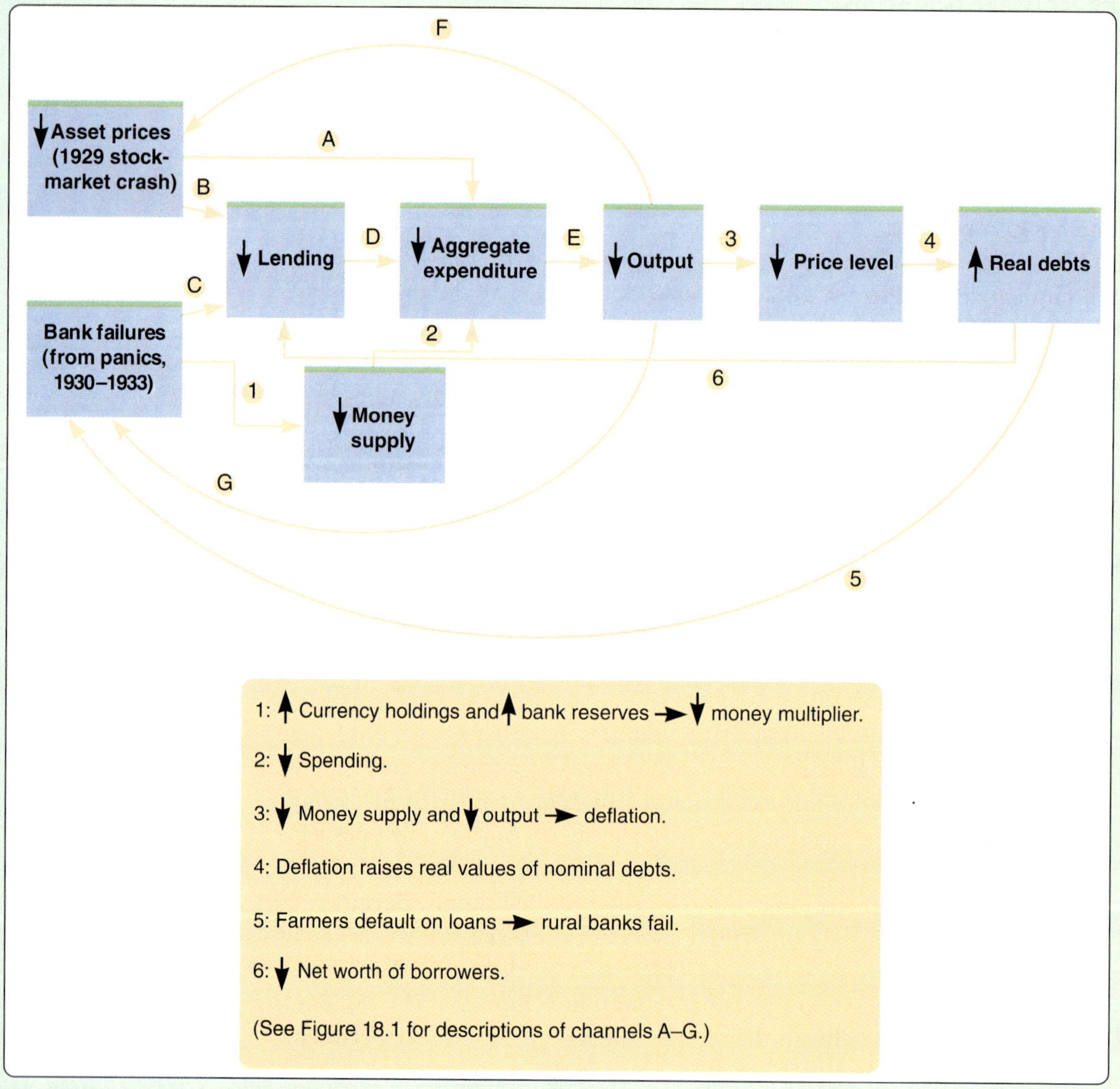

The financial crisis that produced the Great Depression included a stock market crash, bank panics, a fall in the money supply, and deflation.

In turn, higher debt burdens reinforced the crisis. Farmers defaulted on bank loans, contributing to failures of rural banks (channel 5). Throughout the economy, higher real debt reduced the net worth of households and firms, worsening moral hazard and adverse selection in loan markets. The result was a further contraction of bank lending (channel 6).

The worst years of the depression were 1932 and 1933. After that, a recovery began, partly resulting from policies of the Roosevelt Administration.*

* For more on the Great Depression, see Christina Romer, "The Nation in Depression," *Journal of Economic Perspectives*, Spring 1993.

18.2 POLICY RESPONSES TO FINANCIAL CRISES

Governments and central banks would like to prevent financial crises. Some economists think central banks can help prevent asset-price crashes, which are one cause of crises. According to this view, policymakers should use interest-rate increases to dampen the asset-price bubbles that lead to crashes. This idea is controversial, however, and central banks generally don't try to dampen bubbles (review Section 15.7).

Policymakers *do* try to prevent bank failures, another basic cause of crises. Deposit insurance, created after the bank panics of the 1930s, has prevented similar panics since then. Government regulators also restrain risk-taking by banks through capital requirements, restrictions on assets, and supervision. These policies reduce the likelihood that banks will suffer large losses and become insolvent.

Unfortunately, no policies can eliminate financial crises entirely. Even with the best regulation, asset prices will sometimes crash and financial institutions will fail. When these events occur, policymakers try to contain the effects on the financial system and economy. They try to dampen vicious cycles like those shown in Figures 18.1 and 18.2.

Central banks and regulatory agencies have several tools for fighting financial crises. These tools include expansionary monetary policy, liquidity provision, and bailouts of insolvent institutions. We'll see, however, that economists disagree about the best uses of these tools.

Expansionary Monetary Policy

One response to a financial crisis is expansionary monetary policy. When a central bank targets interest rates, this means reducing that target. Lower interest rates boost aggregate expenditure, offsetting the effects of asset-price crashes and lower bank lending.

Lower interest rates also raise asset prices, helping to offset an initial crash. Asset prices rise because lower interest rates raise the present value of expected asset income. By stimulating the economy, lower rates raise the income flow from some assets, such as stocks. In addition, lower rates raise the present value of any given income flow.

In the 1930s, a type of expansionary monetary policy helped spur recovery from the Great Depression—but it was not a policy of the Federal Reserve. At the time, the United States was still on a gold standard, with the value of a dollar set by the government. In 1934, the Roosevelt administration reduced the dollar's value from 0.0484 ounces of gold to 0.0286 ounces. Most European countries kept the values of their currencies fixed, so Roosevelt's action amounted to a devaluation against foreign currencies.

This devaluation made U.S. assets less expensive relative to foreign assets, causing capital inflows. Foreigners who wanted to buy U.S. assets traded gold to the government for dollars, and this increased the money supply. Rapid money growth in the mid-1930s pushed interest rates down, stimulating investment and spending on durable goods. This spending helped reverse the output decline of the early 1930s.

▶ The capital inflows behind the rising money supply were also spurred by political events in Europe. As Hitler came to power and fears of a war increased, Europeans sought safe assets in the United States.

Liquidity Crises and the Lender of Last Resort

Liquidity crises at financial institutions, such as bank panics, are one cause of broader financial crises. A liquidity crisis can cause a financial institution to fail even if it is initially solvent (its net worth is positive), meaning there is no good reason for it to fail. The institution fails simply because depositors or creditors lose confidence and demand payments that exceed its liquid assets. Most economists think policymakers should try to prevent such occurrences.

Fortunately, a central bank has a simple solution for liquidity crises. It can make emergency loans to institutions that are running out of liquid assets, allowing them to avoid fire sales of illiquid assets. That is, the central bank can serve as lender of last resort. A borrowing institution remains solvent and repays the central bank when its liquidity crisis subsides. To ensure repayment, the central bank requires the borrower to pledge some of its assets as collateral for the loan.

The Bank of England developed the role of lender of last resort in the 18th and 19th centuries. When Congress established the Federal Reserve in 1913, the main purpose was to create a lender of last resort for U.S. banks. The U.S. had experienced a series of bank panics in the preceding decades, and the Fed's founders hoped to prevent future panics. Unfortunately, the Fed did *not* stop the panics of the early 1930s, as it did not lend to many banks. In retrospect, Fed officials underestimated the danger to the banking system and the economy. The Fed learned from this mistake and has acted quickly in more recent liquidity crises.

Deposit insurance helps prevent bank runs, reducing the need for a lender of last resort, but it does not eliminate the need entirely. Some banks, especially money-center banks, raise most of their funds through borrowing and deposits that exceed the limit on insurance. These uninsured funds disappear quickly if depositors and lenders lose confidence in a bank. A lender of last resort is needed for such an emergency.

Currently, the Fed lends to banks in two ways. A bank can approach the Fed and request a discount loan, or it can bid for a loan in the periodic auctions of the Term Auction Facility (TAF). In either case, the Fed lends simply by crediting the bank's account at the Fed (review Section 11.2).

These loans are available only to commercial banks and savings institutions, entities that fit the definition of *bank*: they accept deposits and make loans. At times, however, the Fed has stretched its role as lender of last resort by providing liquidity to other financial institutions. After the terrorist attacks of September 11, 2001, the Fed encouraged banks to lend to securities firms facing liquidity crises. In turn, the Fed promised to lend any necessary funds to the banks. The Fed used a similar approach during the stock market crash of October 1987, which also caused liquidity crises at securities firms.

In March 2008, the Fed announced an expansion of its role as lender of last resort. The new policy was a response to the near failure of the investment bank Bear Stearns. The Fed established the *Primary Dealer Credit*

Facility (PDCF), which lends to primary dealers in the government securities market—the dealers that trade with the New York Fed when it performs open-market operations. This group includes major securities firms as well as commercial banks. With the PDCF, the Fed can serve directly as lender of last resort to non-bank financial institutions.

Bailouts of Insolvent Institutions

When a central bank acts as lender of last resort, it helps a solvent institution facing a liquidity crisis. The loan prevents the institution from failing, and it is repaid. Ultimately, there is no cost to the central bank, the government, or taxpayers.

Not all failures of financial institutions are caused by liquidity crises. Sometimes an institution simply loses money, so its assets fall below its liabilities: it becomes insolvent. Normally, this causes the institution to fail and default on its debts. In some cases, however, the central bank or government provides a **bailout.** Instead of lending to an institution, it gives money away. Policymakers may seek to restore the institution's solvency and keep it in business. Alternatively, they may let the institution fail but compensate other institutions and individuals who are hurt by the failure.

Bailout Provision of funds by a government or central bank to prevent an insolvent institution from failing or to compensate other parties for losses from a failure

With deposit insurance, any bank failure leads to a partial bailout: the FDIC compensates each depositor up to some limit ($250,000 as of late 2008). Today few economists question the desirability of deposit insurance, at least in countries with effective bank regulation. The controversial issue is whether bailouts should extend beyond promised insurance payments. When a bank fails, should the government or central bank protect uninsured depositors and creditors? Should they bail out financial institutions with no insurance guarantees, such as investment banks and hedge funds?

The Pros and Cons of Bailouts The purpose of bailouts is to prevent failures from multiplying. As we've discussed, banks and other financial institutions deposit money and lend to one another. If one institution fails, it defaults on debts to other institutions, and their losses can cause them to fail. A rash of failures can produce a financial crisis that damages the economy.

But bailouts have two kinds of costs. The first is the direct costs of payments from the government or central bank. These costs are ultimately borne by taxpayers.

The second cost is a worsening of moral hazard, the problem that financial institutions may misuse the funds they raise. In particular, bailouts make it more likely that institutions will take excessive risks, lose money, and become insolvent. Normally, an institution's creditors and uninsured depositors monitor what happens to their money and cut off funds if the institution misuses them. But if bailouts are common, everyone expects the government to protect them from losses. Nobody has incentives for monitoring, so institutions can easily raise funds to finance gambles. These institutions earn a lot if the gambles succeed, and losses fall largely on taxpayers.

When any given institution is in danger of failing, it's hard to know how badly the failure would damage the financial system. It's also hard to gauge how much a bailout would increase moral hazard in the future. Because of these uncertainties, economists differ sharply on the desirability of bailouts.

Too big to fail (TBTF) Doctrine that large banks facing insolvency must be bailed out to protect the financial system

Commercial Banks: "Too Big to Fail"? Historically, most debates about bailouts have focused on commercial banks. Regulators have argued that the case for bailing out a bank depends on its size. A large bank has more links to other financial institutions than a small bank. It is likely to hold deposits from other banks and to borrow heavily. Consequently, the failure of a large bank threatens other institutions, whereas the failure of a small bank is relatively harmless. Some banks must be bailed out, the argument goes, because they are **too big to fail (TBTF).**

This term was coined by a congressman after a famous bailout, the rescue of Continental Illinois Bank in 1984. One of the largest U.S. banks, Continental Illinois became insolvent through bad loans to energy companies and the governments of developing countries. In May 1984, it was on the brink of failure.

Regulators feared that the failure of Continental Illinois would have widespread effects. Over 2000 smaller banks had accounts at Continental. For 66 of these banks, deposits at Continental exceeded their total capital; for another 113, the deposits were more than half of capital. Regulators feared that many of these banks would fail if they lost their deposits, shaking confidence in the financial system. The comptroller of the currency, the head regulator of national banks, said after the crisis that Continental's failure would have caused "a national, if not international, financial crisis the dimensions of which were difficult to imagine."[1]

Policymakers acted aggressively to save Continental. Despite the bank's insolvency, the Fed lent it $3.6 billion to keep it in operation. The FDIC promised to protect all of Continental's creditors and depositors, waiving the usual limit on insurance. Eventually, the FDIC bought Continental from its shareholders, added capital, and sold it to Bank of America. In the process, the FDIC lost about $1 billion.

During the Continental crisis, the comptroller of the currency announced a general policy that large banks would be treated as too big to fail. He said that the nation's 11 largest banks would be covered by this policy.

These actions were controversial at the time, and remain so. Critics stress the moral hazard problem and argue that policymakers overstated the risks from a failure of Continental. When Congress passed the FDIC Improvement Act in 1991, it imposed limits on the TBTF policy. Regulators can declare a bank TBTF only if its failure would have "serious adverse effects on economic conditions or financial stability." This decision must be approved by the secretary of the treasury, two-thirds of the Federal Reserve governors, and two-thirds of the directors of the FDIC. Since these rules were established, the

[1] Todd Conover, testimony before House Banking Committee, September 19, 1984.

government has not bailed out any commercial banks. When banks have failed, the FDIC has not compensated uninsured depositors or creditors.

Bailouts of Nonbank Institutions Commercial banks are not the only financial institutions that become insolvent. In 1998, the Federal Reserve intervened to prevent the failure of a hedge fund, Long-Term Capital Management (LTCM). Ten years later, the Fed helped rescue an investment bank, Bear Stearns. Both actions were highly controversial.

LTCM was famous for its dream team of managers, which included a former vice chair of the Fed and two Nobel Prize winners in economics. It made huge profits for awhile by borrowing from commercial and investment banks and betting on movements in bond prices. But it suffered disastrous losses in 1998, partly on bonds from emerging economies, whose prices fell when Russia defaulted on its debt. LTCM lost most of its capital and started having trouble making loan payments. It was on the verge of bankruptcy.

The Fed feared a failure of LTCM because the hedge fund owed so much to major financial institutions. Officials organized a meeting with LTCM and its creditors at the Federal Reserve Bank of New York. The creditors agreed to buy 90 percent of LTCM and to add new capital, restoring the firm's solvency. LTCM scaled back its business and eventually closed, but it didn't default on its debts.

The Fed's action was not strictly a bailout, because it didn't provide any money. However, critics think the Fed pressured financial institutions to buy shares of LTCM. The New York Fed has influence over these institutions because they trade with the Fed as primary dealers of government securities. The Fed also regulates some of the institutions.

Critics say the rescue of LTCM worsened the moral hazard problem. The deal benefitted the hedge fund's owners as well as its creditors. The owners received money for selling the firm and kept their high-paying management jobs for awhile. This outcome has encouraged other hedge funds to take excessive risks.

Ten years later, meetings at the New York Fed led to the rescue of another institution, Bear Stearns. The Fed's actions in this case were part of a broader effort to contain a financial crisis that began in 2007. We now turn to this episode.

JUMBO CASE STUDY

The Financial System and the Fed, 2007–2008

Policies to address financial crises have long been a subject of debate. The debate intensified in 2007–2008, when a financial crisis threatened the U. S. economy. The problems began with subprime mortgages. Defaults on these mortgages started rising in 2006, causing losses to mortgage lenders and holders of mortgage-backed securities. In retrospect, these losses reflected lax lending standards, which led to defaults when interest rates rose and house prices fell.

▶ See Section 8.4 for more on the subprime mortgage crisis.

▶As this book was going to press, the U.S. financial crisis was deepening. September 2008 brought the failure of Lehman Brothers, the country's fourth-largest investment bank, and Washington Mutual, the largest savings institution. Both the Fed and the U.S. Treasury responded with new policies aimed at stemming the crisis. This Chapter's online case study gives details.

The summer of 2007 brought signs that the subprime crisis was the beginning of a broader financial crisis. Fears grew that losses on mortgages would push financial institutions into insolvency. In turn, these fears caused a liquidity crisis: financial institutions became reluctant to lend to one another because they were not sure of repayment. Falling confidence in the economy pushed stock prices down, and the decline in house prices accelerated.

The Fed under Ben Bernanke was determined to contain these problems and minimize damage to the economy. As a result, it pursued a series of unorthodox policies: it expanded its role as lender of last resort; it sought to prevent insolvencies, partly through the Bear Stearns rescue; and it lowered interest rates with unusual speed. Let's review these actions, which are summarized in **Table 18.1.**

Online Case Study: An Update on the U.S. Financial Crisis and Policymakers' Responses

Addressing the Liquidity Crisis In August 2007, banks suddenly became afraid of lending to one another. On August 9 and 10, lenders were scarce in the federal funds market, and the low supply of loans pushed the federal funds rate above the Fed's target of 5.25 percent. The Fed used large, expansionary, open-market operations to push the funds rate back down. On August 10, it bought securities at three different times of the day.

International banks lend dollars to one another in the London interbank market. Here, too, lenders suddenly became scarce. The overnight interest rate in the London market, the one-day *LIBOR rate,* spiked up by half a percentage point on August 9.

▶LIBOR stands for London Inter-Bank Offered Rate.

Interest rates on interbank loans stayed high for the rest of the year and into 2008. For example, the 3-month LIBOR rate rose 2 percentage points above the 3-month Treasury bill rate; a more normal spread is half a percentage point. Interest rates also rose on commercial paper issued by banks, and less of this commercial paper was sold. Some banks had serious problems raising funds; in the United Kingdom, Northern Rock's problems triggered a bank run.

The Federal Reserve wanted to head off liquidity crises at U.S. banks. Initially it relied on discount loans, its traditional means of providing liquidity. Before August 2007, the Fed had set the discount rate 1 percentage point above the federal funds rate. It cut this gap to half a point on August 16 and to a quarter point on the following March 16. The Fed also issued statements encouraging banks to request discount loans if they needed funds.

TABLE 18.1 Major Fed Policies, 2007–2008*

Cuts in discount rate
Creation of Term Auction Facility
Bear Stearns rescue
Creation of Primary Dealer Credit Facility
Rapid cuts in federal funds rate

* This list covers actions from August 2007 through August 2008. The online case study for this chapter discusses Fed policies since August 2008.

Yet few banks requested loans. The apparent reason was the stigma attached to this action. Banks feared that loan requests would signal that they were in trouble. In the U.K., depositors lost confidence in Northern Rock when a journalist reported that the bank had approached the Bank of England "hat in hand."

The low level of discount lending prompted the Fed to create the Term Auction Facility in December 2007. Policymakers hoped that borrowing through the TAF would not embarrass banks, because the Fed took the lead in setting up auctions rather than waiting for requests from borrowers. Also, participation in auctions was not publicized as widely as requests for discount loans.

The establishment of the TAF raised Fed lending dramatically. In mid-2008, the Fed was holding auctions every 2 weeks, typically offering \$25–\$75 billion of loans at a time. The auctions were providing a stable source of liquidity for banks.

Bear Stearns and the PDCF The subprime crisis caused the failures of Ameriquest and New Century Financial, finance companies that specialized in subprime mortgages. Through 2007, however, the crisis did not seem to threaten the solvency of major commercial or investment banks. Institutions such as Citigroup lost billions of dollars on mortgage-backed securities but were strong enough to survive.

In early 2008, serious problems arose for Bear Stearns, the country's fifth-largest investment bank. Bear held unusually large quantities of securities backed by subprime mortgages. As the prices of these securities fell, rumors spread that Bear Stearns might become insolvent. These fears produced a liquidity crisis. Bear was one institution that relied heavily on short-term borrowing. In early 2008, much of its funding disappeared; for example, money-market mutual funds stopped buying the firm's commercial paper. As Bear Stearns ran out of liquid assets, its lawyers prepared to file for bankruptcy.

As in the Continental Illinois and LTCM cases, the Fed feared that a failure would damage the financial system. Bear had large debts to other financial institutions. In addition, it had traded trillions of dollars of *credit derivatives,* which meant it insured other institutions against default on bank loans and bonds. If Bear had failed, these institutions would suddenly have been exposed to default risk. They might have responded with large sales of assets, causing asset prices to plummet. The Fed also feared a blow to confidence that would trigger liquidity crises at other financial institutions.

The Fed didn't know how badly a Bear Stearns failure would hurt the financial system, but it didn't want to find out. As in the LTCM case, the Fed brokered a sale of Bear Stearns. The buyer was JP Morgan Chase, the nation's second-largest financial institution. JP Morgan paid \$10 for each share of Bear Stearns stock, which had traded as high as \$172 during 2007. So Bear's stockholders suffered large losses, but its creditors did not.

In contrast to the LTCM case, the Fed helped fund the Bear Stearns deal. It lent \$30 billion to JP Morgan Chase to finance the purchase of Bear. With this action, the Fed blurred the distinction between serving as lender of last resort and bailing out an insolvent institution. The \$30 billion was a loan, not a subsidy. However, the Fed accepted risky assets of Bear Stearns, including mortgage-backed securities, as collateral. And the loan was made "without recourse": if the collateral declines in value, the Fed is entitled only to the collateral, not the \$30 billion it lent. So the Fed took on risk to rescue Bear Stearns.

The Fed believes it is unlikely to lose a significant amount of money, and that its action was needed to protect the financial system. Critics say the Fed's losses could be large, and they cite the usual moral hazard problem. Some of the harshest criticism has come from a former Fed insider, Vincent Reinhart, who directed the Division of Monetary Affairs from 2001 to 2007. In April 2008, Reinhart called the Bear Stearns rescue "the worst policy mistake in a generation."[2] He predicted a new era of harmful government meddling in the financial system.

Notice that the Fed rescued Bear Stearns by lending to JP Morgan Chase. Under its rules at the time, the Fed could lend only to institutions with commercial banking units, which included JP Morgan but not Bear Stearns. However, shortly after the Bear Stearns deal, the Fed established the Primary Dealer Credit Facility. The PDCF allows the Fed to lend directly to securities firms without commercial banking units.

▶ One sign of a credit crunch was a cutback in student loans. Some banks stopped making any student loans, and others dropped them for certain colleges. Citigroup's Student Loan Corporation, for example, stopped lending to students at two-year community colleges.

The Economy and Interest Rates The financial system's problems in 2007 and 2008 threatened to cause a recession. Signs of a credit crunch emerged: banks reduced lending to firms and individuals. One reason was that losses in the subprime crisis reduced banks' capital, and lower capital forces banks to cut back on loans. In addition, banks became more nervous about the risks of lending.

The problems of the financial system also reduced consumer spending. Consumption fell because falling stock and real estate prices reduced wealth. In addition, the daily headlines about financial turmoil shook consumer confidence.

The Fed worried that lower bank lending and consumption would reduce output—and that the output fall could be large if the financial crisis worsened. It responded with rapid cuts in interest rates. It reduced its target for the federal funds rate from 5.25 percent to 2 percent over 7 months, from September 2007 to April 2008. It reduced the target by 3/4 of a percent on January 22 and again on March 18, the largest one-day decreases since the early 1980s.

▶ Section 15.7 expands on the Fed's departure from the Taylor rule in 2007–2008. Chapter 12's online case study gives an update on U.S. output and inflation.

In taking these actions, the Fed deviated from the Taylor rule, which says that interest rates should depend on output and inflation. The inflation rate rose somewhat over 2007–2008 as oil prices rose. Output growth slowed, but only moderately; in mid-2008, it was not clear that a recession would

[2] "What Lies Behind the Credit Crunch," Panel Discussion at American Enterprise Institute, April 28, 2008.

occur. With rising inflation and fairly stable output, the Taylor rule did not prescribe the large interest rate cuts that occurred. This episode shows how a financial crisis can cause a departure from normal monetary policy.

Ben Bernanke and Franklin Roosevelt Why did the Fed act so aggressively in 2007–2008? One explanation is that it learned from the past. Historians blame the Great Depression of the 1930s largely on the passivity of the Fed, which allowed bank failures and a fall in the money supply that it could have prevented. The Fed didn't want to stand by again as a financial crisis occurred.

This interpretation of the Fed's behavior fits with the career of Ben Bernanke. As an economics professor, Bernanke became famous for research on the Great Depression, especially a 1983 paper on how bank failures damaged the economy. Later, Bernanke criticized the Bank of Japan for not doing more to end the Japanese recession of the 1990s and early 2000s. In light of these views, it is natural that Bernanke responded aggressively when he perceived a financial crisis.

Bernanke has praised President Franklin Roosevelt for fighting the depression after taking office in 1933. Roosevelt's policies included the Bank Holiday, the introduction of deposit insurance, the devaluation of the dollar against gold, and the various employment programs of the New Deal. These policies were untested and controversial. Yet, wrote Bernanke in 2000,

> *Roosevelt's specific policy actions were, I think, less important than his willingness to be aggressive and to experiment—in short, to do whatever it took to get the country moving again. Many of his policies did not work as intended, but in the end FDR deserves great credit for having the courage to abandon failed paradigms and to do what needed to be done.*[*]

In advocating new policies for the Bank of Japan, Bernanke urged its leaders to show "Rooseveltian resolve."

In 2007–2008, Bernanke introduced his own array of new policies—the Term Auction Facility, the Primary Dealer Credit Facility, the Bear Stearns rescue, the rapid cuts in interest rates. Bernanke, it appears, was trying to show Rooseveltian resolve in addressing the crisis of his day.

Preventing the Next Crisis Recent events have prompted calls for new government policies to prevent financial crises. Since World War II, a trend has existed toward deregulation of financial institutions, such as the elimination of geographic limits on their operations and the repeal of the Glass-Steagall Act's separation of commercial and investment banks. Now some economists suggest that financial institutions should be "re-regulated." In 2008, the Fed issued rules tightening the standards that banks and finance companies must use in approving mortgages. Many think the Bear Stearns episode shows that regulators need to restrict risk-taking by financial institutions. Proposals for new regulations are sure to be debated in the coming years.

* Ben Bernanke, "Japanese Monetary Policy: A Case of Self-Induced Paralysis," in Ryoichi Mikitani and Adam Posen (eds.), *Japan's Financial Crisis and Its Parallels to U.S. Experience*, Institute for International Economics, 2000.

18.3 FINANCIAL CRISES IN EMERGING ECONOMIES

Financial crises occur all over the world. In the last two decades, they have hit many *emerging-market economies*—countries in the middle of the world income distribution (not as rich as the United States, but not as poor as many African countries). Crises occurred in Mexico in 1994, many East Asian countries in 1997–1998, Russia in 1998, and Argentina in 2001. Each caused major economic damage.

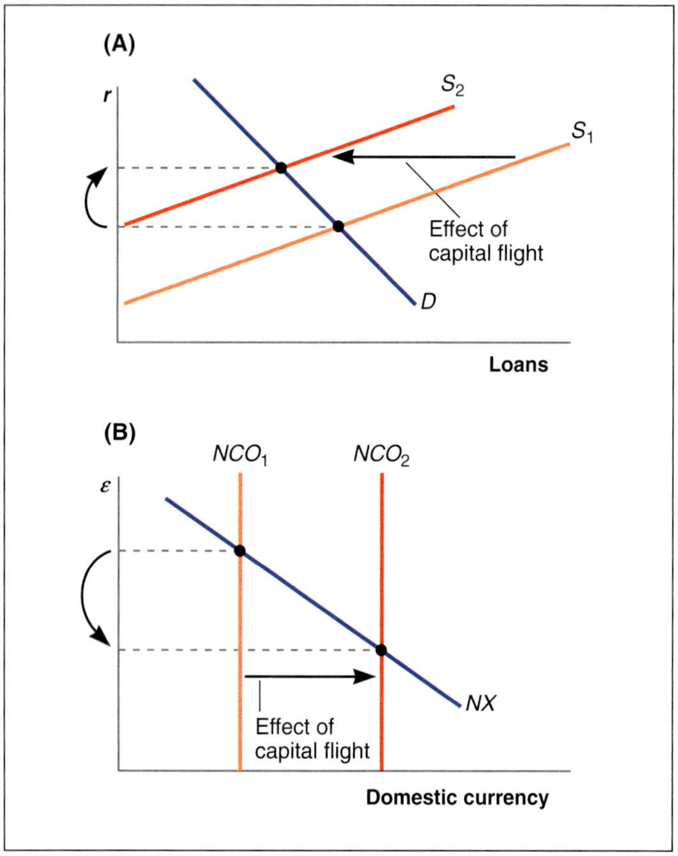

Capital flight reduces the supply of loans, increasing the real interest rate (A). It also raises net capital outflows, decreasing the real exchange rate (B).

Emerging-economy crises have much in common with U.S. crises, including bank failures and asset-price crashes. However, they also have another key element: capital flight. Typically, capital has flowed into a country, but a loss of confidence causes a shift from inflows to outflows. One effect is a sharp fall in the exchange rate. Capital flight and the exchange-rate collapse create additional channels in the vicious cycle of a financial crisis.

Capital Flight

Capital flight means a sharp fall in the demand for a country's assets. In the foreign-exchange market, a rise in net capital outflows (NCO) reduces the real exchange rate. In the country's loan market, the supply of loans falls, raising the real interest rate.

Causes of Capital Flight Various events can shake confidence in an economy, triggering capital flight. Financial crises often involve more than one. Following are some leading causes of capital flight:

- *Government debt.* This was a central factor in the crises in Mexico and Argentina. Rising debt levels created fears that the government would default, so foreign financial institutions stopped buying government bonds. Foreigners also worried that default would hurt the economy, so they stopped buying the securities of corporations.
- *Political risk.* Political instability can bring bad governments to power or produce armed conflicts that disrupt the economy. So signs of instability can spark capital flight. In Mexico, asset holders were

spooked by the assassination of a presidential candidate and a rebellion in the state of Chiapas.

- *Banking problems.* One kind of capital inflow is loans to banks from foreign banks. These loans are cut off if the domestic banks get in trouble. This occurred in East Asian countries, which otherwise weren't candidates for capital flight. (Most countries had stable governments with low budget deficits.) Banks in East Asia made unsound loans because of lax regulation, and because some borrowers had political connections. Default rates were high, threatening the banks' solvency.

The Role of Fixed Exchange Rates Capital flight can hit countries whether their exchange rates are fixed or flexible. However, most recent crises have occurred in countries with fixed rates. Mismanagement of the exchange rate contributed to the crises.

The story was similar in many countries. The central bank fixed the exchange rate to the U.S. dollar to encourage trade and to reduce inflation. Inflation remained above the U.S. level, causing a real appreciation of the currency. So the real exchange rate was rising at the same time capital flight put downward pressure on the exchange rate. At first the central bank intervened in foreign-exchange markets to maintain the fixed rate, but reserves fell and eventually it became clear that the fixed rate was unsustainable. At that point, a speculative attack caused the exchange rate to plummet.

▶ Section 17.4 discusses speculative attacks on fixed exchange rates.

Collapses of fixed exchange rates had bad psychological effects on asset holders. Typically, the fixed exchange rate was a centerpiece of the government's economic policy. Officials promised fervently that they would maintain the fixed rate. So people interpreted collapses in exchange rates as government failures. This reduced asset holders' confidence, which was already shaky because of other problems, and worsened capital flight.

Contagion Just as a bank run can trigger runs at other banks, capital flight can spread from one country to others. This is called **contagion.** Asset holders see that a country's exchange rate and asset prices have fallen. They worry that the same thing could happen in countries in the same region or in countries with similar problems. Capital flight hits these countries as asset holders try to sell before prices fall.

Contagion Spread of capital flight from one country to others

For example, the East Asian financial crisis began in Thailand. A speculative attack on the baht caused a fixed exchange rate to collapse in July 1997. In the following months, capital flight spread to countries including South Korea, Indonesia, and the Philippines, driving down exchange rates throughout the region.

Capital Flight and Financial Crises

Capital flight contributes to broader financial crises. Once again, every crisis is different, but we can sketch a typical story. **Figure 18.3** outlines a crisis involving capital flight in addition to the asset-price crashes and banking problems we examined in Figure 18.1.

FIGURE 18.3 A Financial Crisis with Capital Flight

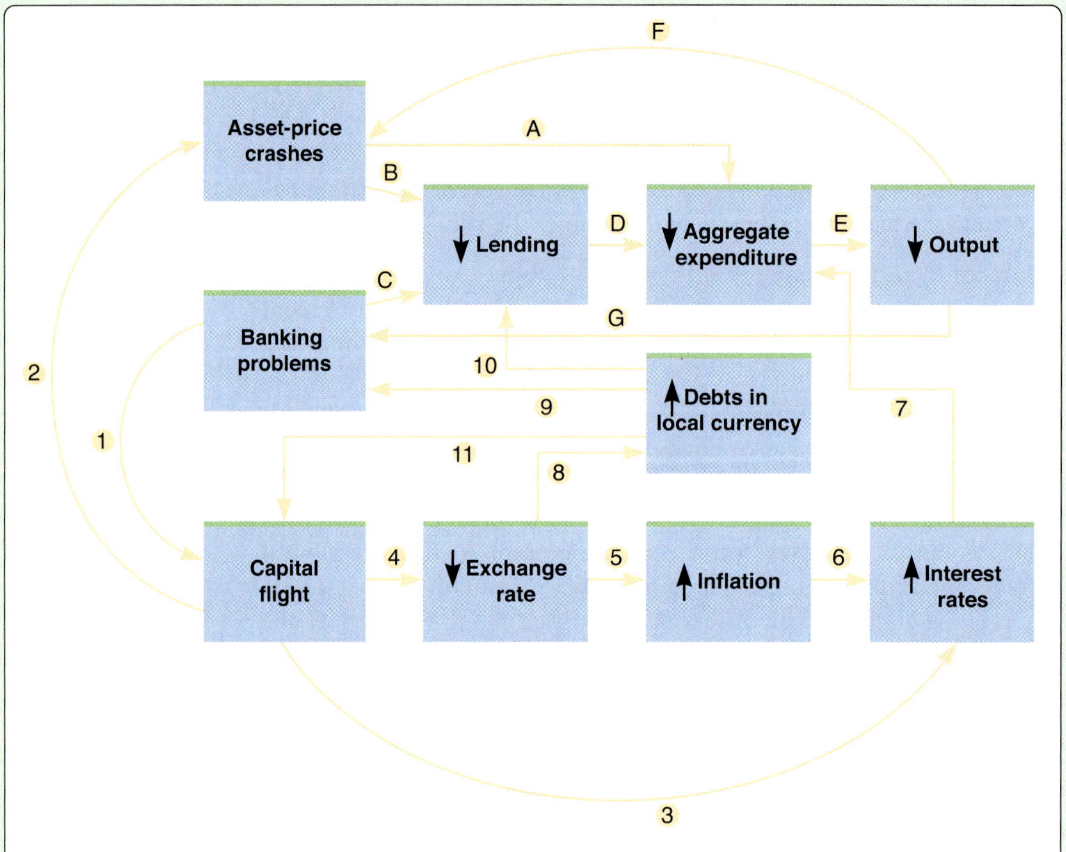

1: Foreign banks cut off loans to domestic banks.
2: Sales of domestic assets reduce their prices.
3: ↓ Supply of loans.
4: ↓ Demand for currency.
5: ↑ Import prices.
6: Central bank tightens to contain inflation.

(See Figure 18.1 for descriptions of channels A–G.)

7: ↓ Spending.
8: ↑ Burden of debt fixed in dollars.
9: ↑ Debts of banks.
10: ↓ Net worth of borrowers.
11: ↑ Government debt → ↑ fears of default.

Financial crises in emerging economies include capital flight, which adds to the channels through which crises damage the economy.

Capital flight interacts with the other basic causes of crises. As we've discussed, banking problems are one cause of capital flight (channel 1 in Figure 18.3). And capital flight triggers crashes in asset prices (channel 2).

Capital flight also raises interest rates, for two reasons. One is the direct effect we've discussed before: a fall in net capital inflows reduces the supply of loans (channel 3). The other involves the effect of capital flight on the exchange rate (channel 4). A large fall in the exchange rate acts as an adverse supply shock: it raises the prices of imported goods (channel 5), pushing up inflation. Central banks respond to higher inflation by tightening monetary policy (channel 6), which raises interest rates. High interest rates reduce aggregate expenditure (channel 7), magnifying the output loss caused by the crisis.

One more set of effects is important. In emerging economies, foreign loans to governments, banks, and firms are usually made in dollars, so debts are fixed in dollars. When the exchange rate falls, each dollar costs more in local currency (channel 8), so debt levels rise when measured in local currency.

Rising debts to foreign banks worsen the problems of domestic banks (channel 9). Rising debt at firms reduces their net worth (channel 10), which reduces bank lending. And higher government debt increases fears of default (channel 11), worsening capital flight.

In sum, capital flight adds a number of feedback loops to financial crises. The vicious cycle becomes more vicious, and economies rarely escape without a deep recession. The next case study gives an example of a particularly traumatic crisis.

CASE STUDY

Argentina's Crisis, 2001–2002

▶ This discussion draws on material on budget deficits and inflation in Section 14.2, currency boards in Section 2.2, and fixed exchange rates in Section 17.5.

Argentina has a long history of economic crises. For decades, a central problem has been large government budget deficits. The government has sometimes financed deficits with bank loans or bonds, but other times it has not been able to borrow. In these periods, it has financed deficits by printing money. Rapid money growth has caused high inflation, which in turn has hurt economic efficiency.

In the 1980s, government budget deficits produced annual inflation rates in the hundreds of percent. The situation deteriorated at the end of the decade, with inflation over 2000 percent in both 1989 and 1990. In 1991, a new president, Carlos Menem, decided that Argentina needed major reforms. His government attacked the budget deficit with spending cuts and higher taxes. It also sought to make the economy more productive by privatizing government-owned industries and eliminating barriers to international trade.

The government's most radical action was to create a currency board, an extreme form of a fixed exchange rate. The currency board set the value of an Argentine peso at 1.0 U.S. dollar, and it held dollar reserves to back all the pesos it created. Policymakers believed that the fixed exchange rate would bring inflation down to U.S. levels. They also thought their reserves would thwart speculative attacks: no matter how many pesos speculators sold, the currency board would have enough dollars to buy them.

Initially, Menem's policies were highly successful. Inflation fell to 25 percent in 1992 and 4 percent in 1994. At the same time, output grew rapidly. Confidence in Argentina's economy soared, and capital flowed into the country. Foreign financial institutions started buying Argentine government debt, which they had shunned in the 1980s.

But then several problems developed:

- Budget deficits started to rise again. This resulted largely from spending by the governments of Argentina's provinces, which the national government could not control.
- The real exchange rate rose, as typically happens when a country fixes the nominal rate to reduce inflation. Although inflation fell, it was well above U.S. levels over 1991–1993; the result, shown in **Figure 18.4,** was a real appreciation of 60 percent. The rise in the real exchange rate reduced net exports, slowing output growth and raising unemployment.
- Mexico's 1994 financial crisis produced contagion. Capital flight occurred throughout Latin America, including Argentina. Capital flight pushed up interest rates, reducing consumption and investment. Combined with the fall in net exports, lower consumption and investment produced a recession in the mid-1990s.

As usual in a financial crisis, different problems reinforced one another. In the late 1990s, the recession reduced tax revenue, worsening the problem of budget deficits. With a currency board, monetary policy was not available to combat the recession, and the unemployment rate rose above

FIGURE 18.4 Argentina's Exchange Rate, 1991–2007

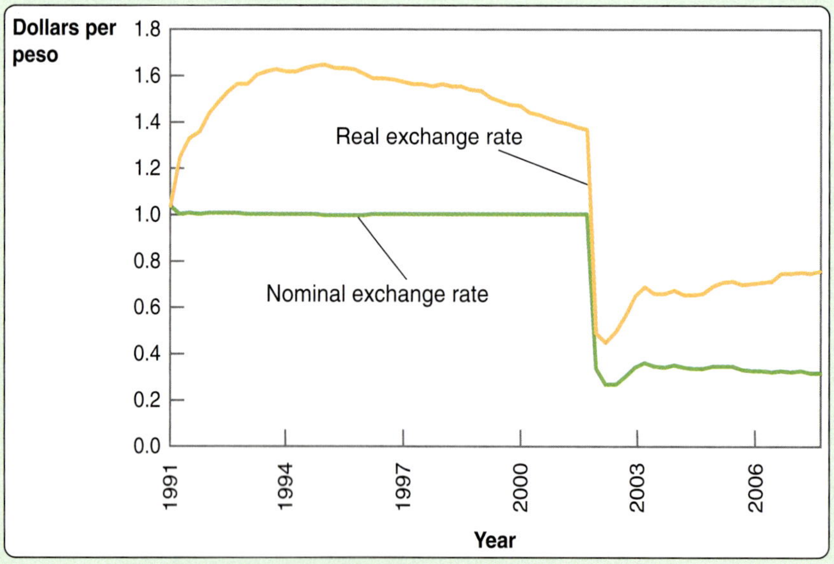

Starting in 1991, Argentina's currency board fixed the nominal exchange rate at 1 peso per dollar. Argentina's inflation exceeded U.S. inflation over 1991–1993, so its real exchange rate rose. The nominal and real exchange rates collapsed with the end of the currency board in 2002.

Source: International Monetary Fund

15 percent. Capital flight increased because of worries about rising government debt and about a possible end of the currency board. In 1999, Fernando de la Rua replaced Carlos Menem as president, but it made little difference for the deteriorating economy.

In late 2001, Argentina's problems spiraled out of control. In October, the government stopped making promised payments on its debt. November brought a banking crisis. Argentina's banks were weakened by the long recession and by losses on holdings of government bonds. Fearing bank failures, and with no deposit insurance, Argentines rushed to withdraw their money.

The government's response to the bank panic was drastic: it imposed a limit on withdrawals. A depositor could withdraw only $250 in cash per week. This policy provoked a political crisis. The long recession had made many Argentines furious at the government, and the denial of access to their money was the last straw. Riots and looting erupted in December 2001, costing 26 lives, and President de la Rua resigned. The following month, an interim president, Eduardo Duhalde, ended the currency board.

The immediate economic consequences were disastrous. As shown in Figure 18.4, the value of a peso fell to 0.27 dollars in 2002. This exchange-rate collapse caused a large rise in import prices, reducing living standards for Argentine consumers. It also caused a huge rise in dollar-denominated debts, leading to a wave of corporate bankruptcies. Output fell by 15 percent from 2000 to 2002, and unemployment rose above 20 percent.

At the time, some economists predicted a long depression for Argentina. However, the fall in the exchange rate set the stage for recovery. It made Argentine goods very cheap relative to foreign goods, and exports boomed. From 2003 to 2007, output grew rapidly and unemployment fell below 10 percent. During this period, the government announced new plans to control budget deficits, the problem underlying Argentina's history of instability. Time will tell whether these plans prove more successful than previous policies.

December 19, 2001: Looters steal merchandise from a supermarket in Buenos Aires during Argentina's financial crisis.

AP Photo/Daniel Luna

The Role of the IMF

When financial crises threaten the United States, the Federal Reserve tries to contain them. When emerging economies experience crises, governments and central banks often don't have the resources to respond. In particular, they lack foreign currency, which is needed to pay debts set in dollars and to replenish international reserves. Therefore, countries in crisis often turn to the **International Monetary Fund (IMF)** for help.

International Monetary Fund (IMF) Institution that lends to countries experiencing financial crises

The IMF was established in 1944 to oversee the Bretton Woods system of fixed exchange rates among 44 nations. Since that system ended, aiding countries in financial crises has been the IMF's primary function. Most of the world's countries are members of the IMF and contribute funds to it, but rich countries provide most of the money. A country's votes on the IMF board of directors are proportional to its financial contribution, so rich countries hold most of the power.

In recent decades, the IMF has intervened in most crises in emerging-market economies, including those in Mexico, East Asia, and Argentina. In the process, the IMF has generated much controversy about its policies.

IMF Loans Countries in crisis approach the IMF for loans, which are made in dollars. Usually the countries' problems make private financial institutions wary of lending to them. The IMF is sometimes called the "international lender of last resort." Countries use IMF loans in various ways:

- The government can use the loans to make payments on its debt, preventing default.
- The central bank can lend dollars to banks to help them repay their dollar debts.
- The central bank can use dollars to buy its currency in foreign-exchange markets. This intervention dampens the fall in the exchange rate.

Each of these actions attacks a part of the financial crisis. In addition, IMF loans are intended to boost confidence in the economy, reducing capital flight. The overall goal is to slow down the vicious cycle shown in Figure 18.3.

IMF loans have strings attached. To obtain a loan, a country must sign an economic agreement with the IMF. The country agrees to reforms that address the problems underlying its crisis. For example, a government with a high debt level may be required to cut spending. Provisions may include stricter bank regulation, monetary tightening to control inflation, or privatization of government-owned industries. The imposition of such requirements is called *conditionality*.

Often the IMF lends money in several installments. It monitors borrowers to see whether they implement the agreed reforms. If progress is slow, the IMF can delay disbursements or cancel the remainder of a loan.

The IMF Debate IMF loans have not cured financial crises. East Asian countries, for example, suffered major recessions in 1997–1998. On the other hand, their economies recovered within a few years. IMF supporters argue that things would have been worse without IMF loans. The vicious cycles of crises would have been more virulent, producing longer recessions.

But the IMF has many critics. Economic conservatives say the institution creates moral hazard. They criticize IMF loans to countries for essentially the same reason they criticize the Fed's rescue of Bear Stearns. Aid to countries that get in trouble encourages other countries to behave the same way. In 2004, Desmond Lachman—like Vincent Reinhart, a fellow at the American Enterprise Institute (AEI)—characterized IMF loans as "huge bailouts that provide incentives for investors and governments alike to behave in an irresponsible fashion, since they assume that they will be saved from the consequences of their mistakes by the IMF's largesse."[3]

The IMF argues that conditionality reduces the moral hazard problem. The IMF helps only countries that promise to follow prudent policies in the future.

Conditionality, however, gets the IMF in trouble with economic liberals. The IMF's loan conditions are often painful. Reducing budget deficits, for example, may force governments to cut spending on antipoverty programs. A monetary tightening to reduce inflation raises unemployment in the short run. The IMF argues that painful reforms are needed for long-run economic growth, but not everyone buys this argument.

Perhaps the most prominent IMF critic is Joseph Stiglitz, a Nobel Prize winner and former chief economist at the World Bank, the IMF's sister institution. After the East Asian crisis, Stiglitz said the IMF's insistence on tight monetary policy had pushed economies into "a vicious downward spiral." In his view, the IMF is not motivated by the best interests of the countries it lends to. Instead, it seeks to contain crises because they are costly to financial institutions that own emerging-economy assets. In a 2002 book, Stiglitz noted that Stanley Fischer, deputy head of the IMF during the Asian crisis, was subsequently named vice chairman of Citigroup. "One could only ask," wrote Stiglitz, "was Fischer being richly rewarded for having faithfully executed what he was told to do?"[4]

Debates about the IMF have died down since Argentina's crisis in 2001–2002, because no major crises have occurred (except recently in the United States, where the Fed can create dollars for itself rather than borrow them). It is likely, however, that a crisis somewhere will eventually return the IMF to prominence.

---

[3] Desmond Lachman, "Go Back to Basics at the IMF," AEI Online, April 1, 2004.

[4] Joseph Stiglitz, *Globalization and Its Discontents*, W.W. Norton, 2002.

Summary

18.1 The Mechanics of Financial Crises

- Financial crises typically begin with crashes in asset prices or failures of financial institutions. Failures can result from insolvency or liquidity crises.
- A financial crisis can reduce bank lending and aggregate expenditure, causing a recession. The recession reinforces the causes of the crisis.
- The U.S. Great Depression was triggered by the 1929 stock market crash and bank panics starting in 1930. The depression was exacerbated by a fall in the money supply and by deflation.

18.2 Policy Responses to Financial Crises

- Expansionary monetary policy can help contain a financial crisis.
- Central banks serve as lenders of last resort to financial institutions facing liquidity crises.
- Sometimes the central bank or government bails out an insolvent financial institution. It provides funds either to prevent the institution from failing or to compensate parties hurt by a failure. Bailouts are controversial.
- The subprime mortgage crisis that began in 2007 evolved into a broader financial crisis. The Federal Reserve responded with a series of new policies.

18.3 Financial Crises in Emerging Economies

- Financial crises in emerging-market economies include capital flight and sharp decreases in exchange rates. Causes of capital flight include high government debt, political instability, banking problems, and mismanagement of fixed exchange rates.
- Capital flight adds new channels to the vicious cycle of a financial crisis.
- Argentina's financial crisis in 2001–2002 included default on government debt, a bank panic, the abandonment of a currency board, and a deep recession.
- The International Monetary Fund lends to countries facing financial crises. Conservative critics of the IMF say it encourages reckless behavior by governments. Liberals criticize the conditions attached to loans.

Key Terms

Bailout, p. 551

Contagion, p. 559

Financial crisis, p. 543

International Monetary Fund (IMF), p. 564

Too big to fail (TBTF), p. 552

Questions and Problems

1. Many economists argue that a bailout of a financial institution should protect the institution's creditors from losses but *not* protect its owners: they should lose their equity. Supporters of this idea say it reduces the moral hazard created by bailouts.
   a. Explain how this approach reduces moral hazard compared to a bailout that protects both creditors and equity holders.
   b. Does this approach eliminate the moral hazard problem completely? Explain.
2. What could U.S. policymakers have done to prevent the Great Depression or at least reduce its severity? Specifically:
   a. What government or Fed policies might have prevented the stock market crash and bank panics that started the financial crisis? (*Hint:* Think of policies that exist today.)

b. Once the crisis began, what could policymakers have done to dampen the series of effects charted in Figure 18.2? Which channels in the figure might have been cut off? Explain.

3. In the United States, commercial banks are regulated more heavily than investment banks. For example, investment banks are allowed to own risky types of assets forbidden to commercial banks. Regulators carry out annual examinations of commercial banks but not investment banks.
   a. What is the traditional rationale for this difference in regulation?
   b. Is this rationale valid today, or should regulators treat investment banks more like they treat commercial banks? Discuss.
4. How can a loan from the IMF reduce the damage from a financial crisis? In Figure 18.3, which channels might be dampened as a result of the loan? Explain.
5. In the late 1990s, some economists advised Argentina to dollarize: it should eliminate the peso and use the U.S. dollar as its currency. Discuss how dollarization might have changed the course of events in 2001–2002.

Online and Data Questions

www.worthpublishers.com/ball

6. When the Fed created the Term Auction Facility in December 2007, it was not clear whether this measure would be temporary or permanent. Link from the text Web site to the Federal Reserve Board site and answer the following questions:
   a. Is the TAF still in operation? Is the current level of lending higher or lower than lending in 2008? What explains any changes?
   b. If the TAF still exists, compare the interest rates determined in recent auctions to recent federal funds rates. Is one type of interest rate higher than the other? Explain what you find.
7. Link through the text Web site to discussions of the Bear Stearns rescue by Vincent Reinhart, who criticizes the action, and by Ben Bernanke, who defends it. Discuss the following questions.
   a. Whose arguments are stronger? Was the Bear Stearns rescue a good decision at the time it was made?
   b. Have developments since the rescue supported the arguments of Reinhart or of Bernanke?

glossary

Accommodative monetary policy: Decision by the central bank to keep the real interest rate constant when a supply shock occurs, allowing inflation to change.

Actively managed fund: Mutual fund that picks stocks based on analysts' research.

Adaptive expectations: Theory that people's expectations of a variable are based on past levels of the variable; also, *backward-looking expectations.*

Adverse selection: The problem that the people or firms who are most eager to make a transaction are the least desirable to parties on the other side of the transaction.

After-tax real interest rate ($\hat{r}$): The interest rate adjusted for both taxes and inflation: $\hat{r} = (1 - \tau)r - \tau\pi$.

Aggregate expenditures (AE): Total spending on an economy's goods and services by people, firms, and governments.

Aggregate expenditure (AE) curve: The negative short-run relationship between the real interest rate and output.

Aggregate expenditure/Phillips curve (AE/PC) model: Theory of short-run economic fluctuations that assumes a negative relationship between the interest rate and output (the AE curve) and a positive relationship between output and inflation (the Phillips curve).

Aggregate price level: An average of the prices of all goods and services.

Appreciation: Rise in a currency's price in terms of foreign currency.

Asset allocation: Decisions by individuals or institutions about what assets to hold.

Asset-price bubble: Rapid rise in asset prices that is not justified by changes in interest rates or expected asset income.

Asset-price crash: Large, rapid fall in asset prices.

Asymmetric information: The problem that one side of an economic transaction knows more than the other.

Bailout: Provision of funds by a government or central bank to prevent an insolvent institution from failing or to compensate other parties for losses from a failure.

Balance sheet: Financial statement that summarizes an entity's assets, liabilities, and net worth at a given date.

Bank: Financial institution that accepts deposits and makes private loans.

Bank charter: Government license to operate a bank.

Bank examination: Visit by regulators to a bank's headquarters to gather information on the bank's activities; part of bank supervision.

Bank panic: Simultaneous runs at many individual banks.

Bank run: Sudden, large withdrawals by depositors who lose confidence in a bank.

Bank supervision: Monitoring of banks' activities by government regulators.

Barter: System of exchange in which goods and services are traded directly, with no money involved.

Basel Accord: 1988 agreement that sets international standards for bank capital requirements.

Behavioral finance: Field that uses ideas from psychology to study how deviations from rational behavior affect asset prices.

Bid-ask spread: Gap between the prices at which a dealer buys and sells a security.

Bimetallism: Monetary system in which money is backed by both gold and silver.

Bond (*fixed-income security*): Security that promises predetermined payments at certain points in time. At *maturity,* the bond pays its *face value*. Before that, the owner may receive *coupon payments*.

Bond rating agencies: Firms that estimate default risk on bonds.

Broker: Firm that buys and sells securities for others.

Budget deficit: A negative level of public saving.

Budget surplus: A positive level of public saving.

Business cycle: Short-run (year-to-year) fluctuations in an economy's output and unemployment.

Call option: An option to buy a security.

Call report: Quarterly financial statement, including a balance sheet and income statement, that banks must submit to regulators as part of bank supervision.

CAMELS ratings: Evaluations by regulators of a bank's insolvency risk based on its capital, asset quality, management, earnings, liquidity, and sensitivity.

Capital: Difference between assets and liabilities; another name for *net worth.*

Capital controls: Regulations that restrict capital inflows or outflows.

Capital crunch: A fall in capital that forces banks to reduce lending.

Capital flight: Sudden decrease in net capital inflows that occurs when foreign savers lose confidence in an economy.

Capital gain: Increase in an asset holder's wealth from a change in the asset's price.

Capital inflows: Funds provided to a country's investors by foreigners.

Capital loss: Decrease in an asset holder's wealth from a change in the asset's price.

Capital outflows: Funds provided to foreign investors by a country's savers.

Capital requirements: Regulations setting minimum levels of capital that banks must hold.

Capital structure: Mix of stocks and bonds that a firm issues.

Central bank: Institution that controls an economy's money supply.

Centrally planned economy *(command economy)*: System in which the government decides what goods and services are produced, who receives them, and what investment projects are undertaken.

Circuit breaker: Requirement that a securities exchange shut down temporarily if prices drop by a specified percentage.

Classical theory of asset prices: The price of an asset equals the present value of expected income from the asset.

Collateral: An asset of a borrower that a bank can seize if the borrower defaults.

Commodity money: Valuable good that serves as the medium of exchange.

Community bank: Commercial bank with less than $1 billion in assets that operates in a small geographic area.

Community Reinvestment Act (CRA): 1977 law requiring banks to lend in low-income areas.

Compensating balance: Minimum checking deposit that a borrower must maintain at the bank that has lent it money.

Conservative policymaker: Central bank official who believes it is more important to keep inflation low than to stimulate output.

Consumption multiplier: Effect of income on consumption that magnifies changes in aggregate expenditure.

Contagion: Spread of capital flight from one country to others.

Core deposits: Banks' inexpensive sources of funds (checking deposits, savings deposits, and small time deposits).

Countercyclical monetary policy: Adjustments of the real interest rate by the central bank to offset expenditure shocks and thereby stabilize output.

Covenant: Provision in a loan contract that restricts the actions of the borrower.

Credit crunch: A sharp reduction in bank lending.

Credit rationing: Refusal of a bank to lend to a borrower at any interest rate.

Credit risk *(default risk)*: The risk that loans will not be repaid.

Credit score: Numerical rating capturing a person's likelihood to repay loans based on her credit history.

Credit union: Nonprofit bank owned by its depositor members, who are drawn from a group of people with something in common.

Currency board: Institution that issues money backed by a foreign currency.

Currency-deposit ratio (C/D): Ratio of currency in circulation to checking deposits.

Currency union: Group of countries with a common currency.

Dealer: Firm that buys and sells certain securities for itself, making a market in the securities.

Dealer market: OTC market in which all trades are made with dealers.

Default: Failure to make promised payments on debts.

Deflation: Sustained period of negative inflation.

Deposit insurance: Government guarantee to compensate depositors for their losses when a bank fails.

Depreciation: Fall in a currency's price in terms of foreign currency.

Derivatives: Securities with payoffs tied to the prices of other assets.

Devaluation: Resetting of a fixed exchange rate at a lower level.

Direct finance: Savers provide funds to investors by buying securities in financial markets.

Discount loan: Loan from the Federal Reserve to a bank made at the bank's request.

Discount rate: Interest rate on discount loans.

Discretionary policy: Monetary policy that is adjusted at each point in time based on the judgment of the central bank.

Disinflation: Monetary policy of reducing inflation by temporarily raising the real interest rate.

Diversification: The distribution of wealth among many assets, such as securities issued by different firms and governments.

Dividend: Payment from a firm to its stockholders.

Dollarization: Use of foreign currency (often U.S. dollars) as money.

Double coincidence of wants: Condition needed for barter: each party to a transaction must have something the other wants.

Economic boom: Period when actual output exceeds potential output.

Economic growth: Increases in productivity and living standards; growth in real GDP.

Economic risk: Risk arising from fluctuations in the economy's aggregate output.

Economies of scope: Cost reductions from combining different activities.

Efficient-markets hypothesis (EMH): The price of every stock equals the value of the stock, so no stock is a better buy than any other.

Electronic communications network (ECN): OTC market in which financial institutions trade securities with one another directly, rather than through dealers.

e-money: Funds in an electronic account used for Internet purchases.

Equity ratio (ER): Ratio of a bank's capital to its assets; $ER = \frac{\text{capital}}{\text{assets}}$.

Eurodollars: Deposits of dollars outside the United States.

Ex ante real interest rate ($r^{\text{ex ante}}$): Nominal interest rate minus expected inflation over the loan period; $r^{\text{ex ante}} = i - \pi^{\text{expected}}$.

Exchange: A physical location where brokers and dealers meet to trade securities.

Expectations theory of the term structure: The n-period interest rate is the average of the current one-period rate and expected rates over the next $n - 1$ periods.

Expenditure shock: Event that changes aggregate expenditure for a given interest rate, shifting the AE curve.

Explicit inflation target: A rate or range that a central bank announces as its long-run goal for inflation.

Ex post real interest rate ($r^{ex\ post}$): Nominal interest rate minus actual inflation over the loan period; $r^{ex\ post} = i - \pi^{actual}$.

Federal Deposit Insurance Corporation (FDIC): Government agency that insures deposits at U.S. commercial banks and savings institutions.

Federal funds: Loans from one bank to another, usually for one day.

Federal funds rate: Interest rate that banks charge one another for one-day loans of reserves, or federal funds; also *overnight interest rate*.

Federal Open Market Committee (FOMC): Body that sets the Fed's targets for the federal funds rate.

Federal Reserve System (the Fed): Central bank of the United States.

Fiat money: Money with no intrinsic value.

Finance company: Nonbank financial institution that makes loans but does not accept deposits.

Financial crisis: Major disruption of the financial system, typically involving crashes in asset prices and failures of financial institutions.

Financial holding company (FHC): Company that owns a group of financial institutions.

Financial institution (*financial intermediary*): Firm that helps channel funds from savers to investors.

Financial market: A collection of people and firms that buy and sell securities or currencies.

Fiscal policy: The government's choice of taxes and spending.

Fisher equation: The nominal interest rate equals the real rate plus expected inflation; $i = r + \pi^e$.

Fixed exchange rate: Policy that holds the exchange rate at a constant level.

Floating exchange rate: Policy that allows the exchange rate to fluctuate in response to economic shocks.

Floating interest rate: Interest rate on a long-term loan that is tied to a short-term rate.

Forbearance: Regulator's decision to allow an insolvent bank to remain open.

Foreign-exchange interventions: Purchases and sales of foreign currencies by central banks.

Free-rider problem: People can benefit from a good without paying for it, leading to underproduction of the good; in financial markets, savers are free riders when information is gathered.

Futures contract: Agreement to trade an asset for a certain price at a future point in time.

Future value: Value of a dollar today in terms of dollars at some future time; \$1 today $= \$(1 + i)^n$ in n years.

Government-sponsored enterprise (GSE): Private corporation with links to the government.

Hedge fund: Variant of a mutual fund that raises money from wealthy people and institutions and is largely unregulated, allowing it to make risky bets on asset prices.

Hedging: Reducing risk by purchasing an asset that is likely to produce a high return if another of one's assets produces low or negative returns.

High-yield spread: Difference between interest rates on BBB and AAA corporate bonds with 10-year maturities.

Hyperinflation: Inflation of more than 50 percent per month (or roughly 13,000 percent per year).

Implicit inflation target: An inflation level that policymakers seek without a formal announcement.

Income statement: Financial statement summarizing income, expenses, and profits over some time period.

Index fund: Mutual fund that buys all the stocks in a broad market index.

Indirect finance: Savers deposit money in banks that then lend to investors.

Industrial loan company (ILC): Financial institution that performs many functions of a commercial bank; may be owned by a nonfinancial firm.

Inflation-indexed bond: Bond that promises a fixed real interest rate; the nominal rate is adjusted for inflation over the life of the bond.

Inflation rate: Percentage change in the aggregate price level over a period of time.

Initial public offering (IPO): Sale of stock when a firm becomes public.

Inside lag: Time between a shock and the policy response.

Insider trading: Buying or selling securities based on information that is not public.

Insolvency: Liabilities exceed assets, producing negative net worth.

Interest: Payment for the use of borrowed funds.

Interest-rate risk: Instability in bank profits caused by fluctuations in short-term interest rates.

Interest-rate smoothing: Central banks' practice of moving interest rates through a series of small changes.

Interest-rate targeting: Approach to monetary policy in which the central bank chooses a level for the nominal interest rate and adjusts it when economic conditions change. The central bank sets the money supply at the level needed to hit the interest-rate target.

International Monetary Fund (IMF): Institution that lends to countries experiencing financial crises.

International reserves: Liquid assets held by central banks that are denominated in foreign currencies.

Inverted yield curve: Downward-sloping yield curve signifying that short-term interest rates exceed long-term rates.

Investment bank: Financial institution that serves as an underwriter and advises companies on mergers and acquisitions.

Investment multiplier: Effect of firms' earnings on investment, which magnifies fluctuations in aggregate expenditure.

Investors: People who expand the productive capacity of businesses.

Junk bond: Corporate bond with an S&P rating below BBB.

Law of one price: Theory that an identical good or service has the same price in all locations.

Lender of last resort: Central bank's role as emergency lender to banks.

Letter of credit: A bank's guarantee, in return for a fee, of a payment promised by a firm.

Leverage: Borrowing money to purchase assets.

Liabilities: Amounts of money owed to others.

Line of credit: A bank's commitment to lend up to a certain amount whenever a borrower asks.

Liquidity: Ease of trading an asset for money.

Liquidity preference theory: The nominal interest rate is determined by the supply and demand for money.

Liquidity risk: The risk that withdrawals from a bank will exceed its liquid assets.

Liquidity trap: Situation in which output is below potential at a nominal interest rate of zero (a real interest rate of $-\pi$), eliminating the central bank's usual ability to raise output and inflation.

Loanable funds theory: Real interest rates are determined by the supply and demand for loans.

Loan guarantee: Government promise to pay off a loan if the borrower defaults.

Loan shark: Lender that violates usury laws and collects debts through illegal means.

Long-run monetary neutrality: Principle that monetary policy cannot permanently affect real variables (variables adjusted for inflation).

M1: The Federal Reserve's primary measure of the money supply; the sum of currency held by the nonbank public, checking deposits, and traveler's checks.

M2: Broad measure of the money supply that includes M1 and other highly liquid assets (savings deposits, small time deposits, and retail money-market mutual funds).

Margin requirements: Limits on the use of credit to purchase stocks.

Market risk: Risk arising from fluctuations in asset prices.

Medium of exchange: Whatever people use to purchase goods and services.

Microfinance: Small loans that allow poor people to start businesses.

Modigliani-Miller Theorem (MM Theorem): Proposition that a firm's capital structure doesn't matter.

Monetarists: School of economists who believe that monetary policy has strong effects on the economy and that policy should be set by a rule.

Monetary aggregate: Measure of the money supply (M1 or M2).

Monetary base (B): Sum of currency in circulation and bank reserves ($B = C + R$); the Federal Reserve's liabilities to the private sector of the economy.

Monetary policy: Central banks' management of the money supply.

Monetary policy rule: A simple rule or formula that tells the central bank how to run policy.

Monetary transmission mechanism: Process through which monetary policy affects output.

Money: Class of assets that serves as an economy's medium of exchange.

Money-center bank: Commercial bank located in a major financial center that raises funds primarily by borrowing from other banks or by issuing bonds.

Money demand: Amount of wealth that people choose to hold in the form of money.

Money multiplier (*m*): Ratio of the money supply to the monetary base; $M = mB$.

Money supply: Total amount of money in the economy.

Money targeting: Approach to monetary policy in which the central bank chooses a level for the money supply and adjusts it when economic conditions change.

Moral hazard: The risk that one party to a transaction takes actions that harm another party.

Municipal bonds: Bonds issued by state and local governments.

Mutual fund: Financial institution that holds a diversified set of securities and sells shares to savers.

NAIRU: Acronym for *nonaccelerating inflation rate of unemployment,* the unemployment rate that produces a constant inflation rate; another name for the *natural rate of unemployment,* U^*.

National bank: Bank chartered by the federal government.

Natural rate of unemployment (U^*): Normal or average level of unemployment; see also *NAIRU.*

Net capital inflows: Capital inflows minus capital outflows.

Net capital outflows (*NCO*): Capital outflows minus capital inflows.

Net exports (*NX*): Exports minus imports.

Net worth *(equity or capital)*: Difference between assets and liabilities.

Neutral real interest rate (r^n): The real interest rate that makes output equal potential output, given the aggregate expenditure curve.

Nominal exchange rate (*e*): Price of one unit of a currency in terms of another currency.

Nominal GDP: The total value of all final goods and services produced in an economy in a given period.

Nominal interest rate (*i*): Interest rate offered by a bank account or bond.

Nonaccommodative monetary policy: Decision by the central bank to adjust the interest rate to offset a supply shock and keep inflation constant.

Off-balance-sheet (OBS) activities: Bank activities that produce income but are not reflected in the assets and liabilities reported on the balance sheet.

Okun's law: Relation between output and unemployment over the business cycle: the output gap falls by 2 percentage points when unemployment rises 1 point above the natural rate; $\frac{(Y - Y^*)}{Y^*} = -2(U - U^*)$.

Open-market operations: Purchases or sales of bonds by a central bank.

Option: The right to trade a security at a certain price any time before an expiration date.

Order flow: In a dealer market, the difference between total buy orders and sell orders over some period.

Output gap: Percentage difference between actual and potential output; $\frac{(Y - Y^*)}{Y^*}$.

Outside lag: Time between a policy response to a shock and its effects on the economy.

Over-the-counter (OTC) market: Secondary securities market with no physical location.

Pawnshop: Small lender that holds an item of value as collateral.

Payday lender: Company that provides cash in return for a postdated check.

Payments system: Arrangements through which money reaches the sellers of goods and services.

Phillips curve: The positive short-run relationship between output and inflation; also, the negative short-run relationship between unemployment and inflation.

Potential output (Y^*): The normal or average level of output, as determined by resources and technology.

Predatory lending: Unfair lending practices aimed at poor and uninformed borrowers.

Present value: Value of a future dollar in terms of today's dollars; \$1 in n years $= \frac{\$1}{(1+i)^n}$ today.

Price-earnings ratio (P/E ratio): A company's stock price divided by earnings per share over the recent past.

Primary markets: Financial markets in which firms and governments issue new securities.

Prime rate: Interest rate banks charge on business loans with the lowest default risk.

Principal–agent problem: Moral hazard that arises when the action of one party (the agent) affects another party (the principal) that does not observe the action.

Printing money: Financing government budget deficits by selling bonds to the central bank.

Private equity firm: Financial institution that owns large shares in private companies; includes takeover firms and venture capital firms.

Private loan: Loan negotiated between one borrower and one lender.

Private saving: Saving by individuals and firms.

Public company: Firm that issues securities that are traded in financial markets.

Public saving: Saving by the government (tax revenue minus government spending).

Purchased funds: Banks' expensive sources of funds (borrowings and large time deposits).

Purchasing power parity (PPP): Theory of exchange rates based on the idea that a currency purchases the same quantities of goods and services in different countries; implies that real exchange rates are constant over time.

Put option: An option to sell a security.

Quantity equation of money: Relationship among the money supply, velocity, and nominal GDP: $MV = PY$.

Random walk: The movements of a variable whose changes are unpredictable.

Rate of return: Return on a security as a percentage of its initial price.

Rate-sensitivity gap: Difference between rate-sensitive assets and rate-sensitive liabilities.

Rational expectations: Theory that people's expectations are the best possible forecasts based on all public information.

Real exchange rate (ε): Measure of the relative prices of domestic and foreign goods $\left(\varepsilon = \frac{eP}{P^*}\right)$.

Real gross domestic product (real GDP): The measure of an economy's total output of goods and services.

Real interest rate (r): Nominal interest rate minus the inflation rate; $r = i - \pi$.

Recession: Period when actual output falls below potential output.

Regional bank: Commercial bank with assets above \$1 billion that operates in one geographic region.

Repurchase agreement *(repo)*: Sale of a security with a promise to buy it back at a higher price on a future date.

Reserve-deposit ratio (R/D): Ratio of bank reserves to checking deposits.

Reserve requirements: Regulations that set a minimum level for banks' reserve-deposit ratios.

Reserves: Vault cash plus banks' deposits at the Federal Reserve.

Return: Total earnings from a security; the capital gain or loss plus any direct payment (coupon payment or dividend).

Return on assets (ROA): Ratio of a bank's profits to its assets; $\text{ROA} = \frac{\text{profits}}{\text{assets}}$.

Return on equity (ROE): Ratio of a bank's profits to its capital; $\text{ROE} = \frac{\text{profits}}{\text{capital}}$.

Revaluation: Resetting of a fixed exchange rate at a higher level.

Risk premium (φ): Payment on an asset that compensates the owner for taking on risk.

Safe interest rate (i^{safe}): Interest rate that savers can receive for sure; also, *risk-free rate.*

Sarbanes-Oxley Act: Federal legislation that strengthens the requirements for information disclosure by corporations.

Savers: People who accumulate wealth by spending less than they earn.

Savings institution: Type of bank created to accept savings deposits and make loans for home mortgages; also known as *savings banks* or *savings and loan associations (S&Ls).*

Secondary markets: Financial markets in which existing securities are traded.

Securities and Exchange Commission (SEC): U.S. government agency that regulates financial markets.

Securities firm: Company whose primary purpose is to hold securities, trade them, or help others trade them; includes mutual funds, hedge funds, brokers and dealers, and investment banks.

Securitization: Process in which a financial institution buys a large number of bank loans, then issues securities entitling the holders to shares of payments on the loans.

Security: Claim on some future flow of income, such as a stock or bond.

Seigniorage revenue: Revenue the government receives from printing money.

Shoe leather costs: Inconveniences that result from holding less money when inflation is high.

Sovereign debt: Bonds issued by national governments.

Specialist: Broker-dealer who manages the trading of a certain stock on an exchange.

Speculation: Using financial markets to make bets on asset prices.

Speculative attack: Strategy of selling a currency with a fixed exchange rate, to force and to profit from a devaluation.

State bank: Bank chartered by a state government.

Stock *(equity)*: Ownership share in a corporation.

Stock market index: An average of prices for a group of stocks.

Stored-value card: Card issued with a prepaid balance that can be used for purchases.

Store of value: Form in which wealth can be held.

Subprime lenders: Companies that lend to people with weak credit histories.

Superregional bank: Commercial bank with assets above \$1 billion that operates across most of the United States.

Supply shock, ν: Event that causes a major change in firms' production costs, which in turn causes a short-run change in the inflation rate.

Suspension of payments: Refusal by a bank to allow withdrawals by depositors.

Sweep program: Banking practice of shifting funds temporarily from customers' checking accounts to money-market deposit accounts.

Takeover firm: Private equity firm that buys entire companies and tries to increase the companies' profits.

Taylor rule: Formula for adjusting the interest rate to stabilize the economy: $r = r^n + a_y\tilde{Y} + a_\pi\pi^T$.

Technical analysis: Set of methods for forecasting prices in financial markets based on the past behavior of prices.

Term Auction Facility (TAF): Program in which the Fed chooses a quantity of loans to make and allocates them to banks that submit the highest interest-rate bids.

Term premium (τ): Extra return on a long-term bond that compensates for its riskiness; τ_n denotes the term premium on an n-period bond.

Term structure of interest rates: Relationships among interest rates on bonds with different maturities.

Thrift institutions *(thrifts)*: Savings institutions and credit unions.

Time-consistency problem: Situation in which someone has incentives to make a promise but later renege on it; because of these incentives, others don't believe the promise.

Too big to fail (TBTF): Doctrine that large banks facing insolvency must be bailed out to protect the financial system.

Trade-weighted real exchange rate: Weighted average of a country's real exchange rates, with weights proportional to levels of trade.

Transaction costs: Costs in time and money of exchanging goods, services, or assets.

Transparency: Provision to the public of clear and detailed information about policy making.

Undervalued asset: Asset with a price below the present value of expected earnings.

Underwriter: Financial institution that helps companies issue new securities.

Unemployment rate (U): Percentage of the labor force without jobs.

Unit of account: Measure in which prices and salaries are quoted.

Usury law: Legal limit on interest rates.

Vault cash: Currency in banks' branches and ATMs.

Velocity of money: Ratio of nominal GDP to the money supply $\left(V = \dfrac{PY}{M}\right)$; shows how quickly money moves through the economy.

Venture capital (VC) firm: Private equity firm that buys shares in new companies that plan to grow.

Yield curve: Graph comparing interest rates on bonds of various maturities at a given point in time.

Yield to maturity: Interest rate that makes the present value of payments from a bond equal to its price.

index

A

Abrams, Burton, 492*n*
Accommodative monetary policy, 368
 supply shock, 370*f*, 372*f*
ACE Cash Express, 236
Actively managed fund, 140
Adaptive expectations, 96, 359
 Phillips curve and, 362–363
Adjustable-rate mortgage, 273. *See* ARMs
Advance America, 236
Adverse selection, 8–9, 190–195
 capital structure, 132–133
 example, 194*f*
 lemons, 192–193
 numerical example, 193–195
 reducing, 11–12
Adverse supply shock, 363
AE/PC. *See* Aggregate expenditure/Phillips curve
Africa
 government-owned banks, 244
After-tax real interest rate, 432
Aggregate expenditure (AE), 351–352
 components of, 352
 countercyclical monetary policy, 357–358
 curve. *See* aggregate expenditure curve
 determination of, 352–358
 effects of, 351*f*
 equilibrium output, 353–354, 355*f*
 exchange rates and, 512–513
 expenditure shocks, 354–356, 355*f*
 financial system and, 390–397
 monetary policy, 353–354, 355*f*
 role of interest rate, 352–353
Aggregate expenditure curve (AE), 344, 353, 353*f*
 Boversian example, 512–513, 513*f*
 combining with Phillips curve, 367–369
 lags in, 401, 405*f*
 mistake, 455–457, 456*f*
Aggregate expenditure/Phillips curve (AE/PC) model, 344, 381
 with time lags, 403*f*
 Taylor rule in, 452–454, 454*f*
Aggregate price level, 22
Akerlof, George, 191
Alesina, Alberto, 488, 488*f*
Alexander the Great, 30
Allfirst Bank, 227
American Bankers Association, 225
American Funds, 121
Ameriquest, 236
Appreciation, 158
 dollar and, 161*t*
 effects of, 160–162
Arbitrage, 169
Arca, 129
Argentina, 34
 crisis, 561–563
 debt, 110
 exchange rate, 562*f*
 seigniorage revenue, 423
ARMs, 273–274
Arthur Andersen, 206
Asia, stored-value cards, 41
Asset allocation, 119, 120
 case study, 138
 choosing, 133
Asset crashes, 27
Asset management, 254
Asset-price bubbles, 63
 evidence of, 66*f*
 Fed policy and, 471
 how they work, 63–65
 looking for, 65–68
 response to, 470–471
 tulip case study, 64–65
Asset-price crash, 68
Asset prices
 bubbles, 63–68
 changing, 60, 391–392
 classical theory of, 57–60, 60*t*
 crashes, 68–71, 544
 expected, 58
 fluctuations in, 60–62
 response to, 470–471
 volatility, 62–63, 63*t*
Asset quality, 304
Asset returns
 measuring, 71–74
 rate of, 72–73
Assets, 252–253
 cash items, 252–253
 loans, 253
 losses to holders of foreign, 162
 restrictions on, 300
 securities, 253
Assumptions, 193
 expected inflation, 359–360, 360*f*
Asymmetric information, 7–10, 195
 adverse selection, 8–9
 banks, 209–212
 in financial markets, 8*f*
 moral hazard, 9–10
 reducing, 198–205
ATMs, 158
 fees and, 265
 reserves and, 330
Auto title loan, 239
Averages, comparing, 183

B

Baby boom
 effect on natural rate, 347
Bacanovic, Peter, 208
Backward-looking expectations, 96, 359. *See* Adaptive expectations
Bailout, 551
 commercial banks, 552–553
 nonbank institutions, 553
 pros and cons of, 551–552
Balance sheet, 250–253
 assets, 317
 consolidated, 250, 250*t*
 Fed and, 317
 liabilities, 317
 restrictions on, 299–303
Ball, Laurence, 347*n*, 500–501, 501*n*
Banc One, 226
Bank, 10
Bank account, risk-return, 136
Bank charter, 224
Bank examinations, 303
Bank Holding Company Act of 1956, 297
Bank holiday, 289
Banking, 49
 business of, 249–278
 crises and deposit insurance, 294–295
 industry, 219–245. *See also* Banks
 international, 228
 investment, 254–255
 lending, effects in monetary transmission mechanism, 398
 private, 254
 problems, 559
 risk, 266–275
 separation of commerce and, 296–297
 unit, 15
Bank of America, 221, 227
Bank of Canada, 515–516
Bank of England, 183, 484, 533
 Northern Rock Bank and, 287–288
 targets, 495–496
Bank of Japan, 484

Bank panic, 288, 547–548
in 1930s, 288–290
Bank run, 283, 284–290, 285*t*
Disney Bank example, 286
example of, 285
Guta Bank example, 286–287
how one occurs, 284
Northern Rock Bank example, 287–288
suspension of payments, 285–286
Bankruptcy
capital structure, 132
Banks, 10–12, 220
asset restrictions, 300
asymmetric information, 209–212
balance sheets, 250–253
branching, 225
central, 26
charters, 296
closing insolvent, 305–308
closure process, 308
commercial, 10, 123, 220*f*, 221–222
community, 222
consolidation, 223–231
creating money, 318–319
deposits, 318–319, 320
dispersion, 223–231
example, 255–258
excess reserves and, 329
failure rate, 289*f*
finance companies, 223
foreign in United States, 228
government-owned banks, 244–245
history of funds, 260–261
investment, 10–11
lending, 356
lending policies, 392–393
loans, 319, 320–321
making profits, 255–258
money-center, 221
national, 225
needs, 12
opening, 295–297
purpose for, 11–12
regional, 221–222
regulation, 47
securitization benefits for, 232–233
setting regulations, 299–300
state, 225
superregional, 221–222
thrift institutions, 222–223
transaction costs, 214–215
types of, 220–223, 221*t*
versus financial markets, 11
Bank supervision, 303–305
CAMELS ratings, 303–305
enforcement actions, 305
information gathering, 303
Barings, LLC, 148–149
Barro, Robert, 137*n*
Barsky, Robert, 136*n*
Barter, 27
case study, 28
money versus, 27
Bartiromo, Maria, 313
Basel Accord, 301
Basel 2, 302–303
Bear Stearns, 236, 545, 550
and PDCF, 555–556
Beckett, Paul, 265*n*
Behavioral finance, 142
Behaviorists, 142
Beige Book, 465, 466
Beneficial supply shock, 363
Bennett, Paul, 330*n*
Berkshire Hathaway, 143–144
Bernanke, Ben, 25–26, 313, 386, 475, 485, 497*n*, 498, 503, 507, 557*n*
appointment of, 483, 497, 502
as Chair of Board of Governors, 46, 314, 336, 446
and Fed policy, 471, 471*n*
and Franklin Roosevelt, 557
stock market and, 60, 61, 62*n*
Bid-ask spread, 129
Bimetallism, 420–421
Black Monday, 69
Blackstone Group, 204
Blinder, Alan, 463, 503–504
Bloomberg, 130
exchange rates on, 159–160*f*
stock prices on, 131*f*
Bloomberg, Michael, 130
Blue Book, 465, 467
Board of Directors, 200–202
captive, 201
elections, 201
shareholder revolts, 201–202
Board of Governors, 46, 314, 336
Boeing, 128, 140
purchasing stock on NYSE, 128*f*
stock prices, 130*f*
Bond, 2–3, 43, 95
borrowing, 252
inflation-indexed, 77
markets, 123–130
municipal, 115–116
prices, 57–58, 63*t*
return on, 73, 73*f*
risk, 105
short versus long, 62
term structure, 103–104
versus stocks, 62–63
Bond markets, 123–130
lemons 192–193
moral hazard, 197–198
Bond rating agencies, 110, 200
Booms, 347–350
economic, 348
permanent, 376–377
Borrowers
screening, 209–210
screening for mortgages, 213
Borrowings, 251–252
short-term, 268–269
Boversia example, 512–513, 513*f*, 513–514, 514*f*, 519, 519*f*
fixed exchange rate, 528–532
Bradsher, Keith, 504*n*
Branching, 225
Brazil
government-owned banks, 244
inflation in, 429–430, 430*f*
intervention, 522
seigniorage revenue, 423
Bretton Woods system, 534–535
Brewster, Mike, 231*n*
Brin, Sergei, 125
Britain, 32
Broad money
measuring, 43–45
Brokers, 121–122, 128
commission, 128
discount, 122
full-service, 121–122
role of, 127–128
Bryan, William Jennings, 421
Bubbles. *See* Asset-price bubbles
Budget deficit, 92, 93*f*
and interest rates, 93–94
Budget surplus, 92
Buffet, Warren, 143, 149
case study, 143–144
Burns, Arthur, 373, 422, 491–492, 498
Bush, George H.W., 83, 343, 483
Bush, George W., 25, 83, 162, 343, 408, 483, 511
Business cycle
aggregate expenditure, 351–352
booms, 347–350, 346*f*
cause of, 375
cost of, 448–449
defined, 345
foreign, 356
long-run output and, 345
recessions, 347–350
reducing, 448*f*
unemployment and, 345–346
Business Cycle Dating Committee, 350

C

C/D. *See* Currency-deposit ratio
C&I. *See* Commercial and industrial loans
Cagan, Phillip, 413*n*
Call option, 146
Call reports, 303
CAMELS ratings, 303–304
Campbell, John, 66
Canada
bonds, 95
monetary policy, 515–516
recession and, 179
targets, 496
Capacity, 212
Capital, 210, 212, 250, 304, 393. *See* Net worth
Capital controls, 523–525
critique of, 525

East Asian crisis, 524–525
effects on exchange rates, 524–525
and exchange rates, 524*f*
Capital crunch, 393
Capital flight, 95, 558–559
causes of, 558–559
contagion, 559
and financial crisis, 559–561, 560*f*
Latin America, 562
role of fixed exchange rates, 559
Capital flows, 85
change in confidence, 94–95
foreign interest rates, 95
net exports and, 172–173
shift in, 94–95, 94*f*
Capital gain, 72
Capital inflows, 85
Capital loss, 72
Capital outflows, 85, 156
shifts in, 174–176, 175*f*
Capital requirements, 300–303, 302*t*
Basel Accord, 301
Basel 2, 302–303
current U.S. requirements, 301
example of, 301–302
Capital structure, 130–133
matter of, 132–133
relevance of, 131–132
Captive boards, 201
Cardoso, Eliana, 429, 430*n*
Carlyle Group, 204
Carter, Jimmy, 343, 413, 483
Case, Karl, 391, 391*n*
Case Study
after-tax real interest rate, 432–433
age and asset allocation, 138
Alan Blinder, 503–504
Argentina's crisis, 561–563
banking crisis of the 1980s, 277–278
bank panics in the 1930s, 288–290
bank runs in fiction and fact, 286–288
barter economies, 28
budget deficits and interest rates, 93–94
Canadian monetary policy, 515–516
Citigroup, 229–231
clean and dirty money, 35–36
Commerce Bank, 261–262
cost of business cycle, 448–449
decline of reserve requirements, 329–330
Dennis Kozlowski, 196–197
deposit insurances and banking crises, 294–295
derivative disasters, 148–149
disaster in the 1930s, 547–548, 548*f*
ECB two pillars, 501–502
Enron collapse, 6–7
euro versus the dollar, 176–178, 177*f*
exchange rates and steel, 167–168, 167*f*
Fed and Great Inflation, 460–462
Fed and 90s, 462–463
Fed and September 11, 47–48
Fed and stock market, 60–62
Fed in 1937, 328–329
fees, 265–266
financial system and the Fed, 553–557
fiscal versus monetary policy, 406
five C's of business lending, 212
fixed- versus floating-rate mortgages, 273–274
free silver movement, 420–421
General Motors bonds, 112–113, 113*f*
George Soros, 533–534
German hyperinflation, 424
Google IPO, 125–126
high-yield spread, 114–115, 114*f*
history of U.S. dollar, 32
inflation and the savings and loan crisis, 77
inflationary Brazil, 429–430, 430*f*
inside traders, 208–209
international differences in shareholder rights, 202–203
interventions, 522–523
inverted yield curves, 109
investment in the Soviet Union, 18–20
Japanese interest rates, 111–112
Japanese slump, 393–396
Japan's liquidity trap, 437–438
Keystone scandal, 292–293
measuring effects of policy on term structure, 389–390, 390*f*
microfinance, 16–18
Millennium boom, 66–68
monetarist experiment, 334–335, 335*f*
money multiplier and the Great Depression, 324–326, 325*f*
natural rate in the United States, 346–347, 346*f*
Nixon and Burns, 491–492
oil prices and inflation, 366–367
Oracle of Omaha, 143–144
payday lending predatory, 237–238
politics of banking in U.S. history, 224–226
politics of the dollar, 162–163
recession, 350–351
regulatory failure in S&L crisis
small firms, 399–400
student loans, 241–243
subprime mortgage fiasco, 234–236
sweep programs, 45–46
targeters and nontargeters, 500–501
technical analysis, 183–184
traditional home mortgages, 212–213
Treasury Bill auctions, 126–127
tulipmania, 64–65
two big crashes, 69–70
tying, 264–265
unit banking and economic growth, 15–16
U.S. economy 1960–2007, 373–375
Wal-Mart Bank, 297–299
worldwide decline in inflation, 425
yuan, 526–527
Cash, 252–253
vault, 252
Cash items in process of collection, 253
CBO. *See* Congressional Budget Office
CCRAA. *See* College Cost Reduction and Access Act
CD, 251, 260. *See* Certificate of deposit
Center for Responsible Lending (CRL), 265
Central bank, 26
clearing payments, 47
communication by, 502–507
conservativism, 487
financial crisis, 543
functions of, 46–48, 46*t*
independence, 483–489, 488*f*, 491
inflation, 488–489, 488*f*
lending, 47
limits of authority, 476
monetary policy, 47
money supply, 100
regulation, 47
reputation, 502–503
targeting, 498
tasks of, 444
transparency, 505
understanding the economy, 463
Central Bank of Russia, 289
Centrally planned economy, 18
market planning versus, 18
CEO. *See* Chief executive officer
Certificate of deposit (CD), 44, 251. *See also* Time deposit, CD
Character, 212
Charles Schwab, 122
Charter
obtaining, 296
Chartering agencies, 269
Office of the Comptroller of the Currency (OCC), 296
Chase, 264
universal default clause, 266
Chase Manhattan Bank, 226
Checking deposits, 251, 260–261
Chemical Bank, 226
Chicago Board of Trade, 145, 149
Chicago Mercantile Exchange, 145, 150
Chief Executive Officer (CEO), 200
Chile
commodity prices, 179
China, 30
foreign-exchange intervention, 526–527
government-owned bank, 244, 245
monetary policy, 511–512
People's Bank of, 485
yuan, 526–527
Chirac, Jacques, 538
Church, Terry, 293
Circuit breakers, 70–71
Citibank, 221, 229
universal default clause, 266
Citicorp, 229, 249

CitiFinancial, 230, 231, 233, 234
Citigroup, 123, 129, 229–231, 236, 249, 264
  history of, 229–230
  purpose of, 230
Citron, Robert, 149
Civil War, 33
Classical theory of asset prices, 57–60, 60*f*
Clinton, Bill, 83, 162, 343, 483, 503
  Federal Banking Commission, 300
  steel exports, 168
Coca-Cola, 144
Coins, 30
Collateral, 210, 212
  asset prices, 392
  example, 210
  mortgages and, 213
College Cost Reduction and Access Act (CCRAA), 243
Colombia
  debt rating, 111
Command economy, 18. *See also* Centrally planned economy
Commerce
  separation of banking and, 296–297
Commerce Bank, 261–262
Commercial and industrial (C&I) loans, 262, 264
  floating rates, 273
Commercial banks, 10, 123, 220*f*, 221–222, 221*t*. *See also* Banks
  average return on equity, 259*f*
  changes in, 258*t*
  community banks, 222
  composition of loans, 263*f*
  consolidation, 226–227
  failures of, 277*f*
  money-center banks, 221
  and money supply, 317–322
  regional banks, 221–222
  regulations, 299–300, 299*t*
  superregional banks, 221–222
  too big to fail, 552–553
Commercial Credit, 229
Commercial letter of credit, 254
Commercial paper, 3
Commodity money, 29, 30–31, 419–420
  coins, 30
  determinants of money growth and inflation, 419*f*
  to fiat money, 32
  paper, 30–31
Commodity prices, 179
Communism, 18
Community banks, 222
Community Reinvestment Act (CRA), 243–244
Compensating balances, 211
Conditionality, 564
Conditions, 212
Confidence
  changes in, 175–176
Congress
  Community Reinvestment Act, 244
  Deficit Reduction Act, 242
  economy stimulation, 375
  FDIC, 290
  FDIC Improvement Act, 308
  Federal Reserve Act, 314
  First and Second Banks, 224–225
  Glass-Steagall Act, 225–226, 255
  Gramm-Leach Bliley Act, 226
  McFadden Act, 223
  National Bank Act, 225
  payday lending, 238
  Resolution Trust Corporation, 307
  Riegle-Neal Act, 224, 226
  Sherman Antitrust Act, 225
Congressional Budget Office (CBO), 93
Conover, Todd, 552*n*
Conservative policymakers, 481
  reputation, 481–482
Conservatorship, 241
Consolidated balance sheet, 250, 250*t*
Consolidation, 223–231
  across businesses, 228–229
  limits to, 227
  motives for, 227
Consumer
  confidence, 356
  loans, 263
Consumer Bankers Association, 243
Consumer price index (CPI), 23
Consumption, 391
  expenditure and, 352
  interest rate and, 352–353
Consumption multiplier, 353
Contagion, 559
  Mexico's crisis, 562
Continental Airlines
  junk bonds and, 112
Continental Congress, 32–33
Continental dollar, 32–33
Continental Illinois bank crisis, 552
Contractionary open-market operation, 315
Core deposits, 259, 260–261
Corporate debt, 112
Countercyclical monetary policy, 357–358, 357*f*
  time lags and, 405–406, 405*f*
Countrywide Financial, 233
Coupon payment, 2
Covenants, 12, 211
  monitoring, 211
  mortgages, 213
Cox, Christopher, 189
CPI. *See* Consumer price index
CRA. *See* Community Reinvestment Act
Cranston, Alan, 307
Crashes
  asset-price, 68–71, 544
  prevention, 70–71
Credit cards, 38
  fees, 266
Credit crunch, 356
Credit derivatives, 555
Credit rationing, 211
Credit risk, 269–270, 270*t*
Credit scores, 213
Credit Suisse, 122, 125
Credit union, 222–223
Crisis. *See* Financial crisis
Critchfield, Tim, 227*n*
CRL. *See* Center for Responsible Learning
Currency. *See* U.S. currency; U.S. dollar
  markets and exchange rates, 156–160
Currency board, 35
Currency-deposit ratio (C/D), 318, 323, 325*f*
Currency futures
  hedging, 163
Currency unions, 35, 535–540
  advantages of, 538
  drawbacks of, 538–539
  economics of, 538–539
  outside of Europe, 540
  politics of, 539
Cynamon, Barry Z., 46*n*

D

Danailova-Trainor, Gergana, 516*n*
Dash, Mike, 13*n*
Davies, Glyn, 32*n*
Dealer, 122
Dealer markets, 127, 129
Dean Witter, 122
Debt
  corporate, 112
  maturity, 133
  sovereign, 110–111
Debt-income ratios, 213
Debt securities, 2. *See also* Bond
Default risk
  on corporate debt, 112
  interest rates and, 110–115
  on sovereign debt, 110–111
Defaults, 3
Defensive open-market operations, 326
Deficit Reduction Act, 242, 243
Deflation, 375, 413
  liquidity trap, 433–438, 435*f*
  role of, 435–436
Dehejia, Rajeev, 16, 16*n*
de la Rua, Fernando, 563
Delta
  junk bonds and, 112
Demand, 87*f*
  money, 98, 101*f*
Demand curve
  money, 101
  shifts in, 89–91
Demirguc-Kunt, Asli, 295*n*
Deposit
  banks and, 318–319, 320
  checking, 251, 260–261
  core, 259, 260–261

excessive risk, 291–292
looting, 292
misuse of, 291–292
Deposit insurance, 290–291
and banking crises, 294–295
limits on, 294
problem with, 293–294
in United States, 290–291
Depreciation, 158
Derivatives, 144–150, 254, 273
disasters, 148–149
futures, 145
hedging with, 146–147
new frontiers, 149–150
options, 145–146
speculating with, 147–148
Detragiache, Enrica, 295*n*
Deutsche Bank, 157
Devaluation, 529
Direct Edge, 129
Direct finance, 11
Direct loan program, 242
Discount broker, 122
Discount loan, 316
Discount rate, 316, 327
changing, 327
Discover Bank, 266
Discretionary policy, 489
Disinflation, 371, 371*f*, 403–404
costs of, 445
Disney bank run example, 286
Dispersion, 223–231
Diversification, 6, 138
Dividends, 58
Division of Monetary Affairs, 467
Division of Research and Statistics, 467
Dollar. *See* U.S. dollar
Dollarization, 34
Dornbusch, Rudi, 375
Double coincidence of wants, 27
Dow Jones, 25, 66–68, 66*f*
market crashes, 69–70
Down payments, mortgages, 213
Duhalde, Eduardo, 563
Duisenberg, Wim, 539
Dutkowsky, Donald, 46*n*

E

Earnings, 304
"East Asian miracle," 13
Ebbers, Bernhard, 206
EBS. *See* Electronic Broking Services
ECB. *See* European Central Bank
Eckholm, Erick, 238*n*
ECN. *See* Electronic communication network
Economic analysis, 182
Economic booms, 348
Economic fluctuations, 343–377
Economic growth, 12
case study, 15–16
evidence on, 14–20
financial development and, 14*f*
financial system and, 12–15
savings and, 13
Economic risk, 274
Economic stability
policies for, 443–471
Economies of scale, 15, 215, 227
Economies of scope, 229
Economy, 49
bank understanding of, 463
complete, 367–375, 367*f*
emerging-market, 558
financial crisis, 545–547, 558–565
and interest rates, 556–557
monitoring, 465–466
output gap, 459–460
over time, 369–372
U.S. 1960–2007, 373–375
without banks, 318
Ecuador, 34
debt rating, 111
Efficient-markets hypothesis (EMH), 139–140
mutual funds and, 140–141
random walk, 139
stock picking, 139–140
Elastic currency, 33
Elections, 201
Electronic Broking Services (EBS), 157, 163
Electronic communication network (ECN), 127, 129
Electronic money. *See* e-money
Electronic payments
payment system and, 40
processing, 40
shift to, 38*f*
El Salvador, 34
Emerging market economies, 558
EMH. *See* Efficient-markets hypothesis
E-money, 40, 42
Empire building, 227
Employment Act, 443
Ence, Ronald, 298
England, Bank of, 183, 287–288, 484
targets, 495–496
Enron, 68, 230
collapse of, 6–7
401(k), 7*n*
scandal, 206
Equilibrium output, 354, 355*f*
Equilibrium real interest rate, 87–89, 88*f*, 90
money and, 98–99
Equity, 3, 250. *See also* Stock
Equity ratio, 275–278
return on equity and, 276
ERM. *See* Exchange Rate Mechanism
E*Trade, 122, 127
Euro, 535–537
area, 537*f*
birth of, 536
countries that use, 536
currency unions, 538–539
growth of area, 536
versus dollar, 176–178, 177*f*
Eurodollars, 228
Europe
monetary policy, 536–537
unemployment rate, 346
European Central Bank (ECB), 35, 177, 178, 484, 493, 536
establishing reputations, 502
inflation target and, 501–502
European Union (EU), euro and, 536
Eurosystem, 536–537
Ex ante real interest rate, 76, 86
Excessive risk, 291–292
Excess reserves, 329
Exchange, 128
Exchange markets
foreign, 155–184
Exchange rate
and aggregate expenditure, 512–513
on Bloomberg.com, 159–160*f*
capital controls, 524–525
changes in, 158, 176
currency markets and, 156–160
equilibrium, 173–174
fixed, 528–535
floating, 528
fluctuations in, 174–180, 174*t*
hedging and risk, 163–164
information on, 158–159
long-run behaviors, 169–172
measuring, 158–160
nominal, 155
offsetting shocks, 513–515
policies, 517–526, 518*t*
purpose of, 160–168
real, 164
real versus nominal, 164–166
and risk, 516–517
and stabilization policy, 512–515, 518*f*
steel, 167–168, 167*f*
U.S.–Canada, 172
volatility, 516–517
Exchange Rate Mechanism (ERM), 533–534, 535, 536
Exchanges, 127, 128
seat on, 128
Expansionary open-market operation, 315
Expectations theory of the term structure, 104–105
Expected inflation, 358
adaptive, 359
assumptions, 359–360
determination of, 358–360
rational, 358–359
Expenditure
components of, 352
effects in the monetary transmission mechanism, 398
Expenditure shocks, 354, 355*f*, 368, 369*f*
example, 354–355
types of, 355–356
Explicit inflation target, 446

Ex post real interest rate, 76, 86
Exxon, 120
  corporate debt rating, 112

F

Face value, 2
Fannie Mae, 231, 233, 240, 253, 267
Fatum, Rasmus, 523, 523*n*
FDIC. *See* Federal Deposit Insurance Corporation
FDIC Improvement Act, 308
Fed, 26. *See* Federal Reserve System
Federal Banking Commission, 300
Federal Deposit Insurance Corporation (FDIC), 290, 552
  in closure process of bank, 308
  regulations, 299
  Wal-Mart and, 298
Federal Family Education Loan (FFEL), 242
Federal funds, 251
Federal funds rate, 335–336, 337*f*
  implementing targets, 336–339
Federal Home Administration (FHA), 241
Federal Home Loan Bank Board (FHLBB), 307
Federal Open Market Committee (FOMC), 336, 385, 386–387, 446
  hitting targets, 339*f*
  implementing targets, 336–339
  meeting, 464, 467–468, 475
  policy change, 388
  Taylor rule, 451–452
  transparency, 506–507, 507*f*
Federal Reserve Act, 314
Federal Reserve Bank, 46–47, 336
  books, 465
  countercyclical policy, 357
  independent, 483–484
  lags, 408
  of New York, 330, 553
  regulations, 299
Federal Reserve Note, 31
Federal Reserve System (Fed), 25, 26, 314, 443, 443*n*
  antitying law, 264, 265
  bubbles and, 471
  balance sheet, 317
  case study on September 11, 47–48
  deposit rates, 260–261
  discount rate and, 327
  economy 1960–2007, 373–375
  establishment of, 33
  in financial crisis, 468, 469
  financial system and, 553–557
  inflation targeting, 497
  interest rates, 384–387
  interest-rate target and, 333–334
  interventions and, 520, 522
  lender of last resort, 550–551
  liquidity crisis, 554–555
  loans from, 252
  monetary aggregate and, 36
  monetary base, 315–317
  monetary policy and yield curves, 109
  monetary tools, 326–330
  money supply, 100
  monitoring the economy, 465–466
  1990s, 462–463
  in 1937, 328–329
  open-market operations, 337–338
  payment systems, 39–40
  policy, 549, 554*t*
  processing electronic payments, 40
  recession, 178
  regulations, 299
  response to crashes, 69–70
  response to financial crisis, 468–469
  secrecy of, 506
  September 11 case study, 47–48
  small time deposits, 44
  stock market case study, 60–62, 61*f*
  stored-value cards, 41
  sweep programs, 45–46
  Taylor rule and, 451, 452*f*
  time-consistency, 482
  trades, 338
  transparency, 506
  2001 recession, 383
Fees, 265–266
  credit card, 266
  overdraft, 265–266
Feldstein, Martin, 445, 445*n*, 446
FFEL. *See* Federal Family Education Loan
FHA. *See* Federal Home Administration
FHC. *See* Financial holding companies
FHLBB. *See* Federal Home Loan Bank Board
Fiat money, 29, 31–32, 33, 35–36
  from commodity money, 32
  determinants of money growth and inflation, 419*f*
  and inflation, 421
Fidelity, 121
  Magellan, 142–143
Finance
  direct, 11
  indirect, 11
Finance companies, 221*t*, 223
Financial crisis, 468–469, 469*f*, 543, 546*f*
  Argentina, 561–563
  asset-price crashes, 544
  capital flight and, 559–561, 560*f*
  and the economy, 545–547
  in emerging economies, 558–565
  Great Depression and, 547–548
  insolvency, 544
  liquidity, 544–545
  mechanics of, 544–547
  policy responses to, 549–553
  preventing, 557
Financial futures, 145. *See also* Futures contract
Financial holding companies (FHC), 228–229
Financial institutions, 10, 122–123
Financial intermediary, 10. *See also* Financial institution
Financial markets, 2, 49
  banks versus, 11
  bond, 2–3
  economics functions, 4–6
  effects in monetary transmission mechanism, 398
  regulation of, 205–208
  stock, 3–4
Financial system, 1–23
  and aggregate expenditure, 390–397
  asymmetric information, 189–215
  economics growth and, 12–15
  and the Fed, 553–557
Fire-sale prices, 267
Firms
  distracted, 428
  information-gathering, 200
  lower sales for, 161–162
  monetary policy, 399–400, 400*f*
  private equity, 203–205
  takeover, 203–204
  venture capital, 204–205
First Bank of the United States, 33, 224–225, 314
First Chicago Bank, 226
Fiscal policy, 407
  versus monetary, 406–408
Fischer, Stanley, 565
Fisher effect, 96
Fisher equation, 95–96, 97, 102
Fisher, Irving, 69, 95
Fixed exchange rates, 528
  and capital flight, 559
  controlling inflation, 530–531
  devaluation, 529
  history of, 534–535
  and inflation, 530–531, 531*f*
  instability of, 531–532, 532*f*
  Israel, 531
  mechanics of, 528–529
  monetary policy, 529–530
  pros and cons, 528*t*
  revaluation, 529
Fixed-income security, 2. *See also* Bond
Flexible target, 495
Floating exchange rate, 528, 535
Floating interest rates, 272–273
FOMC. *See* Federal Open Market Committee
Forbearance, 306
Ford, Gerald, 343, 430
Ford Motor Credit Company, 223
Forecasting
  interest rates, 109
  methods, 182–184

Forecasts, 466
  coordinator, 466
Foreign banks, 228
Foreign-exchange interventions, 519–522, 520*f*
  Brazil, 522
  China, 526–527
  effects of, 520–521
  and exchange rates, 520*f*
  and exchange-rate stabilization, 521*f*
  Japan, 522
  New Zealand, 522–523
  purpose of, 521
  success of, 522–523
  who intervenes, 522
Foreign exchange markets, 155–184
Foreign interest rates, 95
401(k), 6–7
France
  bonds, 95
Frank, Barney, 475, 485–486
Freddie Mac, 231, 233, 240, 267
Free-rider problem, 199–200
Free Silver
  movement, 420–421
Friedman, Milton, 290*n*, 325*n*, 326*n*, 413*n*, 417, 418*n*, 425, 477, 489, 490, 490*n*, 492, 534
Friendly Bank example, 318–321
Friendly takeover, 204
Fujimori, Alberto, 427
Full-service broker, 121–122
Funds
  cheap and expensive, 259
  purchased, 259
  sources of, 258–262
Futures contract, 145
Future value, 54

G

Gambling for resurrection, 306
Garcia, Alan, 426, 427
Gates, Bill, 26
GDP. *See* Gross domestic product
GDP deflator, 23
GEICO, 144
General Electric
  corporate debt rating, 112
  401(k) and, 7
  ILC, 297
General Motors, 12, 53
  bond case study, 112–113, 113*f*
  ILC, 297
  stocks and, 3
General Motors Acceptance Corporation (GMAC), 223
General Theory of Employment, Interest, and Money, The, 351
Germany
  asset restrictions and, 300
  debt rating, 111
  ERM, 533
  hyperinflation, 413, 414, 424–425
Gertler, Mark, 25, 399–400, 400*n*, 471, 471*n*
Gilchrist, Simon, 399–400, 400*n*
Gillette, 144
Glass-Steagall Act, 225–226, 228, 230
  repeal of, 255, 264, 296
GMAC. *See* General Motors Acceptance Corporation
Gold Certificate, 31
Goldman Sachs, 122, 124
  primary dealer, 338
Gold standard, 33, 419–420, 534
Goodfriend, Marvin, 499*n*
Google
  Checkout, 42
  IPO case study, 125
  option example, 146
  and venture capital firms, 204
Governing Council, 537
Government
  action on insolvent banks, 305–306
  debt, 558
  -owned banks, 244–245
  purchases, 352
  role in lending, 239–245
  spending, 356
Government-sponsored enterprise (GSE), 231, 240–241
Graham, Benjamin, 143
Grameen Bank, 17
Gramm-Leach-Bliley Act, 226, 228, 229, 230
Great Depression, 1–2, 33, 351, 425, 543, 549
  financial crisis, 547–548
  and money multiplier, 324–326, 325*f*
Great Inflation
  cause of, 460
  Fed and, 460–462
  output gap and, 461–462
Greece, 30
Greenbacks, 33
Green Book, 465, 466, 467, 507
Greenspan, Alan, 25, 67, 314, 483, 487, 502, 503, 504, 506, 506*n*, 526
Gross domestic product (GDP), 14, 37
  and debt ratings, 111
  money and, 101
  nominal, 22
  private saving and, 92
  real, 13, 23
  Russia, 19
Growth. *See* Economic growth; Money growth
GSE. *See* Government-sponsored enterprise
Guta Bank, 286–287, 291
Guttenberg, Michael, 209

H

Hamilton, Alexander, 33, 224, 225
Harford Bank, 222
Hedge funds, 121, 148
Hedging, 146
  currency futures, 163
  with derivatives, 146–147
  exchange-rate risk, 163–164
  with futures, 146–147
  limits to, 164
  with options, 147
Henderson, Callum, 182*n*
HFC. *See* Household Finance Corporation
Higgins, Bryon, 504*n*
High-inflation trap, 480, 480*f*
High-yield spread, 114–115, 114*f*
Hill, Virgil, 261
Hochschild, Roger, 266
Holden, Sarah, 7*n*
Holland, 64–65
Home Depot, 201–202
Home equity loan, 392
Honda Accord, lemons example, 191
Hong Kong, 35
Horizons, long, 487
Hoshi, Takeo, 396*n*, 438*n*
Hostile takeover, 204
Household Finance Corporation (HFC), 233
Humphrey-Hawkins Act, 443
Hussein, Saddam, 356
Hutchinson, Michael, 523, 523*n*
Hyperinflation, 413, 423–424
  German, 424–425

I

ILC. *See* Industrial loan companies, 297
ImClone Systems, 208
IMF. *See* International Monetary Fund
Implicit inflation target, 446
Imports, 161
Income
  inequality, 429
  present value, 57–58
Income statement, 256–257
  Melvin's Bank example, 257*t*
Income streams, value of, 54–56
Independence
  Federal Reserve, 483–484
  and inflation, 488–489
  opposition to, 485–486
  and time consistency, 487
  traditional case for, 486–487
  world, 484–485
Independent Community Bankers of America, 298
Index fund, 140
India, government-owned banks, 244
Indirect finance, 11
Individuals, 120

Indonesia, 94
Industrial loan companies (ILCs), 297
Industry consolidation, 122, 123
Inflation, 413–438
  balancing, 448
  controlling, 530–531, 531*f*
  costs of, 427–432
  explicit, 497
  fallacy, 427–428
  fiat money and, 421
  fixed exchange rates, 530–531, 531*f*
  high, 478–479
  implicit, 497
  independence and, 488–489, 488*f*
  long run, 414–419
  moderate, 430–432
  money and, 414–419
  money growth rate and, 416–417, 417*f*, 418*f*
  output and, 421–422
  output stability, 446–448
  Phillips curve and, 417–419
  positive, 445–446
  rate. *See* inflation rate
  stability, 447
  target, 446, 446*t*, 493–500
  and taxes, 431–432
  time-consistency problem, 478–480
  trap, 480
  uncertainty, 431
  very high, 422–425, 428–429
  worldwide decline, 425–427, 426*f*
  zero, 444–445
Inflation-indexed bonds, 77–78
Inflation rate, 23, 171, 414*t*
  deriving, 415–416
  effect of output, 360–363
  expected, 358–360
  fluctuations, 358–365
  long-run, 444–446
  and nominal exchange rates, 171*f*
  and nominal interest rates, 97*f*
  oil prices and, 366–367
  output path, 406
  savings and loan crisis, 77
  supply shocks, 363–365
Inflation-surprise decision, 479*f*, 480
Inflation targets, 493–501, 500*f*
  case for, 497–498
  example of, 494–495, 494*f*
  opposition to, 499
  process of, 494–495
  spreading of, 495–497, 496*f*
Information
  disclosure, 205–207
  gathering, 199
Information-gathering firms, 200
  bond-rating agencies, 200
  investment banks, 200
Initial public offering (IPO), 123
Inside lag, 407, 408*f*
Insider trading, 207–208
  example of, 208–209
Insolvency, 275–278, 275*t*
  example, 275
  financial crisis, 544
Insolvent banks
  closing, 305–308
  forbearance, 306
  government action, 305–306
Instinet, 129
Insurance companies, 123
Interbank market, 157
Interest
  bonds, 3
  rates, 59–60
Interest-rate policy
  making, 464–468
Interest-rate risk, 270–273, 271*t*
  example, 271–272
  measuring, 272
  reducing, 272–273
Interest rates, 59–60
  adjusting, 494–495, 518–519
  after tax, 432–433
  budget deficits and, 93–94
  cautious movements, 463–464
  changes in, 100–102, 175
  and credit rationing, 211–212
  default risk and, 110–115
  determination of, 83–116
  economy and, 556–557
  equilibrium, 98–99
  factors that explain differences, 102*t*
  forecasting, 109
  foreign, 95
  high-yield spread and, 114–115
  loanable funds theory, 84–89, 89–97, 89*f*
  lower bounds, 433–435
  measuring, 71–74
  money supply and, 313–339
  nominal, 74–75, 95–97
  policy, 335–339
  politics and, 242–243
  real, 74–77, 84*f*, 86–87, 97. *See also* real interest rate
  relating theories, 102
  rising, 277–278
  role of in aggregate expenditure, 352
  targets, 330–335
  term structure, 102–109
  2004, 389*f*
  yield curve, 107
Interest-rate smoothing, 464
Interest-rate targeting, 331, 331*f*, 333*f*
  choosing, 332
International banking, 228
International Monetary Fund (IMF), 295, 543
  debate, 565
  loans, 564–565
  role of, 564–565
International reserves, 519, 520*f*
Interventions. *See* Foreign-exchange interventions
Inverted yield curve, 108
  case study, 109
  examples of, 108*f*
Investment, 85, 120
  asset prices, 392
  expenditure and, 352
  increase in, 90*f*
  interest rate and, 353
  shifts in, 89–91
Investment bank, 10–11, 122, 200
  need for, 124
Investment banking, 254–255
Investment multiplier, 396–397, 396*n*
Investors, 5
  flow of funds, 11*f*, 190*f*
  matching with savers, 4–5
  reducing costs to, 214–215
IPO. *See* Initial public offering
Israel
  fixed exchange rate, 531
Issing, Ottmar, 502–503, 503*n*
Italy
  debt rating, 111

J

Jackson, Andrew, 224–225, 314, 485
Jansa, Janez, 539
Japan
  asset prices, 470
  asset restrictions and, 300
  Bank of, 484
  deflation and, 413, 433
  exchange rate policies, 526
  forbearance, 306
  interest rate case study, 111–112
  intervention, 522
  liquidity trap, 437–438, 437*f*, 445
  recession, 557
  slump, 393–396, 394–395*f*
  steel, 168
  stored-value cards, 41
  yen and inflation, 172
Jefferson, Thomas, 224
Jevons, William Stanley, 28, 28*n*
Johnson & Johnson, corporate debt rating, 112
Johnson, Lyndon, 343
Jones, Barry E., 46*n*
Jones, Kenneth D., 227*n*
JP Morgan Chase, 129, 221, 226, 229, 264
  Bear Sterns and, 555, 556
  interbank market, 157
  primary dealer, 338
Junk bonds, 112, 262

K

Kashyap, Anil, 396*n*, 438*n*
Keating, Charles, 307
Keating Five, 307

Kennedy, Edward, 243
Kerviel, Jerome, 149, 274, 304
Keynes, John Maynard, 351, 434–435
Keystone, First National Bank of, 292–293, 304
KKR. *See* Kohlberg, Kravis, and Roberts
Kleiner Perkins, 204
Kohlberg, Kravis, and Roberts (KKR), 204
Kohn, Donald, 314, 497, 499, 499*n*
Kozlowski, Dennis, 196–197, 201
Kraushaar, Judah S., 231*n*
Krugman, Paul, 427, 427*n*
Kuttner, Kenneth, 62, 62*n*, 389–390, 390*n*, 396*n*
Kydland, Finn, 478, 479, 480, 481, 482, 487, 490, 502

L

Lachman, Desmond, 565, 565*n*
Lag
  inside, 407, 408*f*
  outside, 407, 408*f*
Langley, Monica, 231*n*
La Porta, Rafael, 203*n*
Laubach, Thomas, 93–94, 94*n*
Law of one price, 169
Lay, Kenneth, 206
Lebanon debt rating, 111
Leeson, Nick, 148
Legg Mason, 143
Lehman Brothers, 554
Lemons
  problem of, 191
  in securities markets, 192–193
Lender of last resort, 47, 550–551
Lenders, subprime, 234–235
Lending, 545–546
  governments role in, 239–245
  policies, 327–328
  predatory, 237–238
  risky, 234–235
Lenin, V.I., 18, 19
Letters of credit, 254
  commercial, 254
  standby, 254
Leverage, 121
Levin, Carl, 266
Liabilities, 250, 251–252, 260, 260*f*
LIBOR rate, 554
Limit order, 128
Lincoln, Abraham, 225
Lincoln Savings and Loan, 307
Lines of credit, 210, 253–254
Liquidity, 42–43, 115, 214, 304
  benefit of, 268*t*
  bonds and, 115
  crisis, 544–545, 550–551, 554–555
  degrees of, 42–43, 43*f*
  need for, 42
  profit trade-off, 268
  risk. *See* liquidity risk
  trap. *See* liquidity trap
Liquidity preference theory, 97–102, 100*t*
Liquidity risk, 267–269, 267*t*, 284
  example, 267–268
Liquidity trap, 433, 434*f*
  avoiding, 445–446
  deflation and, 433–438, 435*f*
  Japan, 437–438, 437*f*, 445
  market for money, 436*f*
Lleras-Muney, Adriana, 16, 16*n*
Loanable funds theory, 84–89, 377
  determinants of interest rates, 89–97, 88*f*
  and neutral interest rate, 381–382
Loan auctions, 327–328
Loan commitments, 253. *See* Lines of credit
Loan guarantees, 241
Loans, 253, 316–317
  auto title, 239
  by banks, 319, 320–321
  commercial and industrial, 262
  consumer, 263
  discount, 316
  effects on demand, 86
  equation, 85
  from the Fed, 252
  IMF, 564–565
  market, 87*f*
  private, 10
  real estate, 262–263
  sales, 272
  student, 241–243
  syndication, 270
Loan sales, 272
Loan sharks, 239
Long-run inflation
  choosing rate, 444–446
  current practice, 446
Long-run monetary neutrality, 376
Long-run output, unemployment and, 345, 376
Long Term Capital Management (LTCM), 468, 469, 553
Looting, 292
LTCM. *See* Long Term Capital Management
Lucas, Robert, 477
Lynch, Peter, 142–143

M

M1, 36–37, 41, 43
  sweep programs and, 45–46, 46*f*
M2, 43–45, 501
M3, 501
M&A. *See* Mergers and acquisitions
M&T Bank, 222, 227
  regulations, 299
Maastricht Treaty, 536
Malaysia
  capital controls, 524–525
Malkiel, Burton, 184
Management, 304
Mankiw, N. Gregory, 347*n*, 427
Manufacturers Hanover, 226
Manugistics Group, 208
Marginal cost, 360
Margin requirements, 70
Market order, 128
Market risk, 274
Markets
  interbank, 157
  primary, 123
  retail, 157
  secondary, 123
  securities, 119–150
  versus central planning, 18
Martin, William McChesney, 450, 491
Mary Poppins, 286
Mastercard, 41
Maturity, 2, 3
McConnell, J Knox, 292
McFadden Act, 223–224, 225
McKinley, William, 420–421
Medium of exchange, 26
Melvin's Bank example, 255–258, 267–270, 271–272, 275
  bank run, 285, 285*t*
  capital requirements, 301–302, 302*t*
Menem, Carlos, 561, 563
Mergers and acquisitions (M&A), 122
Merrill Lynch, 122, 127, 128, 208, 236
Microfinance, 17
  case study, 16–18
  institutions, 17
Microsoft, 6, 12, 53
Miller, Merton, 131
Miller, William, 143, 374, 422
Mishkin, Frederic, 446, 497, 497*n*, 498
Mistakes. *See* Policy mistakes
MMDA. *See* Money-market deposit account
MM Theorem. *See* Modigliani-Miller Theorem
Modigliani, Franco, 131
Modigliani-Miller Theorem (MM Theorem), 131–132
Monetarist, 334–335, 335*f*, 490
Monetary aggregate, 36–37, 44*t*
  M1, 36–37, 41, 43
  M2, 43–45
Monetary base, 325*f*
  creating, 315–317
  Fed and, 315–317
  open-market operations, 326
Monetary policy, 47, 50, 384–389, 468–471
  accommodative, 368
  Canada, 515–516
  countercyclical, 357–358, 357*f*
  European, 536–537
  fiscal versus, 406–408
  inventory and small firms, 399–400
  loss of independent, 529–530
  mistakes, 490–491
  political influence, 491

real rate, 354
rules, 489–493
shifts in, 354, 355*f*
time lags, 400–406
term structure, 384
tightening, 400*f*, 402*f*
two approaches to, 331
Monetary policy rule, 489
money targets, 492–493
time consistency, 492
traditional arguments for, 490–491
Monetary tools, 326–330
lending policies, 327–328
open-market operations, 326
reserve requirements, 328
Monetary transmission mechanism, 384, 397–399, 397*f*
bank lending, 398
expenditure, 398
financial markets, 398
multiplier effects, 398
Money, 26–29, 49
broad, 42–46
clean and dirty, 35
coins, 30
commodity, 29, 30–31, 419–420
demand, 27, 98
determination of growth, 419–427
fiat, 29, 31–32, 421
growth rate data, 416–417, 417*f*, 418*f*
limits to creation of, 321, 322*f*
liquidity, 42–46
market for, 98, 99*f*
medium of exchange, 26
near, 43
new kinds of, 40–42
paper, 31–32
printing, 423
quantity equation of, 415
shifts in demand, 101–102
shifts in supply, 100, 100*f*
spending, 37–38
store of value, 29
supply, 36–42, 98
targets, 330–335
today, 36–42
types of, 29–36
unit of account, 28–29
velocity of, 414–415
versus barter, 27
Money-center bank, 221
Money demand, 27
Money-demand curve
shifting, 332–333, 332*f*
Money growth, 419–427
determinants of, 419*f*
irrelevance of, 436–437
rate data, 416–417, 417*f*, 418*f*
Money-market deposit account (MMDA), 44, 45
Money-market funds, 44–45
Money multiplier, 323, 324*t*
and Great Depression, 324–326, 325*f*
United States, 324
Money supply, 36–42, 325*f*
changes in, 323
commercial banks and, 317–322
deriving formula for, 322–323
formula for, 322–326
and interest rates, 313–339
measuring, 36–37
Money targeting, 331, 331*f*, 333*f*
choosing, 332
Monitoring
covenants, 211
Moody's Investor Services, 110, 200
Moral hazard, 9–10, 195–198, 291–295
in bond markets, 197–198
deposit insurance, 293–294
limits on insurance and, 294
misuse of deposits, 291–292
numerical example, 198
reducing, 12
in stock markets, 196
Morgan Stanley, 122, 125, 231, 471
Mortgage-backed securities, 231
Mortgages
agencies, 240–241
fixed- versus floating-rate, 273–274
home, 212–213
securities and, 233
screening borrowers, 213
subprime fiasco, 234–236
Mugabe, Robert, 423–424
Mullins, David, 503
Multipliers
effects in monetary transmission mechanism, 398
Mundell, Robert, 540
Municipal bonds, 115–116
Muth, John, 477
Mutual banks, 222
Mutual funds, 6, 121
actively managed fund, 140–141
index fund, 140–141

N

NAIRU. *See* Nonaccelerating inflation rate of employment
Nardelli, Robert, 201–202
NASDAQ, 67–68, 67*f*, 129
National Association of Securities Dealers Automated Quotation. *See* NASDAQ
National Bank Act, 225
National banks, 225
National Bureau of Economic Research (NBER), 350–351
National central banks (NCB), 537
National Credit Union Administration, 296
NATO. *See* North Atlantic Treaty Organization
Natural rate of unemployment (U*), 345
in United States, 346–347, 346*f*
NBER. *See* National Bureau Economic Research
NCB. *See* National central banks
NCI. *See* Net capital inflows
NCO. *See* Net capital outflows
Near money, 43
Net capital flows, 85
Net capital inflows (NCI), 85–89, 94*f*, 95, 173, 381–382, 382*f*
Net capital outflows (NCO), 173, 353
capital controls and exchange rates, 524, 524*f*
interventions and, 521
shifts in, 174–176, 175*f*
Net exports (NX), 173
and capital flows, 172–173
expenditures and, 353
interest rates and, 353
shifts in, 178–180, 179*f*
Net worth, 210–211, 250, 251–252. *See also* Capital
asset prices effects on, 392
Neutral real interest rate (r^n), 377, 377*f*
and loanable funds theory, 381–382, 382*f*
New Century Financial, 236
New Deal, 240
New Republic
money in, 33
New York Stock Exchange, 25, 70, 119, 128
purchasing Boeing stock, 128*f*
New Zealand
intervention, 522–523
Nicholas II of Russia, 18
Nikkei stock index, 148, 394
Nixon, Richard, 34, 343, 373, 498
monetary policy and, 491–492
Nominal exchange rate, 155, 180
against dollar, 181*f*
fixed exchange rate, 529
real versus, 164–166
Nominal GDP, 22
Nominal interest rate, 74–75, 75*f*, 95–97
Fisher equation, 95
inflation and, 97*f*, 171*f*
liquidity preference theory, 97
Nominal price, 358
Nominal rate of return, 75
Nonaccelerating inflation rate of employment (NAIRU), 363
Nonaccomodating monetary policy, 369, 370*f*, 372*f*
Nontransaction deposits, 251
Nortel Networks, 264
North Atlantic Treaty Organization (NATO), 539
Northern Rock Bank, 287–288, 291, 294

Norway
  commodity prices, 179
NOW account, 251
NX. *See* Net exports

O

OBS. *See* Off-balance-sheet activities
OCC. *See* Office of the Comptroller of the Currency
October 19, 1987 crash, 68, 69–70, 149
October 28, 1929 crash, 69–70
Ofer, Gur, 20*n*
Off-balance-sheet (OBS) activities, 253–255, 264
  asset management, 254
  derivatives, 254
  investment banking, 254–255
  letters of credit, 254
  lines of credit, 253–254
Office of Management and Budget (OMB), 93
Office of the Comptroller of the Currency (OCC), 296
  regulations, 299
Office of Thrift Supervision, 296, 308
  regulations, 300
Oil prices, 366–367
Okun, Arthur, 348, 373
Okun's law, 348–350, 349*f*, 373, 376, 447, 449, 458
OMB. *See* Office of Management and Budget
O'Neal, Stanley, 236
O'Neill, Paul, 162
One-year rate, 385–386, 386*f*
OPEC. *See* Organization of Petroleum Exporting Countries
Open-market operations, 315–316, 326
  contractionary, 315
  daily operations, 337–338
  defensive, 326
  effects of, 337
  expansionary, 315
  outright, 338
  temporary, 338
Opportunity cost, 98
Option, 145–146
  call, 146
  put, 146
Orange County, 149
Order flows, 182
Organization of Petroleum Exporting Countries (OPEC), 366
Orphanides, Athanasios, 461, 462, 462*n*
Osler, Carol, 184
OTC. *See* Over-the-counter
Output
  balancing, 448
  effect of on inflation rate, 360–363
  fluctuations, 347–348, 348*f*
  gap, 348
  path, 406
  rise in, 421–422
  stability, 447–448
Output gap
  effects on economy, 459–460
  effects on policy, 458
  measurement of, 457–460, 459*f*
  smaller responses, 464
Outright open-market operation, 338
Outside lag, 407, 408*f*
Overnight interest rate, 335. *See* Federal funds rate
Overnight loans, 251
Over-the-counter (OTC) markets, 127, 129
  dealer market, 129

P

P/E ratio, 65–66
Page, Larry, 125
Paper money, 30–31
Paulson, Henry, 163
  Chinese and, 511
Pawnshops, 239
Payday lenders, 236–237
  predatory, 237–238
Payments
  forever, 56
  series of, 55–56
  values of common types, 56*t*
Payments system, 39–40, 39*f*
  check clearing, 39–40
  check imaging, 40
  electronic payments, 40
Payoff method, 308
Paypal, 42
PDCF. *See* Primary Dealer Credit Facility
Penalty rates, 266
Pension funds, 122
Pension Reform Act of 2006, 7
Pentagon, 47
People's Bank of China, 485, 526, 527
Peristiani, Stavros, 330*n*
Perpetuity, 56
Peru, inflation in, 426–427
Pfizer, 401(k) and, 7
Phillips, A.W. ("Bill"), 362
Phillips curve (PC), 344, 361–362, 361*f*, 513*f*
  adaptive expectations, 362–363
  combining with AE curve, 367–369
  equations for, 362
  evidence for, 364*f*
  high inflation, 478–480
  inflation, 417–419
  lags in, 401–402, 404*f*
  mistake, 455–457
  supply shock and, 364–365, 365*f*
  time consistency, 476–477
  unemployment, 363
Plaza Agreement, 526
PLUS Loans, 242
Policy
  coordination, 525–526
  options, 467
  output gap, 458
  responses to financial crisis, 549–553
Policy changes, 387–389
  effects of, 388
  historical example, 388–389
Policymakers
  conservative, 481
  establishing reputations, 502
  rules and, 489–490
Policy mistakes, 454–464
  effects of, 457*f*
  example of, 456
Political risk, 558–559
Politics
  and interest rates, 242–243
Populists, 15
Posen, Adam, 396*n*
Positive inflation, 445–446
Potential output (Y*), 345
Pound, 533–534
PPP. *See* Purchasing power parity
Predatory lending, 237–238
Prescott, Edward, 478, 479, 480, 481, 482, 487, 490, 502
Present value, 55–56
Presidential elections, economy and, 343, 344*f*
Price-earning ratio, 65. *See* P/E ratio
Prices
  asset, 57–78
  bond, 57–58
  stock, 58
  variability, 429
Primary Dealer Credit Facility (PDCF), 550–551
  Bear Sterns and, 555–556
Primary dealers, 338
Primary markets, 123–126
Prime rate, 211
Prince, Charles, 230–231, 236
Principle-agent problem, 196
Printing money, 423
Private banking, 254
Private company, 123
Private equity firms, 203–205
  takeover firms, 203–204
  venture capital firms, 204–205
Private loans, 10
Private saving, 92
  and GDP, 92
Proctor and Gamble, 401(k) and, 7
Productivity growth, effect on natural rate, 347
Profit
  evolving pursuit of, 258–266
  rates, 257–258
Program trading, 70
Prospectus, 123–124
Public company, 123

Public saving, 92
  budget deficit, 92
  budget surplus, 92
Purchase and assumption method, 308
Purchased funds, 259
Purchasing power parity (PPP), 169–170
  evidence for, 170–172
  law across borders, 169–170
  law of one price, 169
  reasonableness, 170
Put option, 146

Q

Quantity equation of money, 415

R

R/D. *See* Reserve-deposit ratio
Rand, 155
Random walk, 139
Rate
  effect of a cut, 387*f*
  historical example, 386–687
  long-term, 386
  1-year, 385–386
Rate of return, 72–73
  nominal, 75
  real, 75
  versus yield to maturity, 74
Rate sensitive, 271
Rate-sensitivity gap, 272
Rational expectations, 58–59, 358–359
  and costless disinflation, 479*f*
  time consistency, 476–477
Reagan administration
  deficits in, 175
  steel crisis, 168
Reagan, Ronald, 483
Real estate
  commercial bust, 278
  loans, 262
Real exchange rates, 164, 166*f*, 180
  against the dollar, 181*f*
  changes in, 165
  defining, 164–165
  effects of, 173
  versus nominal, 164–166
  short run, 172–174, 174*f*
  trade-weighted, 166–167
Real gross domestic product (real GDP), 13
  defined, 23
Real interest rate, 74–75, 75*f*
  after-tax, 432–433
  effects of, 86–87
  equilibrium, 87–89, 88*f*
  ex ante, 76, 86
  ex ante versus ex post, 75–77
  ex post, 79, 86
  fixed exchange rate, 529
  international, 96*f*
  neutral, 377
  rising, 367, 368*f*, 370–372
Real rate of return, 75
Real variables, 376
Reason, Tim, 265*n*
Recession, 347–350, 546
  case study, 350–351
  defined, 348, 350*f*
  foreign, 178–179
  2001, 383
Redlining, 243
Reed, John, 229, 230
Regional bank, 221–222
Regulation, 393
  banks, 47
Regulators, 295
Reinhart, Vincent, 565
Relative price, 358
Renaissance of American Steel, The, 168
Repo, 252. *See* Repurchase agreement
Repurchase agreement, 252
Required reserve ratio, 328
Reserve-deposit ratio (R/D), 319, 323, 325*f*, 328
Reserve requirements, 328
  decline of, 329–330
Reserves, 252–253
Resistance level, 184
Resolution Trust Corporation, 307
Retail market, 157
Retail money-market fund, 44–45
Return, 72
  rate of, 72–73
Return on assets (ROA), 257
Return on equity (ROE), 257–258
  equity ratio and, 276
Reuters, 157, 163
Revaluation, 529
Revolutionary War, 32–33
Riegle-Neal Act, 224, 227
Risk
  accounting for, 105–106
  attitudes toward, 136–137
  credit, 269–270
  default, 110–115
  economic, 274
  and economic integration, 517
  excessive, 291–292
  exchange rates and, 516–517
  interactions among, 274–275
  interest-rate risk, 270–273
  lending, 234–235
  liquidity, 267–269
  managing, 266–275
  market, 274
  perceptions, 392
Risk-adjusted assets, 301
Risk-averse, 136
Risk-free rate, 59. *See* Safe interest rate
Risk perception, 392
Risk premium, 59
Risk-return trade-off, 133–138, 135*f*
  attitudes toward, 136
  bank accounts, 136
  calculating, 134–136
  economists' advice, 136–137
Risk sharing, 5–6
ROA. *See* Return on assets
Roach, Stephen, 471, 471*n*
Road shows, 124
Rodriguez, Alex, 55–56
ROE. *See* Return on equity
Rogoff, Kenneth, 481
Romer, Christina, 402, 402*n*, 427*n*, 445*n*, 548*n*
Romer, David, 402, 402*n*, 427*n*, 445*n*, 449*n*
Roosevelt, Franklin, 33, 240, 547, 548
  bank panic and, 289–290
  Ben Bernanke and, 557
Rubin, Robert, 162
Rules, monetary policy, 489–492
Ruogo, Li, 527
Russia
  bank run, 286–287
  debt, 110

S

S&L. *See* Savings and Loan Association
S&L crisis, 277
S&P. *See* Standard & Poor's
Safe interest rate, 59
Saffer, Barry, 208
Safire, William, 492
Sallie Mae, 242
Salomon Brothers, 229
Salomon Smith Barney, 122, 123
Samuelson, Robert, 504, 504*n*
Sapsford, Jathon, 265*n*
Sarbanes-Oxley Act of 2002, 189, 206–207
Savers, 5
  flow of funds, 11*f*, 190*f*
  matching with investors, 4–5
  reducing costs to, 214
Saving, 85
  allocation of, 13
  growth and, 13
  increase in, 91*f*
  private, 92
  public, 92
  shifts in, 91–94
Saving and Loan Associations (S&L), 10, 222, 277. *See also* Savings institutions
  crisis, 356, 393, 431
  FDIC, 291
  regulatory crisis, 307–308
Savings bank, 222. *See* Savings institution
Savings institutions, 222
SBA. *See* Small Business Administration
Scandals, 206
Scarfo, Jr., Nicodemo, 239
Schwartz, Anna, 290*n*, 325*n*, 326*n*, 418*n*
SEC. *See* Securities and Exchange Commission
Secondary markets, 123, 127–129

Secondary reserves, 253
Second Bank of the United States, 33, 224–225, 314
Secrets of the Temple, 506
Securities, 253
  mortgage-backed, 231–233, 240, 553, 555–556
Securities and Exchange Commission, 205, 207
Securities firms, 121–122
  brokers, 121–122
  dealers, 121–122
  hedge funds, 121
  industry consolidation, 122
  investment banks, 122
  mutual funds, 121
Securities markets, 119–150
  lemons, 192
  major institutions in, 120*t*
  participants in, 120–123
Securitization, 219–220, 231–233
  industry, 231–232
  of loans, 232*f*
  occurrence of, 232–233
Security, 2
  finding information on prices, 130
  fixed-income, 2
Seigniorage, 422–425
Seigniorage revenue, 423
Sensitivity, 304
Separation of banking and commerce, 297
September 11, 2001, 68
  case study on Fed and, 47–48
Sequoia Capital, 204
Serbia
  hyperinflation, 423
Shareholder
  international differences in rights, 202–203, 203*f*
  revolts, 201–202
Sheridan, Niamh, 500–501, 501*n*
Shiller, Robert, 66, 66*n*, 391*n*
Shock
  expenditure, 368, 369*f*
  offsetting exchange-rate, 513–515
  response to, 456–457
  supply, 368–369, 370*f*
Shoe leather costs, 428
Short-run, 19, 345
Siegel, Jeremy, 137, 138
Six Crises, 491
Skilling, Jeffrey, 206
Small Business Administration (SBA), 241
Small time deposit, 44
Smith Barney, 122, 229
Snow, John, 162–163, 526
Societe Generale, 149, 274
Society Islands, 28
Soros, George, 533–534
South Africa, 155–156, 158
  changes in confidence in rand, 176
  exchange rate, 164
  order flow, 182
South Korea, 94, 95
Sovereign debt, 110
  ratings, 110*t*
Soviet Union
  investment in, case study, 18–20
Specialist, 128
Speculation, 147–148
Speculative attack, 532
Spending, 352–353, 545–546
  effects on components of, 515*f*
Stability
  inflation and output, 446–448
Stabilization, 449
  exchange rates and policy, 512–515
  interventions and, 521*f*
  output, 514*f*, 519*f*
Stable prices, 444
Stafford Loans, 242–243
Stalin, Josef, 19
Standard & Poor's (S&P), 110, 112, 200
Standard Oil, 225
Standby letter of credit, 254
State banks, 225
Steel
  exchange rate and, 167–168, 167*f*
  tariffs, 168
Stewart, Martha, 208
Stiglitz, Joseph, 565, 565*n*
Stock, 3–4, 43
  bonds versus, 62–63
  choosing, 138–144
  diversification, 138
  efficient-markets hypothesis, 139–140
  Fed case study, 60–62, 61*f*
  individual ownership, 120
  markets, 123–130. *See also* stock market
  prices, 58, 60, 67*f*, 131*f*
  prices effect on investment, 392
  return on, 73, 73*f*
Stock market
  beating, 141–144
  capitalization, 14, 14*f*
  lemons in, 192
  moral hazard, 196
Stock market index, 130
Stocks for the Long Run, 137
Stone, Amey, 231*n*
Stop Unfair Credit Card Practices Act, 266
Store of value, 29
Stored-value cards, 40, 41
Strict target, 495
Subprime lenders, 220, 233–239, 233*f*
  crash, 236
  finance companies, 233–234
  illegal loan sharks, 239
  mortgage fiasco, 234–236, 235*f*
  pawnshops, 239
  payday lenders, 236–237
Summers, Lawrence, 162, 488, 488*f*
Superregional bank, 221–222
Supervision. *See* Bank supervision
Supply, 87*f*
  effects on, 86–87
  money, 98, 100*f*
Supply curve
  shifts in, 89, 91
Supply shock (v), 363–365, 368–368, 370*f*
  adverse, 363, 371–372
  beneficial, 363
  and Phillips curve, 364–365, 365*f*
Support level, 184
Suspension of payments, 285–286
Sutton, Willie, 292
Sweep program, 45, 46*f*
  case study, 45–46
Symmetric information, 193–195
Syndicate, 123
Syndication, 270

T

TAF. *See* Term Auction Facility
Taiwan, 94
Takeover firms, 203–204
Target
  flexible, 495
  ILC, 297
  inflation, 493–500
  money growth, 492–493
  strict, 495
Tariff, 168
Taxes, 115–116, 356
  capital structure, 132
  and inflation, 431–432
Taylor, John, 450, 450*n*, 461, 462*n*, 490
Taylor rule, 490, 556
  in action, 451–452
  in the AE/PC model, 452–454
  applying, 451
  choosing coefficients, 453–454, 455*f*
  defined, 450
  deviation from, 469*f*
  example, 453, 453*t*
  Fed and, 451, 452*f*
  formula, 450–451
  Martin's metaphor, 450
T-bills, 126–127. *See* Treasury bills
TBTF. *See* Too big to fail
TD Waterhouse, 122
Tearing Down the Walls, 229
Teaser rates, 234
Technical analysis, 183–184
Technology, new, 356
Temporary open-market operation, 338
Term, 102
Term Auction Facility (TAF), 316, 327, 550, 555
Term premium, 105–106
Term structure of interest rates, 102–109
  accounting for risk, 105–106
  case of certainty, 103–104
  expectations theory, 104–105
  and monetary policy, 384–389
  yield curve, 106–109

Terra, Cristina, 430*n*
Texas Rangers, 55–56
Thailand, 559
  capital control, 525
Thaler, Richard, 142
Thatcher, Margaret, 539, 539*n*
3/1 ARM, 273
Thrift institutions, 221*t*, 222–223
  credit unions, 222–223
  savings institution, 222
Time consistency
  independence and, 487
  and inflation, 476–482
  monetary policy, 492
Time-consistency problem, 477–478
  conservative policymakers and, 481
  inflation increase, 478–481
  policy rule, 482
  solving, 481–482
Time deposit, 44, 251
Time lags, 400–403
  effects of policy, 403–406
TIPS. *See* Treasury Inflation Protected Securities
Tobin, James, 6
Toledo, Alejandro, 427
Tommasi, Mariano, 429*n*
Too big to fail (TBTF), 552–553
Trade
  deficit, 173
  surplus, 173
Traders, fast, 141–142
Trade-weighted real exchange rate, 166–167
Trading post, 128
Trading process, 156–158
  interbank market, 157
  retail market, 157
Transaction costs
  and banks, 214–215
Transaction technologies, 102
Transparency, 504–507
  and FOMC, 506–507, 507*f*
  moving toward, 506–507
  secrecy and Fed, 506
Travelers, 229, 249
Treasury bills, 3, 53
  auctions, 126–127
  rate, 270–271, 277–278, 334, 335*f*
Treasury bonds, 225
  futures, 145
  hedging, 147
  options, 145–146
  speculation, 147
Treasury Inflation Protected Securities (TIPS), 78
Trichet, Jean-Claude, 427
Tubbs Jones, Stephanie, 298
Tyco, 196–197
Tying, 264

U

UAW. *See* United Auto Workers
UBS, 209
Uncertainty
  coping with, 463–464
Underpricing, 125
Undervalued asset, 139
Underwriter, 122
  criticism of, 124–125
Unemployment, 343, 345–346
  economy 1960–2007, 373–375
  fluctuations, 348, 348*f*
  natural rate of (U*), 345
  1990s, 462
  Phillips curve, 363
Unemployment rate (U), 345
Unit banking, 15
  case study, 15–16
United Airlines
  junk bonds and, 112
United Auto Workers (UAW), 113
United Kingdom
  bank run, 287–288
  indexed bonds, 78
United States, 31, 32
  bonds, 95
  debt rating, 111
  deposit insurance, 290–291
  dollar, history of, 32–34. *See also* U.S. dollar
  dollar-euro rate, 167
  effects of appreciation, 160–162, 161*t*
  exchange rate policies, 526
  foreign banks in, 228
  growth of potential output, 345
  stored-value cards, 41
  unemployment rate, 346
U.S. currency. *See* U.S. dollar
U.S. Department of Education, 241
U.S. dollar
  classical gold standard, 33
  continental, 32–33
  euro versus, 176–178, 177*f*
  future, 55
  history of, 32–34
  in new republic, 33
  politics of, 162–163
  to present, 33–34
  real and nominal exchange rates against, 181*f*
U.S. Steel, 225
Unit of account, 28–29
Universal default clause, 266
US Airways
  junk bonds and, 112
Usury laws, 237
Uzbekistan, 36

V

Value
  future value, 54
  income stream, 54–56
  present value, 55–56, 57–58
VanDerhei, Jack, 7*n*
Vanguard, 121
Vault cash, 252
VC. *See* Venture capital firms
Velocity of money, 414–415
Venture capital (VC) firms, 123, 204–205
Veterans Administration, 241
Visa, 41
Visclosky, Peter, 527
Vneshtorbank, 287
Volcker, Paul, 334–335, 374, 375, 422, 483, 506, 547

W

Waksal, Sam, 208
Wall Street Journal, 130, 146, 264
Wallace, Mr., 28
Wal-Mart
  Bank, 297–299
  ILC and, 297–299
Wannemacher, Wesley, 266
Washington, George, 224
Washington Mutual (WaMu), 222, 554
Washington Post, 144
Wealth, 391
Weill, Sanford, 229, 230, 249
Withrow, Jason, 238
Woodward, Bob, 504*n*
World Bank, 15, 295
WorldCom, 206, 230, 264
  collapse of, 7
World Trade Center, 47
Write off, 269

Y

Yi, Wu, 511
Yield curve, 106–109, 106*f*, 107*f*
  examples of, 108–109, 108*f*
  forecasting interest rates, 109
  inverted, 108
  shapes of, 106–108
Yield to maturity, 71
  rate of return versus, 74
Yuan, 526–527
Yunus, Mohammed, 17

Z

Zelie, Mademoiselle, 28
Zero-coupon bond, 3
Zero inflation, 444–445
Zimbabwe
  hyperinflation, 423–424

Key Equations

(3.1) **Future Value** $\$1 \text{ today} = \$(1+i)^n \text{ in } n \text{ years}$

(3.2) **Present Value** $\$1 \text{ in } n \text{ years} = \dfrac{\$1}{(1+i)^n} \text{ today}$

(3.5) $$\text{bond price} = \frac{C}{(1+i)} + \frac{C}{(1+i)^2} + \cdots + \frac{(C+F)}{(1+i)^T}$$

(3.6) **An Asset's Rate of Return** $\text{rate of return} = \dfrac{(P_1 - P_0)}{P_0} + \dfrac{X}{P_0}$

(3.7) **Real Interest Rate** $r = i - \pi$

(3.8) **Ex Ante Real Interest Rate** $r^{\text{ex ante}} = i - \pi^{\text{expected}}$

(3.9) **Ex Post Real Interest Rate** $r^{\text{ex post}} = i - \pi^{\text{actual}}$

(4.1) **Fisher Equation** $i = r + \pi^{\text{e}}$

(4.3) **Expectations Theory of the Term Structure**

$$i_n(t) = \frac{1}{n}[\,i_1(t) + Ei_1(t+1) + \cdots + Ei_1(t+n-1)\,]$$

(4.4) **The Expectations Theory with a Term Premium**

$$i_n(t) = \frac{1}{n}[\,i_1(t) + Ei_1(t+1) + \cdots + Ei_1(t+n-1)\,] + \tau_n$$

(6.1) **Real Exchange Rate** $\varepsilon = \dfrac{eP}{P^*}$

(6.4) $NX = NCO$

(11.2) $$m = \frac{(C/D) + 1}{(C/D) + (R/D)}$$

(11.3) $M = mB$

(12.1) **Okun's Law** $(Y - Y^*)/Y^* = -2(U - U^*)$

(12.2) $Y = AE = C + I + G + NX$

(12.3) **Adaptive Expectations** $\pi^{\text{e}} = \pi(-1)$

(12.4) **Output Phillips Curve** $\pi = \pi^{\text{e}} + \alpha(Y - Y^*)/Y^* \quad (\alpha > 0)$

(12.5) **Unemployment Phillips Curve** $\pi = \pi^{\text{e}} - 2\alpha(U - U^*)$

(12.8) **The Phillips Curve with a Supply Shock** $\pi = \pi^{\text{e}} + \alpha(Y - Y^*)/Y^* + \nu$

(14.1) **Quantity Equation of Money** $MV = PY$

(15.1) **The Taylor Rule** $r = r^{\text{n}} + a_{\text{y}}\widetilde{Y} + a_{\pi}(\pi - \pi^T)$